Uniform Investment Adviser Law Exam License Exam Manual

Series 65

11th Edition

At press time, this edition contains the most complete and accurate information currently available. Owing to the nature of license examinations, however, information may have been added recently to the actual test that does not appear in this edition. Please contact the publisher to verify that you have the most current edition.

This publication is designed to provide accurate and authoritative information in regard to the subject matter covered. It is sold with the understanding that the publisher is not engaged in rendering legal, accounting, or other professional services. If legal advice or other expert assistance is required, the services of a competent professional should be sought.

SERIES 65 UNIFORM INVESTMENT ADVISER LAW EXAM LICENSE EXAM MANUAL, 11TH EDITION

©2019 Kaplan, Inc.

If you find imperfections or incorrect information in this product, please visit www.kaplanfinancial.com and submit an errata report.

Published in March 2019 by Kaplan Financial Education.
Revised October 2019.
Printed in the United States of America.

ISBN: 978-1-4754-7471-8

CONTENTS

PART 2 — ECONOMIC FACTORS AND BUSINESS INFORMATION

PART 4   **CLIENT INVESTMENT RECOMMENDATIONS AND STRATEGIES**

INTRODUCTION

Thank you for choosing Kaplan for your educational needs and welcome to the Series 65 License Exam Manual (LEM). This manual applies adult learning principles to give you the tools you'll need to pass your exam on the first attempt.

Why Do I Need to Pass the Series 65 Exam?

Most states require passing a qualification examination by those who give investment advice, or perform certain related functions. The North American Securities Administrators Association (NASAA) has created the Series 65 Uniform Investment Adviser Law Exam as one of the options that may be used to meet that requirement.

Are There Any Prerequisites?

There are no prerequisites to sit for the Series 65 exam. However, the test assumes that the applicant has a broad range of knowledge or experience with investments. Because a significant percentage of our students come to us without that background, this manual attempts to cover all of the basics as well as the more advanced material tested. Those of you with a Series 6 or Series 7 registration will find these basics a good review that will help set the stage for learning the intricate topics you will need to know.

Examination Waivers

Passing the Series 65 normally is a prerequisite to getting licensed as an investment adviser representative. However, most states will allow an individual to substitute one of the following certifications for passing the exam:

- CFP®—CERTIFIED FINANCIAL PLANNER™ (granted by the CFP Board of Standards);
- CIC—Chartered Investment Counselor (granted by the Investment Adviser Association);
- ChFC®—Chartered Financial Consultant® (granted by the The American College of Financial Services);
- PFS—Personal Financial Specialist (granted by the American Institute of Certified Public Accountants); and
- CFA®—Chartered Financial Analyst® (granted by the Chartered Financial Analyst Institute).

The individual applicant still has to go through other state licensing requirements, such as filing a Form U4 or Form U10 and payment of fees.

What Is the Series 65 Exam Like?

The Series 65 is a 3-hour, 140-question exam (130 questions scored) prepared by the North American Securities Administrators Association (NASAA) and administered by FINRA. It is offered as a computer-based exam at Prometric testing centers around the country.

What Score Must I Achieve to Pass?

You need a score of at least 72% (94 questions correct of the 130 scored) on the Series 65 exam to pass and become eligible for registration as a **Registered Investment Adviser Representative**.

What Topics Will I See on the Exam?

The questions you will see on the Series 65 exam do not appear in any particular order. The computer is programmed to select a new, random set of questions for each exam taker according to the preset topic weighting of the exam. Each Series 65 candidate will see the same number of questions on each topic but will see a different mix of questions. The Series 65 exam is divided into four critical function areas.

	Number of Questions	Percentage of Exam
1. Economic Factors and Business Information	20	15
2. Investment Vehicle Characteristics	32	25
3. Client Investment Recommendations and Strategies	39	30
4. Laws, Regulations, and Guidelines, Including Prohibitions on Unethical Business Practices	39	30

When you complete your exam, you will receive either a notification that you **passed** (but no score) or a failing score with a printout that identifies your performance in each area.

PREPARING FOR THE EXAM

How Is the License Exam Manual Organized?

The License Exam Manual consists of four parts (chapters). Each of these parts corresponds to one of the function areas tested. Furthermore, each of the parts is divided into units covering specific areas within the part. Within each unit are a number of learning objectives (LOs) covering the testable material in that unit. The introduction to each unit indicates the LOs and the number of questions you can expect the exam to ask about that Unit's material. For students attending one of our classes, live or online, the class lecture will follow the sequence of these units.

On your dashboard, you will have the opportunity to create a study calendar customized to your personal schedule. Please follow it as it gives step by step details as to how to optimize your learning experience. Think of it as a roadmap; don't take any detours or shortcuts and you will arrive safely at your destination—a passing score.

In following the study calendar, you will be asked to use the SecuritiesPro™ QBank to create a test at the end of each unit. These tests are designed to repeat and reinforce the information presented in the reading.

In order that the material being presented is properly explained, it sometimes happens that a term or phrase is used before its formal introduction in the course. In many cases, the term will be set off to the side with its definition. In other cases, you can consult the glossary for the definition or the index to locate a more complete discussion.

You also may have access to a PDF copy of the LEM. If so, we strongly recommend that you download it, because you can use the search function to find specific terms quickly.

In addition to the regular text, the LEM also has some unique features designed to help with quick understanding of the material. When additional emphasis is valuable to your comprehension, the following distinctions are made:

TAKE NOTE

Each Take Note provides special information designed to amplify important points.

TEST TOPIC ALERT

Each Test Topic Alert reviews content that is especially likely to appear on the exam.

EXAMPLE

Examples provide practical applications that convert theory into understanding.

Additional Study Resources

To accompany and supplement your LEM, your study package may contain additional study resources. Be sure to spend some time on your dashboard, view the best practices video and read the PDF, and understand all that is available to help you study.

SecuritiesPro™ QBank

Coordinating with the LEM, the SecuritiesPro™ QBank includes a large number of questions that are similar in style and content to those you will encounter on the exam. You may use it to generate tests by a specific unit or combination of units. The QBank also allows you to select weighted mock exams that simulate the topical composition of the Series 65 exam. There is no limit on the number of QBank exams you can create.

One thing you should know about the SecuritiesPro™ QBank is that the answer choices are scrambled each time you take a test. That is, if the first time you saw a specific question, the correct answer was choice A, that statement might be choice D the next time. Please keep this in mind if you need to contact us regarding that question.

Another important point is that the online questions are live. That is, unlike this manual, which, once printed, can't be changed, our questions can be updated with a moment's notice. This enables us to keep current with rule changes and, to the extent possible, with new topics as they are added to the Series 65 exam. When we author questions covering new material that is not in this manual, there will be an asterisk (*) placed after the reference number, indicating the general area where this topic belongs and that there is no specific information dealing with it other than this (or similar) questions and the exam tips and content updates link. As a result of their being live, anytime there is a discrepancy between an online question and something in this LEM or one of our videos, the question is always correct.

Practice and Mastery Exams

Depending on the study package purchased, you may also have a fixed practice exam or a fixed practice and mastery exam. These exams are designed to closely replicate the true exam experience, both in terms of the degree of difficulty and topical coverage. They provide scores and diagnostic feedback, but you will not be given access to, or be able to obtain from Kaplan, correct answers or question explanations. The practice and mastery exams are sound indicators of potential actual exam scores—the better you do on these exams, the more likely you are to pass your actual exam. These may only be taken once each.

Video Library

You may also have access to various topics from our video library. These short, engaging videos cover key topics from your manual. If your package includes access to our video library, please review the topics as you complete your reading assignments in the study manual.

Because most of the videos are not exam specific, you may encounter material that is not covered in your LEM. Just skip ahead until the slide shows something familiar.

Exam Tips and Content Updates Link

Don't forget to monitor your Exam Tips and Content Updates (located on your dashboard)—when rules and regulations change, or we want to share new information regarding your exam, it is posted there.

And one more thing. In addition, try as we may, in a text this large, errors are difficult to avoid. When we become aware of them, we acknowledge them in the **Corrections** tab, also located on your homepage.

What Topics Are Covered in the Course?

The License Exam Manual consists of four Parts, each devoted to a particular area of study that you will need to know to pass the Series 65. Each part is divided into study units devoted to more specific areas with which you need to become familiar.

The Series 65 License Exam Manual addresses the following topics:

Part	Topic
1	Laws, Regulations, and Guidelines, including Prohibitions on Unethical Business Practices
2	Economic Factors and Business Information
3	Investment Vehicle Characteristics
4	Client Investment Recommendations and Strategies

How Much Time Should I Spend Studying?

Plan to spend approximately 60–120 hours reading the material and carefully answering the questions. Spread your study time over the four to five weeks before the date on which you are scheduled to take the Series 65 exam. Your actual time may vary depending on your reading rate, comprehension, professional background (those with a securities background will generally require less time and that is the reason for the wide range in recommended study hours), and study environment.

What Is the Best Way to Structure My Study Time?

The following schedule is suggested to help you obtain maximum retention from your study efforts. Remember, this is a guideline only, because each individual may require more or less time to complete the steps included.

Step 1

Read a part, unit by unit, and complete all exercises. Review rationales for all questions whether you got them right or wrong (time will vary based on the size of the unit).

Step 2

In the SecuritiesPro QBank, create exams of the designated length for each unit as you go. Carefully review all rationales. Use the LO number to locate additional or related information on the test topic in your LEM if needed (one to four hours per unit). Be sure to do the Checkpoint Exams following each unit and the Mid-term Exam after you have reviewed the Unit 2 Checkpoint Exam. These tests are generally more challenging than those in the QBank; they have been specifically selected to check your progress and ensure that you are prepared to move forward.

- Do not become too overwhelmed or bogged down in any one unit. You don't want to lose sight of the finish line because you're having trouble with one hurdle. Keep moving forward. It's a steady pace that wins the race.

- View rationales after each question initially and spend time studying each rationale in order to learn the concepts. Later, you will want to create exam scenarios in which scores and rationales are viewed at the end of each exam.

- Perfection is not the goal during the reading phase; a score in the high 60s to low 70s is good initially.

Step 3

When you have completed all the units in the LEM and the unit tests you have created, using the SecuritiesPro QBank, concentrate on comprehensive exams covering all the material. With your comprehensive testing it is best to view correct answers and rationales only after the test is completed. Plan to spend at least one week testing before a scheduled class (four hours for every 130 questions).

- You should complete at least five weighted mock (simulated) exams before class. Review all of your answers and rationales. Also, review your LEM and video library as needed.

- Your goal is to consistently score in the 80s.

Step 4

Complete online practice and mastery exams. The online practice exam and mastery exam present you with questions from the topics covered based on their weighting and emphasis on the actual exam. Remember, you will not receive rationales for the answers you select, nor will you receive immediate feedback as you take the exam—we are simulating actual test conditions. You should complete these exams while observing the time limits for the actual exam. Upon completing the exam, you will receive a diagnostic report that identifies topics for further review (three to four hours per exam).

Note: After completing practice, mastery, and mock exams, be sure to review your Performance Tracker so you can identify areas of weakness. You can then create custom quizzes focused on topics as needed. Also, review your LEM and video library for additional help.

We recommend taking the practice exam shortly after a scheduled class and the mastery exam two to three days before your exam date.

How Well Can I Expect to Do?

The exams prepared by NASAA are not easy. You must display considerable understanding and knowledge of the topics presented in this course to pass the exam and qualify for registration.

If you study diligently, complete all sections of the course, and consistently score in the 80s on the simulated (mock) tests and achieve a passing grade on the practice and mastery exams, you should be well prepared to pass the exam. However, it is important for you to realize that merely knowing the materials will not enable you to pass unless you can apply your knowledge to the questions you are given and understand the essence of the information behind the question.

TEST-TAKING TIPS

Passing the exam depends not only on how well you learn the subject matter, but also on how well you take exams. You can develop your test-taking skills, and improve your score, by learning a few test-taking techniques.

- Read the full question.
- Avoid jumping to conclusions—watch for hedge clauses.
- Interpret the unfamiliar question.
- Look for key words and phrases.
- Identify the intent of the question.
- Memorize key points.
- Use a calculator.
- Beware of changing answers.
- Pace yourself.

Each of these pointers is explained next, including examples that show how to use them to improve your performance on the exam.

Read the Full Question

You cannot expect to answer a question correctly if you do not know what it is asking. If you see a question that seems familiar and easy, you might anticipate the answer, mark it, and move on before you finish reading it. This is a serious mistake. Be sure to read the full question before answering it. Mistakes are often made when assuming too much (or too little).

Avoid Jumping to Conclusions—Watch for Hedge Clauses

The questions on NASAA exams are embellished with distractors as choices. To avoid being misled by seemingly obvious answers, make it a practice to read each question and each answer twice before selecting your choice. Doing so will provide you with a much better chance of doing well on the exam.

Watch out for hedge clauses embedded in the question. Examples of hedge clauses include the terms *if*, *not*, *all*, *none*, and *except*. In the case of *if* statements, the question can be answered correctly only by taking into account the qualifier. If you ignore the qualifier, you will not answer correctly.

Qualifiers are sometimes combined in a question. Some that you will frequently see together are *all* with *except* and *none* with *except*. In general, when a question starts with *all* or *none* and ends with *except*, you are looking for an answer that is opposite to what the question appears to be asking.

Interpret the Unfamiliar Question

Do not be surprised if some questions on the exam seem unfamiliar at first. If you have studied your material, you will have the information to answer all the questions correctly. The challenge may be a matter of understanding what the question is asking.

Very often, questions present information indirectly. You may have to interpret the meaning of certain elements before you can answer the question. Be aware that the exam will approach a concept from different angles.

Look for Key Words and Phrases

Look for words that are tip-offs to the situation presented. For example, if you see the word *prospectus* in the question, you know the question is about a new issue. Sometimes a question will even supply you with the answer if you can recognize the key words it contains. Few questions provide blatant clues, but many offer key words that can guide you to selecting the correct answer if you pay attention. Be sure to read all instructional phrases carefully. Take time to identify the key words to answer this type of question correctly.

Identify the Intent of the Question

Many questions on NASAA exams supply so much information that you lose track of what is being asked. This is often the case in story problems. Learn to separate the story from the question.

Take the time to identify what the question is asking. Of course, your ability to do so assumes you have studied sufficiently. There is no method for correctly answering questions if you don't know the material.

Memorize Key Points

Reasoning and logic will help you answer many questions, but you will have to memorize a good deal of information. Some memorization will be automatic as you go over the material and answer questions; some you will simply have to do systematically.

Use of a Calculator

For the most part, there are only a few questions that will require the use of a calculator. Any math will be simple math; add, subtract, multiply, and divide. We recommend using a calculator for math. A calculator will be supplied upon request.

Avoid Changing Answers

If you are unsure of an answer, your first hunch is the one most likely to be correct. Do not change answers on the exam without good reason. In general, change an answer only if you:

- discover that you did not read the question correctly; or
- find new or additional helpful information in another question.

Pace Yourself

Some people will finish the exam early and some do not have time to finish all the questions. Watch the time carefully (your time remaining will be displayed on your computer screen) and pace yourself through the exam.

Do not waste time by dwelling on a question if you simply do not know the answer. Make the best guess you can, mark the question for Record for Review, and return to the question if time allows. Questions are presented in a bell-shaped curve of difficulty meaning the easiest questions are generally at the beginning and the end of the test; make sure that you have time to read all the questions so that you can record the answers you do know.

THE EXAM

How Do I Enroll in the Exam?

To obtain an admission ticket to a NASAA exam, you or your firm must file an application form and processing fees with FINRA. To take the exam, you should make an appointment with a Prometric Testing Center as far in advance as possible of the date on which you would like to take the exam.

You may schedule your appointment at Prometric 24 hours a day, 7 days a week, on the Prometric secure website at **www.prometric.com**. You may also use **www.prometric.com** to reschedule or cancel your exam, locate a test center, and get a printed confirmation of your appointment. To speak with a Prometric representative by phone, please contact the Prometric Contact Center at **1-800-578-6273**.

What Should I Take to the Exam?

Take one form of personal identification with your signature and photograph as issued by a government agency. No personal items, food, or drink, including coffee and water, are permitted inside the testing room. Personal items include, but are not limited to, pens, pagers, cellular phones, watches, hats, non-medical electronic devices, outerwear, purses, and wallets. Personal items must be kept in your assigned locker or returned to your car before the start of your exam. As the testing vendor is not responsible for any personal items, they encourage you to bring only your identification into the center.

Erasable note boards and pens will be provided to you upon admittance to the testing room. If you need additional note boards or pens, please alert your proctor. The note boards and pens must be returned at the end of your exam.

If you need a calculator for your testing session, please see the test center administrator. You will be provided with a non-programmable, non-printing calculator.

Additional Trial Questions

During your exam, you will see 10 extra trial questions (that is why the test is 140 questions long). These are potential exam-bank questions being tested during the course of the exam. These questions are not identified as such and are not included in your final score.

Exam Results and Reports

At the end of the exam, you will receive either a notification that you **passed** (but no score) or a failing score with a printout that identifies your performance in each area. The testing center will print your results and affix their stamp as physical evidence of your passing.

The next business day after your exam, your results will be mailed to your firm and to the self-regulatory organization and state securities commission specified on your application.

PART

1

Laws, Regulations, and Guidelines, Including Prohibitions on Unethical Business Practices

This part consists of seven units:

Unit 1 Regulation of Investment Advisers, Including State-Registered and Federal Covered Advisers

Unit 2 Regulation of Investment Adviser Representatives

Unit 3 Regulation of Broker-Dealers and their Agents

Unit 4 Regulation of Securities and Issuers

Unit 5 Remedies and Administrative Provisions

Unit 6 Communication With Clients and Prospects

Unit 7 Ethical Practices and Fiduciary Obligations

In total, there will be 39 questions on this material, representing 30% of the Series 65 Exam.

UNIT 1

Regulation of Investment Advisers, Including State-Registered and Federal Covered Advisers

Investment advisers are defined by federal and state securities laws. A person that performs the functions of an investment adviser, as the term is defined in the Uniform Securities Act or the Investment Advisers Act of 1940 and more fully described in Securities and Exchange Commission (SEC) Release IA-1092, is by definition an investment adviser. Investment advisers must conduct business within the regulatory framework prescribed in federal and state securities laws.

The Series 65 exam will include approximately six questions on the material presented in this unit.

LEARNING OBJECTIVES

When you have completed this unit, you will be able to accomplish the following.

U1LO1: Define investment adviser.
U1LO2: Explain the impact of SEC Release IA-1092 on the definition of investment advisers and their activities.
U1LO3: Identify exclusions and exemptions under the Investment Advisers Act of 1940 and the Uniform Securities Act.
U1LO4: Identify the exempt reporting adviser and private fund adviser exemptions.
U1LO5: Describe the investment adviser registration process, required post-registration filings, and business activities.
U1LO6: Recognize that investment adviser representatives must be adequately supervised.

INTRODUCTION

Before we can get started, we need to know a few things. Because this part of the course deals with laws and regulations, it is necessary to know what laws are involved. When it comes to the regulation of investment advisers, on the federal level, we have the Investment Advisers Act of 1940. On the state level, it is the Uniform Securities Act. This exam is the property

3

of NASAA, the North American Securities Administrators Association, the group of state, provincial, and Mexican regulators. Although the exam will ask about state and federal law, if it doesn't specify, the default choice is always state law. Let's investigate that law a bit.

THE UNIFORM SECURITIES ACT OF 1956 (USA)

The USA is Model State Securities Legislation. With the enactment of numerous state securities laws, commonly referred to as *blue-sky* laws, the need for uniformity in securities laws among the states arose. In 1956, the original Uniform Securities Act was drafted as model legislation for the separate states to adopt. As model legislation, the USA is not actual legislation; the USA is a template or guide that each state uses in drafting its securities legislation. The securities laws of most states follow the USA very closely, and, in many cases, almost exactly.

TAKE NOTE

The term state means any of the 50 states, any territory or possession of the United States (such as American Samoa, Guam, and the Virgin Islands), the District of Columbia, and Puerto Rico.

TEST TOPIC ALERT

The exam will test your knowledge of the Uniform Securities Act, not the specifics of your state's securities legislation. The USA is periodically updated to adjust to developments in the securities markets through the passage of Model Rules. You will be tested on the 1956 version of the USA used by the **North American Securities Administrators Association (NASAA)**, the advisory body of state securities regulators responsible for the content of the exam. The Series 65 exam requires that you not only know what the USA says, but also are able to apply the law to concrete situations. General knowledge of the law is not enough to pass the exam; you will be asked to apply the law to situations that may arise in the course of business.

Definition: Administrator

Possibly the most used term in the exam is Administrator. Who or what is this? Although some states may use other terms to describe this position, the exam will only use the word **Administrator** to refer to the office or agency that has the complete responsibility for administering the securities laws of the state.

Therefore, the Administrator has jurisdiction over almost all securities activity that emanates from his state as well as that received in his state. The Administrator has jurisdiction over the registration of securities professionals and securities. He has the power to make rules and issue orders. He can deny, suspend, or revoke registrations. Yes, there are some limitations on the Administrator's powers (and those will be covered in this course), but overall, this is one very powerful person.

U1LO1: Define investment adviser.

The definition of investment adviser is virtually identical under state law (the Uniform Securities Act) and federal law (The Investment Advisers Act of 1940). Here is how it is worded in the Uniform Securities Act:

> Investment adviser means "any person who, for compensation, engages in the business of advising others, either directly or through publications or writings, as to the value of securities or as to the advisability of investing in, purchasing, or selling securities, or who, for compensation and as a part of a regular business, issues or promulgates analyses or reports concerning securities."

Definition: Person

As defined in the Uniform Securities Act, "'Person' means an individual, (a natural person), a corporation, a partnership, an association, a joint-stock company, a trust where the interests of the beneficiaries are evidenced by a security, an unincorporated organization, a government, or a political subdivision of a government." For test purposes, it is easiest to remember the three non-persons. They are, (1) a minor, (2) a deceased individual, and (3) an individual declared mentally incompetent by the courts.

EXAMPLE

A person is basically anyone that can open an account. The test would be looking for you to choose an answer to a question such as this:

1. Which of the following is included in the definition of person?

   A. A minor

   B. The National Basketball Association

   C. A deceased person

   D. A person whom the courts have declared to be mentally incompetent

   Answer: B. Odd to think of the NBA as a person, but, they would be included in the USA's definition. That is why questions are much easier if you just remember the 3 things that are not a person.

The definition of investment adviser is sometimes referred to as the three-prong test. That is, as long as the person involved:

■ gives advice to others on securities;

■ does so as part of a regular business activity; and

■ receives compensation for performing this activity.

Let's examine each of those.

Giving Advice to Others on Securities

Persons will meet the first prong of the test if they provide advice to others about specific securities, such as stocks, bonds, mutual funds, and limited partnerships, as well how to allocate assets among a group of securities. Even indirect advice can be included. Examples of this could be:

■ "Why should you invest in securities as compared to non-securities investments, such as insured bank CDs or rental property?"

■ "Here is our view on future stock market trends."

The advice can be in written or oral form. That is, it can be part of a printed (or online) report or advice given on a phone call. The regulators, both state and federal, have stated that advice on many other types of investments is not advice about securities. Some of the specifically mentioned non-securities investments include:

■ commodities;

■ collectibles, such as coins or stamps;

■ precious metals, such as gold and silver; and

■ real estate.

TAKE NOTE

The list of what is a security and what is not a security will be covered in more detail at Unit 4, LO1.

EXAMPLE

1. A person giving advice on which of the following investments would be deemed to be giving advice on securities?

    A. Gold

    B. Common stock

    C. Rental real estate

    D. Rare stamps

    Answer: B. Common stock is a security; the others are considered non-securities.

In the Business of Providing Advice

Persons are in the business of providing advice and meet the second prong defining one as an investment adviser if they do the following:

■ Give advice on a regular basis such that it constitutes a business activity conducted with some regularity. Although the frequency of the activity is a factor, it is not the only determinant in whether one is in the business of giving advice. Furthermore, providing advice does not have to be the person's principal activity.

■ Advertise investment advisory services and presents himself to the public as an investment adviser or as one who provides investment advice.

EXAMPLE

As an example, a person is an investment adviser if she recommends that a client allocate funds to specific assets, such as high-yield bonds, technology stocks, or mutual funds. Specificity is the term used to describe this activity and invariably fulfills the "in the business" requirement.

A person whose business is to offer only nonspecific investment advice, through publication of a general newsletter, for instance, is not covered by the act. That exclusion will be covered shortly in LO3.

Compensation

A person who receives any economic benefit as a result of providing investment advice meets the third prong. Compensation includes advisory fees, commissions, or other types of fees relating to the service rendered and can be directly or indirectly paid.

EXAMPLE

When a person designs a comprehensive financial plan for an individual, but does not charge a fee for that design, electing to be compensated solely through commissions received on the sale of insurance policies sold as part of the plan, that is considered compensation. Even though that compensation is indirect, it meets the release's definition of compensation for investment advice.

INVESTMENT COUNSEL

One of the terms that may appear on the exam is that of **investment counsel**. Questions dealing with this topic require the student to know that two criteria specified in the Investment Advisers Act of 1940 must be met to use the term to describe the nature of the IA's business. They are as follows:

- The IA's principal business must be giving investment advice. This basically excludes financial planners and others for whom investment advice is only a part of what they do.

- Provide investment supervisory services. This one is a bit harder for most to understand so here are some details as issued by the SEC.

Continuous and Regular Supervisory or Management Services

General Criteria. You provide continuous and regular supervisory or management services with respect to an account if:

(a) you have discretionary authority over and provide ongoing supervisory or management services with respect to the account; or

(b) you do not have discretionary authority over the account, but you have ongoing responsibility to select or make recommendations, based upon the needs of the client, as to specific securities or other investments the account may purchase or sell and, if such recommendations are accepted by the client, you are responsible for arranging or effecting the purchase or sale.

You do not provide continuous and regular supervisory or management services for an account if you:

(a) provide market timing recommendations (i.e., to buy or sell), but have no ongoing management responsibilities;

(b) provide only impersonal investment advice (e.g., market newsletters);

(c) make an initial asset allocation, without continuous and regular monitoring and reallocation; or

(d) provide advice on an intermittent or periodic basis (such as upon client request, in response to a market event), or on a specific date (e.g., the account is reviewed and adjusted quarterly).[1]

EXAMPLE

1. Which of the following investment advisers would be permitted to use the term *investment counsel?*

    A. A financial planner offering a wide range of services to his clients, including tax planning, estate planning, and insurance planning, as well as investment advice

    B. A professional providing a market timing service with an annual subscription fee of $495 (this service attempts to maximize profits by suggesting entry and exit points for over 100 listed stocks)

    C. A firm whose exclusive business is placing their client's assets into model portfolios that are monitored on a daily basis

    D. All of these

    Answer: C. To use the term *investment counsel*, two criteria must be met— the principal business must be giving investment advice and the adviser must provide investment supervisory services. Running model portfolios for clients with daily monitoring would meet both requirements. The financial planner is not principally in the business of offering investment advice because he describes his service as offering a wide range of services, of which advice is only one part. The exam frequently uses that wording to indicate that advice is not the principal activity. While the market timing publisher's principal business activity may be offering advice, nothing about the description indicates that individual client accounts are being monitored.

SEC RELEASE IA-1092

U1LO2: Explain the impact of SEC Release IA-1092 on the definition of investment advisers and their activities.

As a result of the proliferation of persons offering investment advice in the 1980s, Congress directed the SEC to define the activities that would subject a person to the 1940 Investment Advisers Act. The SEC did so in SEC Release IA-1092 in October 1987.

SEC Release IA-1092 interprets the definition of investment adviser under the Investment Advisers Act of 1940 to include financial planners, pension consultants, and others who offer investment advice as part of their financial practices. Much of the Release was a repetition of existing law, such as the three prongs. The biggest impact was the expansion of the definition. Let's look at those who are directly affected.

---

[1]   Appendix B Form ADV: Instructions for Part 1A

Financial Planners

Financial planners who make recommendations regarding a person's financial resources or perform analyses that concern securities are investment advisers if such services are performed as part of a business and for compensation. Under this interpretation, the SEC holds that there is no such thing as a *comprehensive financial plan* that does not involve securities.

Pension Consultants

Consultants who advise employee benefit plans on how to fund their plans with securities are also considered investment advisers by the SEC. In addition, the SEC considers pension consultants who advise employee benefit plans on the selection, performance, and retention of investment managers to be investment advisers.

Sports and Entertainment Representatives

Persons who provide financially related services to entertainers and athletes that includes advice related to investing, tax planning, budgeting, and money management are also investment advisers. As earnings for these celebrities continue to climb, more and more of them use personal managers to handle all of their finances, and those individuals or firms are generally going to be considered investment advisers.

TAKE NOTE

A sports agent who secures a favorable contract for a football player and receives a commission of 10% of the player's salary is not necessarily an investment adviser. However, if the sports agent advises the football player to invest his money in specific securities, the agent is then in the business of offering investment advice and would then be subject to the Investment Advisers Act of 1940 or the Uniform Securities Act.

EXAMPLE

1. Under SEC Release IA-1092, which of the following is most likely to meet the definition of an investment adviser?

    A. A person who sells long-term care insurance

    B. A person who advises businesses on the best location for their stores

    C. A person who assists pension plans in the selection of portfolio managers

    D. A person who manages portfolios of investment grade coins

    Answer: C. This is the role of a pension consultant. Unless the insurance has a securities aspect, selling it would not be considered investment advice. Real estate and coins are not securities.

U1LO3: Identify exclusions and exemptions under the Investment Advisers Act of 1940 and the Uniform Securities Act.

Because terminology is critical to jurisdiction, it is important to know the difference between excluded from a definition and exempt from a provision.

Exclusion means excluded from, or not included in, a definition. For example, if a person is excluded from the definition of an investment adviser, that person is not subject to provisions of state or federal law that refer to investment advisers.

There are a number of exclusions from the investment adviser definition available to persons who might well satisfy all three prongs of the definition, but, because of the provisions of the law, are specifically not defined as investment advisers. An excluded person is not subject to any provisions of the Investment Advisers Act or the Uniform Securities Act (other than antifraud statutes).

Exemption means not being subject to the registration provisions of the acts even though that person meets the definition. For example, a person defined as an investment adviser can be exempt from state registration requirements as an investment adviser because that person enjoys an exemption from state registration under federal law, such as in the case of a federal covered adviser.

Relevant to the previous, a significant portion of the law (and the exam), deals with those who are in either excluded from the definition or who are investment advisers, but exempt from registering as such. Let's begin with those who are excluded from the definition.

EXCLUSIONS

Although the definition of an investment adviser is broad, certain exclusions apply. Under state law (the Uniform Securities Act), there are seven primary exclusions from the definition of an investment adviser.

■ Any bank and bank holding company, savings institution, or trust company. This exclusion is generally limited to U.S. banks and bank holding companies. The exclusion is unavailable to credit unions and investment adviser subsidiaries of banks or bank holding companies.

Definition: Bank Holding Company

A holding company is organized to invest in and manage other corporations. Control can occur through the ownership of more than 50% of the voting rights or through the exercise of a dominant influence. It is sometimes referred to as the parent organization. A bank holding company is a holding company whose primary asset is a commercial bank. Most of the large U.S. banks today are owned by holding companies.

■ Any **lawyer**, **accountant**, **teacher**, or **engineer** whose advice is solely incidental to the practice of his profession is excluded. This exclusion is not available to any of these who have established a separate advisory business. Also, the exclusion would not be available to any of these who holds himself out as offering investment advice. We like to refer to this as the L.A.T.E. exclusion.

 EXAMPLE

When referring to the L.A.T.E. exclusion, it is important to understand the meaning of incidental. A lawyer advising clients to carefully invest a settlement from a legal case is not giving investment advice unless charging a separate fee for helping set up the portfolio. An accountant is not giving investment advice when suggesting to a wealthy client that investing in tax-exempt municipal bonds might be a wise idea, unless charging a separate fee to help select the bonds.

■ Any broker-dealer whose performance of such services is solely incidental to the conduct of its business as a broker-dealer and who receives no special compensation (such as when offering wrap fee programs) is excluded. The exclusion also applies to registered representatives (agents) of broker-dealers.

Definition: Broker-Dealer

A person engaged in the business of executing securities transactions. This is covered in detail at Unit 3.

Definition: Wrap Fee Program

Any advisory program generally established by a broker-dealer, under which a specified fee or fees not based directly upon transactions in a client's account is charged for investment advisory services (which may include portfolio management or advice concerning the selection of other investment advisers) and the execution of client transactions. The exclusion from the definition of investment adviser available under both state and federal law to broker-dealers is not in effect for those offering wrap fee programs. The exam may ask about these programs this way:

> Which two of the following are services provided in a wrap fee program? The correct choice would be: *Investment advisory* and brokerage execution (*transactions*) for a single "wrapped" fee. Don't choose financial planning and recommendations.

TAKE NOTE

Special compensation for investment advice is compensation to the broker-dealer or salesperson in excess of that which he or she would be paid for providing a brokerage or dealer service alone. Consequently, special compensation exists where there is a clearly definable charge for investment advice.

■ Publishers may qualify for an exclusion from the definition, but they must meet certain criteria. Excluded from the definition of investment adviser would be a "publisher of any bona fide newspaper, news magazine, or business or financial publication of general and regular circulation."[2]

To qualify for this exclusion, the publication must be (1) of a general and impersonal nature, in that the advice provided is not adapted to any specific portfolio or any client's particular needs; (2) bona fide, or genuine, in that it contains disinterested commentary and analysis as opposed to promotional material; and (3) of general and regular circulation, in that it is not timed to specific market activity or events affecting, or having the ability to affect the securities industry.

For example, newspapers of general circulation would be eligible for the exclusion.

TEST TOPIC ALERT

An investment newsletter is being published for a subscription fee. Rather than being published on a regular basis (weekly, monthly, quarterly, and so forth), issues are released in response to market events. How do the laws view this publisher? If the publication is issued from time to time in response to episodic market events, the exclusion is lost.

---

2   Section 202(a)(11)D) of the Investment Advisers Act of 1940.

- Certain individuals who are employed by investment advisers—*investment adviser representatives* (described in detail in Unit 2, LO1)

- Any person who is a federal covered adviser is excluded

- Any other person the Administrator specifies is excluded.

The exclusions under the Investment Advisers Act of 1940 mirror the first four we listed for the Uniform Securities Act. In addition, there is a fifth exclusion under federal law:

- any person whose advice, analyses, or reports are related only to securities that are direct obligations of, or obligations guaranteed by, the United States.

TAKE NOTE

For purposes of the exclusion, under both state and federal law, the term *bank* does not include a savings and loan association or a foreign bank, but does include a savings institution.

Because understanding these exclusions is so important, let's look at a few examples.

EXAMPLE

1. The Uniform Securities Act excludes certain persons from the definition of an investment adviser if their performance of advisory services is solely incidental to their professions. This exclusion would apply to all of the following EXCEPT

   A. an accountant

   B. an economist

   C. an electrical engineer

   D. a college professor teaching a course on economics

   Answer: B. As long as the activity is incidental to the professional practice, and no separate fee for the advice is charged, the act specifically excludes accountants, lawyers, any professional engineer (aeronautical, civil, mechanical, or others), and teachers. Economists are not included in this listing (most economists are not teachers).

2. Which of the following would be excluded from the definition of investment adviser under the Uniform Securities Act?

   A. The publisher of a weekly magazine, sold on newsstands, that contains at least 5 stock recommendations per issue

   B. A broker-dealer making a separate charge for investment advice

   C. A civil damages attorney who advertises that she is available to assist clients in suggesting appropriate investments for their successful claim

   D. A finance teacher at a local community college who offers weekend seminars on comprehensive financial planning at a very reasonable price

   Answer: A. Publishers of general circulation newspapers and magazines are excluded from the definition of investment adviser, especially because the entire publication is devoted to impersonal investment advice. An important key here is that it is published regularly, not upon market events. A broker-dealer loses its exclusion the moment it offers advice for a separate charge, as does an attorney who holds herself out as offering investment advice. Normally, a teacher is excluded, but not when charging for advice as would appear to be the case here. On this examination, the term comprehensive (or total) financial planning always includes securities advice.

EXEMPTIONS

When it comes to exemptions, state and federal laws have established rules whereby a person, although meeting the definition of an investment adviser, is not required to register as such. That person is considered to be exempt from registration. Because the state and federal exemptions are not as similar as the exclusions, let's take them separately starting with the exemptions available under the Investment Advisers Act of 1940 (federal law).

Federal Law Exemptions

The Investment Advisers Act of 1940 exempts the following persons who, even though defined as investment advisers, are exempt from the registration requirements of the act.

Intrastate Advisers (Only Within One State)

Investment advisers, other than an investment adviser who acts as an investment adviser to any private fund (defined at LO4), whose clients, are residents of the state in which the adviser has its principal office and only place of business and who do not give advice dealing with securities listed on any national exchange (e.g., New York Stock Exchange), are exempt. For example, an adviser would be exempted under this provision if all of its clients were Georgia residents, its only places of business were in Georgia, and it did not give advice on securities listed on any national exchange.

Advisers to Insurance Companies

Advisers whose only clients are insurance companies are exempt.

 TEST TOPIC ALERT

Please be careful on this last one—the exam frequently asks if the exemption applies when the only clients are banks. As we'll learn shortly, that exemption applies under state law, but not under federal law.

State Law Exemptions

In the same manner as the federal law, the Uniform Securities Act exempts from registration certain persons who, although they fall within the definition of an investment adviser, do not have to register as such in the state.

Investment advisers exempt from registration with the state Administrator are those who have no place of business in the state but are registered in another state, provided their only clients in the state are:

■ broker-dealers registered under the act;

- other investment advisers;
- institutional investors;
- existing clients who are not residents but are temporarily in the state;
- limited to 5 or fewer clients, other than those listed above, resident in the state during the preceding 12 months (called the de minimis exemption); or
- any others the Administrator exempts by rule or order.

Definitions: Institution

The term **institution** would include banks, trust companies, savings and loan associations, insurance companies, investment companies, (e.g., mutual funds), employee benefit plans with assets of not less than $1,000,000, and governmental agencies or instrumentalities. Institutions are included in the term *person*, defined previously. The Act generally affords less protection to these investors owing to their supposed greater investment sophistication.

Retail Client

As you know, terminology is very important on this exam. A few questions use the term *retail client* instead of noninstitutional client. Look for it and remember that retail clients need far more protection than institutional ones. If the question refers to an individual, that will always be a retail client.

TAKE NOTE

This exemption applies to investment advisers who are registered in at least one state, but have clients in another state where the IA does not maintain a place of business.

TEST TOPIC ALERT

One of the previous bullet points refers to an exemption to those investment advisers who have no place of business in the state, but are licensed in another state where they have a place of business, and offer advice in the state only with persons in the state who are existing customers and who are not residents of the state but are just there temporarily. This is sometimes referred to as the *snowbird exemption* because it is frequently used to deal with existing clients who winter in warmer climates. The time limit defining *temporary* is not tested (some folks spend 3–4 months staying warm), but, if the client should change legal residence to that state, the investment adviser has 30 days to register in that state or discontinue doing business with that client (unless qualifying for the de minimis exemption). It is similar to the common experience of moving from one state to another. When you do that, you generally have 30 days to get new license tags for your car and a new driver's license.

TEST TOPIC ALERT

Because these exemptions all apply when the investment adviser does not have a place of business in the state, it is relevant to understand that an investment adviser or one of its representatives who advertises to the public, in any way, the availability of meeting with prospective clients in a hotel, country club, seminar, or any other location in the state is considered to have a place of business in the state. However, an investment adviser or one of its representatives who contacts existing clients who happen to be in the state and notifies them that he will be passing through the state and will be available to meet with them in his hotel room is not considered to have a place of business in the state because the announcement is being made only to existing clients and not to the public.

EXAMPLE

An investment adviser registered in State A, with no business locations in any other state, has, over the preceding 12 months, directed investment advice to five individual investors residing in State B. Is the investment adviser required to register in State B?

The answer is no! Registration is not required because the investment adviser does not have a place of business in State B and directs business to five or fewer individual residents of the state during the previous 12 months (de minimis exemption). If the firm had a place of business in State B, registration would be required in that state even if it had only one client. Also, registration would be required if business had been transacted with 6 or more individual residents (retail clients) of State B during the previous 12 months.

What if the IA gave investment advice to six banks, six insurance companies, and six other investment advisers instead of the individuals? Again, the answer would be no registration. As long as the investment adviser has no place of business in the state and limits its clientele to institutions, broker-dealers, large employee benefit plans, or other investment advisers, it qualifies for this exemption.

U1LO4: Identify the exempt reporting adviser and private fund adviser exemptions.

We've just listed a number of exemptions under federal and then state law. Here is another one that applies to both with only a slight difference between them.

PRIVATE FUND ADVISERS

Title IV of the Dodd-Frank Act of 2010, known as the Private Fund Investment Advisers Registration Act of 2010, contains a comprehensive overhaul of the registration process for investment advisers. The bill provided for the following new exemptions from registration under the Advisers Act:

■ An exemption for advisers solely to private funds with less than $150 million in assets under management (AUM) in the United States, without regard to the number or type of private funds (the private fund adviser exemption)

■ An exemption for certain non-U.S. advisers with no place of business in the United States and minimal AUM (less than $25 million) attributable to U.S. clients and investors (the foreign private adviser exemption)

■ An exemption for advisers solely to venture capital funds (the venture capital fund exemption)

Definition of a Private Fund

Although it is highly unlikely you will be tested on the technical definition, Section 402 of the Dodd-Frank Act defines a private fund as "an issuer that would be an investment company, as defined in section 3 of the Investment Company Act of 1940, but for section 3(c)(1) or 3(c)(7) of that Act."

In more straightforward terms, a 3(c)(1) issuer is one whose outstanding securities are beneficially owned by not more than 100 persons and which is not making and does not presently propose to make a public offering of its securities. With no more than 100 shareholders and no public offering, the term *private fund* seems quite logical.

A 3(c)(7) issuer is one whose outstanding securities are owned exclusively by persons who, at the time of acquisition of such securities, are qualified purchasers (at least $5 million in investments for individuals and generally $25 million in investments for business entities), and which is not making and does not at that time propose to make a public offering of such securities. In this case, the lack of a public offering is logically private, and the fact that the invested wealth requirement limits the potential universe of investors is a factor as well.

The point is, regardless of how it's defined, if one is an adviser solely to private funds, it is possible to qualify for an exemption from registration with the SEC.

Well, what about state law? Their model rule closely parallels the federal exemption with two differences.

Private Fund Adviser Exemption Under State Law

NASAA's Model Rule for the Registration Exemption for Investment Advisers to Private Funds is almost identical to the federal exemption described previously. Here are the two differences that might be testable.

- If qualifying for the exemption as a 3(c)(1) issuer, (no more than 100 investors), NASAA's Model Rule requires that all investors be "qualified clients." That is, they must have either at least $1 million in assets managed by the investment adviser, or a net worth, excluding the value of the primary residence, of at least $2.1 million. The phrase "value of primary residence" means the fair market value of a person's primary residence, minus the amount of debt secured by the property up to its fair market value (net equity). Note that "qualified" for NASAA is significantly less than "qualified" under federal law.

- Neither the private fund adviser nor any of its advisory affiliates are subject to the "bad actor" provisions. Those provisions disqualify anyone who has certain criminal convictions (generally felonies), certain SEC disciplinary orders, or suspension or expulsion from membership in a self-regulatory organization such as FINRA.

Exemption for Foreign Private Advisers

A foreign private adviser is defined in the Dodd-Frank Act as any investment adviser that:

- has no place of business in the United States;

- has, in total, fewer than 15 clients and investors in the United States in private funds advised by the adviser;

- has aggregate AUM attributable to clients in the United States and investors in the United States in private funds advised by the adviser of less than $25 million; and

- does not hold itself out to the public in the United States as an investment adviser or act as an investment adviser to an investment company registered under the Investment Company Act of 1940.

Exemption for Investment Advisers to Venture Capital Funds

The rules define a venture capital fund as a private fund that:

- has limited leverage;

- does not, except in certain limited circumstances, offer its investors redemption rights or other similar liquidity rights;

- represents itself as a venture capital fund to investors; and

- is not registered under the Investment Company Act of 1940.

What really are venture capital funds? What is venture capital? You are probably familiar with the phrase, *startup company*. At one point in time, well known firms like Google, Facebook and Netflix were young and in need of additional capital to expand and grow. Venture capitalists are investors who are willing to take a chance on a new venture, recognizing that there is a high potential for loss as well as potential for gain which can, in some cases, be very high. A venture capital fund is a pooled investment where venture capitalists invest their money and pay an adviser to select opportunities meeting their objectives. If these conditions are met, that investment adviser is exempt from registration under federal (and state) law.

TAKE NOTE

We will have more to say about the operations of private funds and venture capital funds in Part 3, Unit 14, LO5.

Please note that these exemptions are granted on the basis of who you advise, not on what types of securities are the subject of your advice. Note also that **exclusion** means exclusion from a definition, whereas **exemption** means not subject to registration. All of the exemptions mentioned here involve investment advisers; it's just that they qualify for an exemption from registration under federal law.

EXAMPLE

1. Who of the following would NOT qualify for an exemption from registration under the Investment Advisers Act of 1940?

    A. A person whose only advisory clients are insurance companies

    B. A person whose only offices are in a single state, whose only clients are residents of that state, and who does not render advice on securities traded on a national exchange

    C. A person who only gives advice to venture capital funds

    D. An accountant whose advice is incidental to her accounting business and for which no separate fee is charged.

    Answer: D. This is tricky (as is the exam). The accountant is excluded from the definition. Therefore, there is no reason for her to be exempt. The other three choices are investment advisers who qualify for one of the exemptions described previously.

U1LO5: Describe the investment adviser registration process, required post-registration filings, and business activities.

Unless an exemption is available, federal and state law make it unlawful for a person defined as an investment adviser to engage in advisory activity without registration. As we will learn, registration is done on either a federal **or** a state basis, never both. Once registered, there are a number of post-registration activities required, such as recordkeeping, annual filings, and other reports.

REGISTRATION REQUIREMENTS FOR INVESTMENT ADVISERS

At this point, we know who is an investment adviser, who is excluded from the definition and who, although defined as an investment adviser, is exempt from registration. If the person is not excluded and not exempt, then registration is required. In 1996, a major change to the registration requirements took place with the passage of the National Securities Markets Improvement Act (the NSMIA). Up until that time, investment advisers registered with both the federal agency (the SEC) and the appropriate states. However, the NSMIA bifurcated (split in two) those requirements by declaring that investment advisers would register with the SEC or the state(s), but not both. They did this by creating a new definition—*Federal Covered Investment Adviser*, sometimes just referred to as a covered adviser on the exam.

What makes someone a federal covered investment adviser? In most cases, they are the larger firms and are registered with the SEC. The three most tested categories are:

- those registered with the SEC because they are eligible ($100 million in assets under management) or required to register with the SEC because they meet the minimum threshold of assets under management (currently $110 million);

- those under contract to manage an investment company registered under the Investment Company Act of 1940, e.g., a mutual fund, regardless of the amount of assets under management; and

- those not registered with the SEC because they are excluded from the definition of an investment adviser by the Investment Advisers Act of 1940. (The most tested example of this case is the investment adviser whose advice is limited solely to securities issued by the U.S. government or one of its agencies.)

TAKE NOTE

Because so much of this exam deals with interpreting the laws, it is sometimes necessary to review some legal concepts with you. For example, if a person is excluded from the definition of investment adviser under the Investment Advisers Act of 1940, the states, under the NSMIA, cannot define such person as an investment adviser because federal law excluded that person from the definition. In other words, if the separate states could define those persons who were excluded from the federal definition as investment advisers, the federal law would have no meaning.

DODD-FRANK AND ASSETS UNDER MANAGEMENT

As stated previously, the NSMIA eliminated state registration requirements for federal covered advisers, largely based upon assets under management (AUM). Dodd-Frank has created three thresholds: one for the large adviser, one for the mid-size adviser, and, logically, one for the small adviser. Let's examine each of these; their requirements and their exceptions, if any.

Large Investment Advisers

Large advisers, those advisers with at least $100 million or more in assets under management, are eligible for SEC registration; once AUM reach $110 million, registration with the SEC is mandatory. Unless covered by one of the exemptions mentioned previously, all large IAs must register with the SEC. State registration is not required because the federal law preempts state registration.

Small Investment Advisers

This category includes advisers with AUM of less than $25 million. Unless the investment adviser is an adviser to an investment company registered under the Investment Company Act of 1940, registration with the SEC is prohibited and, unless exempted under state rules, registration with the state is required. However, if the adviser would be required to register in 15 or more states, the prohibition is lifted, and registration with the SEC would be permitted instead.

Mid-Size Advisers

This category includes those with AUM of at least $25 million but not $100 million. Generally, these advisers are prohibited from SEC registration and must register with the state. Just as with any other category, advisers to an investment company registered under the Investment Company Act of 1940 register with the SEC. That is true regardless of their size.

A mid-size firm can qualify for SEC registration several other ways. A mid-sized adviser is not prohibited from registering with the SEC:

- if the adviser is not required to be registered as an investment adviser with the securities Administrator of the state in which it maintains its principal office and place of business;

- if registered, the adviser would not be subject to examination as an investment adviser by that securities Administrator;

- if the adviser is required to register in 15 or more states; or

- if the adviser elects to take advantage of the buffer (described following).

Other Exceptions Under Dodd-Frank

The SEC is permitted to grant exceptions to advisers from the prohibition on Commission registration, including small and mid-sized advisers, if the application of the prohibition from registration would be "unfair, a burden on interstate commerce, or otherwise inconsistent with the purposes" of the Act. Under this authority, they have adopted several exemptions from the prohibition on registration with the SEC, including:

- pension consultants, but only those with at least $200 million under control—the SEC picked that number to ensure that, to register with the SEC, if desired, the consultant's activities are "significant enough to have an effect on national markets;"

- those mid-size advisers with at least $100 million in AUM, but less than $110 million in AUM who elect to register with the SEC rather than the state(s) (this buffer will be described following);

■ investment advisers expecting to be eligible for SEC registration within 120 days of filing the application for registration on the Form ADV; and

■ internet advisers.

The $10 Million and $20 Million Buffers

The numbers work like this: A state-registered adviser may, once it has AUM of at least $100 million (subject to certain of the exceptions previously mentioned, everyone needs at least $100 million to initiate registration with the SEC), may choose to remain state-registered or may register with the SEC. Once AUM reach $110 million, registration with the SEC is mandatory—they can no longer stay state-registered. That is the $10 million buffer.

The SEC recognized that market conditions (or obtaining or losing clients) can cause AUM to fluctuate so they established a $20 million buffer to keep advisers from having to switch back and forth. Once registered with the SEC, an investment adviser need not withdraw its SEC registration unless it has less than $90 million of AUM. Having become SEC registered, the IA can remain so as long as AUM remain at or above the $90 million level. Likewise, those investment advisers registered at the state level can choose to remain there until they reach the $110 million level. This buffer is designed to avoid the expense and hassle involved in potentially annual changes to where the investment adviser is registered.

Time for Measuring AUM

These numbers are based on the AUM reported on the IA's annual updating amendment. The effect of this is that a federal-covered adviser's AUM could drop below $90 million during the year without triggering the need to change to state registration, just as long as the annual update showed at least the minimum $90 million required. Of course, the same would be true of a state-registered IA whose AUM peaked above $110 million during the year but then fell at the time of the update. If, at the time of filing the annual updating amendment to the Form ADV by an SEC-registered IA, the reported AUM is less than $90 million, it is necessary for the investment adviser to withdraw its SEC registration and register with the appropriate state(s) within 180 days. On the other hand, if a state-registered adviser's reported AUM exceed $110 million, registration with the SEC must take place within 90 days.

TAKE NOTE

The buffer works because the measurement is made only once per year, at the time of the filing of the firm's annual updating amendment.

Remember these three relevant times:

1. When a state-registered IA reports AUM at $110 million or more on the annual updating amendment, the IA must withdraw from the states and register with the SEC within 90 days.

2. When a new investment adviser files for registration, if that IA believes that it will have at least $100 million in AUM within the first 120 days, it is eligible to register with the SEC, even if their AUM is way below that on day one. This is very common when a large BD decides to open an IA and knows that they'll have billions of dollars in a short time.

3. When an SEC-registered IA reports less than $90 million in AUM on the annual updating amendment, the IA must withdraw its registration with the SEC and register in the appropriate states within 180 days.

Why is the time allowed in #3 twice as long as in #1? Because it takes much less time to register with one agency, the SEC, than to register potentially with a number of states.

TAKE NOTE

As a general rule, the SEC or federal rules involve bigger numbers than the state rules—that is, large investment advisers must register with the SEC, whereas small investment advisers must register with the state.

Adviser managing . . .

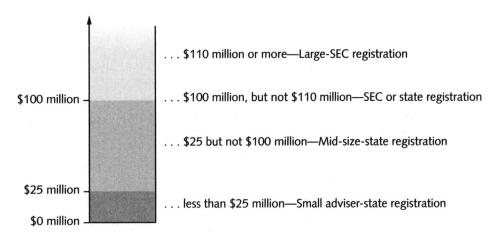

. . . $110 million or more—Large-SEC registration

. . . $100 million, but not $110 million—SEC or state registration

. . . $25 but not $100 million—Mid-size-state registration

. . . less than $25 million—Small adviser-state registration

$100 million

$25 million

$0 million

Registration Process

How does registration take place?

With only a few differences, the procedures for registering as an investment adviser are the same, whether registering with the SEC or with the states. Those differences will be pointed out as we go along.

To register with the state securities Administrator, a person must:

■ submit an application;

■ provide a consent to service of process;

■ pay filing fees;

■ post a bond (if required by the Administrator); and

■ take and pass an examination if required by the Administrator. The examination may be written, oral, or both.

Registration is accomplished using the Form ADV. The Form ADV consists of Part 1A and Part 1B, and Part 2A, and Part 2B. Investment advisers use Form ADV to:

■ register with the Securities and Exchange Commission;

■ register with one or more state securities authorities; or

■ amend those registrations.

Filing in almost all cases is done through the Investment Adviser Registration Depository (IARD). The IARD is an electronic filing system that facilitates investment adviser registration, regulatory review, and the public disclosure information of investment adviser firms.

HOW IS FORM ADV ORGANIZED?

Form ADV contains four parts: Part 1A asks a number of questions about the investment adviser, its business practices, the persons who own and control the firm, and the persons who provide investment advice on behalf of the firm. All advisers registering with the SEC or any of the state securities authorities must complete Part 1A.

Part 1A also contains several supplemental schedules. These include:

- Schedule A, which asks for information about the direct owners and executive officers (control persons); and

- Disclosure Reporting Pages (or DRPs), which are schedules that ask for details about disciplinary events involving the adviser or advisory affiliates.

Part 1B asks additional questions required by state securities authorities. Investment advisers applying for registration or who are registered only with the SEC do not have to complete Part 1B.

Part 2A requires advisers to create narrative **brochures** containing information about the advisory firm. The requirements in Part 2A apply to all investment advisers registered with or applying for registration with the SEC or the states.

Part 2B requires advisers to create **brochure supplements** containing information about certain supervised persons. The requirements in Part 2B apply to all investment advisers registered with or applying for registration with the SEC or the states.

It may help you remember that the **A** in Part 2**A** tells us that that part is for the **A**dviser and the **B** in Part 2 is about the **B**odies (the people) who work there.

We will cover the brochures and brochure supplements in greater detail later in Unit 6.

TEST TOPIC ALERT

Control means the power, directly or indirectly, to direct the management or policies of an investment adviser, whether through ownership of securities, by contract, or otherwise. Under the Investment Advisers Act of 1940 as well as NASAA's Model Rule, each of the firm's officers, partners, or directors exercising executive responsibility (or persons having similar status or functions) is presumed to control the firm.

A person is presumed to control an IA organized as a corporation if the person directly or indirectly has the right to vote 25% or more of a class of the corporation's voting securities; a person is presumed to control one that is a partnership if the person has the right to receive upon dissolution, or has contributed, 25% or more of the capital of the partnership.

Please note that this is a different percentage from the definition of control person under the Securities Exchange Act of 1934 (Unit 7), where having more than 10% of the voting power makes one a control person. Remember that control person is defined three different ways: the Exchange Act requires more than 10%, the Investment Company Act (Unit 14), requires *more than* 25%, and the Advisers Act and the USA require 25% *or more*.

Form ADV

Part 1 contains information about the IA, including:

- location of principal office;

- location of books and records (if not at the principal office);

- form of business organization (sole proprietorship, partnership, corporation, LLC, and so forth);

- method of business;

- other business activities [broker-dealer, registered representative (agent) of a BD];

- maintaining custody of customer assets or exercising discretion;

- details relating to all control persons (officers, directors, partners, etc.);

- disciplinary history; and

- for state-registered IAs, states in which the IA intends to or is already registered.

Part 1B asks additional questions required by state securities authorities. Federal covered advisers do not complete the Part 1B.

Part 2A is known as the investment adviser's brochure and tends to focus on customer related information, such as:

- compensation arrangements (fees, commissions, hourly charge);

- types of clients (individuals, institutions, pension plans);

- type of investments (equities, corporate debt, municipal securities, U.S. treasuries, investment companies);

- types of strategies employed (buy and hold, value, growth);

- methods of analysis used (technical, fundamental);

- educational and business background of those who render advice; and

- an audited balance sheet if a federal or state-registered adviser requires or solicits *substantial* prepayment of fees (defined shortly) or if a state-registered adviser maintains custody (discussed at Unit 7).

The brochure is arranged in a narrative form using plain English.

Part 2B requires advisers to create brochure supplements containing information about certain supervised persons. Together, Part 2A and Part 2B are delivered to the client as described later in this unit.

State-registered advisers file *both* Part 1 and Part 2 with the Administrator of each state in which they are registering.

EXAMPLE

1. If a prospective client wanted to know what type of investment strategies are employed by an investment adviser, that information would be found in the adviser's

   A. Form ADV Part 1A

   B. Form ADV Part 1B

   C. Form ADV Part 2A

   D. Form ADV Part 2B

   Answer: C. The Form ADV Part 2A contains information of most use to clients, such as the type of strategies employed by the adviser. Part 1A contains information needed by the regulators; Part 1B is only for state-registered IAs; Part 2B contains information dealing with those individuals in the firm who manage accounts.

TEST TOPIC ALERT

Although there are no minimum educational or experience requirements, there is a specific area on the Form ADV Part 2 where state-registered advisers must identify each of the principal executive officers and management persons, and describe their formal education and business background. If this information has been supplied elsewhere in the Form ADV, it is not necessary to repeat it in response to this question.

Updating the Form ADV

The Form ADV must be updated each year by filing an annual updating amendment within 90 days after the end of the adviser's fiscal year. This annual updating amendment is used to update the responses to all items on the ADV. Of critical importance is the verification of AUM ensuring that the adviser is eligible to continue being registered with the SEC. One of the requirements relating to the brochure described in Part 2 is that submission must be made of a summary of material changes either in the brochure (cover page or the page immediately thereafter) or as an exhibit to the brochure.

Amendments for Material Changes

In addition to the annual updating amendment, the IA must amend the Form ADV by filing additional amendments promptly if information relating to any of the following changes or becomes inaccurate in any way:

- Change of the registrant's name
- Change in the principal business location
- Change in the location of books and records, if they are kept somewhere other than at the principal location
- Change to the contact person preparing the form
- Change in organizational structure, such as from partnership to corporation and so on
- Information provided in the brochure becomes materially inaccurate
- Change to any of the questions regarding disciplinary actions
- Change in policy regarding custody of the customer funds and/or securities

Fees

In addition to the initial registration, there is a requirement for annual renewal. There are fees for the initial filing and renewals. If an investment adviser changes its form of business organization (e.g., from a sole proprietorship to a corporation), a new ADV, but no fees, would be required.

TEST TOPIC ALERT   Successor Firm

Under both federal and state law, a successor firm registers by filing a new application and, in the case of the SEC, paying the appropriate fee and, under the USA, without additional fee. Please note the difference—one case involves a fee, the other does not.

Notice Filing

While on the topic of fees, it is important to recognize what happened to state revenues after the passage of the NSMIA. Prior to that time, investment advisers registered on both levels and that meant, in many cases, registering with 20, 30 or more states with each state collecting a nice fee. When state lobbyists realized that the NSMIA, by excluding federal covered advisers from the definition, meant that those advisers would no longer have to register, they implored Congress to put some condition into the act that would help recover some of that lost revenue. That is how notice filing came about.

Instead of registering with the state(s), covered advisers pay state filing fees and give notice to the Administrator. The procedure followed is called **notice filing**. As part of the notice filing, the Administrator can require a federal covered adviser to file a copy of whatever has been filed with the SEC, and, of course, pay a filing fee.

TEST TOPIC ALERT

Federal covered advisers must make a notice filing with the state if they have a place of business in the state or have six or more clients in that state in a 12-month period, regardless of place of business.

If a federal covered adviser only deals with institutions, other IAs, other BDs, and so forth, notice filing is not required. This is a similar concept to the USA not requiring registration of state-registered advisers who have no place of business in the state and deal with this same group of clients. We have not heard of this ever being asked on the exam, but, you never know what NASAA has up their sleeve.

Provide a Consent to Service of Process

New applicants for registration must provide the Administrator of every state in which they intend to register with a **consent to service of process**. The consent to service of process appoints the Administrator as the applicant's attorney to receive and process noncriminal securities-related complaints against the applicant. Under the consent to service of process, all legal documents (e.g., subpoenas or warrants) received by the Administrator have the same legal effect as if they had been served personally on the applicant.

TAKE NOTE

The consent to service of process is submitted with the initial application and remains in force permanently. It does not need to be supplied with each renewal of a registration.

Effective Date of Registration and Renewals

Assuming there are no irregularities in the application, registration with the SEC takes effect on the 45th day after filing of a complete application and, as with all securities professionals, at noon of the 30th day in the case of state-registered investment advisers.

TEST TOPIC ALERT

One of the most common questions asked on the exam is the renewal date for the **state** registration of investment advisers (and the other securities professionals—investment adviser representatives [IAR], broker-dealers, and agents). That renewal date is December 31. One of the tricks the exam likes to play is asking about a person who registers in November. When does that registration come up for renewal? Well, even if it is only a month or so later, every registration of a securities professional comes up for renewal on the next December 31, so your first year is always a short one.

Definition: Agent

The USA defines an **agent** as any individual who represents a broker-dealer (legal entity) or an issuer (legal entity) in effecting (or attempting to effect) transactions in securities for their clients. You will learn more about that in Unit 3 LO3.

TEST TOPIC ALERT

Although registration normally takes 30 days, the Administrator has the power to shorten that period, in effect permitting a rush order.

TEST TOPIC ALERT

Although successful completion of the Series 65 examination may satisfy a portion of the requirements of a particular state, it does not convey the right to transact business before being granted a license or registration by that state.

EXAMPLE

While registration as an IAR is pending, the individual may not take part in any activity that would require registration. Clerical work (filing customer records) or assisting internally with research would be permitted.

Just as the exam may ask about registering, it may ask about leaving the business.

Form ADV-W

If an adviser no longer desires to engage in the business, application to withdraw registration is accomplished by filing **Form ADV-W**. Form ADV-W must be filed to withdraw the registration voluntarily.

As is typical, the timing is different under federal and state law. For covered advisers, the withdrawal takes 60 days. In the case of a state-registered adviser, it is 30 days after filing. A testable point is that the Administrator retains jurisdiction over the former registrant for a period of one year.

In Unit 5, we'll discuss the conditions under which a registration may be canceled by the Administrator.

Exempt Reporting Advisers (ERAs)

As described previously, there is an exemption from registration for certain private funds and venture capital funds. However, even though exempt from registration, if designated as ERAs, they are required to complete and electronically file reports using the IARD system on certain items set forth in Form ADV, which will be made publicly available on the SEC's website.

TEST TOPIC ALERT

Exempt Reporting Advisers (ERAs) File an abbreviated Form ADV Part 1 (they don't answer all of the questions), but do not have to prepare a Form ADV Part 2.

FINANCIAL REQUIREMENTS FOR REGISTRATION AS AN INVESTMENT ADVISER

Under the Investment Advisers Act of 1940, no specific financial requirements, such as a minimum net worth, are spelled out. However, as we will see, there are financial disclosures that must be made to clients under certain conditions.

Under the Uniform Securities Act, the Administrator may, by rule or order, establish minimum financial requirements for an investment adviser registered in the state. Those will be discussed shortly.

Substantial Prepayment of Fees

Both state and federal law offer extra protection to those clients of investment advisers who have made substantial advance payment of fees for services to be rendered in the future. The term used is *substantial prepayment of fees.* In the case of a federal covered adviser, it is considered substantial if the IA collects prepayments of more than $1,200 per client, six months or more in advance. Under the NASAA Model Rule, it is more than $500, and again, six months or more in advance.

TEST TOPIC ALERT

When a state-registered investment adviser accepts prepayments of fees of *more* than $500 for a contract period of six months OR more, it is known as a substantial prepayment. However, under the Investment Advisers Act of 1940, it does not become a substantial prepayment until it exceeds $1,200.

This might appear on your exam as:

EXAMPLE

1. Which of the following would an Administrator consider to be a substantial prepayment of fees?

   A. $500 covering the next six months

   B. $800 covering the entire contract year

   C. $800 covering the next calendar quarter

   D. $5,000 covering the next month

   Answer: B. NASAA (state law) defines a substantial prepayment of fees to be more than $500, 6 or more months in advance. While $800 and $5,000 are certainly more than $500, they cover a shorter period than 6 months.

Balance Sheet Requirement for Federal Covered Advisers

Any federal covered investment adviser whose agreement requires *substantial prepayment of fees* (as previously defined) from clients, must include a balance sheet with the adviser's ADV Part 2A for the adviser's most recent fiscal year. The balance sheet must be prepared and audited by an independent public accountant.

Balance Sheet Requirements for State-Registered Advisers

An audited balance sheet must be included with the ADV Part 2A for any state-registered investment adviser whose agreement requires *substantial prepayment of fees* (as defined previously) from clients. In addition, even without the fees, those who maintain custody of client funds and/or securities (covered at Unit 7), must include an audited balance sheet with their ADV Part 2A for their most recent fiscal year with the same requirements. The audited balance sheet is also required when the custodian is a related (affiliated) broker-dealer. Furthermore, state-registered advisers who exercise discretionary authority over client accounts but do not maintain custody must file with the Administrator within 90 days of the end of the adviser's fiscal year a balance sheet, but this one does not have to be audited.

Disclosure of Financial Impairment

Any investment adviser that has *discretionary* authority or *custody* of client funds or securities, or requires or solicits *substantial prepayment of fees*, must disclose any financial condition that is reasonably likely to impair its ability to meet contractual commitments to its clients. As an example, the SEC has indicated that disclosure may be required of any arbitration award "sufficiently large that payment of it would create such a financial condition."

Here is the way it is stated in the Form ADV Part 2:

> "If you have discretionary authority or custody of client funds or securities, or you require or solicit prepayment of more than $1,200 in fees per client, six months or more in advance, you must disclose any financial condition that is reasonably likely to impair your ability to meet contractual commitments to clients."[3]

---

3   Form ADV Part 2 Instructions, Item 18 B

TEST TOPIC ALERT

The Administrator may require an adviser who has *custody* of client funds or securities or has *discretion* over a client's account to post a surety bond or maintain a minimum net worth. Usually, the requirement is higher for custody than for discretion. Typically, the net worth required of investment advisers with discretionary authority is $10,000 and that for those taking custody is $35,000. If the adviser is using a surety bond instead, the requirement in either case is $35,000. An adviser who does not exercise discretion and does not maintain custody, but does accept prepayment of fees of more than $500, six or more months in advance, must maintain a positive net worth at all times.

Definition: Surety Bond

Usually issued by an insurance company (the surety) who guarantees payment of a specified sum to an injured party (either the client or the Administrator) when the securities professional causes damages by his actions or fails to perform.

TEST TOPIC ALERT

Because the USA is only a template, some states have higher net worth or bonding requirements. The exam may want you to know that if an IA meets the net worth or surety bonding requirements of the state where its principal office is located, that is sufficient in any other state in which it may be registered.

Definition: Principal Office

We've used this term several times and it is an important one to know. Both state and federal law define this as "the executive office of the investment adviser from which the officers, partners, or managers of the investment adviser direct, control, and coordinate the activities of the investment adviser."

EXAMPLE

1. Mammon Money Managers (MMM) has its principal office in State A and is also registered in States B, C, and D. MMM exercises discretion in client accounts. As a result, MMM would have to meet the net worth or bonding requirements of

    A. the SEC

    B. State A

    C. the state with the highest requirement

    D. each state

    Answer: B. A state-registered investment adviser need only meet the financial requirements of the state in which its principal office is located. SEC requirements are meaningless here because this is a state-registered firm.

TEST TOPIC ALERT

One of the effects of the NSMIA is to limit the powers of an Administrator over a federal covered adviser. Section 222 of the Investment Advisers Act of 1940 states that when it comes to federal covered advisers, any financial or bonding requirements, as well as rules relating to recordkeeping, are solely under federal jurisdiction.

TEST TOPIC ALERT

The proper term to use when referring to the financial requirements of an investment adviser is *net worth*, while for broker-dealers it is *net capital*. However, we have heard from a number of students that NASAA might be using net capital where they should be using net worth in questions about IAs. So, if you want to get the question right, answer it the way they give it to you. You will see several examples of this in our practice questions.

Failure to Maintain Minimum Net Worth

NASAA's Model Rule specifies the action to be taken by a registered investment adviser whose net worth falls below the required minimum. By the close of business on the next business day, the adviser must notify the Administrator that the investment adviser's net worth is less than the minimum required. After sending that notice, the adviser must file a financial report with the Administrator by the close of business on the next business day. One more item that must be included in the report is the number of client accounts. When the adviser's net worth is below the minimum requirement, the adviser must obtain a bond in an amount of the net worth deficiency rounded up to the nearest $5,000.

EXAMPLE

A state-registered investment adviser discovers on *Monday* that its net worth is below the minimum requirement. No later than the close of business on *Tuesday*, notice must be sent to the Administrator of the state in which the investment adviser has its principal office. Then, no later than the close of business on *Wednesday*, the investment adviser must file a detailed report with the Administrator of its financial condition. Included in the report must be a statement as to the number of client accounts.

EXAMPLE

An investment adviser who maintains custody of customer funds and securities discovers that its net worth is only $23,000. Even though the adviser only needs a net worth of $35,000, this would require immediate surety bonding in the amount of $15,000 because it must be rounded up to the nearest $5,000.

Computing Net Worth

At Part 2, Unit 9, LO1, we'll learn about computing net worth from a corporate balance sheet. For NASAA purposes, the term net worth is the excess of assets over liabilities, (assets minus liabilities). However, NASAA does not permit the investment adviser to include the following as assets:

- Goodwill and all other assets of an intangible nature, home, home furnishings, automobile(s), and any other personal items not readily marketable in the case of an individual

- Advances or loans to stockholders and officers in the case of a corporation

- Advances or loans to partners in the case of a partnership

However, furniture used in the office, such as a sofa in the reception room, or bookcases in the company research library, are considered assets for the purpose of the computation.

BOOKS AND RECORDS REQUIRED BY FEDERAL AND STATE LAW

The Uniform Securities Act virtually duplicates the first 12 items of the recordkeeping requirements of the Investment Advisers Act of 1940 listed following. The major exception is that on the 11th bullet (a copy of each notice), NASAA's Model Rule requires a copy when the material is distributed to two or more persons (other than persons connected with the investment adviser), not 10 or more, as is the case under federal law.

Unless the investment adviser is exempt from registration, the SEC and the states require investment advisers to maintain the following books and records:

- A journal, including cash receipts and disbursement records

- General and auxiliary ledgers reflecting asset, liability, reserve, capital, income, and expense accounts

- A memorandum of each order given by the adviser for the purchase or sale of any security, or any instruction received by the adviser from the client concerning the purchase, sale, receipt, or delivery of a security, and of any modification or cancellation of any such order or instruction

- All checkbooks, bank statements, canceled checks, and cash reconciliations

- All bills or statements (or copies thereof) paid or unpaid

- All trial balances, financial statements, and internal audit working papers

- Originals of all written communications received and copies of all written communications sent by the adviser related to any recommendation or advice given or proposed to be given; any receipt, disbursement, or delivery of funds or securities; or the placing or execution of any order to purchase or sell any security (provided, however, that if the investment adviser sends any notice, circular, or other advertisement offering any report, analysis, publication, or other investment advisory service to more than 10 persons, the investment adviser shall not be required to keep a record of the names and addresses of the persons to whom it was sent; except that if the notice, circular, or advertisement is distributed to persons named on any list, the investment adviser shall retain with the copy of the notice, circular, or advertisement, a memorandum describing the list and its source.)

- A record of all accounts in which the adviser is vested with any discretionary power with respect to the funds, securities, or transactions of any client

- All powers of attorney and other evidences of the granting of any discretionary authority by any client to the adviser, or copies thereof

- All written agreements (or copies thereof) entered into by the adviser with a client or otherwise relating to its investment advisory business

- A file containing a copy of each notice, circular, advertisement, newspaper article, investment letter, bulletin, or other communication, including by electronic media (email), that the investment adviser circulates or distributes, directly or indirectly, to 10 or more persons (other than persons connected with the investment adviser); if the item, including communications by electronic media recommends the purchase or sale of a specific security and does not state the reasons for the recommendation, the adviser must prepare a memorandum indicating the reasons for that recommendation

- A file containing a copy of all written communications received or sent regarding any litigation involving the investment adviser or any investment adviser representative or employee, and regarding any written customer or client complaint

- A file containing a copy of each document that pertains to the registrant or its investment adviser representatives. That file should contain, but is not limited to, all applications, amendments, renewal filings, and correspondence.

- With certain exceptions, a record of all securities transactions in which an investment adviser or any advisory representative has, or by reason of such transaction acquires, any direct or beneficial ownership

In practice, the recordkeeping rule has served as a deterrent to the practice of scalping because it requires all advisory representatives to report all of their security transactions to their affiliated advisory firms on a regular basis; these reports are subject to SEC examination. **Scalping** is the practice whereby an investment adviser, before the dissemination of a securities recommendation, trades on the anticipated short-run market activity that may result from the recommendation.

Time Period for Maintenance of Records

The Investment Advisers Act of 1940, as well as the NASAA Model Rule on recordkeeping requirements for investment advisers, requires that an investment adviser's books and records be maintained in a readily accessible place for five years. The five-year period will run from the end of the fiscal year during which the last entry was made on the record. During the first two years of the five-year period, the rule requires that the records be maintained in the principal office of the adviser. However, after this initial two-year period, the records may be preserved in electronic or microfilm format or any other form of data storage in compliance with the act. Even though the recordkeeping requirements are almost identical, it is important to remember for the test that federal covered advisers only comply with the SEC's requirements while state-registered advisers need only meet the requirements of the state where their principal office is located.

The NASAA Model Rule also states that partnership articles and any amendments thereto, articles of incorporation, charters, minute books, and stock certificate books of the investment adviser and of any predecessor must be maintained in the principal office of the investment adviser and preserved until at least three years after termination of the enterprise.

 TEST TOPIC ALERT

A few pages ago, we gave you a Test Topic Alert that emphasized that as long as state-registered investment advisers met the net worth or surety bond requirements of their home state, that was sufficient for any state in which they are registered. The same is true regarding recordkeeping requirements and the proof is in the following statement copied from the Form ADV:

> 2. State-Registered Investment Adviser Affidavit

> If you are subject to state regulation, by signing this Form ADV, you represent that, you are in compliance with the registration requirements of the state in which you maintain your principal place of business and are in compliance with the bonding, capital, and recordkeeping requirements of that state.

Storage Requirements

The records required to be maintained and preserved may be maintained and preserved for the required time by an investment adviser on:

- paper or hard copy form, as those records are kept in their original form;
- micrographic media, including microfilm, microfiche, or any similar medium; or
- electronic storage media, including any digital (computer disk) storage medium or system as long as the investment adviser establishes and maintains procedures
    - to maintain and preserve the records, so as to reasonably safeguard them from loss, alteration, or destruction,
    - to limit access to the records to properly authorized personnel and the Administrator, and
    - to reasonably ensure that any reproduction of a non-electronic original record on electronic storage media is complete, true, and legible when retrieved.

In all cases, the investment adviser must arrange and index the records in a way that permits easy location, access, and retrieval of any particular record and provide the Administrator with the means to access, view, and print the records.

Here are a couple of examples for you:

EXAMPLE

1. Under the Investment Advisers Act of 1940, all of the following are true regarding adviser recordkeeping EXCEPT

    A. the IA must keep records of transactions made for its own account as well as the account of investment adviser representatives to lessen the likelihood of scalping

    B. computer-generated records may be stored in that format

    C. client account records must be maintained, including a list of recommendations made

    D. records must be maintained for a period of 2 years from the end of the fiscal year in which the last entry was made

    Answer: D. This is the exception because the records must be kept for 5 years. Nothing in the question asked about the 2-year requirement in the office. The 5-year requirement is that records be easily accessible whether in the office or not.

2. An investment adviser registered in State G is obligated to maintain certain books and records as specified by the Uniform Securities Act. Which of the following statements regarding adviser recordkeeping is NOT true?

    A. Records originally created on computer may be stored in electronic media.

    B. Records are subject to surprise audits by the State G Administrator.

    C. Written records may be reduced to microfilm.

    D. Records must be kept for six years.

    Answer: D. Records of an investment adviser must be maintained for five years. Records are subject to surprise audits by the state Administrator, written records may be reduced to microfilm, and records originally created on a company's computer may be stored in electronic media.

TEST TOPIC ALERT

You will need to remember that the record retention requirement for investment advisers is five years from the end of the year in which the record was originally generated.

SUPERVISORY REQUIREMENTS

U1LO6: Recognize that investment adviser representatives must be adequately supervised.

Each registered investment adviser must adopt and implement written policies and procedures designed to prevent violation of the federal and state securities laws, review those policies and procedures **annually** for their adequacy and the effectiveness of their implementation, and designate a **chief compliance officer** (CCO) to be responsible for administering the policies and procedures. An adviser's CCO should be competent and knowledgeable regarding the Advisers Act and the USA and should be empowered with full responsibility and authority to develop and enforce appropriate policies and procedures for the firm. Thus, the compliance officer should have a position of sufficient seniority and authority within the organization to compel others to adhere to the compliance policies and procedures. In fact, the CCO's identity must be disclosed on the Form ADV.

The role of the CCO is particularly important when it comes to ensuring supervision of those individuals referred to as "supervised persons."

Definition: Supervised Person

Any of the IAs officers, partners, directors (or other persons occupying a similar status or performing similar functions), or employees, or any other person who provides investment advice on the investment adviser's behalf and is subject to its supervision or control. The most common example is the investment adviser representative (defined in Unit 2).

Although many supervised persons fall within the definition of "investment adviser," (they meet the three-prong test), the SEC and the states do not require those individuals to register as investment advisers with the regulators. Instead, the advisory firm must register. The adviser's registration covers its employees and other persons under its control, provided that their advisory activities are undertaken on the investment adviser's behalf. However, in most cases, these individuals must register as investment adviser representatives and come under the adviser's supervisory jurisdiction.

This is particularly true in the case of financial planners who have elected to operate as independent contractors, not employees of investment advisory firms. Regardless, they are required to be registered as investment adviser representatives of the firm and must be placed under the same level of supervisory scrutiny as employees. Their business cards may contain the name of their separate planning entity, but must also disclose the name of the entity registered as the investment adviser.

UNIT 2

Regulation of Investment Adviser Representatives

LEARNING OBJECTIVES

When you have completed this unit, you will be able to accomplish the following.

U2LO1: Define investment adviser representative.

U2LO2: Identify exclusions and exemptions under the Investment Advisers Act of 1940 and the Uniform Securities Act.

U2LO3: Describe the investment adviser representative registration requirements and process, post registration filings, and business activities.

INTRODUCTION

In Unit 1, we defined an investment adviser, determined who was excluded from the definition or exempt from registration and, if required to register, with whom and how. In this unit, we will cover those individuals who represent investment advisers—investment adviser representatives. One important regulatory note is that, unlike investment advisers who register either on a federal or a state level, registration requirements of representatives only comes under the jurisdiction of the states. That is why this is a NASAA exam rather than one sponsored by FINRA or the SEC.

The exam will contain four questions on this unit.

INVESTMENT ADVISER REPRESENTATIVES

U2LO1: Define investment adviser representative.

Investment adviser representative (IAR) means any partner, officer, director (or an individual occupying a similar status or performing similar functions), or other individual employed by or associated with an investment adviser and is registered or required to be registered under the Uniform Securities Act. Remember, IARs only register with the states. An individual meets the definition of an IAR by doing any of the following:

- Makes any recommendations or otherwise renders advice regarding securities
- Manages accounts or portfolios of clients
- Determines which recommendation or advice regarding securities should be given
- Solicits, offers, or negotiates for the sale of or sells investment advisory services
- Supervises employees who perform any of the foregoing

EXAMPLE

An individual employed by an investment adviser who manages investment portfolios for clients is considered an investment adviser representative. So is the individual who supervises that person. Under state law, there is no distinct registration for supervisory persons as there is under FINRA's rules for broker-dealers; even the CEO is registered as an IAR.

TAKE NOTE

The use of the term *individual* here is important. Only an individual, or a natural person, can be an investment adviser representative. The investment advisory firm is the legal person (entity) that the IAR (natural person) represents in performing the functions listed above.

TAKE NOTE

An individual may act as both an investment adviser and an investment adviser representative. This is typically the case when the business is organized as a sole proprietorship. However, an individual who acts solely as an investment adviser representative is excluded from the definition of investment adviser.

IAR EXCLUSIONS AND EXEMPTIONS

U2LO2: Identify exclusions and exemptions under the Investment Advisers Act of 1940 and the Uniform Securities Act.

Just as with investment advisers, the laws provide for exclusions for the definition and exemptions for those who are defined as IARs.

Exclusions from the Definition of Investment Adviser Representative

Certain employees of investment advisory firms are excluded from the term *investment adviser representative*, provided their activities are confined to clerical or administrative duties or those activities that are solely incidental to the investment advisory services offered, such as mailing out a research report to an advisory client when directed by an IAR. Should the investment advisory employee "step over the line" as the saying goes, and perform any activity that makes one an IAR, the employee would then have to register as an investment adviser representative.

In addition, an individual is not an investment adviser representative if the person does not on a regular basis solicit, meet with, or otherwise communicate with clients of the investment adviser or provides only impersonal investment advice.

Let's define that last term because you're going to see it a number of times in this course. Impersonal investment advice means investment advisory services provided by means of written material or oral statements that do not purport to meet the objectives or needs of specific individuals or accounts.

EXAMPLE

1. Which of the following individuals would be defined as an investment adviser representative?

    A. Melinda, one of the firm's research analysts, who has no contact with public clients

    B. Johnny, an employee who makes cold calls soliciting for new advisory clients

    C. Mel, who prepares client account statements

    D. Jane, who is the firm's VP of HR services

    Answer: B. One of the functions making a supervised person an IAR is soliciting for new business. Research personnel are not considered IARs unless they have client relationships. Mel's job is purely clerical and, even though Jane is a vice president, the HR department is far removed from anything to do with giving investment advice.

Exemptions from Registration as an Investment Adviser Representative

There are three different exemptions available for those defined as IARs. Two of those are for those who represent state-registered IAs and the other for those who represent federal covered IAs.

■ If the individual represents a state-registered adviser, there is a de minimis exemption. Just as is the case with investment advisers, if an IAR does not maintain a place of business in the state and, during the preceding 12-month period has had no more than five retail clients, registration in the state is not required.

■ The previously mentioned *snowbird* exemption also applies to these IARs.

■ If the individual represents a covered investment adviser, there is a special exemption under Section 203A of the 1940 Act. Keeping it simple, it states that for those performing as IARs for federal covered advisers, IAR registration is required only in those states where that individual has a place of business. Place of business of an investment adviser representative means:

    a. an office at which the investment adviser representative regularly provides investment advisory services, solicits, meets with, or otherwise communicates with clients; and

    b. any other location that is held out to the general public as a location at which the investment adviser representative provides investment advisory services, solicits, meets with, or otherwise communicates with clients.

Let's look at some examples.

EXAMPLE

1. Under the Uniform Securities Act, which of the following is NOT required to register as an investment adviser representative

   A. A director of a state-registered investment advisory firm who determines specific recommendations for clients

   B. An associate in an SEC-registered investment advisory firm who has a place of business in the state and manages the account of only one individual client

   C. A clerk employed by a state-registered investment advisory firm

   D. A vice president of a state-registered investment advisory firm who supervises employees who solicit clients for the firm

   Answer: C. Clerical and ministerial (administrative) personnel are specifically excluded from the definition of investment adviser representative. Specifically included in the definition are directors, officers, partners, associates, and employees of state-registered advisers who carry out investment advisory or solicitation functions or who supervise those functions. Also included in the definition are persons who perform similar functions for SEC-registered advisers and who have a place of business in the state.

Try this one:

EXAMPLE

1. Which of the following individuals would be required to register with the Administrator of a state?

   A. Walter, who represents a state-registered adviser, has no place of business in the state, and only serves existing clients who vacation in the state.

   B. May, who represents a covered adviser, has no place of business in the state and has 38 clients who reside in the state.

   C. Aliza, who represents a state-registered adviser, has no place of business in the state and had fewer than 6 individual clients who were residents of the state during the past 12 months.

   D. Joe, who represents a covered adviser, has a place of business in the state, and had 4 retail clients who were residents of the state during the past 12 months.

   Answer: D. Even though he represents a federal covered adviser, once an IAR maintains a place of business in a state, Joe must register in that state regardless of the number of clients. Walter need not register because he qualifies for the snowbird exemption. May qualifies for the exemption as an IAR of a federal covered investment adviser. She is only required to register in those states where she maintains a place of business. Aliza qualifies for the de minimis exemption (fewer than 6 is the same as 5 or fewer).

   Important note: Even if May's employer had a place of business in the state, she would not have to register because she, the IAR, doesn't. Of course, her employer, being federal covered, doesn't register in any states.

EXAMPLE

1. Wealth Management Experts (WME) is an investment adviser registered in State X, the location of its only offices. During the past 12 months, WME has directed investment advice to 6 individual clients in State Y. This means that WME

    A. is required to register in State Y because it has exceeded the de minimis limit

    B. is not required to register in State Y because it is within the de minimis limit

    C. does not need to register in State Y if that state has a reciprocal licensing arrangement with State X

    D. would be required to register in State Y as soon as advice was directed to a single retail client

    Answer: A. What is the de minimis exemption? It is available to an investment adviser who does not maintain a place of business in the state and limits its business to 5 or fewer retail clients who are legal residents in the state during the preceding 12 months. That would make **A** the correct answer because 6 is above the limit of 5. There is no such thing as a reciprocal licensing arrangement between states. How would things change if the question was worded to say that there were 6 clients, 3 of whom were retail and the other 3 insurance companies? In that case, no registration would be required because the retail clients are within the de minimis limit, and there is no limit on the number of institutional clients an investment adviser can have in a state without the need to register (as long as there is no place of business in the state).

Completing our examples, suppose you had a question like this on your exam:

EXAMPLE

1. An IAR representing a state-registered investment adviser would NOT qualify for the de minimis exemption in a state if, over a 12-month period, she had

    A. 5 retail clients

    B. 5 or fewer retail clients

    C. fewer than 6 retail clients

    D. 6 or fewer retail clients

    Answer: D. Because the maximum is 5 retail clients in a 12-month period, choice D with 6 clients is over the limit. Notice that, "fewer than 6" and "5 or fewer" mean the same thing.

REGISTRATION REQUIREMENTS FOR INVESTMENT ADVISER REPRESENTATIVES

U2LO3: Describe the investment adviser representative registration requirements and process, post registration filings, and business activities.

As we learned with investment advisers, if you are not excluded from the definition of investment adviser representative or if you don't qualify for one of the exemptions, then you have to register. As pointed out earlier, it is only on the state level that an IAR registers so we don't have the issue of comparing state and federal law as we do with IAs.

Unless properly registered, it is unlawful for any registered investment adviser to engage the services of an individual as an investment adviser representative if that individual is required to register. This is true whether the investment adviser is state-registered or federal covered. All IARs must be registered in at least one state. (They have to have a place of business somewhere, right?)

Registration is accomplished by filing a Form U4 (a Form U10 can be used in certain cases, but that is unlikely to be tested) through FINRA's CRD (Central Registration Depository). Most of you have already completed that Form so you know it asks about your personal history and details. One of the most important parts is the DRPs, the Disclosure Reporting Pages. It is on these pages that the applicant discloses past disciplinary events. The Form U4 requires disclosing if you have *ever* been convicted or even just *arrested*, (charged), with no time limit, for any felony or securities-related misdemeanors. In unit 5, we'll discuss how those can affect the application. Another important part of the Form U4 is the Consent to Service of Process, mentioned earlier at Unit 1 LO4 in conjunction with the registration of an IA.

Here are two important items dealing with registration that are frequently tested.

1. The Uniform Securities Act states, "Registration of an investment adviser automatically constitutes registration of any investment adviser representative who is a partner, officer, or director, or a person occupying a similar status or performing similar functions."

It isn't only the title that determines your registration, it is the function performed. Note that this quoted rule states that the partner, officer, or director of the investment adviser is an IAR. Doesn't that mean they are already registered? What is the purpose of "automatic" registration to someone already registered?

When a state-registered IA expands its business so that registration is required in another state (or states), the application process is basically the same as their initial state registration. That is, a Form ADV is filed. That filing includes the names and other pertinent information about all of the partners, officers, or directors who are already acting as IARs. Therefore, when the firm's registration becomes effective in that new state, those individuals included in the filing are granted automatic registration—they don't have to file an individual Form U4. Please note, it is not any IAR, it is only those listed, or, as the rule states, those occupying a similar status, etc., who receive this treatment. Any of the firm's other existing IARs who will need to be registered in the new state, must file an amended Form U4 with the Administrator and wait for their supervisor to tell them that the firm has received the word that their registration is effective with that state.

Here is the way this might be presented on the exam.

EXAMPLE

1. When an investment adviser registers in a new state, who of the following is automatically registered as IARs?

   A. Any employee who is functioning as an IAR in at least one state

   B. Officers, partners, and directors of the firm who are functioning as IARs

   C. Clerical employees stuffing the envelopes with research reports

   D. Any employee who will be soliciting clients for the adviser

   Answer: B. As we just stated, the "automatic registration" provision applies to those officers, partners, and directors of the IA who are already IARs in at least one state.

   Important note: For those of you who have taken a FINRA exam, you know there is a supervisory level of registration—registered principal. No such gradations apply under NASAA rules. So, no matter how high ranking the officer of the investment advisory firm, that individual registers as an IAR. Therefore, anytime you see reference made to your supervisor, remember, that person is an IAR just like you.

2. Testing:

Unless a waiver is granted (see introduction), passing the Series 65 exam (or the Series 66 exam) is a requirement for registration. We do expect you to pass, but, if an applicant is not successful on the first or second attempt, there is a 30-day waiting period before the exam may be retaken. After the third (and subsequent) attempts, the waiting period is 180 days.

Now that you know how to register, what about termination procedures?

IAR Termination Procedures

If an investment adviser representative terminates employment with an investment adviser, notification requirements depend on how the investment adviser is registered.

If the investment adviser is a state-registered adviser, the firm must notify the Administrator. If the investment adviser is a federal covered adviser, the investment adviser representative must notify the Administrator. All notifications must be made promptly.

A clue that might help is to visualize the I in IAR as the number 1 to remember that only one person gives notification. What is the story if the IAR leaves one firm to go to another?

EXAMPLE

1. Zack is an IAR with Unicorn Investment Advisers (UIA), an investment adviser registered in State W. Zack has accepted an employment offer from Elite Research Associates, (ERA), an investment adviser also registered in State W. What are the notification requirements to the State W Administrator?

   A. Zack is the only person who notifies the Administrator

   B. UIA is the only person who notifies the Administrator

   C. ERA is the only person who notifies the Administrator

   D. UIA and ERA notify the Administrator

Answer: D. This is bit sneaky. We've just told you to remember the "I" in IAR resembles the number 1 so only one person must notify. We also stated that if the IAR represents a state-registered investment adviser, the IA does the notification. In this specific instance, because two IA firms are involved, each of them must notify the Administrator; UIA that Zack is no longer under their control and ERA that Zack now is. This is just an example of how every rule has an exception.

Financial Requirements of IARs

Unlike an investment adviser, there are no financial requirements—no net worth or bonding requirements—to register as an investment adviser representative.

Recordkeeping Requirements of IARs

Unlike an investment adviser, there are no ongoing recordkeeping requirements for IARs. Annual renewal on December 31 requires the payment of fees. If there are any material changes, especially of a disciplinary nature, the individual's Form U4 must be updated within 30 days.

TEST TOPIC ALERT

If there should be a change to any material information in the Form U4, (e.g., change of permanent address or change to military status), an amendment must be filed within 30 days.

Here is an example of how that might appear:

EXAMPLE

1. When an investment adviser representative's permanent residence address changes, updates must be made to the information on file with the regulatory bodies. The proper procedure to be followed is

    A. File a Form U4 within 30 days

    B. File a Form U4 within 45 days

    C. File a Form U5 within 30 days

    D. File a Form U5 within 45 days

    Answer: A. Amendments are made to the Form U4 and must be filed within 30 days. The Form U5 is for terminations.

UNIT
3

Regulation of Broker-Dealers and their Agents

LEARNING OBJECTIVES

When you have completed this unit, you will be able to accomplish the following.

U3LO1:   Define a broker-dealer.

U3LO2:   Identify broker-dealer exclusions and exemptions under the Securities Exchange Act of 1934 and the Uniform Securities Act.

U3LO3:   Define an agent.

U3LO4:   Identify agent exclusions and exemptions under the Securities Exchange Act of 1934 and the Uniform Securities Act.

U3LO5:   Describe the initial and post registration requirements of the Securities Exchange Act of 1934 and the Uniform Securities Act regarding broker-dealers, and agents.

INTRODUCTION

We have already discussed two of the four securities professionals covered under the Uniform Securities Act (and federal law)—investment advisers and those who represent them—investment adviser representatives. This unit will cover the other two—broker-dealers and those who represent them—agents.

You can expect four questions from the Unit.

WHO IS A BROKER-DEALER?

U3LO1: Define a broker-dealer.

When describing the exclusions from the definition of an investment adviser (Unit 1 LO1), we gave a brief definition of a broker-dealer. Let's get into more detail.

A **broker-dealer** is defined in the Securities Exchange Act of 1934 (the federal law regulating broker-dealers and their representatives) and in the USA as any *person*, (think back to the broad definition we gave you at the beginning of Unit 1), engaged in the business of effecting transactions in securities for the accounts of others or for its own account. Any person (e.g., a securities firm, even one organized as a sole proprietorship) with an established place of business (an office) in the state that is in the business of buying and selling securities for the accounts of others (customers) and/or for its own proprietary account is a defined as a broker-dealer.

In other words, broker-dealers are firms for which agents (registered representatives) work. They are firms that engage in securities transactions, such as sales and trading. When acting on behalf of their customers—that is, buying and selling securities for their clients' accounts— broker-dealers act in an agency capacity. When broker-dealers buy and sell securities for their own accounts, called proprietary accounts, they act in a principal capacity as dealers. We'll cover their activity in this regard in Part 4, Unit 22.

TAKE NOTE

Individuals who buy and sell securities for their own accounts are not broker-dealers because they are engaged in personal investment activity, not the business of buying and selling securities for others. They are individual investors, not securities dealers.

TEST TOPIC ALERT

One of the roles of a broker-dealer is underwriting (distributing) shares of new securities for issuers. When they do that, they generally earn a spread (the difference between the public offering price and what they pay the issuer) or receive a commission on the sales, which they then use to pay their agents who actually made the sales to the clients. In Unit 4, we'll cover the registration and issuance of securities.

BROKER-DEALER EXCLUSIONS AND EXEMPTIONS

U3LO2: Identify broker-dealer exclusions and exemptions under the Securities Exchange Act of 1934 and the Uniform Securities Act.

Exclusions from the Definition of Broker-Dealer Under the Uniform Securities Act

Broker-dealers are firms that buy and sell securities for others or themselves as a business. There are, however, many persons, legal and natural, that effect securities transactions that are excluded from the definition of broker-dealer for purposes of state regulation. Persons not included in the definition of broker-dealer are:

- agents (those individuals who represent broker-dealers);
- issuers (those entities, such as corporations and governments who raise money by issuing securities); and
- banks, savings institutions, and trust companies.

Today most banks and other financial institutions engage in securities activities through broker-dealer subsidiaries of the bank holding company. The broker-dealer subsidiaries of banks are, as a result, not excluded from the definition of a broker-dealer and therefore subject to the same securities regulations as other broker-dealers. Keep in mind that formation of these subsidiaries eliminates the need for the bank holding companies to register as broker-dealers. Their broker-dealer subsidiaries must, of course, register.

- **Broker-dealers with no place of business in the state.** This exclusion is very much like the one offered to investment advisers. States exclude from the definition of broker-dealer those broker-dealers that:

  - have no place of business in the state and deal exclusively with the issuers of the security involved in the transactions, other broker-dealers, and other financial institutions, such as banks, savings and loan associations, trust companies, insurance companies, investment companies, or employee benefit plans with assets of not less than $1 million; or

  - have no place of business in the state, but are licensed in a state where they have a place of business, and offer and sell securities in the state only with persons in the state who are existing customers and who are not residents of the state.

Similar to the rule for investment advisers and their representatives, the USA also allows broker-dealers and their agents to do business with existing customers who are temporarily in a state to avoid unnecessary multiple registrations.

EXAMPLE

As long as your client has not changed state of residence, there is no time limit. Many people, after a couple of years in the workforce, decide to get an MBA. If they go out of state to a resident program for a year or two, that does not mean they've changed their state of residence, merely that they are not commuter students. Only when official residency is changed (new driver's license or voter registration) does the 30-day rule apply.

TEST TOPIC ALERT

Unlike investment advisers and their IARs, there is no de minimis exemption for broker-dealers. That is, even if the BD does not maintain a place of business in the state, a single retail client means registration is required.

- We'll cover one final exclusion: using the internet. Obviously, there was no internet when the Uniform Securities Act was written in 1956. As with other changes in the way we do business, NASAA has written Model Rules to update the regulatory scheme. A firm's website, considered advertising, can be seen everywhere. Does that mean the firm has a place of business in the state? Without getting too technical, there are several requirements to insure that the person is not deemed to be in the state.

  - The communication clearly states that the person may only do business in this state if properly registered or exempt from registration.

  - Any follow-up individualized responses with prospects in this state that involve either the effecting or attempting to effect transactions in securities, or the rendering of personalized investment advice for compensation, as may be, will not be made without compliance with state broker-dealer, investment adviser, agent or IA representative registration requirements, or an applicable exemption or exclusion.

- The site may only make available general information, not specific advice or recommendations.

- In the case of an agent or IAR

  ■ the affiliation with the broker-dealer or investment adviser of the agent or IAR is prominently disclosed within the communication,

  ■ the broker-dealer or investment adviser with whom the agent or IAR is associated retains responsibility for reviewing and approving the content of any internet communication by an agent or IAR,

  ■ the broker-dealer or investment adviser with whom the agent or IAR is associated first authorizes the distribution of information on the particular products and services through the internet communication, and

  ■ in disseminating information through the internet communication, the agent or IAR acts within the scope of the authority granted by the broker-dealer or investment adviser.

What this basically means is that if you just generally advertise on the internet, you don't have to be registered in the state. But, if you follow up with advice (IAR) or offering securities (agent), you either have to register or find some kind of exemption.

TEST TOPIC ALERT

The exam focuses more on the exclusions from the definition of broker-dealer than on the definition itself. Know these exclusions well.

EXAMPLE   Exclusion from the Definition of Broker-Dealer

First Securities Corporation (FSC) is a broker-dealer registered in State A, the location of its only office. One of their agents contacts a client who is currently on vacation in State B and recommends the purchase of XYZ common stock. The client agrees and purchases 100 shares of XYZ. Neither the broker-dealer nor the agent is registered in State B. Is this a problem? What if the client enjoys being in State B to the extent that it becomes his permanent residence?

When a broker-dealer has no place of business in a state and deals with an existing client who is temporarily in that state, the USA does not define that entity as a broker-dealer in the state. Therefore, FSC would not be required to register in State B, and neither would any of its agents.

Things change, however, if the client becomes a resident of State B. Once that client's residence has officially changed, the relationship can only continue for a maximum of 30 days. After that, both FSC and the agent would have to register in State B if they wanted to keep the client. Let's take the example one step further. A question might appear something like this.

EXAMPLE

1. First Securities Corporation (FSC) is a broker-dealer registered in State A, the location of its principal office. They have begun doing business in State B with the First Fidelity Bank and Trust Company and open a small branch office in State B to service the account. Which of the following statements is CORRECT?

   A. FSC does not need to register in State B because its only client is an institution.

   B. FSC needs to register in State B because it has a place of business in the state.

   C. Broker-dealers are only required to register in the state where their principal office is located.

   D. FSC would have to register in State B even if it didn't have a place of business there.

   Answer: B. We learned that the USA excludes from the definition of broker-dealer, a firm with no place of business in a state whose only clients are, among others, institutions, such as banks. That exclusion only applies when there is no place of business in the state; opening a small branch in State B voids that exclusion. Even if there is no place of business in the state, if they have a single individual (called a retail client on the exam) who resides in the state, then registration is always required.

Federal Exemptions From Registration as a Broker-Dealer

A broker-dealer that conducts all of its business in one state is exempt from registration with the SEC. The exception provided for intrastate broker-dealer activity is very narrow. To qualify, all aspects of all transactions must be done within the borders of one state. This means that, without SEC registration, a broker-dealer cannot participate in any transaction executed on a national securities exchange. Intrastate broker-dealers register with the state in which they are located.

State Exemptions From Registration as a Broker-Dealer

The USA exempts a broker-dealer without a place of business in a state if its only transactions effected in the state are with the issuer of the securities involved in the transaction.

Unit 3

TAKE NOTE

Here is a chart that should help (the "you" here does not mean individuals like yourself—it is referring to the brokerage firm).

Under the USA, you are a broker-dealer if:	Under the USA, you are *not* a broker-dealer if:
1. you have a place of business in the state regardless of the nature of your clients; or	1. you have no place of business in the state *and*
2. you have even one retail client in the state	2. your only clients are: other BDs, institutions, and issuers of the security involved in the transaction; or
	3. you are registered in a state where you do maintain a place of business and only do business in this state with existing clients who are not residents of this state (snowbirds).

WHO ARE AGENTS?

U3LO3: Define an agent.

"Agent" means any individual, other than a broker-dealer, who represents a broker-dealer or issuer in effecting or attempting to effect purchases or sales of securities. As agents, they act— usually on a commission basis—on behalf of others. Other than on this exam, agents are often referred to as **registered representatives**, whether they sell registered securities or securities exempt from registration.

The use of the term *individual* here is important. Only an individual (a natural person) can be an agent. A corporation, such as a brokerage firm, is not a natural person—it is a legal entity. The brokerage firm is the legal person (legal entity) that the agent (natural person) represents in securities transactions.

TAKE NOTE

As just mentioned, *agent* is the term used under state law and that is the only term that will be used on the exam.

Definition: Associated Person

A **person associated with a broker-dealer** is any partner, officer, or director of the broker-dealer (or any individual performing similar functions) or any person directly or indirectly controlling or controlled by the broker-dealer, including any employees of the broker-dealer, except that any person associated with a broker or dealer whose functions are solely clerical or ministerial shall not be included in the meaning of the term.

TEST TOPIC ALERT

Even outside directors or partners whose only connection to the firm is the contribution of capital are considered associated persons of the broker-dealer.

AGENT EXCLUSIONS AND EXEMPTIONS

U3LO4: Identify agent exclusions and exemptions under the Securities Exchange Act of 1934 and the Uniform Securities Act.

Clerical and administrative (sometimes referred to as *ministerial*) employees of a broker-dealer are generally not included in the definition of agent and, therefore, are not required to be registered. The logic for this exclusion from the definition should be obvious. Clerical and administrative employees do not effect securities transactions with the public. They attend to the administration of the broker-dealer as a business organization. Under these circumstances, they are like employees of any other corporation. In fact, if the broker-dealer they work for wishes to pay their employees, including this group, a year-end bonus based on company profits (not related to any individual's sales efforts), it would be allowable and would not require registrations of the clerical personnel.

The situation changes when administrative personnel take on securities-related functions. When they do so, they lose their exemption and must register as an agent.

TAKE NOTE

Secretaries and sales assistants are not agents if their activities are confined to administrative activities, including responding to an existing client's request for a quote. However, if secretaries or sales assistants accept customer transactions or take orders over the phone, they are engaging in securities transactions and are subject to registration as agents.

TEST TOPIC ALERT

Cold callers working for a broker-dealer would be defined as an agent if they did any more than ask if clients wanted to receive information. For example, if they prequalified clients or suggested ways to receive more money for their stocks or bonds, they would be considered agents.

As is customary in other industries, broker-dealers frequently hire summer interns. If these interns received any selling related compensation, such as $10 for each existing client solicited, they would be considered agents and would have to register.

Basically, there is no way for an individual to represent a broker-dealer in a securities sales function without being an agent.

Exclusions From the Definition of Agent for Personnel Representing Issuers

In many cases, individuals who represent issuers of securities are agents and therefore must register as such in the states in which they sell the issuers' securities. When does something like this occur? In many cases, a local company is looking to raise some additional capital—something in the range of several million dollars. Instead of going through the normal investment banking procedure (and paying all of those fees and commissions to the investment bankers), the company (known under the USA as the issuer) either uses its own employees or hires an outside sales force to sell the new security. In general, these individuals are required to register as agents of the issuer. There is an exception as follows. Individuals are excluded from the definition of agent and, therefore, are exempt from registration in a state when representing issuers in effecting transactions:

- in certain exempt securities (the five listed below);
- exempt from registration; or
- with existing employees, partners, or directors of the issuer if no sales-related commission or other remuneration is paid or given directly or indirectly for soliciting any person in this state.

Effecting Transactions in Exempt Securities

Securities exempt from registration are called **exempt securities**. Although there are almost a dozen different securities that qualify for exemption under the Uniform Securities Act (they will be discussed later in Unit 4), an individual is excluded from the term *agent* only when that individual represents an issuer in effecting transactions for the following five exempt securities:

1. Any security issued or guaranteed by the United States, any state, any political subdivision of a state, or any agency of one or more of these or any security issued or guaranteed by Canada, any Canadian province, or any political subdivision of any such province

2. Securities of foreign governments with which the United States has diplomatic relationships

3. Any security issued by, or guaranteed by, any bank organized under the laws of the United States, or any bank, savings institution, or trust company organized and supervised under the laws of any state

4. Commercial paper rated in the top three categories by the major rating agencies with denominations of $50,000 or more with maturities of nine months or less

5. Investment contracts issued in connection with employee's stock purchase, savings, pensions, or profit-sharing plans

Effecting Exempt Transactions

An employee of an issuer is not an agent when representing an issuer in exempt transactions. Transactions exempt from registration are called **exempt transactions**. Some examples are:

- unsolicited brokerage transactions;
- transactions between the issuer and underwriters;
- transactions with financial institutions; or
- private placements.

Exempt securities and exempt transactions will be covered in thorough detail later in Unit 4 so you will probably want to come back and review this information after that.

 TAKE NOTE

An employee of an issuer is not an agent when representing an issuer if the issue is exempt from registration, as long as it is one of the five listed previously. Additionally, the employee is not an agent when representing an issuer in exempt transactions (e.g., transactions between an underwriter and issuer).

An individual employed by a corporation (not a broker-dealer) to sell a new initial public offering (IPO) to the public would be considered an **agent of the issuer** needing registration, even if not paid compensation based on sales. The only exception would be if all transactions were exempt, such as selling the shares only to institutional investors.

TAKE NOTE

Keep in mind that an individual who works for an issuer of securities is excluded from the definition of agent when engaging in transactions with employees involving the issuer's securities, provided that the individual is not compensated for such participation by commissions or other remuneration based either directly or indirectly on the amount of securities sold. In other words, salaried employees engaged in distributing their employers' shares as part of an employee benefit plan would not be required to register as agents because they are, by definition, excluded from the definition. If such employees were compensated on the basis of the number of shares sold, they would be defined as agents and therefore would be subject to registration.

TEST TOPIC ALERT

Individuals representing *broker-dealers* in a sales capacity must register as agents whether they sell registered securities, securities exempt from registration, or securities in an exempt transaction. .

Agent Exemptions from Registration

Just as with broker-dealers, there is no de minimis exemption for agents. If you have a single client in a state, regardless of whether or not you have a place of business there, you are an agent in that state and require registration.

There are only two exemptions. First is the snowbird exemption we've discussed several times before. The second is when the firm is excluded from the definition of BD because it has no place of business in the state and only deals with other broker-dealers and institutions, etc. In that case, the BD's employees who service those clients are not considered to be agents in that state.

EXAMPLE

1. Under the Uniform Securities Act, which of the following would be considered an agent?

   A. An individual who is employed by a small community bank for the purpose of selling stock in the bank

   B. A broker-dealer with a place of business in the state with an extensive retail clientele

   C. An individual whose broker-dealer is registered in the state, but her only clients are institutions

   D. An individual with no place of business in the state dealing with more than 5 existing clients who are vacationing in the state

Answer: C. Even though the individual's only clients are institutions, the fact that her BD is registered in the state means she must register as well. Yes, transactions with institutions are exempt transactions, but that exemption only applies to individuals selling on behalf of the issuer, not when representing a broker-dealer. Individuals selling the securities of certain exempt issuers (like a bank) are excluded from the definition as are broker-dealers. If the individual has no place of business in the state and only deals with existing clients (regardless of the number), who are temporarily in the state, that individual is exempt from registration.

BROKER-DEALER REGISTRATION REQUIREMENTS

U3LO5: Describe the initial and post registration requirements of the Securities Exchange Act of 1934 and the Uniform Securities Act regarding broker-dealers, and agents.

Under the USA, if a person is included in the definition of a broker-dealer, that person, unless meeting one of the exemptions we've discussed, must register as a broker-dealer in the states where it does business. The USA is clear about broker-dealer registration. It states, "It is unlawful for any person to transact business in this state as a broker-dealer... unless he is registered under this Act."

This means every person (legal entity) that falls within the definition of a broker-dealer must register with the Administrator of the state. Again, keep in mind that if a person falls under one of the exclusions from the definition, that person or legal entity does not have to register in the state. The rules are basically the same for agents.

In most jurisdictions, registration is accomplished by filing the SEC's Form BD modified to meet the needs of the state. If any material information on the BD becomes inaccurate, *prompt* notice must be given to the Administrator.

While the exam will focus on state registration requirements, you need to know that almost all broker-dealers register with the SEC. That means, unlike investment advisers who only register with one regulator, you can assume that any broker-dealer referred to in a question (unless something tells you otherwise) registers with the SEC **and** at least one state.

TAKE NOTE

The automatic registration of officers, etc. that we discussed with regard to investment advisers applies here as well to those who are registered with the BD. And, as mentioned before, unlike FINRA, there is no separate principal registration so these individuals are registered as agents.

SUBMITTING AN APPLICATION

All persons must complete and submit an **initial application** (as well as renewals) to the state securities Administrator. For broker-dealers, the application is Form BD and for agents, Form U4. The application must contain whatever information the Administrator may require by rule, and may include:

- form and place of business (broker-dealers);

- proposed method of doing business;

- a list of all jurisdictions in which the applicant is registering (or already registered);

- qualifications and business history (broker-dealers must include the qualifications and history of partners, officers, directors, and other persons with controlling influence over the organization);

- court-issued injunctions and administrative orders;

- adjudications by the SEC or any securities SRO, such as FINRA within the past 10 years;

- convictions of misdemeanors involving a security or any aspect of the securities business, (including charges as well as convictions);

- felony convictions, whether securities related or not (including charges as well as convictions);

- financial condition and history (broker-dealers only, but only of the firm—no credit reports on the officers);

- any current unsatisfied liens and judgments must be shown as well as any declaration of bankruptcy within the past 10 years;

- any information to be furnished or disseminated to any client or prospective client, if the applicant is an investment adviser; and

- in the case of an individual registrant (agent or investment adviser representative), citizenship information.

The Administrator also may require that an applicant publish an announcement of the registration in one or more newspapers in the state.

TEST TOPIC ALERT

Please note that, unlike FINRA registration requirements, individuals applying for registration do NOT have to submit fingerprints.

Before we continue, an important term found in the Securities Exchange Act of 1934 needs to be defined: **Statutory disqualification**.

Because the Exchange Act deals with the registration of persons and exchanges (the "people and places" act), the SEC sets forth certain actions that a person disqualified under statute (law) from becoming registered or associated with a broker-dealer or investment adviser. The person is subject to a **statutory disqualification** if that person:

- has been or is expelled or suspended from membership or being associated with a member of any self-regulatory organization (SRO) (think FINRA);

- is subject to an order of the SEC or other appropriate regulatory agency (think the Administrator) denying, suspending, or revoking his registration as a broker-dealer, or barring or suspending his association with a broker or dealer;

- by his conduct while associated with a broker-dealer, has been found to be a cause of any effective suspension, expulsion, or order of the type described in the two previous points;

- has been convicted within the past 10 years of a securities violation or a misdemeanor involving finance or dishonesty, bribery, embezzlement, forgery, theft, and so forth, or any felony;

- is subject to a temporary or permanent injunction from a competent court of jurisdiction prohibiting him from engaging in any phase of the securities business;

- has willfully violated any federal securities law; or

- has made a false or misleading statement in any filing with information requested by an SRO (omitting important facts is cause as well).

TAKE NOTE

Loss of a civil lawsuit, even involving securities, is not a cause for statutory disqualification.

PAYMENT OF INITIAL AND RENEWAL FILING FEES

States require **filing fees** for initial applications as well as for renewal applications. If an application is withdrawn or denied, the Administrator is entitled to retain a portion of the fee. Filing fees for broker-dealers, investment advisers, and their representatives need not be identical. A registered broker-dealer, covered adviser, or state-registered investment adviser may file an application for registration of a successor, whether or not the successor is then in existence, for the unexpired portion of the year. There is no filing or registration fee until renewal, (December 31), of the firm's license, but the successor firm would have to file a new consent to service of process.

Under normal circumstances, registration becomes effective for all securities professionals at noon of the 30th day after filing. In the case of agents (or IARs), the Administrator will notify the employing firm of effectiveness, and they will tell the new registrants when they are "good to go."

Once registered, broker-dealers are subject to numerous administrative requirements to keep their registrations current and in good order.

Books and Records

Every registered broker-dealer must make and keep such accounts, blotters (records of original entry), correspondence (including emails), memoranda, papers, books, and other records as the state Administrator by rule prescribes. All records so required must be preserved for three years (the first two years easily accessible in the principal office) unless the Administrator specifies otherwise. These records must be current, complete, and accurate. Broker-dealers are obligated to *promptly* file correcting amendments. State securities Administrators cannot impose recordkeeping requirements that are in excess of those prescribed by the SEC.

The records broker-dealers are required to maintain are subject to periodic, special, or other examinations by representatives of the Administrator of the state where the broker-dealer's principal office is located or of any other state in which the broker-dealer is registered as the Administrator deems necessary or appropriate in the public interest.

TEST TOPIC ALERT

Included in the recordkeeping requirements are electronic communications, particularly emails. However, it is not required to maintain emails of a personal nature sent to non-clients (e.g., "Honey, I'm stuck at the office and will be late for dinner.").

Website Storage

Websites are treated as would be any other advertisement. So, the original site design is kept for three years and, whenever revised, the new copy is maintained and starts a new retention requirement for that copy. Therefore, the firm will likely have several different versions in its advertising file at the same time.

TEST TOPIC ALERT

Although broker-dealers (and investment advisers) are required to keep all records relating to customers, there are no requirements to keep copies of the customer's tax returns.

Financial Requirements for Broker-Dealers

The Administrator may establish **net capital requirements** for broker-dealers. Net capital requirements of the states may not exceed those required by federal law, in this case, the Securities Exchange Act of 1934. The Administrator of a state may require those broker-dealers that have custody of, or discretionary authority over, clients' funds or securities to **post surety bonds**. Just as with net capital, the amount of surety bonds required by the states is limited to the amount set by the Securities Exchange Act of 1934. No bond may be required of any broker-dealer whose net capital exceeds the amounts required by the Administrator.

Stated simply, when it comes to broker-dealers, regardless of how many states in which they are registered, other than enforcing antifraud statutes, the Administrator has relinquished most control to the SEC.

TEST TOPIC ALERT

You will have to know that broker-dealers who meet the SEC's net capital or bonding requirements cannot be required to meet higher ones in any state in which they do business.

TEST TOPIC ALERT

In lieu of a surety bond, the Administrator will accept deposits of cash or securities.

AGENT REGISTRATION REQUIREMENTS

The registration requirements for an agent who is not exempt are similar to those for a broker-dealer. An application, generally the Form U4, must be completed. One thing, however, that is on the agent's application that does not apply to a broker-dealer is disclosing *citizenship*.

The USA states, "It is unlawful for any person to transact business in this state as an agent unless he is registered under this act." In other words, an individual may not conduct securities transactions in a state unless that person is properly registered in the state where he conducts business. This is true even when receiving unsolicited orders. If an agent does business in a state, she must be registered in that state, even if there is only one client. This is not like investment advisers and their representatives who enjoy a de minimis exemption. So, what can an individual who has been hired to become an agent of a broker-dealer do while registration is pending? After all, one does not fill out the Form U4 and become an agent immediately. Permitted activities would be those allowed to any other employee of the broker-dealer who is not required to be registered. That would include clerical functions, such as posting trade details to client accounts, or administrative activities, like assisting with research. As long as it does not involve customer contact relating to selling/offering securities or opening accounts, these newbies can hang around the office and try to make themselves useful. Of course, most of their time should be spent preparing to pass the exam.

An agent's registration is not effective during any period when the agent is not associated with a broker-dealer registered in the state. Therefore, if the broker-dealer's registration is terminated, the agent is no longer considered licensed. The terminology depends on the specific state. In some cases, the agent's license is placed in *suspense*. In other states, it is put on *hold* or some such similar language. Whatever the phrase, when the broker-dealer closes up shop, either voluntarily or involuntarily (think revocation of registration by the Administrator), the agent cannot function because there is no broker-dealer affiliation. This is also true of an investment adviser representative when the investment adviser's registration is terminated.

One place where IARs and agents differ is their termination notice procedures. When an agent begins or terminates a connection with a broker-dealer or issuer, or begins or terminates those activities that make him an agent, the agent and the broker-dealer or issuer must *promptly* notify the Administrator.

TEST TOPIC ALERT

If an agent terminates employment with a broker-dealer, both parties must notify the Administrator promptly. If an agent terminates employment with one broker-dealer to join another broker-dealer, all three parties must notify the Administrator. One way to remember this is that in the case of an agent, the first letter, **A**, tells us that **A**ll the parties involved must notify the Administrator. All notifications must be made promptly. Please note how this differs from the termination of an IAR.

EXAMPLE

1. The City of Chicago issues bonds for the maintenance of local recreational facilities. Purchasers have two choices: they can purchase the bonds directly from the city through Regina Stith (an employee of the city responsible for selling the bonds), or they can purchase them from Gary Thompson (an employee of First Allied Securities Corporation). Neither Stith nor Thompson charges a commission, although FASC is remunerated with an underwriting fee. It would be correct to state that

   A. Stith and Thompson must be registered as agents.

   B. Stith must be registered as an agent, but Thompson is excluded.

   C. Thompson must be registered as an agent, but Stith is excluded.

   D. Thompson and Stith are excluded from the definition of agent.

   Answer: C. Any individual selling securities while representing a registered broker-dealer is always defined as an agent, even when the securities are exempt from registration (as are these municipal bonds). When an individual represents the issuer of certain exempt securities, such as municipal bonds, that individual is excluded from the definition of agent and does not register. This means the correct answer is **C**. It is important to remember the 5 categories of exempt issuers to which this exclusion applies.

Exemptions from registration as an agent generally apply to representatives of issuers, rather than to representatives of broker-dealers.

Financial Requirements of Agents

There are no financial requirements, or **net worth requirements**, to register as an agent. The Administrator may, however, require an agent to be bonded, particularly if the agent has discretion over a client's account.

Multiple Registrations

An individual may not act at any one time as an agent for more than one broker-dealer or for more than one issuer, unless the broker-dealers or issuers for whom the agent acts are affiliated by direct or indirect common control or the Administrator grants an exception. In the event an agent does wish to affiliate with a second broker-dealer, the agent would have to go through the registration process with the second firm in the same manner as the original application (filing another Form U4).

LIMITED REGISTRATION OF CANADIAN BROKER-DEALERS AND AGENTS

Provided the limited registration requirements enumerated below are met, a broker-dealer domiciled in Canada that has no office in this state may effect transactions in securities with or for, or attempt to induce the purchase or sale of any security by:

■ a person from Canada who is temporarily a resident in this state who was already a client of the broker-dealer; or

■ a person from Canada who is a resident in this state, whose transaction is in a self-directed, tax-advantaged retirement plan in Canada of which the person is the holder or contributor. In Canada, the equivalent of an IRA is called a Registered Retirement Savings Plan (RRSP).

An agent who will be representing a Canadian broker-dealer who registers under these provisions may effect transactions in securities in this state on the same basis as permitted for the broker-dealer.

For the Canadian broker-dealer to register in this fashion, it must:

■ file an application in the form required by the jurisdiction where it has its principal office in Canada;

■ file a consent to service of process;

■ provide evidence that it is registered in good standing in its home jurisdiction; and

■ be a member of an SRO or stock exchange in Canada.

Requirements for agents are the same, except that membership in an SRO or stock exchange is not relevant.

Unit 3

However, just as with domestic broker-dealers, if there is no place of business in the state, there are no registration requirements if the only securities transactions are with issuers, other broker-dealers, and institutional clients.

TAKE NOTE

Renewal applications for Canadian broker-dealers and agents who file for limited registration must be filed before December 1 each year.

Comparing the Four Securities Professionals

In our many years of preparing applicants for this exam, one thing we have observed is that many students do not have a clear idea of the difference between a broker-dealer and an investment adviser and, similarly, between an agent and an investment adviser representative. Perhaps the following will help:

Broker-dealer	Investment Adviser
■ Primary business function is executing transactions in securities ■ Compensation is earned in the form of commissions and markups (markdowns)	■ Primary business function is giving advice ■ Compensation is earned in the form of fees or other charges, generally based on the amount of assets managed
Agents	**IARs**
■ Individuals employed by brokers/dealers to handle their customer orders to buy or sell securities ■ Separate function from an IAR (although many in large firms wear both hats)	■ Individuals employed by investment advisers to give advice to their clients ■ After an IAR advises a client about a specific security, the next step is to contact the broker-dealer where that client maintains a brokerage account to give the buy/sell order to an agent

TAKE NOTE

Here are 4 important point to remember:

1. IAs register on the federal level (SEC) or state level; never both

2. IARs only register on the state level

3. BDs register on the federal level (through FINRA) *and* the state level

4. Agents register on the federal level (through FINRA) *and* the state level

UNIT 4

Regulation of Securities and Issuers

State securities Administrators regulate securities transactions that occur in their states similarly to the way they regulate persons engaged in those transactions. This unit discusses the procedures for the registration of securities as well as their exemptions from registration. For a securities transaction to be lawful under the USA, the security itself must be registered unless it or the transaction is exempt from registration requirements. In addition, we'll also review some of the SEC's regulations dealing with this subject as found in the Securities Act of 1933.

The Series 65 exam will include two questions on the material presented in this unit.

LEARNING OBJECTIVES

When you have completed this unit, you will be able to accomplish the following.

U4LO1:   Identify instruments that are defined under the Uniform Securities Act as securities.
U4LO2:   Identify those who issue securities.
U4LO3:   Describe the significant securities registration provisions and exemptions from the Securities Act of 1933 and the Uniform Securities Act.
U4LO4:   Describe the applicability of the antifraud provisions of the Uniform Securities Act.

WHAT IS A SECURITY UNDER THE UNIFORM SECURITIES ACT?

U4LO1: Identify instruments that are defined under the Uniform Securities Act as securities.

Perhaps the most important term in the USA is the term *security*. Why is it so important? The reason is simple: the USA applies only to those financial instruments that are securities. The purchase, sale, or issuance of anything that is not a security is not covered by the act. The definition of a security, however, is complex. Over the years, courts have determined case by case what constitutes a security. The U.S. Supreme Court, in the Howey decision, defined the primary characteristics of what constitutes a security by concluding that an investment contract is a security. For an instrument to be a security, the court held, it must constitute (1) an investment of money, (2) in a common enterprise, (3) with the expectation of profits, (4) to be derived primarily from the efforts of a person other than the investor. A common enterprise means an enterprise in which the fortunes of the investor are interwoven with those of either the person offering the investment, a third party, or other investors.

The USA provides a comprehensive list of more than a dozen financial instruments, (many of which you've never heard of), that are securities under the act and therefore covered by its provisions. Rather than waste your time with the list (we've included it in the Glossary), please focus on the six items that are **not** a security and you'll get any question you are given correct. The following six items are not securities under the act:

- An insurance or endowment policy or annuity contract under which an insurance company promises to pay a fixed sum of money either in a lump sum or periodically (this is basically any product from a life insurance company that does not use the word "variable")

- Interest in a retirement plan, such as an IRA or 401(k) plan

- Collectibles

- Commodities such as precious metals and grains, including futures and forward contracts

- Condominiums used as a personal residence

- Currency

TEST TOPIC ALERT

The exam will want you to know what is and what is not a security. We suggest that you concentrate on learning the six that are *not* securities because they are much easier to remember, and you will still be able to answer the questions correctly. Let's try a few questions so that you can see what we mean.

EXAMPLES

1. Which group of instruments is NOT composed of securities?

   A. Stock, treasury stock, rights, warrants, and transferable shares

   B. Voting trust certificates and interests in oil and gas drilling programs

   C. Commodity futures contracts and fixed payment life insurance contracts

   D. Options on securities and interests in multilevel distributorship arrangements

   Answer: C. Commodity futures contracts and fixed payment life insurance contracts are included in our list of 6 items that are not securities.

2. Which of the following is defined as a security under the Uniform Securities Act?

A. A guaranteed, lump-sum payment to a beneficiary under a modified endowment policy

B. Fixed, guaranteed payments made for life or for a specified period under an annuity contract

C. Commodity futures contracts

D. An investment contract

Answer: D. Investment contracts are defined as a security under the Uniform Securities Act. In fact, the term is often used as a synonym for a security. A guaranteed, lump-sum payment to a beneficiary is an insurance policy excluded from the definition of a security. Fixed, guaranteed payments made for life or for a specified period are fixed annuity contracts not defined as securities. Commodity futures contracts and the commodities themselves are not securities. It is much easier to remember what is not a security than what is.

NONSECURITY INVESTMENTS

Although collectibles, fixed annuities, precious metals, grains, real estate, and currencies can be attractive investments, they are not securities. Because these items are not securities, their sale is not regulated by state securities law. Furthermore, if a registered agent commits fraud in the sale of any of these items, he has not committed a violation of any state securities law. He has violated the antifraud provisions of another act prohibiting fraudulent commercial transactions.

An individual's direct ownership of an automobile is not a security—it is just ownership of a car. However, if that individual makes an investment of money in the stock of an automobile manufacturer with the expectation of making money due to the efforts of the company's management skill, he has purchased a security. In the same manner, if a condominium is purchased in a resort area with the goal of placing it into a rental pool and renting it out most of the year, and it is used only for personal vacation time, the condo is considered a security because there is a profit motive, typically reliant on the efforts of a third party—the rental agent. On the other hand, if the individual has chosen to live in the condominium as a personal residence, it is a home, not a security.

TAKE NOTE

Annuities with fixed payouts are not securities, but variable annuities are because they are dependent on the investment performance of securities within the annuity.

ISSUER

U4LO2: Identify those who issue securities.

An **issuer** is any person who issues (distributes) or *proposes* to issue a security. The most common issuers of securities are companies or governments (federal, state, and municipal governments and their agencies and subdivisions).

If an issuer is nonexempt, (not exempt from registering its securities), it must generally register its securities in the states where they will be sold under one of the registration methods described in this unit.

TEST TOPIC ALERT

This is very strange wording, but might well appear on your exam. Under the USA, with respect to certificates of interest; participation in oil, gas, or mining titles or leases; or in payments out of production under such titles or leases, there is not considered to be any issuer.

Issuer Transaction

An **issuer transaction** is one in which the proceeds of the sale go to the issuer. All newly issued securities, such as an initial public offering (IPO), are issuer transactions. In other words, when a company raises money by selling (issuing) securities to investors, the proceeds from the sale go to the company itself.

EXAMPLE

State X issues bonds as a way of borrowing money so that the state government can function. The state is the issuer of those bonds. Typically, they will be purchased by a client of a broker-dealer whose account is handled by an agent of the firm. This would be an issuer transaction because the proceeds of the sale of the bonds would go to State X, the issuer.

Nonissuer Transaction

A **nonissuer transaction** is one in which the proceeds of the sales do not go, directly or indirectly, to the entity that originally offered the securities to the public. The most common instance of this is everyday trading on exchanges such as the New York Stock Exchange or the Nasdaq Stock Market. In a nonissuer transaction, the proceeds of the sale go to the investor who sold the shares. Because the shares are not new, we refer to this as *secondary trading*.

EXAMPLE

Using our previous example, if the investor who purchased those State X bonds decided to sell them, she would contact her agent who would then arrange for a sale to an interested buyer. In this case, because the proceeds of the bond sale would go to the investor, this is a nonissuer transaction, or secondary transaction (like when you sell your old car, it is a secondhand sale; the manufacturer received the money when the product was initially sold [primary] and you receive the money now [secondary]).

INITIAL OR PRIMARY OFFERING

An issuer transaction involving new securities is called a **primary offering**. If it is the first time an issuer distributes securities to the public, it is called an **initial public offering (IPO)**. All primary offerings are issuer transactions because the issuer (the company) receives the proceeds from the investor investing in the company.

> **EXAMPLE**
>
> The first time that ABC Shoe Co. issued shares to the public, ABC Shoe engaged in an IPO or a primary offering because it received the proceeds from distributing its shares to the public. After ABC Shoe went public, subsequent transactions between investors through agents of broker-dealers were nonissuer (secondary) transactions.

SECURITY EXEMPTIONS FROM REGISTRATION UNDER THE UNIFORM SECURITIES ACT

U4LO3: Describe the significant securities registration provisions and exemptions from the Securities Act of 1933 and the Uniform Securities Act.

The **Securities Act of 1933** (also called the **Paper Act**, the **Truth in Securities Act**, and the **Prospectus Act**) regulates the issuing of corporate securities sold to the public. Unless the security or transaction is exempt (covered shortly), the act requires securities issuers to make full disclosure of all material information in their registration materials in order for investors to make fully informed investment decisions. State law, under the Uniform Securities Act, requires similar disclosures as will be detailed in this unit. Depending on the nature of the issuer and/or the type of transaction, a security may or may not have to register under state and/or federal law. The following is a key statement regarding state law:

Under the USA, it is unlawful for any person to offer or sell an unregistered security in a state unless

- it is registered under the Act;
- the security **or** transaction is exempted from registration under the Act; or
- it is a federal covered security.

If the security or transaction is not exempt or is not a federal covered security as defined by the National Securities Markets Improvement Act, it must be registered in the state or it cannot be lawfully sold in the state.

What are federal covered securities?

We introduced you to the NSMIA of 1996 in a previous unit. This law effectively divided the responsibility for regulating investment advisers between the states and the SEC by creating the category of registration known as a federal covered adviser.

Of importance to this unit, the NSMIA also created the term *federal covered security*, a security that was exempt from registration on the state level. State securities registration requirements were preempted with respect to federal covered securities. However, states may require Notice Filings, consisting of filing fees and copies of documents filed with the SEC, primarily in the case of registered investment companies (e.g., mutual funds).

Categories of Federal Covered Securities

The major categories of covered securities (securities covered by federal securities laws), which therefore cannot be regulated by state securities Administrators (except for violating antifraud provisions), include:

■ securities issued by an open-end or closed-end investment company, unit investment trust, or face amount certificate company, that is registered under the Investment Company Act of 1940;

■ securities listed on the New York Stock Exchange, the NYSE American LLC (formerly known as the American Stock Exchange [AMEX]), the Nasdaq Stock Market, and (not tested) several other U.S. exchanges. In addition, any security equal in seniority (rights or warrants) or senior to these securities (bonds and preferred stock) is also considered federal covered;

■ securities offered pursuant to the provisions of **Rule 506(b)** or **506(c) of Regulation D** under the Securities Act of 1933 (qualifying under the private placement transaction exemption); and

■ most securities exempt from registration under the Securities Act of 1933 (you do not have to know the exceptions other than the one we're going to describe following). If the federal government says the security does not have to register, no state can overstep that. Municipal bonds are included in the list of securities exempt from registration under federal (and state) law. However, under the NSMIA, if the municipal issuer is located in the state in which the securities are being offered, that security is not considered a *federal covered security*. Exemptions under the Securities Act of 1933 will be covered after those of the USA.

EXAMPLE

A bond issued by the city of Columbus, OH, is a federal covered security everywhere but in the state of Ohio. The effect of this is that no state regulator can enforce any of their rules against the bond. But, in the state of Ohio, even though the security is exempt under Ohio's securities laws, the Administrator could request that the issuer (the city) furnish certain details about the issue. This Columbus, OH, bond is still exempt from registration under both state and federal law, but, in Ohio, it is not known as a federal covered security (everywhere else, it is).

TAKE NOTE

It is important to note that registering a security with the SEC does not automatically make it federal covered. Yes, that is true of investment companies and those securities listed on certain stock exchanges and the Nasdaq Stock Market, but there are tens of thousands of stocks registered with the SEC that trade on the OTC Bulletin Board or the OTC Link, formerly known as the Pink Sheets, and they are *not* federal covered. Furthermore, a security does not have to be registered with the SEC to be included in the definition of federal covered security. For example, U.S. government and municipal securities are exempt from registration with the SEC and are included in NSMIA's list of federal covered securities.

TAKE NOTE

Although investment company securities such as mutual funds, are federal covered securities, the Uniform Securities Act allows states to impose filing fees on them under a process called notice filing, as described shortly.

Exemptions From Registration

Under the Uniform Securities Act, the exemptions discussed in this unit refer to an exemption from the act's registration and sales literature filing requirements. In certain situations, the USA exempts both securities and transactions. A security, a transaction, or both, can be exempt.

An **exempt security** retains its exemption when initially issued and in subsequent trading. However, justification as an **exempt transaction** must be established before each transaction.

The USA provides for a number of categories of exempt securities and even more categories of exempt transactions. Those securities that are **nonexempt** must register unless sold in exempt transactions. Federal covered securities do not register with the Administrator but may, especially in the case of investment companies, have to Notice File with the Administrator. As mentioned above, an **exempt security** retains its exemption at its initial issue and in subsequent trading.

An exemption for a transaction, on the other hand, must be established with each transaction. Provided it is in the public interest, the state Administrator can deny, suspend, or revoke any securities transaction exemption other than that of a federal covered security. This action may be taken with or without prior notice (summarily).

TAKE NOTE

A security is exempt because of the nature of the issuer, not the purchaser.

An **exempt transaction** is exempt from the regulatory control of the state Administrator because of the manner in which a sale is made or because of the person to whom the sale is made. A transaction is an action and must be judged by the merits of each instance.

EXAMPLE

An agent can sell an unregistered security that is not exempt from registration in the state if the purchaser of the security is a bank or other institutional buyer. Why is that so? Because the sale of securities to certain financial institutions is an exempt transaction (as will be enumerated shortly), the sale can be made without registration. This means that the securities sold in exempt transactions do not have to be registered in the state. If that same nonexempt security was not sold in an exempt transaction, such as to an individual investor, it would have to be registered in the state.

EXEMPT SECURITIES

Securities exempt from state registration are also exempt from state filing of sales literature. Exempt securities include the following.

- **U.S. and Canadian government and municipal securities.** These include securities issued, insured, or guaranteed by the United States or Canada, by a state or province, or by their political subdivisions, (states or provinces, cities, counties, etc.).*

- **Foreign government securities.** These include securities issued, insured, or guaranteed by a foreign government with which the United States maintains diplomatic relations. However, unlike U.S. or Canadian issues, political subdivisions are not included (unless guaranteed by the sovereign government).*

- **Depository institutions.** These include securities that are issued, guaranteed by, or are a direct obligation of a depository institution. The USA divides them into the following categories: (1) any security issued by and representing an interest in or a debt of, or guaranteed by, any bank organized under the laws of the United States, or any bank, savings institution, or trust company organized and supervised under the laws of any state*; (2) any security issued by and representing an interest in or a debt of, or guaranteed by, any federal savings and loan association, or any building and loan or similar association organized under the laws of any state and authorized to do business in this state; and (3) any security issued or guaranteed by any federal credit union or any credit union, industrial loan association, or similar association organized and supervised under the laws of this state. Please note that for categories (2) and (3), if the institution is not federally chartered, then it must be authorized to do business in the state (under the supervision of a regulator in that state).

- **Insurance company securities.** These include securities issued, insured, or guaranteed by an insurance company authorized to do business in the state. Insurance company securities refer to the stocks or bonds issued by insurance companies, not the variable life policies and variable annuities sold by the companies.

- **Public utility and common carrier securities.** These include any security issued or guaranteed by a public utility or public utility holding company, or an equipment trust certificate issued by a railroad or other common carrier regulated in respect to rates by federal or state authority; or regulated in respect to issuance or guarantee of the security by a governmental authority of the United States, any state, Canada, or any Canadian province.

- **Federal covered securities.** These include any security of that issuer equal to or senior to it. This would include rights, warrants, preferred stock, and any debt security.

- **Securities issued by nonprofit organizations.** These include securities issued by religious, educational, fraternal, charitable, social, athletic, reformatory, or trade associations. Nonprofit is the key word.

- **Securities of employee benefit plans.** This includes any investment contract issued by an employee stock purchase, saving, pension, or profit-sharing plan.*

- **Certain money market instruments.** Commercial paper is the most common example.*

TAKE NOTE

The five previous items listed with an asterisk (*) are the only cases where an individual representing the issuer in the sale of its securities is excluded from the definition of an agent. (Described previously at Unit 3 LO4.)

TAKE NOTE

A promissory note (commercial paper), that matures within nine months, is issued in denominations of at least $50,000, and receives one of the three highest ratings by a nationally recognized rating agency is exempt from registration requirements. Please note that this is the only case where a security's rating is part of the registration or exemption under the Uniform Securities Act.

Remembering a list like this is best accomplished through drill and repetition, so let's try a few questions.

EXAMPLES

1. Which of the following securities is NOT exempt from the registration and advertising requirements of the USA?

   A. Shares of Commonwealth Edisin, a regulated public utility holding company

   B. Securities issued by the nonprofit Carnegee Endowment for Peace

   C. Securities issued by a bank that is a member of the Federal Reserve System

   D. Variable annuity contracts issued by Metrodential Insurance Company, licensed to do business in the state

   Answer: D. Variable annuities (whose performance depends on the securities in a segregated fund) are nonexempt, which means they are covered by the act and have to register. Shares in public utilities, charitable foundations, and banking institutions that are members of the Federal Reserve System are included in our list of exempt securities.

2. Which of the following securities is NOT exempt from the registration and sales literature filing requirements of the USA?

   A. Shares of investment companies registered under the Investment Company Act of 1940

   B. Shares sold on the Nasdaq Stock Market

   C. AAA rated promissory notes of $100,000 that mature in 300 days

   D. Bonds issued by Saskatchewan, Canada

   Answer: C. To be exempt, promissory notes cannot have a maturity beyond 270 days. Registered investment companies (think mutual funds), are federal covered securities as are shares of companies listed on the Nasdaq Stock Market. Any security issued by a state or Canadian province (and their subdivisions) is an exempt security.

3. All of the following securities are exempt from the registration provisions of the Uniform Securities Act EXCEPT

   A. an issue of a savings and loan association authorized to conduct business in the state

   B. a U.S. Treasury bill maturing in 52 weeks

   C. a bond issued by a company that has common stock listed on the New York Stock Exchange (NYSE)

   D. common stock listed on the Vancouver Stock Exchange (VSE)

   Answer: D. No exemption from registration is granted to securities listed on the VSE. Federal covered securities are exempt, but they are listed on the NYSE, the NYSE American LLC (formerly known as the American Stock Exchange [AMEX]), and the Nasdaq Stock Market. As long as the S&L is authorized to do business in the state, it is an exempt issuer. U.S. Treasury securities are exempt under both state and federal law (don't be fooled by the 52 weeks—length to maturity is only a consideration for promissory notes like commercial paper).

EXEMPT TRANSACTIONS

Before a security can be sold in a state, it must be registered unless exempt from registration, or traded in an exempt transaction. This section covers exemptions for transactions that take place in a state.

There are many different types of **exempt transactions**. We begin by focusing on those most likely to be on your exam and finish with several others.

- **Isolated nonissuer transactions.** Isolated nonissuer transactions include secondary (nonissuer) transactions that occur infrequently (very few transactions per year; the exact number varies by state). However, these usually do not involve securities professionals. In the same manner that individuals placing a "for sale by owner" sign on their front lawns do not need a real estate license, one individual selling stock to another in a one-on-one transaction is engaging in a transaction exempt from the oversight of the Administrator, because the issuer is not receiving any of the proceeds, and the parties involved are not trading as part of a regular practice.

- **Unsolicited brokerage transactions.** These include transactions initiated by the client, not the agent. This is probably the most common of the exempt transactions. If a client calls a registered agent and requests that the agent buy or sell a security, the transaction is an unsolicited brokerage transaction exempt from state registration. But, the Administrator may by rule require that the customer acknowledge upon a specified form that the sale was unsolicited, and that a signed copy of the form be kept by the broker-dealer for a specified period.

- **Underwriter transactions.** These include transactions between issuer and broker-dealers performing in the capacity of an underwriter (such as a firm commitment underwriting) as well as those between underwriters themselves (as when functioning as members of a selling syndicate).

- **Bankruptcy, guardian, or conservator transactions.** Transactions by an executor, administrator, sheriff, marshal, receiver, guardian, or trustee in *bankruptcy* are exempt transactions. Please note that a custodian under UGMA or UTMA is not included in this list and that the only trustee is one in bankruptcy.

- **Institutional investor transactions.** These are primarily transactions with financial institutions such as banks, insurance companies, and investment companies, and there is no minimum order size used to define these trades.

- **Limited offering transactions.** These include any offering, called a *private placement*, directed at not more than 10 persons (called *offerees*) other than institutional investors during the previous 12 consecutive months, provided that

  - the seller reasonably believes that all of the noninstitutional buyers are purchasing for investment purposes only,

  - no commissions or other remuneration is paid for soliciting noninstitutional investors, and

  - no general solicitation or advertising is used.

Unlike federal law, where the private placement rule restricts the number of purchasers, the USA restricts the number of offers that may be made.

The number 10 is the figure that will be tested. But, an Administrator may want to reduce it, for example, for uranium stocks or oil royalties, or increase it for a closely held corporation that wants to solicit 20 or 30 friends and relatives of the owners for additional capital. As we continue to learn, the Administrator has a great deal of power.

■ **Preorganization certificates.** An offer or sale of a preorganization certificate or subscription is exempt if

– no commission or other remuneration is paid or given directly or indirectly for soliciting any subscriber,

– the number of subscribers does not exceed 10, and

– no payment is made by any subscriber.

You have probably never heard of a preorganization certificate or subscription, so a little explanation is in order. A new corporation cannot receive a charter unless its documents of incorporation provide evidence that minimum funding is assured. Because the purpose of these preorganization certificates is to enable a new enterprise to obtain the minimum amount of capital required by the corporation law of the state, the USA places a limitation on the number of *subscribers* rather than the number of offerees (as in the previously described private placement exemption). Hence, there may be a publicly advertised offering of preorganization subscriptions. But there may be *no payment* until effective registration unless another exemption is available. This tool itself simply postpones registration; it does not excuse registration altogether.

■ **Transactions with existing security holders.** A transaction made under an offer to existing security holders of the issuer (including persons who are holders of convertible securities, rights, or warrants) is exempt as long as no commission or other form of remuneration is paid directly or indirectly for soliciting that security holder.

■ **Nonissuer transactions by pledgees.** A nonissuer transaction executed by a bona fide pledgee (i.e., the one who received the security as collateral for a loan), as long as it was not for the purpose of evading the act, is an exempt transaction. For example, you pledged stock as collateral for a loan and defaulted on your obligation. The lender will sell your stock to try to recoup his loss and, under the USA, this is considered an exempt transaction.

TAKE NOTE

Some students find it helpful to remember that an exempt security is a noun while an exempt transaction is a verb (hence the word "action").

EXAMPLES

1. Which of the following are exempt transactions?

   I.   A nonissuer transaction with a bank in a Nasdaq traded security

   II. An unsolicited request from an existing client to purchase a nonexempt security

   III. The sale of an unregistered security in a private, nonpublicly advertised transaction to 10 noninstitutional purchasers over a period not exceeding 12 months

   IV. The sale of unlisted securities by a trustee in bankruptcy

   A. I and II

   B. I, II, and III

   C. I, II, and IV

   D. I, II, III, and IV

Answer C. Choice III is not an exempt transaction because the private placement exemption is limited to 10 offerees, not 10 purchasers. All of the others are included in our list of exempt transactions.

2. All of the following describe exempt transactions EXCEPT

   A. ABC, a broker-dealer, purchases securities from XYZ Corporation as part of an underwriting commitment

   B. First National Bank sells its entire publicly traded bond portfolio to Amalgamated National Bank

   C. Amalgamated National Bank sells its publicly traded bond portfolio to ABC Insurance Company

   D. Joan Smith, an employee of Amalgamated National Bank, buys securities recommended by her agent at ABC Brokerage Corporation

Answer: D. The purchase of securities from a broker-dealer by an employee of a bank is a nonexempt transaction—it is a sale of a security by a broker-dealer to a member of the public and is therefore not exempt. Transactions between broker-dealers and issuers as part of an underwriting commitment; transactions between banks; and transactions between banks and insurance companies are exempt because they are transactions between financial institutions. Exempt transactions are most often identified by who the transaction is with rather than what type of security is involved.

Try to follow this next point because it is a bit tricky. The Administrator may, by rule or order, deny or revoke the registration exemption of:

■ any security issued by any person organized and operated not for private profit but exclusively for religious, educational, benevolent, charitable, fraternal, social, athletic, or reformatory purposes, or as a chamber of commerce or trade or professional association (your basic nonprofit exemption); and

■ any investment contract issued in connection with an employees' stock purchase, savings, pension, profit-sharing, or similar benefit plan.

Please note that a few pages ago, we gave you a list of nine different exempt securities, from U.S. and Canadian government issues through certain money market instruments. However, the Administrator can only deny exemption to the two in the previous bullet points. On the other hand, with the exception of those involving federal covered securities, the Administrator may deny any exempt transaction. This means that, for example, just because an agent solicited a transaction with an insurance company of a security that was not federal covered, the Administrator has the power, if he feels it is justified, to consider that transaction nonexempt.

Under the USA, the burden of providing an exemption or an exception from a definition falls upon the person claiming it.

TAKE NOTE

There are only two securities exemptions that the Administrator may revoke, while all exempt transactions, other than in federal covered securities, may be revoked.

Before we summarize, let's try a few examples.

EXAMPLES

1. Under the Uniform Securities Act, which of the following persons is responsible for proving that a securities issue is exempt from registration?

   A. Underwriter

   B. The person requesting the exemption

   C. State Administrator

   D. There is no need to prove eligibility for an exemption.

   Answer: B. The burden of proof for claiming eligibility for an exemption falls to the person claiming the exemption. In the event the registration statement was filed by someone other than the issuer (such as selling stockholders or a broker-dealer), that person must prove the claim.

Summary of Exemptions from Registration under the Uniform Securities Act

Let's start our summary with the key statement from the USA:

> It is unlawful for any person to offer or sell any security in this state unless (1) it is registered under this act or (2) the security or transaction is exempted under this act; or (3) it is a federal covered security.[1]

We must point out that these exemptions apply to the security or transaction only, not to the securities professional. So if a security is exempt, such as a government security, it can be sold in this state without any registration. But, the person who sells it must be properly registered in this state (unless that person qualifies for an exemption). Are you confused?

Remember, we learned earlier in this course that broker-dealers with no place of business in the state, dealing exclusively with other broker-dealers or institutional clients, are not considered to be a BD in the state (as long as they are properly registered in at least one state—the location of their principal office). Let's apply that to the following situation.

ABC Securities is a broker-dealer registered in State A. They have no place of business in State B, but they do effect transactions on behalf of a number of banks and insurance companies located in State B. Therefore, they are not considered BDs in State B and are exempt from registering. Should ABC Securities sell some government securities to these clients, neither ABC nor the agents making the sale are required to be registered. This is not because the government securities are exempt (that just means the securities don't have to register with the Administrator), but because, under the USA, ABC does not meet the definition of a broker-dealer in State B, it does not have to register.

However, should ABC decide to have any of their agents sell these government bonds to individual (sometimes referred to as *retail*) clients in State B, then, even though the bonds are exempt securities, both ABC and the selling agents must register in that state.

The same applies to exempt transactions. One of the most common cases is when a client calls an agent to purchase a security that is not exempt and not registered in your state. But, because the transaction has been initiated by the client, as an unsolicited trade, it is an exempt transaction and, therefore, the trade may be made even though the security is not registered.

---

[1]   Section 301, Uniform Securities Act of 1956

One way the exam will try to trick you is by asking about an individual calling an agent from a state in which the agent is not registered. The broker-dealer is registered in that state, and the individual is a client of the firm, but not that particular agent. The individual wishes to enter an unsolicited order—can the agent accept it? No! Although the transaction is exempt (which only means that the security does not have to be registered in that state), an agent can only do business with a resident of a state if the agent is properly licensed in that state. In this case, the agent would have to turn the order over to an agent who is licensed in that other state.

EXEMPTED SECURITIES UNDER THE SECURITIES ACT OF 1933

The exemptions under the federal law are similar to those under state law, but there are some significant differences. As a NASAA exam, the Series 65 exam will focus on the state laws, but you should be familiar with the federal ones as well.

The Securities Act of 1933 makes it unlawful to sell or deliver a security through any instrument of interstate commerce unless a registration statement is in effect. However, certain securities are exempted from the registration requirements of the act. The following issues qualify as exempted securities:

- Any security issued or guaranteed by the United States, any state, or any political subdivision of a state (all federal government issues and municipal securities are exempted securities). Note that Canadian securities are not included in this exemption (NASAA membership includes Canadian Administrators)

- Any commercial paper that has a maturity at the time of issuance of no more than nine months (270 days), with the stipulation that the proceeds are to be used by the issuer to increase working capital and not for the purchase of fixed assets; there is no minimum denomination or rating requirement similar to that found in the Uniform Securities Act

- Any security issued by a person organized and operated exclusively for religious, educational, benevolent, fraternal, or charitable purposes, and not for pecuniary profit

- Any interest in a railroad equipment trust (for purposes of the law, *interest in a railroad equipment trust* means any interest in an equipment trust, lease, or other similar arrangement entered into, guaranteed by, or for the benefit of a regulated common carrier to finance the acquisition of rolling stock, including motive power)

- Any security issued by a federal or state bank, savings and loan association, building and loan association, or similar institution

TAKE NOTE

The exemption described for banks does not apply to bank holding companies. Most of the large U.S. banks today are owned by holding companies.

Rule 147 Exemption

Any security issued under this rule qualifies as an exempt security under federal law but is not exempt under the Uniform Securities Act and will probably have to register with the state.

This exemption from federal registration applies to any security offered and sold only to persons resident within a single state, where the issuer of such security is a person whose principal place of business is located within such state. *Principal place of business* means the location from which the officers, partners, or managers of the issuer primarily direct, control, and coordinate the activities of the issuer.

The Rule 147 exemption is available only if the entire issue is offered and sold exclusively to residents of a single state. If any sales take place to non-residents, the entire issue loses its exemption. The purpose of this exemption is to allow issuers to raise money on a local basis, provided the business is operating primarily within that state.

Exempt Transactions Under the Securities Act of 1933

Unlike the USA, there are only two exempt transactions that might be tested and they are:

- transactions by any person other than an issuer, underwriter, or dealer, (basically private transactions between individuals); and

- transactions by an issuer that do not involve a public offering (private placement under Regulation D).

In a major effort aimed at facilitating the capital formation needs of small businesses, the SEC adopted Regulation D, the private placement exempt transaction. Securities offered and sold in compliance with Regulation D are exempt from registration with the SEC and, as was listed earlier, are considered federal covered securities exempt from registration on the state level as well. Our primary concern is with **SEC Rule 506**, a private placement where there is no dollar limit on the amount sold.

The Jumpstart Our Business Startups Act of 2012, or **JOBS Act**, made several important changes to Rule 506 of Regulation D. Rule 506 consists of two sections, 506(b) and 506(c). A company seeking to raise capital through a private placement under Rule 506(b) can sell the offering to an unlimited number of accredited investors (defined shortly) and up to 35 non-accredited investors. In addition, no advertising may be done on behalf of the offering.

On the other hand, Section 506(c) permits the offering to be advertised. There are two primary (and interrelated) requirements to do this.

- All purchasers are accredited investors, or the issuer reasonably believes that they are accredited investors.

- The issuer takes reasonable steps to verify that all purchasers are accredited investors, which could include reviewing documentation, such as W-2s, tax returns, bank and brokerage statements, credit reports, and the like.

An issuer can elect to make a typical Rule 506 offering without general solicitation or advertising under Section 506(b) to include up to 35 non-accredited investors in the offering or to avoid the heightened verification procedures.

The JOBS Act also included a provision that an issuer is disqualified from using Rule 506 under their "bad actor" provisions. Simply, if the issuer or other relevant persons, (such as underwriters, directors, officers, or significant shareholders of the issuer) have been convicted of securities fraud or certain other securities violations, an offering under Rule 506 may not take place.

SEC Rule 501 Accredited Investors

SEC Rule 501 classifies an accredited investor for the purposes of Regulation D into several categories. Investors are considered to be accredited under the rule only if the issuer or any person acting on the issuer's behalf has reasonable grounds to believe, and does believe after reasonable inquiry, that the investors are included in one of the categories in the definition.

The separate categories of accredited investors under Regulation D include:

- a bank, insurance company, or registered investment company;

- an employee benefit plan if a bank, insurance company, or registered investment adviser makes the investment decisions, or if the plan has total assets in excess of $5 million;

- a charitable organization, corporation, or partnership with assets exceeding $5 million;

- directors, executive officers, and general partners of the issuer;

- any natural person whose individual net worth, or joint net worth with that person's spouse, excluding the net equity in his primary residence, exceeds $1 million at the time of his purchase;

- any natural person who had an individual income in excess of $200,000 in each of the two most recent years or joint income with that person's spouse in excess of $300,000 in each of those years and has a reasonable expectation of reaching the same income level in the current year; and

- entities made up of accredited investors.

The term *accredited investor* applies only to private placements. A favorite phrase of the regulators is, "eligibility does not equal suitability." Therefore, just because one meets the financial requirements of an accredited investor does not mean that suitability standards are ignored.

TEST TOPIC ALERT

Can assets in an account or property held jointly with another person who is not the purchaser's spouse be included in determining whether the purchaser satisfies the net worth test in Rule 501?

Answer: Yes, assets in an account or property held jointly with a person who is not the purchaser's spouse may be included in the calculation for the net worth test, but only to the extent of his percentage of ownership of the account or property.

EXAMPLE

1. Which of the following statements about accredited investors is TRUE?

   A. Taxpayers who report an income in excess of $200,000 on a joint return in each of the last two years and who reasonably expect the same for the current year are included in the definition.

   B. An officer, director, or greater than 10% shareholder of any company listed on the NYSE would be considered an accredited investor for purposes of acquiring a private placement your firm is selling.

   C. The term includes an employee benefit plan with assets in excess of $2 million.

   D. Purchases of securities by accredited investors do not count toward the 35 investor limitation found in Rule 506(b) of Regulation D.

   Answer: D. One of the benefits of this term is that these investors do not count in the numerical limitation placed on private placements made under Rule 506(b). Note that for offerings made under Rule 506(c), *all* investors must be accredited. When filing a joint return, the income requirement is $300,000, and an employee benefit plan must have assets in excess of $5 million. Insiders are only considered accredited investors when it is that issuer's security being offered.

Form D

What is Form D, and when does it have to be filed? Under Rule 503 of Regulation D, an issuer that is issuing securities in reliance on Regulation D must file Form D electronically with the SEC no later than 15 days after the first sale of securities in the offering.

Rule 147 deals with an exempt security and Rule 506 an exempt transaction. Perhaps this example will help solidify your understanding of these.

EXAMPLE

1. A business incorporated in State A, with its principal place of business in that state, would like to take advantage of the intrastate offering exemption found in the Securities Act of 1933. Which of the following would be most appropriate?

   A. Rule 147

   B. Rule 501

   C. Rule 506(b)

   D. Rule 506(c)

   Answer: A. The intrastate offering exemption is found in Rule 147. Rule 501 defines an accredited investor (which has nothing to do with the intrastate exemption). The question must mention private placement, Regulation D, or exempt transaction in order for Rule 506 to be relevant.

REGISTRATION OF SECURITIES UNDER FEDERAL LAW

Just like the rules under state law, if the security is not exempt (a nonexempt security) or the transaction is not exempt (exempt transaction), then the security must be registered with the SEC.

Issuer information must be disclosed to the SEC in a registration statement and published in a **prospectus**. In addition, the act prohibits fraudulent activity in connection with the sale, underwriting, and distribution of securities. The act provides for both civil and criminal penalties for violations of its provisions.

Even though registration under the Uniform Securities Act (the law that deals with regulation by the states) will be covered directly after this, where appropriate, mention will be of the similarities and differences between certain federal and state definitions.

Definition: Prospectus

A **prospectus** is any notice, circular, letter, or communication, written or broadcast by radio or television, that offers any security for sale or confirms the sale of a security. A **tombstone** advertisement published on the effective date (one that simply identifies the security, the price, and the underwriters) is not considered a prospectus nor an offering of the subject security. The term *prospectus* does not include oral communications.

As mentioned earlier, an **issuer** is any person who issues or proposes to issue any security. Most issuers are businesses, and the term *issuer* would also apply to a government entity.

When we described the exclusion from the definition of agent for an individual who represented the issuer in the sale of its security, we said that this was not the usual method of distributing a new issue, but was used by small firms who wished to reduce the cost. In almost all cases, securities are distributed by a broker-dealer (or network of BDs) acting as underwriters of the issue. The term underwriter is defined as any person, usually a broker-dealer, who has purchased a security from an issuer with a view to the distribution of the security, or participates or has a direct or indirect participation in that distribution.[2]

> **TAKE NOTE**
>
> The SEC does not approve securities registered with it, does not pass on the investment merit of any security, and never guarantees the accuracy of statements in the registration statement and prospectus.
>
> In its review process, the SEC merely attempts to make certain that all pertinent information is fully disclosed in the registration statement and prospectus by requiring that:
>
> - the issuer file a registration statement with the SEC before securities are offered or sold in interstate commerce;
> - a prospectus that meets the requirements of the act be provided to prospective buyers; and
> - penalties (civil, criminal, or administrative) be imposed for violations of the act.

REGISTRATION OF SECURITIES

The Registration Statement

An issuer must file a *registration statement* with the SEC disclosing material information about the issue. The registration statement must be signed by the principal executive officer (usually designated the CEO), the principal financial officer (usually designated the CFO), and a majority of the board of directors.

All of the signers are subject to criminal and civil penalties for willful omissions and misstatements of material facts. The information required in the registration statement may be summarized as follows:

- Purpose of issue
- Public offering price (anticipated range, but not the actual price)
- Underwriter's commissions or discounts
- Promotion expenses
- Expected use of the net proceeds of the issue to the company
- Balance sheet
- Earnings statements for the last three years
- Names, addresses, and bios of officers, directors, stockholders owning more than 10% of the outstanding stock (i.e., control persons), and underwriters of the issue
- Copy of underwriting agreements
- Copies of articles of incorporation

---

[2]   SEC. 202. (a)(20) of the Investment Advisers Act of 1940

The Cooling-Off Period

After the issuer files a registration statement with the SEC, a 20-day **cooling-off period** begins. After the issuer (with the underwriter's assistance) files with the SEC for registration of the securities, the cooling-off period begins before the registration becomes effective. The registration can become effective as early as 20 calendar days after the date the SEC has received it. In practice, however, the cooling-off period is seldom the minimum 20 days; the SEC usually takes longer to clear registration statements.

The Three Phases of an Underwriting

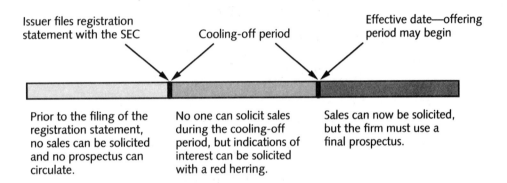

Issuer files registration statement with the SEC

Cooling-off period

Effective date—offering period may begin

Prior to the filing of the registration statement, no sales can be solicited and no prospectus can circulate.

No one can solicit sales during the cooling-off period, but indications of interest can be solicited with a red herring.

Sales can now be solicited, but the firm must use a final prospectus.

The cooling-off period can last several months because of the time it takes to make additions and corrections.

PRELIMINARY (RED HERRING) PROSPECTUS

The preliminary prospectus must be made available to any prospective purchaser who expresses interest in the security from the time the issue is filed with the SEC until it becomes publicly available for sale, the effective date (the previously described cooling-off period).

A red herring is used to acquaint investors with essential facts concerning the new issue. It is also used to solicit indications of buyer interest. However, it cannot be used:

- as a confirmation of sale;
- in place of a registration statement; or
- to declare the final public offering price.

However, along with stating the expected number of shares to be sold, a bona fide estimate of the price range per share must be included.

Under no circumstances may a broker-dealer or one of its agents accept money or orders prior to the effective date. All the agent can do is ask the client for an indication of interest as to whether she might be interested in the security once the registration is declared effective. This indication of interest is non-binding on both parties (the investor and the broker-dealer).

The term *red herring* was given to the preliminary prospectus because the front page contains the following statement printed in red ink.

> A Registration Statement relating to these securities has been filed with the Securities and Exchange Commission but has not yet become effective. Information contained herein is subject to completion or amendment. These securities may not be sold nor may offers to buy be accepted prior to the time the Registration Statement becomes effective.

No person connected with the offering is allowed to make marks on a preliminary prospectus under any circumstances. They cannot write short summaries or reviews on the preliminary prospectus. The preliminary prospectus must be given to customers without any alterations because, as stated previously, information is subject to change.

TAKE NOTE

Two items missing from the preliminary prospectus (red herring) are the public offering price (expected range must be shown) and the effective date.

TEST TOPIC ALERT

During the cooling-off period, underwriters may not:

- take orders; or
- distribute sales literature or advertising material.

However, they may:

- take indications of interest;
- distribute preliminary prospectuses; or
- publish tombstone advertisements to provide information about the potential availability of the securities.

The Final (Effective) Prospectus

A registration statement is normally a very long and complex document for an investor to read. The act requires the preparation of a shorter document called a **prospectus**. The prospectus summarizes the information contained in the registration statement. It must contain all the material facts in the registration statement, but in shorter form. The purpose of a prospectus is to provide the investor with adequate information to analyze the investment merits of the security. Even if an investor does not intend to read a prospectus, it still must be given to him. It is unlawful for a company to sell securities before the effective date of the registration statement.

Effective Date of Registration Statement

On the date a registration statement becomes effective (the SEC has cleared the security for sale), securities may be sold to the public by broker-dealers and their agents. A copy of the final (effective) prospectus must be delivered to each purchaser. This is normally accomplished by including the prospectus along with a confirmation of the trade, although it would certainly be permitted to deliver it earlier. Additional sales literature may be used by the firm as long as the sales literature is preceded or accompanied by a prospectus. Just as with a preliminary prospectus, no markings of any kind may be placed on the prospectus. No areas of special interest may be highlighted or have attention drawn to them by any other method. Money may be accepted by the broker-dealer from customers at this time.

State Securities Registration Procedures

The first step in the registration procedure is for the issuer or its representative to complete a registration application and file it with the state securities Administrator. The person registering the securities is known as the **registrant**. There are some provisions applicable to all registrations regardless of the method used. The exam will want you to know these well.

Filing the Registration Statement

State Administrators require every issuer to supply the following information on their applications:

- Amount of securities to be issued in the state
- States in which the security is to be offered, but not the amounts offered in those other states
- Any adverse order or judgment concerning the offering by regulatory authorities, court, or the SEC
- Anticipated effective date
- Anticipated use of the proceeds (why are we raising this money?)

The Administrator may, by rule or order, permit the omission of any information she considers unnecessary.

TEST TOPIC ALERT

Although most registration statements are filed by the issuer, the exam may require you to know that they may also be filed by any selling stockholder, such as an insider making a large block sale, or by a broker-dealer.

Filing Fee

The issuer (or any other person on whose behalf the offering is to be made) must pay a filing fee, as determined by the Administrator, when filing the registration. The filing fees are often based on a percentage of the total offering price.

If the registration is withdrawn or if the Administrator issues a stop order before the registration is effective, the Administrator may retain a portion of the fee and refund the remainder to the applicant.

TAKE NOTE

A **stop order** is used to deny effectiveness to, or suspend or revoke the effectiveness of, any registration statement. This applies only to securities, not professionals such as broker-dealers, agents, investment advisers, and investment adviser representatives.

Ongoing Reports

The Administrator may require the person who filed the registration statement to file reports to keep the information contained in the registration statement current and to inform the Administrator of the progress of the offering.

TEST TOPIC ALERT

These reports cannot be required more often than quarterly.

Escrow

As a condition of registration under coordination or qualification, the Administrator may require that a security be placed in **escrow** if the security is issued:

- within the past three years;
- to a promoter at a price substantially different than the offering price; or
- to any person for a consideration other than cash.

In addition, the Administrator may require that the proceeds from the sale of the registered security in this state be impounded until the issuer receives a specified amount from the sale of the security either in this state or elsewhere. There have been many instances where companies were unable to raise their targeted goal and just took the money and ran. This impound, or escrow, lessens the likelihood that this will happen.

Special Subscription Form

The Administrator may also require, as a condition of registration, that the issue be sold only on a form specified by the Administrator and that a copy of the form or subscription contract be filed with the Administrator or preserved for up to three years.

METHODS OF STATE REGISTRATION OF SECURITIES

The USA provides two methods for securities issuers to register their securities in a state, plus a special method for certain federal covered securities. They are:

- notice filing;
- coordination; and
- qualification.

Notice Filing

As previously mentioned, the National Securities Markets Improvement Act of 1996 (NSMIA) designated certain securities as federal covered and, therefore, removed from the jurisdiction of the state regulatory authorities. Although the states are preempted from requiring registration for federal covered securities, status as a federal covered security is not a preemption of the licensing or antifraud laws. Any person that sells a federal covered security must be licensed as a broker-dealer or agent (unless otherwise exempted) and must also comply with the antifraud provisions of state laws.

The Uniform Securities Act gives the Administrator the authority to require notice filings with respect to federal covered securities, generally investment companies registered with the SEC under the Investment Company Act of 1940. So, what is this notice filing? Primarily, it is an opportunity for the states to collect revenue in the form of filing fees because, unlike with the two actual methods of registration we are going to discuss, the Administrator has limited powers to review any documentation filed with her department. The fees for notice filing are generally lower than for the two forms of registration.

Under the notice filing procedure, state Administrators may require the issuer of certain federal covered securities to file the following documents as a condition for sale of their securities in the state:

- Documents filed along with their registration statements filed with the SEC

- Documents filed as amendments to the initial federal registration statement
- A report as to the value of such securities offered in the state
- Consent to service of process

TEST TOPIC ALERT

Keep in mind the distinction between federal covered securities and SEC-registered securities. As stated earlier, SEC-registered does not mean federal covered. Many are and many aren't and federal covered also includes those exempt from SEC registration.

TEST TOPIC ALERT

Before the initial offer of any federal covered security in this state, the Administrator, by rule or order, may require the filing of all documents that are part of a federal registration statement filed with the U.S. Securities and Exchange Commission under the Securities Act of 1933, together with a consent to service of process signed by the issuer. However, unless there is an appearance of fraud, the Administrator does not have the power (because of lack of jurisdiction) to prevent the sale of a federal covered security in his state.

TEST TOPIC ALERT

Even though an issuer of a federal covered security (think about a Fortune 500 company listed on the NYSE) may not have to notice file, that does not mean that the company can make misrepresentations during an offer made in any state. To do so would violate the antifraud provisions of the USA.

Registration by Coordination

The most common form of registration for those securities that are not federal covered (typically securities traded on the OTC Bulletin Board or the OTC Link) is coordination. A security may be **registered by coordination** if a registration statement has been filed under the Securities Act of 1933 in connection with the same offering.

In coordinating a federal registration with state registration, issuers must supply the following records in addition to the consent to service of process:

- Copies of the latest form of prospectus filed under the Securities Act of 1933, if the Administrator requires it
- Copy of articles of incorporation and bylaws, a copy of the underwriting agreement, or a specimen copy of the certificate
- If the Administrator requests, copies of any other information filed by the issuer under the Securities Act of 1933
- Each amendment to the federal prospectus promptly after it is filed with the SEC

Effective Date

Registration by coordination becomes effective at the same time the federal registration becomes effective, provided:

- no stop orders have been issued by the Administrator and no proceedings are pending against the issuer;

- the registration has been on file for at least the minimum number of days specified by the Administrator, a number that currently ranges from 10 to 20 days, depending on the state; and

- a statement of the maximum and minimum offering prices and underwriting discounts have been on file for two business days.

Registration by coordination is by far the most frequently used method and, from a practical standpoint, is the only sensible way to register a multi-state offering.

Registration by Qualification

Any security can be **registered by qualification**. Registration by qualification requires a registrant to supply any information required by the state securities Administrator. Securities not eligible for registration by another method must be registered by qualification. In general, securities that will be sold only in one state (intrastate) will be registered by qualification.

To register by qualification, an issuer must supply a consent to service of process and the following information:

- Name, address, form of organization, description of property, and nature of business

- Name and address of any person owning 10% or more of the outstanding shares of any class of equity security of the issuer;

- Estimated proceeds and the use to which the proceeds will be put

- Type and amount of securities offered, offering price, and selling and underwriting costs

- Copy of any prospectus, pamphlet, circular, or sales literature to be used in the offering

- A specimen copy of the security's certificate

The Administrator may require additional information by rule or order. The Administrator may require that a prospectus be sent to purchasers before the sale and that newly established companies register their securities for the first time in a state by qualification.

TAKE NOTE

As we've noted previously, to register, even by notice filing, there must be a consent to service of process filed with the Administrator. However, a person (remember the broad definition) who has filed such a consent in connection with a previous registration or notice filing need not file another. A practical effect of this is if a company decides to raise additional capital by issuing more stock, a new consent is not required.

Effective Date

Unlike coordination, where the effective date is triggered by SEC acceptance of the registration, a registration by qualification becomes effective whenever the state Administrator so orders.

Regardless of the method used, every registration statement is effective for one year from its effective date. Unlike the registration of securities professionals, the date December 31 is of no consequence. One interesting facet of the law is that the registration may continue in effect past the first anniversary if there are still some unsold shares remaining, as long as they are still being offered at the original public offering price by either the issuer or the underwriter.

Although the one year effective period applies to all methods of registration, as a practical matter, it would rarely apply other than in a security registered by qualification. Those registered by coordination are also obviously registered with the SEC and therefore are sold by the major investment banking houses. Unless the issue is a real dog, it will sell out rather quickly. Even those that are not popular are usually completely subscribed to in a week or two.

On the other hand, what if the issue, regardless of the method of registration, is in very high demand? Is it possible to increase the number of shares in the offering without having to file a new registration statement? Yes. A registration statement may be amended after its effective date so as to increase the securities specified to be offered and sold if two conditions are met:

- The public offering price is not changed from the amount stated in the original registration statement
- The underwriters' discounts and commissions are not changed from the respective amounts stated in the original registration statement

TEST TOPIC ALERT

A registration statement may be amended after its effective date to change the number of shares to be offered and sold if the public offering price and underwriter's discounts and commissions are unchanged.

EXAMPLE

1. XYZ Corporation has been in business for over 20 years. They need additional capital for expansion, and determine that a public offering in their home state and neighboring states is appropriate. Which method of securities registration would most likely be used to register this initial public offering?

    A. Coordination

    B. Notice filing

    C. Qualification

    D. Registration

    Answer: A. Because this offering is being made in more than one state, SEC registration is necessary. The state registration method would be coordination, which is the simultaneous registration of a security with both the SEC and the states.

2. KAPCO Dividend Yield Fund, a closed-end investment company registered under the Investment Company Act of 1940, wishes to commence offering its shares in States A, B, C, and D. It could be required to

   A. coordinate its federal registration with each of the four states

   B. notice file

   C. register by qualification in each of the states

   D. do none of these because investment companies registered under the Investment Company Act of 1940 are federal covered securities and are exempt from registration

   Answer: B. Although these are federal covered securities and exempt from traditional registration, as a registered investment company, you can expect that it will be required to engage in a notice filing.

3. Registration is effective when ordered by the Administrator in the case of registration by

   A. coordination

   B. integration

   C. notice filing

   D. qualification

   Answer: D. Registration by qualification is the only registration method where the Administrator sets the effective date. The effective date under registration by coordination is set by the SEC, and notice filing is merely the filing of certain documents by certain federal covered securities.

4. In general, registration statements for securities under the Uniform Securities Act are effective for

   A. a period determined by the Administrator for each issue

   B. 1 year from the effective date

   C. 1 year from the date of issue

   D. 1 year from the previous January 1

   Answer: B. On the state level, securities registration statements are generally effective for 1 year from the effective date. However, the effective date may be extended for a longer period during which the security is being offered or distributed in a nonexempt transaction by the issuer or other person on whose behalf the offering is being made or by any underwriter who is still offering part of an unsold allotment or subscription taken by him as a participant in the distribution.

ANTIFRAUD

U4LO4: Describe the applicability of the antifraud provisions of the Uniform Securities Act.

Under all regulatory bodies, in order for an action to be fraudulent, it must committed willfully and knowingly. There is no such thing as "accidental" fraud. Although the SEC has antifraud statues as well, the exam will focus on those of the Uniform Securities Act. The applicability of the antifraud provisions is almost universal. For example, here is a statement about *investment advisers*:

"It is unlawful for any person who receives, directly or indirectly, any consideration from another person for advising the other person as to the value of securities or their purchase or sale, whether through the issuance of analyses or reports or otherwise,

(1) to employ any device, scheme, or artifice to defraud the other person,

(2) to engage in any act, practice, or course of business which operates or would operate as a fraud or deceit upon the other person."[3]

For *broker-dealers*:

"It is unlawful for any person, in connection with the offer, sale or purchase of any security, directly or indirectly

(1) to employ any device, scheme, or artifice to defraud,

(2) to make any untrue statement of a material fact or to omit to state a material fact necessary to make the statements made, in the light of the circumstances under which they are made, not misleading, or

(3) to engage in any act, practice, or course of business which operates or would operate as a fraud or deceit upon any person."[4]

For *securities*:

"The antifraud provisions, apply regardless of whether the security is registered, exempted, or sold in violation of the registration requirements."

What these statements indicate that that no securities professional and no security is exempt from the antifraud rules. But, what if the person is excluded from the definition of, say, an investment adviser? Or what if the investment is excluded from the definition of a security? What then?

"There are no exemptions from fraud. For example, persons availing themselves of the de minimis exemption as investment advisers would remain subject to the antifraud provisions."

A common example of fraudulent behavior is the use of material nonpublic information (insider trading).

EXAMPLE

The distinction between exemptions and exceptions (or exclusions) from definitions is important in view of the fact that an exempt security is not exempt from the antifraud provisions of the Uniform Securities Act.

As we covered earlier in this unit, the typical life insurance policy or fixed annuity is not a security, and is not covered under the antifraud statutes of the Uniform Securities Act. On the other hand, we know that securities issued by insurance companies are exempted from registration under the conditions of the Act. Even though these securities are exempt from registration and the filing of advertising

---

3   Uniform Securities Act, Section 102

4   Uniform Securities Act, Section 101

and sales literature with the Administrator, they are still subject to the antifraud provisions. Therefore, one could be charged with fraudulent behavior in the sale of stock in an insurance company (or any other exempt security).

Using the same logic, a federal covered investment adviser, although not registered in any state, can be charged by the state Administrator when there is an alleged violation of the antifraud provisions of the USA.

Is there ever a time when the antifraud provisions do not apply? Yes. They do not apply to an investment that is excluded from the definition of a security. An example of this would be a rare coin dealer who falsifies the dates on coins sold to a client. That certainly is fraud, but doesn't come under the USA's antifraud provisions because rare coins are not securities. We previously mentioned the sale of a fixed annuity—it is not a security so the antifraud provisions of the Uniform Securities Act do not apply. Of course, the state insurance department would have something to say about any fraudulent activity with insurance products, but, if they were not a security, the USA doesn't apply.

UNIT 5

Remedies and Administrative Provisions

This unit addresses the administrative provisions of the act and the remedies available to the Administrator. Under the USA, the state Administrator has jurisdiction over securities transactions that originate in, are directed into, or are accepted in the Administrator's state.

When a securities transaction falls within the Administrator's jurisdiction, the Administrator has power to make rules and orders; conduct investigations and issue subpoenas; issue cease and desist orders; and deny, suspend, or revoke registrations.

Both civil liabilities and criminal penalties exist for violating the act.

The Series 65 exam will include two questions on the material presented in this unit.

LEARNING OBJECTIVES

When you have completed this unit, you will be able to accomplish the following.

U5LO1:   Recognize the jurisdiction and authority of the state securities Administrator.

U5LO2:   Identify the administrative actions that may be taken by the Administrator.

U5LO3:   Describe the civil rights of recovery for a security's sale or for investment advice purchased in violation of the Uniform Securities Act.

U5LO4:   Identify criminal penalties for violation of the Uniform Securities Act.

ADMINISTRATOR'S JURISDICTION

U5LO1: Recognize the jurisdiction and authority of the state securities Administrator.

The jurisdiction and powers of the Administrator extend to activities related to securities transactions originated in the state, directed to the state, or accepted in the state. Securities transactions involve an offer and a sale so we need to know what those terms mean and then we can focus on the Administrator's jurisdiction.

TAKE NOTE

The SEC's authority does not extend over state securities regulation (the Uniform Securities Act).

Sale or Sell and Offer or Offer to Sell

The USA defines **offer** or **offer to sell** as every attempt or offer to dispose of, or solicitation of an offer to buy, a security or interest in a security for value. For test purposes, you should know that:

- any security given or delivered with, or as a bonus on account of, a purchase of securities or anything else (a car, jewelry, and so forth) is considered to constitute part of the subject of the purchase and to have been offered and sold for value;

- a purported gift of *assessable* stock is considered to involve an offer and a sale (assessable stock is stock issued below par for which the issuer or creditors have the right to assess shareholders for the balance of unpaid par); or

- a sale or offer of a warrant or right to purchase or subscribe to another security of the same or another issuer, as well as every sale or offer of a security which gives the holder a present or future right or privilege to convert into another security of the same or another issuer, is considered to include an offer of the other security.

If a car dealer, as an essential part of a car sale, offers $1,000 in corporate bonds as an incentive, this would be considered a bonus under the act and, therefore, this now becomes a securities sale and falls under the jurisdiction of the state securities Administrator. As a result, to do this, and I know it is hard to believe, the car dealer would have to register with the state as a broker-dealer.

Sale or Sell

The USA defines **sale** or **sell** as every contract of sale, contract to sell, and disposition of a security or interest in a security for value. This means that any transfer of a security in which money or some other valuable consideration is involved is covered by this definition and subject to the act.

TAKE NOTE

You must be able to distinguish between a sale and an offer to sell. The offer is the attempt; a transaction has not taken place. In a sale, there has been an actual transaction involving money or another form of consideration for value. One must be properly registered to both make the offer and then the sale.

Gifts of Assessable Stock

When assessable stock is given as a gift, the Administrator has jurisdiction over the transaction because there is a potential future obligation in that either the issuer or, more likely, creditors can demand payment for the balance of the par value.

TAKE NOTE

If an individual owned assessable stock and felt that the issuer was on the verge of bankruptcy, that person could give the stock as a present. If the bankruptcy occurred, the new owner would then be subject to the assessment.

TEST TOPIC ALERT

Assessable stock no longer exists, but the exam may ask about it. Look for this direct quote from the Uniform Securities Act: "A purported gift of assessable stock is considered to involve an offer and sale."

Exclusions From the Definition of Sale/Sell and Offer/Offer to Sell

The terms *sale* or *sell* and *offer* or *offer to sell* do not include any:

- bona fide pledge or loan (pledging stock as collateral for a loan, such as for a loan at the bank, is not a sale; you expect to get your stock back when the loan is paid off—you haven't sold it);

- gift of nonassessable stock (this is the way all stocks are today);

- stock dividend, whether the corporation distributing the dividend is the issuer of the stock or not, if nothing of value is given by stockholders for the dividend (and this would include stock splits);

- class vote by stockholders, pursuant to the certificate of incorporation or the applicable corporation statute, or a merger, consolidation, reclassification of securities, or sale of corporate assets in consideration of the issuance of securities of another corporation; or

- act incident to a judicially approved reorganization with which a security is issued in exchange for one or more outstanding securities, claims, or property interest, or partly in such exchange and partly for cash.

TEST TOPIC ALERT

Because you have just learned that the gift of nonassessable stock is not considered a sale, you have to be careful not to be tricked by a question on the exam in which shares of nonassessable stock are given free as a bonus with the purchase of something else (e.g., a security, a car, a house). This would not be a gift and would, in fact, be an offer or a sale.

Legal Jurisdiction of the Administrator

Under law, for any agent of a state (e.g., the Administrator) to have authority over an activity such as a sale or offer of securities, he must have legal jurisdiction to act. **Jurisdiction** under the USA specifically means the legal authority to regulate securities activities that take place in the state.

The USA describes activities considered to have taken place in the state as any offer to buy or sell a security, as well as any acceptance of the offer, if the offer:

- originated in the Administrator's state;

- is directed to the Administrator's state; or

- is accepted in the Administrator's state.

TAKE NOTE

Because securities transactions often involve several states, more than one Administrator may have jurisdiction over a security or a transaction.

Let's work through some examples to see how this might appear on your exam.

EXAMPLE

1. Jane is an agent registered in States A and B. While sitting in her office in State A, she contacts a client who lives in State B with a recommendation to buy ABC stock. The client agrees to make the purchase. Jurisdiction here would belong to

    A. the State A Administrator

    B. the State B Administrator

    C. both the State A and State B Administrators

    D. neither Administrator because this is an existing client

    Answer: C. In this case, it would be the Administrators of both States A and B (choice **C**). Why is that? Remember that the Administrator has jurisdiction over any offer that originated in his state and clearly this offer originated from Jane in State A. Recall that the Administrator has jurisdiction over any offer that was accepted in his state and this client who accepted the offer lives in State B. The status of the client, existing or prospective, does not affect the Administrator's jurisdiction.

Let's take a look at another possible question:

EXAMPLE

1. Jane has another State A-based client, Sally, who spends the winters in State C, a state where neither Jane nor her broker-dealer have a place of business or any retail clients. Jane sends Sally a research report with a strong buy recommendation for XYZ stock. Sally calls Jane with an order to purchase 100 shares of XYZ. Jurisdiction over this transaction belongs to

    A. the State A Administrator

    B. the State C Administrator

    C. both the State A and State B Administrators

    D. both the State A and State C Administrators

    Answer: D. Just as with the previous question, we have an offer being made from State A resulting in that Administrator having jurisdiction. Although the client lives in State A, the offer was accepted while she was in State C, so the State C Administrator has jurisdiction making the correct choice **D**. Although not related to the issue of jurisdiction, for review purposes, we should ask ourselves, "Can this transaction legally take place?" Jane is not registered in State C—how can she make the offer to a client who is there and how can she (and her broker-dealer) accept a retail order when neither of them are registered in State C? As noted in Unit 3, a broker-dealer with no place of business in a state who deals with existing clients (such as Sally) who are temporarily in the state (as Sally is), is not defined as a broker-dealer in that state and, therefore, does not register (nor do their agents).

TAKE NOTE

The Administrator's authority does not stop at the state line. The Administrator of any state where the registrant is registered may demand an inspection during reasonable business hours with whatever frequency the Administrator deems necessary.

TAKE NOTE

To avoid unnecessary duplication of examinations, the Administrator may cooperate with the securities administrators of other states, the SEC, and any national securities exchange or national securities association registered under the Securities Exchange Act of 1934.

Publishing and Broadcast Exceptions to Jurisdiction

There are special rules regarding the Administrator's jurisdiction over offers made through a TV or radio broadcast or a bona fide newspaper.

The Administrator would not have jurisdiction if the offer were made under any of the following circumstances:

- Television or radio broadcast that originated outside of the state
- Bona fide newspaper or periodical published outside of the state
- Newspaper or periodical published inside the state but with more than two-thirds (66.7%) of its circulation outside the state in the last year

TAKE NOTE

A bona fide newspaper is a newspaper of general interest and circulation, such as *The New York Times*. Private investment advisory newsletters, usually distributed by subscription, are not bona fide newspapers and therefore are not included in the publishing exception.

TEST TOPIC ALERT

A radio or television program is considered to originate in the state where the microphone or television camera is located.

EXAMPLE

Let's take a look at how this publishing exemption might appear on the exam:

1. Wayne and Grayson, LTD., is a broker-dealer with offices in Gotham, New Jersey. They place an ad for a new securities issue in the Gotham Gazette. Approximately 55% of the Gazette's readership is in Delaware. Under the Uniform Securities Act, jurisdiction over this ad would lie with

    A. the Administrator of New Jersey

    B. the Administrator of Delaware

    C. the Administrator of both New Jersey and Delaware

    D. the Administrator of neither New Jersey nor Delaware

Answer: A. Although more than half the readers of the Gazette live in Delaware, under the terms of the publishing and broadcasting exemption of the USA, the offer is not made in Delaware because the paper is not published there. Therefore, the Administrator of New Jersey has sole jurisdiction over the offering. No dual or multiple jurisdiction applies in this case, unless the offer is actually accepted in Delaware. What would the answer be if the question stated that more than ⅔ of the circulation was outside of New Jersey? Once that happens, believe it or not, no state has jurisdiction.

ADMINISTRATOR'S ACTIONS

U5LO2: Identify the administrative actions that may be taken by the Administrator.

The USA not only establishes the jurisdiction of the Administrator but also outlines the powers or the actions that the Administrator can take within its jurisdiction.

The four broad powers the Administrator has to enforce and administer the act in his state are to:

■ make, amend, or rescind rules and orders and require the use of specific forms;

■ conduct investigations and issue subpoenas;

■ issue cease and desist orders and seek injunctions; and

■ deny, suspend, cancel, or revoke registrations and licenses.

Because the Administrator has the power to enforce the act for the benefit of the public, the Administrator, as well as his employees, have an obligation not to use the office for personal gain. Administrators are, as a result, prohibited from using, for their own benefit, any information derived from their official duties that has not been made public.

Rules, Orders, and Forms

To enforce the USA, the Administrator has the authority to make, amend, or rescind rules, forms, and orders necessary to administer the act. The USA requires that all rules and forms be published. A rule or order of the Administrator has the same authority as a provision of the act itself, but these rules and orders are not part of the USA itself. The difference between a rule and an order is that a rule applies to everyone, whereas an order applies to a specific instance.

EXAMPLE

The Administrator may decide to issue a rule requiring all agents to pay an annual registration fee of $250. This rule applies to everyone. Or, the Administrator may find that a specific agent has violated a provision of the law and orders a 30-day suspension. This order applies only to that particular agent.

Although the Administrator has the power to make and amend rules for compliance with his state's blue-sky law, he does not have the power to alter the law itself.

The composition or content of state securities law is the responsibility of the state legislature, not of administrative agencies. Rules for administration and compliance with the law are the responsibility of the securities Administrator.

EXAMPLE   Rules and Orders of the Administrator

Situation: The Administrator of State R requires by rule that all companies registering their securities in State R must supply financial statements in a specific form and with content prescribed by the Administrator. However, the Administrator does not publish the rule because the rule is too long and complex.

Analysis: The USA allows state Administrators to issue rules and orders in carrying out their regulatory functions, and the State R Administrator acted properly in designing the form and content for financial reports. However, it is required by the USA that Administrators publish all rules and orders. The Administrator, despite the latitude given him in administering the USA, cannot suspend any provision of the USA itself. The State R Administrator acted within his authority in designing the forms but acted without authority—that is, he violated the USA—by suspending the requirement that all rules and orders be published.

Conduct Investigations and Issue Subpoenas

The Administrator has broad discretionary authority to **conduct investigations** and **issue subpoenas**. These investigations may be made in public or in private and may occur within or outside of the Administrator's state. Normally, these investigations are open to the public, but when, in the opinion of the Administrator and with the consent of all parties, it is felt that a private investigation is more appropriate, that investigation will be conducted without public scrutiny.

In conducting an investigation, the Administrator, or any officer designated by him, has the power to:

- require statements in writing, under oath, as to all matters relating to the issue under investigation;
- publish and make public the facts and circumstances concerning the issue to be investigated;
- subpoena witnesses and compel their attendance and testimony; and
- take evidence and require the production of books, papers, correspondence, and any other documents deemed relevant.

TEST TOPIC ALERT

If the Administrator of State A wishes to investigate a BD registered in State A, but whose principal office is located in State B, does he need the okay of the State B Administrator? No! When can he go in? The Administrator can go in during normal business hours and doesn't need to make an appointment.

Contumacy

So, what happens if a person who is the subject of an investigation refuses to furnish the required evidence or just ignores the subpoena? After all, the Administrator is not a police officer—he doesn't wear a badge and cannot arrest anyone. There is a legal term that describes this type of disobedience. That term is *contumacy* and here is what the USA says about that:

> In case of contumacy by, or refusal to obey a subpoena issued to, any person, the Administrator may apply to the appropriate court in his state and ask for help. Upon application by the Administrator, the court can issue an order to the person requiring him to appear before the Administrator, or the officer designated by him, to produce documentary evidence if so ordered or to give evidence touching the matter under investigation or in question. Failure to obey the order of the court may be punished by the court as a contempt of court.[1]

Contempt of court can, of course, lead to jail time.

TAKE NOTE

In addition to having the power to conduct investigations, the Administrator may enforce subpoenas issued by Administrators in other states on the same basis as if the alleged offense took place in the Administrator's state. However, the Administrator may issue and apply to enforce subpoenas in his state at the request of a securities agency or administrator of another state only if the activities constituting an alleged violation for which the information is sought would be a violation of the securities laws of that state if the activities had occurred in his state.

Issue Cease and Desist Orders

Whenever it appears to the Administrator that any person has engaged or is about to engage in any act or practice constituting a violation of any provision of this act or any rule or order hereunder, she may in her discretion bring either or both of the following remedies:

■ issue a cease and desist order, with or without a prior hearing, against the person or persons engaged in the prohibited activities, directing them to cease and desist from further illegal activity; or

■ bring an action in the appropriate court to obtain enforcement of the order through the issuance of a temporary or permanent injunction. If necessary, the court may appoint a receiver or conservator for the defendant or the defendant's assets.

The Administrator is granted this power to prevent potential violations before they occur. It is sometimes said that the Administrator can act when she "smells the smoke, even without seeing the fire." Sometimes a tipster or whistleblower will divulge information to the Administrator that might be relevant to a serious infraction. To prevent any further damage to investors, a cease and desist order can be entered.

Although the Administrator has the power to issue cease and desist orders, she does not have the legal power to compel compliance with the order. To compel compliance in the face of a person's resistance, the Administrator must apply to a court of competent jurisdiction for an injunction. Only the courts can compel compliance by issuing injunctions and imposing penalties for violation of them. You will need to know that **enjoined** is the legal term that is used to refer to a person who is the subject of an injunction.

---

[1]   Source Section 407 (c) of the USA

TAKE NOTE

Cease and desist orders are not the same as stop orders. **Cease and desist orders** are directed to persons, requiring them to cease activities. Stop orders are directed to applications regarding registration of a security.

EXAMPLE   Cease and Desist Orders

Situation: Althea Thomas is registered to conduct business in State C and makes plans to sell a security within the next few days. The Administrator considers this security ineligible for sale in the state. The Administrator orders Thomas to stop her sales procedures immediately.

Analysis: The Administrator of State C issued a cease and desist order to Thomas because there was insufficient time to conduct a public hearing before the sale to determine whether the security was eligible for sale in the state.

Deny, Suspend, Cancel, or Revoke Registrations

The Administrator has the power to deny, suspend, cancel, or revoke the registration of broker-dealers, investment advisers, and their representatives as well as the registration of securities issues.

Broker-Dealers, Investment Advisers, and Their Representatives

To justify a denial, revocation, or suspension of the license of a **securities professional**, the Administrator must find that the order is in the public interest and also find that the applicant or registrant, or in the case of a broker-dealer or investment adviser, any partner, officer, or director, or any person occupying a similar status or performing similar functions:

- has filed an incomplete, false, or misleading registration application;
- has willfully violated the USA;
- has been disqualified from membership in any securities or commodities regulatory body due to a conviction of a securities-related misdemeanor as a result of action brought within the last 10 years;
- has been convicted of any felony within the last 10 years;
- has been enjoined by law from engaging in the securities business;
- is subject to another Administrator's denial, revocation, or suspension;
- is engaged in dishonest or unethical securities practices;
- is insolvent;
- is the subject of an adjudication that the broker-dealer has willfully violated the Securities Act of 1933, the Securities Exchange Act of 1934, the Investment Advisers Act of 1940, the Investment Company Act of 1940, or the Commodities Exchange Act;
- has, in the case of a broker-dealer or investment adviser, been found guilty on the charge of failure to supervise;
- has failed to pay application filing fees; or
- is not qualified on the basis of training, lack of experience, and knowledge of the securities business.

TEST TOPIC ALERT

Because of a lack of uniformity in state criminal laws, it can happen that a person is convicted of a misdemeanor in one state and then moves to a state where that same crime is a felony. If the person were to then apply for registration, the Administrator must consider the crime under the statutes of the state where it occurred, not his own. In other words, the Administrator may only consider what is on the person's record.

TEST TOPIC ALERT

If a person is subject to a disqualification by any SRO, even the NASD (before it became FINRA), for something that was *not* a violation of the Uniform Securities Act, that would still be a cause for denial.

TEST TOPIC ALERT

Denial is generally limited to convictions for any felony or investment-related misdemeanors within the past 10 years. However, as pointed out in a previous unit, these convictions (and even just being charged) must always be disclosed on the application for registration—there is no time limit.

TAKE NOTE

The public's best interest is not reason enough for the denial, suspension, or revocation of a registration. There must be a further reason, as described previously.

Other than when acting summarily, no order to deny, suspend, or revoke may be entered without:

- appropriate prior notice to the applicant or registrant (as well as the employer or prospective employer if the applicant or registrant is an agent or investment adviser representative);
- opportunity for hearing; and
- written findings of fact and conclusions of law.

The Administrator may not suspend or revoke a registration on the basis of facts that were known to the Administrator at the time the registration became effective (unless the proceedings are initiated within 90 days).

Lack of Qualification

An Administrator may not base a denial of a person's registration solely on his lack of experience. However, the Administrator may consider that registration as a broker-dealer does not necessarily qualify one for a license as an investment adviser and may restrict that applicant's registration as a broker-dealer conditional upon its not functioning as an investment adviser.

To better understand these two points, let's look at the wording in the Act itself.

1. *The Administrator may not enter an order denying registration solely on the basis of lack of experience if the applicant or registrant is qualified by training or knowledge or both.*[2]

Obviously, a new applicant for registration as an agent or IAR is not going to have any experience selling securities. So, the Act says that this lack of experience by itself is not enough to deny the registration as long as the Administrator feels assured that the individual will receive adequate training and/or has the requisite knowledge. One could suppose that passing this exam demonstrates the necessary knowledge.

2. *The Administrator may consider that an investment adviser is not necessarily qualified solely on the basis of experience as a broker-dealer or agent. When she finds that an applicant for initial or renewal registration as a broker-dealer is not qualified as an investment adviser, she may, by order, condition the applicant's registration as a broker-dealer upon the firm's agreeing to not engage in business in this state as an investment adviser.*[3]

In this case, the Act is dealing with a person who has experience, albeit not necessarily in the giving of advice. Just because a person has been a broker-dealer, or an agent for a broker-dealer, does not mean that the person is qualified to be an investment adviser. So, the registration will be limited to acting only in their stated capacity as long as one does not cross over the line and give investment advice.

Summary Powers

One of the powers of the Administrator is known as acting **summarily**. This means that she may order, without having to go through the hearing process, a postponement or suspension of a registration pending final determination of any proceeding based upon actions described previously. Once the summary order is entered, the Administrator will promptly notify the applicant or registrant, as well as the employer or prospective employer if the applicant or registrant is an agent or investment adviser representative, that it has been entered and of the reasons for it. If the applicant wishes a hearing, written request must be made and, within 15 days after the receipt of the written request, the matter will be set down for hearing. If no hearing is requested and none is ordered by the Administrator, the order will remain in effect until it is modified or vacated by the Administrator.

Final Orders

A **final order** is one that ends litigation (usually). Under the Uniform Securities Act, it is when the Administrator (or a court) renders a judgment in an action (guilty or innocent). Regardless of whether we're referring to persons, exemptions, or registration, as stated previously (and repeated because it is likely to be on the exam), other than when the Administrator has acted summarily as described previously, no final order may be issued without the Administrator:

- giving appropriate prior notice to the affected persons;
- granting an opportunity for a hearing; and
- providing findings of fact and conclusions of law.

---

[2]   Uniform Securities Act, Section 204 (b) (3)

[3]   Uniform Securities Act, Section (b) (5)

Securities Issues

As is the case with a securities professional, a securities Administrator may deny, suspend, cancel, or revoke a security's registration if the order is in the public's interest and the securities registrant:

- files a misleading or incomplete registration statement;

- is engaged in an offering that is fraudulent or made on unfair, unjust, or inequitable terms;

- charges offering fees that are excessive or unreasonable;

- has a control person convicted of a securities-related crime;

- is subject to a court injunction;

- is engaged in a method of business that is illegal; or

- is subject to an administrative stop order of any other state.

In addition, the Administrator may deny a registration if the applicant fails to pay the filing fee. When the fee is paid, the denial order will be removed provided the applicant is in compliance with all registration procedures.

TEST TOPIC ALERT

When the conditions that led to the issuance of the stop order have changed for the better, the legal term (remember, this is a law exam) used to describe the lifting of the stop order is **vacated** (e.g., "the order has been vacated").

It is important that you be able to recognize the difference between a cease and desist order and a stop order. Look at the following examples:

EXAMPLES

1. An agent of a broker-dealer solicits clients to purchase unregistered promissory notes. The agent claims that promissory notes are not securities and, therefore, do not need to be registered. The Administrator disagrees with that position and would issue

   A. a cease and desist order against the agent

   B. a cease and desist order against the issuer of the note

   C. a stop order against the agent

   D. a stop order against the issuer

   Answer: A. Unless we had reason to believe that the issuer was the one claiming that its notes were not securities, the only person guilty here is the agent. Stopping the agent from continuing to solicit the purchase of unregistered securities is done by issuing a cease and desist order, choice **A**. Alternatively, if the question went like this:

2. Palterer Products, Inc. (PPI), headquartered in State J, has sent an announcement to a number of broker-dealers in the state promoting their 8% promissory notes as a high interest nonsecurity alternative to a

bank CD. The compliance officer of your firm forwards this to the State J Administrator. What action would the Administrator likely take?

A. Issue a cease and desist order against the compliance officer with or without a hearing

B. Issue a cease and desist order against PPI with or without a hearing

C. Issue a stop order against the compliance officer after giving opportunity for a hearing

D. Issue a stop order against PPI after giving opportunity for a hearing

Answer: D. Promissory notes are securities and, therefore, PPI must stop soliciting the sale of them as non-securities. The method of doing so is through the issue of a stop order, choice **D**. No order would be forthcoming against the compliance officer; she was only doing her job correctly. Remember, cease and desist orders are against registered securities professionals and stop orders against issuers. Finally, the cease and desist order can be issued with or without a hearing and the stop order only after a hearing.

NONPUNITIVE TERMINATIONS OF REGISTRATION

A registration can be terminated even if there has not been a violation of the USA. A request for withdrawal and lack of qualification are both reasons for cancellation.

Withdrawal

A person may request on his own initiative a withdrawal of a registration. The withdrawal is effective 30 days after the Administrator receives it, provided no revocation or suspension proceedings are in process against the person making the request. In that event, the Administrator may institute a revocation or suspension proceeding within one year after a withdrawal becomes effective.

Cancellation

If an Administrator finds that an applicant or a registrant no longer exists or has ceased to transact business, the Administrator may cancel the registration.

TEST TOPIC ALERT

For any of the four securities professionals, the Administrator retains jurisdiction for a period of one year after the effective date of withdrawal of registration. That means that an action can commence for a violation discovered during that period. Note—FINRA has the same rule, but their jurisdiction lasts for two years.

TEST TOPIC ALERT

You may encounter this type of question regarding cancellation: "What would the Administrator do if mailings to a registrant were returned with no forwarding address?" The answer is, "Cancel the registration."

The Administrator may also cancel a registration if a person is declared mentally incompetent.

TEST TOPIC ALERT

Be familiar with the distinctions between cancellation and denial, suspension, or revocation. Cancellation does not result from violations or a failure to follow the provisions of the act. Cancellation occurs as the result of death, dissolution, or mental incompetency.

TEST TOPIC ALERT

Because an agent's (or IAR's) registration is dependent on being associated with a broker-dealer (or IA), when the employer's registration is suspended or revoked, that of the registered individual is placed into suspense or some other term with essentially the same effect. When the period of suspension of the firm is over, registration of the individuals is reactivated. If the firm's registration has been revoked, then the individual will either have to find a new affiliation or the license will be canceled. Individual agents or IARs who withdraw their registration must re-affiliate within two years or will be required to retake the exam to re-qualify.

RIGHTS OF RECOVERY FROM IMPROPER SALE OF SECURITIES

U5LO3: Describe the civil rights of recovery for a security's sale or for investment advice purchased in violation of the Uniform Securities Act.

If the purchaser of securities feels that the sale has been made in violation of the USA, that purchaser may file a complaint with the Administrator. If the Administrator investigates the claim and finds it has merit, then a case will be opened against the offending broker-dealer and/or agent.

If the client's case is proven, at the direction of the Administrator, the client may recover:

- the original purchase price of the securities ("made whole"); plus
- interest at a rate determined by the Administrator (generally referred to as the state's *legal rate*); plus
- all reasonable attorney's fees and court costs; minus
- any income received while the securities were held.

TAKE NOTE

The exam may refer to the interest paid to the client as being at the state's legal rate.

Right of Rescission for Security Sales

If the seller of securities discovers that a sale has been made in violation of the USA, the seller may offer to repurchase the securities from the buyer. In this case, the seller is offering the buyer the **right of rescission**. To satisfy the buyer's right of rescission, the amount paid back to the buyer must include the original purchase price and interest, as determined by the Administrator.

By offering to buy back the securities that were sold in violation of the act, the seller can avoid a lawsuit (and legal fees and court costs) through a **letter of rescission**. The buyer has 30 days after receiving the letter of rescission to respond. If the buyer does not accept or reject the rescission offer within 30 days, the buyer gives up any right to pursue a lawsuit at a later date.

TAKE NOTE

If the client rejects the offer within the 30-day period, he may sue. But, if the offer is not accepted or rejected within that 30-day period, it becomes void.

How might this play out on the exam? Let's take a look at a sample question:

EXAMPLE

1. Martha is an agent with Rapid Execution Services (RES), a broker-dealer registered in all 50 states. Martha offers an IPO of a nonexempt security to a client without realizing that the security has not been registered in the client's state. The client purchases 500 shares of the new issue and, 6 months later, sells the stock at price 70% below the original purchase price. Because the stock was not registered in the client's state, the client could claim

   I. payment of the difference between the proceeds and the purchase price

   II. interest at the state's legal rate, minus any income received from the security

   III. court costs and lawyer's fees if the client has to go to court

   IV. punitive damages equal to the amount of the loss

   A. I and II

   B. I, II, and III

   C. IV only

   D. I, II, III, and IV

   Answer: B. When a security is sold in violation of the USA (a nonexempt security must be registered under this scenario), the client can claim to be "made whole" plus interest, plus the expenses of going to court and paying for legal representation. In general, to avoid the legal costs (and publicity), when a case like this is uncovered, the broker-dealer will present an offer of rescission, which gives the client all of this except the court and legal fees (because it is not necessary to go to court). Punitive damages are not part of the client's recovery rights.

Rights of Recovery From Improper Investment Advice

A person who buys a security as the result of investment advice received in violation of the USA also has the right to file a complaint. In the case of securities purchased as a result of improper investment advice, if the client's case is proven, at the direction of the Administrator, the advisory client may recover:

■ cost of the advice; plus

■ loss as a result of the advice; plus

■ interest at a rate determined by the Administrator; plus

- any reasonable attorney's fees; minus
- the amount of any income received from the advice.

Right of Rescission for Investment Advice

Similar to the right of rescission described previously for improper securities sales, an investment adviser who realizes that he has given advice that will subject him to civil action may avoid legal expenses by offering the client the same package as he would receive if he had sued. That is, refunding the cost of the advice, losses from the advice, and interest at the state's predetermined rate, less any income received on recommended securities.

TEST TOPIC ALERT

Unlike some federal laws, there is no provision for receiving treble damages. That is, in addition to receiving back your investment, you receive payment equal to three times what you lost. That is primarily found in the federal laws regarding insider trading, but that is not relevant to the Uniform Securities Act.

Scope of Liability

Under the USA, the actual seller of the securities or the advice is not the only person liable for the violation of the act. Every person who directly or indirectly controls the person who sold the securities or the advice is also liable to the same extent as the person who conducted the transaction.

The effect of this is that if an agent makes a sale in violation (or IAR gives improper advice), but it can be shown that officers or partners of the broker-dealer or IA were irresponsible, action can be taken against them as well, and they can be found civilly liable.

Claims Against the Surety Bond

Earlier in this course, we discussed the need for securities professionals to post a surety bond under certain conditions. The USA states:

> Every bond shall provide for suit thereon by any person who has a cause of action under this Act and, if the Administrator by rule or order requires, by any person who has a cause of action not arising under this act. Every bond shall provide that no suit may be maintained to enforce any liability on the bond unless brought within the time limitations of the Act.[4]

TEST TOPIC ALERT

In other words, in order for a surety bond to meet the requirements of the USA, it must provide that any customer who can prove a violation (and does so within the statute of limitations) is entitled to collect against the bond.

---

[4] Uniform Securities Act, Section 202 (f)

Statute of Limitations

The time limit, or statute of limitations, for violations of the civil provisions of the USA is three years from the date of sale (or rendering of the investment advice) or two years after discovering the violation, whichever comes first. It is unlikely to be tested, but, just in case, under federal law, the statute of limitations for bringing action is the earlier of **one** year after discovery of the violation or three years after the date of the action.

TEST TOPIC ALERT

The USA provides that every cause of action under this statute survives the death of any person who might have been a plaintiff or defendant. Therefore, any bond required must provide that suit may be brought for the specified statute of limitations even though the person who is bonded dies before the expiration of that period.

U5LO4: Identify criminal penalties for violation of the Uniform Securities Act.

We need to define two terms:

Civil Liability

The accused person has not violated a state criminal code (the law). The aggrieved party has the right to sue for losses incurred. Damages are generally monetary and/or administrative (no jail sentence).

Criminal Liability

The accused person has violated the state's criminal code (broken the law). This could result in jail time.

TAKE NOTE

There are cases where the same action could result in both civil and criminal liability.

Civil Liabilities

These have been covered previously in the discussion of the rights of recovery. The successful claim of the client must be paid by the securities professional.

Criminal Liabilities

Upon conviction for willfully violating any provision of the USA, a person may be fined, imprisoned, or both. The maximum penalty is a fine of $5,000, a jail sentence of three years, or both. It is important to note that no person may be imprisoned for the violation of any rule or order if he proves that he had no knowledge of the rule or order. In other words, you have to know that you are willingly in violation to get jail time. It is also important to note that while the Administrator does not have the power to arrest anyone, he may apply to the appropriate authorities in his state for the issuance of an arrest warrant. The appropriate state prosecutor, usually the State Attorney General, may decide whether to bring a criminal action under the USA, another statute, or, when applicable, common law. In certain states, the Administrator has full or limited criminal enforcement powers. To be convicted of fraud, the violation must be willful and the registrant must know that the activity is fraudulent.

TAKE NOTE

Fraud is the deliberate or willful concealment, misrepresentation, or omission of material information or the truth to deceive or manipulate another person for unlawful or unfair gain. Under the USA, fraud is not limited to common-law deceit.

Judicial Review of Orders (Appeal)

Any person affected by an order of the Administrator may obtain a review of the order in an appropriate court by filing a written petition within 60 days. In general, filing an appeal does not automatically act as a stay of the penalty. The order will go into effect as issued unless the court rules otherwise.

SEC Enforcement Powers

What about the SEC's powers? As mentioned previously, the SEC has no jurisdiction over state securities laws (although federal law always supersedes state law). However, this exam deals with many areas of federal law, so we need to know about those powers.

Enforcement and administration of the federal securities laws, such as the Investment Advisers Act of 1940 (our focus here) is the responsibility of the SEC. As of the date of publication, there is no self-regulatory organization (SRO) for investment advisers. If that situation should change and become testable, it will be posted in the Exam-tips and Content Updates. In other words, FINRA, the NYSE, and the like have no jurisdiction over federal covered investment advisers; only the SEC does. If the SEC suspects a violation of the law or its rules, it may take the following actions:

- Subpoena witnesses
- Acquire evidence
- Subpoena books and records
- Administer oaths
- Go to a competent court of jurisdiction to obtain an injunction enjoining a person from continued activity until the results of a hearing
- Refer to the appropriate court for criminal prosecution

The SEC has the power to censure, place limitations on the activities, functions, or operations of, suspend for a period not exceeding 12 months, or revoke the registration of any investment adviser if it finds, after a hearing, that the penalty is appropriate. If it is necessary to go to court, all hearings are held in the federal court system. If a defendant is found guilty, he may appeal an SEC order against him by filing that appeal in the U.S. Court of Appeals with jurisdiction where the violation occurred.

If the violation is one in which the SEC seeks criminal penalties, the act provides for a fine of no more than $10,000, imprisonment for no more than five years, or both.

There is nothing in the USA that specifies a maximum suspension as there is in the federal law. Another difference is that, in the case of an appeal, it is made through the state court system, not the federal one. In both cases, the appeal must be filed within 60 days of the court's decision.

Another difference is in the level of penalties. Under the USA, the maximum penalties for a criminal infraction are a fine of up to $5,000, or a prison sentence not to exceed three years, or both. However, imprisonment is only an option when the violation is committed knowingly.

TEST TOPIC ALERT

You may be asked about either or both of these penalties on your exam and must be able to keep them straight. Federal law is $10,000 and 5 years. State law is $5,000 and three years.

UNIT
6

Communication With Clients and Prospects

INTRODUCTION

Before a person can become a customer, the person is first a prospect. Knowing what can and what cannot be said at all stages of the relationship is critical to not only the protection of the client, but to the securities professional as well. One of the most important communication requirements is disclosure of all material information, especially potential conflicts of interest. Failure to abide by the required practices can lead to suspension or a more severe penalty such as a revocation or bar from the industry.

The Series 65 exam will contain 10 questions on the material presented in this unit.

LEARNING OBJECTIVES

When you have completed this unit, you will be able to accomplish the following.

U6LO1:   Identify the disclosures that must be made to clients and prospects.
U6LO2:   Indicate the unlawful representations concerning registrations.
U6LO3:   Recall the restrictions on performance guarantees.
U6LO4:   Identify the required elements of the investment advisory contract, client disclosure brochure, wrap-fee programs, and solicitor's brochure.
U6LO5:   Describe the proper use of correspondence and advertising.

DISCLOSURE OF CAPACITY

U6LO1: Identify the disclosures that must be made to clients and prospects.

When asked about the three most important factors affecting the value of real estate, invariably, the response is "Location, Location, Location." In this industry, the three most important factors involved in avoiding disciplinary actions are Disclosure, Disclosure, Disclosure. There is very little that a securities professional cannot do as long as proper disclosure is made.

As stated in Unit 3, broker-dealers can operate either in a principal or agency capacity when executing transactions for their clients. When acting in a principal capacity, the BD is the *contra party* to the trade. That is, they are on the other side of the trade of the client. When the client is buying a security, the broker-dealer is selling it out of inventory. In this case, the firm's profit comes from a markup. If the client is selling a security and the broker-dealer purchases it for its inventory, once again, the firm is acting as a principal (every trade has two principals—the buyer and the seller) and, in this case, the profit comes from a markdown.

When acting in an agency capacity, the firm is acting like any other broker or agent (real estate broker, insurance agent, or employment agent) in that they are simply putting the buyer and seller together. And, like all agents or brokers, they earn a commission.

For the exam, it is important to know that broker-dealers must always indicate their capacity on the trade confirmation, sent no later than completion of the trade (settlement date). They will indicate if they acted as a broker (and always disclose the amount of commission) or if they acted as a principal (and, depending on the circumstances—not tested—may have to indicate the markup or markdown).

TAKE NOTE

This discussion will be revisited at Part 4 Unit 22.

Disclosure of Capacity by Investment Advisers

As stated in Unit 1, the business of an investment adviser is giving advice. That is why they get compensated; they're not in the business of executing securities transactions—that is the role of the broker-dealer.

However, on rare occasions, an investment adviser might buy from or sell to an advisory client in the capacity of a principal. Or, the adviser might put together a buyer and seller acting in the capacity of an agent.

The regulators have recognized that both principal and agency transactions create the potential for advisers to engage in self-dealing. Principal transactions, in particular, may lead to abuses such as price manipulation or the placing of unwanted securities into client accounts. When an adviser engages in an agency transaction on behalf of a client, it is primarily the incentive to earn additional compensation that creates the adviser's conflict of interest. Although recognizing the potential for these abuses, the regulators did not prohibit advisers entirely from engaging in all principal and agency transactions with clients. Rather, they chose to address these particular conflicts of interest by imposing the following disclosure and client consent requirements.

- The client receives full written disclosure as to the capacity in which the adviser proposes to act.
- Client consent is obtained.

Consent, which can be oral or written, may be obtained before or after the execution of the trade, but both of these must be done prior to completion of the transaction. This is unlike a broker-dealer who, when acting as a principal in a trade with a customer or as the customer's agent, need only indicate that capacity on the trade confirmation; consent is not required.

TAKE NOTE

Completion of the transaction is considered to be the day the trade settles. Under current industry practice, that is the second business day after the trade is made.

It is important to remember that:

- an adviser may obtain client consent to a principal or agency transaction after execution, but must prior to settlement of the transaction; and

- an adviser is not "acting as broker" within the meaning of the acts if the adviser receives no compensation (other than its advisory fee) for effecting a particular agency transaction between advisory clients. It is primarily the incentive to earn additional compensation that creates the adviser's conflict of interest when effecting an agency transaction between advisory clients.

TEST TOPIC ALERT

What happens if the investment adviser is also registered as a broker-dealer? The requirements just described do not apply to any transaction with a customer of a broker-dealer if such broker-dealer is not acting as an investment adviser in relation to such transaction. In other words, the transaction is not as a result of a recommendation from the adviser.

TAKE NOTE

What is really going on here? As stated previously, the function of an investment adviser is to be compensated for giving investment advice, not trading securities. Buying and selling securities is the job of a broker-dealer. This discussion deals with the odd case where an investment adviser wears two hats, as it were, and, in addition to giving advice, also trades the security.

Agency Cross Transactions

A similar case to the situation just described is the agency cross transaction where the investment adviser acts as an agent for both sides of the trade (hence the term, agency cross transaction).

In an **agency cross transaction**, the adviser (or IAR acting on behalf of the firm) acts as agent for both its advisory client and the party on the other side of the trade. Both state and federal law will permit an adviser to engage in these transactions provided the advisory client executes a written consent prospectively (in advance) authorizing the investment adviser to effect agency cross transactions for such clients and the adviser discloses the following:

- The adviser will be receiving commissions from both sides of the trade.

- There is a potential conflict of interest because of the division of loyalties to both sides.

- On at least an annual basis, the adviser will furnish a statement or summary of the account identifying the total number of such transactions and the total amount of all remuneration from these transactions.

- In a conspicuous manner, indicates that this arrangement may be terminated at any time.

- No transaction is effected in which the same investment adviser or an investment adviser and any person controlling, controlled by, or under common control with that investment adviser recommended the transaction to both any seller and any purchaser.

These requirements do not relieve advisers of their duties to obtain best execution and best price for any transaction.

In addition to the prior written consent, at or before the completion of each agency cross transaction, the client must be sent a written trade confirmation that includes:

- a statement of the nature of the transaction;

- the date, and if requested, the time of the transaction; and

- the source and amount of any remuneration to be received by the IA (or IAR) in connection with the transaction.

EXAMPLE

An adviser has a client who is conservative and another who generally looks for more aggressive positions. The conservative client calls and expresses concerns about the volatility of First Tech Internet Services, Inc., stating that he thinks this may be the best time to exit his position. The adviser agrees and mentions that he has a risk-taking client for whom First Tech is suitable and he'd like to "cross" the security between the two clients, charging a small commission to each of them. He then contacts the other client and recommends the purchase of First Tech. With the prior written consent of both parties, this is not a violation because the recommendation was only made to one side (the buyer).

TEST TOPIC ALERT

In an agency cross transaction, the adviser may not recommend the transaction to both parties of the trade.

TAKE NOTE

In the case of agency cross transactions, permission to engage in them must be obtained in writing before, (the law says, prospectively), the first transaction. In essence, the client is giving blanket authority to engage in this activity. In the case of acting as a principal or agent, as described previously, no blanket authorization is permitted and client consent (can be oral or written) must be obtained before completion of the transaction.

GENERAL DISCLOSURE REQUIREMENTS

To provide some assurance that the disclosure requirements of the acts will not be violated, the regulators have recommended that each of the adviser's advisory clients be given a written statement (the brochure described shortly) prepared by the adviser that makes all appropriate disclosures.

The securities laws do not prohibit a registered investment adviser representative from being an employee of a registered broker-dealer. However, there would be a duty on the part of both the broker-dealer and the soliciting advisers to inform advisory clients of their ability to seek execution of transactions with broker-dealers other than those who have employed the advisers.

Disclosure must be made to all current clients and to prospective clients regarding material disciplinary action. The broadest definition of *material* would include any actions taken against the firm or management persons by a court or regulatory authority within the past 10 years. Required disclosure would include the following:

■ State or regulatory proceedings in which the adviser or a management person was found to have violated rules or statutes that led to the denial, suspension, or revocation of the firm's or the individual management person's registration

■ Court proceedings, such as a permanent or temporary injunction, against the firm or management person pertaining to an investment-related activity or any felony

■ SRO proceedings in which the adviser or management person caused the business to lose its registration or the firm or individual was barred, suspended, or expelled, or a fine in excess of $2,500 or a limitation was placed on the adviser or management person's activities

Examples of failures to disclose material information to clients would include the following:

■ An adviser fails to disclose all fees that a client would pay in connection with the advisory contract, including how fees are charged and whether fees are negotiable.

■ An adviser fails to disclose its affiliation with a broker-dealer or other securities professionals or issuers.

■ If a state-registered adviser has discretionary authority or custody over a client's funds or securities, or requires prepayment of advisory fees of more than $500 from a client, six or more months in advance, the adviser fails to disclose a financial condition that is reasonably likely to impair the ability of the adviser to meet contractual commitments to those clients. In the case of a federal covered adviser, the dollar limit is more than $1,200.

■ An adviser may defraud its clients when it fails to use the average price paid when allocating securities to accounts participating in bunched trades and fails to adequately disclose its allocation policy. This practice violates the act if securities that were purchased at the lowest price or sold at the highest price are allocated to favored clients without adequate disclosure.

■ Any material legal action against the adviser must be disclosed to existing clients promptly. If the action occurred within the past 10 years, it must be disclosed by a state-registered adviser to prospective clients not less than 48 hours before entering into the contract, or no later than the time of entering into such contract if the client has the right to terminate the contract without penalty within five business days. In the case of a federal covered adviser, the 48-hour rule does not apply; disclosure is part of the brochure delivered no later than commencing the advisory agreement.

 EXAMPLES

1. Fiduciary Investment Group (FIG), an investment adviser registered in 6 states, from time to time acts as a principal in trades recommended to advisory clients. Under the provisions of the Uniform Securities Act,

   A. FIG is engaging in an unlawful practice.

   B. FIG must receive consent of the clients and disclose its capacity no later than execution of the trade.

   C. FIG must receive consent of the clients and disclose its capacity no later than completion of the trade.

   D. FIG does not need consent because the trade was recommended to existing advisory clients.

Answer: C. This practice is not unlawful as long as the investment adviser obtains the required consent and makes the appropriate disclosures on a timely basis. That time limit is no later than the completion of the trade (the settlement date). If FIG is also a broker-dealer and a client makes a trade that is not initiated through an advisory recommendation, then acting as a principal only requires disclosure of capacity, not consent.

2. The BJS Advisory Service maintains no custody of customer funds or securities, requires no substantial prepayments of fees, and does not have investment discretion over clients' accounts. Which of the following would have to be promptly disclosed to clients?

    I.   The SEC has entered an order barring the executive vice president of the firm from association with any firm in the investment business.

    II. BJS has just been fined $3,500 by the NYSE.

    III. A civil suit has just been filed against BJS by one of its clients alleging that BJS made unsuitable recommendations.

    A. I and II.

    B. I and III.

    C. II and III.

    D. I, II, and III.

Answer: A. Material disciplinary violations must be reported by all investment advisers, regardless of whether they keep custody. The first two answers fit the definition of material actions, but not the third. If the suit goes in favor of the client and the adviser is found guilty, disclosure would need to be made. However, there is something that investment advisers who do not maintain custody or receive substantial prepayments avoid having to do. What is that? They do not have to notify their clients about any financial situation that might impair their ability to meet contractual commitments to clients.

Disclosure of Conflicts of Interest

What is a conflict of interest? One legal definition goes something like this: "A term used to describe the situation in which a person in a position of trust, contrary to the obligation and absolute duty to act for the benefit of a designated individual, exploits the relationship for personal benefit, typically pecuniary."

Because of the fiduciary relationship, clients of investment advisers expect them to do what is best for them, not for the person they're trusting with their money. Broker-dealers have always had the suitability rules where potential conflicts must be taken into consideration. The best way to avoid these conflicts of interest is to disclose them so that the customer can decide what to do. Some examples of potential conflicts of interest are:

- offering a proprietary product, such as a house fund (a mutual fund where the underwriter or adviser is affiliated with the broker-dealer);

- offering a limited partnership offering (DPP) where the sponsor is an affiliate of the broker-dealer;

- program sponsors, such as investment companies or insurance companies, providing incentives or rewards to agents for selling the sponsors' products;

- a securities professional having a financial interest in any security being recommended;

- a broker-dealer going public and placing shares of its own stock into discretionary accounts; and

- a broker-dealer publishing a favorable research report after underwriting the issuer's stock offering.

This is just a sample. The key point is, if there is any doubt about the transparency of the recommendation or transaction, be sure to make full disclosure.

TAKE NOTE

Shortly before releasing this edition, the SEC proposed *Regulation Best Interest*. If enacted, this rule will require a broker-dealer to act in the best interest of a retail customer when making a recommendation of any securities transaction or investment strategy involving securities to a retail customer. Regulation Best Interest is designed to make it clear that a broker-dealer may not put its financial interests ahead of the interests of a retail customer in making recommendations and is more stringent than the current suitability requirements. When and if this regulation becomes relevant to the exam, we will post the information to the Content Updates and it will be reflected in the online questions.

TEST TOPIC ALERT

Suppose you were selling shares of a company where your sister was a control person. Do you think you'd have to disclose that potential conflict to your clients? Yes!

Disclosure of Fees

Many years ago, NASAA declared that it is a prohibited business practice for a broker-dealer to charge unreasonable and inequitable fees for services performed, including miscellaneous services such as collection of monies due for principal, dividends or interest, exchange or transfer of securities, appraisals, safekeeping, or custody of securities and other services related to its securities business. However, as long as these charges are not unreasonable, they would be permitted for performing these services. But, if clients were not aware of those fees, or didn't understand them, firms could take unfair advantage.

NASAA recognizes that not all broker-dealers offer the same level of services and that those who offer a large array of services to their clients may charge more without it being considered an unethical business practice. In other cases, a particular transaction may involve more expense to the broker-dealers, particularly in a thinly traded security, generally defined as one with very low trading volume, and that too would justify a charge that is higher than normal. Of course, all charges must be clearly disclosed to clients. If not, a violation has occurred.

In 2015, NASAA published an investor advisory regarding fees charged by broker-dealer firms for services and maintenance of investment accounts. The advisory followed research from NASAA, showing that investors are confused about brokerage services and maintenance fees and want clear and easy access to fee information from their broker-dealer firms. A national public opinion poll commissioned by NASAA found that fees are important to investors, but a general lack of standardization and clarity in their disclosures has left investors unaware of how much their broker-dealer firms charge for the service and maintenance of their investment accounts. Here are some ways that broker-dealers can make the disclosures easier for customers to follow:

- Fees are typically disclosed when a customer account is opened. If the firm changes the fee schedule, be clear about it, and be sure to use appropriate methods to give advance notification of the changes to the customer.

- Minimize the fine print, or at least make the fees and charges clear. Whether using a table, a chart, or a list, make sure it is easy for customers to determine what the fees and charges are and how they are computed.

- Use standardized and uncomplicated terms to describe service and maintenance fees to help clients compare fees between different firms.

TAKE NOTE

A working group convened by NASAA has developed a model fee disclosure schedule and related accessibility guidelines to help investors better understand and compare various broker-dealer service and maintenance-related fees. The template and guidelines make fee disclosure easily accessible for retail investors to use to understand and compare fees. Under that guideline broker-dealers should provide retail customers at account opening written notification of all service charges and fees. In addition, firms should provide retail customers with written notification at least 30 calendar days before the implementation or increase of any service charge or fee. These notifications may be made by electronic means.

Typical Broker-Dealer Fees

Examples of the more common fees that might be charged by a broker-dealer include the following:

- **Issuance of a stock certificate.** Although most securities are kept in street name, there could be instances where the customer wants delivery of the physical certificate. There is usually a charge for this service.

- **Transferring an account.** When a client decides to move the account from one broker-dealer to another, there is usually a charge to cover the administrative expenses of the transfer.

- **Wiring funds.** Although frequently waived for those with large account balances, if the client needs money wired out of the account, a charge, similar to that made by most banks, is levied against the account.

- **Margin account interest.** When purchasing on margin, money is borrowed, and the rate of interest charged on the borrowed funds must be disclosed.

- **Account maintenance fees.** Similar to the monthly charge on your bank statement, many firms charge an annual account fee, particularly if a small account.

- **Safekeeping of funds/securities.** This is the charge made for maintaining custody of client assets, which is usually waived for larger accounts.

- **Late settlement fee.** This is similar to the late fee on a credit card. When a client's payment arrives after settlement date (or is returned due to insufficient funds), the broker-dealer may assess a fee.

- **Postage and handling.** Although many firms absorb the cost of normal mailings, express or overnight delivery at the request of the client is usually subject to a charge.

This is not a complete list, but it includes the most common charges. What is most important for the exam is that these fees must be disclosed.

TEST TOPIC ALERT

Not included in the fee disclosure documents are:

- commissions,

- markups and markdowns, and

- advisory fees.

Those disclosures are made in other documents, not the fee disclosure schedule.

MISREPRESENTING A SECURITIES PROFESSIONAL'S REGISTRATION

U6LO2: Indicate the unlawful representations concerning registrations.

Misrepresentation is a prohibited practice. There are two areas covered: registration of the securities professional and registration of a security.

Once you are registered, what can you say about that? Can you say the Administrator has *approved* of you or your registration? Not at all! Representing that your registration implies any kind of approval of you or your qualifications is a prohibited practice. What you can state is that you are a registered agent of ABC Broker-Dealer, or you are a registered investment adviser representative of the XYZ Investment Adviser.

Misrepresenting a Security's Registration

Similar to the above, it is prohibited to imply that registration of a security means that the Administrator (or any regulatory body) has *approved* of the issue. In fact, on the front page (or inside cover) of every prospectus is a statement called the disclaimer, which states that the security has not been approved or disapproved, and any representation to the contrary is a criminal offense.

EXAMPLE

1. Which of the following statements may be made by an issuer selling securities to the public that are registered with the Administrator?

   A. The Administrator has cleared this issue for sale to the public.

   B. The Administrator has passed on the adequacy of the information provided in the prospectus.

   C. The Administrator has approved the accuracy of the information contained in the prospectus.

   D. The Administrator has affirmed the merits of the security as an investment.

   Answer: A. The Administrator does not approve or disapprove of securities. Rather, the Administrator reviews registrations for omission of material facts and clarity of information and makes certain that all supporting documentation is included. If these requirements are met, the Administrator clears or releases the security for sale to the public.

2. LMN Securities, a broker-dealer registered with the SEC in more than a dozen states, has just become a member firm of the New York Stock Exchange. It would be permitted for LMN to tell its customers that

   A. the membership in the NYSE is a testimony to the integrity of the firm

   B. they are now members of the NYSE

   C. they are now federal covered and will no longer have to register in those states where they do not maintain a place of business.

   D. this adds one more level of approval of the firm's business

   Answer: B. When it comes to the registration of any securities professional, any statement relating to approval or something similar is prohibited. There is no such thing as a federal covered broker-dealer, and becoming a member of a national stock exchange has no impact on the state registration of a broker-dealer.

PERFORMANCE GUARANTEES

U6LO3: Recall the restrictions on performance guarantees.

Little can be guaranteed in this industry.

Guaranteed Security

A guaranteed security is where a party other than the issuer guarantees the payment of principal and interest (on a debt security) or dividend (on an equity security). The important thing about that guarantee is that there is no guarantee on the performance of the investment. That is, gains cannot be part of the guarantee.

Guarantee Against Loss

Unfortunately, it is not uncommon in the industry for a securities professional to tell a client something to the effect of, "If this stock doesn't earn X% within the next three months, I'll make up the difference," or, "I am so sure you won't lose on this investment that I'll buy it back from you at your cost plus 10%." Both of these are considered performance guarantees and are prohibited actions.

Perhaps the simplest statement regarding guarantees is found in the NASAA Model Rule on Unethical Business Practices of Investment Advisers, Investment Adviser Representatives, and Federal Covered Advisers, where it lists, "Guaranteeing a client that a specific result will be achieved (gain or no loss) with advice which will be rendered" as one of the prohibitions.

TAKE NOTE

Although performance guarantees are prohibited, under certain circumstances, investment advisers can receive performance-based compensation. That means the advisory contract with the client can provide that investment return that is better than that of a selected index can result in a higher fee to the adviser. Of course, it must go both ways; if the performance of the account is below that of the index, the fee is reduced. This topic will be covered in detail in the next unit.

TEST TOPIC ALERT

If justified, a broker-dealer, but not an associated person of the firm, may correct a bona fide error. An associated person of a broker-dealer cannot do this because of the concern that any such payment may conceal individual misconduct.

INVESTMENT ADVISORY CONTRACT

U6LO4: Identify the required elements of the investment advisory contract, client disclosure brochure, wrap-fee programs, and solicitor's brochure.

The primary relationship between a client and an investment adviser is evidenced by an investment advisory contract. There are three major differences between federal and state law. The USA prohibits entering into, extending, or renewing any advisory services, unless the contract is in writing, while federal law permits the contract to be written or oral. Another difference concerns the amount of the fees. The USA requires that fees be competitive while federal law only requires that they be reasonable in view of the services rendered. Finally, the NASAA Model Rule on performance-based compensation is a bit more stringent than that of the SEC as we will cover in the next unit.

Under both acts, the contract must disclose:

- the services to be provided, including custody if appropriate;
- the term of the contract (contracts can be of any length, not necessarily annual, but all renewals under **state law**, just as with initial contracts, must be in **writing**);
- the amount of the advisory fee or the formula for computing the fee;
- the amount or manner of calculation of the amount of any prepaid fee to be returned in the event of contract termination;
- whether the contract grants discretionary power to the adviser or its representatives;
- that no assignment of the contract may be made by the adviser without the consent of the other party to the contract (the client); and
- that, if the adviser is organized as a partnership, any change to a minority interest in the firm will be communicated to advisory clients within a reasonable period of time. A change to a majority of the partnership interests would be considered an assignment.

TAKE NOTE

It is necessary for you to understand the technical definition of *assignment* as used in the acts. When an advisory firm is sold, what do you think its major asset is? Furniture? Computers? No. It is the advisory contracts with clients and, legally, that sale means the contracts have been assigned to the new buyer. This does not mean that the clients have to approve of the sale; they only have to approve of letting the new owner(s) manage their money. They can decide to take their money elsewhere. Assignment also includes any direct or indirect transfer or pledge of an investment advisory contract by the adviser or of a controlling block of the adviser's outstanding voting securities by a stockholder of the adviser. If the investment adviser is a partnership, no assignment of an investment advisory contract is considered to result from the death or withdrawal of a minority of the partners or from the admission to the adviser of one or more partners who, after admission, will be only a minority interest in the business while a change to a majority would be considered an assignment. However, a reorganization or similar activity that does not result in a change of actual control or management of an investment adviser is not an assignment.

TEST TOPIC ALERT

If a broker-dealer forms a subsidiary to start an investment adviser, existing clients of the BD wishing to become clients of the IA must enter into a new contract for advisory services.

The acts also prohibit waiving fees in the event of losses in the client's account. The Model Rule states that "Indicating, in an advisory contract, any condition, stipulation, or provisions binding any person to waive compliance with any provision of the Uniform Securities Act or of the Investment Advisers Act of 1940" is an unethical business practice.

One final prohibition found in both state and federal law deals with performance-based compensation. That is, including in the advisory contract, a provision where the adviser's fee will be increased for good performance and decreased for poor performance. On the exam, unless the question refers to one of the exceptions we're going to learn about in the next unit, you should always take the attitude that performance-based compensation is prohibited.

TEST TOPIC ALERT

This point (waivers) sometimes comes up on the exam. What you have to know is that in all cases on the test (remember, this course is about the test world and not the *real* world), waivers are not permitted. For exam purposes, if you are given a question where clients agree to waive their rights to sue, the agreement is null and void.

EXAMPLES

1. The Investment Advisers Act of 1940 would permit investment advisory contracts to provide for

    I. assignment without the client's consent

    II. changes to be made in a partnership with notification to clients within a reasonable period of time

    III. compensation based on average assets under management over a particular time period

    A. I and II

    B. I and III

    C. II and III

    D. I, II, and III

    Answer: C. A client's contracts, whether written or oral (technically, the Investment Advisers Act of 1940 does not require written contracts), may not be assigned without the client's consent under any circumstances. If the adviser is a partnership, notice must be made to clients of any changes in the membership of the partnership within a reasonable period. It is always permitted to charge a fee based on the average value of assets under management.

2. Which 2 of the following statements regarding investment advisory contracts demonstrate compliance with the Uniform Securities Act?

   I. ABC Investment Advisers, organized as a partnership with 5 equal partners, admits 2 additional partners on a proportionate basis, but fails to obtain consent of its clients.

   II. DEF Investment Advisers, organized as a partnership with 7 equal partners, has 4 of those partners simultaneously leave, but the firm continues to operate as before while failing to obtain consent of its clients.

   III. GHI Investment Advisers, organized as a corporation with 5 equal shareholders, has 3 of them pledge their GHI stock as collateral for a bank loan, but the firm fails to obtain consent of its clients.

   IV. JKL Investment Advisers, organized as a corporation with 5 equal shareholders, has 3 of them sell their shares to the remaining 2 owners, but the firm fails to obtain consent of its clients.

   A. I and III.

   B. I and IV.

   C. II and III.

   D. II and IV.

   Answer: B. The addition of 2 equal partners to a 5-person firm does not constitute a majority change so all that is necessary is notice within a reasonable period, not consent. In the case of a corporation, a change in stock ownership is never required to be disclosed unless there is an actual change to the control or management of the adviser and such is not indicated here. Pledging a majority stock interest in an adviser structured as a corporation is considered an assignment and, therefore, requires client consent.

3. Which of the following fee arrangements is legal under the Investment Advisers Act of 1940?

   A. Adviser A charges an annual fee of 0.5% of the value of the client's account, due on the first day of the client's fiscal year.

   B. Adviser B charges an annual fee of 0.75%, guaranteed to be waived if the value of the account does not increase during the year.

   C. Adviser C charges an annual fee of 0.5% to be waived if the account does not grow by at least 5% during the year.

   D. Adviser D guarantees the annual fee will be waived if the account decreases in value while under her management.

   Answer: A. An adviser's fee may not be based on portfolio appreciation or capital gains, except under certain circumstances that are not detailed in the question. Advisory fees may be based on a percentage of AUM There should be no question on the exam where "waiving" something will be permitted.

Summary of Notice and Consent

- Investment advisers organized as a partnership must notify clients when there is a change involving a minority of the partners (e.g., five equal partners, one dies, one retires—notification within a reasonable period).

- Investment advisers organized as corporations do not have to notify clients of changes to shareholders.

- Investment advisers may only assign client contracts with client permission. Assignment occurs when there is a change to a majority of the partners (in our previous example, if one more of the partners left, that would be 3 out of 5—a majority). In the case of a corporation, if a majority of the stock is pledged as collateral for a loan, then that is considered an assignment.

INVESTMENT ADVISER BROCHURE RULE

As mentioned earlier, the Form ADV Part 2 is a disclosure document that, under state and federal securities laws, is required to be given to clients.

The Part 2 consists of the following three parts:

- Part 2A of Form ADV: Firm Brochure
- Part 2A Appendix 1 of Form ADV: Wrap Fee Program Brochure
- Part 2B of Form ADV: Brochure Supplement (describes certain supervised persons)

Under SEC and similar state rules, investment advisers are required to deliver to clients and prospective clients a brochure disclosing information about the firm. They also may be required to deliver a brochure supplement disclosing information about one or more of their supervised persons. Part 2 of Form ADV sets out the minimum required disclosure that the brochure (Part 2A for a firm brochure, or Appendix 1 for a wrap fee program brochure) and brochure supplements (Part 2B) must contain. Here are some of the key points of which you should be aware:

- *Narrative Format.* Part 2 of Form ADV consists of a series of items that contain disclosure requirements for the firm's brochure and any required supplements. The items require narrative responses. If an item does not apply to their business, they must indicate that item is not applicable. There are 18 items on the ADV Part 2 (with a 19th one for state-registered advisers only). Remember, this is for clients to use to understand what the IA does so the information disclosed relates to the way the IA operates the business. Some of the items include

  - a description of the types of advisory services provided,
  - fees and compensation,
  - methods of analysis, investment strategies, and risk of loss,
  - disciplinary information,
  - how you select or recommend broker-dealers for client transactions,
  - custody practices, and
  - investment discretion.

- *Plain English.* The items in Part 2 of Form ADV are designed to promote effective communication between the firm and their clients. The brochure and supplements must be written in plain English, taking into consideration the clients' level of financial sophistication. Specifically, the SEC states that the brochure should be concise and direct.

The brochure should discuss any conflicts the adviser has or is reasonably likely to have and practices in which it engages or is reasonably likely to engage.

■ *Disclosure Obligations as a Fiduciary.* Under federal and state law, IAs act in a fiduciary capacity and must make full disclosure to their clients of all material facts relating to the advisory relationship. As a fiduciary, they also must seek to avoid conflicts of interest with their clients, and, at a minimum, make full disclosure of all material conflicts of interest between them and their clients that could affect the advisory relationship.

■ *Full and Truthful Disclosure.* Obviously, all information in the brochure and brochure supplements must be true and may not omit any material facts.

■ *Filing.* The investment adviser must file the brochure(s) (and amendments) through the IARD system. If the IA is federal covered or in the process of registering with the SEC, it is not required to file the brochure supplements through the IARD or otherwise. However, a copy of the supplements must be preserved and made available to SEC staff upon request. If the IA is registered with or is in the process of registering with one or more state securities authorities, a copy of the brochure supplement (Part 2B) must be filed for each supervised person doing business in that state.

TAKE NOTE

Only in the case of state-registered investment advisers is it required to file the brochure supplements. If you think about it, it makes sense because virtually all of the supervised persons described in the supplements are investment adviser representatives and they are always registered on a state level only, not with the SEC.

The cover page of the brochure must state the name, business address, contact information, website address (if there is one), and the date of the brochure. Furthermore, the cover page of the brochure must state the following (or other clear and concise language conveying the same information) and identify the document as a brochure:

> This brochure provides information about the qualifications and business practices of [firm name]. If you have any questions about the contents of this brochure, please contact us at [telephone number and/or email address]. The information in this brochure has not been approved or verified by the United States Securities and Exchange Commission or by any state securities authority.
>
> Additional information about [firm name] also is available on the SEC's website at www.adviserinfo.sec.gov.

Brochure Supplement Disclosing Individual Advisory Personnel

As has been mentioned earlier, Part 2B is a brochure supplement that must contain certain information about "advisory personnel on whom clients rely for investment advice." The brochure supplement is also a narrative format in plain English and includes six required disclosure categories:

■ **Cover page** identifying the supervised person (or persons) covered by the supplement as well as the advisory firm

■ **Educational background and business experience**, including disclosing if the supervised person has no high school education, no formal education after high school, or no business background

- **Disciplinary information** about material events within the past 10 years, although the SEC says that even if more than 10 years have passed since the date of the event, you must disclose the event if it is so serious that it remains currently material to a client's or prospective client's evaluation

- **Other business activities**, including disclosing if the supervised person receives commissions, bonuses, or other compensation based on the sale of securities or other investment products, including as a broker-dealer or registered representative (agent), and including distribution or service (trail) fees from the sale of mutual funds

- **Additional compensation** beyond that paid by the client (such as a sales award or other prize)

- **Supervision**, including providing the name, title, and telephone number of the individual responsible for supervising the supervised person's advisory activities on behalf of the firm

The investment adviser must prepare a brochure supplement covering the following supervised persons:

- Any supervised person who formulates investment advice for a client and has direct client contact

- Any supervised person who has discretionary authority over a client's assets, even if the supervised person has no direct client contact

Wrap Fee Programs

The rules on disclosure are somewhat different for wrap fee programs. A **wrap fee program** is a program under which a client is charged a specified fee, or fees, not based directly on transactions in a client's account, for investment advisory services (which may include portfolio management or advice concerning the selection of other investment advisers) and for execution of client transactions.

Any registered investment adviser compensated under a wrap fee program for sponsoring, organizing, or administering the program, or for selecting, or providing advice to clients regarding the selection of, other investment advisers in the program, does not use the normal brochure or Part 2A of the ADV. Instead, that adviser furnishes clients and prospective clients Part 2A, Appendix 1.

If the entire advisory business is sponsoring wrap fee programs, the firm does not need to prepare a firm brochure separate from the wrap fee program brochure(s). In other words, if all the IA does is sponsor wrap fee programs, it must prepare and deliver a completed Part 2A, Appendix 1, but not a Part 2A.

Some of the required disclosures required under Appendix 1 include:

- a statement on the cover page of the wrap fee program brochure must state the following (or other clear and concise language conveying the same information) and identify the document as a wrap fee program brochure:

    > This wrap fee program brochure provides information about the qualifications and business practices of [firm name]. If you have any questions about the contents of this brochure, please contact us at [telephone number and/or email address]. The information in this brochure has not been approved or verified by the United States Securities and Exchange Commission or by any state securities authority.

    > Additional information about [firm name] also is available on the SEC's website at www.adviserinfo.sec.gov.

- the amount of the wrap fee charged for the program;

- whether the fees are negotiable;

- the services provided under the program, including the types of portfolio management services;

- a statement that the program may cost the client more or less than purchasing these services separately;

- a description of the nature of any fees that the client may pay in addition to the wrap fee;

- if the person recommending the wrap fee program to the client receives compensation as a result of the client's participation in the program, disclose this fact

  - explain, if applicable, that the amount of this compensation may be more than what the person would receive if the client participated in the firm's other programs or paid separately for investment advice, brokerage, and other services,

- describe how portfolio managers are selected and reviewed, the basis for recommending or selecting portfolio managers for particular clients, and the criteria for replacing or recommending the replacement of portfolio managers for the program and for particular clients; and

- disclose whether any of the firm's related persons act as a portfolio manager for a wrap fee program described in the wrap fee program brochure.

TEST TOPIC ALERT

It is generally agreed that "buy and hold" clients are not suitable for a wrap fee account because they don't do enough trading to benefit from the fact that commissions are included in the program fee.

Brochure Delivery Requirements

Both federal and state-registered advisers must prepare and deliver a brochure to their clients. If the question does not specify federal or state-registered (or refer to the Investment Advisers Act of 1940 or the USA), you should assume they are asking about a state-registered adviser. It is, after all, NASAA's exam.

Delivery Requirements for SEC-Registered Advisers

A firm brochure must be delivered to each client. It must be delivered even if the advisory agreement with the client is oral (under federal law, contracts may be oral or in writing; under state law, they must be in writing).

The firm brochure must be given to each client before or at the time an advisory agreement is entered into with that client. Thereafter, each year, within 120 days of the end of the fiscal year, a free, updated brochure must be delivered to each client that either includes a summary of material changes or is accompanied by a summary of material changes, or alternatively, it would be permitted to deliver to each client a summary of material changes that includes an offer to provide a copy of the updated brochure and information on how a client may obtain the brochure.

TAKE NOTE

If there are no material changes, then nothing—not the brochure nor the brochure supplement, nor the summary—must be sent.

Although, as we will see shortly, the brochure must be updated promptly when something becomes materially inaccurate, the only time that an interim amendment must be delivered to clients is when there is a disciplinary action. This interim amendment can be in the form of a document describing the material facts relating to the amended disciplinary event.

Delivery Requirements for State-registered Advisers

The brochure delivery requirements for state-registered advisers are essentially the same as that for covered advisers with one very important exception. Under the NASAA Model Rule on adviser brochures, advisers are required to deliver the brochure to the client at least 48 hours before entering into an advisory contract or at the time of entering into an advisory contract, if the advisory client has the right to terminate the contract without penalty within five business days after entering into the contract. Some advisers charge a startup or setup fee. Any new client who does not receive a brochure at least 48 hours before entering into an advisory agreement may terminate the agreement and be refunded the setup fee. However, it would not be considered a penalty for the adviser to make a pro rata charge for management services rendered during that five-business-day period.

Exemptions From the Brochure Rule

There are two exemptions under both state and federal law from the delivery requirements of the rule.

▪ Contracts with an investment company registered under the Investment Company Act of 1940 (e.g., mutual funds) are exempted because those contracts are covered by that act.

▪ Advisers entering into a contract providing solely for impersonal advisory services—that is, publishers of market letters—are exempt from the rule's initial delivery requirements. But, if the annual charge for this service is $500 or greater, delivery of the brochure must be offered with the same two timing options listed previously.

Updating the Brochure

The brochure must be updated:

▪ each year at the time of filing the annual updating amendment; and

▪ promptly, whenever any information in the brochure becomes materially inaccurate.

It is not required to update the brochure between annual amendments solely because the amount of client assets under management has changed or because the fee schedule has changed. However, if the brochure is being updated for a separate reason in between annual amendments (a disciplinary action, some other material change, and so forth), the IA should update that item(s) as part of the interim amendment.

If, when preparing the annual updating amendment, there are no material changes to the previous brochure, and there have been no interim amendments making material changes to the brochure that was filed with the previous year's annual updating amendment, a summary of material changes does not have to be prepared (because there is nothing to say). Read what the SEC has to say about that: "If you do not have to prepare a summary of material changes, you do not have to deliver a summary of material changes or a brochure to your existing clients that year. If you are a state-registered adviser, you should contact the appropriate state securities authorities to determine whether you must make an annual offer of the brochure."

That means that a new brochure doesn't even have to be offered (in the case of federal covered advisers) if there has been no material change.

Finally, if the IA has no clients to whom delivery of a brochure is required, a brochure does not have to be prepared.

Summary

Form ADV facts: Part 1B is only filed by state-registered advisers; only state-registered advisers file Part 2 with their regulators—federal covered advisers must keep theirs on hand for inspection; Part 2A is the brochure which must be delivered to clients of all IAs within 120 days of the end of the fiscal year. A brochure supplement may be delivered instead showing the material changes. If there are no material changes, there is no need to send a brochure. The Part 1A annual amendment must be sent to the SEC or Administrator within 90 days after the end of the fiscal year.

Many students get confused over the 90-day and 120-day requirements. This example should help:

EXAMPLE

1. Which two of the following statements accurately describes the time limits for investment adviser documents?

    I.   Filing of the annual updating amendment to the Form ADV with the appropriate regulatory body is within 90 days of the end of the adviser's fiscal year

    II. Filing of the annual updating amendment to the Form ADV with the appropriate regulatory body is within 120 days of the end of the adviser's fiscal year

    III. Delivery of the investment adviser's brochure to the customer is due within 90 days of the end of the adviser's fiscal year

    IV. Delivery of the investment adviser's brochure to the customer is due within 120 days of the end of the adviser's fiscal year

    A. I and III
    B. I and IV
    C. II and III
    D. II and IV

    Answer: B. The answer would be choices **I** and **IV**. Some logic here might help. The investment adviser must get its paperwork into the state (or SEC) prior to the end of the 90 day period. Then, the IA has another 30 days to get the information into the brochure to be sent to the clients.

Here are some examples.

EXAMPLES

1. With regard to the brochure rule of the Investment Advisers Act of 1940, which of the following are exempt from the delivery requirements of that rule?

   A. An adviser whose only clients are registered investment companies

   B. An adviser whose only clients are insurance companies

   C. An adviser who only provides impersonal advisory services at an annual charge of less than $500

   D. All of these

   Answer: D. An adviser to investment companies and an adviser who provides only impersonal advisory services are specifically listed as being exempt from the delivery requirements of the brochure rule (impersonal advice with a charge of $500 or more would require an offer to deliver). Under the federal law, an adviser who provides advice only to insurance companies is exempt from registration as an investment adviser and therefore would also be exempt from the requirements of the brochure.

2. With regard to a federal covered investment adviser, which of the following statements regarding the Form ADV Part 2A is CORRECT?

   A. It must be delivered no later than 48 hours before entering into an advisory contract.

   B. It must be delivered no later than upon receipt of a client's funds.

   C. It must accompany the ADV Part 1A when being delivered to new clients.

   D. An investment adviser must deliver to each client, a copy of the most recent ADV Part 2A no later than at the time of entering into the advisory agreement.

   Answer: D. Delivery of the ADV Part 2A, or brochure, must be made to each client no later than the commencement of the advisory agreement. If the adviser wishes to deliver before that, there is no problem, but it is not required. For a state-registered adviser, there is a requirement to deliver the brochure at least 48 hours in advance, unless the contract calls for a penalty-free termination. The ADV Part 1 is used when registering and is not furnished to clients

3. Under the Investment Advisers Act of 1940, a registered investment adviser who provides investment advisory services to individuals must

   A. have a minimum net worth of $100,000

   B. limit the giving of advice to securities listed on major exchanges

   C. avoid maintaining control or custody of client funds and securities

   D. provide each new client with a disclosure statement or brochure no later than when entering into the advisory agreement

   Answer: D. The brochure rule requires that each client be given a written disclosure statement by the adviser no later than the time of entering into the advisory agreement. It may consist of a copy of Part 2A and 2B of Form ADV or another document providing similar information. There are no minimum net worth requirements for SEC-registered investment advisers.

Solicitor's Brochure

In the next unit, we will study cash referral fees and the role of solicitors, but, in the context of our present discussion, the exam may want you to know what is included in the solicitor's brochure. You will probably want to come back to this information after you have learned more about solicitors.

The disclosure document must include:

■ the name of the solicitor,

■ the name of the investment adviser, and

■ the nature of the relationship between the solicitor and the investment adviser.

In addition, this document must disclose the fact that the solicitor will receive compensation, the terms of the compensation arrangement, and indicate whether the client will pay a specific charge or a higher advisory fee because a solicitor recommended the investment adviser to the client. Why is it important to include the terms of the compensation arrangement? Here is what the SEC said about that:

> "[T]he Commission believes that the terms of the compensation paid or to be paid to the solicitor are relevant to a prospective client's evaluation of the solicitor's recommendation. Thus, if a specific amount of compensation were being paid, that amount would be required to be disclosed. If the solicitor's compensation was to take the form of a percentage of the total advisory fee over a period of time, that percentage and the time period would have to be disclosed. If all, or part, of the solicitor's compensation is deferred or contingent upon some future event, such as the client's continuation or renewal of the advisory relationship or agreement, such terms would also have to be disclosed."(SEC Release No. IA-688, July 12, 1979)

In the next unit, we'll present this information in a sample question format.

SOCIAL MEDIA INCLUDING ELECTRONIC COMMUNICATIONS (EMAILS AND TEXT MESSAGES)

U6LO5: Describe the proper use of correspondence and advertising.

Correspondence and Social Media

It should be clear that disclosure and fairness are the primary themes underlying all communications with customers. Use of social media websites for business purposes should be treated no differently from any other business-related electronic communication. Firms must ensure they have sufficient systems, policies, and procedures to supervise, review, and retain business communications made using social media sites. In this final segment of this unit, we will address several of the specific methods used to communicate with both existing and prospective clients.

Definition

The SEC's definition of social media is:

> "Social media" is an umbrella term that encompasses various activities that integrate technology, social interaction, and content creation. Social media may use many technologies, including, but not limited to, blogs, microblogs, wikis, photo and video sharing, podcasts, social networking, and virtual worlds. The terms "social media," "social media sites," "sites" and "social networking sites" are used interchangeably in the industry.[1]

Communication with customers has historically been through written correspondence, while the traditional way of reaching prospects has been through print, TV, and radio advertising. In the 21st century, however, snail mail has given way to email, texting, and the broker-dealer's website. Prospects are being reached through various social networks as well as the internet.

At the time of this printing, NASAA's primary concern with social media has been alerting investors to the risks. Although some of that may be tested, it is probable that the exam's focus will be on usage of social media by securities professionals. As has been done with other topics not directly addressed by NASAA, we will rely on the policies adopted by other regulators. But first, let's look at some of NASAA's comments regarding investor awareness.

Investor Concerns Regarding Social Media

Social networking in the internet age allows people to connect to one another more quickly and easily than ever before. Investment promoters increasingly are logging on to find investors and their money.

The role of the securities professional is to help protect clients from falling prey to the many phony schemes found on social networks.

While social networking helps connect people with others who share similar interests or views, con artists infiltrate these social networks looking for victims. By joining and actively participating in a social network or community, the con artist builds credibility and gains the trust of other members of the group. In online social networks, a con artist can establish this trust and credibility more quickly. The scammer has immediate access to potential victims through their online profiles, which may contain sensitive personal information such as their dates or places of birth, phone numbers, home addresses, religious and political views, employment histories, and even personal photographs.

The con artist takes advantage of how easily people share background and personal information online and uses it to make a skillful and highly targeted pitch. The scam can spread rapidly through a social network as the con artist gains access to the friends and colleagues of the initial target.

TAKE NOTE

Social media generally takes two forms: static and interactive. **Static content** remains posted until changed by the person who established the account on the site. Generally, static content is accessible to all visitors to the site. Examples of

---

static content typically available through social networking sites include company websites, profiles, backgrounds, or walls.

Interactive content, as the name implies, has input from both the creator and the viewer. Common examples include Facebook, Twitter, Instagram, and LinkedIn.

Online Red Flags for Investors

- **Promises of high returns with no risk.** Many online scams promise unreasonably high short-term profits. Guarantees of returns around 2% a day, 14% a week, or 40% a month are too good to be true. Remember that risk and reward go hand in hand.

- **Offshore operations.** Many scams are headquartered offshore, making it more difficult for regulators to shut down the scam and recover investors' funds.

- **E-currency sites.** If investors have to open an e-currency account to transfer money, use caution. These sites may not be regulated, and con artists use them to cover up money trails.

- **Recruit friends.** Most cons will offer bonuses if investors recruit their friends into the scheme.

- **Professional websites with little to no information.** These days anyone can put up a website. Scam sites may look professional, but they offer little to no information about the company's management, location, or details about the investment.

- **No written information.** Online scam promoters often fail to provide a prospectus or other form of written information detailing the risks of the investment and procedures to get the investor's money out.

- **Testimonials from other group members.** Scam artists frequently pay out high returns to early investors using money from later arrivals. This type of scam is a Ponzi scheme. Fraud aimed at groups of people who share similar interests is called affinity fraud.

EXAMPLE

1. One of your clients approaches you to get your evaluation of an investment opportunity that was received through a Facebook post sent by a friend. The investment promises a monthly return in excess of 1% and claims that it is registered with an offshore regulatory body. You should explain to your client that

   A. these are reasonable expectations based on the investment and the location of the issuer

   B. your firm does not sell that security and, as a result, you cannot make any comments about the issue

   C. it is important to check with the friend to find out more about the deal

   D. these are red flags and are a clear warning to stay away from this investment

   Answer: D. Unreasonably high returns and not being registered in the United States are two items on the list of red flag warnings to investors published by NASAA.

Regulatory Concerns About Social Media

Both the SEC and FINRA have established policies, most of which are used as the basis for disciplinary actions when the Administrator's staff conducts an examination of broker-dealers and investment advisers located in his state.

FINRA has offered guidance to broker-dealers and registered personnel in their notices to members regarding the use of different technologies and devices for the delivery of business communications. As the technology, communications platforms, and devices are ever-changing, so will be the guidance, and FINRA will continue to supply interpretive materials to assist in that respect. Currently, the use of email, instant messaging, chat rooms, blogs, bulletin boards, and websites—including social networking sites such as Facebook, LinkedIn, and Twitter—are all included within FINRA's guidance.

While the challenge is generally to determine which category of public communication any piece falls under to determine its supervisory and filing requirements FINRA has said that it will always be the **content** delivered that ultimately determines this, and not the technology, platform, or device used to deliver it. In this light, FINRA reminds broker-dealers that compliance responsibilities when communicating via the internet or other electronic media are the same as in face-to-face discussions or in written communications with the public. Therefore, all existing FINRA rules and regulations applicable to communications with the public would also be applicable to communications delivered electronically by any technology or device if the content is business related. In addition, registered representatives (agents) must be aware of internal firm policies and procedures that may restrict or prohibit the use of certain electronic communications, and in those instances, FINRA directs that employees of the firm must abide by the firm's internal policies.

Although social media has been around for some time, it has now caught the attention of the SEC (and every other regulator, for that matter). You might ask, "Why should I be concerned with my emails or Facebook posts?" Well, here are just a couple of examples of how and why the regulators react.

The problem for regulated financial institutions is that inappropriate use of email and other social media can mean non-compliance with government and industry regulations, resulting in hefty fines, potential loss of business, and fraud. A few years ago, a major international bank lost nearly €4.9 billion in fraudulent trades by a rogue employee that used instant messaging to manage the transactions. On a smaller level, in early 2016, an agent was fined $15,000 and suspended from association with any broker-dealer for a period of two years for sending an unapproved email to prospective clients. During the same time period, a broker-dealer was fined $1.1 million, and one of its agents was fined $50,000, for failure to retain emails as required. So, this is serious business to the regulators.

You need to know that agents are duty bound to follow the rules and regulations surrounding electronic communications, even during their own time, if they are identifiable as a representative of the securities firm. Members of the marketing team might understand what is appropriate to post to Facebook or what process to follow to post, but, without proper training, average agents may not. Their posts or photographs from weekend parties might not be suitable content.

Review and Supervision of Electronic Communications

When it comes to review and supervision, it is important to note that the terms electronic communications, email, and electronic correspondence may be used interchangeably and can include such forms of electronic communications as instant messaging and text messaging.

This is particularly important for those firms that permit their agents or investment adviser representatives to maintain social media platforms.

ADVERTISING

NASAA considers it to be an unethical business practice to use any advertising or sales presentation in such a fashion as to be deceptive or misleading. An example of such practice would be:

- a distribution of any nonfactual data;
- any material or presentation based on conjecture;
- unfounded or unrealistic claims in any brochure, flyer, or display by words, pictures, or graphs; or
- anything otherwise designed to supplement, detract from, supersede, or defeat the purpose or effect of any prospectus or disclosure.

One way in which this violation occurs is when a broker-dealer or agent prepares a sales brochure for a new issue but includes only the positive information from the prospectus. Leaving out risk factors and other potentially deal-killing information is prohibited. Somewhat related, and also prohibited, is **highlighting** or making any other marks on a prospectus to draw attention to key points.

Broker-Dealer Advertising

Included in advertising is a firm's website.

Whether through the website or other social media, an important form of communications with the public is the making of recommendations.

A logical question is, do recommendations made through social media come under the same suitability constraints as any other recommendation? The reply is just what you would expect: of course they do. But it is not always obvious when a particular communication constitutes a recommendation for purposes of the suitability rule. Because so much hinges on what is considered to be a recommendation, let's look further at some examples of what is and what is not a recommendation.

In addition to when a broker-dealer acts merely as an order-taker regarding a particular transaction (an unsolicited transaction, which we know is an exempt transaction—exempt from the registration and advertising filing requirements under the USA), the policy generally would view the following activities and communications as falling outside the definition of *recommendation*.

- A broker-dealer creates a website that is available to customers or groups of customers. The website has research pages or electronic libraries that contain research reports (which may include buy-sell recommendations from the author of the report), news, quotes, and charts that customers can obtain or request.

- A broker-dealer has a search engine on its website that enables customers to sort through the data available about the performance of a broad range of stocks and mutual funds, company fundamentals, and industry sectors. The data is not limited to, and does not favor, securities in which the BD makes a market or has made a buy recommendation. Customers use and direct this tool on their own. Search results from this tool may rank securities using any criteria selected by the customer, and may display current news, quotes, and links to related sites.

■ A broker-dealer provides research tools on its website that allow customers to screen through a wide universe of securities (e.g., all exchange-listed and Nasdaq securities) or an externally recognized group of securities (e.g., certain indexes) and to request lists of securities that meet broad, objective criteria (e.g., all companies in a certain sector with 25% annual earnings growth). The BD does not impose limits on the manner in which the research tool searches through a wide universe of securities, nor does it control the generation of the list to favor certain securities. For instance, the BD does not limit the universe of securities to those in which it makes a market or for which it has made a buy recommendation. Similarly, the algorithms for these tools are not programmed to produce lists of securities based on subjective factors that the BD has created or developed, nor do the algorithms, for example, produce lists that favor those securities in which the BD makes a market or for which the BD has made a buy recommendation.

■ A broker-dealer allows customers to subscribe to emails or other electronic communications that alert customers to news affecting the securities in the customer's portfolio or on the customer's watch list. Such news might include price changes, notice of pre-scheduled events (such as an imminent bond maturation), or generalized information. The customer selects the scope of the information that the firm will send to him.

On the other hand, the regulators generally would view the following communications as falling within the definition of *recommendation*:

■ A broker-dealer sends a customer-specific electronic communication (e.g., an email or pop-up screen) to a targeted customer or targeted group of customers, encouraging the particular customer(s) to purchase a security.

■ A broker-dealer sends its customers an email stating that customers should be invested in stocks from a particular sector (such as technology) and urges customers to purchase one or more stocks from a list with buy recommendations.

■ A broker-dealer provides a portfolio analysis tool that allows a customer to indicate an investment goal and input personalized information such as age, financial condition, and risk tolerance. The BD, in this instance, then sends the customer a list of specific securities the customer could buy or sell to meet the investment goal the customer has indicated.

■ A broker-dealer uses data-mining technology (the electronic collection of information on website users) to analyze a customer's financial or online activity—whether or not it is known by the customer—and then, based on those observations, sends (or "pushes") specific investment suggestions that the customer purchase or sell a security.

It is important to keep in mind that these examples are meant only to provide guidance and are not an exhaustive list of communications that are or are not considered to be recommendations. They recognize that many other types of electronic communications are not easily characterized. In addition, changes to the factual suppositions upon which these examples are based (or the existence of additional factors) could alter the determination of whether similar communications may or may not be viewed as recommendations.

Broker-dealers, therefore, should analyze all relevant facts and circumstances to determine whether a communication is a recommendation, and they should take the necessary steps to fulfill their suitability obligations.

Investment Adviser Advertising

When it comes to investment advisers, the NASAA Model Rule states that publishing, circulating, or distributing any advertisement that does not comply with the Investment Advisers Act of 1940 would be prohibited.

The SEC has defined the term *advertisement* to include any notice, circular, website, letter, or other written communication addressed to more than one person, or any notice or other announcement in any publication or by radio or television, that offers:

- any analysis, report, or publication concerning securities;
- any graph, chart, formula, or other device to be used in making any determination concerning securities; or
- any other investment advisory service with regard to securities.

The term *advertisement* has generally been broadly construed. For example, an investment adviser's proposed publication of lists of past securities recommendations for a specific period constitutes an advertisement. Similarly, investment advisory material that promotes advisory services for the purpose of inducing potential clients to subscribe to those services is advertising material. In keeping with the changing times, an investment adviser's website is considered advertising.

An investment adviser should not publish, circulate, or distribute any advertisement that is inconsistent with federal rules governing the use of advertisements. Included in the prohibition are advertisements:

- containing untrue statements of material fact;
- that refer directly or indirectly to any testimonial of any kind;
- that represent that a chart, formula, or other device being offered can, by itself, be used to determine which securities are to be bought or sold;
- that contain a statement that any analysis, report, or service will be furnished for free when that is not the case;
- that refer to past specific recommendations of an adviser, which were or would have been profitable to any person. However, the Rule does not prohibit an advertisement which sets out or offers to furnish a list of all recommendations made by such investment adviser during the preceding year, provided that the advertisement or the list contains certain specific disclosures about the recommendations. Those disclosures would include stating that past performance is no guarantee of future results and explaining the effect of material market or economic conditions on the results advertised;
- that advertise gross performance data (i.e., performance data that does not reflect the deduction of various fees, commissions, and expenses that a client would pay) unless the adviser also includes net performance information in an equally prominent manner; and
- that represent or imply that the adviser has been sponsored, recommended, or approved, or that its abilities or qualifications have in any respect been passed upon by the SEC or the Administrator (the SEC has taken the position that the use of the initials *R.I.A.* following a name on printed materials would be misleading because, among other things, it suggests that the person to whom it refers has a level of professional competence, education, or other special training, when in fact there are no specific qualifications for becoming a registered investment adviser; the term *registered investment adviser* may be used, but not the initials).

TEST TOPIC ALERT

In the same manner that the use of the designation RIA is prohibited, investment adviser representatives may not use the initials IAR on business cards or any other literature. Yes, the exam will frequently use IAR, but you can't. What you can use on your business card are certain recognized professional or academic designations (assuming you've earned them). Examples would include CPA, CLU°, CFA°, CFP°, MBA, JD, or PhD.

These prohibitions are fundamental and sound standards that all investment advisers should follow.

An advertisement under state law is defined as a communication to more than one person. In addition, although the rules do not prohibit **testimonials** for broker-dealers, they are strictly forbidden for use by IAs. One thing to look for on the exam deals with investment advisers who advertise a charting or similar system—they must indicate that there are *limitations and difficulties* inherent in using such programs.

TAKE NOTE

In March 2014, the SEC published an interpretive release dealing with testimonials for investment advisers using social media. Included in that release is the statement that third-party use of the "like" feature on an investment adviser's social media site could be deemed to be a testimonial if it is an explicit or implicit statement of a client's experience with the adviser.

Issues Related to Agents

While much of the supervisory burden revolves around broker-dealer use of various social media tools, the nitty-gritty, day-to-day work relates to their agents. Some things to be aware of include the following.

- In addition to computers in the office, personal devices (Blackberry, iPhone, Android, etc.) used to communicate with clients in a social media setting are covered by the rules.

- Depending on the nature of the media, prior approval by a supervisory person may or may not be required. For example, an "unscripted" participation in an interactive electronic forum (such as Twitter) generally does not require prior supervisory approval. On the other hand, a LinkedIn page would probably require pre-approval.

- Look out for the red flags. Certain activities, such as linking to third-party sites or receiving data feeds from outside sources could contain information that NASAA considers objectionable.

- It is not the device or technology that determines if a piece delivered by a broker-dealer or any agent is subject to approval and recordkeeping. Rather, it should always be the *content* that determines if a piece delivered by an agent is subject to approval and recordkeeping.

It is suggested that Twitter posts are easy to monitor, but sites such as Facebook are not, given what they've termed *entanglement* issues (i.e., the firm or its personnel is involved with the preparation of a third-party post) and the challenges they pose. Essentially, who is responsible for links to a third-party site, and who is responsible for third-party postings to an agent's Facebook page?

Definitions

Adoption is a social media term meaning that a securities firm links to a third-party site and indicates that it endorses the content on that site.

Entangled is a social media term meaning that a securities firm has participated in the development of content on a third-party site to which it publishes links.

TAKE NOTE

Two related terms may appear on your exam. If a firm permits a third-party post on its website or it provides links to a third-party site, it will be considered that the firm is entangled with that post or link if the firm participates in the development or preparation of the content. A firm may be deemed to "adopt" a third-party post or content on a third-party site if the firm or its personnel explicitly or implicitly endorses or approves the post or the content. The key to entanglement is that your firm had a part in its authorship whereas *adoption* is the use of content or a link that is solely the creation of someone else—your firm is just using it.

Specifically regarding Twitter, posts do *not* need supervisory pre-approval except for an agent's initial tweet.

LinkedIn is considered different from Facebook, as it is more of a business networking site than a social site. With that, it is believed that information limited to your current position, past positions, and job responsibilities allow the site to be left unmonitored as the firm would have no responsibility regarding that content for any individual. However, if testimonials are used on the site ("Joe is the best stockbroker in the world," or "I've made a ton of money because of Sheila's recommendations"), or if recommendations are posted on the site, then that would make it a business site that the firm is now responsible for.

EXAMPLE

1. The regulatory bodies are concerned about agents using social media to communicate with clients when they are using their

    I. office desktop computers

    II. personal tablets

    III. smartphones

    IV. personal laptop from homes

    A. I and II

    B. I and IV

    C. II, III, and IV

    D. I, II, III, and IV

    Answer: D. The format is not what counts; it is the content that matters.

Supervisory Actions to Be Taken by the Broker-Dealer or Investment Adviser

Before allowing associated persons to use social media for business purposes, a firm's policies and procedures must provide for personnel training and education relating to the parameters of permitted use. Both supervisory personnel and agents need to understand the difference between interactive and static content, between business and non-business communications, and whether the communication is a retail communication requiring pre-approval. A firm should consider requiring training in the use of social media before permitting use. At a minimum, a firm that permits use of social media sites must hold annual training as part of its continuing education obligations. Any such training will reinforce personnel understanding of the firm's policies and procedures as applied to this continuously evolving technology and, in turn, limit the firm's compliance risks.

One of the unintended consequences of the growth of social media has been exposure to privacy issues. The firm's social media policies should include relevant privacy issues. We will cover those in the next unit when we discuss cybersecurity and data protection.

To summarize, because the technology behind social media continues to advance at such a rapid pace, potential damage to both the firm and employee exist. To mitigate these, it is suggested that firm policies should:

- be committed to writing and communicated firmwide;

- be written in a clear and concise manner so as to eliminate confusion;

- define the responsibilities of all concerned parties to minimize confusion and maximize expectations; and

- clearly describe the monitoring tools to be used by the firm.

Because social media technology continues to evolve, the potential for reputational and financial loss from any employee or firm mistake is difficult to quantify. Before venturing into any form of social media, firm policies should (1) be firmly established, (2) be precise, (3) clearly define the employees' responsibilities, (4) and explain how they are to be monitored on each electronic platform used by the firm. Until the law catches up with technology, a useful way to reduce and manage unforeseeable social media risk is to create a work environment that fosters a strong culture of compliance.

EXAMPLE

1. Which of the following is NOT a factor when a communication to be distributed to the public is either being reviewed or approved by the investment adviser?

   A. Whether statements of benefits are balanced with statements of potential risks

   B. The nature of the audience to which the communication is intended to be distributed

   C. Whether the piece will be distributed in written form or on the firm's website

   D. Whether the communication is targeting existing customers or prospective ones

   Answer: C. The format is not what counts; it is the content that matters.

UNIT 7

Ethical Practices and Fiduciary Obligations

The Uniform Securities Act was drafted for two primary reasons: (1) to eliminate conflicts in state securities legislation and make state securities laws uniform, and (2) to protect the public from unethical securities practices and fraud. Understanding ethical practices, and securities professionals' obligations to follow them, is the subject of this unit. This unit addresses what constitutes unethical and prohibited business practices, as defined in the Statement of Policy on Dishonest or Unethical Business Practices of Broker-Dealers and Agents issued by NASAA (the North American Securities Administrators Association), The NASAA Model Rule on Unethical Business Practices of Investment Advisers, Investment Adviser Representatives, and Federal Covered Advisers, as well as what are considered unethical practices under federal securities laws. It will also examine the fiduciary responsibilities of investment advisers and their representatives.

Recognizing that the industry is a dynamic rather than static one, this unit will also deal with the modern challenges of cybersecurity and data protection.

Dishonest and unethical practices are heavily tested topics. You must know what these practices are and be able to apply the principles that guide ethical behavior to specific situations presented in the exam.

The Series 65 exam will include 11 questions on the material presented in this unit.

LEARNING OBJECTIVES

When you have completed this unit, you will be able to accomplish the following.

U7LO1: Identify the important ethical considerations and fiduciary responsibilities in providing investment advisory services.

U7LO2: Recognize how investment advisers and broker-dealers protect client funds and securities.

U7LO3: Describe how the Prudent Investor Rule applies to investment advisers and their representatives when making suitable recommendations.

U7LO4:   Identify the implications of the NASAA Model Rule on Unethical Business Practices of Investment Advisers, Investment Adviser Representatives, and Federal Covered Advisers and the NASAA Statement of Policy on Dishonest or Unethical Business Practices of Broker-Dealers and Agents.

U7LO5:   Recognize the potential criminal (fraud) or unethical activities.

U7LO6:   Identify the kind of reporting required of investment advisers.

U7LO7:   Recognize that investment advisers and their representatives must practice good cyber security, privacy, and data protection.

U7LO8:   Recall what constitutes an adequate business continuity plan.

FIDUCIARY RESPONSIBILITY OF INVESTMENT ADVISERS

U7LO1: Identify the important ethical considerations and fiduciary responsibilities in providing investment advisory services.

Unlike broker-dealers and their agents, investment advisers and their IARs have a fiduciary responsibility to their customers. That obligates these advisers and their representatives to put their clients' interests ahead of their own. That is the primary reason why advisers need their clients' consent when acting as agents or principals in trades with them (as covered in the previous unit). As fiduciaries, investment advisers must identify and address all material conflicts of interest by eliminating or disclosing such conflicts. Clients rely on the advice of their advisers and must feel confident that those advisers are working in the clients' best interests.

If the adviser also engages in non-securities-related activities, such as selling auto insurance or real estate, these represent potential conflicts of interest (time taken away from "watching the market") and must be disclosed.

 EXAMPLE

1. Investment advisers and their representatives have an obligation to place their clients' needs ahead of their own. This is legally known as

    A. avoiding conflicts of interest

    B. making full disclosure

    C. fiduciary responsibility

    D. playing fair

    Answer: C. The obligation of investment advisers and IARs to place clients' interests ahead of their own is known as acting in a fiduciary capacity.

Another responsibility is recognizing your capabilities. It is an unethical business practice to promise to provide services that you know can't be provided. And, one other relevant idea is criticizing the work of other professionals. This is not to say that you can't point out suggestions you would have made differently, such as a different clause in a will, but, unless you are an attorney or an accountant, be careful criticizing legal or accounting work performed by those professionals.

Hedge Clauses

A constant concern of the regulators is any attempt by an investment adviser to waive the implied fiduciary responsibilities inherent in the client/adviser relationship. One of the most common methods of doing so is through the use of the hedge clause, sometimes referred to as an exculpatory clause. This test is consistent with the Investment Advisers Act of 1940 which states that "any condition, stipulation, or provision binding any person to waive compliance with any provision of this Act or with any rule, regulation or order thereunder shall be void."

In a recent example, one state took issue with a contract that stated: "It is understood that we will extend our best efforts in the supervision of the portfolio, but we assume no responsibility for action taken or omitted in good faith if negligence, willful or reckless misconduct, or violation of applicable law is not involved."

So, here's the bottom line for the exam. You will be presented with a question or two containing a statement to the effect of, "the client agrees to waive rule violations by the IA (or other securities professional)." The answer to choose is the one that states, "waivers are never permitted."

This is not to say that the acts prohibit the use of all hedge clauses. For example, the SEC has not objected to clauses that limit the investment adviser's liability for losses caused by conditions and events beyond its control, such as war, strikes, natural disasters, new government restrictions, market fluctuations, communications disruptions, and so forth. Such provisions are acceptable because they do not attempt to limit or misstate the adviser's fiduciary obligations to its clients; but, it is highly unlikely that one of these choices will be on your test.

 EXAMPLES

1. An investment adviser runs an advertisement in the business section of the local newspaper. The ad describes the nature of the firm's model portfolio and indicates that it has outperformed the overall market by 800% over the past 10 years, and, therefore, they guarantee that their clients will more than keep pace with inflation. At the bottom of the ad in smaller print is the following statement: "Results are not guaranteed. Past performance is not indicative of future results. These results are not normal and cannot be expected to be repeated." This is an example of

    A. a properly worded disclaimer

    B. an improper hedge clause

    C. a violation of an investment adviser's fiduciary responsibility

    D. a wrap fee account

    Answer: B. Hedge clauses may not be used to disclaim statements that are inherently misleading—no ad can state a guarantee like that.

2. Which of the following statements regarding the use of a hedge clause by an investment adviser is CORRECT?

   A. The adviser's brochure must always contain at least one hedge clause.

   B. A properly worded hedge clause may be used to minimize the investment adviser's fiduciary responsibility.

   C. A hedge clause that limits the investment adviser's liability for losses caused by conditions and events beyond its control, such as war, strikes, and natural disasters, would generally be acceptable to the Administrator.

   D. A hedge clause that limits liability to acts done in bad faith or pursuant to willful misconduct but also explicitly provides that rights under state or federal law cannot be relinquished would generally be acceptable to the Administrator.

   Answer: C. The regulators have not objected to clauses that limit the investment adviser's liability for losses caused by conditions and events beyond its control, such as war, strikes, natural disasters, new government restrictions, market fluctuations, communications disruptions, and so forth. Such provisions are acceptable because they do not attempt to limit or misstate the adviser's fiduciary obligations to its clients. Limiting liability to acts done in bad faith might cause the unsophisticated client to fail to understand that he still has a right to take action, even when the acts are committed in good faith. Fiduciary responsibility cannot be limited by hedge clauses.

Disclosure of Compensation

One of the areas where the importance of the fiduciary relationship comes into play deals with compensation.

As we covered when discussing advisory contracts, compensation details must always be disclosed. This would include:

- the method of computing compensation;
- refunding of prepaid fees;
- the type of compensation (hourly fees, fees based on AUM, commissions, etc.); and
- any incentives or other compensation from the issuer of securities recommended.

That last bullet point is particularly important because of the fiduciary relationship. Incentives or bonuses will undoubtedly present a potential conflict of interest and the IA must always put the interest of the client first.

We learned in the previous unit that performance-based compensation is prohibited under all circumstances unless there is a qualifying exception. Now, we'll look at those exceptions.

Under state and federal law, the exceptions from the performance fee prohibition apply to contracts with a qualified client, defined as:

- a natural person or company that immediately after entering into the contract has at least $1 million under the management of the investment adviser; or

- a natural person or company that the IA has reason to believe that immediately prior to entering into the contract has a net worth exclusive of the primary residence (in the case of individuals, assets held jointly with a spouse, but no one else, can be used) in excess of $2.1 million; or

- a natural person who is an officer or director of the investment adviser or one of their IARs who has been employed in the industry at least 12 months.

TAKE NOTE

Please notice the inconsistency in the rule. It is at least $1 million in AUM with the adviser, or net worth *in excess* of $2.1 million. Why couldn't they both be *at least*, or *in excess* of? Makes the test tougher, doesn't it?

The test may want you to know that a fee based on the average amount of money under management over a particular period is *not* considered to be a performance fee.

There is one significant difference between the rules for state-registered IAs and federal covered IAs. In order for a state-registered IA to enter into, extend, or renew an investment advisory contract that provides for compensation to the investment adviser on the basis of a share of capital gains upon or capital appreciation of the funds of the client, the investment adviser must disclose the following in writing to the client:

- That the fee arrangement may create an incentive for the investment adviser to make investments that are riskier or more speculative than would be the case in the absence of a performance fee

- Where relevant, that the investment adviser may receive increased compensation with regard to unrealized appreciation as well as realized gains in the client's account

- The periods that will be used to measure investment performance throughout the contract and their significance in the computation of the fee

- The nature of any index that will be used as a comparative measure of investment; and performance, the significance of the index, and the reason the investment adviser believes that the index is appropriate

None of these disclosures apply to federal covered advisers; although, from a practical standpoint (not on the exam), most of these are made to clients.

The most common type of performance fee is known as a fulcrum fee. In this case, the fee is averaged over a specified period (at least 12 months) with an increase or decrease in proportion to the investment performance in relation to the performance of a specified securities index (the S&P 500 is a very popular example). For example, for each 5% that the client's account outperforms the specified index, the adviser would receive an increase to the fee of 10 basis points (.10%). Of course, negative performance would have the same results.

TEST TOPIC ALERT

There are two additional points related to performance-based compensation that you must know. Firstly, the adviser must use net performance, that is, consider both gains and losses. Secondly, as with so many other rules, the Administrator has the power to authorize this type of fee even when the client doesn't meet the financial requirements.

CASH REFERRAL FEES

No discussion of compensation would be complete without mentioning payments for referrals. The SEC has not prohibited payment of cash referral fees by investment advisers to persons who solicit business for them. The Investment Advisers Act of 1940 permits payment of cash referral fees to solicitors, providing four conditions are met. The first three conditions apply to all cash referral fee payments.

The first condition requires that the investment adviser be registered under the Advisers Act. Thus, the rule prohibits cash referral fee payments to a solicitor by an investment adviser required to be registered but who is not registered. The second condition prohibits payment of cash referral fees to a solicitor who is subject to a statutory disqualification (e.g., a solicitor who is subject to an SEC order or convicted of certain crimes within a 10-year period). The third condition requires cash referral fees to be paid pursuant to a written agreement to which the investment adviser is a party.

Even if the first three conditions are satisfied, cash referral fee payments are prohibited unless they are made in one of three circumstances. In the first circumstance, payments are for the provision of impersonal advisory services. The second circumstance is where the adviser pays a referral fee to a person affiliated with the adviser (e.g., a partner, officer, director, or employee of the adviser and this is likely the only case where the individual will be registered as an investment adviser representative of the IA). The third circumstance, and generally the most tested, in which cash referral fees may be paid involves third-party solicitors who are not persons affiliated with the adviser.

When the cash referral fees are paid to third-party solicitors who are not affiliated with the adviser, the following disclosures must be made:

- Unless for impersonal advisory services, the fact that it is a third party must be disclosed (this is usually accomplished by requiring that a separate solicitor brochure be delivered along with the adviser's brochure).

- Any script or sales approach used by the third party is the responsibility of the adviser.

According to the SEC staff, failure to adequately inform clients of a referral fee arrangement may be a violation. The amount of the remuneration and the basis on which it is paid must be disclosed, together with the fact that the finder is being compensated specifically for referring clients to the adviser.

Finally, the SEC requires investment advisers to keep copies of the following material pertaining to solicitors and referrals:

- Evidence of a written agreement to which the adviser is a party related to the payment of such fee

- A signed and dated acknowledgment of receipt from the client evidencing the client's receipt of the investment adviser's disclosure statement and a written disclosure statement of the solicitor

- A copy of the solicitor's written disclosure statement

- Copies of the investment adviser's disclosure documents (e.g., Form ADV Part 2A) delivered to the solicited client by the solicitor

The rules are much simpler for state-registered advisers. Under the Uniform Securities Act, in almost every case, anyone who solicits on behalf of an investment adviser must be registered as an IAR.

TEST TOPIC ALERT

You might have to know the contents of the solicitor's brochure. They are:

- the name of the solicitor;

- the name of the investment adviser;

- the nature of the relationship between the solicitor and the IA; and

- the fact that the solicitor will receive compensation, the terms of the compensation arrangement, and indicate whether the client will pay a specific charge or a higher advisory fee because the solicitor recommended the IA to the client.

EXAMPLE

1. Capital Asset Planning & Management, (CAPM), a registered investment adviser, has decided to employ the services of Optimized Lead Generators, (OLG), a third-party solicitor. To be in compliance, OLG's disclosure document must include the:

    I. name of the solicitor (OLG)

    II. name of the investment adviser (CAPM)

    III. nature of the relationship between OLG and CAPM

    IV. fact that OLG will receive compensation, the terms of the compensation arrangement, and indicate whether the client will pay a specific charge or a higher advisory fee because OLG recommended CAPM to the client

    A. I, II, III, and IV

    B. I and II

    C. I, III, and IV

    D. II, III, and IV

    Answer: A. SEC Release IA-688 contains the specifications for required inclusions in a third-party solicitor's disclosure document (brochures). This document, which includes all of the information in these choices, must be delivered along with the IA's brochure. Although not in this question, you should know that the investment adviser must receive from the client, before or at the time of entering into any written or oral investment advisory contract with such client, a signed and dated acknowledgment of receipt of the investment adviser's brochure and the solicitor's written disclosure document.

TEST TOPIC ALERT

Many good investment advisers are successful at networking. As a result, they may refer to, and/or receive referrals from, other professionals, such as attorneys, accountants, and insurance agents. Depending on the nature of the relationship, there may even be a fee paid by the investment adviser for the referral. The rules we've previously discussed regarding cash referral fees deal with those who are focused on soliciting clients for an investment adviser. However, when a lawyer, accountant, or insurance agent refers a client to an IA, it would be permitted for the IA to offer a nominal fee (something in the range of several hundred dollars) as a thank you. What would be prohibited would be to have the size of the fee based on the size of the client account or the fees generated by managing that account.

EXAMPLES

1. Which of the following statements regarding cash referral fees to solicitors are correct under the Investment Advisers Act of 1940?

    I.   If the solicitation involves anything other than impersonal advisory services, disclosure must be made to the client regarding any affiliation between the adviser and the solicitor.

    II. The agreement must be in writing.

    III. The solicitor must not be subject to a statutory disqualification.

    IV. The adviser's principal business activity must be the rendering of investment advice.

    A. I and II

    B. I, II, and III

    C. III and IV

    D. I, II, III, and IV

    Answer: B. To make cash payments to solicitors, the agreement must:

    — be in writing;

    — provide for disclosure of any affiliations between the adviser and the solicitor (unless the solicitation is being made for impersonal advisory service);

    — provide that no one subject to statutory disqualification be compensated;

    — follow a script approved by the adviser; and

    — provide that, in addition to the adviser's brochure, a solicitor brochure be delivered as well (third party).

    Nothing in the rules refers to how much of the adviser's time must be spent giving advice. The only time there is a requirement that a substantial portion of the adviser's business be giving investment advice is when using the term investment counsel.

2. Omerta Transparent Advisers, Inc., (OTA), registered with the SEC as an investment adviser, wishes to pay an individual to act as a third-party solicitor to solicit or refer new advisory clients. Under the provisions of the Investment Advisers Act of 1940, which of the following statements is TRUE regarding this relationship?

    A. The individual would be required to register as an IAR of OTA, Inc.

    B. The individual would not be required to register as an IAR of OTA, Inc.

    C. The individual would be prohibited from registering as an IAR of OTA, Inc.

    D. The individual would only be required to register as an IAR of OTA, Inc. if compensated for the solicitation activities.

Answer: B. The Investment Advisers Act of 1940 and the associated SEC rules do not require the solicitor to register as an investment adviser representative as long as the solicitor's activities are strictly limited to merely referring clients to a registered investment adviser in compliance with SEC rules. However, the majority of state securities regulators define the solicitation or referral of investment advisory clients as an investment advisory activity requiring the registration of the solicitor as an investment adviser or investment adviser representative. But remember to read the question—it only asks about the federal law.

SECTION 28(E) SAFE HARBOR

One specific form of compensation that is unique to investment advisers is *soft dollar* compensation from broker-dealers. This subject is dealt with in Section 28(e) of the Securities Exchange Act of 1934.

Research is the foundation of the money management industry. Providing research is one important, long-standing service of the brokerage business. Soft dollar arrangements have developed as a link between the brokerage industry's supply of research and the money management industry's demand for research. What does that mean and how does it work? To find the answers, we must review the provisions of Section 28(e) of the Securities Exchange Act of 1934 and its "safe harbor."

Definition: Safe Harbor

The original use was a maritime one referring to a safe place for a ship to enter, especially during a storm or a war. In the business world, it has come to mean a method of behavior which avoids running afoul of the law. In our case, the Section 28(e) safe harbor describes compensation to an investment adviser from a broker-dealer that will generally not be considered unethical.

Broker-dealers typically provide a bundle of services, including research and execution of transactions. The research provided can be either proprietary (created and provided by the broker-dealer, including tangible research products as well as access to analysts and traders) or third party (created by a third party but provided by the broker-dealer). Because commission dollars pay for the entire bundle of services, the practice of allocating certain of these dollars to pay for the research component has come to be called *soft dollars*. The SEC has defined soft dollar practices as arrangements under which products or services other than execution of securities transactions are obtained by an investment adviser from or through a broker-dealer in exchange for the direction by the investment adviser of client brokerage transactions to the broker-dealer, frequently referred to as *directed transactions* on the exam. Under traditional fiduciary principles, a fiduciary cannot use assets entrusted by clients to benefit itself. As the SEC has recognized, when an adviser uses client commissions to buy research from a broker-dealer, it receives a benefit because it is relieved from the need to produce or pay for the research itself.

Because of the conflict of interest that exists when an investment adviser receives research, products, or other services as a result of allocating brokerage on behalf of clients, the SEC requires advisers to disclose soft dollar arrangements to their clients. Section 28(e) provides that a person who exercises investment discretion with respect to an account will not be deemed to have acted unlawfully or to have breached a fiduciary duty solely by reason of his having caused the account to pay more than the lowest available commission if such person determines in good faith that the amount of the commission is reasonable in relation to the value of the brokerage and research services provided.

In adopting Section 28(e), Congress acknowledged the important service broker-dealers provide by producing and distributing investment research to money managers. Section 28(e) defines when a person is deemed to be providing brokerage and research services, and states that a person provides brokerage and research services insofar as he:

■   furnishes advice directly or through publications or writing about the value of securities, the advisability of investing in, purchasing, or selling securities, or the availability of purchasers or sellers of securities;

■   furnishes analyses and reports concerning issuers, industries, securities, economic factors and trends, portfolio strategy, and performance of accounts; or

■   effects securities transactions and performs functions incidental thereto (such as clearance, settlement, and custody).

An adviser is obligated under both the Investment Advisers Act of 1940 and state law to act in the best interests of its client. This duty generally precludes the adviser from using client assets for its own benefit or the benefit of other clients, without obtaining the client's consent based on full and fair disclosure. In such a situation, the antifraud provisions of the federal securities laws also would require full and fair disclosure to the client of all material facts concerning the arrangement. As the SEC has stated, "the adviser may not use its client's assets for its own benefit without prior consent, even if it costs the client nothing extra." Consent may be expressly provided by the client; consent also may be inferred from all of the facts and circumstances, including the adviser's disclosure in its Form ADV.

Section 28(e) does not relieve investment advisers of their disclosure obligations under the federal securities laws. Advisers are required to disclose, among other things, the products and services received through soft dollar arrangements, regardless of whether the safe harbor applies.

Registered investment advisers must disclose certain information about their brokerage allocation policies to clients in Item 12 of Part 2A of Form ADV. Specifically, if the value of products, research, and services provided to an investment adviser is a factor in selecting brokers to execute client trades, the investment adviser must describe in its Form ADV:

■   the products, research, and services;

■   whether clients may pay commissions higher than those obtainable from other brokers in return for the research, products, and services;

■   whether research is used to service all accounts or just those accounts paying for it; and

■   any procedures that the adviser used during the last fiscal year to direct client transactions to a particular broker in return for products, research and services received.

The purpose of this disclosure is to provide clients with material information about the adviser's brokerage selection practices that may be important to clients in deciding to hire or continue a contract with an adviser and that will permit them to evaluate any conflicts of interest inherent in the adviser's policies and practices. In this respect, the SEC and courts have stated that disclosure is required, even when there is only a potential conflict of interest.

Here is an example of a statement found in one adviser's brochure:

"We may direct transactions for your account to registered broker-dealers in return for research products and services that assist us in making decisions about investments. The research products will be used to generally service all of our clients, so the brokerage commissions you pay may be used to pay for research that is not used in managing your account."

Finally, the SEC believes that an adviser accepting soft dollar benefits must explain that:

- the adviser benefits because it does not have to produce or pay for the research or other products or services acquired with soft dollars; and
- the adviser therefore has an incentive to select or recommend brokers based on the adviser's interest in receiving these benefits, rather than on the client's interest in getting the most favorable execution.

TEST TOPIC ALERT

What this all comes down to is knowing what is and what is not included in the safe harbor. Here are some of the items that, if received as soft dollar compensation, would likely fall under 28(e)'s safe harbor:

- Research reports analyzing the performance of a particular company or stock
- Financial newsletters and trade journals could be eligible research if they relate with appropriate specificity
- Quantitative analytical software
- Seminars or conferences with appropriate content
- Effecting and clearing securities trades

On the other hand, likely to fall out of the safe harbor would be:

- telephone lines;
- office furniture, including computer hardware;
- travel expenses associated with attending seminars;
- rent;
- any software that does not relate directly to analysis of securities;
- payment for training courses for this exam; and
- internet service.

EXAMPLES

1. Which of the following would NOT be included in the safe harbor provisions of Section 28(e) of the Securities Exchange Act of 1934?

   A. Proprietary research

   B. Third-party research

   C. Rent

   D. Seminar registration fees

   Answer: C. Section 28(e) provides a safe harbor for those expenses paid with soft dollars that offer a direct research benefit. Rent is not included in the list of acceptable items coming under that safe harbor.

2. When an investment adviser with discretion over a client's account directs trade executions to a specific broker-dealer and uses the commission dollars generated to acquire software that analyzes technical market trends, it is known as

   A. hard-dollar compensation

   B. indirect compensation

   C. investment discretion

   D. soft dollar compensation

   Answer: D. Soft dollar compensation is when an investment adviser derives an economic benefit from the use of a client's commission dollars. Software of the type mentioned here is allowable under the safe harbor provisions of Section 28(e) of the Securities Exchange Act of 1934. It is true that this is indirect compensation and that this is a discretionary account, but the answer that best matches the question is soft dollar. Many times on the exam, you have to select best of the choices given.

OTHER BROKERAGE PRACTICES

In addition to disclosing how soft dollars are handled, there are several other practices involving broker-dealers and investment advisers where disclosure is required. Investment advisers must describe the factors that they consider in selecting or recommending broker-dealers for client transactions and determining the reasonableness of the broker-dealer's compensation.

Client Referrals

It is not an uncommon practice for broker-dealers to recommend their clients to investment advisers. Naturally, the investment adviser is happy to receive the referral, and the broker-dealer hopes to continue to execute the client's trades. This is considered as if the IA is compensating the broker-dealer for the referral. It is not illegal, but the IA must disclose the practice and, as a fiduciary, take steps to ensure that the charges for the services being rendered by the broker-dealer are reasonable.

Directed Brokerage

Directed brokerage is the practice of asking or permitting clients to send trades to a specific broker-dealer for execution. When the IA suggests the client use a specific broker-dealer(s), disclosure of any possible conflicts of interest must be made. There is nothing wrong with urging clients to use specific firms because of the quality of service received, even if the IA is doing so in response to referrals or soft dollars. As long as it is disclosed and the services rendered bear a reasonable relationship to their cost, directed brokerage should be a good deal for both the client and the IA. On the other hand, if the adviser permits the client to direct the brokerage firm to use, certain other disclosures are required. For example, the IA must explain that it may be unable to achieve most favorable execution of client transactions or that directing brokerage may cost clients more money. For example, in a client-directed brokerage account, the client may pay higher brokerage commissions because the IA may not be able to aggregate orders to reduce transaction costs, or the client may receive less favorable prices because the IA has arranged a preferred commission rate with a preferred broker-dealer. Here is an example of how that might appear in the brochure:

"It is important to note that if you do not give KAPCO Advisers discretion to direct trades, you may limit our ability to negotiate favorable commissions and seek best execution for trades in your account. You may also be excluded from block trades and average price transactions."

Trade Aggregation and Allocation

This is the practice of bundling (sometimes called *bunching*) trades to obtain volume discounts on execution costs. It occurs most often when an IA with discretion over accounts has several of them for whom the same security is appropriate and, instead of entering separate orders, enters them as one larger order. This invariably saves on execution costs. Sometimes, the order cannot be filled in one transaction or at a single price. In that case, it is generally considered that the fairest method of allocating the security's cost is on an average basis.

RULES ON CUSTODY OF FUNDS AND SECURITIES

U7LO2: Recognize how investment advisers and broker-dealers protect client funds and securities.

For the most part, the custody rules are identical under federal and state law. Our text will focus on the rule stated in the Investment Advisers Act of 1940 and, where the NASAA model rule differs, a notation will be made.

Safekeeping required

If you are an investment adviser registered under either federal or state law, it is a fraudulent, deceptive, or manipulative act, practice, or course of business within the meaning of the act for you to have custody of client funds or securities unless the following conditions are met.

- You have a qualified custodian. A qualified custodian maintains those funds and securities in a separate account for each client under that client's name, or in accounts that contain only your clients' funds and securities, under your name as agent or trustee for the clients.

- You give notice to your clients. If you open an account with a qualified custodian on your client's behalf, either under the client's name or under your name as agent, you must notify the client in writing of the qualified custodian's name and address and the manner in which the funds or securities are maintained, promptly when the account is opened and following any changes, such as a change in the location of the assets, to this information.

- Account statements are delivered to clients, either:
  - by qualified custodian: you have a reasonable basis for believing that the qualified custodian sends an account statement, at least quarterly, to each of your clients for which it maintains funds or securities, identifying the amount of funds and of each security in the account at the end of the period and setting forth all transactions in the account during that period; or
  - by adviser: if you (the investment adviser) maintain custody, or if you have custody because a related person maintains client funds or securities pursuant to this rule, you send a quarterly account statement to each of your clients for whom you have custody of funds or securities, identifying the amount of funds and of each security of which you have custody at the end of the period and setting forth all transactions

during that period. An independent public accountant must verify all of those funds and securities by actual examination at least once during each calendar year, at a time that is chosen by the accountant without prior notice or announcement to you and that is irregular from year to year, and file a copy of the auditor's report and financial statements with the SEC/Administrator stating that it has examined the funds and securities and describing the nature and extent of the examination: If the independent public accountant finds any material discrepancies during the course of the examination, the accountant must promptly notify the SEC/Administrator.

■   Under the NASAA model rule, in the absence of a rule prohibiting custody, the investment adviser notifies the Administrator promptly in writing on Form ADV that the investment adviser has or may have custody.

Definitions

For the purposes of this rule, **custody** means holding, directly or indirectly, client funds or securities, or having any authority to obtain possession of them. Custody also includes:

■   possession of client funds or securities (but not of checks drawn by clients and made payable to third parties) unless you receive them inadvertently and you return them to the sender promptly but in any case within three business days of receiving them: therefore, you should remember that the SEC never considers the receipt of a third-party check to constitute custody, while the Administrator will if the check is not sent on within three business days (NASAA—Under state law, the receipt of checks drawn by clients and made payable to unrelated third parties is considered custody unless forwarded to the third party within three business days of receipt and the adviser maintains a record of the event). If by mistake, a client leaves a stock certificate in an investment adviser's office, it would not be considered custody if the certificate was **returned** to the client within three business days; and

■   any arrangement (including a general power of attorney) under which you are authorized or permitted to withdraw client funds or securities maintained with a custodian upon your instruction to the custodian.

A **qualified custodian** is a bank or savings association that has deposits insured by the Federal Deposit Insurance Corporation under the Federal Deposit Insurance Act, a registered broker-dealer holding the client assets in customer accounts, and a foreign financial institution that customarily holds financial assets for its customers, provided that the foreign financial institution keeps the advisory clients' assets in customer accounts segregated from its proprietary assets.

TEST TOPIC ALERT

Most investment advisers do not take custody and, therefore, are unable to accept direct delivery of customer securities or funds except under the limited conditions described in this section. However, broker-dealers are not constrained by this rule; they are only required to provide receipts anytime they accept customer assets.

TAKE NOTE

There are two major benefits to an investment adviser using a qualified custodian.

■   Because the custodian is sending the quarterly reports to the client, that administrative burden is lifted from the investment adviser.

■   There is no requirement for a surprise annual audit by an independent accountant.

The NASAA model rule also adds language dealing with direct fee deduction. An adviser who has custody because the adviser's fees are directly deducted from client's accounts must also provide the following safeguards.

■ Written authorization—the adviser must have written authorization from each client to deduct advisory fees from the accounts held with the qualified custodian.

■ Notice of fee deduction—each time a fee is directly deducted from a client account, the adviser must concurrently:

  − send the qualified custodian notice of the amount of the fee to be deducted from the client's account, and

  − send the client an invoice itemizing the fee. Itemization includes the formula used to calculate the fee, the amount of assets under management the fee is based on, and the time period covered by the fee.

■ Notice of safeguards—the investment adviser notifies the Administrator in writing on Form ADV that the adviser intends to use the safeguards provided above.

TAKE NOTE

If the previously stated three requirements are satisfied, then the IA who is only considered to have custody because of direct deduction of fees will receive a waiver from the financial requirements for the net worth and bonding requirements described earlier in this unit (usually $35,000). In addition, just as with the IA who uses a qualified custodian, they will be relieved of the obligation to file an audited balance sheet.

EXAMPLE

Let's look at three examples of custody given by the SEC.

■ An adviser that holds clients' stock certificates or cash, even temporarily, puts those assets at risk of misuse or loss. The rule, however, expressly excludes inadvertent receipt by the adviser of client funds or securities, so long as the adviser returns them to the sender within three business days of receiving them. The rule does not permit advisers to forward clients' funds and securities without having custody, although advisers may certainly assist clients in such matters. In addition, the rule makes clear that an adviser's possession of a check drawn by the client and made payable to a third party is not possession of client funds for purposes of the custody definition. (Note, this is only true under NASAA rules if forwarded within three business days).

■ An adviser has custody if it has the authority to withdraw funds or securities from a client's account. An adviser with power of attorney to sign checks on a client's behalf, to withdraw funds or securities from a client's account, or to dispose of client funds or securities for any purpose other than authorized trading has access to the client's assets. An adviser authorized to deduct advisory fees or other expenses directly from a client's account has access to, and therefore has custody of, the client funds and securities in that account. These advisers might not have possession of client assets, but they have the authority to obtain possession.

■ An adviser has custody if it acts in any capacity that gives the adviser legal ownership of, or access to, the client funds or securities. One common instance is a firm that acts as both general partner and investment adviser to a limited partnership. By virtue of its position as general partner, the adviser generally has authority to dispose of funds and securities in the limited partnership's account and thus has custody of client assets.

Custody is a popular topic for exam questions so here are a few to try:

EXAMPLES

1. Which of the following advisers would be deemed to have custody of customer funds or securities as defined in the Investment Advisers Act of 1940?

   A. The adviser receives the proceeds of sales in the customer's account.

   B. The adviser receives a fee of $1,500 as a prepayment for the next contract year.

   C. The adviser has investment discretion over the account.

   D. All of these.

   Answer: A. Under the Investment Advisers Act of 1940, discretion and substantial prepayments are not considered custody. Access to funds in the client's account, choice **A**, is one of the standard tenets of custody.

2. An investment adviser registered with the state wishes to take custody of client's funds or securities. Which of the following statements best describes NASAA rules regarding notification to the Administrator?

   A. The adviser must supply prompt notification to the Administrator by immediately updating its Form ADV.

   B. The adviser must notify the Administrator within 90 days of the end of its fiscal year by updating its Form ADV.

   C. If the adviser will be using a qualified custodian, no notification is necessary.

   D. Prompt notification to the Administrator is made by the independent accounting firm performing the adviser's annual surprise audit.

   Answer: A. Taking custody is considered to be of such significance that it requires prompt notification to the Administrator, choice **A**, by the investment adviser by updating the Form ADV. Using a qualified custodian still constitutes a form of custody and requires notification to the Administrator.

3. An investment adviser takes custody of client's funds and securities. Client account statements must be sent no less frequently than

   A. monthly

   B. quarterly

   C. semiannually

   D. annually

   Answer: B. Whether custody is maintained by the investment adviser itself or by a qualified custodian, statements must be sent at least quarterly, choice **B**.

4. Under the NASAA Model Custody Rules, an investment adviser is deemed to have custody of customer funds or securities when

   A. securities inadvertently received are returned to the customer within 3 business days of receipt

   B. checks made payable to the investment adviser are returned to the customer within 3 business days of receipt

   C. checks made payable to an unrelated third party are returned to the customer within 3 business days of receipt

   D. checks made payable to an unrelated third party are forwarded to that third party within 3 business days of receipt

   Answer: C. Under the NASAA Model Custody Rule, whenever an investment adviser receives customer checks made payable to an unrelated third party, failure to **forward**, not return, the check to that third party within 3 business days of receipt, choice **C**, is considered to be maintaining custody. Unlike the other cases where the money or securities are returned to the client, third party checks must be forwarded.

5. Foster Advisers operates as an investment adviser that is registered in a state where the Administrator, by rule, prohibits investment advisers from holding custody of client funds and securities. This means that Foster Advisers may NOT

   A. refer clients to an affiliated broker-dealer

   B. manage client accounts on a discretionary basis

   C. examine customers' stock certificates

   D. have physical custody over its clients' monies and certificates

   Answer: D. Under the Uniform Securities Act, custody indicates that the adviser has physical possession over its clients' certificates and monies. If there is a rule prohibiting it, no investment adviser registered in that state can act in contravention of that rule, choice **D**. A prohibition against custody in a given state does not prohibit the adviser from holding investment discretion over clients' accounts, provided such discretion is granted under a suitable authorization or power of attorney. Merely examining customers' stock certificates is certainly not the same as holding custody or possession of such certificates. As long as the affiliation is disclosed, there is nothing improper about an IA referring advisory clients to that affiliated BD.

TEST TOPIC ALERT

Although the general rule is that state-registered investment advisers having custody must maintain a minimum net worth of $35,000 (or an equivalent surety bond), he net worth/bonding requirements are waived in two cases:

- Advisers having custody solely due to direct fee deduction and who keep the required records and make the required notifications to clients

- Advisers having custody solely due to advising pooled investment vehicles and who keep the required records and make the required notifications to clients

Form ADV-E

Investment advisers that have custody of client funds or securities are required to undergo an annual surprise examination by an independent public accountant to verify client funds and securities. Form ADV-E is used as a cover page for a certificate of accounting of securities and funds of which the investment adviser has custody (surprise exam report). Form ADV-E contains both information about the adviser and the surprise exam conducted.

The Form ADV-E is filled out by the investment adviser and then submitted along with the surprise examination report or statement by the independent public accountant after a surprise inspection of the adviser.

TEST TOPIC ALERT

Filing of the Form ADV-E is required only when the investment adviser, rather than a qualified custodian, maintains custody of customer funds/securities.

INVESTMENT DISCRETION

Investment discretion is frequently lumped together with custody. They are not the same thing and the exam will want you to know the differences.

A **discretionary account** is an account set up with preapproved authority for a securities professional to make transactions without having to ask for specific approval.

Discretion is defined as the authority to decide:

- which security;
- the number of shares or units; or
- whether to buy or sell.

Normally, an order to buy or sell a security is at the direction of the client, generally via a telephone call (firms will not accept emailed orders without oral verification from the client). Many clients prefer the convenience of letting their securities professional "call the shots." Obviously, the ability to determine the trading activity in a client's account presents a potential conflict of interest. In the case of broker-dealers and agents, their compensation is transaction-based—the more trading, the more income. In the case of investment advisers and their IARs, the conflict is less prominent, (they are rarely compensated for trading), but, especially with the fiduciary responsibility they carry, there is a burden on them not to incur unnecessary trading costs in their client's accounts.

TEST TOPIC ALERT

To identify a discretionary order, try this method: an order is discretionary if any one of the **three As** is missing. The three As are:

- **A**ctivity
- **A**mount
- **A**sset

Both state and federal law prohibit the exercise of any discretionary power by a broker-dealer or agent in a customer's account unless the customer has given prior written authorization (a power of attorney/trading authorization) to a stated individual or individuals and the account has been accepted by the brokerage firm, as evidenced in writing by the firm. No discretionary transactions can take place without this document on file. Once authorization is given, the firm is legally empowered to make trading decisions for the account, although the customer may also continue to enter orders on her own if she wishes.

Time or Price Discretion

There is an exception to this requirement that applies to the exercise of time or price discretion—which is discretion orally granted by the customer to purchase or sell a specific amount of a particular security (e.g., "Buy 100 shares of ABCD and get the best price you can.").

An oral grant of time or price discretion is limited to the end of the business day on which the customer grants it. An extension of such time or price discretion requires explicit signed and dated customer instructions. Any exercise of time or price discretion must be reflected on the order ticket (as is the case with regular discretion).

Why is it necessary to have written instructions if the discretion is to carry beyond the date of the order? The concept of time or price discretion has been subject to abuse and/or misunderstanding. At one time, there was no time limit placed on a grant of oral time or price discretion by a customer. This became problematic in instances where an agent was granted such discretion but did not exercise it for an extended period, sometimes several weeks. This led to claims of unauthorized trading by customers who may have forgotten that they granted the discretion, or who assumed it was not valid for such an extended period. The written extension requirement under the rules is intended to prevent such misunderstandings.

EXAMPLE

An order from a customer, worded, "Buy 100 shares of ABC for my account whenever you think the price is right," is not a discretionary order, because the client has specified the action (buy), the amount (100 shares) and the asset (ABC). Time or price are not considered discretion.

Discretion for Investment Advisers

Like anyone else, an investment adviser must have written authorization to exercise discretion in a client's advisory account. However, there is a unique provision found in the NASAA Model Rules which permits oral discretionary authority to be used for transactions in a customer's account during the first 10 business days after the date of the first discretionary transaction. After that time, if the written authorization has not been received, no further discretionary activity can take place.

TEST TOPIC ALERT

Be aware of the calendar. The 10-business-day period is equal to two normal work weeks. If a client opens a discretionary account with an investment adviser and gives the OK orally, but three weeks has passed by since the initial trade and the written authorization has not been received, the IA can't exercise discretion in the account, even if not taking action would cause disastrous results to the client's portfolio.

TEST TOPIC ALERT

Probably the greatest concern of the regulators when it comes to discretionary accounts is the possibility of the account being churned. **Churning** can be described as a securities professional effecting transactions in a discretionary account that are excessive in size or frequency, in view of the financial resources, objectives, and character of the account. To safeguard against the possibility of churning, a designated supervisor or manager must review all trading activity in discretionary accounts frequently and systematically. We will discuss churning again later in this unit.

Third Party Trading Authorization

In addition to granting a securities professional discretionary trading authorization, there is another common case where clients allow others to exercise control over their account. In Unit 18, we will discuss these in greater detail, but, at this point what you need to know is that executing a transaction on behalf of a customer without authorization to do so is a prohibited practice.

Securities professionals may never enter an order from a party other than the client, for a client without proper written authorization, even when it is in the best interest of the client. You may be asked a question where a spouse of a client or other person with a strong personal relationship contacts an agent with transaction instructions, allegedly on behalf of the client. Unless there is a written third-party trading authorization on file, no activity can take place.

Somewhat related to this activity is deliberately failing to follow a customer's instructions. In this case, the client has given the specific terms of the order and if the agent decides to purchase more or less than ordered, or in any other way change the nature of the order, it is a prohibited practice.

Commingling of Customer and Firm Assets

Broker-dealers and investment advisers must segregate customers' free securities or securities held in safekeeping. Customer's "free" securities are those which have no lien against them (just like one might have a lien against your car). Securities pledged as collateral in a margin account have a lien against them (we'll cover that in Unit 22).

Securities that are held in a customer's name must not be **commingled** (mixed) with securities of the firm.

If a firm has 100,000 shares of ABCD common stock in its own proprietary account and its clients separately own an additional 100,000 shares, the firm may not place customer shares in the firm's proprietary account.

To mix shares together would give undue leverage or borrowing power to a firm and could jeopardize the security of client securities in the event of default.

Improper Hypothecation

It is unethical to hypothecate (pledge as collateral) a customer's securities unless the broker-dealer secures from the customer a properly executed written consent promptly after the initial transaction in the client's margin account. This will be explained fully at Part 4, Unit 22.

MONEY LAUNDERING

Money laundering involves disguising financial assets so they can be utilized without detecting the illegal activity that produced them. Through money laundering, a criminal transforms the proceeds of illicit activities into funds that appear to have been generated by legal means. Money laundering enables criminals to hide and legitimize the proceeds derived from illegal ventures.

Currency Transaction Reports (CTRs)

The Bank Secrecy Act requires every financial institution to electronically file through the Department of the U.S. Treasury, a currency transaction report (CTR) on FinCEN Form 112 for each cash transaction that exceeds $10,000 within 15 days of receipt of the currency. This requirement applies to cash transactions used to pay off loans, the electronic transfer of funds, or the purchase of certificates of deposit, stocks, bonds, mutual funds, or other investments. The act also requires the reporting of wire transfers of $3,000 or more.

If anyone designs deposits to fall under the $10,000 radar this is a prohibited activity known as structuring. Financial institutions should have systems in place to monitor for and recognize such attempts.

 EXAMPLE

A customer makes 25 $500 cash deposits to pay for a $12,500 transaction. This should be recognized at an attempt to structure payments to fall under the $10,000 radar to avoid the filing of a CTR.

THE PRUDENT INVESTOR RULE

U7LO3: Describe how the Prudent Investor Rule applies to investment advisers and their representatives when making suitable recommendations.

Beginning with the dynamic growth of the stock markets in the late 1960s, the investment practices of fiduciaries experienced significant change. As a result, the Uniform Prudent Investor Act (UPIA) was adopted in 1994 as an attempt to update trust investment laws in recognition of those many changes. One of the major influences on this legislation was the growing acceptance of modern portfolio theory. The UPIA (now used in almost every state) makes five fundamental alterations in the former criteria for prudent investing. Those changes are as follows.

- The standard of prudence is applied to any investment as part of the total portfolio, rather than to individual investments. In this context, the term *portfolio* means all of the trust's or client's assets.

- The trade-off in all investments between risk and return is identified as the fiduciary's primary consideration.

- All categorical restrictions on types of investments have been removed; the fiduciary can invest in anything that plays an appropriate role in achieving the risk/return objectives of the account and that meets the other requirements of prudent investing.

■ The well-accepted requirement that fiduciaries diversify their investments has been integrated into the definition of prudent investing.

■ The much-criticized former rule forbidding the trustee to delegate investment functions has been reversed. Delegation is now permitted, subject to safeguards and the requirement that the fiduciary act with reasonable care, *skill*, and *caution*.

Because the most practical common application of the UPIA deals with retirement plans covered by ERISA, we'll go into more detail when that topic is covered in Unit 24.

STATEMENT OF POLICY ON DISHONEST OR UNETHICAL BUSINESS PRACTICES OF BROKER-DEALERS AND AGENTS

U7LO4: Identify the implications of the NASAA Model Rule on Unethical Business Practices of Investment Advisers, Investment Adviser Representatives, and Federal Covered Advisers and the NASAA Statement of Policy on Dishonest or Unethical Business Practices of Broker-Dealers and Agents.

NASAA's Model Rule for investment advisers and Statement of Policy for broker-dealers contain most of the prohibitions on unethical business practices of securities professionals. Most of them are the same or very similar and we'll point out where there are differences. Many of these practices have already been discussed in previous text so we'll limit this coverage largely to new items. Even so, this is a lengthy list, but important because of the large number of questions drawn from this information.

In 1983, NASAA released a Statement of Policy enumerating a large number of business practices that, when engaged in by broker-dealers or agents, they deemed dishonest or unethical. Subsequently, they have issued several Model Rules that have expanded the list. Most students report seeing at least five questions on their exam relating to this material. In most cases, the listed prohibition is logical common sense, "don't lie, don't cheat, and don't steal." However, due to the nature of this exam and their legal interpretations, particularly for those of you without a securities or law background, further explanations will be supplied.

The premise of the NASAA Policy is that each broker-dealer and agent shall observe high standards of commercial honor and just and equitable principles of trade in the conduct of their business. Acts and practices, including but not limited to those enumerated following, are considered contrary to such standards and may constitute grounds for denial, suspension or revocation of registration or such other action authorized by the Uniform Securities Act.

Likewise, NASAA issued their Model Rule on Unethical Business Practices of Investment Advisers, Investment Adviser Representatives, and Federal Covered Investment Advisers.

It is a dishonest or unethical business practice when doing any of the following:

Delivery Delays

A broker-dealer engaging in a pattern of unreasonable and unjustifiable delays in the delivery of securities purchased by any of its customers and/or in the payment upon request of free credit balances reflecting completed transactions of any of its customers. A free credit balance is just like a credit balance on your charge card—it is your money and must be sent to you upon request. In the event that the client requests a certificate for the security purchased, it would be considered an unethical business practice for the firm to delay delivering it to the client.

Unsuitable Recommendations

Recommending to a customer the purchase, sale, or exchange of any security without reasonable grounds to believe that such transaction or recommendation is suitable for the customer based upon reasonable inquiry concerning the customer's investment objectives, financial situation and needs, and any other relevant information known by the securities professional.

Securities professionals must always have reasonable grounds for making recommendations to clients. Before making recommendations, the securities professional must inquire into the client's financial status, investment objectives, and ability to assume financial risk. What about the client who refuses to give any financial information or discuss objectives? In that case, all a broker-dealer or agent can do is accept unsolicited orders because there is no basis for making any recommendation. As far as investment advisers and their representatives—because they are paid for their advice, if they don't have the requisite information, they won't open the advisory account.

TEST TOPIC ALERT

An unethical business practice is making blanket recommendations. That is when the investment adviser recommends the same security to most or all clients without regard to individual suitability.

TAKE NOTE

So, what do you do when you think you've made a totally appropriate recommendation to your client, but your client is not happy with it. Upon reflection, you realize the client's problem is a lack of understanding of both the recommendation and the marketplace. What should you do? Most would agree that the first step would be to attempt to impart some education to the client in an effort to make your recommendation clearer. However, as with all customer issues, the client is the one who has to make the final decision.

Free Lunch Seminars

Although not specifically included in the NASAA Statement of Policy, a Model Rule regarding unfair business practices, especially with regard to seniors, may be included on your exam. The most common instance is the so-called free lunch seminar. These seminars are widely offered by financial services firms seeking to sell financial products and they often include a free meal for attendees. Even though many of these seminars are promoted as being educational or workshops accompanied by the statement, "nothing will be sold at this meeting," the seminars are clearly intended to result in the attendees' opening new accounts with the sponsoring firm and, ultimately, in the sale of investment products, if not at the seminar itself, then in follow-up contacts with the attendees.

If not clearly presented, NASAA will consider that both the sponsoring firm and those individuals involved in the delivery of the seminar are committing a prohibited business practice.

Withholding Shares of a Public Offering

Failing to make a bona fide public offering of all of the securities allotted to a broker-dealer for distribution, whether acquired as an underwriter, a selling group member, or from a member participating in the distribution as an underwriter or selling group member. If the firm is fortunate to be part of the underwriting of one of these IPOs that rockets in price because the issue is oversubscribed, they better be sure to allocate the shares to clients in an equitable manner and not keep any for themselves.

Responding to Complaints

Failing or refusal to furnish a customer, upon reasonable request, information to which he is entitled, or to respond to a formal written request or complaint.

When a written complaint is received by the firm (and only written complaints are recognized), action must be taken. The complainant (customer) would be notified that the complaint had been received and an entry would be made in the firm's complaint file. If an agent were the subject of the complaint, the agent would be notified, but would *not* be given a copy of the complaint (agents do not have recordkeeping requirements). If the complaint is received by the agent rather than the firm, the agent must report the complaint to the appropriate supervisor. If the complaint is sent by email, that is considered *in writing*.

TEST TOPIC ALERT

A complaint received by electronic means (email) is considered a written complaint.

EXAMPLE

1. A customer is upset with her agent for not servicing her account properly and sends him a complaint via text message about his actions. Under the Uniform Securities Act, the agent should

    A. call the customer, apologize, and attempt to correct the problem

    B. tell the customer he is willing to make rescission

    C. do nothing because the complaint is not in writing

    D. bring the customer complaint to his employer immediately

    Answer: D. Any written customer complaint (and email or text message is considered written) must be brought to the attention of the agent's supervisor without hesitation.

TAKE NOTE

Written complaints must be kept on file by broker-dealers for three years and by investment advisers for five years.

Reporting Errors

To keep from generating complaints, any trade or other operational error, once discovered, must be reported by the agent to the appropriate supervisory person.

Front Running

Front running is the unethical business practice of a securities professional placing a personal order ahead of a previously received customer order. It occurs most frequently when the firm has received an institutional order of sufficient size to move the market. By running in front of the order, the firm or representative can profit on that movement. This may also be called *trading ahead.*

Spreading Rumors

Any agent or IAR hearing a rumor must report it to the appropriate supervisor. Firms must ensure that rumors they become aware of are not spread or used in any way, particularly not as the basis for recommendations.

EXAMPLE

1. An IAR hears a rumor concerning a security and uses the rumor to convince a client to purchase the security. Under the USA, the IAR may

   A. recommend the security if it is an appropriate investment

   B. recommend the investment if the rumor is based on material inside information

   C. recommend the security if the source of the rumor came from a reliable source

   D. not recommend the security

   Answer: D. Rumors must be promptly reported to the appropriate supervisory personnel and may never be used as the basis for a recommendation.

Backdating Records

All records and documents must reflect their actual dates. Although there can be tax or other benefits to clients when their trade confirmations are backdated, it is an unethical business practice to do so.

Lending or Borrowing

Engaging in the practice of lending to or borrowing money or securities from a customer.

Securities professionals may not borrow money or securities from a client unless the client is a broker-dealer, an affiliate of the professional, or a financial institution engaged in the business of loaning money.

Securities professionals may not loan money to clients unless the firm is a broker-dealer or financial institution engaged in the business of loaning funds or the client is an affiliate.

EXAMPLE

An agent purchases a used car from an individual client for $10,000 with a $3,000 down payment. The balance is to be paid over the next 36 months. This is prohibited because it is borrowing money from a client who is not in the money–lending business.

TEST TOPIC ALERT

As a former President of the United States once said, "Let me make one thing perfectly clear." When it comes to borrowing or lending money, you cannot borrow from *any* client (including your mother), unless that client is a lending institution such as a bank or credit union. Be careful, mortgage brokers are **not** in the business of lending money—they put the borrower and the lender together, which is why they are called *brokers*. Likewise, as an agent or IAR, you can never lend money to any client unless the client has some kind of affiliation with your firm. If your broker-dealer handles margin accounts, then, of course, money can be loaned to clients. Don't take this personally; just get the questions right on the exam.

EXAMPLE   **Borrowing Money or Securities from Clients**

One of the more confusing areas relates to borrowing money from (or lending money to) clients. Part of the reason for the confusion is that FINRA rules (many students taking this exam have taken a FINRA test) permit borrowing (lending) to clients under certain conditions that are more liberal than those of NASAA.

The first point to emphasize is that this prohibition only applies when the other side is a client. Securities professionals may borrow (or lend) as much as they want to those who are not clients, but once there is a client relationship, the NASAA policy takes effect. So, which **clients** can you borrow from?

- A bank or other financial institution in the business of making loans (e.g., credit union)
- A broker-dealer in a margin account
- A person affiliated with your firm

Which **clients** can't you borrow from?

- The employee at the lending institution who processes or approves your loan
- The agent at the broker-dealer who services your margin account
- A mortgage broker (only arranges the loan)
- A family member

PRACTICES RELATING SOLELY TO AGENTS

Fictitious Accounts

Establishing or maintaining an account containing fictitious information to execute transactions which would otherwise be prohibited. Examples of this kind of conduct sometimes given on the exam are "beefing up" a client's net worth to enable him to engage in margin or options trading, or making him appear to have more investment experience than is true.

Sharing in Accounts

Sharing directly or indirectly in profits or losses in the account of any customer without the written authorization of the customer and the broker-dealer which the agent represents.

Agents cannot share in the profits or losses of client accounts unless the client and the broker-dealer supply prior written approval. In such a situation, it would be permissible to commingle the agent's and the customer's funds if they have a joint account. Unlike FINRA rules, a joint account is not required nor is the sharing required to be proportionate to the agent's financial contribution.

TEST TOPIC ALERT

Unlike agents, broker-dealers, investment advisers, and investment adviser representatives are never permitted to share in the profits or losses in their client's accounts.

Splitting Commissions

Dividing or otherwise splitting the agent's commissions, profits, or other compensation from the purchase or sale of securities with any person not also registered as an agent for the same broker-dealer, or for a broker-dealer under direct or indirect common control. Interestingly enough, they can do this without disclosing the split to their clients, *unless* it increases the transaction cost to the client. This is one of the very rare cases where disclosure is not necessary.

NASAA MODEL RULE ON UNETHICAL BUSINESS PRACTICES OF INVESTMENT ADVISERS, INVESTMENT ADVISER REPRESENTATIVES, AND FEDERAL COVERED ADVISERS

Unethical Practices Relating Solely to Investment Advisers and Their Representatives

(See Appendix B for the complete list)

Misrepresenting to any advisory client, or prospective advisory client, the qualifications of the investment adviser or any employee of the investment adviser, or to misrepresent the nature of the advisory services being offered or fees to be charged for such service, or to omit to state a material fact necessary to make the statements made regarding qualifications, services or fees, in light of the circumstances under which they are made, not misleading.

EXAMPLE

When an investment adviser offers its services to a prospective client or when it provides services to an existing client, the qualifications of the investment adviser or any employee of the investment adviser and the nature of the advisory services and the fees to be charged must be disclosed in such a way as to not mislead. Overstating the qualifications of the investment adviser or disclosing inaccurately the nature of the advisory services to be provided or fees to be charged are not ethical ways to either acquire or retain clients.

Providing a report or recommendation to any advisory client prepared by someone other than the adviser without disclosing the fact. (This prohibition does not apply to a situation where the adviser uses published research reports or statistical analyses to render advice or where an adviser orders such a report in the normal course of providing service.)

EXAMPLE

If an investment adviser provides a report to a client that is prepared by a third party, the adviser has a responsibility to disclose the fact to the client. By entering into an investment advisory agreement, the client relies on the expertise of the adviser to provide the advisory service. Thus, if the advice is provided by a third party, it is imperative that the adviser disclose this fact to the client so the client is not misled. That would be something like turning in a term paper written by someone else and putting your name on it. The prohibition does not apply when an investment adviser gathers and uses research materials before making its recommendation to a client.

SEC Release IA-1092 warns against effecting transactions in which the adviser has a personal interest in a manner that could result in preferring his own interest to that of his advisory clients.

EXAMPLE

Some of the ways this applies are:

■ an investment adviser structures his personal securities transactions to trade on the market impact caused by his recommendation to clients without disclosing this to clients;

■ an investment adviser fails to disclose if his personal securities transactions are inconsistent with advice given to his clients;

■ an investment adviser must disclose compensation received from the issuer of a security being recommended; and

■ the SEC staff has taken the position that an investment adviser who sells non-securities investments, such as insurance products, to clients must disclose to clients and prospective clients all its interests in the sale to them of such non-securities investments.

CRIMINAL OR UNETHICAL ACTIVITIES

U7LO5: Recognize the potential criminal (fraud) or unethical activities.

As with the previous learning objective, it is easiest to list these activities with explanations or comments.

Client Confidentiality

Investment advisers and their representatives must respect the confidentiality of the relationship with their clients. It would be an unethical business practice to disclose the identity, affairs, or investments of any client, unless required by law to do so, or unless consented to by the client.

EXAMPLE

An investment advisory firm has a responsibility to ensure that all information collected from a client be kept confidential. The only exception to the rule should be in those instances where the client or a joint owner authorized the release of such information, or when the investment advisory firm is required by law to disclose such information.

TEST TOPIC ALERT

If the advisory account is held in joint name, consent may be granted by any of the joint owners. On the exam, the most common example is from a spouse. Speaking of a spouse, the most common time when the firm could be required by law to disclose account information would be during a divorce proceeding in court. Another time would be during an IRS investigation when you receive a subpoena from a court to testify.

Using Inside Information

Making recommendations on the basis of material inside information about an issuer or its securities is prohibited. Should an agent or IAR come into possession of inside information, she must report the possession of the information to a supervisor or compliance officer. Even the use of a broker-dealer or investment adviser's internally generated research report before public release can be considered use of inside information.

TAKE NOTE

Material nonpublic inside information (MNPI) under securities law is any information about a company that has not been communicated to the general public and that would likely affect the value of a security. Even if you acquire the information "accidentally," you cannot use it until it becomes public.

As detailed earlier in this course, **insider** or **control person** is defined as an officer, director, or owner of more than 10% of the voting stock of the company, or the immediate family of any of these persons. After the tremendous insider abuses of the mid-1980s, the SEC took steps to beef up its enforcement of insider trading, hence passage of the Insider Trading and Securities Fraud Enforcement Act of 1988 (ITSFEA). This act incorporated all of the other prohibitions against the activities of insiders and the use of inside information and also increased the penalties that could be levied and made the recipient of inside information as guilty as the insider who passed on that information. In other words, the tippee would be just as guilty as the tipper.

An insider is in violation of SEC rules when he trades securities on the basis of MNPI, or when he passes on this information to another who subsequently acts on this information. It is critical to remember that no chargeable violation has occurred unless a transaction has taken place.

Even persons who do not meet the definition of an insider are subject to the rules governing the use of nonpublic information and could be liable for any actions taken. When it comes to who could potentially be an insider—that is, who could possibly possess material inside information—the list is virtually endless. One could therefore say that a potential insider could be anyone coming across information dealing with a company, other than those individuals who, by virtue of their title or other circumstance, are definitely insiders.

ITSFEA gave the SEC authority to seek *civil* penalties against persons violating the provisions of the act in amounts up to the greater of $1 million or treble damages. **Treble damages** means that the guilty party could be fined up to three times any ill-gotten gains or up to three times any losses avoided by using inside information to get out before a market drop. The Federal Civil Penalties Inflation Adjustment Act of 2015 changed the way the civil penalty is applied for insider trading. The new penalties are applied as of August 1, 2016. The $1,000,000 is now indexed for inflation to $1,978,690 and represents the maximum civil penalty for insider trading to be compared to the treble damages. Historically, the exam stays away from numbers that change such as this one.

These civil penalties are in addition to any disgorgement of profits made or losses avoided as a result of the insider trading. From this fine, the SEC is authorized to award bounties to informants. If the SEC should elect to pursue *criminal* action, then penalties would include potential jail time with a maximum sentence of 20 years.

Chinese Wall Doctrine

It is plain that the regulators wish to maintain a level playing field for all and if those with material nonpublic information were to let it leak out to favored interests, a prohibited activity would be taking place. This is particularly an issue with those broker-dealers who engage in investment banking, especially mergers and acquisitions. To do their job, they must have access to confidential information that is not publically available—at least not yet. Therefore, to ensure that this information does not become available, for example, to the research department or the retail sales staff, these firms must erect (figuratively) a wall as impenetrable as the Great Wall of China between these departments. In essence, a Chinese Wall is the term used to describe the procedures followed by these firms to insulate information from reaching the wrong hands.

TAKE NOTE

Although you might see the term *Chinese Wall* on your exam, the preferred term in the industry is *Information Barrier*.

EXAMPLE   Using Inside Information

Because the potential rewards are so great, this is one of the most commonly violated rules by both investors and securities professionals. Some go to extreme lengths to try to hide the activity in an effort to make it difficult to uncover.

As an example of the type of returns that can be made, Mr. H, a convenience store employee, has a sister whose boyfriend worked for a company that was about to be bought out by another company. The boyfriend mentioned that to the sister who told her brother. The day before the announcement was made public, Mr. H. took his life savings of $8,000 and invested in options in that company. The next day, after the announcement and the jump in price, he sold and reaped a profit of over $295,000 (almost 37 times his investment in one trading day). He was caught (which is how we know the story) and had to return his profits and then some interest.

Another case involved getting access to a law firm's computer. The law firm specialized in mergers and acquisitions, and those with access were able to learn of upcoming takeover bids being made at prices significantly higher than the current trading price. To avoid being noticed, the trades were placed through the account of one of the participant's mother who was based in China. Total penalties in this case were almost $6 million plus interest of about $125,000.

In our first example, Mr. H wasn't looking for the information, but when it came his way, he used it. In the second example, the perpetrators hacked into the computers with malice aforethought.

The exam might present a question about insider trading in the following manner:

EXAMPLE

1. Which of the following employees of a publicly traded company would most likely have access to MNPI?

   A. VP of Human Resources

   B. Receptionist

   C. Chief Financial Officer (CFO)

   D. VP of Marketing

   Answer: C. Although any of these employees could obtain access to MNPI, because the CFO is the individual who sees the financial numbers first, it is part of the job to have access to earnings numbers before anyone else.

TEST TOPIC ALERT

The exam may ask you to identify who is guilty of insider trading violations—a corporate officer of the issuer who divulges material inside information to a friend, but no transaction takes place, or an agent who executes a trade for a client who is acting on inside information? Simply giving someone inside information, although imprudent, is not a violation of the law. Only when the information is used for trading does a violation occur. In our question, the agent is in violation for accepting an order on the basis of material nonpublic information that results in a trade.

Selling Away

Effecting securities transactions not recorded on the regular books or records of the broker-dealer which the agent represents, unless the transactions are authorized in writing by the broker-dealer prior to execution of the transaction.

TEST TOPIC ALERT

The exam may refer to this as a trade made off the books of the broker-dealer. Just remember that it is considered to be a prohibited practice anytime an agent engages in a securities transaction not recorded on the regular books or records of the broker-dealer the agent represents, unless the transaction is authorized in writing by the broker-dealer before execution of the transaction.

EXAMPLE

An agent was approached at a party by a friend and was asked if he knew anyone that might like to invest in a movie he was making. One of the agent's clients was there and was interested, so much so that she ended up writing a check for $50,000. When the investor received her next account statement, she called the agent's broker-dealer because she didn't see the $50,000. The call was escalated up to the compliance officer and the agent lost his license for selling away; engaging in a transaction off the books of the firm without prior authorization.

Churning

Churning is generally defined as inducing trading in a customer's account which is excessive in size or frequency in view of the financial resources, objectives, and character of the account. A key here is the word *excessive*. By definition, anytime something is excessive, it is too much. The regulators understand that different clients have different needs and ability to take risks, so what is excessive for the 80-year-old pensioner is probably not going to be so for the 40-year-old partner in a major law firm.

TEST TOPIC ALERT

Excessive trading may be used on the exam instead of the word churning.

Market Manipulation

Effecting any transaction in, or inducing the purchase or sale of, any security by means of any manipulative, deceptive, or fraudulent device, practice, plan, program, design, or contrivance is generally considered a fraudulent practice.

Securities legislation is designed to uphold the integrity of markets and transactions in securities. However, market integrity is violated when transactions misrepresent actual securities prices or market activity. The most common forms of market manipulation are matched orders and wash trades.

Matched orders occur when an order to buy or sell securities is entered with knowledge that a matching order on the opposite side of the transaction has been or will be entered for the purpose of (1) creating a false or misleading appearance of active trading in any publicly traded security or (2) creating a false or misleading appearance with respect to the market for any such security.

Increased volume in a security can induce unsuspecting investors to purchase the security, thereby bidding up the price. As the price rises, participants who initiated the matched orders sell their securities at a profit.

A **wash trade** is an order to buy or sell securities resulting in no change of beneficial ownership for the purpose of (1) creating a false or misleading appearance of active trading in any publicly traded security; or (2) creating a false or misleading appearance with respect to the market for any such security. This is typically done by an investor buying in one brokerage account and simultaneously selling through another. No real change in ownership has occurred, but to the marketplace, it appears that volume and/or price is increasing.

■ A **wash sale** for tax purposes is not related to this in any way. A wash sale for tax purposes occurs when a person sells a security and repurchases it within 30 days before or after the sale and is covered in Unit 21 of this course.

Accurate recording of orders and subsequent trades is one way the regulators monitor for attempts to manipulate the market.

TAKE NOTE

So, what is the difference between a matched order and a wash trade? Keeping it simple (because the exam only wants you to know they're both illegal), *wash trades* are trades in which the (natural or legal) person who is the beneficial owner of the traded securities does not change, even though this is the impression conveyed to the public. In other words, in a wash trade, it is the same investor trading in two or more accounts owned or controlled by that single investor. In the case of *matched orders*, these are prearranged entries of equal but opposite buy and sell orders in the same security made between different parties with the intention to distort the public impression of actual liquidity or prices. There is a change in ownership, but the attempt is to deceive.

TAKE NOTE

Arbitrage is the simultaneous buying and selling of the same security in different markets to take advantage of different prices; it is not a form of market manipulation. Simultaneously buying a security in one market and selling it in another forces prices to converge and, therefore, provides uniform prices for the general public.

Due Diligence

SEC studies have indicated that investment advisers, including pension consultants, are increasingly recommending alternative investments, such as leveraged exchange-traded funds (ETFs), (covered in Unit 17) to their clients. Investment advisers are fiduciaries and thus must act in their clients' best interests. An adviser that exercises discretion to purchase alternative investments on behalf of its clients, or that relies on a manager to perform due diligence of alternative investments, must determine whether such investments:

■ meet the clients' investment objectives; and

■ are consistent with the investment principles and strategies that were disclosed by the manager to the adviser in the offering materials provided by the manager.

The due diligence process can be more challenging for alternative investments due to the characteristics of private offerings, including the complexity of certain alternative investment strategies.

COMPLIANCE PROGRAMS

We have just completed a very comprehensive description of the many rules and regulations imposed upon investment advisers. How do the regulators ensure compliance with these rules? The Investment Advisers Act of 1940 requires each investment adviser registered with the SEC to adopt and implement written policies and procedures designed to prevent violation of the federal securities laws, review those policies and procedures **annually** for their adequacy and the effectiveness of their implementation, and designate a **chief compliance officer** (CCO) to be responsible for administering the policies and procedures. However, the SEC does not set a standard of competency such as a specific qualification exam or number of years of experience. By and large, the states have followed suit for investment advisers registered with them.

Under rule 206(4)-7, it is unlawful for an investment adviser registered with the Commission to provide investment advice unless the adviser has adopted and implemented written policies and procedures reasonably designed to prevent violation of the Advisers Act by the adviser or any of its supervised persons. The rule requires advisers to consider their fiduciary and regulatory obligations under the Advisers Act and to formalize policies and procedures to address them.

Each adviser, in designing its policies and procedures, should first identify conflicts and other compliance factors creating risk exposure for the firm and its clients in light of the firm's particular operations, and then design policies and procedures that address those risks. The

SEC and the Administrators expect that an adviser's policies and procedures, at a minimum, should address the issues covered in this unit to the extent that they are relevant to that adviser

Although the rule requires only annual reviews, advisers should consider the need for interim reviews in response to significant compliance events, changes in business arrangements, and regulatory developments.

INVESTMENT ADVISER REPORTING

U7LO6: Identify the kind of reporting required of investment advisers.

In addition to the reporting related to updating the Form ADV and the brochure, here are several other cases where investment advisers must report to the regulators.

Section 13(f) Filings

There is a reporting requirement that applies to SEC-registered investment advisers. Section 13(f) of the Securities Exchange Act of 1934 requires that any institutional investment manager that exercises investment discretion over an equity portfolio with a market value on the last trading day in any of the preceding 12 months of $100 million or more in 13(f) securities, must file a **Form 13F** with the SEC quarterly, within 45 days of the end of each quarter.

The purpose of this rule is to require institutional investment managers who exercise investment discretion over accounts holding certain levels of securities to make periodic public disclosures of significant portfolio holdings.

What Are 13(f) Securities?

At the end of each calendar quarter, a list of these securities—called the Official List of Section 13(f) Securities—may be found on the SEC's website.

Generally, the list includes exchange-traded (e.g., NYSE) or Nasdaq-quoted stocks, equity options and warrants, shares of closed-end investment companies, and certain convertible debt securities. Shares of open-end investment companies (i.e., mutual funds) are not included. Shares of some ETFs, however, are on the official list and would be reported on Form 13F.

Investment Adviser Code of Ethics

To ensure that investment advisers and their representatives will act in an ethical manner, all advisers are required to prepare a Code of Ethics. Although this code is part of the Investment Advisers Act of 1940, NASAA considers it binding on state-registered advisers as well. This Code is under the jurisdiction of the CCO.

Rule 204A-1, Investment Adviser Code of Ethics, requires each adviser's code of ethics to require an adviser's access persons (defined in the following paragraph) to report their personal securities transactions and holdings to the adviser's chief compliance officer or other designated persons on a quarterly basis. The code of ethics must also require the CCO or her designee to review those reports. Reviewing these reports will allow advisers as well as the SEC's examination staff to identify improper trades or patterns of trading by access persons.

Access Person

An **access person** is any of the adviser's supervised persons who (1) has access to nonpublic information regarding any clients' purchase or sale of securities, or (2) is involved in making securities recommendations to clients, or who has access to such recommendations that are nonpublic. If providing investment advice is the adviser's primary business, all of the firm's directors, officers, and partners are presumed to be access persons. The rule requires that the firm maintain a record of the names of persons who are currently, or within the past five years were, access persons of the investment adviser. It is also required to keep a record of any decision, and the reasons supporting the decision, to approve the acquisition of securities by access persons, for at least five years after the end of the fiscal year in which the approval is granted

These procedures are designed to prevent violations by IARs and others in the firm who have access. Advisory firms should include the following elements, or address the following issues, when crafting their procedures for employees' personal securities trading:

- Prior written approval before access persons can place a personal securities transaction (i.e., preclearance)

- Maintenance of lists of issuers of securities that the advisory firm is analyzing or recommending for client transactions, and prohibitions on personal trading in securities of those issuers. Remember, the regulators consider the use of a firm's internal research before public release to be potential insider trading.

- Maintenance of restricted lists of issuers about which the advisory firm has inside information, and prohibitions on any trading (personal or for clients) in securities of those issuers

- Reminders that investment opportunities must be offered first to clients before the adviser or its employees may act on them, and procedures to implement this principle

Several exceptions exist where access persons may be permitted to trade in securities, such as when the person is participating in an automatic dividend reinvestment program (and does not alter the program to take advantage of the IA's recommendations or other information), but it is unlikely that these will be tested.

EXAMPLE

1. Alberto is an IAR with Exceptional Analysis and Results, (EAR), an investment adviser registered in 3 Southwestern states. Although Alberto relies heavily on the recommendations furnished by EAR's research department, he occasionally does his own research for his personal account. As an access person, Alberto

   A. would be prohibited from trading in his personal account

   B. would be prohibited from trading these securities in his personal account until his research was publicly available

   C. must report any personal transactions on a quarterly basis

   D. can only use personal research to benefit clients

Answer: C. Alberto is considered an access person. As such, any personal securities transactions must be reported on a quarterly basis. Alberto could not use research reports developed by the firm until they were made publicly available, but his own personal research doesn't come under that requirement.

Political Contributions by Investment Advisers (Pay to Play Rule)

This is an SEC rule that prohibits investment advisers from receiving compensation for advisory services to a government entity, (any agency, authority, of instrumentality of a state or political subdivision), for **2** years after the advisory firm or any covered employee makes a political contribution to a public official or candidate who is or would be in a position to influence the award of investment advisory business by public retirement funds. Please note that the advisory relationship can continue, just without any compensation. There are some exceptions, listed below.

De Minimis Exception

The rule allows covered employees to make contributions up to **$350** per official or candidate per election in which they can vote, or **$150** for other elections. Contributions by investment firms in any amount would trigger a violation of the rule.

Covered Associates

Covered individuals include:

- any general partner, managing member or executive officer, or other individual with a similar status or function;
- any employee who solicits a government entity for the investment adviser and any person who supervises, directly or indirectly, such employee; and
- any political action committee controlled by the investment adviser.

New Hire Exception

When an investment adviser hires a new covered associate, political contributions made by that individual more than six months before coming on board do not trigger the ban. However, if the new person's role is soliciting clients on behalf of the investment adviser, rather than rendering advice or other functions, this exception does not apply. In that case, there is a two-year "look back" period.

Returned Contributions Exceptions

An investment adviser can be excepted from the prohibition if the contribution is returned under certain conditions.

- The investment adviser must have discovered the contribution that resulted in the prohibition within four months of the date of such contribution.
- The contribution must not have exceeded $350.
- The contributor must obtain a return of the contribution within 60 calendar days of the date of discovery of such contribution by the investment adviser.

Although unlikely to be tested, an investment adviser with more than 50 employees is entitled to no more than three exceptions and one with 50 or fewer employees is limited to two exceptions during any single calendar year

CYBERSECURITY, DATA PROTECTION, AND PRIVACY

U7LO7: Recognize that investment advisers and their representatives must practice good cyber security, privacy, and data protection.

Hardly a day goes by without news of a hacking attempt that has compromised the security of a company, its clients, or both. There are steps that can be taken by securities professionals to reduce the potential for loss to the firm and its clients.

Cybersecurity Points to Be Addressed

In September 2014, NASAA released results of a pilot survey designed to better understand the cybersecurity practices of state-registered investment advisers. Based on that survey, in setting up a cybersecurity program, NASAA suggests addressing the following points:

- **Cyber preparedness:** Has the firm addressed which cybersecurity threats and vulnerabilities may impact its business?

- **Cybersecurity compliance program:** Does the firm have written policies, procedures, or training programs in place regarding safeguarding client information?

- **Cybersecurity and social media:** Does the firm have written policies, procedures, or training programs in place relating to the use of social media for business purposes (e.g., LinkedIn, Twitter, and Facebook)?

- **Cyber insurance:** Does the firm maintain insurance coverage for cybersecurity?

- **Cyber expertise:** Has the firm engaged an outside consultant to provide cybersecurity services for your firm?

- **Cyber confidentiality:** Does the firm have confidentiality agreements with any third-party service providers with access to the firm's information technology systems?

- **Cyber incident:** Has the firm ever experienced a cybersecurity incident where, directly or indirectly, theft, loss, unauthorized exposure, use of, or access to customer information occurred? If so, has the firm taken steps to close any gaps in its cybersecurity infrastructure?

- **Cyber disposal:** Does the firm have a procedure for the disposal of electronic data storage devices? It is required that broker-dealers and investment advisers properly dispose of sensitive information by taking reasonable measures to protect against unauthorized access to or use of the information. However, disposal shall not take place until the end of the required holding period.

- **Cyber continuation:** What are the plans for your firm's continued operation during a cyber-event or cybersecurity incident?

- **Cyber losses:** Are there plans for treating the loss of electronic devices (e.g., loss of a laptop containing personal and confidential client information)?

- **Cybersecurity safeguards:** Does the firm use safeguards, such as encryption and antivirus or anti-malware programs? Does the firm contact clients via email or other electronic messaging, and if so, does the firm use secure email or any procedures to authenticate client instructions received via email or electronic messaging, to work against the possibility of a client being impersonated?

Safeguarding Client Information

Broker-dealers have a great deal of information about their clients that would be highly valuable to persons with evil intentions. Our primary concern here is with identity theft, which may be used to falsify client requests for funds and/or securities. To combat identity theft, securities professionals must be aware of the red flags.

TAKE NOTE

Identity theft means a fraud committed or attempted using the identifying information of another person without authority. Red flag means a pattern, practice, or specific activity that indicates the possible existence of identity theft.

The regulators are concerned when broker-dealers (or other financial professionals) maintain what are referred to as covered accounts. The term *covered account* is defined as:

■ an account that a financial institution offers or maintains—primarily for personal, family, or household purposes—that involves or is designed to permit multiple payments or transactions (not a business account—it is felt that there is much less identity theft risk there); and

■ any other account that the financial institution offers or maintains for which there is a reasonably foreseeable risk to customers or to the safety and soundness of the financial institution from identity theft, including financial, operational, compliance, reputation, or litigation risks.

TAKE NOTE

The definition includes a margin account as an example of a covered account. Also included is a brokerage account with a broker-dealer or an account maintained by a mutual fund (or its agent) that permits wire transfers or other payments to third parties.

Investment advisers who have the ability to direct transfers or payments from accounts belonging to individuals to third parties upon the individuals' instructions, or who act as agents on behalf of the individuals, are susceptible to the same types of risks of fraud as other financial institutions. If such an adviser does not have a program in place to verify investors' identities and detect identity theft red flags, another individual may deceive the adviser by posing as an investor.

It is required that each financial institution that offers or maintains one or more covered accounts must develop and implement a written program designed to detect, prevent, and mitigate identity theft in connection with the opening of a covered account or any existing covered account. These provisions also require that each program be appropriate to the size and complexity of the financial institution and the nature and scope of its activities.

The program must include reasonable policies and procedures to:

■ identify relevant red flags for the covered accounts that the financial institution offers or maintains and incorporate those red flags into its program;

■ detect red flags that have been incorporated into the program of the financial institution;

- respond appropriately to any red flags that are detected to prevent and mitigate identity theft; and

- ensure the program (including the red flags determined to be relevant) is updated periodically to reflect changes in risks to customers and to the safety and soundness of the financial institution or creditor from identity theft.

Identity Theft Red Flags

Following is a list of some of the most common warnings that firms should include in their identity theft programs as is appropriate to the nature of the firm's business:

- Alerts, notifications, or other warnings received from consumer reporting agencies or service providers, such as fraud detection services or a notice of credit freeze in response to a request for a consumer report

- Presentation of suspicious documents, such as documents that appear to have been altered or forged

- The photograph or physical description on the identification is not consistent with the appearance of the applicant or customer presenting the identification

- Presentation of suspicious personal identifying information, such as a suspicious address change

- Unusual use of, or other suspicious activity related to, a covered account

- Notice from customers, victims of identity theft, law enforcement authorities, or other persons regarding possible identity theft in connection with covered accounts held by the financial institution

- Personal identifying information provided by the customer is not consistent with other personal identifying information provided by the customer (e.g., there is a lack of correlation between the SSN range and date of birth)

- Personal identifying information provided is of a type commonly associated with fraudulent activity as indicated by internal or third-party sources used by the financial institution. For example
  - The address on an application is fictitious, a mail drop, or a prison, or
  - The phone number is invalid or is associated with a pager or answering service

- For financial institutions that use challenge questions (what is the name of your first pet, etc.), the person opening the covered account or the customer cannot provide authenticating information beyond that which generally would be available from a wallet or consumer report

- Mail sent to the customer is returned repeatedly as undeliverable although transactions continue to be conducted in connection with the customer's covered account

Please note, this is not meant to be an exhaustive list. Your firm will make you aware of its program and the specific red flags they are addressing. The exam is more concerned about concept than an actual list, although you should be able to recognize obvious patterns of misuse in an account.

EXAMPLE

1. A great concern to broker-dealers is the theft of the identity of a client. To reduce the possibility of a client's assets being improperly taken, most firms would consider all of these to be a red flag EXCEPT

   A. almost 1 year since your last contact with your client, you receive a phone call requesting that funds be wired to an offshore account

   B. a client regularly visits your office to pick up a check representing the proceeds of recently settled transactions

   C. when running a credit report on a new client's applications, there is a discrepancy between the home address listed on the report and the one on the new account form

   D. the photograph on the identification documents provided does not resemble the individual opening the account

   Answer: B. There is nothing wrong with a client picking up a check for the proceeds of a securities transaction, choice **B**, even if done on a regular basis (some folks don't trust the mail). Each of the other choices should raise a red flag as being something needing further investigation.

METHODS FOR PROTECTING THE FIRM AND ITS CUSTOMERS

What are the methods of authentication used by customers or employees to access electronic data storage devices, which allow access to client communications, client information, or both?

- Single-factor authentication (e.g., ID/password)
- Dual-factor authentication (e.g., key fobs, secure IDs)
- Adaptive-factor authentication (e.g., challenge questions)
- Biometric authentication (e.g., fingerprint scan)
- Antivirus software installed on electronic devices used to access client information

Some questions to ask regarding the security methods used include the following.

- How often are updates downloaded to antivirus software?
- Does your firm utilize encryption on its files or devices?
- Does your firm utilize online or remote backup of electronic files?
- Does your firm allow remote access to servers or workstations via a virtual private network (VPN) or similar technology?
- Does your firm use free Cloud services such as iCloud, Dropbox, or Google Drive, to store personal and confidential client information?
- Does your firm utilize your firm's website to use or access client information data?
- Does your firm's website include a client portal?

As you can see from the many questions posed, protecting data is not a simple issue. Although the decision as to what will be used and how it will be used is that of the firm, agents must be aware of the tools being employed and how they work. That is why so much emphasis is placed on initial and continual training.

TEST TOPIC ALERT

Broker-dealers and investment advisers backing up client data should make sure it is *encrypted*.

PRIVACY—REGULATION S-P

Regulation S-P, mandated by the Gramm-Leach-Bliley Act, requires that firms take identity theft seriously and have adequate safeguards in the form of privacy policies to protect nonpublic personal information from unauthorized access or use. Member firms must provide an initial privacy notice to new customers when an account is opened and must provide an annual privacy notice to all customers. Regulation S-P permits firms to disclose nonpublic personal information to unaffiliated third parties unless the customer has elected to opt out of the disclosure. Examples of nonpublic personal information include a customer's Social Security number, account balances, transaction history, the fact that the individual was at one time a customer, and any information collected through a consumer reporting agency or an internet cookie. Furthermore, the regulation requires that the customer be given 30 days to opt out before disclosure of nonpublic personal information may be made.

TAKE NOTE

An internet cookie is created with a view that allows the member firm to collect information about the customer and is an example that illustrates one of the many ways that any financial institution may obtain information about a consumer in connection with providing a financial product or service to that specific consumer. If the information is not specific, it is known as blind data or aggregate information that contains no personal identifiers. It is not deemed to be personally identifiable information and, therefore, not subject to Regulation S-P requirements.

Regulation S-P distinguishes between a consumer and a customer. A consumer is an individual who obtains a financial product or service from a firm and has no further contact with the firm. A customer is an individual who has an ongoing relationship with a firm. Consumers are given an initial privacy notice only, while customers must be given both an initial and annual privacy notice. Only individuals, not businesses or institutions, are covered by the regulation.

Regulation S-P also requires members to adopt policies and procedures that provide adequate safeguards of confidential customer information and records. Before permitting employees to access customer information remotely, members must implement and update appropriate measures to secure customer information.

TAKE NOTE

Reasonable opt-out methods available to members include providing a reply form with the opt-out notice, an electronic means to opt out if the customer has agreed to the electronic delivery of information, and a toll-free number that customers may call.

The SEC has stated that members are not providing a reasonable means to opt out if the only method to do so is by writing a letter to the member.

These three questions should give you a taste of what you'll need to know for the exam.

EXAMPLES

1. Protection of customer confidential information is an obligation of the

   I.   agent servicing the customer's account

   II. broker-dealer maintaining the account

   III. customer

   IV. investment adviser in an advisory account

   A. I and II

   B. II and IV

   C. III and IV

   D. I, II, III, and IV

   Answer: D.. Although any securities professional handing a customer account is obligated to follow all necessary procedures to protect client data, customers themselves also bear a responsibility. Customers ignoring the cybersecurity safeguards put not only their own data at risk, but also that of other customers, by potentially opening the door to hackers.

2. A broker-dealer's cybersecurity procedures should address all of the following EXCEPT

   A. the music played while customers are placed on hold

   B. office desktop computers

   C. agent's personal smartphones used on occasion to communicate with clients

   D. remote access to servers or workstations via a virtual private network (VPN)

   Answer: A. It is hard to imagine how the music on hold, choice **A**, would present a security risk. All of the others clearly offer potential for loss.

3. Under Regulation S-P, if an investment adviser sends a customer an initial privacy notice that contains an opt-out provision, the firm may NOT disclose nonpublic, personal information about that customer for how many days from the mailing?

   A. 10

   B. 15

   C. 20

   D. 30

   Answer: D. An investment adviser (or broker-dealer) must give a customer 30 days, choice **D**, to implement any opt-out provision in the privacy notice.

BUSINESS CONTINUITY AND SUCCESSION PLANS

U7LO8: Recall what constitutes an adequate business continuity plan.

TAKE NOTE

As mentioned several times, NASAA does not have a separate principal's registration category like FINRA does. This means that registrants passing the Series 65 exam can go to the Administrator's office with a completed Form ADV and, in most states, a check for $200 and become a registered investment adviser. Because there is no way for NASAA to know if you will be opening your own IA firm or simply working as an IAR, some of the information tested goes into detail one would expect to be limited to the owners of the firm. This next portion is an example of that.

In April 2015, NASAA released a Model Rule dealing with business continuity plans for state-registered investment advisers. In most respects, it mirrors FINRA Rule 4370 dealing with their member broker-dealers. The rule requires that every investment adviser shall establish, implement, and maintain written procedures relating to a Business Continuity and Succession Plan (BCP). The plan should be based upon the facts and circumstances of the investment adviser's business model, including the size of the firm, type(s) of services provided, and the number of locations of the investment adviser. The plan shall provide for at least the following:

- The protection, backup, and recovery of books and records

- Alternate means of communications with customers, key personnel, employees, vendors, service providers (including third-party custodians), and regulators, including, but not limited to, providing notice of a significant business interruption or the death or unavailability of key personnel or other disruptions or cessation of business activities

- Office relocation in the event of temporary or permanent loss of a principal place of business

- Assignment of duties to qualified responsible persons in the event of the death or unavailability of key personnel

- Otherwise minimizing service disruptions and client harm that could result from a sudden significant business interruption

Purpose of a BCP

The most common purpose of a BCP is to have processes and procedures in place to ensure that critical business functions can continue during and after a disaster or other significant business interruption. BCPs outline actions advisers should take if utility outages, catastrophic natural disasters, national emergencies, acts of terrorism, or other types of disturbances disrupt day-to-day business operations. Advisers' BCPs should reflect comprehensive approaches to reduce and manage risks associated with disasters, significant business interruptions and work stoppages. All BCPs should include Succession Plans. Advisers have a fiduciary duty to act in the best interest of their clients, and it is in the best interest of clients for advisers to adopt a Succession Plan with procedures to ensure continuity of services and the day-to-day operations of the business, or to smoothly wind down advisers' businesses in the event of death, disability, or incapacity. Without proper planning, the unexpected loss of executives, key personnel, or owners can be disastrous to the business and to clients.

Succession Issues

Planning for an unexpected succession situation is an important part of a BCP. While there are some succession issues that apply to every adviser (e.g., every Adviser needs a designated regulatory contact person), each adviser must also tailor its succession plan to the adviser's needs. An adviser's business entity structure will affect the types of items that should be addressed in the adviser's succession plan.

For example, in a sole proprietorship, the client's legal relationship is with the sole proprietor, who is often the only investment adviser representative. With the death or permanent disability of the IAR, the sole proprietorship itself may legally terminate as an entity, as would any powers of attorney, advisory contracts, and other client agreements. The deceased (or otherwise incapacitated) sole proprietor is likely to be the only regulatory contact and may be the only person who would be able to access electronic client files or authorize rebates of prepaid fees. There are many additional issues, such as probate, that are unique to sole proprietorships and that affect the implementation of a succession plan. Therefore, the adviser should have a succession plan that will immediately address these issues when an IAR becomes unavailable. Regardless of who takes over, a person cannot provide advisory services for compensation unless she is registered with the state's securities regulator(s) or exempt from registration.

Advisers should consider the following items when drafting a succession plan to ensure that the succession plan adequately accounts for the risks related to the business entity.

- Are the clients' investment advisory contracts with an individual or a legal entity?

- Does an IAR's death or unavailability affect the advisory agreement?

EXAMPLE

1. A BCP should be designed to protect the firm's clients in the event of which of the following?

    I. A natural disaster such as a hurricane or tornado

    II. Acts of terrorism

    III. Pregnancy of one of the firm's IARs

    IV. Climate change

    A. I and II

    B. I and IV

    C. II and III

    D. III and IV

    Answer: A. Business Continuity Plans are designed to provide for the sudden unexpected events that can disrupt day-to-day business operations and that makes choice **A** the correct answer.

PART

2

Economic Factors and Business Information

This part consists of four units:

Unit 8 Basic Economic Concepts

Unit 9 Financial Reporting

Unit 10 Analytical Methods

Unit 11 Types of Investment Risk

In total, there will be 20 questions on this material, representing 15% of the Series 65 Exam.

UNIT

8

Basic Economic Concepts

Investment decisions are made within the context of the general economic climate and are based on the specific merits of the selected investments. This unit will deal with basic economic concepts, such as monetary and fiscal policy, the business cycle, yield curves, and measuring inflation.

The Series 65 exam will include approximately six questions on the material presented in this unit.

LEARNING OBJECTIVES

When you have completed this unit, you will be able to accomplish the following.

U8LO1:   Identify fundamental economic principles, including the difference between monetary and fiscal policy.

U8LO2:   Analyze the four stages of the business cycle.

U8LO3:   Differentiate between inflation and deflation and how they are impacted by the major economic indicators.

U8LO4:   Identify the three types of yield curves and how they reflect interest rates.

FUNDAMENTAL ECONOMIC PRINCIPLES

U8LO1: Identify fundamental economic principles, including the difference between monetary and fiscal policy.

The economic climate has an enormous effect on the conditions of individual companies and, therefore, the securities markets. In addition to a company's earnings and business prospects, any changes in government policy, business cycles, the money supply, and Federal Reserve Board (FRB) actions affect securities prices and trading and the markets at large. In today's global economy, economic conditions abroad can influence the conditions domestically and in turn will also impact our securities markets. This unit will explore some of these factors.

Fiscal policy refers to a government's use of spending and taxation to influence economic activity. The budget is said to be *balanced* when tax revenues equal government expenditures. A **budget surplus** occurs when government tax revenues exceed expenditures, and a **budget deficit** occurs when government expenditures exceed tax revenues.

Monetary policy refers to the central bank's actions that affect the quantity of money and credit in an economy to influence economic activity. Monetary policy is said to be **expansionary** (or *accommodative* or *easy*) when the central bank increases the quantity of money and credit in an economy. Conversely, when the central bank is reducing the quantity of money and credit in an economy, the monetary policy is said to be **contractionary** (or *restrictive* or *tight*). Monetary policy is under the control of the Federal Reserve Board (the Fed).

TAKE NOTE

It is important for you to know that the fiscal policy of the United States is determined by the President and Congress through the process of budgeting and taxation. The budget is presented by the President and approved by the Congress. Monetary policy is determined by the Board of Governors of the Federal Reserve System. Unlike monetary policy, the Federal Reserve has nothing to do with fiscal policy.

MAJOR SCHOOLS OF ECONOMICS

Keynesian Economics

Named after the economist John Maynard Keynes (pronounced "Canes"), Keynesian economists recognize the importance of government intervention. In 1936, Keynes published *The General Theory of Employment, Interest, and Money*, in which he revolutionized the way economists think about macroeconomics. He laid out how and why recessions happen and what must be done to recover from them. His strategy for recovery from a recession was for government to run deficits to stimulate demand and employment. In other words, he suggested lower levels of taxation and more government spending.

Classical and Supply-Side Economics

Classical economists favor a school of thought referred to as supply-side economics. The most notable feature of this idea is the belief that lower taxes and less government regulation benefits consumers through a greater supply of goods and services at lower costs. **Supply-side economics** holds that supply creates demand by providing jobs and wages. The prices of goods of which there is excess supply will fall, and the prices of goods in demand will rise.

Monetarist Theory

Monetarists, such as the late Milton Friedman, believe that the quantity of money, or **money supply**, determines overall price levels and economic activity. Too many dollars chasing too few goods leads to inflation, and too few dollars chasing too many goods leads to deflation. One of the principal roles of the FRB is monitoring the money supply and making adjustments when necessary.

Tools of the Federal Reserve Board

Because the Federal Reserve Board (the Fed) determines how much money is available for businesses and consumers to spend, its decisions are critical to the U.S. economy. The Fed uses three primary tools to affect the money supply.

- **Changes in reserve requirements.** By raising the amount of funds commercial banks must leave on deposit with the Fed, the amount of money available for these banks to lend out is decreased. This shrinkage of the money supply generally translates into higher interest rates. The reverse is true when reserve requirements are eased.

- **Changes in the discount rate.** This is the rate the Fed charges member banks when lending them money. Higher rates discourage borrowing, reducing the money supply with lower rates having an opposite effect.

- **Open-market operations.** The Fed buys and sells U.S. Treasury securities in the open market under the direction of the Federal Open Market Committee (FOMC). When Treasuries are purchased, it adds to the money supply. This is because the FOMC is purchasing these securities from commercial banks causing the banks to have greater reserves. When the FOMC sells Treasuries, the money supply is reduced because funds are pulled out of the bank's reserves to pay for those securities. This is the most actively used Fed tool.

There is a fourth rate which, although not set by the Fed, is highly influenced by their actions. That rate is the Fed Funds rate. The **federal funds rate** is the rate banks that are members of the Federal Reserve System charge each other for overnight loans of $1 million or more. The rate is considered a barometer of the direction of short-term interest rates. The federal funds rate is listed in daily newspapers and is the most volatile rate; it can fluctuate drastically under certain market conditions.

TAKE NOTE

The FRB establishes the discount rate. The discount rate, unlike the federal funds rate, is a managed rate. It is one of the tools of monetary policy. In contrast, the **federal funds rate** is a market rate determined by the demand for bank reserves on the part of deposit-based financial institutions.

One final rate to discuss is the prime rate. The **prime rate** is the most preferential interest rate on corporate loans at large U.S. money center commercial banks. Each bank sets its own prime rate, with larger banks generally setting the rate that other banks follow. Banks lower their prime rates when the Fed eases the money supply and raise rates when the Fed contracts the money supply.

EXAMPLE

1. Which of the following statements regarding significant interest rates in the U.S. economy is NOT true?

   A. Federal funds rate is the rate the Federal Reserve charges for overnight loans to member commercial banks.

   B. The prime rate is the interest rate that large U.S. money center commercial banks charge their most creditworthy corporate borrowers.

   C. The discount rate is the rate the New York Federal Reserve Bank charges for short-term loans to member banks.

   D. The most active tool used by the Fed is the buying and selling of Treasury securities by the FOMC.

   Answer: A. The federal funds rate is the rate that member banks charge each other for overnight loans of $1 million or more; it is not the rate that the Federal Reserve charges member banks for overnight loans.

TEST TOPIC ALERT

Although the Fed's actions certainly impact all interest rates, you'll need to know that the Fed does not set the prime rate—that is done by the major commercial banks.

TEST TOPIC ALERT

Know the fundamentals of fiscal and monetary policy.

Fiscal policy:

- Actions of Congress and the President
- Government spending and taxation

Monetary policy:

- Policy of the FRB
- Discount rate (set by the Fed)
- Reserve requirement (most drastic)
- Open-market operations (most frequently used)

BALANCE OF PAYMENTS

The **balance of payments** measures all the nation's import and export transactions with those of other countries for the year. The balance of payments account contains all payments and liabilities to foreigners (debits) and all payments and obligations (credits) received from foreigners.

TEST TOPIC ALERT

When you receive interest on your bank account, what happens to that account? It's simple: your balance is credited; it goes up. When foreign money is received here, such as interest received on money loaned to foreign business enterprises, there is a credit to the foreign account balance of the United States. Conversely, a debit (reduction) to the foreign account balance of the United States occurs when money leaves our shores, such as loans made to foreign governments or dividends paid on foreign investment in the United States.

TAKE NOTE

The value of the dollar against foreign currencies affects the balance of trade. If the dollar is weak, foreign currency buys more U.S. goods, so exports increase. When the dollar is strong, foreign currency buys fewer U.S. goods. The dollar buys more foreign goods, so imports increase.

TEST TOPIC ALERT

One way an investor can protect against a weakening U.S. dollar is to invest in foreign securities. In Unit 12, we'll discuss the American Depositary Receipt (ADR), the simplest way to invest in foreign securities.

Balance of Trade

The largest component of a country's balance of payments is usually its balance of trade. That is, comparing the country's exports to its imports.

Trade Deficit

A **trade deficit** is an excess of one country's imports over its exports and is reported as part of the balance of payments figures. Over time, an excessive trade deficit can lead to the devaluation of a country's currency because the country will be converting, or selling, its currency to obtain foreign currency to pay for its increasing imports.

Trade Surplus

The opposite of a trade deficit, a **trade surplus** is an excess of one country's export over its imports and is reported as part of the balance of payments figures. Over time, an excessive trade surplus can lead to the strengthening of a country's currency.

EXAMPLE

On the U.S. credit side are sales of American products to foreign countries. On the debit side are American purchases of foreign goods that cause American dollars to flow out of the country. When debits exceed credits, a deficit in the balance of payments occurs; when credits exceed debits, a surplus exists.

Balance of Trade	
Debit Items	**Credit Items**
Imports	Exports
U.S. spending abroad	Foreign spending in the United States
U.S. investments abroad	Foreign investments in the United States
U.S. bank loans abroad	
U.S. foreign aid	

EXAMPLE

Assume the dollar value of French perfume imported into the United States is greater than the dollar value of Kentucky bourbon exported to France. That difference results in a negative trade balance creating a debit to the U.S. trade account and a credit to France's.

TOP DOWN AND BOTTOM UP ANALYSIS

There are two popular methods used by analysts to help them determine where the best investment opportunities lie.

Top Down Analysis

If we were to draw a picture of top down analysis, it would look like an inverted isosceles triangle: broad on top and narrow on the bottom. The analyst starts with the broadest measure of the overall economy and then successively narrows it down to finally select the company or companies that best fit the objectives.

Bottom Up Analysis

This is the direct opposite of top down. In this case, we merely start at the bottom (the point) of the triangle with the specific company and work our way up through the industry and then the economy. This analyst starts with the narrowest indicator and then steadily broadens the search.

Let's look at the items that these analysts use, regardless of which of these two methods are used.

THE BUSINESS CYCLE

U8LO2: Analyze the four stages of the business cycle.

Business Cycles

Business cycles reflect fluctuations in economic activity as measured by the level of activity in such variables as the rate of unemployment and the GDP. Periods of economic expansion have been followed by periods of contraction in a pattern called the **business cycle**. Business cycles go through four stages:

- Expansion
- Peak
- Contraction
- Trough

Definition: Gross Domestic Product (GDP)

The market value of all final goods and services produced within a country in a given period. To account for inflation, GDP in the United States is based on a constant dollar, currently the value in 2005.

Expansion

Expansion, or recovery, is characterized by increasing business activity—in sales, manufacturing, and wages—throughout the economy. When GDP increases rapidly and businesses reach their productive capacity, the nation's economy cannot expand further. At this point, the economy is said to have reached its **peak**. When business activity declines from its peak, the economy is **contracting**.

Economists call mild short-term contractions **recessions**. Longer, more severe contractions are **depressions**. When business activity stops declining and levels off, the cycle makes a **trough**.

According to the U.S. Department of Commerce, the economy is in a recession when a decline in real output of goods and services—the **GDP**—continues for two or more consecutive quarters. It defines a depression as a decrease in GDP for six consecutive quarters.

Real GDP

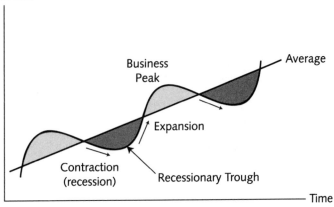

The Four Stages of the Business Cycle

To determine the economy's overall direction, economists consider many trends in business activity. Expansions are characterized by increasing consumer demand for goods and services, possibly leading to an:

- increasing rate of inflation; and
- increasing industrial production, generally leading to
    - a decreasing unemployment rate as hiring accelerates,
    - falling inventories,
    - rising stock markets,
    - rising property values, and
    - increasing GDP.

Peaks are characterized by:

- a decrease to the GDP growth rate;
- a decrease to the unemployment rate, but a slowdown in hiring;
- a slower rate of growth in consumer spending and business investment; and
- an increase to the inflation rate.

Contractions/recessions in the business cycle tend to be characterized by:

- rising numbers of bankruptcies and bond defaults;
- decreasing hours worked, increasing unemployment rate;
- decreasing consumer spending, home construction, and business investment;
- falling stock markets;
- a decrease to the inflation rate;
- rising inventories (a sign of slackening consumer demand); and
- a negative growth rate for the GDP.

Troughs tend to be characterized by:

- a change from negative to positive GDP growth rate;
- a high unemployment rate, increasing use of overtime and temporary workers;
- spending on consumer durable goods and housing may increase; and
- a moderate or decreasing inflation rate.

EXAMPLE

1. If the Consumer Price Index (CPI) is down but consumer demand is up, the economy is likely in which stage of the business cycle?

    A. Recovery to expansion

    B. Peak to contraction

    C. Recovery to trough

    D. Contraction to trough

Answer: A. As prices trend downward and consumer demand increases, the economy is moving from recovery to expansion, choice **A**. As demand continues to increase, assuming supply remains constant, upward pressure will be put on prices through the expansion to the peak.

Analysts will frequently make investment decisions based upon where we are in the business cycle. Certain industries outperform while others underperform at different points in the cycle. Following are several examples.

Cyclical Industries

Cyclical industries are highly sensitive to business cycles and inflation trends. Most cyclical industries produce durable goods, such as heavy machinery and automobiles, as well as raw materials, such as steel.

During recessions, the demand for durable goods declines as manufacturers postpone investments in new capital goods and consumers postpone purchases of automobiles. On the other hand, **countercyclical industries** tend to turn down as the economy heats up and to rise when the economy turns down. Gold mining has historically been a countercyclical industry.

Growth Industries

Most industries pass through four phases during their existence: introduction, growth, maturity, and decline. An industry is considered in its growth phase if the industry is growing faster than the economy as a whole because of technological changes, new products, or changing consumer tastes. Social media and bioengineering are examples of current growth industries. Because many growth companies retain nearly all of their earnings to finance their business expansion, growth stocks usually pay little or no dividends.

Defensive Industries

Defensive industries are least affected by normal business cycles. Companies in defensive industries generally produce nondurable consumer goods, such as food, pharmaceuticals, tobacco, and energy. Public consumption of such goods remains fairly steady throughout the business cycle.

During recessions and bear markets, stocks in defensive industries generally decline less than stocks in other industries. During expansions and bull markets, defensive stocks may advance less. Investments in defensive industries tend to involve less risk and, consequently, lower investment returns. Those using sector rotation will *rotate* into defensive issues when it appears the business cycle is headed into the contraction phase.

Let's make sure you understand these terms.

Unit 8

EXAMPLE

1. An investor fears a coming recession. She would probably invest in

   A. biotech

   B. steel producers

   C. drug companies

   D. home builders

   Answer: C. In a recessionary period, business activity slows, and one should take a defensive position. Drug companies, (pharmaceuticals), tend to have steady earnings, even in bad economic times. After all, those taking needed prescription drugs will not stop. Even OTC drugs like headache remedies and anti-acids will continue to be sold (some say even more in a downturn). People generally don't buy a new home when things slow down, nor to the buy new cars (much of the steel produced goes into the manufacturing of autos). Biotech companies will find that funding for experimental treatments dries up.

INFLATION AND DEFLATION

U8LO3: Differentiate between inflation and deflation and how they are affected by the major economic indicators.

Inflation is a general increase in prices as measured by an index such as the **Consumer Price Index (CPI)**, described in detail shortly. Mild inflation can encourage economic growth because gradually increasing prices tend to stimulate business investments. High inflation reduces a dollar's buying power, which can reduce demand for goods and services. A term that may appear on your exam is *inflation inertia*. This is the concept that the rate of inflation does not immediately react to unexpected changes in economic conditions. Rather, it lags behind, sometimes for several quarters, before there is an effect.

Sometimes the term inertial rate of inflation or *inertial inflation* is used. This is the persistent rate of inflation that continues at the same rate until an economic shock leads to a change. One of the results of this is that prices rarely go down. After all, what company wants to lower the prices of its goods or services and how many workers are willing to accept wage cuts? So, prices generally continue to advance, hopefully at a slow rate.

TEST TOPIC ALERT

Because inflation is a global issue, not just confined to the United States and our dollar, a universal definition would be "a decrease in the value of the monetary unit."

Causes of Inflation

Excessive demand occurs when aggregate demand exceeds the aggregate supply and prices rise.

Monetary expansion is a rapid increase in a nation's money stock in excess of the nation's growth rate.

Increased inflation drives interest rates higher and drives bond prices lower. Decreases in the inflation rate have the opposite effect: bond yields decline and bond prices rise as you will learn shortly.

TAKE NOTE

An increase in real income means the percentage increase in income is greater than the rate of inflation. Buying power has increased.

Deflation

Though rare, **deflation** is a general decline in prices. Deflation usually occurs during severe recessions when unemployment is on the rise.

Causes of Deflation

Deflation is caused by conditions opposite those that cause inflation. Basically, when the demand for goods and services is substantially below the supply of those goods or services, prices tend to drift downward (certainly not increase) to encourage an increased demand. One other possible cause of deflation is a severe shrinkage in the money supply.

If . . .	And . . .	Then . . .	Thus . . .
inflation increases	interest rates go up	bond prices go down	bond yields go up
inflation decreases	interest rates go down	bond prices go up	bond yields go down

TEST TOPIC ALERT

It is not unusual to experience deflation during recessionary periods. At those times, investors tend to flee to safe havens such as U.S. government securities because unlike stocks, real estate, and commodities, Treasuries will likely not only hold their value but may even show some capital appreciation.

EXAMPLES

1. The contraction phase of the business cycle is least likely accompanied by decreasing

   A. consumer spending

   B. economic output

   C. inflation pressure

   D. unemployment

   Answer: D. An economic contraction is likely to feature increasing unemployment (i.e., decreasing employment), along with decreasing consumer spending, declining economic output, and decreasing inflation pressure.

2. Which of the following statements reflects the monetarist economic position?

   A. The amount of money in the economy is not significant because economic activity reflects the value of real goods and services and, therefore, the Federal Reserve should not attempt to manage the money supply.

   B. The total amount of money in the economy is the result of the level of interest rates.

   C. The amount of money in the economy determines the overall price level over time and, therefore, the Federal Reserve should control the growth in the amount of money in the economy in a gradual and predictable way.

   D. The best way to control the money supply is to raise taxes, which, in turn, will reduce the amount of money in the economy and lower prices.

   Answer: C. Monetarists believe that the economy and inflation are best controlled through the management of the money supply rather than through fiscal policy stimulation.

Certain statistical **indicators** are used to measure the economic health of a country at a given time. Some of the primary indicators used are discussed here.

Gross Domestic Product (GDP)

Gross domestic product (GDP) expresses the total value of all final goods and services produced within the United States during the year. GDP includes personal consumption (by far the largest component), government spending, gross private investment, foreign investment, and the total value of net exports. If imports exceed exports, that negatively affects GDP and that net amount is subtracted. The GDP measures a country's output produced within its borders regardless of who generated it. When the GDP is negative, it is generally a sign of deflation.

 EXAMPLE

A U.S.-based firm assembles electronic equipment using parts imported from Singapore. Its income statement looks like this:

Sales:	$60 million
Wages:	30 million
Parts:	16 million
Expenses:	46 million
Net Income:	14 million

1. What is this firm's contribution to the U.S. GDP?

   A. $14 million

   B. $30 million

   C. $44 million

   D. $60 million

   Answer: C. The question is how we measure this firm's contribution to U.S. output. At first glance, the answer would seem to be $60 million, the total value of its sales. However, $16 million of this was produced somewhere else, so it shouldn't be counted as part of the firm's—or the United States'—output. Thus, the correct answer is $44 million, the amount of value the firm has added to the imported parts.

   TEST TOPIC ALERT

   The exam may want you to know that net exports will lead to an **increase** in GDP.

Employment Indicators

The unemployment level is a key indicator of a country's economic health and bears a relationship to inflation. The two most common employment indicators are the average weekly initial claims for unemployment compensation and the average workweek in manufacturing. Both measures serve to predict the direction of economic activity. Many economists believe an unemployment level of about 4% reflects full employment, the point at which wage pressures do not create undue inflation.

Consumer Price Index (CPI)

The **Consumer Price Index (CPI)** is a measure of the general retail price level. By comparing the current cost of buying a basket of goods with the cost of buying the same basket a year ago, we can get an indication of changes in the cost of living. In doing so, the CPI figure attempts to measure the rate of increase or decrease in a broad range of prices, such as food, housing, transportation, medical care, clothing, electricity, entertainment, and services. The CPI is published on a monthly basis by the Bureau of Labor Statistics (BLS) and is the most commonly used measurement of the rate of inflation.

   TAKE NOTE

   The index for all items, less food and energy, is often unofficially referred to as the core CPI, a term created by the media and not the BLS. The reasoning behind excluding food and energy prices when computing core inflation is because of their high short-term volatility.

Barometers of Economic Activity

Certain aspects of economic activity serve as barometers, or **indicators**, of business cycle phases. There are three broad categories of economic indicators: **leading**, **coincident**, and **lagging**. These indicators are published on a monthly basis by The Conference Board, a non-governmental, not-for-profit research organization.

Unit 8

Leading Indicators

Leading indicators are economic activities that tend to turn down before the beginning of a recession or turn up before the beginning of a business expansion. These indicators are used by economists to predict the future direction of economic activity four to six months hence. The leading economic indicators include the following:

- Money supply
- Building permits (housing starts)
- Average weekly initial claims for unemployment insurance
- Average weekly hours, manufacturing
- Manufacturers' new orders for consumer goods
- Manufacturers' new orders for nondefense capital goods
- Index of supplier deliveries—vendor performance
- Interest rate spread between 10-year Treasury bond and the federal funds rate
- Stock prices (e.g., S&P 500)
- Index of consumer expectations

Not all leading indicators move in tandem. Positive changes in a majority of leading indicators point to increased spending, production, and employment. This will generally result in an increase to the rate of inflation. Negative changes in a majority of indicators can forecast a recession.

Coincident (or Current) Indicators

Coincident, or **current**, **indicators** are economic measurements that change directly and simultaneously with the business cycle. Widely used coincident indicators include the following:

- Nonagricultural employment
- Personal income, minus Social Security, veteran benefits, and welfare payments
- Industrial production
- Manufacturing and trade sales in constant dollars

Lagging Indicators

Lagging indicators are measurements that change four to six months after the economy has begun a new trend and serve to confirm the new trend. Lagging indicators help analysts differentiate long-term trends from short-term reversals that occur in any trend. Lagging indicators include the following:

- Average duration of unemployment
- Ratio of consumer installment credit to personal income
- Ratio of manufacturing and trade inventories to sales
- Average prime rate
- Change in the CPI for services
- Total amount of commercial and industrial loans outstanding
- Change in the index of labor cost per unit of output (manufacturing)

TAKE NOTE

Simply stated, these indicators attempt to tell us where we're going (Leading), where we are (Coincident), and where we've been (Lagging). As an IAR, we suspect you'd be most interested in knowing where we're going so you'd pay most attention (as everyone else does) to the leading indicators.

EXAMPLES

1. Core inflation is best described as an inflation rate

   A. for producers' raw materials

   B. the central bank views as acceptable

   C. that excludes certain volatile goods prices

   D. that represents a market basket of consumer items

   Answer: C. Core inflation is measured using a price index that excludes food and energy prices.

2. The Conference Board has released information indicating an increase in the Help Wanted Index. Most analysts would take this as a sign of

   A. an impending recession

   B. likely wage inflation in the future

   C. an increase in manufacturing inventories

   D. a rising trade deficit

   Answer: B. An increase in the Help Wanted Index signifies that employers are hiring—business is good. Competition for qualified workers will usually result in paying higher wages and that will translate to higher prices for goods and services (inflation).

YIELD CURVES AND INTEREST RATES

U8LO4: Identify the three types of yield curves and how they reflect interest rates.

Although interest rates in general reflect investor expectations about inflation, short-term rates reflect the policy decisions of the Federal Reserve Board (FRB) as it implements the nation's monetary policy.

Interest Rates

An **interest rate** is the cost of borrowing money. The rate a borrower pays for funds is determined by the supply and demand for loanable funds, the credit quality of the borrower, and the length of time for which money is borrowed. In addition, the cost of funds is influenced by factors not related to the borrower, such as current and expected inflation.

When a company borrows money by issuing bonds, the bonds have a fixed interest rate, or coupon payment. As interest rates fluctuate, the price of the bonds in the secondary market also fluctuates. When interest rates increase, the bond prices decrease; when interest rates decrease, bond prices increase. Thus, there is an inverse relationship between interest rates and bond prices.

Nominal Interest Rates

The **nominal rate of interest** is the actual rate of interest a borrower pays on the borrowed money. If inflation is expected, it is likely that interest rates are going to increase. This means that new loans, e.g., bonds, will carry a nominal rate higher than the bonds currently available. As a result, as interest rates rise, market forces will lead to the price of those older, lower interest rate bonds to decline. That is because an investor's rate of return needs to be equivalent to current market conditions.

EXAMPLE

A bond has a nominal yield of 5%. That means it is paying 5% interest annual on the loan, or $50 on each $1,000 bond. If interest rates rise to 7%, where a newly issued bond is paying $70 per year, would you pay $1,000 to buy the bond paying $50 per year? Probably not. To make the old bond attractive to investors, the price will have to decline. In this case, it might sell for approximately $700. Why? Because receiving $50 per year (the loan rate is a fixed percentage of the $1,000 loan) on an investment of $700 give you a return of just a bit over 7% (50 / 700 = 7.14%). We will spend much more time on this concept later in the course.

Yield Curve Analysis

An important tool in gauging investor sentiment towards future interest rates is analyzing the *yield curve.*

Plotted on a graph, the difference between short- and long-term interest rates normally reflects an upward sloping line known as the **yield curve**. When it is an upward sloping curve it is a positive, or normal, yield curve. Long-term interest rates are normally higher than short-term rates for a number of reasons. Lenders must be compensated for the:

- time value of money;
- reduced buying power of money resulting from inflation;
- increased risk of default over long periods; and
- loss of liquidity associated with long-term investments.

The yield curve is also a reflection of investor **expectations** about inflation. If investors expect high inflation rates, they will require higher rates of return to compensate for the reduction in purchasing power over time.

TAKE NOTE

When the yield curve is normal, long-term interest rates are higher than short-term interest rates. On a graph, the normal yield curve is upward sloping.

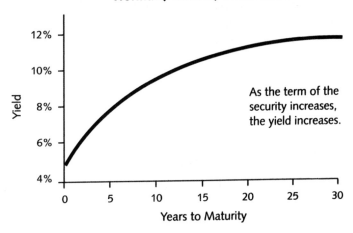

Normal (Positive) Yield Curve

As the term of the security increases, the yield increases.

In unusual circumstances, the yield curve can be inverted, or downward sloping. An inverted or negative yield curve can be the result of high current demand for money relative to the available supply. Short-term interest rates tend to be more sensitive to Fed policy than long-term rates. An inverted yield curve may occur because of a sharp increase in short-term rates. Therefore, when you notice a negative yield curve, you can expect that interest rates have rapidly risen and, according to most analysts, they will soon retreat.

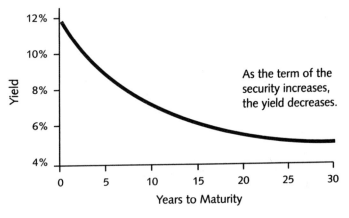

Inverted (Negative) Yield Curve

As the term of the security increases, the yield decreases.

When short-term and long-term rates are the same, it is called a **flat** yield curve.

TEST TOPIC ALERT

You will need to be able to recognize the different yield curves from their shape. A normal (positive) curve slopes upward. An inverted (negative) curve slopes downward. And, there is such a thing as a flat yield curve which, as the name implies, is level throughout all of the maturities.

Unit 8

TAKE NOTE

The shape of the yield curve varies with changes in the economic cycle.

- A normal, or ascending, yield curve occurs during periods of economic expansion—it generally predicts that interest rates will rise in the future.

- A flat yield curve occurs when no change in interest rates is expected.

- An inverted, or descending, yield curve occurs when the FRB has tightened credit in an overheating economy; it predicts that rates will fall in the future.

- Yield curves for issuers with different risk levels can be compared to make economic predictions.

Yield Spread (Credit Spread)

It should be obvious that the greater the risk, the higher the yield on the bond. Many analysts compare the difference between yields on bonds with the same maturity, but different quality (rating) to get a sense of the market sentiment. One common measurement is the difference in yields between Treasuries and corporate bonds. This difference is called the yield spread and tends to widen when economic conditions sour and narrow when they get better.

Yield spread can also be used between issues of the same issuer. For example, one of the most popular measurements of attitudes regarding future economic conditions is the yield spread between the 2-year Treasury note and the 10-year Treasury bond. When investors are feeling optimistic about the economy, the yield spread narrows; when pessimistic, the yield spread widens.

EXAMPLE

How is the yield spread predictive?

- If the yield spread between corporate bonds and government bonds is widening, a **recession** is expected. Investors have chosen the safety of government bonds over higher corporate yields, which occurs when the economy slows down.

- If the yield between corporate bonds and government bonds is narrowing, an economic **expansion** is expected and investors are willing to take risks. They will sell government bonds to buy higher-yielding corporates.

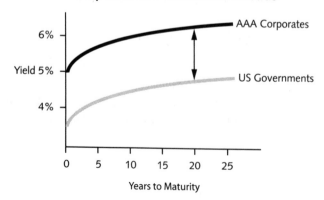

Corporate and Government Bonds

TEST TOPIC ALERT

When constructing a yield curve, the most common method is to use bonds of a single issuer over varying maturities. Specifically, most rely on the curve drawn when plotting yields on U.S. Treasury securities, starting with the 91-day T-bill and ending with anything from the 10-year note to the 30-year bond.

EXAMPLE

1. A bond analyst is plotting a yield curve and notices that short-term maturities have higher yields than intermediate and long-term maturities. This is an example of

   A. an inverted yield curve

   B. a positive yield curve

   C. a normal yield curve

   D. an algorithmic yield curve

   Answer: A. An inverted, or negative, yield curve is one that results when debt with short-term maturities has higher yields than those with maturities that are longer. A positive, or normal, yield curve results when the yields increase as maturities do.

UNIT 9

Financial Reporting

This unit deals with the methods used by publicly traded companies to report their financial results. Just as a credit card company evaluates your financial condition when determining if you are worthy of their credit card (and the amount of your credit limit), analysts view the company's financial statement to determine the strength of the issuer and growth and/or income opportunities for investors.

The Series 65 exam will include approximately four questions on the material presented in this unit

LEARNING OBJECTIVES

When you have completed this unit, you will be able to accomplish the following.

U9LO1:   Recognize balance sheet and income statement items.
U9LO2:   Identify the use of the statement of cash flows.
U9LO3:   Distinguish between the different forms used in SEC reporting.

FINANCIAL STATEMENTS

U9LO1: Recognize balance sheet and income statement items.

A corporation's **financial statements** provide a fundamental analyst with the information needed to assess that corporation's profitability, liquidity, financial strength (ability of cash flow to meet debt payments), and operating efficiency. By examining how certain numbers from one statement relate to prior statements and how the resulting ratios relate to the company's competitors, the analyst can determine how financially viable the company is.

Publicly traded companies issue quarterly and annual financial reports to the SEC. A company's balance sheet and income statement are included in these reports.

Balance Sheet

The **balance sheet** provides a snapshot of a company's financial position at a specific point in time. It identifies the value of the company's **assets** (what it owns) and its **liabilities** (what it owes). The difference between these two figures is the corporation's **owners' equity**, or **net worth**.

The **balance sheet equation** is:

assets – liabilities = owners' equity; or

assets = liabilities + owners' equity.

The balance sheet gets its name from the fact that its two sides must balance. The balance sheet equation mathematically expresses the relationship between the two sides of the balance sheet. Simply stated, everything that is owned (assets) minus everything that is owed (liabilities) is equal to the net worth (owners' or shareholders' equity) of the entity.

Assets

Assets appear on the balance sheet in order of liquidity, which is the ease with which they can be turned into cash. Assets that are most readily turned into cash are listed first, followed by less liquid assets. Balance sheets commonly identify three types of assets: **current assets** (cash and assets easily turned into cash), **fixed assets** (physical assets that could eventually be sold), and **other assets** (usually intangible and only of value to the corporation that owns them).

Current Assets

Current assets include all cash and other items expected to be converted into cash within the next 12 months, including the following.

- **Cash and equivalents** include cash and short-term safe investments, such as money market instruments that can be readily sold, as well as other marketable securities.

- **Accounts receivable** include amounts due from customers for goods delivered or services rendered, reduced by the allowance for bad debts.

- **Inventory** is the cost of raw materials, work in process, and finished goods ready for sale.

- **Prepaid expenses** are items a company has already paid for but has not yet benefited from, such as prepaid advertising, rents, insurance, and operating supplies.

Fixed Assets

Fixed assets are property, plant, and equipment. Unlike current assets, they are not easily converted into cash. Fixed assets, such as factories, have limited useful lives because wear and tear eventually reduces their value. For this reason, their cost can be **depreciated** over time or deducted from taxable income in annual installments to compensate for loss in value.

Other Assets

Intangible assets are nonphysical properties, such as formulas, brand names, contract rights, and trademarks. Goodwill, also an intangible asset, reflects the corporation's reputation and relationship with its clients.

> **TAKE NOTE**
>
> Although intangible assets may have great value to the corporation owning them, they generally carry little value to other entities.

Liabilities

Total liabilities on a balance sheet represent all financial claims by creditors against the corporation's assets. Balance sheets usually include two main types of liabilities: **current liabilities** and **long-term liabilities**.

Current Liabilities

Current liabilities are corporate debt obligations due for payment within the next 12 months. These include the following:

- **Accounts payable**—amounts owed to suppliers of materials and other business costs
- **Accrued wages payable**—unpaid wages, salaries, commissions, and interest
- **Current long-term debt**—any portion of long-term debt due within 12 months
- **Notes payable**—the balance due on equipment purchased on credit or cash borrowed
- **Accrued taxes**—unpaid federal, state, and local taxes

Long-Term Liabilities

Long-term debts are financial obligations due for payment after 12 months. Examples would include bonds and mortgages.

> **TAKE NOTE**
>
> Long-term debts include mortgages on real property, long-term promissory notes, and outstanding corporate bonds.

Figure 9.1:   Sample Balance Sheet

Balance Sheet

Amalgamated Widget

as of Dec. 31, 2017

ASSETS			
Current assets	Cash and equivalents	$ 5,000,000	
	Accounts receivable	15,000,000	
	Inventory	19,000,000	
	Prepaid expenses	1,000,000	
	Total current assets		$ 40,000,000
Fixed assets	Buildings, furniture, and fixtures		
	(at cost less $10 million accumulated depreciation)	$40,000,000	
	Land	15,000,000	
	Total fixed assets		$ 55,000,000
Other (intangibles, goodwill)		$5,000,000	
Total assets			$100,000,000
LIABILITIES AND NET WORTH			
Current liabilities	Accounts payable	$5,000,000	
	Accrued wages payable	4,000,000	
	Accrued taxes payable	1,000,000	
	Total current liabilities		$ 10,000,000
Long-term liabilities	8% 20-year convertible debentures		$ 50,000,000
Total liabilities			$ 60,000,000
Net worth	Preferred stock $100 par ($5 noncumulative convertible 200,000 shares issued)	$20,000,000	
	Common stock $1 par		
	(1 million shares)	1,000,000	
	Capital in excess of par	4,000,000	
	Retained earnings	15,000,000	
Total net worth			$ 40,000,000
Total liabilities and net worth			$100,000,000

Shareholder Equity

Shareholder equity, also called **net worth** or **owners' equity**, is the stockholder claims on a company's assets after all of its creditors have been paid. Shareholder equity equals total assets less total liabilities. On a balance sheet, three components of shareholder equity are identified: capital stock at par, capital in excess of par, and retained earnings.

Capital Stock at Par

Capital stock includes preferred and common stock, listed at par value. **Par value** is the dollar value per share assigned when a corporation's owners (the stockholders) first contributed capital. Par value of common stock is an arbitrary value with no relationship to market price. As you will see in Unit 12, it plays an important role with preferred stock.

Capital in Excess of Par

Capital in excess of par, often called **additional paid-in capital** or **paid-in surplus**, is the amount of money over par value that a company received when issuing its common stock. For example, if the par value was $1 per share and the stock was issued at $5 per share, there is a paid-in surplus of $4 per share.

Retained Earnings

Retained earnings, sometimes called **earned surplus** or **accumulated earnings**, are profits that have not been paid out in dividends. Retained earnings represent the total of all earnings held since the corporation was formed less dividends paid to stockholders. Operating losses in any year reduce the retained earnings from prior years.

TEST TOPIC ALERT

Treasury stock is stock that has been issued and then reacquired by the issuing corporation. Those shares are no longer considered outstanding in the hands of the public because they are, so to speak, held in the corporation's treasury. When a company has done this, the cost of those reacquired shares is shown in the owner's equity portion of the balance sheet as a negative number. This has the effect of reducing the company's net worth.

Capital Structure

A company's **capitalization** is the combined sum of its long-term debt and equity securities. The **capital structure** is the relative amounts of debt and equity that compose a company's capitalization. Some companies finance their business with a large proportion of borrowed funds; others finance growth with retained earnings from normal operations and little or no debt.

Looking at the balance sheet, a corporation builds its capital structure with equity and debt including the following four elements:

- Long-term debt
- Capital stock (common and preferred)
- Capital in excess of par
- Retained earnings (earned surplus)

EXAMPLE

(See the following table for reference and explanation of the following terms.) The total capitalization on the sample balance is $90 million ($50 million in long-term debt, $20 million in preferred stock, and $20 million in common shareholders' equity). Remember, capital stock + capital in excess of par + retained earnings = shareholders' equity (net worth).

Unit 9

Figure 9.2: Capitalization Table

Long-term debt	$50 million
Preferred stock (1 million shares @ $20 par value)	$20 million
Common stock (1 million shares @ $1 par value)	$1 million
Capital surplus (Common stock issue price $5 per share)	$4 million
Retained earnings	$15 million
Total equity capital	$40 million
Total Capitalization (long-term debt + equity)	$90 million

If a company changes its capitalization by issuing stock or bonds, the effects will show up on the balance sheet.

Issuing Securities

The example balance sheet indicates the company issued 1 million shares of $1 par common stock at a price of $5 per share. If it issues another 1 million shares, the net worth (shareholders' equity) will increase by the additional capital raised, and the amount of cash on the asset side of the balance sheet will increase.

Convertible Securities

When an investor converts a convertible debt security into shares of common stock, the amount of liabilities decreases, and the owners' equity increases. The changes are on the same side of the balance sheet, so there is no change to the assets.

Definition: Convertible Security

A corporate security which includes the provision that the owner may elect to convert (exchange) that security for a specified number of shares of the company's common stock. We'll have more to say about this in Part 3.

Bond Redemption

When bonds are redeemed, that is, the debt is repaid, liabilities on the balance sheet are reduced. The offsetting change would be a decrease in cash on the asset side of the balance sheet. The company would have less debt outstanding, but it would also have less cash. The balance sheet balances. Therefore, because the current asset (cash) was used to redeem the long-term liability (bond), working capital is reduced. However, because there would no longer be semiannual interest payments due on the debt, the future effect of the retirement of the bonds would be to increase the company's cash flow.

Dividends

When a cash dividend on the company's stock is declared, retained earnings are lowered and current liabilities are increased. The declaration of a cash dividend establishes a current liability until it is paid. Once paid, it reduces cash in current assets and also reduces current liabilities.

Stock Splits

A **stock split** does not affect shareholders' equity. On the balance sheet, only the par value per share and number of shares outstanding change.

Financial Leverage

Financial leverage is a company's ability to use long-term debt to increase its return on equity. A company with a high ratio of long-term debt to equity is said to be **highly leveraged**.

Stockholders benefit from leverage if the return on borrowed money exceeds the debt service costs. But leverage is risky because excessive increases in debt raise the possibility of default in a business downturn.

In general, industrial companies with debt-to-equity ratios of 50% or higher are considered highly leveraged. However, utilities, with their relatively stable earnings and cash flows, can be more highly leveraged without subjecting stockholders to undue risk. If a company is highly leveraged, it is also affected more by changes in interest rates.

EXAMPLE

1. As a result of corporate transactions, a company's assets remain the same and its owners' equity decreases. Which of the following statements is TRUE?

   A. Prepaid expenses decrease

   B. Total liabilities increase

   C. Accrued expenses decrease

   D. Net worth increases

   Answer: B. Sometimes questions are best answered by analyzing the question before we even look at the answer choices. We are told in the question that assets have remained the same, but, somehow the net worth (owners' equity) has gone down. If the balance sheet formula is assets minus liabilities = net worth, then somehow the liabilities must have increased. That seems to make choice **B** a straightforward answer, but let's just check the others to be sure. Prepaid expenses are an asset—can't be that because we know assets haven't changed. Choice D is so simple that students sometimes choose it because they think there is a trick somewhere. No trick here—if owners' equity goes down, that is the net worth so we can't choose "net worth increases." Finally, accrued expenses are a liability so if they decrease, net worth goes up, not down. If you take these questions step by step, they tend to be very logical.

Footnotes

Footnotes to the financial statements identify significant financial and management issues that may affect the company's overall performance, such as accounting methods used, extraordinary items, pending litigation, and management philosophy.

Typically, a company separately discloses details about its long-term debt in the footnotes. These disclosures are useful for determining the timing and amount of future cash outflows.

The disclosures usually include a discussion of the nature of the liabilities, maturity dates, stated and effective interest rates, call provisions and conversion privileges, restrictions imposed by creditors, assets pledged as security, and the amount of debt maturing in each of the next five years.

Also disclosed in the footnotes would be *off the books* financing arrangements such as debt guarantees.

Footnotes are generally found on the bottom of the financial statements and can be several pages long. Here is an example of how you might be asked about footnotes on your exam:

EXAMPLE

1. Potential litigation for patent infringement would appear on a corporation's

    A. balance sheet as a deferred asset

    B. footnotes

    C. income statement as an expense

    D. statement of potential litigation

    Answer B. The footnotes to the financial statements carry information such as potential legal actions, accounting methods used, and off-book debt.

TAKE NOTE

The balance sheet reports what resources (assets) a company owns and how it has funded them. How the firm has financed the assets is revealed by the capital structure—for example, long-term debt and owners' equity (preferred stock, common stock, and retained earnings).

Income Statement

The **income statement**, sometimes referred to as the profit and loss or P&L statement, summarizes a company's revenues (sales) and expenses for an accounting period, usually quarterly, year to date, or the full year. It compares revenue against costs and expenses during the period. Fundamental analysts use the income statement to judge the efficiency and profitability of a company's operation. Just as with the balance sheet, technical analysts generally ignore this information—it is not relevant to their charting schemes.

Components of the Income Statement

The various operating and nonoperating expenses on the income statement are discussed here.

Revenues indicate the firm's total sales during the period (the money that came in).

The **cost of goods sold (COGS)** is the costs of labor, material, and production (including depreciation on assets used in production) used to create finished goods. Subtracting COGS from revenues shows the gross operating profit or gross margin. This *gross margin* is usually divided by the net sales or revenues and is shown as a percentage, sometimes referred to as the *margin of profit*. Pretax margin is determined by subtracting COGS and other operating costs (rent and utilities) from sales to arrive at net operating profit. The resulting figure is earnings before interest and taxes (EBIT).

Interest payments on a corporation's debt is not considered an operating expense. However, interest payments reduce the corporation's taxable income. **Pretax income**, the amount of taxable income, is operating income less interest payment expenses.

If dividends are paid to stockholders, they are paid out of net income after taxes have been paid. After dividends have been paid, the remaining income is added to retained earnings and is available to invest in the business.

TEST TOPIC ALERT

Please note the three terms that we have put in boldface for you. **Revenue** (or sales), **COGS**, and **pretax income** are the three primary components of an income statement.

Think of it simply like this: the income statement shows (1) what came in, (2) what went out, and (3) how much is left (before taxes).

TAKE NOTE

Interest payments reduce a corporation's taxable income, whereas dividend payments to stockholders are paid from after-tax dollars. Because they are taxable as income to stockholders, dividends are taxed twice, whereas interest payments are taxed once as income to the recipient.

Accounting for Depreciation

As mentioned earlier when reviewing the balance sheet, fixed assets are shown at their cost minus accumulated depreciation. For these assets, which wear out over time, tax law requires that the loss of value be deducted over the asset's useful life, longer for some assets, shorter for others (you won't have to know depreciation schedules). On the income statement, the allowable portion for the year is shown as an expense and, for our purposes, will generally be part of COGS. Remember, if the company uses accelerated depreciation, the expenses will be higher in the early years resulting in lower pretax income (and lower income taxes) but higher income later on.

Fiscal Year Accounting

Many business entities prefer to end their accounting year on a date other than December 31 (calendar year accounting). Any 12-month period used by a business that ends other than on December 31 is known as a fiscal year (the term fiscal is generally defined as something that pertains to financial matters). This term was used many times when referring to required filings by investment advisers.

Unit 9

EXAMPLE

The following table should help you see some of the differences between balance sheet and income statement items.

Balance Sheet	Income Statement
current liabilities	revenues
net worth	COGS
retained earnings	net income
cash	interest paid

1. XYZ Corporation issues 1 million shares of common stock at a price of $6 per share. As a result of this, all of the following will be true EXCEPT

    A. net worth will increase by $6 million

    B. financial leverage will decrease

    C. net income will increase by $6 million

    D. current assets will increase by $6 million

    Answer: C. The issuance of common stock brings cash into the company without any offsetting liability. Therefore, current assets and net worth increase by the amount of the securities sold. Because stock is equity capitalization, the ratio of debt to equity capital is reduced. This reduces the financial leverage. Income is not generated by issuing stock; the company needs sales or revenues for that. That reasoning makes choice **C** the correct answer because it is the exception.

ACCOUNTING FUNDAMENTALS

In addition to the information thus far presented, there are two additional accounting concepts you may be required to understand.

Audited vs. Unaudited Financial Statements

Businesses must know their financial position at all times. With today's technologies, it is much easier than only a few decades ago when all bookkeeping was done manually. It is rare to find a business that does not produce financial information at least monthly and many do so even more frequently. These financial reports are generally done by in-house staff and, even when done by an outside accounting firm, they are considered unaudited. That is, specific care has not been taken to examine every item. For normal operating purposes, these unaudited statements do the job. However, for formal reporting to the SEC (or other regulators) and to shareholders, an audited report is required. In an audited report, an independent (and independence is critical) auditor, most commonly a representative, or in the case of a large entity, a number of representatives, of a CPA firm spends many hours poring over the books and records to verify and count everything.

Cash vs. Accrual Accounting

Smaller business enterprises tend to use the cash method of accounting while larger ones base their financial reporting on the accrual method. How do these two methods differ? Primarily, it is the timing of when revenue and expenses are recognized. In the cash method, everything is "as received," while in the accrual it is when "booked." Let's look at an example.

EXAMPLE

ABC Comfort Systems sells home heating and air conditioning systems. They install a system in a home for $3,000 in May and, because they offer "90 days same as cash" terms, they receive the payment in August. Under the cash method, the $3,000 would not be entered on their books until actually received in August. Under the accrual method, the $3,000 would be recorded when the sale took place in May.

CASH FLOW STATEMENT

U9LO2: Identify the use of the statement of cash flows.

The cash flow statement reports a business' sources and uses of cash and the beginning and ending values for cash and cash equivalents each year. There are three components generating cash flow:

- operating activities;
- investing activities; and
- financing activities.

TEST TOPIC ALERT

Most financial professionals add revenues and expenses that do not involve cash inflows or outflows (e.g., cost allocations such as depreciation and amortization) back to the company's net income to determine the cash flow. As listed previously, the cash flow statement will also reflect money from operations, financing, and investing, but not accounting changes.

Cash Flow From Operating Activities

Operating activities (all transactions and events that normally enter into the determination of operating income) include cash receipts (money coming in) from selling goods or providing services, as well as income from items such as interest and dividends. Operating activities also include cash payments (money going out) such as cost of inventory, payroll, taxes, interest, utilities, and rent. The net amount of cash provided (or used) by operating activities is the key figure on a statement of cash flows. Even though it would seem that interest and dividends received would belong in investing activities, the accounting gurus put them here.

EXAMPLE

You will recall that, included in our list of COGS was that year's depreciation. However, the company didn't write a check for that—it was merely an accounting entry shown as an expense. In reality, our net income reflects a deduction for an expense that was never paid. The true operating cash flow of the business was not only its net income, but also that depreciation expense. Adding the two numbers results in the total cash flow from operations. Let's take a personal example. Perhaps you, or someone you know, uses a car for business. The IRS permits a deduction for the expenses of operating the vehicle. Those expenses would include gas, oil, insurance, repairs, and so forth. In addition, a deduction would also be allowed for that year's depreciation. Sure, you know the car is worth less as it is a year older and has more mileage, but, did you write a check for that loss in value? No, but tax law permits you to deduct that depreciation as if you had.

Cash Flow From Investing Activities

Investing activities include transactions and events involving the purchase and sale of securities, land, buildings, equipment, and other assets not generally held for resale as a product of the business. It also covers the making and collecting of loans. Investing activities are not classified as operating activities because they have an indirect relationship to the central, ongoing operation of the business (usually the sale of goods or services).

Cash Flow From Financing Activities

All financing activities deal with the flow of cash to or from the business owners (equity financing) and creditors (debt financing). For example, cash proceeds from issuing stock or bonds would be classified under financing activities. Likewise, payments to repurchase stock (treasury stock) or to retire bonds and the payment of dividends are financing activities as well.

TEST TOPIC ALERT

Cash flow from operations will only use items from the income statement, while cash flow from financing activities will use balance sheet items. Make sure you know which one the question is asking about. For example, liquidating an outstanding bond issue (paying off the debt) will have a profound impact on cash flow and that uses information from the balance sheet (cash for the payoff, and no more debt remaining).

Here is how a question might appear on the exam.

EXAMPLE

1. A corporation's cash flow will increase as a result of

   A. paying dividends to preferred stockholders

   B. collecting on past due receivables

   C. paying overdue bills

   D. increasing inventory on hand

Answer B. Cash flow increases when more money comes in than goes out. When receivables are collected, the company receives money. When dividends or bills are paid, someone else receives money. When we buy more inventory, we use cash to do so.

SEC REPORTING FORMS

U9LO3: Distinguish between the different forms used in SEC reporting.

One of the best sources of financial information is found in the reports required to be filed with the SEC by publicly traded companies. This information is available online at the SEC's website. The location is at EDGAR, which stands for Electronic Data Gathering, Analysis, and Retrieval of SEC filings. Among those filings, there are generally three that are used by fundamental analysts.

Form 8-K

This form is used to report newsworthy events to the SEC, thereby making them available to the public. Included are items such as change in management, change in the company's name, mergers or acquisitions, bankruptcy filings, and major new product introductions or sale of a product line. A Form 8-K even has to be filed when a member of the board of directors resigns over a disagreement. The 8-K is filed within four business days of the occurrence. This form is used only by domestic issuers, foreign issuers are exempt. Although ADRs are registered with the SEC, they too are exempt because the underlying security is a foreign issue.

TEST TOPIC ALERT

One thing that would not trigger a Form 8-K is the relocation of a wholly owned subsidiary. However, sale of that subsidiary would require a filing and that, like any other Form 8-K filing, must be done within four business days of the event.

Form 10-K

Most domestic public issuers must file an annual report to the SEC on Form 10-K. This report is a comprehensive overview of the company's business and financial condition and includes financial statements that have been audited by an independent accountant. Do not confuse this with the annual report to shareholders, which also contains an audited statement and is sent to shareholders. The Form 10-K will generally contain more detailed financial information than the annual report, while the annual report will have much more detail about the company itself and its future plans.

The filing deadlines depend upon the company's public float. You don't have to know this information for the exam, but, for those companies with a float of $700 million or more, the Form 10-K deadline is 60 days after the close of the fiscal year; $75 million, but not $700 million, it is 75 days; and less than $75 million is due at 90 days.

Form 10-Q

Because one year between filings is a long time and a lot can happen quickly, we also have this form, and it is filed quarterly (Q for quarterly). It contains unaudited financial statements and for all but the companies with a public float of less than $75 million, it must be filed within 40 days of each of the first three fiscal quarters of the year (no 10-Q is filed at the end of the fourth quarter—that information is taken care of by the filing of the 10-K). Those smaller firms file theirs within 45 days of the end of the quarter.

Annual Reports

When it comes to publicly traded companies, in general, all shareholders must receive a copy of the issuer's annual report. For those too lazy to access EDGAR, this is the most detailed information they can get on the company's financial position. Unlike the Form 10-K, this is usually a professionally prepared piece which is just as much used for marketing purposes as it is for providing information. There is usually a welcoming letter from the CEO and/or Chairman of the Board, and it is generally loaded with beautiful pictures of smiling people (employees and customers) and the company's facilities. New plans for products and programs are discussed and voting proxies are included.

TEST TOPIC ALERT

SEC rules provide that a company may provide shareholders with a copy of the Form 10-K instead of sending an annual report.

EXAMPLE

1. A publicly traded corporation keeps its books on a calendar year basis. An investor wanting the most up-to-date financial information in late August would view the company's

   A. June 30 Form 10-Q

   B. June 30 Form 8-K

   C. December 31 Form 10-K

   D. July 31 Form 10-Q

   Answer: A. Form 10-Q is the quarterly financial information document filed with the SEC. Because this is a calendar year company, 10-Qs are prepared as of March 31, June 30, and September 30. The Form 10-K is prepared as of December 31 in lieu of another Form 10- Q. Form 8-K is event driven, not a routine financial report.

UNIT
10

Analytical Methods

Analytical Methods primarily involve mathematical concepts in an attempt to assist in making better investment decisions. Because the testing center only permits the use of a simple four-function calculator, any computations you will be asked to perform will be relatively straightforward. In general, it will be more important to understand the concept than do the computation.

The Series 65 exam will have approximately four questions on the material covered in this unit.

LEARNING OBJECTIVES

When you have completed this unit, you will be able to accomplish the following.

U10LO1: Describe the different time value concepts including use of the rule of 72 to determine the return on an investment.

U10LO2: Select the proper measure of central tendency when presented with a group of numbers.

U10LO3: Compute income in perpetuity and exhausting the principal.

U10LO4: Identify alpha and beta.

U10LO5: Recall how standard deviation relates to volatility.

U10LO6: Recognize the relationship between correlation and diversification.

U10LO7: Compute liquidity and valuation ratios of a common stock.

TIME VALUE OF MONEY

U10LO1: Describe the different time value concepts including use of the rule of 72 to determine the return on an investment.

There is no question that investing is a numbers business. In the previous unit, we discussed financial statements as a tool for evaluating a company and those are almost entirely number oriented. In this unit, we'll go further by looking at the overall market and examining some of the tools that quantitative analysts (known as *quants* in the industry) use to assist them in making investment decisions. The first place to start is understanding the time value of money.

We've all heard the famous saying, "Time is money." The concept certainly applies to investments. For example, if a person promises to pay a certain sum 10 years from now, what is it worth to have the money today so that the investor will have use of it over the next 10 years instead of having to wait? If the investor could earn 10% on the money, compounded annually, having about $38.55 today would be equivalent in value to receiving $100 in 10 years. That is known as the *present value* of a future sum. The second view of time value relates to computing the amount necessary to be invested today, using an assumed rate of return, so that it will have a defined amount in the future. Using the previous example, an investor depositing $38.55 today earning 10% compounded annually, would have $100 in 10 years. We call that the *future value* computation.

TAKE NOTE

Although this can be proven in less than 10 seconds using a financial calculator, you may have to do a compound return computation on the exam but won't have the benefit of such a fancy tool. Using the basic four-function calculator issued at the testing center, you would take the initial $38.55 and multiply that by 110% and continue to do that for a total of 10 times. I'll just get you started to show you what it looks like:

38.55 × 110% = 42.405 × 110% = 46.6455 × 110% = 51.31 and so forth seven more times will get to you approximately $100.00. This is the same concept we will show you with the TIPS bond in Unit 13.

Future Value

Future value (FV) is the formal term that indicates what an amount invested today at a given rate will be worth at some period in the future. The FV of a dollar invested today depends on the:

■ rate of return it earns (r); and

■ number of years over which it is invested (n).

The equation to calculate the FV of an investment is expressed as:

$$FV = PV \times (1 + r)^n$$

EXAMPLE

In these two examples, we will demonstrate how these values are calculated. However, you will NOT be required to know the formula or how to do these computations.

Assuming we invest $11,348.54 today and expect to earn 12% compounded annually for five years. What will it be worth then? Its FV is calculated using the previous formula as follows:

$$FV = \$11{,}348.54 \text{ (the PV)} \times 1.12^5 = \$20{,}000$$

The FV expressed here reflects a **compound rate of return** on the original $11,348.54 invested. The compound return assumes that the interest earned (12% in this case) in a given period (five years), is reinvested at the identical rate for the number of years in which it is invested.

TAKE NOTE

To find PV, you must already know the FV.

To find FV, you must already know the PV.

Present Value

Present value (PV) is the formal term for value today of the future cash flows of an investment discounted at a specified interest rate to determine the present worth of those future cash flows.

Intuitively, investors recognize that a dollar in hand is worth more than a dollar in the future. The difference between the value today and sometime in the future is a function of the time elapsed and the rate of interest earned.

The formula used to calculate present value is as follows:

$$PV = FV / (1 + r)^n$$

In this formula, **PV** stands for the present value, **FV** stands for the future value, r is the interest rate, and n is the number of time periods the money is compounded.

This formula says that the present value of an investment equals the investment's FV discounted at (divided by) an interest rate over a time period specified by n. The factor $(1 + r)^n$ is known as the **discount factor**.

EXAMPLE

What is the present value of $20,000 that will be received 5 years (n) from today? If the investor requires a 12% return (r) for the $20,000, the value of that $20,000 today (PV) to be received in 5 years is calculated as follows:

$$PV = \frac{FV}{(1 + 0.12)^5} = \frac{\$20{,}000}{1.7623416} = (\$11{,}348.54)$$

The $20,000 to be received in 5 years discounted by the required 12% interest rate is worth $11,348.54 today.

TEST TOPIC ALERT

When computing present value (or future value), we are using an estimated rate of return. What happens if the actual return is different from the estimated? If our actual return is less, we don't make out as well. That means that the PV (the required initial deposit) is going to be higher than we computed. On the other hand, if the actual return was higher than the PV (we did better than we thought), the PV (the amount we would have had to deposit), is less.

The same logic holds true for FV. If the actual return is higher than projected, the FV will be higher (we made more on our money than we thought we would). Logically, if the actual return is lower, our FV winds up lower. Here is how that might look in question format:

EXAMPLE

1. Present value is a computation that is frequently used to determine the amount of a deposit needed now to meet a future need, such as a college education. If an investor uses an expected return of 8% but the actual return over the period is 10%, the future value will be

   A. lower than anticipated

   B. higher than anticipated

   C. the same as anticipated

   D. too varying to tell

   Answer: B. Present value is the amount deposited to meet a future goal based on an expected rate of return. If the return is higher than expected, the ending result will be greater (a good thing).

Rule of 72

The rule of 72 is a shortcut method for determining the number of years it takes for an investment to double in value assuming compounded earnings. To find the number of years for an investment to double, simply divide the number 72 by the interest rate the investment pays. For example, an investment of $2,000 earning 6% will double in 12 years (72 / 6 = 12).

Here is another example of the rule of 72. A savings account with $1,000 in it bearing 4% compounded per year in interest would double (i.e., the account would be worth $2,000) in 18 years; 72 / 4 = 18.

EXAMPLE

Suppose an investment of $1,000 was worth $4,000 in 16 years. Under the rule of 72, what is the compounded earnings rate?

You figure this by realizing that the account has quadrupled. That means it has doubled twice. So, if it took 16 years to double twice, it takes 8 years to double one time. Dividing 72 by 8 tells us that our account must be earning 9%.

The rule of 72 also works in reverse. That is, if you know the number of years you have, you can compute the required earnings rate to double by, once again, using 72 as the numerator and this time the number of years as the denominator. For example, if you have nine years before your child is going to enter college, what will you have to earn in order for a deposit made today to double? Simply divide 72 by 9 and the result is that an 8% earnings rate will have your money double.

Net Present Value (NPV)

Net present value (**NPV**) is the difference between an investment's present value and its cost. A positive NPV of $10 means that an investment that cost $100 must have a discounted PV of $110, for an NPV of $10. Note that the difference between the cost ($100) and the PV of the investment's future returns ($110) equals the NPV ($10). If the PV is $90, there is a negative NPV of $10 because the price is above the present value.

TAKE NOTE

NPV is expressed in dollar amounts and not as a rate of return.

An investment adviser could use the NPV concept to evaluate a client's investment in any investment vehicle with a projected income stream. The adviser would project the cash flows from the investment and then discount them to their present value at the investor's required rate of return. If the NPV is positive, the investment is a worthwhile addition to the investor's portfolio.

EXAMPLE

This concept is very important on the exam—at least 2 or 3 questions worth so let's try to make it as simple as possible. Don't worry about how we got the following numbers—that won't be tested. What will be tested is understanding what they mean.

Several years ago, the XYZ Corporation issued a bond with a nominal yield (interest rate) of 5% per year. The bond matures in exactly 20 years. As of the date of this example, comparable bonds are being issued with nominal rates of 4%. In this type of computation, the *required* rate of return = the current market rate (which is 4%). Using a financial calculator (which, as stated before, you won't have at the test center), the PV of this bond (using these assumptions), is $1,136.78. I hope you are not surprised that this bond's expected value is above the $1,000. After all, we learned in Unit 8 that when interest rates decline, the price of outstanding bonds increases.

Now, here is where we get to the critical test question: If this bond is currently available from your broker-dealer for $1,100, what is its NPV? The answer is $36.78 because NPV is computed by subtracting the market price from the PV. In this case, we have a positive NPV and that means we're able to buy the bond for less than what it is theoretically worth. If, on the other hand, the bond was available for $1,150, it would have a NPV of minus $13.22, or a negative NPV, and would not be one you would likely purchase.

Internal Rate of Return (IRR)

The **internal rate of return** (**IRR**) is the discount rate (r) that makes the NPV of an investment equal to zero. The IRR can be thought of as the *r* in the present and FV calculations. The IRR is difficult to calculate directly; it must be determined by a trial-and-error process called **iteration**. IRR takes into consideration the time value of money. Although IRR may be used for almost any investment, its practical use for common stock is limited to those companies paying stable dividends.

TAKE NOTE

The IRR calculation can be used to determine whether an investment meets the investor's required rate of return. If an investor requires an investment return of 10% and the IRR for a proposed investment is 12%, the investor will view that investment as attractive because it returns a higher rate than the investor's required rate.

TEST TOPIC ALERT

NPV and IRR are far and away the most difficult mathematical concepts you'll encounter on this exam. These are most important points to remember.

■ IRR is the method of computing long-term returns that takes into consideration *time value* of money.

■ The yield to maturity of a bond reflects its IRR.

■ The investment is a good one if it has a positive NPV; stay away if the NPV is negative.

■ NPV is generally considered more important than IRR.

— When an investment's IRR is equal to the discount rate (sometimes call the required rate of return), the NPV = zero. In an efficient market (Unit 20) bonds should be priced so that their NPV is zero.

— The quickest way, to identify IRR versus NPV is that IRR is always expressed as a percentage, NPV never is. It is usually shown as a dollar amount. So, one is a rate (%), the other is a value ($).

EXAMPLE

Let's go back to that NPV example to show you how IRR fits in. We established that the required rate of return was one that equaled the market rate of 4%. If the XYZ bond in our question was available from the broker-dealer at a price of $1,136.78, then its PV and the market price would be the same, giving us a NPV of zero. At that price, bond's yield to maturity and the IRR are equal to the market rate of 4%.

We are going to elaborate further on this in Unit 13 when we show how this is a **discounted cash flow (DCF)** computation, (and you might want to come back here after that).

MEASURES OF CENTRAL TENDENCY

U10LO2: Select the proper measure of central tendency when presented with a group of numbers.

There are a number of other numerical tools used that do not involve time value. The following are those most likely to appear on your exam.

We are going to continue this section on quantitative measurements with a discussion dealing with the method of determining how one might approach figuring the logical outcome of a securities investment. Central tendency is usually defined as the center or middle of a distribution. There are many measures of central tendency. Let's take a look at some of them.

Mean or Arithmetic Mean

When we use the word average, this is what we are really speaking about. Of all the different measures, this is the one most commonly used to measure central tendency. You've been computing this for years—all you do is take the sum of the variables and divide by the number of occurrences. For example, if a stock returned 5%, then 8%, then 9%, and then 2%, the mean would be 6% (5 + 8 + 9 + 2 = 24 / 4 = 6). Even though is the most used (probably because it is so simple to do), the mean may not be an appropriate measure of central tendency for skewed distributions. The term *mean* by itself will always refer to the arithmetic mean.

Median

The median is a midpoint of a distribution. That is, there are as many variables below as there are above. To find the median of a number of returns, list them in order, and then find the number in the middle. For example, the median of 11, 7, 4, 13 and 8 is 8 (4, 7, 8, 11, and 13). If the number of variables is even, then take the average of the middle two. If we use the numbers given previously for computing the mean (2, 5, 8, and 9), the average of the middle two is 6.5 (5 + 8 = 13 divided by 2 = 6.5). Note that the median is not the same number as the mean. The median is often more appropriate than the mean in skewed distributions or in situations with variables that fall far outside the normal range, (outliers).

Mode

The mode is determined much differently than the prior two. Mode measures the most common value in a distribution of numbers. For example, the mode of 2, 2, 2, 6, 7, 7, 9 is 2. The mode is likely to be quite unlike the mean or median. For example, using the numbers just shown, the mean is 5 (35 / 7) and the median is 6.

Geometric Mean

This one takes some math skills and probably won't be a correct choice on the exam and certainly not something you'll have to compute. The geometric mean of any given set of numbers (n) is obtained by multiplying all of them together, and then taking the nth root of them.

TEST TOPIC ALERT

When comparing the arithmetic mean to the geometric mean, the arithmetic mean will always be higher, unless all of the numbers being used are the same (e.g., figuring the mean of 6, 6, and 6), in which case they will be equal. The reason is because the geometric mean uses imputed **compounding**.

Range

Range is the difference between the highest and lowest returns in the sample being viewed. When there are many values at either extreme of the range, the results tend to be skewed in that direction. Some look at the mid-range value which, as the name implies, is the number that is exactly in the middle of the range. The simplest way to do this is to reorder the data set from smallest to largest and then subtract the first element from the last element.

For example, if we look at the numbers we used to determine median, we reorder the numbers: 4, 7, 8, 11, and 13. This makes the range 9 (13–4) and the mid-range is 8.5, close to, but not the same as the median. Using our mode example, the range is 7 (9–2) and the mid-range is 5.5.

EXAMPLE

Over the past seven years, a security has produced annual returns of 10%, 4%, –5%, 10%, 12%, –2%, and 6%.

In this example, the mean return (the average) is 5% (adding these 7 returns totals +35% and dividing by 7 results in an average of 5%). The median return, the one with as many returns above as below, is 6%. The mode, the return with the most occurrences, is 10% and the range, the difference between the lowest and highest returns, is 17% (–5% to +12%).

Here is a sample question:

1. An investor is looking at the past performance of a security over the past three years. In year one, it returned 10%; year two it returned 15%; and year three it returned –4%. This computes to an average rate of return of 7%. This would be properly referred to as the

   A. arithmetic mean

   B. internal rate of return

   C. median return

   D. range

   Answer: A. When a true average return is shown, that is the arithmetic mean. The median return (the number in the middle of the group of three) is 10%, and the range is 19% (–4 to +15).

TEST TOPIC ALERT

You may have a question that shows four portfolios listing the mean, the median, and the mode for each one. The question will ask: Which one had some investments that significantly outperformed the average of the other investments? The answer will be the one with the highest mean. To show how that works, let's say that you have seven securities in the portfolio with the following returns: A: 5%; B: 5%; C: 8%; D: 10%; E: 12%; F: 40%; and G: 60%. The mode (the number that appears the most frequently) is 5%. The median (the number with the same number of returns above and below it) is 10% and the mean (the average of the seven returns) is 20% (140 divided by 7). The two outliers (F at 40% and G at 60%) caused the mean (average) to be significantly higher than the mode or the median because those two performed significantly better than the other five holdings.

INCOME IN PERPETUITY

U10LO3: Compute income in perpetuity and exhausting the principal.

As an investment adviser representative, a client may approach you about a method for providing an annual income "forever" for a relative or perhaps a charity. This is known as income in perpetuity. If you know the average expected rate of return and the desired annual income, divide that income by the rate of return and you will arrive at the lump sum required to throw off that income perpetually.

EXAMPLE

1. A rich aunt wishes to provide $1,000 per month in perpetuity to her favorite nephew. If the account can be invested to earn 5% per annum, what is the required deposit?

    A. $20,000

    B. $24,000

    C. $200,000

    D. $240,000

    Answer: D. The first step is to take the monthly income and convert it to a yearly number: $1,000 per month is $12,000 per year. Then, divide that $12,000 by the 5% rate of return, and you arrive at a lump-sum deposit of $240,000.

EXHAUSTING THE PRINCIPAL

Unlike the previous example where the income was to last forever, what happens when the client has a fixed sum and wants to know how long money can be withdrawn before it is exhausted?

This is a simple computation when one has a financial calculator available, but all they give you at the test center is a simple four-function one, and that makes the task highly laborious.

Let's take a look at an example of the kind that may be presented on the Series 65 exam.

EXAMPLE

1. An investor has $100,000 to invest. If the account is estimated to earn at a rate of 5% per year and the investor wishes to withdraw $12,000 at the end of each year, approximately how long will the money last?

    A. 5 years

    B. 8 years

    C. 11 years

    D. 16 years

Answer: C. Here is the correct math, where BOY means Beginning of the Year and EOY is End of the Year:

Year	BOY Value	EOY Value
1	100,000	105,000
2	93,000	97,650
3	85,650	89,933
4	77,933	81,829
5	69,829	73,321
6	61,321	64,387
7	52,387	55,006
8	43,006	45,156
9	33,156	34,814
10	22,814	23,955
11	11,955	12,552
12	552	580

This shows that one taking the money out at the end of the year, will have exhausted all but a bit over $550 by the end of the 11th year. You can do this with the calculator furnished at the test center as follows:

- 100,000 × 105% = 105,000 − 12,000 = 93,000

- 93,000 × 105% = 97,650 − 12,000 = 85,650

- 85,650 × 105% = 89,933 − 12,000 = 77,933 and continue

Obviously, this takes a lot of time. Because the answer choices shown on the test will be so far apart, I would suggest taking a shortcut. Take the initial principal, $100,000; divide by the annual withdrawal rate, $12,000 (100 / 12 = 8.33); and choose the next highest number (because you have to realize that the account is earning 5% on whatever assets remain).

EXAMPLE

1. Your 50-year-old client has just inherited $50,000 from a relative and wishes to invest it into a single payment deferred variable annuity. What computation would be used to approximate the value of the account when the client reaches 70?

   A. Future value

   B. Present value

   C. Net present value

   D. Internal rate of return

   Answer: A. This is what the future value (**A**) computation is used for. We take a sum of money available now, consider the time the money will be invested, estimate a rate of return, and arrive at the expected value (assuming the earnings are equal to the estimated rate).

BETA COEFFICIENT

U10LO4: Identify alpha and beta.

Beta and *beta coefficient* mean the same thing. In the securities industry, *coefficient* is ordinarily dropped for purposes of convenience. Beta is used to measure the variability between a particular stock's (or portfolio's) movement and that of the market in general. A stock with a beta of 1.00 will tend to have a market risk similar to that of the market as a whole. Most frequently, beta is measured against the Standard & Poor's 500 composite index. A stock with a beta of 1.50 will be considerably more volatile than the market; a stock with a beta of 0.70 will be much less volatile than the market. Although most assets have a positive beta, it is possible to find some with a negative beta. Assets with a negative beta can be an important component when diversifying a portfolio. For example, if beta is –1.2, a 10% up move in the market's return will cause the stock return to decline by 12%. On the other hand, if the general market were to suffer a decline, a stock with a negative beta would generally show positive returns. Know that conservative clients need securities with low positive betas, whereas aggressive clients will find betas in excess of 1.00 to be quite suitable. In the next unit, we'll have more to say about beta and *systematic* risk.

TAKE NOTE

If the S&P 500 rises or falls by 10%, a stock with a beta of 1 rises or falls by about 10%, a stock with a beta of 1.5 rises or falls by about 15%, and a stock with a beta of .75 rises or falls by about 7.5%.

EXAMPLE

1. Adding investments with a negative beta to a well-diversified portfolio that currently has a beta of +1.0 will

   A. cause the expected performance of the portfolio to improve in declining markets

   B. cause the expected performance of the portfolio to decline in declining markets

   C. cause the portfolio to experience more volatility in times of a rising market

   D. cause the portfolio to experience more volatility in times of a declining market

   Answer: A. A negative beta means that the investment will move in an opposite direction from the overall market. Therefore, if the market is declining, then the asset should increase in value, thereby increasing the expected performance of the portfolio.

ALPHA

For portfolio managers, good news is when they can say that they have generated *positive alpha*. Basically, that means that their investment performance is better than what would have been anticipated, given the risk in terms of volatility that was taken. That generally means the manager has been adept at security selection and timing.

You may be asked to compute how much alpha was generated for a particular stock or portfolio based on the amount of risk taken. Alpha can be positive, negative, or zero. If the alpha is negative, then the portfolio is underperforming the market; if higher, the portfolio is outperforming the market (and the manager is doing a good job).

The most common formula for computing alpha goes like this:

(total portfolio return – risk-free rate) – (portfolio beta × [market return – risk-free rate])

In essence, what is being done is comparing performance after eliminating the risk-free rate.

This is one item where it's easier to understand if we show you the numbers.

Definition: Risk-Free Rate

The risk-free rate used on the exam will always be the 91-day (or 13-week) U.S. Treasury bill. Because their price movements are not generally related to the stock market, those T bills are said to have a beta of zero.

EXAMPLES

Example #1

Portfolio return 10%

Risk-free rate 2%

Market return rate 8%

Beta 1.2

The computation of alpha would be:

(10% – 2%) = 8%. Then (1.2 × [8 – 2]) which is 1.2 × 6 = 7.2

Plug that into the formula, giving us 8 – 7.2 or an alpha of 0.8 (positive alpha).

Example #2

Same numbers except the beta is 0.8.

(10% – 2%) – (0.8 × 6) = 8 – 4.8 = positive alpha of +3.2

Let's review for a moment. Both portfolios earned the same 12%, but the second one did it with a much lower beta—we would not have expected that portfolio to do as well as the one with the higher beta (remember, more risk, more reward). The fact that it did means the portfolio manager(s) did a great job.

Example #3

Same numbers as example #1 except the portfolio returned 9%.

(9% − 2%) − (1.2 × 6) = 7 − 7.2 = alpha of −0.2 (negative)

This portfolio underperformed; for the additional risk taken, it should have returned at least 9.2%.

Example #4

The most common alpha question on the exam will compare a portfolio (or stock) to the market's beta of 1.0. It is also possible to compare two portfolios (or securities) based on their relative betas. Portfolio T has a beta of 1.50 and has returned 20% while portfolio Z, with a beta of 1.20 has returned 12%. If the RF is 2%, what is T's alpha?

Because we are not comparing to a beta of 1.0 (the market beta), we have an additional step and that is determining the relationship (ratio) between the two betas. T's beta is given as 1.50 and Z's as 1.20. That means we should expect Portfolio T's performance to be 1.50/1.20 better than Portfolio Z's. That converts to 1.25 or 125% better. In the formula, instead of the market return, we use the return of Portfolio Z. It looks like this:

T's return minus the RF (20% − 2%) = 18%. Subtract from that, the beta ratio of 1.25 times (Z's return − RF).

That comes out to be 18% − (1.25 × 10%) = 18% − 12.5% = +5.5% alpha.

Take a look in the Glossary to see one additional alpha example.

TEST TOPIC ALERT

It is possible on the exam that you will have an alpha computation where the RF (risk-free return) is not given. In that case, the computation is the same, but without the RF being subtracted from both the actual return and the market return. For example, in our first case, the computation would be 10% − (1.2 × 8%) or 10% − 9.6% for an alpha of +0.4.

STANDARD DEVIATION

U10LO5: Recall how standard deviation relates to volatility.

Standard deviation is a measure of the volatility of an investment's projected returns, computed by using historical performance data. Standard deviation is a statistical term that measures the amount of variability or dispersion around an average. The larger this dispersion or variability is, the higher the standard deviation. The higher the standard deviation, the larger the security's returns are expected to deviate from its average return, and, hence, the greater the risk.

EXAMPLE

This simple example should give you a basic understanding of the concept behind using standard deviation as a tool to predict price volatility. Let's compare the returns generated by the common stock of two unrelated companies over the past three years.

	2016	**2017**	**2018**
Company A	8%	12%	10%
Company B	–4%	25%	9%

For an investor who held shares in Company A for those three years, the mean return on investment was 10%. This is calculated, just like any other average, by adding together the three annual returns (8 + 12 + 10 = 30) and dividing that by 3.

For an investor who held shares in Company B for those three years, the mean return on investment was exactly the same 10% (25 + 9 – 4 = 30 / 3). However, which one of the shares had a greater dispersion (or variance) from the mean? Clearly, Company B's. You will not have to compute it, but you should be able to see from this that Company B would have a much higher standard deviation (its returns have deviated far greater from the average) than Company A. If you were asked on your exam to choose which of these two would be more suitable for the conservative investor (the one who likes to sleep well at night), you'd better pick Company A, the one with the lower standard deviation.

Standard deviation is expressed in terms of percentage. It is generally accepted that a security will vary within one standard deviation about two-thirds of the time and within two standard deviations about 95% of the time. A standard deviation of 7.5 means that the return of a stock for a given period may vary by 7.5% above or below its predicted return about two-thirds of the time and within 15% about 95% of the time.

EXAMPLE

A security has an expected return of 12% and a standard deviation of 5%. Investing in a security with an expected 12% return, an investor can expect returns to range within 7% to 17% about 67% of the time and within 2% to 22% about 95% of the time.

TAKE NOTE

An investor can use standard deviation to compare the volatility between investments. Simply, the higher the standard deviation, the greater the volatility (and the reverse).

EXAMPLE

If an investor had a choice between an investment that historically returned 12% with a standard deviation of 6% and another investment that also returned 12% but had a standard deviation of 10%, the investor would probably choose the first one. In effect, he would expect to receive an equal return in the future return with less risk.

Beta vs. Standard Deviation

Beta is a volatility measure of a security compared with the overall market, measuring only systematic (market) risk. Standard deviation is a volatility measure of a security compared with its expected performance and includes both systematic and unsystematic risk. Another way to put that is that standard deviation measures the total risk of a security or portfolio. After studying the next unit, you might want to re-read this because you will have a better understanding of these two types of risk.

CORRELATION COEFFICIENT

U10LO6: Recognize the relationship between correlation and diversification.

Correlation means that securities move in the same direction. A **strong** or **perfect correlation** means two securities prices move in a perfect positive linear relationship with each other.

EXAMPLE

Two securities are correlated if one security's price rises by 5% and the other security's price then rises by 5%, or if one declines by 4% and the other also declines by 4%.

The correlation coefficient is a number that ranges from –1 to +1. Securities that are perfectly correlated have a correlation coefficient of +1. Securities whose price movements are unrelated to each other have a correlation coefficient of 0. If prices move in perfectly opposite directions, they are negatively correlated or have a correlation coefficient of –1. Generally speaking, correlation coefficients of 0.80 and up are considered to be a very high correlation.

TAKE NOTE

Index funds attempt to achieve perfect correlation (+1) with the index they are mirroring (e.g., the Standard & Poor's 500). The goal of an index fund manager is to come as close as possible to matching the performance of the underlying index. It is not a goal to exceed the performance, only to match it.

TEST TOPIC ALERT

One of the best ways to increase the diversification of a portfolio is to include investments with a negative correlation. The logic is that those negatively correlated assets will go up when the rest of the portfolio is going down. One of the best examples of a negatively correlated asset is an investment in gold stocks. Bonds frequently have a negative correlation as well which is one of the reasons for creating a balanced allocation.

EXAMPLE

1. Take a look at this example: One of your clients has a portfolio that has a correlation of 0.91 with the overall market. A stock with which correlation coefficient would most likely offer the greatest diversification to this client?

   A. 0.91

   B. 0.51

   C. 0.01

   D. −0.51

   Answer: D. Remember, the best way to diversify is to include securities with a negative correlation and, the only one here that meets that requirement is choice **D**.

BALANCE SHEET RATIOS

U10LO7: Compute liquidity and valuation ratios of a common stock.

One of the key tools in fundamental analysis is the corporation's financial statements. We have viewed the balance sheet and income statement in a previous unit and now are going to focus on the most testable calculations derived from those documents. We will begin with the three ratios that evaluate liquidity as determined by examining the company's balance sheet.

Working Capital

Working capital is the amount of liquid capital or cash a company has available. Working capital is a measure of a firm's liquidity, which is its ability to quickly turn assets into cash to meet its short-term obligations.

The formula for working capital is:

current assets − current liabilities = working capital

Factors that **increase** working capital include increases in cash from:

■ issuing securities (long-term debt or equity);

■ profits from the business operations; and

■ the sale of noncurrent assets, such as equipment no longer in use.

Factors that **decrease** working capital include increasing current liabilities such as:

■ declaring cash dividends;

■ paying off long-term debt whether at maturity or, if called, earlier; and

■ net operating losses.

Current Ratio

Knowing the amount of working capital is useful, but it becomes an even better indicator when paired together with the current ratio. This computation uses the same two items, current assets and current liabilities, but expresses them as a ratio of one to the other. Simply divide the current assets by the current liabilities and the higher the ratio, the more liquid the company is.

Quick Asset Ratio (Acid Test Ratio)

Sometimes it is important for the analyst to use an even stricter test of a company's ability to meet its short-term obligations (as such, "pass the acid test"). The quick asset ratio uses the company's quick assets instead of all of the current assets. Quick assets are current assets minus the inventory. Then divide these quick assets by the current liabilities to arrive at the quick ratio.

TAKE NOTE

Liquidity measures a company's ability to pay the expenses associated with running the business.

As with most arithmetic, there are two ways to get to the correct answer. The standard formula for the quick asset ratio is: current assets minus inventory divided by current liabilities. The same result is achieved by adding together all of the current assets *except* the inventory and then dividing by the current liabilities. It might look like this on your exam:

EXAMPLE

1. The balance sheet of the DEF Corporation shows that included in its $15 million in current assets is $4 million in cash and $2 million in accounts receivable. If DEF's current liabilities are $4 million, the quick asset ratio is

    A. 1.0:1

    B. 1.5:1

    C. 2.5:1

    D. 3.0:1

    Answer: B. We aren't told what the inventory is, but we are given the other current assets. So, we can add together the $4 million in cash to the $2 million in receivables resulting in $6 million divided by the $4 million in current liabilities for a 1.5 to 1 (choice **B**) answer. It wasn't necessary for the question to tell us the inventory—we didn't have to subtract it because we never included it in the first place.

Here are two additional computations relying on the balance sheet:

Debt-to-Equity Ratio

The best way to measure the amount of financial leverage being used by the company is by calculating the debt-to-equity ratio. It is really a misnomer—it should be called the debt-to-total capitalization ratio because that is what it is. For example, using the numbers in the following capitalization table, we see that the total capital used in the business is $90 million. Of that, $50 million is long-term debt. So, we want to know how much of the $90 million total is represented by debt capital. The answer is simple: $50 million of the $90 million, or 55.55%. That is the debt-to-equity ratio.

Capitalization Table	
Long-term debt	$50 million
Preferred stock (1 million shares @ $20 par value)	$20 million
Common stock (1 million shares @ $1 par value)	$1 million
Capital surplus (Common stock issue price $5 per share)	$4 million
Retained earnings	$15 million
Total equity capital	$40 million
Total Capitalization (long-term debt + equity)	$90 million

Book Value Per Share

A fundamental analyst is described as one who focuses on the company's books. Therefore, one of the key numbers computed is the book value per share.

In the case of a corporation, it is basically the liquidation value of the enterprise. That is, let's assume we sold all of our assets, paid back everyone we owe, and then split what is left among the stockholders. But, remember, before we can hand over anything to the common shareholders, we must take care of any outstanding preferred stock. So, from the funds that are left after we pay off all of the liabilities, we give the preferred shareholders back their par (or stated) value and the rest belongs to the common stockholders.

But there is one more thing. In the case of liquidation, some of the assets on our books might not really be worth what we're carrying them at. In particular, those that are known as intangible assets (goodwill, patents, trademarks, copyrights, etc.). That is why the analyst uses only the tangible assets, computed by subtracting those intangibles from the total assets.

Expressed as a formula, book value per share is:

$$\frac{\text{tangible assets} - \text{liabilities} - \text{par value of preferred}}{\text{shares of common stock outstanding}} = \text{book value per share}$$

 TEST TOPIC ALERT

Book value reflects the *liquidating* value of the company, not its *intrinsic* value.

There are a number of important ratios that can be computed using information from the income statement. We'll take a look at several of them.

Earnings Per Share (EPS)

Among the most widely used statistics, EPS measures the value of a company's earnings for each common share:

$$\text{EPS} = \frac{\text{earnings available to common}}{\text{number of shares outstanding}}$$

Earnings available to common are the remaining earnings after the preferred dividend has been paid. EPS relates to common stock only. Preferred stockholders have no claims to earnings beyond the stipulated preferred stock dividends.

Figure 10.1:   Simplified Income Statement

	Net Revenues (Sales)		$10,000,000
−	Cost of Goods Sold (including $500,000 of depreciation)		5,500,000
=	Gross Profit		4,500,000
−	Other Operating Expenses (rent, utilities)		500,000
=	Operating Profit		4,000,000
−	Interest Expense		750,000
=	Income After Interest Expense (Pretax Income)		3,250,000
−	Income Tax		1,000,000
=	Net Income		2,250,000
	EPS (1,000,000 common shares outstanding)		2.25
	Dividends per Share ($1.50)		1,500,000
	Balance Credited to Retained Earnings		750,000

Earnings Per Share After Dilution

EPS after dilution assumes that all convertible securities, such as warrants, convertible bonds, and preferred stock, have been converted into the common. In most cases, because there is now more common stock outstanding sharing in the earnings, EPS is reduced (diluted). Because of tax adjustments, the calculations for figuring EPS after dilution can be complicated and will not be tested.

Current Yield (Dividend Yield)

A common stock's **current yield**, expresses the annual dividend payout as a percentage of the current stock price:

$$\text{current yield} = \frac{\text{annual dividends per common share}}{\text{market value per common share}}$$

EXAMPLE

LMN Corporation pays a quarterly dividend on its common stock of $0.50 per share. If the current market price of LMN common stock is $80 per share, the current yield is? The first step is to recognize that quarterly dividends of $0.50 total $2.00 annually. Then, we plug the numbers into the formula:

$$\frac{\$2.00}{\$80.00} = 0.025 \text{ or } 2.5\% \text{ current yield}$$

One way to remember this is that we are computing the return on your investment. So take the return ($2) and put it "*on*" your investment ($80).

Dividend Payout Ratio

The **dividend payout ratio** measures the proportion of earnings paid to stockholders as dividends:

$$\text{dividend payout ratio} = \frac{\text{annual dividends per common share}}{\text{earnings per share (EPS)}}$$

In general, older companies pay out larger percentages of earnings as dividends. Utilities as a group have an especially high payout ratio. Growth companies normally have the lowest ratios because they reinvest their earnings in the businesses. Companies on the way up hope to reward stockholders with gains in the stock value rather than with high dividend income.

EXAMPLE

Using the simple income statement above, we see that the company paid dividends of $1.50 per share out of the earnings of $2.25 per share. That is a ratio of 2 to 3 or 66.7%. Simply, the computation is:

Dividends paid over (divided by) earnings made

MARKET PRICE RELATED RATIOS

Price-to-Earnings Ratio (P/E)

The widely used **price-to-earnings (P/E) ratio** provides investors with a rough idea of the relationship between the prices of different common stocks compared with the earnings that accrue to one share of stock:

$$\text{P/E ratio} = \frac{\text{current market price of common share}}{\text{earnings per share (EPS)}}$$

EXAMPLE

In our income statement, we see that the EPS are $2.25. If the stock's current market price is $45, what is the P/E ratio? Simply take the price (45) and place it on the earnings (2.25) and that computes to 20. So, we say the P/E ratio is 20 to 1, or 20:1.

Growth companies usually have higher P/E ratios than do cyclical companies. Investors are willing to pay more per dollar of current earnings if a company's future earnings are expected to be dramatically higher than earnings for stocks that rise and fall with business cycles. Companies subject to cyclical fluctuations generally sell at lower PEs; declining industries sell at still lower PEs. Investors should beware of extremely high or extremely low PEs. Speculative stocks often sell at one extreme or the other.

If a stock's market price and P/E ratio are known, the EPS can be calculated as follows:

$$\text{EPS} = \frac{\text{current market price of common stock}}{\text{P/E ratio}}$$

EXAMPLE

If the price of the stock is $45 and that is 20 times the earnings, the earnings must be 45/20 or $2.25 per share.

TAKE NOTE

A company's stock trades for $30 per share and has earnings of $1.50 per share. It has a PE (multiple) of 20 ($30 / 1.5 = 20). If the average PE of the company's industry is 11, this stock is high priced. If the average PE is 35, this company is low priced.

TEST TOPIC ALERT

Some fundamental analysts feel that the company's price to sales ratio is more valuable than the PE ratio because different accounting methods can impact earnings much more than sales.

Price-to-Book Ratio

The **price-to-book ratio** reflects the market price of the common stock relative to its **book value** per share. **Book value** is the theoretical value of a company (stated in dollars per share) in the event of liquidation and bears little or no relationship to the stock's current trading price.

TAKE NOTE

A quick rundown of the most testable points about ratios follows.

- Book value is the company's theoretical liquidation value expressed on a per share basis.

- Growth companies have higher PE ratios than do cyclical or defensive companies.

- Earnings per share relates only to common stock; it assumes preferred dividends were paid.

EXAMPLE

1. RMBN common stock is currently selling for $60, which gives the stock a P/E ratio of 20:1. Based on that information, the earnings per share are

   A. $2.00

   B. $3.00

   C. $5.00

   D. $20.00

   Answer: B. This is simply telling us that the price of $60 is 20 times the earnings. That would make the earnings 60/20 or choice **B**, $3.00.

UNIT 11

Types of Investment Risk

The concepts discussed in this unit are types of risk that both businesses and investors bear. Though not a comprehensive list, they are among the most common.

Although we routinely use the term risk, we often have difficulty defining it precisely. In finance, **risk** is defined as the uncertainty that an investment will earn its expected rate of return. There are two basic categories of risk, systematic and unsystematic. We will address both of them and their subcategories one at a time.

The Series 65 exam will include approximately six questions on the material presented in this unit.

LEARNING OBJECTIVES

When you have completed this unit, you will be able to accomplish the following.

U11LO1:   Identify the different systematic risks.
U11LO2:   Identify the different unsystematic risks.
U11LO3:   Identify opportunity cost.
U11LO4:   Recall the sequence of priority of claims in the event of a corporate liquidation.

SYSTEMATIC RISKS

U11LO1: Identify the different systematic risks.

Systematic risk is the risk in the return of an investment that is associated with the macroeconomic factors that affect all risky assets. Stated another way, systematic risk is the risk that changes in the overall economy will have an adverse effect on individual securities regardless of the company's circumstances. It is generally caused by factors that affect all businesses, such as war, global security threats, or inflation. Primary examples would include market risk, interest rate risk, and purchasing power risk, each of which will be dealt with separately. You might also see this referred to as nondiversifiable risk because, as we'll learn, systematic risk cannot be avoided through diversification.

Market Risk

The first example of systematic risk that generally comes to mind is market risk. When the market tanks, virtually all securities lose value. This is a classic example of a nondiversifiable risk because, regardless of the number of different stocks in your portfolio, when you encounter a stock market such as we had from late 2007 until early 2009, chances are most of those assets will have declined in price. In the previous unit, we discussed *correlation*. One way to protect against market risk is to have some negatively correlated securities in your portfolio. Remember, they go up when the others go down.

TAKE NOTE

Market risk is measured by a security's beta.

EXAMPLE

Should a war break out between two major oil-producing countries, the stock market could decline dramatically. The stocks of individual companies would likely decline as well, regardless of whether the war directly affected their businesses.

TAKE NOTE

Market risk cannot be diversified away. In Part 4, we will discuss several strategies that might be used to protect portfolios against this risk.

Interest Rate Risk

Interest rates fluctuate in the market all the time. If market conditions or the Federal Reserve push interest rates higher, the market price of all bonds will be affected. When interest rates rise, the market price of bonds falls and that is why this is a systematic risk. This risk is sometimes referred to as the market risk for bonds. Rising interest rates can be bearish for some common stock prices as well, particularly those of highly leveraged companies such as public utilities. Having a diversified portfolio of bonds won't help because an increase in interest rates will cause all bonds to decline in price. In Unit 20, we'll discuss three strategies that may be used to reduce interest rate risk.

TAKE NOTE

Interest rate risk is intrinsic to all types of fixed-income investments, such as debt securities and preferred stock, whether from an emerging market issuer or a triple-A issuer. It is the risk that a security's value will decline as a result of an increase in market interest rates. In general, the longer the term to maturity, the greater the price fluctuation when interest rates change.

EXAMPLE

If the Federal Reserve increases interest rates dramatically, the market price of all bonds, regardless of credit quality, will decline.

Reinvestment Risk

A variation of interest rate risk is reinvestment risk. There is reinvestment risk as to interest and reinvestment risk as to principal.

An investor receiving a periodic cash flow from an investment, such as interest on a debt security, may be unable to reinvest the income at the same rate as the security itself is paying. For example, if an investor purchased a bond with a 10% coupon and several years later comparable securities were only paying 7%, the investor would not be able to compound the investment at the original rate. Zero-coupon bonds avoid this risk because there is nothing to reinvest.

This risk also occurs at maturity. If the fixed-income investor was enjoying a 10% return on the previous bond, when it matured, the investor was only able to reinvest the principal in a 7% security.

Inflation Risk (Purchasing Power Risk)

This is another systematic risk. Inflation reduces the buying power of a dollar (or whatever currency is used where you live). A modest amount of inflation is inherent in a healthy, growing economy, but uncontrolled inflation causes uncertainty among individual investors as well as corporate managers attempting to evaluate potential returns from projects. Treasury Inflation Protection Securities are one investment vehicle designed to protect against inflation risk.

Fixed-income securities are the most vulnerable to this risk; equity securities are historically the least susceptible. In Part 3 of this course, we will learn that tangible assets, such as real estate and precious metals such as gold are also good inflation hedges.

EXAMPLE

As we stated, purchasing power risk is a systematic risk, meaning that diversifying your portfolio is of little or no help. Let's assume that an individual nearing retirement took $1 million and, seeking income with safety, invested $100,000 into each of 10 different corporate bonds, all maturing in 20 years. For sure, this diversification does give some protection against financial risk (if one of the bonds defaults due to bankruptcy of the issuer, the other nine should still pay off). However, if the cost of living rises, 20 years from now, when each of those bonds pays back the $100,000 principal, the investor will have $1 million, but how much will that $1 million purchase compared to what it would have 20 years earlier?

UNSYSTEMATIC RISKS

U11LO2: Identify the different unsystematic risks.

Unlike systematic risk which is nondiversifiable, these risks can be reduced through diversification. They are risks that are unique to the specific industry or business enterprise and would include things such as labor union strikes, lawsuits, and product failure. Let's look at the most testable examples here.

Business Risk

This is an operating risk, generally caused by poor management decisions (e.g., Edsel, New Coke, or more recently, RIMM failing to pay attention to the success of the iPhone—remember when everybody had to have a Blackberry?). At best, earnings are lowered; at worst, the company goes out of business and common stockholders probably lose their entire investment.

Financial Risk

Often confused with business risk (it is similar), financial risk relates primarily to those companies that use debt financing (leverage). An inability to meet those debt obligations could lead to bankruptcy and, once again, total loss for the stockholders.

Credit (Default) Risk

Anytime debt financing is involved, there is always the possibility that the debtor will be unable to make timely payment of interest, principal, or both. This is primarily a risk to investors in debt securities, but can sometimes be viewed as a sub-category of financial risk for equity investors. When investing in the stock of a company that is highly leveraged (borrowed money), there is the risk that the company might default on its obligations which may lead to bankruptcy and a significant (or possibly total) loss of value to its equity securities. That said, if a test question should ask for the security without credit risk, it is common stock because there is no obligation to pay back a debt.

TEST TOPIC ALERT

Unsystematic risk can be minimized through portfolio diversification. For example, a client who owns 1,000 shares of XYZ sells those shares and invests the proceeds into an S&P Index fund eliminates (or greatly reduces) business risk (but not market risk). In similar fashion, owning a diversified portfolio of bonds, such as is offered in a bond fund, offers protection against financial risk.

TEST TOPIC ALERT

Business risk is highest for investors whose portfolios contain stock in only one issuer or in lower rated bonds.

Regulatory Risk

A sudden change in the regulatory climate can have a dramatic effect on the performance or risk of a business and entire business sectors. Overreaching bureaucrats and court judgments that change the rules a business must comply with can devastate individual companies and industries almost overnight. A very common example of this is rulings by the EPA (Environmental Protection Agency), which can sometimes play havoc with the oil and gas industry.

Legislative Risk

It is common to lump together regulatory and legislative risk, but there is a difference. Whereas regulatory risk comes from a change to regulations, legislative risk results from a change in the law. And, because there is frequently a political agenda behind legislation, this risk is sometimes referred to as political risk, although most consider political risk to be of its own making. A governmental agency, state or federal, may pass certain regulations, but only a legislature can pass a law. Changes to the tax code are the most obvious legislative risks.

Political Risk

It might seem like we are splitting hairs here, but each of these, although potentially interrelated, does have a different basis in the source of the risk. In the case of political risk, most attribute this to potential instability in the political underpinnings of the country (think of a coup). This is particularly true in emerging economies, but, as history has shown, political insurrections can occur even in highly developed societies.

Sovereign Risk

Sovereign risk ratings capture the risk of a country defaulting on its commercial debt obligations. Headlines were made several years ago when the credit rating of the United States was reduced from AAA (it didn't take long before the United States was back up to AAA). That is an example of the perceived increased sovereign risk that existed at the time. More recent examples with Greece point out that even countries can have difficulty paying their obligations.

Country Risk

Country risk monitors the political and economic stability of countries. Country risk is the total risk of investing in the obligations of that country and includes political and sovereign risk.

 EXAMPLE

Investments that could be affected by regulatory changes include "green" industries (and those that tend to pollute), oil and gas exploration, airlines, and pharmaceutical manufacturers. The most common regulatory risk comes from governmental agency attempts to control or influence product prices or the competitive structure of a particular industry through the passage and enforcement of regulations.

EXAMPLE

An example of legislative risk is how the domestic boat-building business in the United States was nearly wiped out in the early 1990s after the government instituted a luxury tax for yacht purchases.

EXAMPLE

A recent example of political risk was the actions of the Chavez government in Venezuela several years ago, where nationalization took place in many industries from cement to supermarkets. Those investors in what were previously privately owned (not government) businesses saw much, if not all, of their investment lost.

Liquidity Risk

Liquidity measures the speed or ease of converting an investment into cash without causing a price disruption. **Liquidity risk** is the risk that when an investor wishes to dispose of an investment, no one will be willing to buy it, or that a very large purchase or sale would not be possible at the current price. Although there is technically a difference, for exam purposes, you may also refer to this as **marketability risk**.

EXAMPLE

The Treasury bill market is a highly liquid market because investors can sell a Treasury bill within seconds at the quoted prices. Real estate investments, however, can take months or years to sell if you want to get close to your asking price. The longer it takes to convert an investment into cash without having a fire sale, the greater the liquidity risk.

TAKE NOTE

Listed stocks and mutual funds have virtually no liquidity risk. Thinly traded stocks, many municipal bonds, and most tangible assets have a greater degree of inability to liquidate rapidly at your price.

Currency or Exchange Rate Risk

Purchasers of foreign securities, whether through direct ownership or ADRs, face the uncertainty that the value of either the foreign currency or the domestic currency will fluctuate. For example, as of the date of publication, the Euro (€) is up over 13% against the U.S. dollar in the past 12 months. As a result, someone who invested one year ago in the stock of a company domiciled in the Eurozone will find that, even if the stock has remained level or slightly lower on its local market, in terms of dollars, the value has increased. On the other hand, if your funds are in domestic cash, or cash equivalents, you have little if any exposure to currency or exchange rate risk.

TEST TOPIC ALERT

On an individual level, the exam may even ask you about exchange rates and vacationers. For example, you take a trip to Country A and purchase a dinner on your credit card for 200 units of the local currency. Then, on the final night of your stay, you go to the same restaurant, order the same meal and, once again, the bill is for 200 units. When you get home, you check your credit card statement and see that you were billed $100 for the first meal and $110 for the second. What happened? The value of the foreign currency rose against the U.S. dollar from $0.50 ($100 / 200) to $0.55 ($110 / 200). Even though no prices changed in the foreign country, you encountered currency risk.

TAKE NOTE

When an investment's systematic risk and unsystematic risk are added together, we have the total risk. This was discussed previously at standard deviation (U10LO5).

OPPORTUNITY COST

U11LO3: Identify opportunity cost.

Opportunity cost is the foregone return, or the return given up, on an alternative investment. In economic terms, opportunity cost is defined as the highest valued alternative that must be sacrificed as a result of choosing among alternatives. More simply, one can invest in short-term U.S. Treasury bills, incurring virtually no risk. That is the risk-free alternative that can be earned by basically doing nothing. Any return that deviates from the risk-free return represents your opportunity gained or lost.

EXAMPLE

The 91-day Treasury bill is currently yielding 6%. An investor decides to purchase a stock with an expected return of 11%. If that stock's actual return is 2%, the opportunity cost is 4% (6% − 2%) because that is the rate that the investor gave up, risk free, to assume the risk of investing in the alternative choice.

TEST TOPIC ALERT

You may need to know that the three primary systematic risks are:

- market;
- interest rate; and
- inflation or purchasing power.

There are also five primary unsystematic risks:

- Business
- Financial
- Liquidity
- Political
- Regulatory

EXAMPLE

1. All of the following risks are considered diversifiable EXCEPT

   A. currency risk

   B. liquidity risk

   C. purchasing power risk

   D. sovereign risk

   Answer: C. Purchasing power risk, also known as inflation risk, is a systematic risk and, as such, is one that cannot generally be lessened through diversification.

LIQUIDATION PRIORITY

U11LO4: Recall the sequence of priority of claims in the event of a corporate liquidation.

As discussed previously in this unit, a corporation's capital structure is the way it raises its capital. Think of it like the building blocks of the company. All corporations build the base, as it were, with common stock. They may or may not issue preferred stock. If they wish to employ leverage, they will borrow money by issuing debt securities. Those securities may be issued with collateral, such as a mortgage bond, or merely on the general credit of the issuer (a debenture). In terms of looking at risks, it is critical to understand where the investor's position is in the event of a bankruptcy.

When examining the capital structure of a corporation, it is important to know the liquidation priority:

- Secured creditors (e.g., mortgage bonds, equipment trust certificates, and collateral trust bonds)
- Unsecured creditors (e.g., general creditors including debenture holders)
- Subordinated debt holders
- Preferred stockholders
- Common stockholders

Regardless of how low on the totem pole a debt security is, such as a subordinated debenture, it still has priority in terms of payment of interest and principal ahead of any equity security. Look for a question asking, in essence, "In the event of a corporate liquidation, who comes first: A senior, prior lien preferred stock or a junior, unsecured subordinated debenture?" Now, you may not see all of those adjectives, but no matter what, a debt security always has priority over an equity security.

PART 3

Investment Vehicle Characteristics

This part consists of six units:

Unit 12 Types and Characteristics of Equity Securities Including Methods Used to Determine Their Value

Unit 13 Types and Characteristics of Fixed Income (Debt) Securities and Methods Used to Determine Their Value

Unit 14 Types and Characteristics of Pooled Investments

Unit 15 Insurance-Based Products

Unit 16 Types and Characteristics of Derivative Securities

Unit 17 Alternative Investments and Other Assets

In total there will be 32 questions on this material, representing 25% of the Series 65 exam.

UNIT 12

Types and Characteristics of Equity Securities Including Methods Used to Determine Their Value

Because equity is such an important capital market security, the fundamentals that you learn in this unit will lay the groundwork for your success in future units. This unit will cover common stock, preferred stock, and related equity securities.

The investment world is divided between owners (stock, or equity securities) and lenders (bonds, or debt securities). Owning equity in a company is perhaps the most visible and accessible means by which wealth is created. Individual investors become owners of a publicly traded company by buying stock in that company. In so doing, they can participate in the company's growth over time and, in many cases receive a share of the company's profits in the form of dividends.

The Series 65 exam will include approximately eight questions on the material presented in this unit.

LEARNING OBJECTIVES

When you have completed this unit, you will be able to accomplish the following.

U12LO1:   Describe the characteristics of equity securities.
U12LO2:   Identify the basic features of equity securities.
U12LO3:   Describe how incentive stock options differ from nonqualified ones.
U12LO4:   Contrast restricted stock and non-restricted stock.
U12LO5:   Identify the unique features of American Depositary Receipts (ADRs) and the risks of investing in foreign securities.
U12LO6:   Evaluate the methods used to determine the value of equity securities.

EQUITY SECURITIES

U12LO1: Describe the characteristics of equity securities.

As covered in Part 1 of this course, in the simplest terms, a **security** is an investment that represents either an ownership stake or a debt stake. An investor becomes part owner in a corporation by buying shares of the company's stock. A debt security is usually acquired by buying an issuer's (company or government) bonds. A debt investment is a loan to the issuer in exchange for interest income and the promise to repay the loan at a future maturity date. It does not confer ownership (equity) as does the purchase of stock.

When investors become owners of a corporation by purchasing stock in that company, they can participate in the company's prosperity by sharing in earnings through the receipt of dividends and, particularly in the case of common stock, benefit from an increase in the price of the shares.

COMMON STOCK

Common stock is equity (ownership) in a corporation. A company issues stock to raise capital, and investors who buy the stock are buying a share of ownership in the company. Whatever a business owns (its assets) less its creditors' claims (its liabilities) belongs to the owners (its stockholders).

Each share of stock entitles its owner to a portion of the company's earnings and dividends and a proportionate vote in major management decisions, such as electing members to the board of directors at the annual meeting. Most corporations are organized in such a way that their common stockholders regularly vote for and elect a few individuals to a **board of directors** to oversee company business. By electing a board of directors, these stockholders have an indirect say in the company's management but are not involved in the day-to-day details of its operations.

 EXAMPLE

If a corporation issues 100 shares of stock, each share represents an identical 1/100—or 1%—ownership position in the company. An investor who owns 10 shares of stock would own 10% of the company; an investor who owns 50 shares of stock would own 50% of the company.

Corporations may issue two types of stock: **common** and **preferred**. When speaking of stocks, people generally mean common stock. **Preferred stock** also represents equity (ownership) in a corporation but usually does not have the same voting rights or appreciation potential as common stock. Preferred stock normally pays a fixed quarterly dividend and has **priority claims** over common stock; that is, common stockholders cannot receive a dividend until the preferred shareholders have been paid theirs and, in the event the company goes bankrupt, preferred stockholders have a prior claim on any remaining assets

Preferred Stock

Preferred stock is an equity security because it represents a class of ownership in the issuing corporation. However, it does share some characteristics with a debt security. Just as with debt securities, the rate of return on a preferred stock is fixed rather than subject to variation as with common stock. As a result, its price tends to fluctuate with changes in interest rates rather than with the issuing company's business prospects unless, of course, dramatic changes occur in the company's ability to pay dividends. This concept, known as interest rate or money rate risk, was covered in the previous unit.

TAKE NOTE

Unlike common stock, most preferred stock is nonvoting.

TEST TOPIC ALERT

Like common stock, preferred stock represents ownership in a company, but its price reacts to the market more like a bond because with its fixed dividend payment, its price is sensitive to interest rate changes.

EXAMPLE

1. Holders of each of the following are creditors EXCEPT investors owning

   A. preferred stock

   B. corporate bonds

   C. municipal bonds

   D. government bonds

   Answer: A. Remember all stockholders (even preferred stockholders) are owners of a corporation, not creditors.

BASIC FEATURES OF EQUITY SECURITIES

U12LO2: Identify the basic features of equity securities.

Growth (Capital Gains)

An increase in the market price of securities is **capital appreciation**. Historically, owning common stock has provided investors with returns in excess of the inflation rate. For this reason, most investors with a long-term investment horizon have included common stock in their portfolios as a hedge against inflation. Of course, it must be mentioned that stock prices can decline, particularly over the short run.

EXAMPLE

An investor buys shares of RST for $60 per share on January 1, 2017. On December 31, 2017, the shares are worth $90, an increase of 50% in the market price.

Income

Many corporations pay regular quarterly cash dividends to stockholders. A company's dividends, in the case of common stock, may increase over time as profitability increases. Dividends, which can be a significant source of income for investors, are a major reason many people invest in stocks. Because stock is an equity security, unlike interest payments on debt, dividends are not obligatory, and are declared at the discretion of the company's board of directors.

Issuers may also pay **stock dividends** in additional shares of common stock in the issuing company, or **property dividends**, shares in a subsidiary company, or in product.

EXAMPLE

RST paid a dividend of $2 per share during 2017, which provided the investor with a dividend yield of 3.3% ($2 / $60 = 3.33%) in addition to the price appreciation.

TAKE NOTE

The increase in the price of RST stock in the previous example is an **unrealized gain** until the stock is sold; when it is sold, it becomes a **realized gain**. Capital gains are not taxed until they are realized. Under current tax law, most dividends and long-term capital gains are taxed at a rate not in excess of 15%. Taxation will be covered in more detail in Unit 21.

Definition: Stock Dividend

One option a corporation has is to pay common stockholder a dividend in additional shares of the stock. This saves the cash that would be used in a normal dividend while giving stockholders something at no cost. For example, if an investor owned 100 shares of the stock and the company declared a 20% stock dividend, that investor would receive 20 additional shares bringing the total holding up to 120 shares. There are two important facts to know:

- As a result of the additional shares being distributed where the company receives no new money, the price of the stock will drop so that the overall value remains the same. Using our numbers from above, if, before the distribution, the market price was $48 per share, the investor has $4,800 worth of stock. After the stock dividend is paid, the investor still has $4,800 of stock, but now owns 120 shares. That would make the current market price approximately $40 per share ($4,800 divided by 120).

- Stock dividends are not taxed when received. As you will learn in Unit 21, they are not taxed until sold and have the effect of reducing the investor's cost basis per share.

Do not confuse a stock dividend with a **stock split**. A split is an accounting process whereby the corporation exchanges new shares for old ones while changing the number of shares outstanding in the market place. For example, in a 2 for 1 stock split, the investor now owns twice as many shares worth half as much each. Conceptually, it is the same as changing large bills for small ones. If you had a $20 bill and changed it for two $10 bills, in essence, you've just had a 2 for 1 split. Do you have any more money? No, just 2 bills worth the same as the previous one. If you changed your $20 bill for four $5 bills, that would be the equivalent of a 4 to 1 split.

Rights of Stockholders

As mentioned earlier, common stockholders have the right to vote for the corporation's board of directors at the corporation's annual meeting. Stock, whether common or preferred, is freely transferable (permission of the company is not required) to anyone who wants to buy it or receive it as a gift. Without this feature, there would be no stock markets. The owner (or broker-dealer holding the stock) sends the stock certificate to the issuer's *transfer agent* with instructions to issue a certificate in the new owner's name. The concept is similar to transferring title when you sell a car. Because of the opportunities for fraud, transfer agents (usually large commercial banks), must be registered as such with the SEC under the Exchange Act. Shareholders also have the right to receive an audited set of financial statements of the company's performance each year (annual reports). Common, but not preferred stockholders usually have the preemptive right to maintain their proportionate share of ownership in the corporation. The word *preempt* means to put oneself in front of another. We will have a further discussion on preemptive rights in Unit 16.

EXAMPLE

1. Which of the following statements regarding rights is TRUE?

    A. Common stockholders would not generally receive preemptive rights

    B. Preferred stockholders would not generally receive preemptive rights

    C. Both common and preferred stockholders would generally receive preemptive rights

    D. Neither common nor preferred stockholders would generally receive preemptive rights

    Answer: B. Preferred stockholders have no right to maintain a percentage of ownership when new shares are issued (no preemptive rights), choice **B**. However, they do receive preference in dividend payment and company liquidation.

TEST TOPIC ALERT

Before a vote or a payment of dividend, the company establishes a *record date*. This is the date by which an investor must be an owner of record (shown as an owner on the company's records) in order to vote or receive the announced dividend.

Limited Liability

One of the most important features of equity ownership (common stock or preferred stock) is limited liability. In the event of the bankruptcy of a corporation, when corporate assets are not adequate to meet corporate obligations, the stockholder's personal assets are not at risk. One cannot be forced to sell any personal assets to help pay the debts of the business.

An individual investing $5,000 in the stock (common or preferred) of a corporation that goes bankrupt may lose the entire $5,000 if the company is not salvaged, but will not be forced to pay out any more money to take care of the corporation's debts. That investor is personally at risk only for the amount that was invested. This is different from a business organized as a sole proprietorship or partnership where the owner's personal assets are placed at risk should the business not be able to pay off its obligations. This concept will be discussed later in Unit 18.

Liquidity

In almost all cases, shares of common and preferred stock are freely transferrable. This means that shareholders do not need the permission of the issuer, or anyone else, to sell their stock in the open market. This is especially true in the case of shares traded on the major stock exchanges. One exception is restricted stock (covered shortly), where sales are contingent upon meeting the requirements of SEC Rule 144.

Unit 12

BENEFITS AND RISKS OF OWNING COMMON STOCK

Regardless of their expectations, investors have no assurances that they will receive the returns they expect from their investments so the risks must be balanced against the rewards.

TAKE NOTE

In owning common equity, the investor stands to lose current income through dividend reduction or suspension, as well as capital loss, should the market price decline. In return, however, the shareholder has limited liability; that is, the liability is limited to the amount invested and theoretically unlimited potential for future price appreciation and/or dividend growth.

In summation, why would you include common stock in a client's portfolio?

- Potential capital appreciation
- Income from dividends
- Hedge against inflation

In doing so, the client would be incurring the following risks:

Market Risk

The chance that a stock will decline in price is one risk of owning common stock (known as **market risk**). A stock's price fluctuates daily as perceptions of the company's business prospects change and influence the actions of buyers and sellers. Investors have no assurance whatsoever that they will be able to recoup the investment in a stock at any time.

Business Risk

As described in the previous unit, poor management decisions or other conditions unique to the company could cause it to lose money and even go out of business. This could lead to a large or total loss to the investor.

Low Priority at Dissolution

If a company enters bankruptcy, the holders of its bonds and preferred stock have priority over common stockholders. A company's debt and preferred shares are considered **senior securities**. Common stockholders have **residual rights** to corporate assets upon dissolution.

EXAMPLES

1. Among the benefits of owning common stock are

    I. it has historically been a hedge against inflation

    II. voting rights

    III. access, as owners, to information about corporate earnings before the general public

    IV. dividends

    A. I and II

    B. I, II, and IV

    C. II and IV

    D. I, II, III, and IV

    Answer: B. One does not have access to insider information solely by becoming a shareholder. Even if one did receive material nonpublic information, such as prior access to earnings, no benefit may be received from that information. All of the other choices are among the reasons to purchase common stock.

2. Limited liability regarding ownership in a U.S. corporation means all of the following EXCEPT

    A. investors might lose more than the amount of their investment

    B. investors might lose their investment

    C. creditors of the corporation cannot seek relief from the shareholders

    D. investors are not liable to the full extent of their personal property

    Answer: A. An advantage of owning stock is that an investor's liability is limited to the amount of money invested when the stock was purchased.

TEST TOPIC ALERT

Because the primary objective met by investing in preferred stock is *income*, when analyzing a specific preferred stock, the most important determination should be the ability of the company to meet its dividend payments.

TYPES OF PREFERRED STOCK

There are several different types of preferred stock starting with straight preferred (think of "plain vanilla") and expanding depending on which and how many adjectives we use to describe the security. However, all maintain preference over common stock. Remember, preferred stock is an equity security and, just as with common stock, dividends are paid at the discretion of the Board of Directors. What is special about preferred stock is that no dividend can ever be paid to the common stockholders unless the preferred is satisfied first. Preferred stock may have one or more of the following characteristics.

Straight (Noncumulative)

Straight preferred has no special features beyond the stated dividend payment. Missed dividends are not paid to the holder.

Unit 12

Cumulative Preferred

Cumulative preferred stock accrues payments due its shareholders in the event dividends are reduced or suspended.

Dividends due cumulative preferred stock accumulate on the company's books until the corporation's board of directors decides to pay them. When the company resumes dividend payments, cumulative preferred stockholders receive current dividends plus the total accumulated dividends—dividends **in arrears**—before any dividends may be distributed to common stockholders.

EXAMPLE

In 2013, RST Corp. had both common stock and cumulative preferred stock outstanding. The common paid a dividend of $1, and the preferred paid a $2 dividend. Because of financial difficulties, the company stopped paying dividends after 2013. Having resolved its problems in 2018, the company resumed dividend payments and paid the cumulative preferred holders an $8 dividend for the arrears in years 2014, 2015, 2016, and 2017 plus the current year's (2018) $2 dividend before paying any dividends to the common stockholders.

TEST TOPIC ALERT

Because of this unique feature, found only with cumulative preferred stock, an investor seeking steady income would find this to be the most suitable of the different types of preferred stock.

Callable Preferred

Corporations often issue **callable** (or **redeemable**) **preferred**, which a company can buy back from investors at a stated price after a specified date. The right to call the stock allows the company to replace a relatively high fixed dividend obligation with a lower one when the cost of money has gone down. This is similar to refinancing a mortgage.

When a corporation calls a preferred stock, dividend payments cease on the call date. In return for the call privilege, the corporation may pay a premium exceeding the stock's par value at the call, such as $103 for a $100 par value stock. This can create a problem for your client who purchased callable preferred shares issued at a time when market conditions dictated relatively high dividend rates. If the cost of new money comes down, the company will call in the preferred and the investor will now have to reinvest the proceeds at a lower rate. This is an example of reinvestment risk.

Having the call price at a premium over par is one way to compensate for this additional risk (and inconvenience). Another is that the dividend rate on callable preferred stock is generally a bit higher than other preferred stock issued by the corporation.

Convertible Preferred

A preferred stock is **convertible** if the owner can exchange the shares for a fixed number of shares of common stock of the issuing corporation.

TAKE NOTE

Because the value of a convertible preferred stock is linked to the value of a common stock, the convertible's preferred price tends to fluctuate in line with the common.

Convertible preferred is generally issued with a lower stated dividend rate than nonconvertible preferred of the same quality because the investor may have the opportunity to convert to common shares and enjoy greater capital gain potential. The concept of a convertible security will be discussed in greater detail later in the next unit when we cover convertible bonds.

Adjustable-Rate Preferred

Some preferred stocks are issued with adjustable (or variable) dividend rates. Such dividends are usually tied to the rates of other interest rate benchmarks, such as Treasury bills and money market rates, and can be adjusted as often as quarterly. Because the payment adjusts to current interest rates, the price of the stock remains relatively stable.

TEST TOPIC ALERT

For investors looking for fixed income through preferred stocks, adjustable-rate would be their least appropriate choice.

TAKE NOTE

A preferred stock could be cumulative and callable, callable and convertible, or any combination of these adjectives. If none are listed, it is just a straight preferred.

EXAMPLES

1. An investor who has purchased preferred stock with the goal of receiving steady quarterly income would be most interested in the

    A. seniority of the stock compared to other securities

    B. ability of the company to continue paying the stated dividend

    C. voting power of the shares

    D. par value of the shares

    Answer: B. Investors in preferred stock with the goal of income are most concerned that the company will be able to sustain the dividend making choice **B** the correct answer. For exam purposes, all preferred stock is nonvoting and it makes no difference if the par value is $10, $25, or $100 because the dividend is fixed as a percentage return. The fact that the preferred stock has seniority over the common is important, but that concept is included in the ability of the company to pay its dividend.

2. A company that has issued cumulative preferred stock

    a. pays past and current preferred dividends before paying dividends on common stock

    b. pays the preferred dividend before paying the coupons due on its outstanding bonds

    c. pays the current dividends on the preferred, but not the past dividends on the preferred, before paying a dividend on the common

    d. forces conversion of the preferred that is trading at a discount to par, thereby eliminating the need to pay past-due dividends

Answer: A. The concept behind cumulative preferred stock is that dividends in arrears accumulate and must be paid, along with the current year's dividend, before anything can be paid to common stockholders, choice **A**. Bond interest is always paid before dividends.

BENEFITS AND RISKS OF OWNING PREFERRED STOCK

In summation, why would you include preferred stock in a client's portfolio?

- Fixed income from dividends

- Prior claim ahead of common stock

- Convertible preferred sacrifices income in exchange for potential appreciation. Although it is generally regarded as a fixed-income investment, preferred stock, unlike debt securities, usually has no preset date at which it matures and no scheduled redemption date. Preferred stock is thus a perpetual security.

In doing so, the client would be incurring the following risks:

- Market risk—in an economic downturn, fear of an inability to maintain the dividend will cause the price to drop

- Possible loss of purchasing power

- Interest rate (money rate) risk

- Business difficulties leading to possible reduction or elimination of the dividend and even bankruptcy leading to loss of principal

EMPLOYEE STOCK OPTIONS

U12LO3: Describe how incentive stock options differ from nonqualified ones.

Most of the questions on the exam deal with securities purchased by investors. There are, however a few questions where stock in a corporation is purchased from the company by its employees through the granting of stock options.

Employee stock options give an employee the right to purchase a specified number of shares of the common stock of her employer at a stated price over a stated time period. Unlike qualified retirement plans (discussed in Unit 24), there are no non-discrimination requirements for these plans. For publicly traded stock, the strike price (also called the grant or exercise price) must be at least the market price of the stock at the time the option is granted. In most cases, there is a minimum time the employee must remain with the company to be able to use the option (the vesting period). The hope of the employee is that the market price of the employer's stock will increase in value. Then, the employee will be able to purchase the stock by exercising the option (purchasing the stock) at the lower strike price and then sell the stock at the current market price. There are two principal kinds of stock option programs, each with their own rules and tax consequences: nonqualified stock options (NSOs) and incentive stock options (ISOs). Don't confuse these with publicly traded puts and calls described later in Unit 16—these are available only to employees of the issuing company. Most states require that the stock option plan be approved by the board of directors.

Nonqualified Stock Options (NSOs)

These are the more common of the two varieties of employee stock options. Unlike the ISO, which is limited to employees only, NSOs can also be offered to board members and even suppliers. NSOs are basically treated as a form of compensation. When NSOs are exercised, the difference between the current market price, (or fair market value for stock that isn't actively traded), at the time of exercise and the strike price, referred to as the *bargain element*, is reported as wages on the tax returns of the employer and the employee. Therefore, instead of capital gains treatment, the employee is taxed as ordinary income while the company receives a tax deduction as salary expense for the difference between the current market price and the strike price.

EXAMPLE

1. Four years ago, Susan was granted enough NSOs to purchase 500 shares of her employer's stock at $20 per share. Assuming Susan exercises all of her options when the fair market value of the stock is $30 and her ordinary income tax rate at the time is 28%, how much income tax will be due?

    A. $280

    B. $1,400

    C. $5,600

    D. $8,400

    Answer: B. The exercise cost of the NQSO is $10,000 (500 shares × $20 per share). She will have to pay ordinary income taxes of $1,400, choice **B**, on the bargain element [($30 FMV − $20 exercise price) × 500 shares × 28%. In addition, that $5,000 will also be subject to the same taxes as her regular salary, e.g., Social Security tax.

TAKE NOTE

Because the spread between the market price and the strike price is considered salary, it is subject to payroll taxes as well as income tax.

Incentive Stock Options (ISOs)

You might see these called *qualified* as a way of distinguishing them from NSOs. Unlike the NSO, there are generally no tax consequences to the employer with an ISO, but, if done properly, they can be more advantageous than NSOs to the employee. As mentioned, the employee's profits from NSOs are taxed as ordinary income. However, as long as stock purchased through exercise of an ISO is held at least two years after the date of grant and one year after the date of exercise, any profits are reported as long-term capital gains. If these time limits are broached, the ISO is taxed like an NSO. There is one other time stipulation—there is a maximum 10-year limit for exercise.

But, there is a catch. When an ISO is exercised, the difference between the market value at time of purchase and the strike price is a preference item used in calculating the Alternative Minimum Tax (AMT) (covered in Unit 21).

Incentive Stock Options (ISOs)

No income recognized when option is granted

No tax due when option is exercised

Tax is due when stock is sold

- Gain is capital if held at least one year and sold at least two years after grant
- Otherwise—ordinary income

Difference between option price and the FMV on date of exercise is an add back for AMT purposes

---

EXAMPLE

Jeff's employer grants him an ISO on January 1, 2015, with an exercise (strike) price of $25 per share. Jeff exercises the option on January 1, 2016, when the market price of the stock is $40 per share. Because this is an ISO and the stock has not yet been sold, there is no salary income or capital gains taxation. But, there is a $15 per share adjustment for purposes of computing the AMT.

Jeff sells the stock two years later for $60 per share. Now that the sale has been recognized and Jeff has followed the required holding periods, the $35 per share profit is taxed as long-term capital gain.

RESTRICTED STOCK

U12LO4: Contrast restricted stock and non-restricted stock.

At the beginning of this unit, we stated that one of the characteristics of stock is that it is freely transferable. That is, once purchased, it may be sold (or gifted) at any time to anyone. As is with most of this course, there are exceptions. The two that are testable deal with the sale of stock that is restricted and the stock owned by control persons.

Going back to Part 1 of this course, we discussed the exemption from registration for securities sold as part of a private placement (the limited offering exemption). In general, retail investors cannot sell these securities until having held them for a certain period; they are *restricted* from immediate resale and, therefore, are referred to as **restricted securities**. The length of that restriction is generally **6 months** and there are volume restrictions as well applying to those who are affiliates of the issuer. You probably will not be tested on those; just know that restricted stock has time limit for all investors and may also have a volume limit (for affiliates) on the amount that may be resold.

The other case is with control stock. **Control stock** is stock held by a control person. What makes it control stock is who owns it, not how it was acquired. For purposes of this discussion, a **control person** is a corporate director, officer, large stockholder, or the immediate family of any of the preceding. They are generally referred to as **affiliates** because of their unique status within the issuer. In general, purchases and sales of control stock must be reported to the SEC. Control stock always has volume limits (not tested).

TAKE NOTE

The Securities Act of 1933, unlike the Exchange Act, never defines a control person by a specific percentage of ownership. For testing purposes, assume that ownership of more than **10%** of the voting stock is considered control.

The mechanism for reporting the sale of control stock as well as the sale of restricted stock is found in SEC Rule 144 of the Securities Act of 1933. SEC Rule 144 was created so that certain resales of already existing securities could be made without having to file a complete registration statement with the SEC. The time and money involved in having to file such a registration are usually so prohibitive as to make it uneconomical for the individual seller. In almost all cases, those who wish to sell control stock or restricted stock must do so by filing a Form 144.

EXAMPLE

1. A man owns 15% of the stock of a company. His wife owns 5% of the stock of the same company. If the wife wishes to sell the stock she owns, which of the following statements are TRUE?

    I.   Both the husband and the wife are control persons.

    II. He is a control person, but she is not.

    III. She must file a Form 144.

    IV. She does not have to file a Form 144.

    A. I and III

    B. I and IV

    C. II and III

    D. II and IV

    Answer: A. His 15% ownership is control. Her 5% is not, but the fact that she is the spouse of an insider makes her one, causing this to be a sale of control stock. All sales of control stock (unless an exemption applies) must be accompanied by a Rule 144 filing on Form 144.

AMERICAN DEPOSITARY RECEIPTS

U12LO5: Identify the unique features of American Depositary Receipts (ADRs) and the risks of investing in foreign securities.

American Depositary Receipts (ADRs), also known as **American Depositary Shares (ADSs)**, facilitate the trading of foreign stocks in U.S. markets because everything is done in English and in U.S. dollars. ADRs are bought and sold (traded) in U.S. dollars, and dividends are paid out in U.S. dollars.

An **ADR** is a negotiable security that represents a receipt for shares of stock in a non-U.S. corporation. ADRs are bought and sold in the U.S. securities markets like any domestic stock.

Rights of ADR Owners

Most of the rights that common stockholders normally hold, such as the right to receive dividends, also apply to ADR owners. In fact, if the owner wishes, the ADR can be exchanged for the foreign shares upon request (although that would eliminate the benefits of the ADR).

Currency Risk

In addition to the normal risks associated with stock ownership, ADR investors are also subject to currency risk. **Currency risk** is the possibility that an investment denominated in one currency (such as the Mexican peso) could decline if the value of that currency declines in its exchange rate with the U.S. dollar. Because ADRs represent shares of stock in companies located in foreign countries, currency exchange rates are an important consideration.

TAKE NOTE

The banks collect the dividend payments, convert them into U.S. funds for U.S. owners, and withhold any required foreign tax payments. Owners of ADRs can claim a U.S. tax credit for these withholdings.

TEST TOPIC ALERT

The exam will want you to know that ADRs are issued by domestic branches of U.S. banks and that, even though they are traded in U.S. dollars, they still bear currency risk.

EXAMPLES

1. ADRs are used to facilitate

    A. foreign trading of domestic securities

    B. foreign trading of U.S. government securities

    C. domestic trading of U.S. government securities

    D. domestic trading of foreign securities

    Answer: D. Because everything is in U.S. dollars and in English, ADRs make trading in foreign securities (choice **D**) much easier for those who live here.

2. Which two of the following risks would be of greatest concern to the holder of an ADR?

    I.   Currency

    II. Liquidity

    III. Market

    IV. Purchasing power

    A. I and II

    B. I and III

    C. II and IV

    D. III and IV

    Answer: B. ADRs represent ownership in a foreign security so there is always going to be currency risk, (I). These ADRs trade in the market and have market risk (III). Because most ADRs are traded on the exchanges, there is little liquidity risk and, because they represent equity, they are usually a good hedge against inflation. Choice **B** is correct.

INVESTING IN FOREIGN MARKETS

Although foreign securities offer investors the potential for substantial gains, they bear a variety of risks that are not present with domestic investments. There are two broad market classifications of foreign markets: emerging and developed.

Emerging Markets

Emerging markets are markets in lesser developed countries. They are generally associated with:

- low levels of income, as measured by the country's gross domestic product (GDP);
- low levels of equity capitalization;
- questionable market liquidity;
- potential restrictions on currency conversion;
- high volatility;
- prospects for economic growth and development;
- stabilizing political and social institutions;
- high taxes and commission costs for foreign investor;
- restrictions on foreign ownership and on foreign currency conversion; and
- lower regulatory standards resulting in a lack of transparency.

Despite primitive market infrastructures, many emerging markets have rapid growth rates that make their securities attractive to foreign investors whose local markets experience more modest growth.

Developed Markets

Developed markets are those associated with countries that have highly developed economies with stable political and social institutions. These are characterized by:

- large levels of equity capitalization;
- low commission rates;
- few, if any, currency conversion restrictions;
- highly liquid markets with many brokerage institutions and market makers;
- many large capitalization securities; and
- well-defined regulatory schemes leading to transparency similar to that enjoyed by those investing in U.S. securities.

In summation, why would you include foreign securities in a client's portfolio?

- You have expanded the potential investment universe leading to greater diversification.

- Foreign securities sometimes outperform domestic ones.
- Foreign securities are usually not highly correlated with domestic ones (correlation was covered in Unit 10) and, as a result, the overall risk of the portfolio is reduced.

In doing so, whether investing in the securities of emerging or developed foreign markets, the investor faces, in addition to the normal risks involved in investing, the following risks not present in domestic investing:

- Country risk
- Exchange controls
- Currency risk
- Withholding taxes and fees

Country Risk

Country risk is a composite of all the risks of investing in a particular country. These may include political risks, such as revolutions or military coups, and structural risks, such as confiscatory policies toward profits, capital gains, and dividends. Economic policies, interest rates, and inflation are also elements of risk of investing in emerging countries.

Exchange Controls

Foreign investors can also be subject to restrictions on currency conversion or movement.

Withholding, Fees, and Taxes

Some foreign countries may withhold a portion of dividends and capital gains for taxes. Some also impose heavy fees and taxes on securities that the investor must bear in addition to generally higher brokerage commissions.

FUNDAMENTAL ANALYSIS

U12LO6: Evaluate the methods used to determine the value of equity securities.

The two approaches most commonly used to select investments are fundamental and technical analysis. Both fundamental and technical analysts attempt to forecast prices or values of securities and markets.

Fundamental analysts evaluate broad-based economic trends, current business conditions within an industry, and the quality of a particular corporation's business, finances, and management. **Technical analysts** attempt to predict the direction of prices on the basis of charts reflecting price and trading volume patterns of specific securities without regard to the issuer's profitability.

Fundamental analysis is the study of the business prospects of an individual company within the context of its industry and the overall economy. They do this by examining the company in detail, including the financial statements and company management. We could compare this to an individual receiving a full physical examination which, in addition to all kinds of tests, would include a detailed family medical history. With a company, the financial statement analysis is like the blood tests, X-rays, stress test, and so forth, and the evaluation of the company's management is like the medical history. In U10LO7, we described the P/E ratio, one of the most popular tools for evaluating the reasonableness of a stock's market price. Another of the ways these analysts attempt to determine the value of common stock is through the use of dividend models.

Dividend Models

Some analysts believe that the value of a stock can be determined based upon current or anticipated dividends. The models work best with a company with dividends that are paid with regularity, so it is more popular with larger, well-established organizations than smaller companies with irregular dividend distributions. Two models used are the dividend discount model and the dividend growth model.

Dividend Discount Model

This model states that the current market value of a stock should be equal to the present value of all future dividends. There are several methods to use, such as assuming constant or variable dividends, but the concept is still the same. We take the investor's expected future returns (the dividends), and then discount that amount to compute the present value. It is not necessary to know the formula for the exam; however, it can be calculated by dividing the annual dividend by the expected return, sometimes referred to as the required rate of return. For example, if a stock pays a $1.20 dividend and the required rate of return in the marketplace is 6%, the stock should be worth $20 (1.20 / 0.06). If it is priced above that, it might be overvalued; if less, undervalued.

This tool may also be used to value preferred stock. Let's take a look at the following example.

EXAMPLE

If you have a $100 par, 6% preferred stock and the required rate of return is 8%, what should the current market price of the stock be? You might encounter a question similar to this on the exam and you solve it by dividing the $6 dividend (6% of the $100 par) by the 8% required rate of return: $6.00 / 0.08 = $75. In other words, if this preferred stock is selling for $75 per share, the $6 annual dividend will produce an 8% return on your investment.

Dividend Growth Model

This model assumes that the amount of the annual dividend will grow at a constant rate. Because projections of future growth can be hazy, this model is best used in conjunction with other forecasting tools. It is not necessary to know the formula for the exam; however, it should be obvious that the computed value will be higher when dividends are expected to grow rather than remain the same.

TEST TOPIC ALERT

If you are asked on the exam, "Which model computes a higher current stock price?" it should be common sense that the answer that factors in growth is the correct answer. Remember, you will never have to do this computation on the test.

EXAMPLE

1. Among the popular methods of valuing equity securities is the dividend growth model. One could expect to see an analyst using this to value any of these EXCEPT

   A. common stock

   B. ADRs represent common stock in a foreign company

   C. preferred stock

   D. none of these are exceptions

   Answer: C. To use the dividend growth model, there must be a possibility of dividend growth. Because preferred stock dividends are fixed, this tool would not make any sense.

TECHNICAL ANALYSIS

While fundamental analysis looks at the company, technical analysis looks at the market. A fundamental analyst attempts to measure the business or financial risk inherent in investing in a particular security, whereas technical analysis is used by an analyst to measure the market risk assumed when investing in a particular security. You have to know the goal of technical analysis and several of the more popular technical systems.

Technical analysis is a method of attempting to predict stock price trends over the near term, generally four to six weeks. The prediction is based on current stock price trends and the relationship of the present trend to prior trends. These trends are measured through charts of price movements; therefore, it would be correct to say that a technician uses charts to attempt to predict future price movements in an effort to reduce timing risk (buying a stock at the wrong time). In using these charts of price movements, a technician also uses the trading volume of the stock in an attempt to validate the trends. Let's start by defining some key terms.

TAKE NOTE

A technical analyst **charts** a stock's **price** and **volume** over a period of **time**.

Trendlines

In an effort to see where the price of stock may be going, the technician charts where it has been. He attempts to determine from his chart what the trend has been by drawing a trendline. A popular saying is, "the trend is your friend."

Support and Resistance

Chartists believe that one can understand more about a stock by studying its chart. Two of the most important conclusions drawn from a chart are the support levels and resistance levels. The **support level** is that price where the stock price bottoms. That is, once it gets that low, there becomes an imbalance between buyers and sellers (more investors seek to buy than sell) and the price begins to rise. The opposite is the **resistance level** where the stock's price reaches a high enough level where there are now more sellers than buyers and the stock no longer rises in price. Just think of the English definitions of the terms and it makes sense. That is, support is where you stop falling and resistance is where you can't go any higher.

Breakout

When the price movement penetrates the support or the resistance level, it is known as a **breakout**. The analyst believes that once a breakout has been confirmed, there will be rapid price movement in the direction of the break until a new support or resistance level is established. The technician believes that if a breakout through **resistance** can be spotted, it represents a good buying opportunity for those quick enough to take advantage. Conversely, a breakout through the support level would represent a good opportunity for short sellers able to move quickly.

Moving Averages

To avoid the volatility frequently present in stock price trends, analysts will use the moving average. A **moving average** attempts to modify the fluctuations of stock prices into a smoothed trend; the distortions are reduced to a minimum. For example, to plot a 13-week moving average on a particular stock, take the Friday closing price for each of the previous 13 weeks, add them together, and divide by 13. That number will be the average closing price for the last 13 weeks and that number is plotted. The next week you would add the new closing price for that week and delete the closing price for the first week used, 14 weeks ago. This average would be plotted on the same chart as the actual current price movement of the stock. Changes in the trend of the stock being plotted are identified, not by a change in the direction of the moving average, but by the price of the security crossing over the moving average. If the stock price moved below the moving average, it is usually a signal of a change from a rising to declining market. The reverse is also true.

TECHNICAL MARKET THEORIES

Technical analysts follow various theories regarding market trends.

Short Interest Theory

Short interest refers to the number of shares that have been sold short. Because short positions must be repurchased eventually, some analysts believe that short interest reflects mandatory demand that creates a support level for stock prices. It seems counterintuitive, but high short interest is a bullish indicator, and low short interest is a bearish indicator.

Odd-Lot Theory

Typically, small investors engage in **odd-lot trading**, which is transactions of fewer than 100 shares. **Odd-lot theorists** believe that small investors invariably buy and sell at the wrong times. When odd-lot traders buy, odd-lot analysts are bearish. When odd-lot traders sell, odd-lot analysts are bullish.

Advance/Decline Theory

The number of issues closing up or down on a specific day reflects market breadth. The number of advances and declines can be a significant indication of the market's relative strength. When declines outnumber advances by a large amount, the market is bearish even if it closed higher. In bull markets, advances substantially outnumber declines. Technical analysts plot daily advances and declines on a graph to produce an advance/decline line that gives them an indication of market breadth trends.

EXAMPLES

1. In the assessment of a company's stock, a technical analyst takes into consideration all of the following EXCEPT

   A. earnings

   B. market price

   C. price trends

   D. volume

   Answer: A. Remember our key phrase: A technical analyst *charts* a stock's *price* and *volume* over a period of *time*. It is the fundamental analyst who focuses on the company's performance, such as earnings.

2. Proponents of which of the following technical theories assume that small investors are usually wrong?

   A. Advance/decline

   B. Moving averages

   C. Odd lot

   D. Short interest

   Answer: C. Odd lots are usually traded by small investors; some analysts believe small investors are generally wrong, making choice **C** correct.

Types and Characteristics of Fixed Income (Debt) Securities and Methods Used to Determine Their Value

In addition to raising capital through the issuance of equity securities (stock), many corporations fund their business efforts through borrowing by issuing debt securities. Long-term borrowing is usually in the form of bonds and debentures, while cash equivalents, such as commercial paper and Treasury bills, are the primary source of short-term financing for corporations and the U.S. government.

Governmental bodies can only issue debt securities (you cannot buy stock in the U.S. Treasury or your state).

The Series 65 exam will include seven questions on the material presented in this unit.

LEARNING OBJECTIVES

When you have completed this unit, you will be able to accomplish the following.

U13LO1: Recognize the unique features of U.S. Government and Agency issues including TIPS bonds.

U13LO2: Compute the price of government and corporate bonds.

U13LO3: Differentiate between secured (collateralized) and unsecured corporate debt.

U13LO4: Identify the relevance of a bond's rating.

U13LO5: Describe the unique features of municipal bonds.

U13LO6: Compute the tax-equivalent yield of municipal bonds.

U13LO7: Describe the advantages and disadvantages of investing in foreign bonds.

U13LO8: Recall the methods of repayment of principal.

U13LO9: Compute the parity price of a convertible security.

U13LO10: Compare current yield, yield to maturity, and yield to call.

U13LO11: Evaluate the effect of a bond's duration on its market price.

U13LO12: Describe how discounted cash flow is used to estimate the value of an investment.

U13LO13: Identify the special characteristics of money market instruments and the risks and benefits of adding them to a client's portfolio.

U13LO14: Contrast demand deposit accounts (DDAs) with time deposits accounts.

FIXED INCOME (DEBT SECURITIES)

Debt capital represents money loaned to an issuer by investors purchasing that issuer's bonds. A **bond** represents the issuer's indebtedness. There is, in essence, a contract between the borrower (the issuer) and the lender (the investor). The terms of the loan are expressed in a document known as the bond's **indenture**. The indenture, sometimes also referred to as the deed of trust, states the issuer's obligation to pay back a specific amount of money on a specific date. The indenture also states the issuer's obligation to pay the investor a specific rate of interest for the use of the funds as well as any collateral pledged as security for the loan and all other pertinent details. An investor purchasing a bond is lending the issuer money for a set period at a fixed annual interest rate. That rate is frequently referred to as the *coupon* rate because, years ago, bonds were issued with detachable coupons that were presented for collection of the interest. That is no longer the case, but the term coupon is still in common use.

It is important to understand that debt capital refers to **long-term debt** financing. Long-term debt is money borrowed for a minimum of five years, although more frequently the length of time is 20–30 years.

There are three major issuers of debt securities. The largest issuer of debt securities is the U.S. government. Corporations issue bonds to finance their operations and substantial sums are also borrowed by state governments and those political entities that are subdivisions of a state, such as cities, counties, towns, and so forth. These issues from state and local political entities are called **municipal bonds**.

Let us begin this adventure by explaining the different types of bonds and their issuers.

U.S. GOVERNMENT SECURITIES

U13LO1: Recognize the unique features of U.S. Government and Agency issues including TIPS bonds.

Whenever the word government is used in conjunction with a security on the exam, it means the federal government. U.S. Government bonds are the safest of all. There are two primary types of backing; direct government backing or guarantee, as in the case of Treasury issues, and the moral guarantee as in the case of federal agencies.

U.S. Treasury Bills

Treasury bills are direct short-term debt obligations of the U.S. government. They are issued every week by using a competitive bidding process. Each week, T-bills, as they are known, with maturities of 4 weeks, 8 weeks, 13 weeks, 26 weeks, are issued and once each 4 weeks, 52 week bills are issued.

Treasury bills pay no interest; they are issued at a discount from their par value. An investor might purchase a $10,000, 26-week T-bill at a price of $9,800. No interest would be received, but, at maturity, the Treasury would send the investor a check for $10,000. The difference between the $9,800 paid and the $10,000 received would be considered interest income even though a separate interest check was never received.

TAKE NOTE

Key points to remember regarding T-bills include: (1) Treasury bills are always issued and traded at a discount; (2) Treasury bills are the only Treasury security issued without a stated interest rate; (3) Treasury bills are highly liquid; and (4) 13-week (also referred to as 91-day) Treasury bills are used in market analysis as the stereotypical "risk-free" investment, especially in computations that refer to the risk-free rate. We discussed that in Unit 10 with alpha and will have more about that in Part 4.

U.S. Treasury Notes

U.S. Treasury notes are direct debt obligations of the U.S. Treasury with the following characteristics.

- They pay semiannual interest as a percentage of the stated par value.
- They have intermediate maturities (2, 3, 5, 7, and 10 years).
- They mature at par value.
- They are noncallable.

U.S. Treasury Bonds

U.S. Treasury bonds are direct debt obligations of the U.S. Treasury with the following characteristics.

- They pay semiannual interest as a percentage of the stated par value.
- They have long-term maturities, generally 10–30 years.
- They mature at par value.

TAKE NOTE

When doing any calculations relating to bonds on the exam, the par or face value will always be $1,000. This is true even though the previous three Treasury issues are available in denominations as low as $100. Furthermore, all government securities are only available in book entry form. That means there are no certificates issued—records of the investor's ownership are "on the books" of the Treasury Department.

EXAMPLE

1. When Treasury bills are issued, they are quoted at

    A. a premium over par

    B. 100% of the par value

    C. par value with interest coupons attached

    D. a discount from principal with no coupons attached

    Answer: D. Treasury bills are always issued at a discount, they pay no interest. The investor profits by receiving back par value and makes the difference between the discounted purchase price and the par received at maturity. All government bonds are now book entry (electronic record); there has not been a Treasury note or bond issued since July 1986 with interest coupons attached.

Treasury Inflation Protection Securities (TIPS)

A special type of Treasury issue, **Treasury Inflation Protection Securities (TIPS)**, helps protect investors against purchasing power risk. These notes are issued with a fixed interest rate, but the principal amount is adjusted semiannually by an amount equal to the change in the Consumer Price Index, the standard measurement of inflation. They are issued with maturities of 5, 10, and 30 years.

The interest payment the investor receives every six months is equal to the fixed interest rate times the newly adjusted principal. During times of inflation, the interest payments increase, while during times of deflation, the interest payments fall. These notes are sold at lower interest rates than conventional fixed-rate Treasury notes because of their adjustable nature.

Like other Treasury securities, TIPS are exempt from state and local income taxes on the interest income generated, but are subject to federal taxation. However, in any year when the principal is adjusted for inflation, that increase is considered reportable income for that year even though the increase will not be received until the note matures.

TEST TOPIC ALERT

Interest payments from TIPS, and increases in the principal of TIPS, are subject to federal tax, but exempt from state and local income taxes.

EXAMPLE

If you have a TIPS bond with a 3% coupon and the annual inflation rate is 4% for the next two years, here is what happens:

Each six months, you will receive 1.5% (half of the annual 3% coupon) of the principal value as adjusted for the inflation rate. If the inflation rate is 4% per year, that is 2% each six months. So, after the first semiannual period, the principal value of the bond is now $1,020 ($1,000 + 2% of $1,000, or 102% × $1,000). Therefore, the first interest check will be 1.5% × $1,020, or $15.30. Six months later, the adjusted principal value is $1,040.40 (102% × $1,020), so that interest check will be for $15.61 ($1,040.40 × 1.5%). As we continue into the next year, the principal will increase to $1,061.21 ($1,040.40 × 102%) and the interest check will be for $15.92. Because we're only looking at two years, the ending principal value will be $1,082.43 with the final interest check of $16.24. As you can see, both the income from the TIPS and its principal value are increasing at a compounded rate based upon inflation.

We know that some of you may be mathematically challenged so here is a shortcut that will always work. The key to the increased principal value of the TIPS is that the interest is compounding. But, you don't have to do that. In this example, the inflation rate is 4%. Using just simple interest would mean that the principal would increase by $40 (4% of $1,000) per year. After two years, that would be $80 or a new principal amount of $1,080. However, we know that compounding will give us more so we choose the first number given in the answers that is above $1,080. The same trick can be used to determine the final interest payment. We take 1.5% of $1,080 ($16.20) and look for an answer choice that is slightly higher.

TEST TOPIC ALERT

The Series 65 exam may ask questions similar to the following.

EXAMPLES

1. A customer wishes to buy a security providing periodic interest payments, safety of principal, and protection from purchasing power risk. The customer should purchase

   A. TIPS

   B. TIGRS

   C. CMOs

   D. STRIPS

   Answer: A. TIPS offer inflation protection and safety of principal because they are backed by the U.S. government.

2. A client has a TIPS with a coupon rate of 4.5%. The inflation rate has been 7% for the last year. What is the inflation-adjusted return?

   A. −2.5%

   B. 4.5%

   C. 7.0%

   D. 11.5%

   Answer: B. TIPS adjust the principal value every 6 months to account for the inflation rate. Therefore, the real rate of return will always be the coupon.

GNMA SECURITIES

There is one more security guaranteed by the full faith and credit of the U.S. Government. The Government National Mortgage Association (Ginnie Mae or GNMA) is a wholly owned government corporation. The primary difference between GNMA securities and the agency securities that we will cover next is the backing of the federal government.

Ginnie Maes are known as modified pass-through certificates. They represent an interest in pools of FHA-insured mortgages or Veterans-Administration-guaranteed mortgages. The term *pass-through* is used because, as the homeowners make their monthly mortgage payments, those payments are collected in the pool and proportionately passes through to the investor. This payment received by the investor differs from most other securities in two respects.

First, payments are received monthly, because underlying the security is a pool of home mortgages, which are paid for monthly. Second, each monthly payment the investor receives consists partly of interest and partly of principal. Because payments on home mortgages consist of interest and some principal and, because that money goes into the pool for all the investors, as it is paid out monthly, some of each monthly payment to the investor represents principal, and the balance of each payment represents interest. The portion of each monthly payment representing interest is subject to state and local taxation and, of course, federal income tax as well. Ginnie Maes carry a minimum denomination of $25,000 and then in $1,000 increments.

U.S. Federal Agency Securities

In addition to those securities issued directly by the U.S. Treasury, the exam covers those issued by U.S. government agencies. These are known as government-sponsored enterprises (GSEs). These are quasi-governmental organizations with the power to raise funds by borrowing (which does not carry the full faith and credit of the Federal Government) or to guarantee the debt of others. Although there are a number of agencies authorized to issue securities, the exam is most likely to limit its coverage to those issuing mortgage-backed securities. Although the securities do not have direct Treasury backing, they are considered moral obligations of the U.S. government. As such, they are generally considered second only to government securities in terms of safety.

Federal National Mortgage Association

The Federal National Mortgage Association (Fannie Mae) purchases and sells real estate mortgages—primarily those insured by the Federal Housing Administration (FHA) or guaranteed by the Veterans Administration (VA). Then, Fannie Mae issues bonds backed by those mortgages. They are issued at par and pay semiannual interest. That interest is taxable at all levels; state, local, and federal. Like the other federal issues, they come out in book entry form. Stock in Fannie Mae is publicly traded.

Whether a Ginnie Mae or a Fannie Mae, the debt obligation is backed by a pool of mortgages. In reality, only a small percentage of mortgages last the full term. People move and sell their home or they may refinance the mortgage. Whatever the reason, most mortgages are paid off early. This leads to an unusual risk for those owning mortgage-backed securities—*prepayment risk*. Why do people refinance their mortgage? Usually, it is because interest rates have fallen and they can get a new mortgage with a lower interest cost. In that case, the investor receives back the principal ahead of schedule and now has to reinvest at the current lower rates available. Prepayment risk is a form of reinvestment risk.

Benefits to Investors

The primary advantage of investing in mortgage-backed securities is that, compared with other debt securities with similar ratings, they pay a higher rate of return.

Risks to Investors

There are a number of risks faced by investors in these securities:

- they are among the most complicated instruments and are, therefore, difficult to understand;
- prepayment risk due to mortgages being refinanced when rates drop;
- default risk, particularly if the mortgages are subprime;
- reinvestment risk; and
- liquidity risk.

Tennessee Valley Authority (TVA)

One final agency that might be tested is the TVA. The TVA is the nation's largest public power provider and a corporation of the U.S. government. TVA bonds are not backed by the U.S. government. Instead, they're backed by the revenues generated by the agencies' projects.

However, credit-rating agencies perceive that there is an "implicit government guarantee of TVA bonds." If push came to shove, it's a good bet that Uncle Sam would make that guarantee explicit.

EXAMPLE

1. All of the following debt instruments pay interest semiannually EXCEPT
   A. Ginnie Mae pass-through certificates
   B. U.S. Treasury notes
   C. U.S. Treasury bonds
   D. TIPS

   Answer: A. A unique feature of Ginnie Maes (choice **A**) is that they pay interest on a monthly basis, not semiannually. In addition to the interest, investors receive their share of that portion of the mortgage payments that represented principal repayment.

BOND PRICING

U13LO2: Compute the price of government and corporate bonds.

It is important to understand how the market prices of bonds are quoted. Look at the following examples to see how corporates, municipals, and governments are quoted. Remember, par or face value is always $1,000.

Corporates and Municipal

- Corporate and municipal bonds are quoted as a percentage of par where 100% = $1,000.
- Each bond point represents $10, and the fractions are in eighths: each 1/8 = $1.25.
  - A bond quoted at 90¼ = $902.50.
  - A bond quoted at 101¾ = $1,017.50.

Governments

- Government bonds are quoted as a percentage of par.
- Each point is $10, and each .1 represents 1/32 of $10 ($0.3125).
  - A government bond quoted at 90.8 (or 90.08) = $902.50.
  - A government bond quoted at 101.24 = $1,017.50.

TAKE NOTE

In recent years, some quote systems have added a 0 for prices between .1 and .9 to avoid confusion (similar to the way you enter the expiration date for your credit card as 01/2020 instead of 1/2020). That is why, in the previous example, we show you both 90.8 and 90.08—they both mean 90 8/32.

EXAMPLE

When you see a corporate bond quoted at 103½, it represents a market price of $1,035. The 103 is 103% of $1,000, or $1,030, and the ½ is half of a $10 point, or $5. On a Treasury bond, that same price would be shown as 103.16 where the .16 is 16/32s or ½.

BOND LISTINGS

If you were to look up a bond in the newspaper or other source for a quote, you might see something like this:

DEF 5s35 @106.

What does that mean? The DEF is the issuer, the 5 is the nominal or coupon rate, the 35 is the maturity date of 2035 and the 106 is the price ($1,060). So, what is the "s"? It is nothing but a separation between the coupon and the maturity date.

SECURED DEBT

U13LO3: Differentiate between secured (collateralized) and unsecured corporate debt.

Corporate debt securities, like any other loan, may be either secured or unsecured. **Secured debt securities** are backed by various kinds of assets of the issuing corporation, whereas **unsecured debt securities** are backed only by the reputation, credit record, and financial stability of the corporation. Regardless of whether secured or unsecured, the interest on debt securities is always paid before dividends on stock (preferred and common).

Mortgage Bonds

Just as the owner of a home pledges a real asset (the home and land) as collateral for the mortgage, a corporation will borrow money backed by real estate and physical assets of the corporation. Just as a home ordinarily would have a market value greater than the principal amount of its mortgage, the value of the real assets pledged by the corporation will be in excess of the amount borrowed under that bond issue. If the corporation develops financial problems and is unable to pay the interest on the bonds, those real assets pledged as collateral are generally sold to pay off the mortgage bondholders. There may be a situation where foreclosing on the property results in a sale below the outstanding mortgage balance. In that case, the mortgage holder becomes a general creditor for the unsatisfied balance.

Equipment Trust Certificates

Corporations, particularly railroads and airline companies, finance the acquisition of their rolling stock, locomotives, or airplanes by issuing an equipment trust certificate. The company makes a down payment, usually 20% of the cost of the rolling stock, and finances the balance over the course of time, for example, 15 years. Because the equipment does wear out, the railroad will pay off a portion of the loan on an annual basis. At no time, theoretically, is the value of the assets (the rolling stock, locomotives, or planes) worth less than the amount of the principal remaining on the loan. When the company has finished paying off the loan, it receives clear title to its equipment from the trustee. If the company does not make the payments, the lender repossesses the collateral and sells it for his benefit. If you have ever financed the purchase of a car, it is basically the same concept.

Collateral Trust Bonds

Sometimes a corporation wants to borrow money and has neither real estate (for a mortgage) nor equipment (for an equipment trust) to use as collateral. Instead, it deposits securities it owns into a trust to serve as collateral for the lenders. The securities it deposits can be securities in that corporation or any other securities as long as the securities are marketable, that is, readily liquidated. Obviously, the better the quality of the securities deposited as collateral, the better the quality and rating of the bond. You might see these called collateral trust certificates.

Debentures

A **debenture** is a debt obligation of the corporation backed only by its word and general creditworthiness. Debentures are written promises of the corporation to pay the principal at its due date and interest on a regular basis. Although this promise is as binding as a promise for a mortgage bond, debentures are not secured by any pledge of property. They are sold on the general credit of the company; their security depends on the assets and earnings of the corporation. Although debentures are unsecured, there are issuers whose credit standing is so good that their debentures are safer than mortgage bonds of less creditworthy companies. This is similar in concept to the extension of credit on your credit cards; the better your credit rating, the higher the limit and the lower the interest rate.

Guaranteed Bonds

A **guaranteed bond** is a bond that is guaranteed as to payment of interest, or both principal and interest, by a corporate entity other than the issuer. The value of the guarantee is only as good as the strength of the company making that guarantee. Guaranteed bonds were particularly popular in the railroad industry in which a major railroad seeking to lease trackage rights from a short line would guarantee that smaller company's debt. A more recent example is the ExxonMobil Corporation guaranteeing the debt issues of the Exxon Pipeline Company.

Senior

The word *senior* is used to describe the relative priority of claim of a security. Every preferred stock has a senior claim to common stock. Every debt security has senior claim to preferred stock. Secured bonds have a senior claim to unsecured debt, such as debentures. The term *senior securities* means bonds and preferred stock, because they have a claim senior to common stock. If an exam question described a corporation as having issued senior bonds, the answer would have to state that there were mortgage bonds and/or collateral trust bonds and/or equipment trust certificates issued by that corporation with prior claim ahead of unsecured creditors.

Subordinated

The term *subordinated* means "belonging to a lower or inferior class or rank; secondary." It is usually describing a debenture. A subordinated debenture has a claim that is behind (junior to) that of any other creditor. However, no matter how subordinated the debenture, it is still senior to any stockholder.

EXAMPLE

1. A debenture is issued based on

    A. the general credit of the corporation

    B. a pledge of real estate

    C. a pledge of equipment

    D. the ability to levy taxes

    Answer: A. There are no pledged assets behind a debenture, merely the credit standing of the corporation, choice **A**. It is a corporate IOU.

TEST TOPIC ALERT

When examining the capital structure of a corporation, it is important to know the liquidation priority:

■ Secured creditors, (e.g., mortgage bonds, equipment trust certificates, collateral trust bonds)

■ Unsecured creditors, (e.g., general creditors including debenture holders)

■ Subordinated debt holders

■ Preferred stockholders

■ Common stockholders

RATINGS

U13LO4: Identify the relevance of a bond's rating.

The purchase of a debt security is only as safe as the strength of the borrower and what is received for collateral. Because safety of the bond will frequently be a very important consideration for clients, most investors consult the rating services. The two primary rating organizations for debt securities are Standard & Poor's and Moody's. Both organizations have highly qualified personnel who analyze all the details of the debt issue and arrive at a letter rating indicating their opinion of the debt's quality (safety). The following chart should give you all the information you need for the exam.

Standard & Poor's Bond Ratings		Moody's Ratings	
AAA	Bonds of highest quality	Aaa	Bonds of highest quality
AA	High-quality debt obligations	Aa	Bonds of high quality
A	Bonds that have a strong capacity to pay interest and principal but may be susceptible to adverse effects	A	Bonds whose security of principal and interest is considered adequate but may be impaired in the future
BBB	Bonds that have an adequate capacity to pay interest and principal but are more vulnerable to adverse economic conditions or changing circumstances	Baa	Bonds of medium grade that are neither highly protected nor poorly secured
BB	Bonds of lower medium grade with few desirable investment characteristics	Ba	Bonds of speculative quality whose future cannot be considered well assured
B	Primarily speculative bonds with great uncertainties and major risk if exposed to adverse conditions	B	Bonds that lack characteristics of a desirable investment
CCC	Bonds in poor standing that may be defaulted	Caa	Bonds in poor standing that may be defaulted
C	Income bonds on which no interest is being paid	Ca	Speculative bonds that are often in default
D	Bonds in default	C	Bonds with little probability of any investment value (lowest rating)

Note:	Note:
Plus (+) and minus (−) are used to show relative strength within a rating category.	For ratings Aa through B, 1 indicates the high, 2 indicates the middle, and 3 indicates the low end of the rating class.

Investment-Grade Debt

In the industry, bonds rated in the top four categories (BBB or Baa and higher) are referred to as investment grade. Investment-grade bonds are generally the only quality eligible for purchase by the institutions (e.g., banks or insurance companies) and by fiduciaries and, therefore, have greater liquidity than lower-grade instruments.

High-Yield Bonds

Lower-grade bonds, known in the industry as junk bonds, are now more commonly called high-yield bonds. Because of their lower ratings (BB or Ba or lower) and additional risk of default, high-yield bonds may be subject to substantial price erosion during slow economic times or when a bond issuer's creditworthiness is questioned. Their volatility is usually substantially higher than investment-grade bonds, but they may be suitable for sophisticated investors seeking higher returns and possible capital appreciation from speculative fixed-income investments.

There is a critical relationship in all investments known as the risk-reward relationship. The more risk an investor takes, the greater must be the reward. The less creditworthy the borrower, the more risk to the lender, so the greater reward the lender must receive to compensate for that risk. That is why lower-rated bonds carry higher rates of return.

It is important to understand that when the raters evaluate a bond they look at all the factors, including collateral. A mortgage bond is not necessarily safer than any debenture.

EXAMPLE

1. According to Standard and Poor's rating system, the four highest grades of bonds (from best to lowest grade) are

   A. Aaa, Aa, A, and Baa

   B. A, Aa, Aaa, and B

   C. B, A, AA, and AAA

   D. AAA, AA, A, and BBB

Answer: D. Choice A would be correct if the question referred to Moody's.

MUNICIPAL BONDS

U13LO5: Describe the unique features of municipal bonds.

Whenever the phrase "municipal security" is used on the exam, it is referring to a debt security issued by a state or political subdivision, e.g., city, county, school district. Although there are short-term obligations, the exam will likely only deal with long-term debt (bonds). Among the key investment features of municipal bonds are the tax treatment (the interest is generally free from federal income tax—covered shortly) and the safety. The record of safety of principal and interest payments of municipal bonds is second only to that of government issues. There is another unique feature of these securities. You can purchase municipal bonds where the scheduled payment of interest and repayment of the principal at maturity are insured—the issuer has taken out an insurance policy from one of several consortiums that offers this kind of protection. There are two basic types of municipal bonds.

General Obligation Bonds (GOs)

GOs bonds are backed by a pledge of the issuer's full faith and credit for prompt payment of principal and interest. Most city, county, and school district bonds have the further distinction of being secured by a pledge of unlimited ad valorem (property) taxes to be levied against all taxable property. Because GOs are geared to tax resources, they are normally analyzed in terms of the size of the resources being taxed. They are generally very safe.

Revenue Bonds

Revenue bonds are payable from the earnings of a revenue-producing enterprise, such as a water, sewer, electric or gas system, toll bridge, airport, college dormitory, or other income-producing facility.

Authorities and agencies are created by states or their subdivisions to perform specific functions, such as the operation of water, sewer, or electric systems, bridges, tunnels, or highways, and in some states, to construct schools or public facilities. In some cases, the authority has the right to levy fees and charges for its services. In other cases, it receives lease rentals, which may be payable from specific revenues. The yield, generally, is higher for this type of bond than for a GO (taxes are more secure than revenues).

TAX-EQUIVALENT YIELD

U13LO6: Compute the tax-equivalent yield of municipal bonds.

One final factor to be considered in the analysis of debt securities is taxability. When it comes to taxation, the interest on corporate bonds is taxed as ordinary income on both state and federal tax returns, while the interest on Treasury debt is only taxable on the federal level. Municipal bonds have one important characteristic that sets them apart from all other securities. In most cases, interest received from municipal bonds is free of federal income tax, and if the investor resides in the issuer's state, it is generally free of state income tax as well.

Assume an investor has $2,000 to invest. If he purchases, at par, one corporate or government bond of standard size ($1,000) with a 10% nominal (coupon) yield, he would receive $100 per year paid by two semiannual interest checks of $50. For purposes of this example, assume that he is in the 28% federal income tax bracket. An individual in the 28% tax bracket pays tax on any additional income earned at a rate of 28%. Therefore, on the $100 in interest he received, he would pay the IRS $28 (28%) and keep the other $72.

The other $1,000 he had available to invest was used to purchase a $1,000 par-value municipal bond with a 7.5% nominal yield. He would receive $75 annually on that bond paid by two semiannual interest checks of $37.50. The 10% bonds, on which the interest is taxable, would net $72 per year after taxes. Of the $75 interest received for the 7.5% municipal, none of it is taxed; the whole amount is kept. Therefore, a client in the 28% bracket should purchase 7.5% municipals before 10% corporates. The taxable equivalent yield of a 7.5% tax-free bond for this investor in the 28% tax bracket would be the tax-free yield divided by (100% minus the tax bracket). In this case, 7.5 / (100 − 28), or 0.72. That equals 10.42%, so it is obvious that the 7.5% municipal bond will provide a higher after-tax return.

There are two ways to work with tax-equivalent yield (TEY). The first we've just done. That is, given the coupon on a municipal bond and the investor's tax bracket, divide that coupon by (100 − tax bracket) to determine what a taxable security would have to pay to give the same after-tax return.

Alternatively, we might know the taxable security's coupon and the investor's tax bracket and we want to know what the tax-free bond must yield to give us an equivalent yield. For example, a taxable bond is paying 8% interest and the investor is in the 30% tax bracket. Therefore, the investor will pay taxes equal to 2.4% (30% of the 8%). After paying taxes, the investor will keep the other 5.6% (8% − 2.4%). So, a tax-free bond paying 5.6% will offer a TEY equal to the 8% one.

TEST TOPIC ALERT

The TEY for a municipal bond issued by an entity within a state with a state income tax will have a higher TEY to a resident of that state due to the "double" tax exemption.

TAKE NOTE

The formula for computing TEY is:

Municipal bond coupon divided by (100%—investor's tax bracket).

Therefore, if the coupon rate (nominal yield) of the municipal bond is 4.2% and the investor is in the 40% tax bracket, you would divide 4.2% by (100% − 40%) or 4.2% by 60% and arrive at a TEY of 7%. That is, in order to receive the same after-tax benefit, this investor would have to purchase a taxable bond (corporate or government) with a coupon of 7%. This can be easily proven by taking the 7% yield and reducing it by the 40% tax which results in 7% minus 2.8% tax or 4.2%.

EXAMPLE

1. If an investor in the 27% federal income tax bracket invests in municipal general obligation bonds selling at par with a coupon of 4.5%, what is the tax equivalent yield?

    A. 3.29%

    B. 5.72%

    C. 6.16%

    D. 16.67%

    Answer: C. The formula for computing tax equivalent yield is: nominal (coupon) yield divided by (1 − federal income tax rate) 0.045 / (1 − 0.27) = 6.16%.

FOREIGN BONDS

U13LO7: Describe the advantages and disadvantages of investing in foreign bonds.

Many investors choose to diversify their portfolios by investing in bonds issued by sovereign foreign governments. Some, such as the *gilts* (a gilt is a U.K. liability issued by the British Treasury and listed on the London Stock Exchange), are extremely safe. Others, especially those issued by countries with a less established financial structure, can be very risky, and may even carry a rating equivalent to a junk bond. In addition, it is also possible to invest in corporate debt securities issued by foreign business entities. Once again, there is a great variation in risk. The advantages of investing in foreign bonds include:

- Potentially higher returns
- Diversification
- Hedging against a drop in value of the U.S. dollar

Risks would include those found with all debt securities plus:

- Currency risk (if the foreign currency falls in value against the dollar)
- Potentially higher risk of default
- Generally less liquidity
- Generally higher trading costs

In a later unit, we will discuss how most investors use pooled investment vehicles, such as mutual funds, to invest in foreign debt securities.

Eurobonds and Eurodollar Bonds

A **eurobond** is any long-term debt instrument issued and sold outside the country of the currency in which it is denominated. A U.S. dollar-denominated eurobond, or Eurodollar bond, is a bond issued by a non-American company (or government), sold outside the United States and the issuer's country, but for which the principal and interest are stated and paid in U.S. dollars. Foreign corporations, foreign governments, domestic corporations, and domestic governments (including municipalities) can issue Eurodollar bonds. The U.S. government does not issue Eurodollar bonds. These bonds are not limited to European issuers; that's just where they originated. For example, if an Indian bank held dollar-denominated bonds issued by a Korean company, the term *Eurodollar bond* would still apply.

TEST TOPIC ALERT

Test questions sometimes ask you to contrast eurobonds and Eurodollar bonds. The name of the instrument tells you how principal and interest is paid. Eurodollar bonds pay in U.S. dollars; eurobonds pay in foreign currency. Note that these instruments must be issued outside of the United States. The primary reason for issuing these bonds is that they are free from the requirement to register with the SEC, resulting in lower issuance costs. However, because the liquidity is not as great as with domestic issues and because the political and country risks tend to be higher, yields are generally higher.

TEST TOPIC ALERT

What is a Yankee bond? There are a number of cute names given to bonds in an attempt to signify where they are issued, in what currency they are denominated, and by whom they are issued. The Yankee bond is a first cousin to the Eurodollar bond discussed previously.

Just as a Eurodollar bond is a U.S. dollar-denominated bond issued by a non-U.S. entity outside the United States, a Yankee bond is a U.S. dollar-denominated bond issued by a non-U.S. entity in the U.S. market. Because they are issued in the U.S., they come under the registration requirements of the Securities Act of 1933. Another example of this is the Maple bond, a Canadian dollar-denominated bond issued by a non-Canadian entity in the Canadian market. Can you guess what a Matilda bond is? (Clue—it takes its name from a song that had waltzing in the title.) The answer will be found later in this course.

TAKE NOTE

If you purchase a bond issued in a foreign currency, you will receive your fixed rate of interest in that currency. However, when converting to U.S. dollars, you will be subject to currency risk. The same is true at maturity. For example, if you purchase £100,000 of U.K. gilts (the term given to their government bonds) with a 4% coupon, you would always receive £4,000 per year in interest. At the exchange rate in effect when this is being written (£1 = $1.41), the bonds would cost you $141,000 and you would be receiving the equivalent of $ 5,640 in interest. At maturity you would receive £100,000, but if the value of the pound had fallen, say to $1.25, then

Unit 13

the value of the matured bonds would only be $125,000. The same would be true about your interest payments if, during the holding period, the pound changed in value. Remember, currency values can fluctuate up or down; that is the nature of currency risk.

TEST TOPIC ALERT

Three advantages of Eurodollar bonds to investors are:

■ because they are U.S.-dollar-denominated, they bear no currency risk to U.S. investors;

■ they are rated by U.S. rating agencies so the risk is clear; and

■ they may offer higher yields than domestic bonds from the same issuer.

Disadvantages of Eurodollar bonds (as with foreign bonds in general) are that:

■ because they are not registered with the SEC, there may be a lack of transparency;

■ they have political and country risk (taken into consideration by the rating agencies);

■ they have less liquidity than domestic issues; and

■ currency risk (if denominated in a currency other than one's home country).

BRADY BONDS

Brady bonds, named after former U.S. Treasury Secretary Nicholas Brady initiated a plan in 1989 to exchange defaulted commercial bank loans issued in less-developed countries, particularly in Latin America, with a security that could be carried on the bank's books as a performing asset. The first Brady agreement was reached with Mexico and the bonds were first issued in March, 1990. Partners in the program were the International Monetary Fund (IMF) and the World Bank. Most are denominated in U.S. dollars. Maturities range from 10 to 30 years and may be interest bearing or discounted or even zero coupon. The safety of a Brady bond largely depends on the pledged collateral, frequently a U.S. Treasury zero-coupon bond. The Brady bond market was the largest and most actively traded emerging market asset class, but, as most of the countries involved have matured, they are only a small fraction today. Because of their relatively high safety, Brady bonds are generally more liquid than other debt issues from emerging markets.

The Brady Plan offered several important benefits:

■ Those countries who participated were able to reduce both their overall debt level as well as the debt servicing cost

■ For the bank's portfolio, their sovereign risk was diversified

■ The Plan encouraged emerging markets countries to undertake economic reforms

■ With the added safety and promise of economic reforms, emerging markets countries would now have a broader access to the financial markets.

TEST TOPIC ALERT

No Brady bond carries a U.S. government guarantee.

EXAMPLES

1. Advantages of Brady bonds to an American investor include all of the following EXCEPT

   A. tax-free interest

   B. greater liquidity than found in most emerging market securities

   C. greater safety than most emerging market debt because of the collateral

   D. higher yields than on U.S. Treasury securities

   Answer: A. The interest on Brady bonds is fully taxable to a U.S. investor. All of the other statements are true.

2. Which of the following statements is NOT true?

   A. A country wishing to restructure its debt using Brady bonds would do so to save on debt servicing costs.

   B. One of the benefits of holding convertible preferred stock is the option to convert into the corporation's common stock.

   C. A resident of England has no currency risk when holding U.K. gilts.

   D. A resident of France purchasing Eurodollar bonds does not incur currency risk.

   Answer: D. As the name implies, Eurodollar bonds are denominated in U.S. dollars. That means that someone in France, choice **D**, will have the risk that the euro, the home currency in France, will rise against the dollar and, as a result, interest payments will be worth less as will the ultimate payback at maturity. Only U.S. residents have no currency risk with Eurodollar bonds. One of the benefits of Brady bonds is the ability of the sovereign government to borrow at a lower cost because of the collateral behind the bond. Currency risk is when investors hold securities denominated in a currency other than their home country. Convertible preferred shares are convertible into the issuer's common stock which is a benefit if the stock rises in price.

REPAYING DEBT PRINCIPAL

U13LO8: Recall the methods of repayment of principal.

As stated in the beginning of this unit, in addition to receiving regular income from the investment, the investor does want to receive a return of the loan principal. Normally, one expects to be paid off when the debt matures. However, there are cases when the issuer pays off the debt before maturity.

Zero-Coupon Bonds

The nominal (coupon) rate on a zero-coupon bond is zero. Zero-coupon bonds are issued at a substantial discount from par. They pay no interest, but the difference between the discounted price paid and the par value received at maturity makes up for the lack of a current interest coupon. For example, investors purchasing new zero-coupon bonds for $500 that matured at par in 10 years would receive a profit of $500 in 10 years or an average of $50 per year on an out-of-pocket expenditure of $500. Here are the key things to remember about zero-coupon bonds.

- They are always issued at a discount.

- There is no reinvestment risk because there are no interest payments to worry about reinvesting.

- They are more volatile than other bonds of similar quality.

- Even though no periodic interest payments are received, the IRS requires the issuer to send a Form 1099-OID indicating the taxable interest to be reported each year. This is generally referred to as *phantom income* because you don't "see" it, but pay tax on it.

- This investment is particularly useful when there is a target goal, such as a college education or a qualified retirement plan. This is particularly true because of the tax treatment mentioned in the previous bullet. Unless a large quantity, the child generally incurs little, if any, tax liability, and the earnings in the retirement plan are tax-deferred.

In the case of zero-coupon corporate or municipal securities, there is a somewhat higher level of credit risk. (On a 20-year bond, the investor receives nothing until the maturity date, and if the issuer is insolvent at that time, the investor has received nothing during the entire 20 years.) However, no credit risk exists in the case of zero-coupon treasuries (known as STRIPS for Separate Trading of Registered Interest and Principal of Securities) because the risk of default on a U.S. government security, (at least for purposes of this exam), is nonexistent.

The major attraction of this type of investment is that it allows an investor to lock in a yield (or rate of return) for a predetermined, investor-selected time with no reinvestment risk. Because all zeroes are sold at discounts and have no current return, there is a great deal of price volatility. This point will be reviewed again later in this unit at the discussion on duration.

Callable Bonds

Most of the questions on the exam dealing with early payback of principal are about callable bonds. Bonds can be either callable or noncallable. The call feature permits the issuer to redeem its bonds (pay off the principal) before maturity if it so desires. The call feature is most often exercised when interest rates (borrowing costs) have declined. In this case, the issuer could take advantage of the lower cost of borrowing by issuing new bonds at the lower rate prevailing in the market and using those proceeds to call in the old bonds with their higher coupons. This is similar to refinancing a home mortgage, but in this business we use the term refunding. An issuer would not be interested in redeeming its bonds when interest rates have gone up and the bond prices have gone down; the cheapest way for the issuer to retire its debt is to buy it in the open market.

TAKE NOTE

The comments made previously at Unit 12 LO2 about callable preferred stock relating to the call price and the yields applies here as well.

Call Protection

Before purchasing a bond, determine the extent of its call protection. **Call protection** is the number of years into the issue before the issuer may exercise the call provision. The best call protection a bond may have is if a bond is noncallable; in other words, the issuer cannot call it early, and the investor has the best protection against a call.

EXAMPLES

1. A bond issue that may be retired in advance of maturity at the option of the issuer is said to have

   A. a callable feature

   B. an optional reserve

   C. a conversion feature

   D. a cumulative feature

   Answer: A. A bond that is callable, choice **A**, has a provision that the issuer, at its option, may redeem that bond at a specified price known as the call or redemption price. As we will see in the next topic, the conversion feature may be exercised by the investor, not the issuer.

2. Which of the following statements about zero-coupon bonds is NOT true?

   A. Zero-coupon bonds are sold at a deep discount from face value.

   B. Zero-coupon bonds pay periodic interest payments.

   C. The owner of a zero-coupon bond receives the face value only at maturity.

   D. Zero-coupon bonds have greater price volatility than interest-bearing bonds.

   Answer: B. The key distinguishing feature of zero-coupon bonds, and the reason for their name, is that there is no periodic interest payment made during the life of the bond (choice **B** is the untrue statement). Without interest payments, the bonds must sell at a discount and the investor receives payment of the face value at maturity. The lack of periodic interest payments causes the price volatility even with the safest zero-coupon bond—the Treasury STRIPS.

CONVERTIBLE BONDS

The exam also deals with bonds paid off before maturity that have a convertible feature. These convertible bonds are issued by corporations only. Because they may be converted or exchanged for the company's common stock, there are no convertible municipal or government bonds. The conversion privilege is exercised at the discretion of the investor. The ratio of conversion varies from one company's bond to another according to the terms set forth in the indenture at the time the bonds are issued. The exact number of shares (or method of computing the number) that a particular bond will be convertible into at any point is printed in the bond indenture at the time of issue. Most convertibles are debentures.

In many cases, the indenture merely tells you the number of shares into which the bond is convertible. For example, the bond may be convertible into 50 shares; thus, it would have a conversion ratio of 50:1, 50 shares for 1 bond. If a bond is convertible into 25 shares, it would have a conversion ratio of 25:1.

Frequently, instead of telling the number of shares into which the bond is convertible, the indenture will give the conversion price. That conversion price is the price per share that the corporation will sell their stock in exchange for the bond one is holding. Regardless of the current market price of the bond, the bond always represents a debt of the corporation of $1,000. Therefore, if the conversion price is given, to compute the number of shares into which the bond is convertible, always divide the par value ($1,000) by the conversion price. For example, a bond convertible at $20 per share is convertible into 50 shares ($1,000 / $20 = 50 shares).

If the bond has a conversion price of $50, the conversion ratio is 20 shares ($1,000 / $50 = 20 shares). If the JRP 6s of '31, currently selling at 120, were convertible at $40, how many shares would one get when one converted the bond? The answer is not 30. The current market has nothing to do with the computation. The bond conversion is fixed at issuance, and the market fluctuates all the time. The correct answer is 25 shares ($1,000 / $40 = 25 shares).

The bond's price will rise along with the stock. Most convertible bonds contain a call provision. If the market price of the bonds becomes sufficiently high, the company can force the investors to convert by exercising the call provision. This is known as forced conversion. The reason the bond price went up was because the underlying stock went up. If a bond is called at a price significantly lower than its current market, it will be to the bondholder's advantage to convert the bond into the stock. Once that occurs, the issuer owes nothing because there is stock now where there once were bonds.

COMPUTING PARITY PRICE

U13LO9: Compute the parity price of a convertible security.

All of the comments we've made about convertible bonds (or convertible preferred) moving in relation to the underlying common stock is due to the concept of parity. According to the dictionary, when two things are at parity, they are equal. How does that work here? If you think about it, when holding a convertible security, we have a choice of two actions: we can either continue to hold the bond (or preferred), or, we can decide to convert it into the common. If the convertible security and the common stock we would get upon conversion are worth the same, we say they are at parity.

 EXAMPLE

On the Series 65 exam, there may be questions on parity. Here are two methods to help you solve the problem.

RST's 6% debenture is convertible to common at $50. If the debenture is currently trading for $1,200, what is the parity price of the common?

Method One: Parity means equal. Solve for the conversion ratio as follows:

Par value: $1,000

Conversion price: $ 50

Conversion ratio: 20

The parity stock price is found by dividing $1,200 by 20. The parity price of the common is $60 because 20 shares of the stock at $60 each equals the value of one bond trading at $1,200.

Method Two: If you prefer to think in percentages, identify that the debenture's price of $1,200 is 20% greater than the original $1,000 price. To be at equivalence, the stock price must also increase by 20%. So add 20% to 50 and the problem is solved; 20% of 50 is 10; 10 + 50 = parity price of $60.

Here is another style of parity question.

RST's 6% debenture is convertible to common at $50. If the common is trading for $45, what is the parity price of the debenture? Start by solving for the conversion ratio.

Par value: $1,000

Conversion price: $50

Conversion ratio: 20

The debenture's parity price is found by multiplying 20 × 45 which is $900. Using the percentage method, you can determine that the market price of the common stock is 10% below that of the conversion price (5 / 50 = 10%). Reducing the debenture's price of $1,000 by 10% results in a parity price of the debenture of $900.

It is important to remember that parity is a theoretical concept—we're looking for the price that would make the bond and stock equal. In actuality, convertible securities, whether bonds or preferred stock, almost always have a market price that is somewhat above the parity price.

ADVANTAGES AND DISADVANTAGES TO CONVERTIBLE SECURITIES

Advantages to Investors

Downside Protection

The investor is a creditor. If the company's business does not prosper and the stock does not go up, or declines in value, the investor becomes, as a bondholder, a creditor. Interest must be paid semiannually, and the principal must be repaid at maturity. The investor has assured income, as long as the company is solvent, and has a bondholder's claim, in the event of financial difficulty. Convertibles carry a lower interest rate than non-convertibles because of the added bonus of the convertibility factor. If the underlying common stock declines to a point where the convertibility factor is worth nothing, then the bond will sell on the basis of its yield alone like any other debt security.

Upside Potential

If the company's business prospers, the underlying stock will increase in market value. Because the bondholder can convert to stock, the bond will go up parallel to the increase in the common stock price.

A convertible bondholder, therefore, has all the upside potential of the common stockholder with less downside risk.

Unit 13

Disadvantages to Investors

The only disadvantages to investors in convertible bonds are that they receive a lower interest rate than a nonconvertible debt and, of course, the possibility that the convertible bond may be called away before one is ready to convert.

Anti-Dilutive Protection

One of the concerns of any holder of a convertible security (bond or preferred stock) is protection against the potential dilution resulting from a stock split or a stock dividend. For example, if you owned a bond convertible into 20 shares and the issuer declared a 2-for-1 stock split, in order for you to have the same conversion powers, you would need to be able to convert into 40 shares. If the conversion privilege were expressed as a conversion price, the new price would now be half the former one allowing you to convert into twice as many new shares.

TEST TOPIC ALERT

The following are key points to remember about convertible securities:

- They give the owner the opportunity to participate in the company's growth through the ability to acquire common stock

- The coupon (interest) rate will invariably be lower than for non-convertibles of the same quality. In other words, investors sacrifice income for the growth opportunity. That means if a question asks about choosing an investment for income, you don't select the convertible security.

- They offer the potential stability of a debt security with the upside potential of an equity security

- Convertible securities generally sell at price somewhat above the parity price

BOND YIELD COMPUTATIONS

U13LO10: Compare current yield, yield to maturity, and yield to call.

The nature of fixed income, usually being debt rather than equity, involves somewhat different methodology in determining proper valuation. After all, in most cases, these securities are purchased for their income rather than future capital appreciation. The first thing we will look at is the various yield computations that are applicable to debt securities.

Yield Computations

The interest rate will always be stated as a percentage of the par value. The interest stated on the face of the bond is called the **nominal yield**. Sometimes it is referred to as the coupon rate. To compute the annual interest payments in dollars, multiply this nominal yield by the face amount of the bond ($1,000 unless stated otherwise). A bond with a 5% coupon rate pays $50 per year. One with an 8% nominal yield pays $80 per year. One with a coupon of 13.5% pays $135 per year. Because, on any particular bond, this interest payment is the same every year, it is referred to as a fixed charge.

TEST TOPIC ALERT

When a question states that a bond pays interest at a rate of 6% semiannually, that does not mean two payments of $60 per year. The interest rate is always stated on an annual basis ($60 per year), and it is paid twice per year, $30 every 6 months.

Current Yield

Investors always want to know the return on their investment. The most straightforward way to do that is to place the return on the investment as follows.

$$\frac{\text{Return}}{\text{Investment}}$$

The return will always be the annual interest in dollars (if referring to a stock, the dividend in dollars) divided by the current market price (the amount of investment required to own the security). This calculation is called current yield or current return.

Although bonds are issued with a face, or par, value of $1,000, bond prices do fluctuate in the market. As stated earlier, the interest a bond pays is called its coupon rate or nominal yield. Look at this example: The DBL 10s of '39. DBL is the name of the issuer, 10s means the nominal yield is 10%, and '39 means that the bonds mature in 2039. The letter *s* is added because it is easier to say "the 10s" than to say "the 10". These bonds pay $100 a year ($50 semiannually) for each $1,000 of face value. Regardless of what the market price of the bonds may be, DBL has an obligation to pay annual interest of 10% of the $1,000 face they borrowed.

If an investor were to buy these bonds for more than $1,000 or less than $1,000, the return on the investment would not be 10%. For example, if these bonds had a current market value of $800, their current yield would be 12.5% ($100 / $800). Similarly, someone paying $1,200 for the bonds will receive a current yield of 8.33% ($100 / $1,200). Please notice, the $100 interest received is the same in all cases regardless of the current market price.

Bond prices and yields move in opposite directions: as interest rates rise, bond prices fall, and vice versa. When a bond trades at a discount, its current yield increases; when it trades at a premium, its current yield decreases.

Discount and Premium

When a bond is selling at a price above par (or face), it is selling at a premium; when it is selling below par, it is selling at a discount. The two following statements are critical to remember.

If you pay more, you get less.

If you pay less, you get more.

An investor buying a bond at a premium will always receive a rate of return less than the coupon (or nominal) yield stated on the face of the bond (8.33% is less than 10%). Conversely, any time an investor purchases a bond at a discount, the return will be more than the rate stated on the face of the bond (12.5% is greater than 10%).

In addition to being the dollar amount on which the annual interest was based, par value was also the dollar amount that would be returned to the investor at maturity. Therefore, an investor purchasing a bond at a discount knows that holding the bond until maturity date will result in a return of the par value, an amount which will be more than what was paid for the

Unit 13

bond. An investor purchasing a bond at a premium, and holding it until the maturity date, knows that the par value received will be less than what was paid for the bond. To accurately reflect this gain or loss that an investor will have upon maturity, there is another yield to consider—the yield to maturity, or true yield.

TEST TOPIC ALERT

Another way you may be tested is by giving you a quoted yield and asking you for the price relative to par. For example, if a bond with a 5% coupon is currently yielding 6%, is it selling at a discount, a premium, or par? Well, anytime you are getting a yield higher than the coupon rate, the bond has to be selling at a discount from par. Conversely, if the bond had a 5% coupon, but the current return was 4%, the bond must be selling at a premium to par.

Yield to Maturity or Basis

This measurement takes into account the gain or loss the investor will have when the bonds are redeemed at maturity. The person who buys the bonds mentioned previously at $800 will get back $1,000 if the bonds are held to maturity, in addition to receiving $100 per year interest (a current yield of 12.5% on his money). Consequently, this investor will have a gain of $200 on top of the annual interest. The individual paying $1,200 for the bonds will have a $200 loss at maturity when receiving the face value for them at maturity.

Whenever an investor pays less (buys at a discount), there will be a profit in addition to the annual interest, and whenever the investor pays more (buys at a premium), there will be a loss if held to maturity. Try to understand these key facts:

- A bond is issued at par ($1,000) because that is how much the issuer is borrowing.
- The interest paid on the bond is always fixed as a percentage of the par (face) value.
- Regardless of changes in the market value of the bond, the interest checks remain the same.
- The current market price of a bond is determined by supply and demand.
- The current market price will fluctuate.
- The current market price may be at par, above par, or below par.
- A bond always matures at par.
- Purchasing a bond at par will always result in getting back the same as the original investment at maturity.
- Purchasing a bond at a discount (below par) will always result in getting back par, which means more (a profit) than the original investment.
- Purchasing a bond at a premium (above par) will always result in getting back par, which means less (a loss) than the original investment.

You may also be asked to determine which is higher (or lower), the current yield or the yield to maturity. Because yield to maturity (YTM) accentuates the return by adding a profit to a bond bought at a discount or subtracting the loss on a bond bought at a premium, the YTM on a discounted bond will always be higher than that bond's current yield, and the reverse is true regarding a bond bought at a premium.

Although you will probably not have to do a YTM computation on the exam, some students find that seeing the numbers played out gives them a better understanding of the concept. Try to follow this example:

EXAMPLE

An investor who buys a 10% coupon bond at 105 ($1,050 per bond) with 10 years remaining to maturity can expect $100 in interest per year. If the bond is held to maturity, the bondholder loses $50, the amount of the premium. This loss is included in the YTM approximation.

The actual YTM calculation for this bond selling at a premium follows:

$$\frac{\text{annual interest} - (\text{premium}/\text{years to maturity})}{\text{average price of the bond}}$$

A bond's average price is the price paid plus the amount received at maturity (par) divided by two. Alternatively, the average price is that price midway between the purchase price and par.

$$\frac{100 - (50/10)}{1025} = \frac{95}{1025} = 0.093, \text{ or } 9.3\%$$

The YTM of a bond bought at a premium is always lower than both the coupon rate (nominal yield) and the current yield. In this example, the nominal yield is 10%, and the current yield is 9.52% (100 / 1,050).

If an investor buys a 10-year bond with a 10% coupon for 95 ($950 per bond), $100 per year in coupon interest payments is received and a gain of $50 (the amount of the discount) at maturity. This gain is included in the YTM approximation.

The actual YTM calculation for this bond selling at a discount follows:

$$\frac{\text{Annual interest} + (\text{discount}/\text{years to maturity})}{\text{Average price of the bond}}$$

$$\frac{100 + (50/10)}{975} = \frac{105}{975} = 0.1077, \text{ or } 10.77\%$$

The YTM of a bond bought at a discount is always higher than both the coupon rate (nominal yield) and the current yield. In this example, the nominal yield is 10%, and the current yield is 10.53% (100 / 950).

If these calculations seem complicated, do not worry. You will have at most one question requiring a YTM calculation. Focus on the relationship between YTM and CY based on the price of the bond.

TAKE NOTE

YTM is also called the **market-driven yield** because it reflects the internal rate of return from the bond investment.

Yield to Call (YTC)

A bond with a call feature may be redeemed before maturity at the issuer's option. Unless the bond was bought at par, and is callable at par, **yield to call** (YTC) calculations reflect the early redemption date and consequent acceleration of the premium loss from the purchase price.

A bond's YTC, similar to YTM, is the rate of return the bond provides from the purchase date to the call date and price. This calculation generates a lower return than does the YTM and should be considered by investors when evaluating a callable bond trading at a premium.

TEST TOPIC ALERT

The reason why we've only referred to a bond selling at a premium being called for redemption is because it is highly unlikely that an issuer would call in a bond that was available in the marketplace at a discount. If that were to happen, the YTC would be higher than the YTM because the profit resulting from the discount would be accelerated.

The following example and chart will help you follow the discussion of the various bond yields.

Current Yield, Yield to Maturity, and Yield to Call

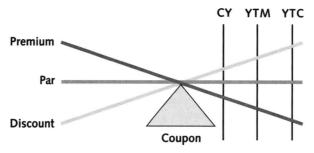

CY = Current Yield YTM = Yield to Maturity YTC = Yield to Call

1. What is the current yield of a 6% bond trading for 80 ($800)?

    Current yield = annual income / current market price

    Find the solution as follows: $60 / $800 = 7.5%. This bond is trading at a discount. When prices fall, yields rise. The current yield is greater than the nominal yield when bonds are trading at a discount.

2. What is the current yield of a 6% bond trading for 120 ($1,200)?

    Find the solution as follows: $60 / $1,200 = 5%. This bond is trading at a premium. The price is up so the yield is down. The current yield is less than the nominal yield when bonds are trading at a premium.

    It is critical to understand the inverse relationship between price and yield. An effective way to visualize it is through the chart. When bonds are at par, coupon and current yield are equal. When bonds are at a premium, the CY is less than the coupon. When bonds are at a discount, the CY is greater than the coupon.

Current market value (CMV) of bond with 10 years to maturity

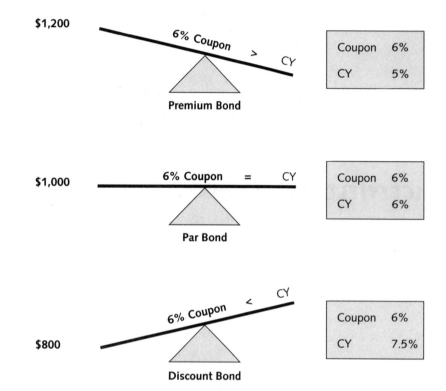

$1,200

6% Coupon   >   CY

| Coupon | 6% |
| CY | 5% |

Premium Bond

$1,000

6% Coupon   =   CY

| Coupon | 6% |
| CY | 6% |

Par Bond

$800

6% Coupon   <   CY

| Coupon | 6% |
| CY | 7.5% |

Discount Bond

TAKE NOTE

Know how to calculate the CY of a bond or a stock. Expect to see one question on the calculation of CY.

The CY of common stock is calculated by dividing the current dividend by the current price of the stock. For instance, a stock with a $2 dividend trading on the market for $40 has a 5% CY ($2 / $40 = 5%).

EXAMPLE

Answer the following questions with **premium**, **par**, or **discount**.

1. If the bond has a YTC lower than its CY, it is trading at

2. If the bond has a YTM and CY that are equal, the bond is trading at

3. If the bond has a YTM less than its YTC, the bond is trading at

4. If a bond has a YTM greater than its coupon, the bond is trading at

The answers are: 1. premium; 2. par; 3. discount; and 4. discount.

TEST TOPIC ALERT

Memorize the following chart for the exam:

Ranking Yields from Lowest to Highest

Discounts	Premiums
Nominal	YTC
CY	YTM
YTM	CY
YTC	Nominal

Once you understand the yield ranking for discounts, the ranking for premium is easy—it is the exact opposite.

PRICE/YIELD RELATIONSHIP SUMMARY

There are many reasons interest rates rise and fall. The main concern for the exam, at this point, is the effect that interest rates have on the price fluctuations of bonds. As a general rule, keep in mind that interest rates and bond prices move counter to each other. That is, when interest rates are going up, the price of older bonds will be going down. When interest rates are going down, the price of older bonds will be going up.

When most people hear this for the first time, they have difficulty understanding it. Simply stated, when newly issued bonds are paying a higher rate of interest than ones currently in the market place, those older bonds are not as attractive. After all, if a new bond came out with a 6% coupon, your 4% or 5% bond would not be as valuable (this always assumes equal quality or rating). Conversely, if you were holding a bond with an 8% coupon, and newly issued bonds were only offering 6%, your bond is more valuable.

EXAMPLE

1. When a bond with a 6% coupon is selling for 90, each of the following statements is correct, EXCEPT

    A. the current yield is approximately 6.67%

    B. the bond is selling at a discount

    C. the bondholder will receive two semiannual interest payments of $27 each

    D. the yield to maturity is slightly higher than the current yield

    Answer: C. A bond with a 6% coupon is going to make two semiannual interest payments of $30 each, regardless of the bond's market price. After all, the loan was $1,000 at 6% interest and that won't change. A price of 90 is 90% of the $1,000 par—clearly a discount. The current yield is the $60 annual interest divided by the $900 price, or 6.67%, and that is a bit lower than the yield to maturity, because if we hold the bond to maturity, we're going to get back the full $1,000, which will represent a $100 profit. Please see the chart at the previous Test Topic Alert.

DURATION

U13LO11: Evaluate the effect of a bond's duration on its market price.

In the financial industry, the term *duration* is used to measure the sensitivity of a debt security when faced with changes in interest rates. The longer the duration, the greater the market price movement, and vice versa.

It is a complicated computation, but, to try to simplify things, it is basically a measurement of the time it takes for the cash flow (interest payments) to repay the invested principal. That being the case, in general the higher the coupon rate, the shorter the duration, or the lower the coupon, the longer the duration.

Just remember that there are two components to the computation: the interest rate and the maturity date. If the maturity dates are about the same (the difference between a 20-year maturity and a 22-year one is almost insignificant), then the bond paying the highest coupon rate will always have the shortest duration and that with the lowest coupon, the longest. However, if the coupon rates are approximately the same, then the bond that will mature first will have the shortest duration, and the one that will mature last will have the longest duration.

The way to compute the duration (calculation not tested) is: the present value of a bond's future cash flows (interest and repayment of principal), weighted by length of time to receipt and divided by the bond's current market value. We're talking about that same present value covered in Unit 10. There, we learned that when a bond's coupon rate was higher than the current market rate, the bond's present value was greater than the face amount and it should sell at a premium. Here, the effect of that higher present value results in a shorter duration and less market volatility.

TAKE NOTE

One way to keep things straight is to think about the zero-coupon bond. With no periodic interest payments (that's why it's called zero-coupon), the duration of a zero-coupon bond will always equal its length to maturity. In other words, if we're trying to compute how long it will take for the income payments to return your principal, without any interest payments, you can't expect to get your money back until maturity date. If that is the case with a zero-coupon bond, then as we find bonds paying interest, the more they're paying every six months, the quicker the payback.

TEST TOPIC ALERT

The general characteristics of duration follow.

- The lower the coupon rate, the longer a bond's duration; the higher the coupon rate, the shorter the duration.

- The longer a bond's maturity, the longer the bond's duration.

- For coupon bonds, duration is always less than the bond's maturity.

- Duration for a zero-coupon bond is always equal to its maturity.

- The longer a bond's duration, the more its value will change for a 1% change in interest rates; the shorter the duration, the less it will change.

TEST TOPIC ALERT

If you were managing a portfolio of bonds and expected interest rates to decline (bond prices will rise), you would lengthen the average duration of the portfolio. On the other hand, if you were of the opinion that interest rates were going to rise, (bond prices will decline), you would want to shorten the average duration.

TAKE NOTE

The approximate average duration of a bond portfolio can be estimated by finding the mean (average) of the individual bonds' durations. If the portfolio consisted of Bond A, duration 5 years, Bond B, duration 6 years, Bond C, duration 9 years, Bond D, duration 11 years, and Bond E, duration 14 years, the average duration would be 9 years (5 + 6 + 9 + 11 + 14 = 45 divided by 5 = 9).

TAKE NOTE

A five-year, zero-coupon bond has a duration of five because it takes five years to make the money back; the buyer gets a single payment (par) at maturity five years after purchase.

Convexity

If you took geometry in school, you learned that curves could be convex (bulging to the outside) or concave (curving to the inside). It's been over 60 years, but I still remember the key to the difference by the statement, "you can hide in a cave." Now, what does that have to do with our discussion?

Convexity is the measurement of the curve that results when plotting a bond's price movements in response to changes in interest rates. It is a more accurate representation than duration of what will happen to a bond's price as interest rates change, especially when the changes are great. Should you have a question about convexity on your exam, here's what you have to know:

- Duration is a linear (straight-line) measurement, while convexity follows a curve.
- Comparing two bonds, the one with the higher convexity will show a greater price increase when yields fall and a smaller decrease when yields rise (that is a good thing).
- If we find two bonds with the same duration, the one with the higher convexity offers greater interest rate risk protection.

TEST TOPIC ALERT

If you should be asked, "Which of the following is the most useful in determining the price volatility of a bond to a significant change in interest rates?" the correct choice is *convexity*.

DISCOUNTED CASH FLOW (DCF)

U13LO12: Describe how discounted cash flow is used to estimate the value of an investment.

One way of assessing the value of a fixed-income security is by looking at the future expected free cash flow (the interest payments plus the eventual return of the principal) and discounting it to arrive at a present value. In its simplest iteration, this is nothing more than taking the all the money you are scheduled to receive over a given future period and adjusting that for the time value of money. The concept is used as well in some equity projections, such as the dividend discount and dividend growth models described previously. Therefore, to compute the future value of the cash flow from a bond, you would have to know the:

- principal amount;
- coupon rate; and
- number of interest payments.

TAKE NOTE

The higher the discounted cash flow (DCF), the more valuable the investment.

EXAMPLE

There will be no computations regarding DCF, but there is a common example that may help you understand the concept better. We all wish we could be a winner of those huge Powerball or Mega Millions jackpots. Winners have the choice of receiving a series of payments over a number of years (about 29 currently), or taking the money in cash. If they take the cash, they'll receive around 65% of the announced total prize. Why is there a difference? The cash represents the present value of those future payments and that is why you get less by taking it now instead of over time. In fact, years ago, when interest rates were higher than they are at the time of this printing, the lump-sum payment was only about 60% of the prize. That is because the higher the market interest rates, the higher the discount rate. This is the same concept used in valuing a bond using DCF. When you buy a bond, you are expecting semiannual interest payments (cash flow) until the maturity date. When you compare those interest rates to the current market rates (the discount rate in the equation), you get an idea of a fair value of the bond. To better help you understand, take a look at this question.

EXAMPLES

1. A client interested in fixed income is viewing different bonds with the same rating and a coupon of 6%. Using the DCF method, which bond should have the highest market value?

    A. 5-year maturity when the discount rate is 4%

    B. 5-year maturity when the discount rate is 8%

    C. 10-year maturity when the discount rate is 4%

    D. 10-year maturity when the discount rate is 8%

    Answer: C. Remember, the discount rate is just another way of stating the current interest rate in the marketplace. If the discount rate is *higher* than the coupon rate, the present value (the expected market price) will be *below* par. Conversely, if the discount rate is lower than the coupon rate, the present value will be ***above*** the par value. Now, there is nothing new for you here—when the current interest rate in the market place (that is what the discount rate represents) is less than the coupon, the bond price is higher (as interest rates go down, bond prices go up). And, if the current market interest rate is higher than the coupon rate, the bond's price will be lower (when interest rates increase, bond prices fall). That would narrow the choices to the two 4% bonds. That is, a bond with a 6% coupon should sell at premium when current interest rates are at 4% and when interest rates are at 8%, the 6% bond should be selling at a discount. Then, as we've just learned with duration, when interest rates change, the longer the time to maturity, the greater the effect on the market price of a bond.

2. An analyst would use the discounted cash flow method in an attempt to find

   A. the fair value of a security

   B. the current market price of a security

   C. the current rate of return of a security

   D. the cash flow from operations

   Answer: A. DCF uses the present value of future cash flows, based on a specified discount (interest) rate, to evaluate the price that a security should be selling for in the market. If the current market price of the security is less than this value, it has a positive net present value (NPV) and should be a good investment. The opposite is true if there is a negative NPV (the market price is higher than that computed under the DCF method).

3. Being concerned about price volatility, a bond investor wishes to compute the duration of a bond being considered for her portfolio. Which of the following is NOT a necessary component of that calculation?

   A. Coupon rate

   B. Current market price

   C. Rating of the bond

   D. Time until maturity

   Answer: C. Although it is true that lower-rated bonds tend to have greater price volatility than high-rated ones, the rating has nothing to do with the calculation of the bond's duration so our exception here is choice **C**. Duration is simply the weighted average of the cash flows an investor will receive over time, discounted to the bond's present value. Those cash flows come from the coupon and the return of the par value at maturity.

EXAMPLE

Here is something that may help. The current rate of interest (the *discount* rate) on new AA-rated bonds with a 20-year maturity is 4%. If you have an older AA bond with 20 years until it matures and a coupon of 6%, how does all of this apply?

If your bond is priced so the yield to maturity (YTM) on your bond is 4.4%, it has a *positive* NPV (its yield is above the market rate of 4% so this bond is selling at a price below its present value).

If your bond is priced so the YTM on your bond is 3.6%, it has a *negative* NPV (its yield is below the market rate of 4% so this bond is selling at a price above its present value).

If your bond is priced so the YTM on your bond is 4%, it has a *zero* NPV (its yield is equal to the market rate of 4% so this bond is selling at its present value).

Unlike the other debt securities we've discussed, trying to project your client's cash flow on a portfolio of mortgage-backed securities has its challenges. Although they do have default risk (other than GNMAs), as do other debt securities, the specific risk due to the possible (some would say, likely) prepayments, complicates the computation.

TEST TOPIC ALERT

When doing cash flow analysis on a mortgage-backed pass-through security, you would want to know the average maturities.

You might want to go back and review the discussion of present value at Part 2, Unit 10.

MONEY MARKET INSTRUMENTS

U13LO13: Identify the special characteristics of money market instruments and the risks and benefits of adding them to a client's portfolio.

As we will learn when discussing asset allocation programs later in this course, one important asset is cash. Now, we don't mean greenbacks buried in the mattress or the backyard; we're referring to places to keep funds that are in the bank or in securities that are considered to be the same as cash. When it comes to cash equivalents, the exam will include money market instruments with a maturity of up to one year.

Money Market

The **money market** may be defined as the market for buying and selling short-term loanable funds in the form of securities and loans. It is called the money market because that is what is traded there, money not cash. The buyer of a money market instrument is the lender of the money; the seller of a money market instrument is the entity borrowing the money.

Although there are many different kinds of money market instruments, there are several common factors. For example, they all have a maturity date of one year or less. In fact, most money market instruments mature in less than six months. Another factor that many (but not all) money market instruments share is that they are issued at a discount; they do not pay interest because debt securities generally pay interest semiannually and because most money market instruments have a maturity of six months or less, the administrative costs of paying out interest would be very high. Therefore, the solution is to issue the security at a discount with the investor being paid back par at maturity, that difference being what he is paid for the use of his money. Money market instruments are safe. Although some are not quite as safe as others (e.g., commercial paper is not as safe as a Treasury bill), they are all considered to be low-risk securities.

EXAMPLE

1. Money market instruments are

    A. short-term equity

    B. intermediate debt

    C. short-term debt

    D. long-term debt

    Answer: C. The definition of a money market instrument is that of high-quality, short-term debt—choice **C**.

Treasury Securities

Because there is so much Treasury debt outstanding, the level of activity in Treasury bills and other short-term government issues is by far the highest and most carefully watched. Governments with short terms also refer to U.S. Treasury notes or U.S. Treasury bonds that are in their last year before maturity because, at that time, they would trade like any other security with one year or less to maturity.

Negotiable Certificates of Deposit

These Certificates of Deposits (CDs) are unsecured time deposits (no asset of the bank is pledged as collateral), and the money is being loaned to the bank for a specified period. A negotiable CD allows the initial investor, or any subsequent owner of the CD, to sell the CD in the open market before the maturity date. The bank that issues the CD redeems the CD at face value plus interest on maturity date. CDs are the only money market instrument that pays periodic interest, usually semiannually. To be considered a negotiable CD, such CDs must have a face value of $100,000 or more, with $1 million and more being most common. Although maturities can run as long as 10 years, it is those with the one year or less maturity that are considered money market instruments.

TAKE NOTE

In the industry (and sometimes on the exam), these are referred to as Jumbo CDs. Although covered by FDIC insurance, these are not the CDs you purchase at your local bank branch. We'll discuss them shortly.

TEST TOPIC ALERT

■ Negotiable CDs do not have a prepayment penalty

■ FDIC insurance applies up to $250,000

■ Jumbo CDs pay interest semiannually

Commercial Paper

Another money market instrument is commercial paper. This is short-term unsecured paper issued by corporations (especially finance companies), primarily to raise working capital. In other words, for current rather than long-term needs. As you saw when we covered securities exemptions in Part 1, commercial paper is exempt from registration on both the federal and state level as long as the maximum maturity is 270 days. While negotiable CDs are interest bearing and issued at face amount, commercial paper is generally issued at a discount—instead of receiving interest, the investor receives the face amount at maturity.

Eurodollars and the Foreign Currency Markets

The cost of raising money and doing business is not restricted by national boundaries. International monetary factors, such as changes in foreign currency exchange rates, Eurodollars, eurosecurities, and the interbank market, can also affect U.S. money markets and businesses.

Eurodollars

Eurodollars are U.S. dollars deposited in banks outside the United States; that is, the deposits remain denominated in U.S. dollars rather than the local currency.

EXAMPLE

Euroyen are Japanese yen deposited in banks outside Japan. In other words, when a currency is preceded by the prefix *euro*, it refers to a bank deposit outside of the currency's home country.

Eurodollar time deposits tend to be short term, ranging from overnight to 180 days. European banks lend Eurodollars to other banks in much the same way that U.S. banks lend federal funds. The interest rate is usually based on the **London Interbank Offered Rate** (**LIBOR**).

London Interbank Offered Rate (LIBOR)

LIBOR, sometimes referred to as the ICE LIBOR, is derived from a survey of banks conducted each day in London, U.K., on behalf of the Intercontinental Exchange (ICE). Lenders are asked how much it would cost them to borrow from each other for 15 different periods, from overnight to one year, in currencies including dollars, euros, yen, and Swiss francs. Rates are based on actual transactions for which records are kept. After a set number of quotes are excluded, those remaining are averaged and published for each currency by the ICE before noon.

TAKE NOTE

The exam may expect you to know that the LIBOR is the world's most widely used benchmark for short-term interest rates.

TAKE NOTE

Scandals in London have raised doubts about the future use of LIBOR. Alternative measurements have been proposed and it is likely that by 2020 or so, there will be a new tool. When that happens and LIBOR is no longer the answer to the questions, our QBank will be updated and the new information will be posted to the Content Updates.

Unit 13

EXAMPLES

1. The LIBOR rate is established on a daily basis in

   A. Liberia

   B. Libya

   C. London

   D. New York

   Answer: C. LIBOR is the London Interbank Offered Rate (technically the ICE-LIBOR now) and, as shown, the L stands for London, U.K.

2. A company realizes money from the sale of surplus equipment. It would like to invest this money but will need it in 4–6 months and must take that into consideration when selecting an investment. You would recommend

   A. preferred stock

   B. Treasury bills

   C. AAA rated bonds with long-term maturities

   D. common stock

   Answer: B. For this client, the appropriate investment is a money market instrument (choice **B**) and nothing is safer than a T-bill.

In summation, why would you place money market securities in a client's portfolio?

■ Highly liquid

■ Very safe

■ The best place to store money that will be needed soon

In doing so, the client would be incurring the following risks:

■ Because of their many advantages, the rate of return is quite low, so these are not suitable for long-term investors.

■ Fluctuating income—due to short-term maturities, principal is potentially being reinvested at a different rate each time the instrument matures.

BANK DEPOSIT ACCOUNTS

U13LO14: Contrast demand deposit accounts (DDAs) with time deposits accounts.

As mentioned, when referring to cash as part of one's asset allocation, in addition to cash equivalents in the form of money market instruments, one might keep the proverbial "cash in the bank." The term *insured* will frequently be used on the exam because, at least up to the legal limits, the funds involved are insured by the FDIC. There are several ways this may be done.

Demand Deposits

This is legal term for a checking account. This is the favorite repository for funds that will be needed in the very near term.

TEST TOPIC ALERT

What we normally refer to as "cash in the bank" is, in banking terms, known as a **demand deposit**. To bankers, the term *demand deposit* refers to a type of account (usually just shown by the initials DDA) held at banks and financial institutions that may be withdrawn at any time by the customer. Historically, the term referred only to checking accounts, but it now commonly includes savings accounts and money market accounts (not money market mutual funds—those are not banking products).

When analyzing a client's financial profile, it should be understood that these are considered *short-term* funds (readily available) and provide safe, but *low* returns.

Certificates of Deposits (CDs) (Time Deposits)

In the money market segment, we introduced you to the Jumbo (negotiable) CD. Here, we're referring to the non-negotiable (you can't sell it to anyone, you can only redeem it at the bank) certificate of deposit available at your local branch (or online). These are typically available with a minimum deposit of as little as $500 and maturities of anywhere from 3 months to 5 years. In most cases, withdrawal before the maturity date will result in a penalty. Here are some key facts to remember for the exam:

■ If capital preservation is the goal with no risk, the answer is an insured bank CD.

■ Insured bank CDs have no interest rate risk (they don't fluctuate in value as interest rates change).

■ Even with the potential early withdrawal penalty, these are considered liquid assets, but certainly not as liquid as a DDA.

There are risks, however

■ As fixed-income investments, they bear purchasing power (inflation) risk

■ Yields tend to be quite low so they should not be a major portion of a long-term investment.

EXAMPLE

1. One would expect to have checkbook access to

    A. a CMO

    B. a DDA

    C. a GNMA

    D. a LIBOR

Answer: B. DDA stands for demand deposit account, most often a checking account at a bank.

UNIT 14

Types and Characteristics of Pooled Investments

In addition to equity and debt, other investments related to stocks and bonds are available to investors. Such investment products include packaged products such as mutual funds, exchange-traded funds (ETFs), variable contracts of insurance companies (variable annuities and variable life insurance), and real estate investment trusts (REITs). These packaged products are generally referred to as pooled investments because they represent a pool of funds contributed by a number of investors.

The Series 65 exam will include approximately six questions on the material presented in this unit.

LEARNING OBJECTIVES

When you have completed this unit, you will be able to accomplish the following.

U14LO1: Identify the legal requirements of investment companies.

U14LO2: Compare the difference between the method of capitalization of open-end investment companies and closed-end investment companies.

U14LO3: Identify the difference in pricing between open-end and closed-end investment companies.

U14LO4: Contrast the different mutual fund share classes and how that relates to the different types of loads charged to fund investors.

U14LO5: Identify the characteristics of private funds and venture capital funds.

U14LO6: Identify the structure, compensation arrangements, and suitability requirements of a hedge fund.

U14LO7: Recall the special features of unit investment trusts.

U14LO8: Identify the distinguishing characteristics of exchange-traded funds (ETFs).

U14LO9: Identify the unique features of REITs.

U14LO10: Explain the benefits and risks of pooled investments in client portfolios.

THE INVESTMENT COMPANY ACT OF 1940

U14LO1: Identify the legal requirements of investment companies.

The first of the pooled investment vehicles we'll cover are investment companies. An **investment company** is a corporation or a trust through which investors may acquire an interest in large, diversified portfolios of securities by pooling their funds with other investors' funds. People often invest in investment companies because they believe a professional money manager should be able to outperform the average investor in the market.

As with all investments, there are benefits and risks. This unit will close with a discussion of the benefits and risks for most of the pooled investments covered. Investment companies raise capital by selling shares to the public. Investment companies must abide by similar registration and prospectus requirements imposed by the Securities Act of 1933 on every other issuer.

Investment companies are also subject to regulations regarding how their shares are sold to the public. The **Investment Company Act of 1940** provides for SEC regulation of investment companies and their activities.

TYPES OF INVESTMENT COMPANIES

The Investment Company Act of 1940 classifies investment companies into three broad types: face-amount certificate companies, management investment companies, and unit investment trusts (UITs which will be covered a bit later at LO7).

Face-Amount Certificate Companies (FACC)

A **face-amount certificate** is a contract between an investor and an issuer in which the issuer guarantees payment of a stated (or fixed) sum to the investor at some set date in the future. In return for this future payment, the investor agrees to pay the issuer a set amount of money either as a lump sum or in periodic installments.

■ The most important fact you need to know about this security is that it is one of the three types of investment companies listed in the Investment Company Act of 1940.

Management Investment Companies

The most familiar type of investment company is the **management investment company**, which actively manages a securities portfolio to achieve a stated investment objective. A management investment company is either closed-end or open-end. Mutual funds are open-end investment companies. Initially, both closed-end and open-end companies sell shares to the public; the difference between them lies in the way they raise capital and how investors buy and sell their shares—in the primary or secondary market.

TAKE NOTE

Open-end and closed-end investment companies have far more similarities than differences. One of these is the term net asset value per share, generally shown as NAV. This value is the result of the fund valuing all of its assets (the largest of which is the portfolio), subtracting its liabilities, and then dividing that by the number of shares outstanding. This NAV per share computation is critical to the purchase and sale of open-end companies, and, as we'll see, has little relationship to the buying and selling price of closed-end funds.

TEST TOPIC ALERT

It is important for you to know that the definition of investment company does not include holding companies

EXAMPLE

1. Which of the following would NOT be considered an investment company under the Investment Company Act of 1940?

    A. Face-amount certificate company

    B. Unit investment trust

    C. Management company

    D. Holding company

    Answer: D. Holding companies are specifically excluded from the definition of investment company so choice **D** is correct.

The sale of investment companies, especially mutual funds, is highly regulated through the provisions of the Investment Company Act. Some of the testable regulations are:

1. Board of Directors

In general, investment companies cannot have a board of directors that consists of more than 60% of persons who meet the definition of interested persons of the investment company.

TAKE NOTE

Another way of stating that no more than 60% of the directors may be interested persons is to say that at least 40% must be noninterested, that is, *outside* directors. These are individuals who have no connection to the fund other than a position on the board (and maybe owning some shares of the fund as would any investor). Typically outside directors are academics or prominent community members.

2. Prohibited Activities

Investment companies are prohibited from engaging in several activities. Investment companies may not:

- purchase any security on margin;

- participate on a joint basis in any trading account in securities (i.e., an investment company cannot have a joint account with someone else);

- sell any security short; or

- acquire more than 3% of the outstanding voting securities of another investment company.

There are exceptions to these prohibitions, but, for the purposes of the exam, you may disregard any exceptions.

Unit 14

EXAMPLE

1. The Investment Company Act of 1940 prohibits registered open-end investment companies from engaging in any of the following practices EXCEPT

   A. issuing common stock

   B. selling short or purchasing securities for the company's portfolio on margin

   C. owning more than 3% of the outstanding voting securities of another investment company

   D. opening a joint account with another investment company

   Answer: A. The one thing that all open-end investment companies must do is issue common stock, choice **A**. That is the form of ownership. All of the other activities are prohibited.

3. Changes in Investment Policy

In order for an investment company's board to make fundamental investment policy changes, a majority vote of the outstanding voting stock is required. Examples of fundamental changes would include:

■ a change in subclassification, such as from an open-end to a closed-end company or from a diversified to a nondiversified company;

■ deviation from any fundamental policy in its registration statement, including a change in investment objective; and

■ changing the nature of its business so as to cease to be an investment company.

In other words, because the investment company is supposed to function for the benefit of the shareholders, any of these changes would require the vote of a majority of the shareholders.

4. Size of Investment Companies

No registered investment company is permitted to make a public offering of securities unless it has a net worth of at least $100,000.

5. Investment Advisory and Underwriter Contracts

A majority vote of the shareholders is required to approve the contract between the investment company and its investment adviser and the contract with its principal underwriter. These contracts must be in writing and provide that the contract:

■ precisely describes all compensation to be paid;

■ will be approved at least annually by the board of directors or by majority vote of the shareholders if it is to be renewed after the first two years; and

■ provides that it may be terminated at any time, without penalty, by the board of directors or by majority vote of the shareholders on not more than 60 days' written notice to the investment adviser.

In addition, it is unlawful for any registered investment company to enter into or renew any contract with an investment adviser or principal underwriter unless the terms have been approved by majority vote of directors who are not parties to such contract as affiliated persons (i.e., directors who are not affiliated with the adviser or the underwriter, who in the aggregate must comprise at least 40% of the directors).

TAKE NOTE

The effect of this final paragraph is that no advisory contract, whether initial or renewal, may take effect without approval of the noninterested members of the board.

6. Transactions of Certain Affiliated Persons and Underwriters

Those individuals who are affiliated with the investment company or its underwriter have certain restrictions when it comes to dealing with the fund. These individuals cannot

- sell any personally owned security to the fund except redeeming personally owned shares of the fund (like any other investor);
- borrow money from the fund; or
- purchase from that investment company any security other than the fund's shares.

TEST TOPIC ALERT

An **affiliated person** is defined as any person directly or indirectly owning, controlling, or holding with power to vote, **5%** or more of the outstanding shares of the investment company. An affiliated person also includes any person directly or indirectly controlling, controlled by, or under common control with the investment company or any officer, director, partner, or employee of the investment company. However, while technically considered an affiliated person, no person is deemed to be an interested person for purposes of the maximum percentage of interested persons on the board solely by reason of his being a member of the fund's board of directors or an owner of its securities. A person is deemed to be a **control** person when owning or controlling more than **25%** of the outstanding shares.

7. Custodian

It is required that every registered investment company keeps its assets with a custodian. In most cases, that custodian is a bank, hence the common use of the term *custodian bank*. Although the Act specifies certain financial requirements for that bank, it does not require that the bank have FDIC coverage. Alternatively, the investment company may use a broker-dealer that is a member firm of a national securities exchange.

8. Redemption of Shares—Mutual Funds

Upon request of the investor, the Investment Company Act of 1940 requires that the proceeds be sent in no more than seven days. The investor receives the next computed NAV per share using the forward pricing principle (described at LO3).

9. Periodic and Other Reports

All investment companies must file **annual** financial reports with the SEC. These reports contain an audited balance sheet and income statement. In addition, shareholders must be sent financial information **semiannually**.

Knowing what is prohibited and what is required is often tested on the exam. Here are two examples expressing ideas that are likely to be tested:

EXAMPLES

1. ABC is an FINRA member broker-dealer. Among other functions, it serves as the principal underwriter of the XYZ Mutual Fund. Which of the following transactions of ABC would be prohibited?

    A. ABC tenders, from its investment account, 500 shares of the XYZ Mutual Fund for redemption.

    B. ABC purchases, for its investment account, 500 shares of XYZ Mutual Fund.

    C. ABC purchases some securities directly from XYZ's portfolio.

    D. All of these.

    Answer: C. It would be a violation of the Investment Company Act of 1940 for any affiliated person, such as the principal underwriter, to purchase any security from an investment company other than shares of the fund itself. Investing in the fund's shares would be permitted, not prohibited.

2. Which of the following statements correctly expresses requirements under the Investment Company Act of 1940?

    I.   A registered open-end investment company using a bank as custodian must choose one that has FDIC coverage.

    II. If an affiliated person of a registered investment company wishes to borrow money from the fund, there must be at least 300% asset coverage.

    III. No investment advisory contract may be entered into that does not provide for termination with no more than 60 days' notice in writing.

    IV. No registered investment company may acquire more than 3% of the shares of another investment company.

    A. I and II

    B. I and IV

    C. II and III

    D. III and IV

    Answer: D. The Investment Company Act of 1940 requires that all advisory contracts contain a provision that the contract may be terminated upon no more than 60 days' notice in writing, choice III. The Act prohibits any registered investment company from owning more than 3% of the shares of another investment company, choice IV making choice **D** the correct answer. There are no circumstances under which an affiliated person can borrow from the fund, and it is not a requirement that the custodian bank have FDIC insurance.

CAPITALIZATION OF MANAGEMENT INVESTMENT COMPANIES

U14LO2: Compare the difference between the method of capitalization of open-end investment companies and closed-end investment companies.

Open-End Investment Companies Initial Capitalization

An open-end investment company, or **mutual fund**, does not specify the exact number of shares it intends to issue. It registers an open offering with the SEC. The open-end investment company can raise an unlimited amount of investment capital by continuously issuing new shares. As a consequence, investors in mutual funds are always purchasing a new issue; a primary offering with the money going to the issuer (the mutual fund). One other point is that open-end companies can only issue common stock. The money raised from the issuance of that common stock is then used by the portfolio manager(s) to invest in securities meeting that fund's objectives. For example, a mutual fund seeking income would likely invest a substantial portion of its capital into bonds and/or preferred stock. Don't confuse the limitation on only issuing common stock to raise capital with what it can invest with that capital—bond funds will use the proceeds from the sale of the common shares issued to buy bonds.

EXAMPLE

1. An investor is always purchasing newly issued shares of common stock when investing in

    A. a closed-end investment company

    B. an open-end investment company (mutual fund)

    C. a unit investment trust (UIT)

    D. a holding company

    Answer: B. A unique characteristic of mutual funds is that they are capitalized by a continuous offering of new shares, choice **B**. Whenever an investor adds to her portfolio, she is buying new shares of common stock issued by that fund. In a UIT, the investor is purchasing units, not shares.

TEST TOPIC ALERT

Because mutual funds are a continuous new offering, the **prospectus** must be distributed to a prospective investor before or during any solicitation for sale.

Closed-End Investment Companies Initial Capitalization

As we stated, the primary difference between the two categories of management companies (closed-end and open-end) is the way in which they raise capital and subsequently trade. To raise capital, a closed-end investment company conducts a common stock offering. For the initial offering, the company registers a fixed number of shares with the SEC and offers them to the public for a limited time through an underwriting group in a manner the same as any corporate stock offering. The fund's capitalization is fixed unless an additional public offering is made at a later time. Closed-end investment companies can also issue bonds and preferred stock. Therefore, the capital structure of a closed-end company can resemble that of any other corporation—common stock, preferred stock, and bonds.

PRICING OF MANAGEMENT INVESTMENT COMPANIES

U14LO3: Identify the difference in pricing between open-end and closed-end investment companies.

Closed-end investment companies are commonly known as **publicly traded funds**. After the stock is distributed, anyone can buy or sell shares in the secondary market, either on an exchange or over the counter (OTC). Supply and demand determine the **bid price** (price at which an investor can sell) and the **ask price** (price at which an investor can buy). Closed-end fund shares usually trade at a premium or discount to the shares' NAV.

TEST TOPIC ALERT

Please remember the following points:

1. Closed-end investment companies trade based upon supply and demand for their shares. As a result, their buying and selling price does *not* have a direct relationship to the NAV of the shares. Put another way, the market price of a closed-end fund is independent of the fund's NAV.

2. Country funds are funds that concentrate their investments in the securities of companies domiciled in foreign countries. Well-known examples are the Korea Fund, the New Germany Fund, and the Mexico Fund. These country funds are generally organized as closed-end (rather than open-end) companies because it is often difficult to liquidate the foreign securities to get their value into the United States.

When it comes to open-end investment companies (mutual funds), any person who wants to invest in the company buys shares directly from the company or its underwriters (or a broker-dealer with a selling agreement) at the public offering price (**POP**). A mutual fund's POP is the **NAV** per share plus any applicable sales charges. A mutual fund's NAV is calculated daily by deducting the fund's liabilities from its total assets. NAV per share is calculated by dividing the fund's NAV by the number of shares outstanding.

An open-end investment company sells **redeemable securities**. When an investor sells shares, the company redeems them at their NAV. For each share an investor redeems, the company sends the investor money for the investor's proportionate share of the company's net assets. Therefore, a mutual fund's capital shrinks when investors redeem shares.

Each investor's share in the fund's performance is based on the number of shares owned. Mutual fund shares may be purchased in either full or fractional units, unlike stock, which may be purchased in full units only. Because mutual fund shares can be fractional, the investor can think in terms of dollars rather than number of shares owned. Because closed-end funds trade like any other corporate stock, fractional shares are not available.

	Open-End	**Closed-End**
Capitalization	Unlimited; continuous offering of shares	Fixed; single offering of shares
Issues	Common stock only; no debt securities	May issue: common stock, preferred stock, debt securities
Shares	Full or fractional	Full only
Offering and trading	Sold and redeemed by fund only	Initial primary offering
	Continuous primary offering	Secondary trading OTC or on an exchange
	Must redeem shares	Does not redeem shares
Pricing	NAV + sales charge	Current market value + commission
	Selling price determined by formula in the prospectus; the price can never be below the NAV	Price determined by supply and demand so it can be above, below, or the same as the NAV

TEST TOPIC ALERT

We said earlier that closed-end funds also compute NAV; however, because their price is determined by supply and demand and, as a consequence, may be more than, the same as, or less than the NAV, it does not have the relevance that it does with open-end funds. Therefore, instead of daily computation, it is generally only done once per week.

Forward Pricing

Open-end investment companies (mutual funds) must compute their net asset value per share (NAV) at least once per day (very few compute more than that) as of the close of the markets (generally 4 p.m. ET). Price determination for purchases and sales is based upon the forward pricing principle. That is, whenever an order, whether to purchase or redeem shares, is received, the price is based upon the next computed NAV per share. For example, any order received (and time stamped) prior to 4 p.m. ET will be executed at the price computed as of that day's market close. If the order is received at 4 p.m. (or later), it will be executed based upon the NAV computed as of 4 p.m. the next business day.

EXAMPLE

If NavCo Mutual Fund shares are $15 per share, a $100 investment buys 6.667 shares ($100 / $15 = 6.667).

An investment company's portfolio is elastic. Money is simultaneously invested into the fund and paid out when shares are redeemed. The mutual fund portfolio's value and holdings fluctuate as money is invested or shares redeemed and as the value of the securities held by the portfolio rises and falls. The investor's account value fluctuates proportionately with the mutual fund portfolio's value.

EXAMPLE

1. Daniella has a number of investment company products within her retirement portfolio. One of these investments trades on an exchange and may trade at a premium or discount to its net asset value. These features are most likely found in what type of investment?

    A. Closed-end investment company

    B. Unit investment trust

    C. Open-end investment company

    D. Face-amount certificate company

    Answer: A. A closed-end investment company (closed-end fund, or CEF), choice **A**, is a type of investment company whose shares trade in the secondary market. It is critical to remember for the exam that the price of a closed-end company is based on supply and demand and, therefore, can sell at, above, or below the fund's NAV.

MUTUAL FUND SHARE CLASSES AND LOADS

U14LO4: Contrast the different mutual fund share classes and how that relates to the different types of loads charged to fund investors.

FINRA prohibits its members who underwrite fund shares from assessing sales charges *in excess of 8.5%* of the POP on the purchase of open-end investment company shares. The actual schedule of sales charges is specified *in the prospectus*. Sales loads, management fees, and operating expenses reduce an investor's returns because they diminish the amount of money invested in a fund. Historically, mutual funds have charged **front-end loads** of up to 8.5% of the money invested (the POP).

Alternatively, funds may charge a **back-end** load when funds are withdrawn. Some funds charge ongoing fees under section 12b-1 of the Investment Company Act of 1940. These funds deduct annual fees to pay for marketing and distribution costs.

A fund's expense ratio expresses the management fees and operating expenses as a percentage of the fund's net assets. All mutual funds, load and no-load, have expense ratios.

The expense ratio is calculated by dividing annual operating expenses by the average dollar value of the fund's assets under management.

The sales charge is not considered an expense when calculating a fund's expense ratio.

EXAMPLE

An expense ratio of 1.72% means that the fund spends $1.72 per year for every $100 of invested assets.

Typically, more aggressive funds have higher expense ratios.

EXAMPLE

An aggressive growth fund's expense ratio is usually higher than that of an AAA bond fund because more trading occurs in the growth fund's portfolio.

Closed-End Funds

Closed-end funds do not carry sales charges. An investor pays a brokerage commission in an agency transaction or pays a markup or markdown in a principal transaction.

Open-End Funds

All sales commissions are paid from the sales charges collected. Sales charges include commissions for the managing underwriter, broker-dealers, and their agents who sell the fund, as well as all expenses incurred in communications with the public. The sales charge of a mutual fund is stated as a percentage of the POP per share.

Mutual fund distributors use three different methods to collect the fees for the sale of shares:

- **Front-end loads** (difference between POP and net NAV)
- **Back-end loads** (contingent deferred sales loads)
- **12b-1 fees** (asset-based fees, technically not a sales charge)

Front-End Loads

Front-end sales loads are reflected in a fund's POP. The charges are added to the NAV at the time an investor buys shares. They are frequently referred to as Class A shares and have lower operating expense ratios than other classes.

Back-End Loads

A back-end sales load, also called a *contingent deferred sales charge or load* (*CDSC*), is charged at the time an investor redeems mutual fund shares. The sales load, a declining percentage charge that is reduced annually (for instance, 8% the first year, 7% the second, 6% the third, and so forth), is applied to the proceeds of any shares sold in that year. The back-end load is usually structured so that it drops to zero after six to eight years at which time they are converted to Class A shares with their lower operating expense ratios. They are frequently referred to as Class B shares.

12b-1 Asset-Based Fees

Mutual funds cannot act as distributors for their own fund shares except under Section 12b-1 of the Investment Company Act of 1940. This provision permits a mutual fund to collect a fee for promotion or sales-related activities in connection with the distribution of its shares. The fee is determined as a percentage of the fund's average total NAV during the year. The fee is disclosed in the fund's prospectus.

The percentage of net assets charged must be reasonable (typically 0.5% of net assets—this annual fee cannot exceed 0.75% of net assets), and the fee must reflect the anticipated level of distribution services. If the fee exceeds 0.25%, the fund cannot use the term *no-load*.

In order to charge a 12b-1 fee, there are several specific requirements in the law. There must be a written plan and this written plan must meet the following requirements:

- The plan has been approved initially by a vote of at least a majority of the outstanding voting securities of the investment company.

■ The plan, together with any related agreements, has been approved initially and reapproved at least annually by a vote of the board of directors of the company, and of the directors who are not *interested persons* of the company (the *outside* directors).

■ The plan may be terminated at any time by a vote of the majority of the members of the board of directors of the company who are not *interested persons* of the company, **or** by a vote of the majority of the shareholders of the company.

Classes of Fund Shares

Mutual funds may offer several classes of shares to allow investors to select how they pay the sales charges. The following is a typical method by which firms may classify fund shares by fee type: Class A, B, and C shares.

■ **Class A** shares (*front-end load*): investors pay the charge at the time of purchase.

■ **Class B** shares (*back-end load*): declines over time so investors pay the charge at redemption.

■ **Class C** shares (*level load*): no sales charge to purchase, generally a 1% CDSC for one year, with a continuous 12b-1 charge.

The class of shares determines the type of sales charge as well as operating expenses with Class A having lower costs (usually a low or no 12b-1 fee) than Class B and Class C shares. All other rights associated with mutual fund ownership remain the same across each class.

TAKE NOTE

In recent years, a number of other share classes have emerged. As of the printing of this text, the only ones we are aware of possibly appearing on the exam are the following:

■ Class I shares, which would be sold only to institutional investors (hence the letter, I), and usually have lower fees and expenses.

■ Class R shares, which would be sold only to participants in retirement plans, such as a 401(k), and have no front-end or back-end load, but may have a 12b-1 fee.

Reductions in Sales Charges

There are two ways that an investor can take advantage of reduced sales charges available on Class A shares for larger purchases.

■ Breakpoints—a scale of declining sales charges based on the amount invested

■ Rights of accumulation—permits an investor to aggregate shares owned in related accounts in some or all funds in the fund family to reach a breakpoint discount with no time limit.

Breakpoints

The schedule of discounts a mutual fund offers is called the fund's **breakpoints**. Breakpoints are available to any person. For a breakpoint qualification, the term *any person* includes married couples, parents and their *minor* children, and corporations. Investment clubs or associations formed for the purpose of investing do *not* qualify for breakpoints.

Figure 14.1: Sample Breakpoint Schedule

Purchase Amount	Sales Charge
$0–$24,999	6.5%
$25,000–$49,999	5.5%
$50,000–$99,999	5%
$100,000–$249,999	3%
$250,000–$499,999	2%
$500,000–$999,999	1%
$1,000,000 +	0%

An investor can qualify for breakpoints in several ways. A large, lump-sum investment is one method. Mutual funds offer additional incentives for an investor to continue to invest and qualify for breakpoints through a **letter of intent**.

Breakpoint Sales

Both state and federal regulators prohibit registered personnel from making higher commissions by selling investment company shares in a dollar amount just below the point at which the sales charge is reduced. This is known as a **breakpoint sale** and this practice is considered contrary to just and equitable principles of trade. For example, using the above chart, if an order for $24,000 was taken without indicating to the investor that an additional $1,000 would save $250 in sales charges (1% reduction on $25,000) would likely be considered a violation.

 TAKE NOTE

Although not specifically listed as a violation, regulators scrutinize large purchases of Class B shares. A purchase large enough to reach a significant Class A share breakpoint results in a low enough sales charge that, in just a few years, the lower operating expenses of the Class A shares will more than make up the difference in front-end cost. In practice, very few firms will accept an order for Class B shares in excess of $100,000, particularly if the investor intends to maintain the position for a number of years.

Letter of Intent (LOI)

A person who plans to invest more money with the same mutual fund company may decrease overall sales charges by signing a **letter of intent (LOI)**. In the LOI, the investor informs the investment company that he intends to invest the additional funds necessary to reach the breakpoint within 13 months.

The LOI is a one-sided contract binding on the fund only. The customer must complete the intended investment to qualify for the reduced sales charge. The fund holds the extra shares purchased as a result of the reduced sales charge in escrow. If the customer deposits sufficient money to complete the LOI, he receives the escrowed shares. Appreciation and reinvested dividends do not count toward the LOI.

EXAMPLE

Using the sample breakpoint schedule previously listed, a customer investing $20,000 is under the $25,000 breakpoint. The customer might sign a LOI promising an amount that will qualify for the breakpoint within 13 months from the date of the letter. An additional $5,000 invested in the fund within 13 months qualifies the customer for the reduced sales charge. Each deposit is charged the reduced sales charge at the time of purchase.

If the customer has not completed the investment within 13 months, he will be given the choice of sending a check for the difference in sales charges or cashing in escrowed shares to pay the difference.

Backdating the Letter

A fund often permits a customer to sign an LOI as late as 90 days after an initial purchase. The LOI may be backdated by up to 90 days to include prior purchases but may not cover more than 13 months in total. This means that if the customer signs the LOI after 60 days, he has 11 months to complete the letter.

EXAMPLE

1. When discussing investment companies, the term, sales load, most commonly refers to

    A. the fund's sales charge, expressed as a percentage of the NAV

    B. the fund's sales charge, expressed as a percentage of the public offering price

    C. the commission earned by the broker-dealer making the sale

    D. the 12b-1 fee

    Answer: B. Class A shares of an open-end investment company, (mutual fund) have a "front-end" sales charge, or sales load, which is computed as a percentage of the POP, choice **B**. That is, if the fund's POP is $10 and the NAV is $9.50, the 50 cent sales charge is 5% of the $10 offering price. In general, most of the sales load is paid to the broker-dealer making the sale as compensation. The 12b-1 fee is never referred to as a sales load because it is not related to the sale of shares.

2. Barbara wishes to invest in the KAPCO Growth Fund, an open-end investment company. She expects to hold the shares for at least 10 years. If she purchases KAPCO's Class A shares, each of these would be a way for her to receive a reduction on the sales charge EXCEPT

    A. a single investment that reaches a breakpoint

    B. joining together with her sister to make a purchase at a breakpoint level

    C. signing a letter of intent

    D. benefiting from the right of accumulation

    Answer: B. Reaching a breakpoint is the way in which investors can receive a break on the sales load charged when purchasing Class A shares. Purchases may be combined with spouses and dependent children, but not other family members, such as siblings, making the exception here choice **B**. The three ways to reach a breakpoint are:

1. a lump-sum purchase;

2. using a LOI granting 13 months to reach the breakpoint; or

3. taking advantage of rights of accumulation (no time limit).

3. An investor who initially makes a small investment in a mutual fund may have the advantage of a lower sales charge on investments made over a 13-month period through

    A. a breakpoint letter

    B. a Class A letter

    C. a letter of intent

    D. a sponsor's letter

    Answer: C. Investors who sign a LOI, (choice **C**), stating they will invest a specified amount over a 13-month period are eligible for a reduced sales load if they invest enough to reach the breakpoint within that time. Breakpoints entitle investors to reduced sales charges.

PRIVATE FUNDS

U14LO5: Identify the characteristics of private funds and venture capital funds.

In Part 1, we discussed the exemption from registration offered under both state and federal law for those who are investment advisers to private funds and venture capital funds. At that time, we explained the legal definitions and at this point, we're going to discuss the primary characteristics of these two.

Private funds, generally referred to as private equity funds, limit their ownership so as not to be considered investment companies. Remember, as a 3(c)(1) fund, there can be no more than 100 investors and, under state law, all of them must be *qualified clients*. If exempt under the 3(c)(7) provision, all investors must be *qualified purchasers* and the fund is limited to a maximum of 1,999 investors (most almost never approach anywhere near that number). Most private funds are organized as partnerships rather than corporations. One special kind of private fund is the hedge fund and that will be covered in the next unit. One difference between hedge funds and the other private funds is the anticipated holding period of the investments. Hedge funds tend to take a more active trading role where their positions are traded actively over a short time period. Conversely, private funds generally hold their investments for the long run.

Private funds can be separated into two different categories; those which make **direct** investment and those which make **portfolio** investments. What is the difference? In the first case, the funds have a 10% or greater voting interest in an operating company (one that is actually in operations) with the goal of influencing management and operations. The latter case, the fund does not acquire a control position and builds a portfolio that may be stock, bonds, derivatives, or any combination of these.

One specific type of private fund that is becoming increasingly more popular is the *private liquidity fund*. The SEC defines private liquidity funds as "any private fund that seeks to generate income by investing in a portfolio of short-term obligations to maintain a stable net asset value (NAV) per unit or minimize principal volatility for investors." If that sounds like a money market mutual fund, (MMF), it should. In 2014, a number of restrictions, such as requiring a floating NAV (probably not tested), were placed on certain money market funds. In order to avoid those, the industry developed these private funds which, being exempt from SEC registration, are also exempt from those restrictions. Because they are unregistered, less information is publicly available about these funds compared to a traditional MMF that reports its holdings on a monthly basis.

Venture capital (VC) funds are also generally organized as limited partnerships where the investment decisions are made by the general partner with the capital coming from the limited partners (LPs). Those LPs can be wealthy individuals, pension and endowment funds, and even hedge funds. VC funds look for young, promising companies with an expectation of high returns in exchange for the high risk. Unlike private equity funds, it more typical that venture capital fund investments are made in businesses that are not yet fully operational. The funding (and sometimes management guidance) provided has the goal of developing an exit strategy in 10 years or less.

One common characteristic of private equity and venture capital funds is the compensation to the fund manager. Typically, the annual management fee is 2% of committed capital plus 20% of the profits when the business is sold. This is usually referred to as the *carried interest*.

EXAMPLE

1. One of your friends is an entrepreneur who is looking for a way to raise capital for her fledgling business. Because the enterprise has no operating history, it is most likely that her best bet would be to approach

   A. a hedge fund

   B. a mutual fund

   C. a private equity fund

   D. a venture capital fund

   Answer: D. When the business is in the pre-operating stage, it is of most interest to venture capitalists, choice **D**. Private equity funds, including hedge funds, invariably invest in going concerns and mutual funds are almost always limited to purchasing securities that are marketable.

HEDGE FUNDS

U14LO6: Identify the structure, compensation arrangements, and suitability requirements of a hedge fund.

These are a form of fund generally organized as a limited partnership with no more than 100 investors that does not have to register with the SEC, although the portfolio managers generally are required to register as investment advisers. Because there is no registration requirement, one of the differences between a mutual fund and a hedge fund is the hedge fund's lack of transparency; a mutual fund is offered via a prospectus filed with the SEC while a hedge fund is offered via a private placement memorandum containing significantly less information.

Hedge funds are free to adopt far riskier investment policies than those permitted to open and closed-end funds, such as arbitrage strategies and massive short positions during bearish markets. In addition, they may use leverage (borrowed money) and derivatives such as options and futures. Even though these risky techniques are employed, the primary aim of most hedge funds is to reduce volatility and risk while attempting to preserve capital and deliver positive returns under all market conditions.

Another important factor is that management fees tend to be much, much higher than with other investments. Almost all hedge funds charge performance-based fees. The typical fee structure is known by the vernacular "2 & 20"—most funds take a 2% management fee and 20% of any profits. Fund compensation agreements may also contain a **hurdle rate**, where the incentive fee will only be paid if the fund return exceeds a set threshold return (e.g., 4%).

Many hedge funds also require that investors maintain the investment for a minimum length of time (e.g., one year) and, to that extent, they can be considered illiquid. These requirements are known as *lock-up* provisions. This provision provides that, during a certain initial period, an investor may not make a withdrawal from the fund—the investor's capital is *locked up*. Generally recognized as one way the manager of the hedge fund portfolio can have capital retained in the fund, it is also seen to be another factor adding to the unique risk of hedge funds—in this case, shares being illiquid for that specified length of time.

Therefore, because of the higher risk, investment in these vehicles is limited to institutional clients and wealthy individuals, known as accredited investors (defined in Unit 1).

TEST TOPIC ALERT

Most hedge funds are organized as limited partnerships with the portfolio managers investing along with the investors. As they say in the industry, they have "skin in the game," so they have a greater motivation to succeed. The partnership is the issuer of the ownership units.

EXAMPLE

1. Which type of investment company is most often organized as a limited partnership?

   A. Face-amount certificate company

   B. Exchange-traded fund

   C. Hedge fund

   D. Unit investment trust

   Answer: C. For various legal reasons, mostly related to the need to avoid registration with the SEC, hedge funds are generally structured as limited partnership entities, choice **C**, with the organizers invariably sinking their own funds into a few units.

Hedge funds are indirectly available to ordinary investors through mutual funds called funds of hedge funds. Because hedge funds themselves have limited liquidity, purchasing a mutual fund of hedge funds offers not only diversification but also, in many, but not all cases, the liquidity of the mutual fund.

TEST TOPIC ALERT

You may be required to know what hedge funds and mutual funds have in common. Which of the following would you choose?

- A high degree of transparency
- Relatively low management costs
- A pooled investment with other investors
- High liquidity

From what we've covered, you should have seen that hedge funds do not offer the transparency of mutual funds. The key to getting that point is that they are not registered with the SEC so the disclosures that must be made are limited. The management fee structure for hedge funds is much higher than mutual funds and, due to the lock-up period, their liquidity is questionable. However, the common characteristic is that they are pooled investments.

UNIT INVESTMENT TRUSTS (UITs)

U14LO7: Recall the special features of unit investment trusts.

The third of the entities meeting the definition of an investment company under the Investment Company Act is the unit investment trust (UIT). A UIT is an **unmanaged** investment company organized under a trust indenture. UITs:

- do not have boards of directors;
- do not employ an investment adviser; and
- do not actively manage their own portfolios (trade securities).

A unit investment trust issues only redeemable securities, known as **units** or **shares of beneficial interest**, each of which represents an undivided interest in a portfolio of specified securities. The trustees use the investor's money to purchase securities designed to meet the UIT's stated objective. Without an investment adviser (management), once compiled, the portfolio remains fixed. An example of a UIT is one solely invested in municipal bonds where the trust liquidates after the final bond in the portfolio matures. There are also equity trusts where, because stock doesn't mature, the portfolio is liquidated at a predetermined date and the proceeds distributed to unit holders or reinvested into a new trust at the investor's option.

Under the Investment Company Act of 1940, the trustees must maintain secondary markets in the units, thus allowing unit holders the ability to redeem their units at NAV. Some ETFs (covered later in this unit) are organized as UITs and trade, as the name implies, on exchanges or the Nasdaq Stock Market.

TAKE NOTE

Know the following features of UITs.

- UITs are not actively managed; there is no board of directors or investment adviser.
- UIT shares (units) must be redeemed by the trust.
- UITs are investment companies as defined under the Investment Company Act of 1940.

EXAMPLE

1. Louis owns an investment that is an unmanaged portfolio in which the money manager initially selects the securities to be included in the portfolio and then holds those securities until they mature or the investment portfolio terminates. This statement best describes which type of investment?

   A. Closed-end investment company

   B. Face-amount certificate company

   C. Open-end investment company

   D. Unit investment trust

   Answer: D. A unit investment trust (UIT) is a type of investment company, choice **D**, which is generally unmanaged as the money manager initially selects the securities to be included in the portfolio and then holds those securities until they mature or the UIT terminates.

EXCHANGE-TRADED FUNDS (ETFs)

U14LO8: Identify the distinguishing characteristics of exchange-traded funds (ETFs).

An ETF registers with the SEC under the Investment Company Act of 1940 either as a unit investment trust (a "UIT ETF") or as an open-end management company (an "open-end ETF"). In both cases, the ETF computes its net asset value daily just as would any other UIT or open-end company.

This type of fund generally invests in a specific index, such as the S&P 500. Any class of asset that has a published index around it and is liquid can be made into an ETF so that there are ETFs for real estate and commodities as well as stocks and bonds. In this way, an ETF is similar to an index mutual fund. The difference is that the exchange-traded fund trades like a stock on an exchange or Nasdaq and, in this way, is similar to a closed-end investment company. The investor can take advantage of price changes that are due to the market, rather than just the underlying value of the stocks in the portfolio.

TAKE NOTE

Although, as stated, most ETFs are passive in that they are based on some index, in recent years, there has been a growth in actively traded ETFs where, instead of attempting to mirror an index, the managers select individual assets based upon expected performance. This concept will make more sense after you read Unit 20, which explains passive and active portfolio management styles.

ETFs can be purchased on margin and sold short, (covered in Unit 22), just like any other listed stock. This is another difference between ETFs and mutual funds. Expenses tend to be lower than those of mutual funds as well because all the adviser has to do is match up to the specified index, so the fees are minimal. In addition, there can be tax advantages to owning ETFs.

However, because there are brokerage commissions on each trade (in and out), ETFs are generally not competitive with a no-load index fund for the small investor making regular periodic investments such as in a dollar cost averaging plan (described in Unit 20).

TAKE NOTE

There are now some U.S.-listed ETFs that are available for commission-free trading on certain select platforms (these are typically proprietary funds). These products can be bought and sold without traditional brokerage commissions for investors with certain accounts and subject to certain restrictions. For exam purposes, these are the exceptions rather than the rule.

Many ETFs are legally classified as UITs with the rest as open-end companies (although those cannot be referred to as mutual funds because shares are not redeemable).

Unlike the CEF (closed-end fund) where the market price will generally vary quite a bit from the NAV because those prices are determined by supply and demand, there are occasions where persistent small premiums and discounts arise in ETFs, but that is due to a structural inconsistency. Under normal circumstances, the premium and discount that arises between an ETF's NAV and its trading price at the end of the day is the result of late in the day market activity and will narrow at the opening on the following trading day.

EXAMPLE

1. Which of the following is NOT touted as an advantage to purchasing ETFs instead of index mutual funds?

    A. Intra-day trading

    B. Typically lower expense ratios

    C. Performance is generally better than the underlying index

    D. Can be purchased on margin

    Answer: C. One thing that neither of these products can claim is performance better than the underlying index, choice **C**. Think about it— the index has no management fees. Even though the management fees on index funds are very low and those on ETFs generally lower than that, there are still expenses making it unlikely that their performance can beat that of the index. The fact that an investor can trade the ETF during the day instead of accepting whatever the next computed price is, can be a benefit for those who are trying to time the market. And, for those who wish to add the leverage of margin trading (explained more fully in Unit 22), that can only be done with ETFs, not index mutual funds.

REAL ESTATE INVESTMENT TRUSTS (REITs)

U14LO9: Identify the unique features of REITs.

A **real estate investment trust** (**REIT**, pronounced *reet*) is a company that manages a portfolio of real estate investments to earn profits and/or income for its shareholders. Like many other pooled investment vehicles, REITs offer professional management and diversification. REITs are normally publicly traded and serve as a source of long-term financing for real estate projects. A REIT pools capital in a manner similar to an investment company. Shareholders receive dividends from investment income or capital gains distributions. REITs normally:

■   own commercial property (**equity REITs**);

- own mortgages on commercial property (**mortgage REITs**); or

- do both (**hybrid REITs**).

REITs are organized as trusts in which investors buy and sell shares either on stock exchanges or in the over-the-counter market. They are not redeemable, as is the case with mutual funds or UITs.

REITs enjoy a unique hybrid status for federal income tax purposes. A REIT shareholder generally is taxed only on dividends paid by the REIT and on gains upon the disposition of REIT shares. A REIT is a corporation for U.S. tax purposes, but because it receives a dividends paid deduction, the REIT generally is not subject to corporate tax if it distributes to its shareholders substantially all of its taxable income for each year.

How much is *substantially* all? Under the guidelines of Subchapter M of the Internal Revenue Code, a REIT can avoid being taxed as a corporation by receiving 75% or more of its income from real estate and distributing **90%** or more of its taxable income to its shareholders.

TEST TOPIC ALERT

Five important points to remember about REITs follow.

- An owner of REITs holds an undivided interest in a pool of real estate investments.

- REITs are liquid because they trade on exchanges and OTC.

- REITs are not investment companies (mutual funds).

- REITs offer dividends and gains to investors but do not flow through losses like limited partnerships, and therefore are not considered direct participation programs (DPPs—Unit 17).

- The key numbers are: (1) at least **75%** of a REIT's assets must be represented by real estate assets such as real property or loans secured by real property, cash, and U.S. government securities; (2) at least **75%** of the REIT's annual gross income must be from real estate-related income, such as rents from real property and interest on obligations secured by mortgages on real property; and (3) in order to qualify as a REIT, the REIT must distribute at least **90%** of its taxable income.

TAKE NOTE

In recent years, there has been substantial growth in the number of "non-traded" REITs (limited liquidity). However, for exam purposes, assume the REIT is publicly traded unless the question states otherwise.

BENEFITS AND RISKS OF POOLED INVESTMENTS

U14LO10: Explain the benefits and risks of pooled investments in client portfolios.

As you have seen, there are many different types of pooled investment vehicles. In general, they all share some important characteristics:

- Diversification: By pooling assets with many others, investors have the opportunity to own an interest in a far greater number and range of securities than available to almost any individual investor

- Professional management: In almost all cases, someone with expertise (we hope) is "minding the store." Even in the case of the UIT where there is no ongoing management, the initial portfolio is constructed by experts.

The exam tends to focus on the most popular investments, such as mutual funds, so we will start with those.

Mutual Funds

What are the **benefits** of including mutual funds in a client's portfolio?

- Diversification: The old saying, "don't put all of your eggs in one basket" certainly applies to the benefits of diversifying one's portfolio assets. Mutual funds are probably the easiest way to accomplish this. Although diversification may help to reduce risk, it will never completely eliminate it. It is possible to lose all or part of your investment.

- Professional management: Those individuals in charge of managing a mutual fund's portfolio must be registered as investment advisers with the SEC. The Investment Company Act of 1940 requires that they follow the stated objectives set forth in the prospectus. Taking into consideration prevailing market conditions and other factors, the mutual fund manager will decide when to buy or sell securities. Rare is the individual who has the time, knowledge, or resources to compete with these professionals.

- Choice of objectives: Whatever an investor's investment objectives are, there are mutual funds available to match. There are many shades of growth funds, from highly aggressive to very conservative, but all with the goal of growing the investment. The same is true with income funds where the goal is to generate current income with varying degrees of risk from government bonds to high-yield bonds. If the objective is capital preservation, money market funds fit the bill and then there are funds that combine objectives, such as growth and income funds. There are even specialized funds (sector funds) that concentrate at least **25%** of their portfolio into specific industries or geographic areas, such as a biotech fund or a Southeast Asia fund.

- Convenience: With most mutual funds, buying and liquidating shares, changing reinvestment options, and getting information can be accomplished conveniently by going online at the fund's website, by calling a toll-free phone number, or by mail.
  - Although a fund's shareholder is relieved of the day-to-day tasks involved in researching, buying, and selling securities, an investor will still need to evaluate a mutual fund on the basis of investment goals and risk tolerance before making a purchase decision. Investors should always read the prospectus carefully before investing in any mutual fund.

- Liquidity: The Investment Company Act of 1940 requires that an open-end investment company stand ready to redeem shares at the next computed NAV per share. Payment must be made within 7 days of the redemption request. Although there may be a redemption charge, and, of course, the value of the shares may be less than their cost, liquidity is assured.

- Minimum initial investment: As mentioned previously, it doesn't take a great deal of wealth to get started investing in funds and, generally, once you are a shareholder, most funds permit additional investments of $100 or even less.

- Convenient tax information: Tax liabilities for an investor are simplified because each year the fund distributes a 1099 form explaining taxability of distributions.

- Combination Privilege: A mutual fund company frequently offers more than one fund and refers to these multiple offerings as its family of funds. An investor seeking a reduced sales charge may be allowed to combine separate investments in two or more funds within the same family to reach a breakpoint.

EXAMPLE

Joe Smith has invested $15,000 in the ACE Growth Fund for retirement and $10,000 in the ACE Income Fund for his children's education. The sponsor may view the two separate expenditures as one investment totaling $25,000 when calculating the sales charge.

Exchanges Within a Family of Funds

Many investment companies offer the **exchange** or **conversion privilege** within their families of funds. **Exchange privileges** allow an investor to convert an investment in one fund for an equal investment in another fund in the same family at NAV without incurring an additional sales charge. For example, someone who started investing when in their 30s or 40s by placing their money into an aggressive growth fund might consider moving into something more conservative when they reach their 50s. Once they hit their 60s and 70s, they would want to have a greater percentage of their money in income funds. By staying in the same family of funds and using the exchange or conversion privilege, all of these changes could be made free of sales loads.

TAKE NOTE

Any exchange of funds is considered a sale for tax purposes. Any gains or losses are fully reportable at the time of the exchange.

TEST TOPIC ALERT

It is generally agreed that the #1 advantage to investing in mutual funds is the *diversification* offered.

In doing so, the client would be incurring the following risks:

- Even with the benefits offered by diversification and professional management, market prices do fluctuate. Equity funds have market risk, whereas bond funds may be subject to interest rate risk. Unlike an individual bond that ultimately repays principal at maturity, a bond fund doesn't have a maturity date. The only mutual fund that generally does not fluctuate in price is the money market fund, but there is a tradeoff in lack of growth and low income. Not only that, but the income of a money market fund will vary, unlike that of a bank CD, which is fixed and FDIC insured.

- Fees and expenses: One must carefully analyze all of the costs involved. These include:
  - Sales charges, 12b-1 fees, and possible redemption fees.
  - Management fees (probably the largest expense on an ongoing basis).
  - The investor has no control over the manager's timing of purchases and sales, so tax efficiency could become an issue.
  - Prospectuses will not contain all the costs that affect the net return on the fund. This is why it is important to compare net returns after all expenses, including taxes to the investor.
- Other factors: When comparing funds with similar objectives, the investor should review information regarding funds':
  - services offered;
  - costs;
  - taxation;
  - tenure of management—is the management team unproven or is there a long track record; and
  - performance compared to an appropriate benchmark (see Unit 23).

Net Redemptions

It can sometimes happen, particularly during declining markets, that there is an excess of shareholder redemptions over new share purchases. This is known as *net redemptions*. When that occurs, the portfolio manager is put in the difficult position of having to decide which assets to liquidate when prices are falling. A fund suffering with net redemptions is probably not going to deliver your clients the performance they are seeking.

Private Funds

What are the benefits of including private funds in a client's portfolio?

- By investing before the company matures enough for a public offering, there is an opportunity for very large profits
- Many private funds are structured so as to give the investors a say in the management and development of the company
- Added diversification, because these usually have a low correlation to the overall market

In doing so, the client would be incurring the following risks:

- Business risk—a high percentage of start-ups do not succeed and the investors lose most or all of their investment
- Liquidity risk—there is rarely an opportunity to find a secondary market and even when the company has a public offering, these investors' shares are likely to be restricted
- Lack of transparency—Being unregistered securities, no regulatory body has reviewed the offering documents

Hedge Funds

What are the **benefits** of including hedge funds in a client's portfolio?

- The designed strategy of many hedge funds is to generate positive returns in both rising and falling markets.

- With a large variety of available investment styles, investors have a plethora of choices to assist them in meeting their objectives.

- As part of an asset allocation class, hedge funds may reduce overall portfolio risk and volatility, and increase returns.

- A proper selection of hedge funds can create uncorrelated returns, adding a level of diversification.

In doing so, the client would be incurring the following risks:

- Expenses can be quite high.

- The risky strategies could backfire leading to significant loss of capital.

- Liquidity risk: during the lock-up period, the investor is locked-in to the investment. Furthermore, even after that period, there is no active secondary market for these unregistered securities; they are not listed on any exchanges.

- Finally, as is generally the case with limited partnership investments, the sale of partnership interests may require approval of the general partner.

EXAMPLES

Julia, an IAR, is analyzing various policies utilized by hedge funds recommended by her firm. Julia has summarized the policies as follows:

Policy 1: During the fund raising period, each new investor must contribute a minimum of $500,000 to the fund.

Policy 2: The hedge fund manager will return incentive fees to investors in the event that the minimum required return is not met.

Policy 3: Investors must provide redemption requests to the hedge fund manager at least 60 days before the funds are to be withdrawn.

Policy 4: New investors may not withdraw funds during the first six months that the funds are invested with the hedge fund manager.

1. Which of the policies identified by Julia specifies a lock-up period?

    A. Policy 1

    B. Policy 2

    C. Policy 3

    D. Policy 4

Answer: D. A lock-up period refers to a set period, such as six months (choice **D**) that an investor's funds must remain invested in the hedge fund. During that time period, withdrawal requests are not permitted.

2. One of your clients wishes to invest in a hedge fund. You should explain which of the following points?

    A. Shares of these funds are easy to redeem.

    B. The fund can be expected to generate a profit whether the markets trend up or trend down.

    C. These funds purchase a large amount of preferred stock.

    D. Expenses for these funds tend to be higher than those for traditional mutual funds.

    Answer: D. One of the distinguishing characteristics of hedge funds is their high fee structure when compared to mutual funds, choice **D**. Hedge funds typically use risky strategies to generate profit regardless of market direction, but there is no assurance that the objective will be realized. Redemption may be difficult with these funds.

REITs

What are the benefits of including REITs in a client's portfolio?

■ The opportunity to invest in real estate without the degree of liquidity risk found in direct ownership

■ Properties are selected by professionals with greater negotiating power than an individual

■ A negative correlation to the general stock market, because real estate prices and the stock market frequently move in opposite directions

■ Reasonable income and/or potential capital appreciation

In doing so, the client would be incurring the following risks:

■ Lack of control because much of the risk in investing in REITs lies with the quality of the management.

■ REITs generally have greater price volatility than direct ownership of real estate because they are influenced by stock market conditions

■ Dividends are not considered qualified for purposes of the 15% maximum tax rate and are taxed at full ordinary income rates.

■ If the REIT is not publicly traded, liquidity is very limited. While a portion of total shares outstanding may be redeemable each year, subject to limitations, redemption offers may be priced below the purchase price or current price. As a result, there is the need for more stringent suitability standards and the regulators give greater scrutiny to trades in unlisted REITs.

■ Failure to meet the distribution rules could cause the REIT to be taxed.

■ Problem loans in the portfolio could cause income and/or capital to decrease.

EXAMPLE

1. In order for a REIT to avoid being taxed like a corporation, it must distribute at least

   A. 75% of its taxable income

   B. 90% of its taxable income

   C. 95% of its taxable income

   D. 100% of its taxable income

Answer: B. In order to qualify under IRS regulations, REITs must distribute at least 90% (choice **B**) of their taxable income in the form of dividends to shareholders. At least 75% of the REIT's income must come from real estate investments.

Insurance-Based Products

In the previous unit, we discussed a number of different pooled investment vehicles. In this unit, we're going to cover two more: variable annuities and variable life insurance. But those are not the only insurance-based products that are relevant to this exam. Even though the others we'll discuss are not securities, understanding what they are and their basic features are testable items.

The Series 65 exam will include approximately two questions on the material presented in this unit.

LEARNING OBJECTIVES

When you have completed this unit, you will be able to accomplish the following.

U15LO1: Contrast the difference between fixed and variable annuities.
U15LO2: Compare the differences between variable annuities and mutual funds.
U15LO3: Compute the account return for an index annuity.
U15LO4: Compare the different purchase and settlement options for annuities.
U15LO5: Calculate the tax on an early withdrawal from an annuity.
U15LO6: Compare the major types of life insurance.
U15LO7: Identify the special features applicable to a variable life policy.

TYPES OF ANNUITIES

U15LO1: Contrast the difference between fixed and variable annuities.

Although many products offered by insurance companies are not securities, the securities professional should be aware of the features of both securities and non-securities offerings.

An **annuity** is generally a contract between an individual and a life insurance company, usually purchased for retirement income. An investor, the **annuitant**, pays the premium in one lump sum or in periodic payments. At a future date, the annuitant can either elect to surrender the policy and receive a lump-sum payout or begin receiving regular income distributions that will continue for life.

Because all earnings are tax-deferred, many individuals looking to accumulate additional funds for retirement find annuities to be a valuable tool. Unlike IRAs and qualified retirement plans (covered in Unit 24) which limit the amount that can be contributed, there is no legal limit to the amount that can be invested in an annuity (the insurance company may place a limit, generally in the range of $1–$3 million that it will accept).

Annuity contracts are classified into two major types (depending on the payout the annuity makes):

■   Fixed annuities

■   Variable annuities

Fixed Annuities

A **fixed annuity** guarantees a fixed rate of return. When the individual elects to begin receiving income, the payout is determined by the account's value and the annuitant's life expectancy based on mortality tables. A fixed annuity payout remains constant throughout the annuitant's life.

TAKE NOTE

Because the insurance company guarantees the return and the annuitant bears no risk, a fixed annuity is an insurance product and not a security. A salesperson must have a life insurance license to sell fixed annuities but does not need to be securities licensed.

Although principal and interest are not at risk, a fixed annuity risks loss of purchasing power because of inflation.

EXAMPLE

An individual who annuitized a contract in 1990 may have been guaranteed a monthly payout of $800. Decades later, this amount may prove insufficient to live on.

VARIABLE ANNUITIES

Instead of purchase payments being directed to the insurance company's general account, money deposited in a variable annuity is directed into one or more subaccounts of the company's separate account. Although the options include money market securities and bonds, purchase payments are frequently invested in a stock portfolio, which has a better chance of keeping pace with inflation than fixed-income investments.

The greater potential gain of a variable annuity involves more potential risk than a fixed annuity because it invests in securities rather than accepting the insurance company's guarantees. Payouts may vary considerably because an annuity unit's worth fluctuates with the value of the selected subaccount(s).

Fixed Annuities	Variable Annuities
Monthly payout is fixed	Monthly payout varies
Guaranteed interest rate	Variable rate of return
Investment risk assumed by insurance company	Investment risk assumed by annuitant
Portfolio of fixed-income securities and mortgages	Portfolio of equities, debt, money market instruments
General account	Separate account
Vulnerable to inflation	Resistant to inflation
Insurance regulation	Insurance and securities regulation

EXAMPLE

1. The key difference between a fixed annuity and a variable annuity is that the fixed annuity

    A. offers a guaranteed return

    B. offers a monthly payment that may vary in amount

    C. will always pay out more money than a variable annuity

    D. attempts to offer protection to the annuitant from inflation risk.

    Answer: A. If an annuity is fixed, it means the return to the investor is guaranteed, (choice **A**), whereas with a variable annuity, there are no guarantees as to the amount of return. It is the variable annuity whose annuity payment will vary and, because of the growth opportunity, offers potential inflation protection.

Separate Account

The contributions that investors make to a variable annuity are kept in a **separate account** from the insurance company's general funds. Investors determine which of the subaccounts into which their money will be placed. Some insurance company separate accounts offer 25, 30, or even more subaccounts from the most aggressive to the most conservative.

Because the investor rather than the insurance company bears the risk, a variable annuity is considered to be a security. As a consequence, variable annuity salespersons must have both a securities license (registered with a broker-dealer member of FINRA and the applicable state or states) and an insurance license issued by the appropriate state(s).

TEST TOPIC ALERT

It is the performance of the specific subaccount(s) selected by the investor that determines the investment return.

IS A VARIABLE ANNUITY A MUTUAL FUND?

U15LO2: Compare the differences between variable annuities and mutual funds.

In the eyes of many novice investors, there doesn't seem to be very much difference between a mutual fund and a variable annuity. Although there are many similarities, there are critical differences. The following chart is a good place to begin.

Figure 15.1: Principal Features of Mutual Funds vs. Variable Annuities

Mutual Funds	Variable Annuities
Investment company	Insurance company product
Shares	Units
Investment objectives: varied	Investment objectives: varied
No guarantees	Some guarantees
Redeemed by issuer	Redeemed by issuer
Price based on formula	Price based on formula
Voting rights	Voting rights

Looking at the above chart, there doesn't seem to be much difference other than one being an insurance product with some guarantees and the other not. Let's look a bit deeper:

Advantages to Investing in Variable Annuities Compared to Mutual Funds

- **Tax-deferred growth:** All income and capital gains generated in the portfolio of the separate account are free from income tax until the money is withdrawn. Over time, this tax-deferred compounding can make a significant difference in the value of the account.

- **Guaranteed death benefit:** Most variable annuities offer an option stating that if the investor dies during the accumulation period, the beneficiary will receive the greater of the current value of the account or the amount invested. Therefore, the estate is assured of getting back at least the original investment.

- **Lifetime income:** Although a variable annuity cannot guarantee how much will be paid, choosing a payout option with lifetime benefits gives assurance that there will be a check every month as long as the annuitant is alive. This benefit protects against *longevity risk*, the uncertainty that one will outlive one's money. Be sure that you don't refer to this as guaranteed income—that would be an incorrect statement on the exam, because the income is variable.

- **IRS Section 1035 exchanges:** If you don't like the annuity you're in, you can exchange into another one without any tax consequences. However, it is possible there will be a surrender charge. This is unlike mutual funds, for which use of the exchange privilege is a taxable event.

- **No age 70½ restrictions or requirements:** Unlike traditional retirement plans that have required minimum distributions after the age of 70½, an investor can delay withdrawals as desired and, in fact, can continue to contribute.

- **No contribution limits:** Unlike retirement plans, where the annual contribution is limited, no IRS ceiling is placed on the amount that may be invested into a fixed or variable annuity.

- **Tax-free transfer between subaccounts:** Unlike mutual funds where the exchange between funds is a taxable event, the investor can transfer from one subaccount to another without any current tax liability.

- **No probate:** Because the annuity calls for direct designation of a beneficiary, upon death, the asset passes directly without the time and expense of probate.

Disadvantages to Investing in Variable Annuities Compared to Mutual Funds

- Earnings are taxed as ordinary income: Even though it is possible that most of the increase in value is generated through long-term capital gains, all earnings will be taxed at the higher ordinary income rate.

- The administrative and insurance-related expense fees are typically much higher than the fees incurred by owning a mutual fund.

- Withdrawals made before age 59½ will generally incur a 10% penalty, in addition to the ordinary income tax.

- Most variable annuities carry a conditional deferred sales charge. Therefore, surrender in the early years will usually involve additional costs.

TEST TOPIC ALERT

A variable annuity offers an investor the opportunity to have tax-deferred participation in the equity markets, albeit with expenses that are generally higher than for a mutual fund with a similar objective.

The Test Topic Alert shown above represents an idea that is commonly tested. It could look something like this:

EXAMPLE

1. When comparing mutual funds and variable annuities, it would be correct to state that

   A. both offer tax-deferred growth of earnings

   B. both require the salesperson to possess a securities and an insurance license

   C. the surrender charges on a mutual fund are usually higher than on a variable annuity

   D. the expense ratio of the variable annuity is usually higher than that of a comparable mutual fund

   Answer: D. It is generally correct to state that variable annuities offer a way to accumulate funds on a tax-deferred basis, although generally with operating expenses somewhat higher than mutual funds with the same investment objective. There is no tax-deferral with mutual funds and no insurance license is required to sell them. Only Class B and C shares have redemption fees, a form of surrender charge, and they are invariable lower and/or run for fewer years than annuity surrender charges.

INDEX ANNUITY

U15LO3: Compute the account return for an index annuity.

In an effort to overcome the purchasing power risk of fixed annuities, but without the market risk of the variable annuity, the industry developed the index annuity (IA). This product is sometimes called an equity index annuity or a fixed index annuity.

Indexed annuities (IAs) are currently popular among investors seeking market participation but with a guarantee against loss. Unlike a traditional fixed annuity, an IA credits interest to the owner's account using a formula based on the performance of a particular stock index such as the S&P 500. If the index does well, the annuitant is credited with a specified percentage of the growth of the index—typically 80% or 90% of the growth. This is known as the participation rate. If, over the life of the annuity, the index does poorly, the annuitant may receive the IA's minimum guaranteed return—typically 1 to 3%.

In addition to the participation rate, there is usually a cap rate. A typical cap might be 8%. This means that if your annuity was pegged to the S&P 500 and that index increased 20% during the year, your gain would be capped at 8%. One other negative characteristic of these products is that they tend to have longer surrender charge periods (as long as 15 years) than other annuities, especially if there is a front-end bonus.

EXAMPLE

To give you an idea of how an IA might work, consider one with a participation rate of 80%, a cap rate of 8%, and a minimum guarantee of 2%. If the index shows growth of 9% during the IA's measurement period, the annuitant would be credited with 7.2% growth (80% of 9%, which is less than the cap of 8%). However, if the index grew at a rate of 12%, the participation rate of 80% would yield 9.6%, but, because that is over the 8% cap, the account would only be credited with 8%. In any year where the index declines, the annuitant's account is not credited with any earnings, but, and this is the real benefit, the account does not lose any value either. The 2% guaranteed rate would apply if, over the term of the annuity, performance was less than 2%.

TAKE NOTE

Although index annuity is the preferred term in the industry, your exam may refer to this product as an equity index annuity.

TEST TOPIC ALERT

In NASAA's never-ending battle to try to baffle potential investment adviser representatives with questions about products they will most likely never handle, we are hearing from students that you should know the different crediting methods used for index annuities.

Without going into the technicalities (it seems all you have to know is the different types, not a lot about how they work), the purchaser can be offered the following choices as to how growth in the underlying index will be credited in the form of interest to the account:

- Annual reset. In this method, the interest to be credited to the account is computed by comparing the index value at the end of the year to the value at the beginning of the year (hence the term annual).Annual reset generally has a lower participation rate than point to point.

- High-water mark. In this method, the highest value reached by the index between anniversary dates of the annuity is compared to the value at the beginning of the year. This option can provide the highest gains.

- Point-to-point. In this method, the interest is computed based on the value of the index at the end of the contract compared to the beginning. A variation is annual point-to-point.

- Averaging. The most common is a monthly average and this can be the best options when markets are expected to be highly volatile.

PURCHASING ANNUITIES

U15LO4: Compare the different purchase and settlement options for annuities.

Insurance companies offer a number of purchase options to make it easy for annuity owners to accumulate money.

Deferred Annuity

An annuity may be purchased with a single lump-sum investment (with payout of benefits deferred until the annuitant elects to receive them). This type of investment is referred to as a **single-premium deferred annuity**.

Periodic Payment Deferred Annuity

A **periodic payment deferred annuity** allows a person to make periodic payments. The contract holder can invest money on a monthly, quarterly, or annual basis (with payout of benefits deferred until the annuitant elects to receive them).

Immediate Annuity

An investor may purchase an **immediate annuity** contract by depositing a single lump sum. The insurance company begins to pay out the annuity's benefits immediately—usually within 60 days.

Accumulation Stage

The pay-in period for a deferred annuity is known as the **accumulation stage** (there is no accumulation period for an immediate annuity). During the accumulation stage of an annuity contract, the contract terms are flexible. An investor who misses a periodic payment is in no danger of forfeiting the preceding contributions.

The contract holder can terminate the contract at any time during the accumulation stage, although the contract holder is likely to incur surrender charges on amounts withdrawn in the first five to 10 years after issuance of the contract.

Accumulation Units

An **accumulation unit** is an accounting measure that represents an investor's share of ownership in the separate account. An accumulation unit's value is determined in the same way as the value of mutual fund shares. The unit value changes with the value of the securities held in the separate account.

The names of various purchase options are quite descriptive of how they operate and should not be difficult to follow. Just to be sure, let's try the following question:

EXAMPLE

1. Insurance companies selling annuities offer a variety of purchase options to owners. Which of the following definitions regarding these annuity options is NOT true?

   A. Accumulation annuity—an annuity that allows the investor to accumulate funds in a separate account before investment in an annuity

   B. Single-premium deferred annuity—an annuity with a lump-sum investment, with payment of benefits deferred until the annuitant elects to receive them

   C. Periodic payment deferred annuity—allows a person to make periodic payments over time. The contract holder can invest money on a monthly, quarterly, or annual basis

   D. Immediate annuity—allows an investor to deposit a lump sum with the insurance company. Payout of the annuitant's benefits starts immediately, usually within 60 days

   Answer: A. Accumulation does not refer to a purchase option. The pay-in period for an annuity is known as the accumulation stage. A single-premium deferred annuity is an annuity with a lump-sum investment, with payment of benefits deferred until the annuitant elects to receive them. Periodic payment deferred annuities allow a person to make periodic payments over time. Immediate annuities allow an investor to deposit a lump sum with the insurance company payout of the annuitant's benefits starting immediately, usually within 60 days.

Bonus Annuities

It is not uncommon for index annuities (and variable annuities) to offer a bonus on top of the investor's initial contribution. For example, investing $60,000 into a single-premium annuity with a 5% bonus would result in an initial account balance of $63,000. Usually, bonus annuities have surrender charges lasting longer than those without the bonus.

RECEIVING DISTRIBUTIONS FROM ANNUITIES

The payout period for an annuity is known as the **annuity stage**. It happens when the owner of the annuity *annuitizes*.

Annuity Payout Options

It is now time for the contract holder to decide on the **settlement option**. An annuity offers several payout options for amounts accumulated in the annuity contract. The investor can let the money accumulate in the annuity, withdraw the accumulated funds in a lump sum, or withdraw the accumulated funds periodically by **annuitizing** the contract. Annuitizing occurs when the investor converts from the accumulation (pay-in) stage to the distribution (payout) stage.

The decision to annuitize the contract locks in the specified payout option. The contract holder may not change it. Annuity payout options, in order from largest monthly payout to smallest monthly payout, follow.

Life Annuity/Straight Life/Pure Life

Under this option, the payout is structured so that the annuitant receives periodic payments (usually monthly) until death. No added options or benefits exist; therefore, for a given amount of funds, this option provides the largest periodic payment. This is because it carries the greatest risk. The annuitant could get "hit by a truck" one month after annuitizing and all payments cease.

Life Annuity With Period Certain

Under the life annuity with period certain payout option, an annuitant receives payments for life, with a certain minimum period guaranteed. If the annuitant dies before the period certain expires, payments continue to the annuitant's named beneficiaries for the period certain. If the annuitant lives beyond the period certain, payments continue until the annuitant's death.

EXAMPLE

A client purchases a life annuity with a 10-year period certain payout. The insurance company guarantees payments for the life of the annuitant or 10 years, whichever is longer. If the annuitant lives for only one year after payments begin, the company continues to make payments to the annuitant's beneficiaries for nine more years. If the annuitant dies after receiving payments for 13 years, payments cease at death.

Joint Life With Last Survivor Annuity

With this option, the annuity covers two or more people, and payout is conditioned on both (all) lives.

EXAMPLE

A married couple owns an annuity jointly with a last survivor clause. The contract pays benefits as long as one of the annuitants remains alive. The payment may be the same as when both were alive, or it may be reduced for the surviving annuitant, depending on the contract. If this option includes more than two annuitants, payments cease at the last survivor's death.

Refund Annuity

Sometimes referred to as a unit refund annuity, under this settlement option, payments will continue after death of the insured until the full value of the initial premium (principal) has been returned. In some cases, the payment to the beneficiary will be a lump sum of cash, in others, a series of monthly payments.

Mortality Guarantee

Annuity companies guarantee payments for as long as annuitants live. If a change occurs in life expectancy and annuitants live longer than originally anticipated, the insurance companies assume the increased mortality cost—the **mortality guarantee**. Among the annual charges against the account is that for M&E (mortality and expense).

TEST TOPIC ALERT

The M&E charge ceases once the contract is annuitized.

EXAMPLES

1. Which of the following types of annuity settlement options provides a lifetime income to the annuitant regardless of how long he lives and the highest monthly payment amount?

   A. Straight life annuity

   B. Life annuity with period certain

   C. Installment refund annuity

   D. Joint and survivor annuity

   Answer: A. A straight life annuity, (choice **A**), provides a lifetime income to the owner/annuitant regardless of how long he lives. If the annuitant is fortunate to outlive his anticipated life expectancy, he has made a wise distribution choice. However, if he dies shortly after beginning distribution, he has made an imprudent choice because, after the annuitant dies, the issuer makes no further payments. Nevertheless, for a given purchase price, a single life annuity provides the highest monthly payment amount because the annuity provides no guarantees beyond the annuitant's life.

2. Peter and Connie are thinking about selecting a settlement option for their variable annuity. If their objective is to have the annuity provide income until both of them are deceased, which of the following settlement options will best meet their needs?

   A. Straight life annuity

   B. Joint and survivor annuity

   C. Installment refund annuity

   D. Life annuity with period certain

   Answer: B. The joint and survivor annuity (choice **B**) will allow the couple to have the annuity provide income until both of them are deceased. The payment will be lower than on a straight life annuity because two lives are involved rather than one—more risk for the insurance company; less risk for the annuitants. For a given purchase price, a straight life annuity generally provides the highest monthly payment amount because the annuity provides no payments beyond the annuitant's life. It is the old rule of the risk-reward relationship—the more risk you take, the higher the reward.

Annuity Units

When a variable annuity contract is annuitized, accumulation units are exchanged for annuity units. An **annuity unit** is a measure of value used only during an annuitized contract's payout period. It is an accounting measure that determines the amount of each payment to the annuitant during the payout period.

The number of annuity units is calculated when an owner annuitizes the contract. The number of annuity units liquidated each month does not change—it is fixed at the time of annuitizing based on the value of the contract when the payout period begins and on other variables (such as the payout option selected, the individual's age and sex, and assumed interest rate). The payment the annuitant will receive each month varies because each unit's value fluctuates with the separate account portfolio's value. This is, after all, a variable annuity.

Assumed Interest Rate (AIR)

The **AIR** is a basis for determining distributions from a variable annuity. The rate, usually estimated conservatively, provides an earnings target for the separate account. Simply, if the actual earnings exceed the AIR, the annuity payments increase; if they fall short of the AIR, the payments decrease.

EXAMPLE

An investor who annuitized a variable annuity in 1990 and began with a monthly payout of $375 might now be receiving $2,275 per month because of an increase in the value of the annuity unit.

TAXATION OF ANNUITIES

U15LO5: Calculate the tax on an early withdrawal from an annuity.

Contributions to an annuity that is not part of an employer-sponsored retirement plan (qualified annuities) are made with after-tax dollars, (nonqualified). Because contributions have been taxed already, when the account is annuitized, the portion of each payment representing a return of the original principal is not taxed. As with other investments, the money invested in an annuity represents the investor's cost basis.

The primary advantage of an annuity as an investment is that the tax on interest, dividends, and capital gains is deferred until the owner withdraws money from the contract. On withdrawal, the amount exceeding the investor's cost basis is taxed as ordinary income.

Random Withdrawals

Since 1982, random withdrawals from annuity contracts have been taxed under the **last in, first out** (**LIFO**) method. The IRS takes the view that earnings are the last monies to be received in the account. The earnings are considered to be withdrawn first from the annuity and are taxable as ordinary income. After the withdrawal of all earnings, contributions representing cost basis may be withdrawn without tax.

Lump-Sum Withdrawals

Lump-sum withdrawals are taken by using the **LIFO** accounting method. This means that earnings are removed before contributions. If an investor receives a lump-sum withdrawal before age 59½, the earnings portion withdrawn is taxed as ordinary income and is subject to an additional 10% tax penalty under most circumstances.

The penalty does not apply if the funds are withdrawn after age 59½, are withdrawn because of death or disability, or are part of a life-income option plan with fixed payouts.

EXAMPLE

A contract with a $100,000 value consists of $40,000 in contributions and $60,000 in earnings. If the investor withdraws all $100,000 at once, the $60,000 in earnings is taxed as ordinary income and the $40,000 cost basis is returned tax free. If the investor is at least 59½, there is no 10% tax penalty; if younger, the 10% tax penalty applies. However, the penalty only applies to the taxable portion ($60,000)—there is never a penalty tax on money that is not taxable. If the investor withdraws $10,000, (or any amount up to $60,000), under the LIFO rule, it is considered a withdrawal of earnings and will be taxed as ordinary income. There is never a capital gain with an annuity.

TEST TOPIC ALERT

Yes, it is true. Even when the distribution is from a nonqualified annuity, if it is made before the age of 59½, it is subject to the 10% additional tax (unless it meets one of the exceptions listed above).

Annuitized payouts are typically made monthly and are taxed according to an exclusion ratio. The **exclusion ratio** expresses the percentages of the annuity's value upon annuitization of contribution basis to the total.

EXAMPLE

If $50,000 in after-tax dollars was contributed to an annuity contract worth $100,000 at annuitization, 50% of each payment will be treated as ordinary income, whereas the other 50% of each payment will be treated (for tax purposes) as nontaxable return of basis.

Under certain circumstances, the annuitant's life expectancy may also factor in the exclusion ratio, but that is unlikely to be tested—we're just keeping it simple.

TEST TOPIC ALERT

Upon annuitization, there is never a 10% tax penalty, even if annuitization commences before age 59½.

Some additional tax concepts related to annuities are demonstrated here.

EXAMPLES

1. An annuity contract owner, age 45, surrenders the annuity to buy a home. Which of the following best describes the tax consequences of this action?

    A. Ordinary income taxes and a 10% early withdrawal penalty will apply to all money withdrawn.

    B. Capital gains tax will apply to the amount of the withdrawal that represents earnings; there will be no tax on the cost basis.

    C. Ordinary income taxes and a 10% early withdrawal penalty will apply to the amount of the withdrawal that represents earnings; there will be no tax on the cost basis.

    D. Ordinary income taxes apply to the amount of the withdrawal that represents earnings; the 10% early withdrawal penalty does not apply to surrendering an annuity.

    Answer: C. Interest earnings are taxable as ordinary income. They are also subject to the 10% early withdrawal penalty when withdrawn before age 59½. The contract holder recovers the cost basis without tax.

2. After the death of the annuitant, beneficiaries under a life and 15-year period certain option are subject to

    A. capital gains taxation on the total amount of payments received

    B. ordinary income taxation on the total amount of payments received, plus a 10% withdrawal penalty if the annuitant was under age 59½

    C. ordinary income taxation on the amount of the payout that exceeds the cost basis based on the exclusion ratio

    D. tax-free payout of all remaining annuity benefits

    Answer: C. Payments from the annuity to the beneficiary through a period certain option are taxed in the same way as other periodic annuity payments; benefits over the amount of the cost basis are taxable as ordinary income. However, no 10% penalty applies in this situation.

LIFE INSURANCE

U15LO6: Compare the major types of life insurance.

A life insurance policy is a contract between an insurance company and an individual that is designed to provide financial compensation to the named beneficiaries in the event of the insured's death. In exchange for payment of premiums, the insurance company agrees to pay the proceeds of the policy (the death benefit) upon the death of the insured.

Many types of life insurance contracts are available; each type serves a different need. We will focus more attention on those contracts that use separate accounts to fund the death benefits and those that are considered securities, as defined by the Uniform Securities Act.

Unit 15

Term Insurance

Term insurance is protection for a specified period, hence the description, *term*. Term insurance provides pure protection and is the least expensive form of life insurance.

The important facts about term life insurance policies include the following.

■ They provide temporary insurance protection for a specified period (the policy term). For example, the term may be 1 year, 5 years, 10 years, 30 years, or to a specified age (such as age 65).

■ They pay the death benefit only if the insured dies during the term of coverage. For example, a person buying a 20-year term policy at age 35 who dies at 56 will receive nothing.

■ They do not accumulate cash value.

– The death protection and premium remain level for the specified term, e.g. a $100,000 5-year term policy provides a death benefit of $100,000 anytime during that 5-year term.

– If renewed at the end of the term, the face amount remains the same, but, because the new premium is based upon the insured's attained age, renewal premiums always increase.

Uses of Term Insurance

Term insurance has a variety of useful applications. One of the most common uses for term is to provide a substantial amount of coverage at a minimum cost. Because term insurance provides pure protection, it allows a person with a limited income to purchase more coverage than might otherwise be affordable. This is particularly important when there is a clear need for additional protection, particularly in the case of younger people, married with children.

TEST TOPIC ALERT

For test purposes, younger people with children are better off purchasing term insurance because the lower premiums allow significantly more protection. For those age 60 and older, the rates are generally prohibitive.

Whole Life Insurance (WLI)

A type of permanent or cash value insurance, **whole life insurance** (**WLI**) provides protection for the whole of life. Coverage begins on the date of issue and continues to the date of the insured's death, provided the premiums are paid. The benefit payable is the face amount, or face value, of the policy, which remains constant throughout the policy's life. The premium is set at the time of the policy's issue and it, too, remains level for the policy's life. As with all life insurance policies, the insured can choose how to spread out the premium payments (known as the *mode*). Premiums can be paid annually, semiannually, quarterly, or monthly.

Cash Values

Unlike term insurance, which provides only a death benefit, WLI combines a death benefit with an accumulation, or a savings element. This accumulation, commonly referred to as the policy's **cash surrender value**, increases each year the policy is kept in force. In traditional WLI, the insurer invests reserves in conservative investments (e.g., bonds, real estate, mortgage loans).

Because of the low risk of such investments, the insurer can guarantee the policy's cash value and the nonforfeiture options that are based on that cash value. Traditional life insurance reserves are held in the insurer's **general accounts**.

Policy Loans

Once an insured has accumulated cash value, it cannot be forfeited. An insured may cash in a policy at any time by surrendering it in exchange for its cash value. An insured may also borrow a portion of the cash value in the form of a **policy loan**, but this must be paid back (with interest) to restore policy values. When a policyowner takes a cash value loan, the amount borrowed, and any accumulated interest due on the loan become an indebtedness against the policy. If the insured dies before the loan has been repaid, any indebtedness will reduce the face amount of the policy accordingly—it will be subtracted from any death benefit.

Uses of Whole Life

The principal advantage of whole life is that it is permanent insurance and accordingly can be used to satisfy permanent needs such as the cost of death, dying, and final burial expenses. The level premium allows the policyowner to always know exactly what the cost of insurance will be, and basically offers a form of forced savings. Whole life builds a living benefit through its guaranteed cash value that enables the policyowner to use some of this cash (through policy loans) for emergencies, as a supplemental source of retirement income, and for other living needs. The principal disadvantages of WLI are that the premium paying period may last longer than the insured's income-producing years, and it does not provide as much protection per dollar of premium as term insurance.

Whole Life vs. Term	
Guaranteed interest rate on cash value buildup	Term insurance will provide the highest face amount for the lowest premium
Builds cash value with ability to borrow	Term insurance does not build cash value
Remains in effect until age 100 as long as premiums are paid	Term insurance provides coverage for a specific period; it is pure protection

EXAMPLE

1. A 30-year-old client indicates that he needs $500,000 of life insurance coverage for the next 20 years. The lowest out-of-pocket cost would be if he purchased a

   A. 20-pay life policy

   B. 20-year level term policy

   C. whole life policy

   D. variable annuity with an extended death benefit

   Answer: B. In almost all circumstances, certainly for short to immediate time periods, term life will be the least expensive form of insurance. A 20-pay life is a permanent policy where the premiums are paid in a 20-year period rather than until death. Variable annuities are not life insurance policies even though they are issued by life insurance companies.

Surrendering the Policy

If the policyowner decides to stop paying the premiums, the policyowner may:

- surrender the policy for its cash value;

- take a reduced paid-up policy where the death benefit is decreased and future premiums are no longer required; or

- take extended term insurance which pays the beneficiaries the full face amount if death occurs within a specified time period.

Universal Life

Universal life insurance was developed in the late 1970s in response to the relatively low interest rates (generally 3.5–5%) earned by traditional whole life insurance cash values, which made the whole life product less attractive during periods of high inflation. To be more competitive, insurers introduced universal life policies that might pay higher interest rates (such as 8%, 10%, or even 12%) during inflationary times. These policies also provide greater flexibility, because they allow policyowners to adjust the death benefits and/or premium payments based on current needs assessment.

A universal life policy is similar to a whole life policy in the sense that it has the same two components—death protection and cash value. However, instead of being fixed and guaranteed amounts, the death protection resembles one-year renewable term insurance and the cash value grows according to current interest rates.

Characteristics of Universal Life

- Premium payments are separated first being paid toward the insurance protection, with the remaining balance being used to build the cash value (with interest).

- The policyowner may increase or decrease the death benefit during the policy term, subject to any insurability requirements.

- Premium amounts may be changed as long as enough premium is paid to maintain the policy. This is why universal life is known as flexible premium life. In fact, it is even possible to skip premium payments as long as there is sufficient cash value in the policy to keep it in force.

- The interest earned by the cash account will vary, subject to a guaranteed minimum.

Universal Life Interest Rates

Universal life contracts are subject to two different interest rates: the current annual rate and the contract rate.

- The **current annual rate** varies with current market conditions, and may change every year.

- The **contract rate** is the minimum guaranteed interest rate, and the policy will never pay less than that amount.

For example, if the guaranteed contract rate is 5% and the current rate is 8%, the cash account would grow by the higher 8% during that year. But if the current rate falls below 5%, the cash account would still grow by the minimum rate of 5% during that year.

Universal Life Death Benefits

Generally, two options are available regarding the death benefit payable under a universal life policy.

- Option 1 (also known as option A) provides a level death benefit equal to the policy's face amount. As the policy's cash value increases, net death protection actually decreases over the life of the policy, which makes the policy structure similar to a whole life contract. The major advantage of Option 1 is that the premiums are lower for the same face amount of death coverage. The tradeoff is that the level death benefit will not keep pace with inflation.

- Option 2 (also known as option B) provides for an increasing death benefit equal to the policy's face amount plus the cash account. In terms of policy structure, this contract is more like a combination of level term insurance and increasing cash value than WLI. The primary advantage of universal life insurance option B is that cash values grow more quickly over time. The cash values accumulate more quickly because of the higher initial premiums, and lower initial death benefit. Because the premiums are higher and the death benefit is initially lower, a greater portion of the premium is added to the policy cash value, which then grows interest free inside the contract.

TAKE NOTE

With the original universal life policies, it was common that the flexibility of premium payments caused policies to lapse with the result that one could not truly say there was a guaranteed death benefit. Because of this, most insurers today offer a guaranteed death benefit universal life where the policy is guaranteed not to lapse if the sum of the premiums paid (less any loans or partial withdrawals and partial withdrawal fees) is greater than or equal to the sum of the minimum monthly premiums required. As a result, one can say that a universal life insurance policy has at least some guaranteed death benefit.

Universal Life Policy Loans

Universal life provides for cash value loans in the same manner that whole life or any permanent plan of insurance does. If a loan is taken, it is subject to interest and, if unpaid, both the interest and the loan amount will reduce the face amount of the policy.

Uses of Universal Life

This is a form of permanent insurance that can build cash values, hopefully at a rate greater than with traditional whole life. There is typically a guaranteed minimum interest rate stated in the policy (usually around 2%) which means that, no matter how the investments perform, there will be a known minimum return on the investment. The unique feature is the flexibility to adjust the death benefit as needs change, as well as the flexibility to pay smaller or larger premiums as financial conditions dictate. However, if the premium payments are reduced to the point where they can no longer support the policy, lapse could occur. Another use of the flexibility of the premium payments is to "overfund" the policy, particularly when Option 2 has been chosen. That is, pay premiums in excess of those required with that excess going into the savings portion of the policy. This can have the effect of greatly increasing the cash value—money that may be borrowed out of the policy without tax consequences if done properly. (This is beyond the coverage of this course.)

EXAMPLE

1. All of the following are advantages of universal life insurance EXCEPT

   A. ability to adjust the amount of premium payments

   B. the policy is guaranteed never to lapse

   C. ability to change death benefit amount

   D. when the cash value is sufficient, no premium payment is required

   Answer: B. A universal life policy may lapse if the accumulation fund drops below a specified level and an additional premium is not paid. Universal life has flexible premiums and, when there is sufficient cash value in the policy, premiums may be skipped (with the premium payments taken from that cash value).

VARIABLE LIFE INSURANCE

Variable life insurance differs from WLI in that the premiums are invested not in the insurance company's general account, whose investments are determined by the insurance company, but in a separate account, in whose investments the insured has some choice—common stock, bonds, money market instruments, and so on. The purpose is to let the customer assume some investment risk in an attempt to get inflation protection for the policy's death benefit.

Cash value in the policy fluctuates with the performance of the chosen subaccounts in the separate account and is not guaranteed. Variable life policies provide policy owners with a **minimum guaranteed death benefit**. The benefit may increase above this minimum amount depending on investment results but may never fall below.

Also, remember what was said earlier about variable annuities being securities requiring those who sell them to be dually licensed (insurance and securities); the same is true for those who wish to sell variable life insurance.

Scheduled (Fixed) Premium Variable Life

A **scheduled-premium** (or **fixed-premium**) **VLI contract** is issued with a minimum guaranteed death benefit. (The premiums for some variable life contracts are flexible; this is discussed next under Variable Universal Life.) A scheduled-premium VLI contract's death benefit is determined at issue, and evidence of insurability is required.

The premium is calculated according to the insured's age and sex and the policy's face amount (guaranteed amount) at issue. Once the premium has been determined and the expenses have been deducted, the net premium is invested in the separate account subaccount(s) the policyowner selects.

Flexible Premium Variable Life (Universal)

Universal variable life insurance (UVL or VUL) is a type of variable life insurance with flexible premiums (and thus flexible death benefit). Premiums are invested only in a separate account, and there is only a variable death benefit. The insured has the option to increase, skip, or reduce premium payments, though he must maintain a minimum cash value, and the death benefit is adjusted appropriately.

Deductions from the Premium

Deductions from the gross premium normally reduce the amount of money invested in the separate account. The greater the deductions, the less money available for the investment base in the separate account. Charges deducted from the gross premium include:

■ the administrative fee;

■ the sales load; and

■ state premium taxes (if any).

The administrative fee is normally a one-time charge to cover the cost of processing the application.

The maximum allowable sales load on variable life insurance is the equivalent of an average of 9% of premium per year, computed over a 20-year period. The sales charge may be front-end loaded to 50% of the first year's premium, but must average out to 9% over a 20-year period. Because of the front-end loading, there are special sales charge refund rights for the first two years spelled out in the Investment Company Act of 1940.

Deductions from the Separate Account

Deductions from the separate account normally reduce the investment return payable to the policyowner. Charges deducted from the separate account include:

■ mortality risk fee (cost of insurance);

■ expense risk fee; and

■ investment management fee.

The **mortality risk fee** covers the risk that the insured may live for a period shorter than assumed. The **expense risk fee** covers the risk that the costs of administering and issuing the policy may be greater than assumed. And, of course, the investment management fee is the cost of the management of the chosen separate account subaccounts.

TAKE NOTE

The exam may ask you which charges are deducted from the gross premium and which are deducted from the separate account (the net premium). Remember the acronym **SAS** to make it simple. The charges deducted from the gross premium are:

■ **s**ales load;

■ **a**dministrative fee; and

■ **s**tate premium taxes.

Any other charges; such as cost of insurance, expense risk fees, and investment management fees, are deducted from the net premium, which is invested in the separate account.

Variable Life Insurance Death Benefit

The death benefit payable under a variable life insurance policy consists of two parts: a guaranteed minimum provided by the portion of funds invested in the general account and a variable death benefit provided by those invested in the separate account. The guaranteed minimum does not change, but total benefit, including the variable portion of the death benefit, must be recalculated at least annually.

The effect that a change in earnings has on the contract's variable death benefit depends on a comparison of actual account performance and the performance assumed by the insurance company. If the separate account returns are greater than the assumed interest rate (AIR), additional funds are available to the insured. These extra earnings are reflected in an increase in the death benefit. If the separate account returns equal the AIR, actual earnings meet estimated expenses, resulting in no change in benefit levels. Should the separate account returns be less than the AIR, the contract's death benefit may decrease; however, it may never fall below the amount guaranteed at issue.

TAKE NOTE

If a variable life insurance policy has a minimum stated death benefit, the premiums necessary to fund this part of the death benefit are held in the insurer's general account. Any policy benefit that is guaranteed is invested in the insurer's general account.

Any premium above what is necessary to pay for the minimum death benefit is invested in the separate account. This portion of the premium is subject to investment risk. The death benefit will grow above the minimum guaranteed amount if the separate account performs positively. The death benefit will never be less than the minimum guarantee, even if the separate account performs poorly.

TAKE NOTE

With positive performance in the separate account, the death benefit will increase. If this is followed by several periods of performance that fails to equal the AIR, the death benefit will decline (but never below the minimum guarantee). If the decline has been steep enough, it may take several periods of positive results before the death benefit increases again.

Variable Life Insurance Cash Value

The policy's cash values reflect the investments held in the separate account. Unlike the death benefit, the individual policy's cash value must be calculated at least monthly.

The cash value, like the death benefit, may increase or decrease depending on the separate account's performance. However, because the cash value is not based on any AIR, any positive performance will result in cash value growth. If performance has been negative, the cash value may decrease to zero, even if the contract has been in force for several years. The cash value cannot be negative, but the insurance company keeps track of negative performance. Therefore, like the death benefit, the cash value may not increase until prior negative performance has been offset.

TEST TOPIC ALERT

The AIR has no effect on cash value accumulation in a variable life policy. The cash value will grow whenever the separate account has positive performance. The AIR, however, does affect the death benefit.

- If the separate account performance for the year is greater than the AIR, the death benefit will increase.
- If the separate account performance for the year is equal to the AIR, the death benefit will stay the same.
- If the separate account performance for the year is less than the AIR, the death benefit will decrease (but never below the guaranteed minimum).

TEST TOPIC ALERT

You may see a question that asks about the frequency of certain calculations associated with variable life insurance policies. Know that:

- death benefits are calculated annually;
- cash value is calculated monthly; and
- separate account unit values are calculated daily (in the event there is a withdrawal of cash value).

Figure 15.2: Comparison of Whole Life and Variable Life Policies

Whole Life	Variable Life (VLI)	Universal Variable Life (UVL or VUL)
Scheduled premium	Scheduled premium	Flexible premium
Fixed death benefit	Minimum guaranteed plus variable death benefit	Variable death benefit
Premiums to general account	Premiums to general and separate account	Premiums to separate account
Guaranteed cash value	No guaranteed cash value	No guaranteed cash value

It must be emphasized that variable life insurance must be sold as life insurance, not as an investment. However, the ability to commit a portion of the premium to investor selected separate account subaccounts, makes this form of insurance unique. There is a guaranteed minimum death benefit, but if separate account performance merits such, the death benefit can increase to keep pace with inflation. Cash values, although not guaranteed, can also increase based upon that performance. As with any variable product, the investor bears the investment risk rather than the insurance company.

EXAMPLE

1. Which of the following is indicative of the primary difference between variable life insurance and straight whole life insurance?

   A. Amount of insurance that can be issued

   B. Cost of the insurance

   C. Tax treatment of the death proceeds

   D. Way in which the cash values are invested

Answer: D. Variable life insurance allows the policyowner to decide how the cash value is invested (choice **D**) through a number of subaccounts. With a whole life policy, all investment decisions are made by the insurance company.

VARIABLE LIFE SPECIAL FEATURES

U15LO7: Identify the special features applicable to a variable life policy.

Variable Life Policy Loans

Like traditional WLI, a VLI contract allows the insured to borrow against the cash value that has accumulated in the contract. However, certain restrictions exist. Usually, the insured may only borrow a percentage of the cash value. The minimum percentage that must be made available is 75% after the policy has been in force for three years. If the death benefit becomes payable during any period that a loan is outstanding, the loan amount is deducted from the death benefit before payment. The interest rate charged is stated in the policy.

TEST TOPIC ALERT

Several testable facts about policy loans are as follows.

- A minimum of 75% of the cash value must be available for policy loan after the policy has been in force three years.

- The insurer is never required to loan 100% of the cash value. Full cash value is obtained by surrendering the policy to the insurer.

- If the insured dies with a loan outstanding, the death benefit is reduced by the amount of the loan.

- If the insured surrenders the contract with a loan outstanding, cash value is reduced by the amount of the loan.

EXAMPLE

1. On July 15, 2015, your client purchased a variable life insurance policy with a death benefit of $500,000. The November 2017 statement showed a cash value of $30,000. If the client wanted to borrow as much as possible, the insurance company would have to allow a loan of at least

   A. $0

   B. $15,000

   C. $22,500

   D. $27,000

   Answer: A. Until a variable life policy is in force for a minimum of 3 years (this one is a bit less than 2½ years), there is no requirement to make the loan provision available. Once the 3-year mark is reached, that minimum becomes 75% of the computed cash value

Variable Life Insurance Contract Exchange

A unique feature of variable life insurance is the ability for the insured to have a change of heart. During the early stage of ownership, you have the right to exchange a VLI contract for a form of permanent insurance issued by the company with comparable benefits (usually whole life). The length of time this exchange privilege is in effect varies from company to company, but under no circumstances may the period be less than 24 months (federal law).

The exchange is allowed without evidence of insurability. If a contract is exchanged, the new permanent policy has the same contract date and death benefit as the minimum guaranteed in the VLI contract. The premiums equal the amounts guaranteed in the new permanent contract (as if it were the original contract).

TEST TOPIC ALERT

Three testable facts about the contract exchange provision are listed here.

- The contract exchange provision must be available for a minimum of two years.
- No medical underwriting (evidence of insurability) is required for the exchange.
- The new policy is issued as if everything were retroactive. That is, the age of the insured as of the original date is the age used for premium calculations for the new policy.

Variable Life Insurance Voting Rights

Unlike any other type of life insurance, variable life contract holders have voting rights. Contract holders receive one vote per $100 of cash value funded by the separate account. As with other investment company securities, changes in investment objectives and other important matters may be accomplished only by a majority vote of the separate account's outstanding shares or by order of the state insurance commissioner.

TEST TOPIC ALERT

Do not confuse the voting rights of variable annuities and variable life. Variable annuities and mutual funds are the same: one vote per unit (share). Variable life is one vote per $100 of cash value.

UNIT 16

Types and Characteristics of Derivative Securities

This unit discusses both securities and non-securities derivatives. The term derivative is used to describe investment vehicles that derive their value from an underlying asset, whether that asset be a security, such as a stock, or a physical commodity, such as wheat. You can expect to see five questions about derivatives on the Series 65 exam.

LEARNING OBJECTIVES

When you have completed this unit, you will be able to accomplish the following.

U16LO1: Recognize the common characteristics of all derivatives.
U16LO2: Identify the difference between a put option and a call option and their strategies.
U16LO3: Contrast calls, rights, and warrants.
U16LO4: Describe the difference between futures and forwards contracts.
U16LO5: Identify the costs, benefits, and risks of derivative securities.

DERIVATIVE SECURITIES—OPTIONS

U16LO1: Recognize the common characteristics of all derivatives.

Options are **derivative securities**. That means they derive their value from an underlying instrument, such as a stock, stock index, interest rate, or foreign currency. Option contracts offer investors a means to **hedge**, or protect, an investment's value, or speculate on the price movement of individual securities, markets, foreign currencies, and other instruments.

An **option** is a contract that establishes a price and time frame for the purchase or sale of a particular underlying instrument. Two parties are involved in the contract: one party receives the right to exercise the contract to buy or sell the underlying asset; the other is obligated to fulfill the terms of the contract.

In theory, options can be created on any item with a fluctuating market value. The most familiar options are those issued on common stocks; they are called **equity options**.

The exam is going to deal solely with standardized options traded on an exchange such as the Chicago Board Options Exchange, or Nasdaq. They are called standardized options because each options contract has three standardized terms:

- The underlying asset. That is, all options on XYZ stock are for 100 shares of the XYZ common stock

- The expiration date. All options that expire in June (or July or whatever month) have the same date and time of expiry

- The exercise or strike price. Strike prices are set at standardized intervals.

It is this standardization that makes secondary trading in options possible.

EXAMPLE

1. Your customer is long 10 ABC Jul 50 calls at 4.50. How many shares of stock will change hands if the option is exercised?

   A. 10

   B. 100

   C. 1,000

   D. 10,000

   Answer: C. One of the three standardized terms of equity options is that each contract is for 100 shares. Therefore, the exercise of 10 calls (or puts, for that matter), will involve 10 × 100 or 1,000 shares, choice **C**.

Later in this unit, we will discuss non-securities derivatives—forwards and futures contracts. These derive their value from an asset that is not a security, most commonly a commodity. The concept is the same; there are two parties, a buyer and a seller, and can be used by speculators or those who wish to protect (hedge).

The two most important factors influencing the price of a derivative are the price movement of the underlying asset and the length of time until the contract expires (the longer the time, the greater the *time value*).

PUTS AND CALLS

U16LO2: Identify the difference between a put option and a call option and their strategies.

There are two types of option contracts: **calls** and **puts**.

- A **call** option gives its holder the right to buy a stock for a specific price within a specified time frame. A call buyer buys the *right to buy* a specific stock, and a call seller takes on the *obligation to sell* the stock.

- A **put** option gives its holder the right to sell a stock for a specific price within a specified time frame. A put buyer buys the *right to sell* a specific stock, and a put seller takes on the *obligation to buy* the stock.

Each stock option contract covers 100 shares (a round lot) of stock. An option's cost is its **premium**. Premiums are quoted in dollars per share.

EXAMPLE

Because a contract covers 100 shares, a premium of $3 means $3 for each share multiplied by 100 shares, which equals $300.

EXAMPLE

1. Which of the following statements regarding derivative securities is NOT true?

   A. Derivatives can be sold on securities and non-securities.

   B. An option contract is a derivative security because it has no value independent of the value of an underlying security.

   C. An option contract's price fluctuates in relationship to the time remaining to expiration as well as with the price movement of the underlying security.

   D. An owner of a put has the obligation to purchase securities at a designated price (the strike price) before a specified date (the expiration date).

   Answer: D. An owner of a put has the **right**, not the **obligation**, to sell, not purchase, a security at a designated price (the strike price) before a specified date (the expiration date). That makes choice **D** the untrue statement. It is the only the seller of an option who has an obligation.

Here is another way that point might be asked:

EXAMPLE

1. Choose the term that best describes the following situation: A customer has the right to sell 100 shares of MNO at 60 any time between July and October.

   A. Long call

   B. Long put

   C. Short call

   D. Short put

   Answer: B. The put buyer (long position) has the right to sell stock to a put writer who is obligated to buy that stock (choice **B**).

Option Transactions

Because two types of options (calls and puts) and two types of transactions (buying and selling) exist, four basic transactions are available to an option investor:

- Buy calls
- Sell calls
- Buy puts
- Sell puts

Option buyers are *long* the positions; option sellers are **short** the positions.

An option conveys rights and obligations for a limited time. Therefore, each transaction has a beginning and an end—an open and a close. For instance, an option position opened by an investor buying a call is closed when the call is exercised, is sold, or expires. An option position opened by an investor selling a call is closed when the call is exercised, is bought, or expires.

The owner (long position) of a put or call option contract has three ways to close a position:

- **sell** the option contract before the expiration date;
- **exercise** the option to buy or sell the security specified in the contract; or
- let the option **expire**.

The simplest and most common way to close an option position is entering the transaction opposite of the opening transaction. The following table summarizes potential opening and closing positions.

Open	To Close
Buy call	Sell call
Sell call	Buy call
Buy put	Sell put
Sell put	Buy put

Exercising an Option

In some cases, the holder of the option (only owners can exercise—it is one of their rights) will decide to exercise the option. Exercising a call means purchasing the underlying stock at the strike price; exercising a put means selling the underlying stock at the strike price. For example, if you were long an ABC 50 call and the current market price of ABC is 60, you would be able to exercise and purchase stock worth $60 per share at the exercise price of $50. Or, if you were long an XYZ $45 put and the current market price of XYZ is $35, you might wish to purchase 100 shares of XYZ at $35 per share and then exercise your option to *put* the stock at $45. The test may ask you the difference between American- and European-style exercises. American style means the option can be exercised at any time the holder wishes, up to the expiration date. European-style options may only be exercised on the last trading day before the **expiration** date.

TAKE NOTE

A tool for remembering the difference between American and European exercise is to look at the first letter.

A for American means **A**nytime

E for European means **E**xpiration date

TEST TOPIC ALERT

Now that you have become so focused on the exercise date differences between American and European styles, be prepared for a question stem like, "A European option is a derivative because," and the first answer choice will probably be, "it can only be exercised on the expiration date." Although that is true about exercise, it has nothing to do with why options are derivatives. Please select an answer choice similar to, "its value is based on some underlying asset."

TAKE NOTE

Perhaps you noticed an inconsistency. First, we told you that European style means the option can only be exercised on the day prior to its expiration date. Then, we told you it is only exercised on its expiration date. In the industry, there seems to be much confusion about this, and for exam purposes, either statement is correct (and you won't have to choose between them).

Length of an Option Contract

Options are available that are issued with an expiration date of as short as one week to as long as three years. The short ones are called Weeklys[SM], and the long-term are known as LEAPS (Long-Term Equity Anticipation Securities). Most standard options are issued with expiration days of a maximum of nine months.

TEST TOPIC ALERT

You must remember that all options, regardless of their length, are derivative securities.

Options Greeks

Many of our students tell us that when it comes to understanding options, "it is all Greek to me." Maybe that is why options strategists use a number of Greek letters to describe various properties of an option. There are four commonly used *Greeks*, Delta, Gamma, Theta, and Vega. It is highly unlikely that you will have to know anything about them, but we've given a short definition of each in the glossary.

OPTIONS STRATEGIES

Options strategies are either **bullish** or **bearish positions** on the underlying stock. Bulls believe the price of a security will go up and bears believe the price of a security will go down. The primary reasons for buying or selling options are to profit from or hedge (protect) against price movement in the underlying security.

A bullish investor may buy calls seeking profit if the price of the underlying stock rises. A bearish investor buy puts seeking profit if the price of the underlying stock declines. Likewise a bullish investor may write (sell) puts which will make money if the stock price is stable or rises and a bearish investor may write (sell) calls which will make money if the stock price is stable or declines.

Figure 16.1: Bullish and Bearish Options Positions

	Long	Short
Calls	Right to buy Bullish	Obligation to sell Bearish
Puts	Right to sell Bearish	Obligation to buy Bullish
	(Buyer, Holder, Owner)	(Seller, Writer, Grantor)

TAKE NOTE

A phrase that is invaluable for figuring out options questions is "Call up and put down." That is, you would buy a call because you are hoping (or are afraid) the price of the stock will go *up*, and buy a put because you are hoping (or are afraid) the price of the stock will go *down*.

Buying Calls

Investors expecting a stock to increase in value speculate on that price increase by buying calls on the stock.

By buying a call, an investor can profit from the increase in the stock's price while investing a relatively small amount of money. The most a call buyer can lose is the money paid for the option. The most a call buyer can gain is unlimited because there is no limit to how high the stock price can go. Owners of options (puts or calls) do not receive dividends on the underlying stock.

As we will show you in Unit 20, buying calls is also a hedging (protection) strategy when the investor is afraid the stock price will rise.

TEST TOPIC ALERT

Remember those employee stock options we discussed in Unit 12? No, they are not at all like these puts and calls, but the employer (the company issuing the stock) might want to use call options to protect against market risk. You see, when granting employees the option (the right) to buy shares at a set price, the company is obligated to deliver the shares at that agreed upon price. What happens if the company's stock price soars, the employees exercise their options, and the company has to go out into the stock markets and buy stock at a price far in excess of what they're going to be selling it for? That hurts. One way to protect themselves is to buy call options on the stock so that if this were to happen, they could use their options to buy the stock at whatever exercise price was part of the contract.

Writing Calls

A neutral or bearish investor can write (sell) a call and collect the premium. An investor who believes a stock's price will stay the same or decline can write a call to:

■   generate income from the option premium;

- *partially* protect (hedge) a long stock position by offsetting any loss on the sale of the stock by the premium amount; or

- if the stock price increases, the call may be exercised. In addition to the premium received when the option was sold, the writer will be paid the strike price for the stock. If the option writer owns the stock on which the call is being written, it is known as a covered call and the risk is limited, because no matter how high the stock price rises (meaning the call will certainly be exercised), the writer merely uses the stock already owned (which has been deposited with the broker-dealer) to make delivery. However, if the writer does not own the stock, the option is uncovered (usually referred to as "naked" in the industry). That's when the risk is unlimited, because the writer must pay the going market price (and there is theoretically no limit as to how high a stock's price can go) to acquire the stock needed to fulfill the obligation to deliver. That is why naked call writing is the most risky option strategy.

Buying Puts

A **bearish investor**—one who believes a stock will decline in price—can speculate on the price decline by buying puts. A put buyer acquires the right to sell 100 shares of the underlying stock at the strike price before the expiration date.

EXAMPLE

Here is how that might work. An investor following ABCD common stock believes that it is grossly overpriced at $75 per share and when the next earnings report is released, the stock will drop at least 10 points. If the investor were to purchase an ABCD 75 put for a premium of $3 and was correct, once the stock was at $65 (the 10-point drop), a purchase could be made at that price for $65 per share and then the put could be exercised at the $75 per share strike price. This would give the investor a profit of $7 per share (the $10 difference between the cost of $65 and the sale at $75, minus the $3 premium paid). A $700 profit on a $300 investment is a very handsome percentage return on investment.

As we will show you in Unit 20, buying puts is also a hedging (protection) strategy when the investor is afraid the stock price will fall.

Writing Puts

Generally, investors who write puts believe that the stock's price will rise or remain stable. A put writer (seller) is obligated to buy stock at the exercise price if the put buyer puts it to the put writer. If a stock's price is above the put strike price at expiration, the put expires unexercised, allowing the put writer to keep the premium. Just as with writing calls, receiving that premium is a source of income. Put writers will lose if the stock price falls (the buyer wins), but the loss is limited, because the stock price can never fall below zero.

Straddles

When an investor is not sure which direction the market will move but has a strong opinion that there will be dynamic movement, a strategy that might be employed is the purchase of a straddle. This is the combining of a put and a call on the same stock with the same exercise price and expiration date. If the stock moves up, a profit is made on the call; if down, a profit is made on the put.

TEST TOPIC ALERT

Those who buy a straddle will profit from volatility while those who sell a straddle will profit if the market is stable because the options will expire unexercised.

RIGHTS AND WARRANTS

U16LO3: Contrast calls, rights, and warrants.

Although generally treated as equity securities, in truth, rights and warrants are derivatives because their value is derived from the common stock which they may acquire by exercising that right or warrant. Because rights and warrants give the holder the option (but not the obligation) to buy a stock at a specific price during a specific time period, they can be compared in most respects to a call option. There are some differences, however. Let's start with rights.

Rights, sometimes referred to as preemptive rights, are a privilege extended to existing holders of a company's common stock. When the company is going to issue additional shares of common stock, to prevent dilution of ownership by the current owners, they are given the right to preempt (come ahead of) any members of the general public and have the first shot at the new stock. The right permits them to purchase enough shares to keep their proportionate interest in the company. Here is a very simple example:

Steve has 100 shares of DEF Corporation common stock. DEF has 10,000 shares of stock outstanding so it is clear that Steve owns 1% of the company (100 / 10,000) = 0.01). DEF wishes to raise additional capital by issuing 5,000 new shares of stock. Steve will receive rights to purchase how many of those 5,000 shares?

In order to keep his 1% ownership, Steve will receive stock rights to purchase 50 shares of the new issue. As an incentive, rights offerings always have an exercise price slightly below the current market price of the existing stock. Also, because the company needs to raise the money, they limit the time in which you have to decide to exercise your right, usually no more than 45–60 days. If Steve decided he did not want to exercise his rights, he could sell them, and because the exercise price is below the market price, they would have a value.

The key points to remember about rights are the following:

- They are given (not sold) to existing holder of the common stock.
- They are exercisable at a price below the current market.
- They have a short lifespan—they will expire in 45–60 days.
- They can be sold and then the buyer can exercise them.
- Although generally unwise to do, they can be left to expire.

Warrants

Unlike rights, warrants have an exercise price above the current market price and, again, unlike rights, warrants have no relationship to an existing stockholder's proportionate interest. Another difference is that warrants have a long expiration period, sometimes as much as 10 years or even longer. They are usually attached to a bond issue (their attractiveness *sweetens* the issue, frequently allowing for a lower interest rate on the bond), or attached to a new stock offering where the package is considered a *unit*, such as one share of stock with a warrant to purchase another share. In most cases, the warrants can be detached and sold separately.

The key points to remember about warrants are:

- They are exercisable at a price above the current market. Why would anyone be interested in that? Because you might have a 5 year expiration period and have the right to buy the stock at $45 when it is selling at $40 today. If you think there is a chance that the stock's price will move more than five points in five years, you can make money; sometimes lots of money because of the leverage. This is known as having time value.

- Their life is considerably longer than rights and longer than call options as well.

- When detached, they can be traded like any other security (they are usually traded on the same exchange as the company's common stock).

- Most securities professionals view warrants as call options with a very long time to expiration.

- Warrants do not have voting rights, the same as any other derivative.

One major difference between call options and rights/warrants is that options originate on the exchange on which they are traded where rights and warrants originate with the issuer of the stock. The effect of this is that new shares are issued when a right or warrant is exercised while exercise of a call option requires the assigned seller to deliver existing shares.

EXAMPLE

1. GEMCO Manufacturing Company, traded on the NYSE, has announced that it will be issuing 10 million new shares of common stock to raise new capital for the purchase of new equipment. Your client owning 1,000 shares of GEMCO common stock would probably receive

    A. an advance invitation to purchase some of the new shares

    B. options to purchase some of the new shares

    C. preemptive rights to purchase some of the new shares

    D. warrants to purchase some of the new shares

    Answer: C. Commonly, when a publicly traded company issues new shares of common stock, existing shareholders receive rights, sometimes called stock rights, enabling them to purchase shares in proportion to their current ownership, usually at a reduced price (choice **C**). These rights rarely last longer than 45 days and must be exercised or sold within that time or they'll just expire worthless. Warrants are not sent to shareholders; they are either purchased in the open market or come attached to a new issue of securities as a sweetener.

NON-SECURITIES DERIVATIVES: FORWARD CONTRACTS

U16LO4: Describe the difference between futures and forwards contracts.

Forward Contracts

Forward contracts were developed as a means for commodity users and producers to arrange for the exchange of the commodity at a time agreeable to both. Used in Europe as early as the Middle Ages, typically for agricultural items (grains and so forth), forward contracts evolved to eliminate the problem of finding a buyer or seller for an upcoming cash market transaction. They also reduce the price risk inherent in changing supply and demand relationships. How so? Because the seller knows exactly how much he will receive for his product. Of course, he may wind up contracting to sell too cheaply if market prices at delivery are much higher, but he is protected against receiving too little if the harvest is plentiful and prices plunge.

A forward contract is a direct commitment between one buyer and one seller. If the position is held until the closing date, the forward seller is obligated to make delivery; the forward buyer is obligated to take delivery. A forward contract is nonstandardized. Its unique terms are defined solely by the contract parties, without third-party intervention. This arrangement ensures a ready market or supply source because it presumes delivery.

Because forward contracts are direct obligations between a specific buyer and seller (the user and producer), they are not easily transferred and are considered illiquid (there is no secondary market for forward contracts). Further, each party risks the credit and trustworthiness of the other.

The five components of a typical forward contract are:

- quantity of the commodity;
- quality of the commodity;
- time of delivery;
- place for delivery; and
- price to be paid at delivery.

Futures

In contrast to forward contracts, futures contracts are exchange-traded obligations. The buyer or seller is contingently responsible for the full value of the contract. A buyer goes long, or establishes a long position, and is obligated to take delivery of the commodity on the future date specified. A seller goes short, or establishes a short position, and is obligated to deliver the commodity on the specified future date. If the seller does not own the commodity, his potential loss is unlimited because he has promised delivery and must pay any price to acquire the commodity to deliver.

As prices change, gains or losses are computed daily for all open futures positions on the basis of each day's settlement price. Gains are credited and losses are debited for each open position, long or short. All accounts for firms and traders must be settled before the opening of trading on the next trading day.

Buyers and sellers benefit from organizations that act as clearinghouses for the contracts. Clearinghouses enable futures positions to be offset easily before delivery. To offset, close, or liquidate a futures position before delivery, an investor must complete a transaction opposite to the trade that initiated (opened) the futures position. The offsetting transaction must occur in the same commodity, for the same delivery month, and on the same exchange. About 98% of futures contracts are offset before delivery. Futures may be highly leveraged.

If, at expiration, the settlement price is higher than the delivery price, a long position results in a profit while a short position loses. Conversely, if the settlement price is lower than the delivery price, shorts profit and longs lose.

Typically, there are five standardized parts to an exchange-traded futures contract:

- Quantity of the commodity (e.g., 5,000 bushels of corn or 100 oz. of gold)
- Quality of the commodity (specific grade or range of grades may be acceptable for delivery, including price adjustments for different deliverable grades)
- Delivery price (similar to exercise or strike price with options)
- Time for delivery (e.g., December wheat to be delivered)
- Location (approved for delivery)

TEST TOPIC ALERT

Futures are most commonly used by speculators while forwards are used by producers. That explains why such a small percentage of futures contracts every end with delivery.

EXAMPLE

1. Forwards are commonly used by producers (farmers) to hedge the risk of the price of the commodity falling before it is able to be harvested and sold. For example, if a farmer has planted soybeans and wishes to hedge against a possible decline in the spot or cash price at delivery, the farmer could

   A. buy forward contracts in a size equal to the amount of soybeans expected to be harvested

   B. buy futures contracts in a size equal to the amount of soybeans expected to be harvested

   C. sell futures or forward contracts in a size equal to the amount of the soybeans expected to be harvested

   D. sell the soybeans for cash today

   Answer: C. Hedging a commodity yet to be harvested is done by selling a forward or a futures contract on that commodity. In that way, the price is guaranteed in the event of a market decline. However, the producer is giving up any potential gain in the event the prices rise above the futures/forward agreed upon one.

Regulation of Futures and Forwards

Because these are not securities, they do not come under the jurisdiction of the SEC. The SRO that is in charge of regulating the futures markets and their participants is the Commodity Futures Trading Commission (CFTC). Forward contracts are not regulated by any agency.

EXAMPLE

1. Commonly traded on a regulated exchange would be any of the following EXCEPT

   A. ETFs

   B. forward contracts

   C. futures

   D. warrants

Answer: B. A forward contract, choice **B**, is a direct commitment between one buyer and one seller. This makes each contract different, and lack of standardization makes exchange trading a virtual impossibility.

INVESTING IN DERIVATIVES

U16LO5: Identify the costs, benefits, and risks of derivative securities.

Using derivatives can be a useful strategy for investors if the circumstances warrant it. There is no cost, per se, to open an options account, although, as we will learn in Unit 18, the account opening procedure is somewhat more involved than opening a regular account at a broker-dealer.

For those who buy options (long position), the only cost is the premium to purchase the option plus whatever the brokerage firm charges in commissions. With a very limited, and probably not tested, exception, options cannot be purchased on margin (covered in Unit 22) so, without any borrowed money, no interest is charged.

Selling options, (short position) brings in money from the sale and the seller receives all of that premium, less the brokerage charges. If the call or put being written (sold) is uncovered, there is a margin requirement, but that is beyond the scope of the exam.

The costs to carry forwards and futures is much more complicated and we are not aware of the topic ever being tested.

As with any investment, there are benefits and risks. We'll look at those most likely to be on your exam.

Leverage

One of the key benefits to using derivatives is that of leveraging your investment.

Because an option's cost is normally much less than the underlying stock's cost, option contracts provide investors with leverage: relatively little money allows an investor to control an investment that would otherwise require a much larger capital outlay. And, if you purchase a call and "guess right," the potential profit is unlimited (theoretically, there is no limit as to how high the stock's price can go).

EXAMPLE

An investor can buy the common stock of RST Corporation for $58 per share, investing $5,800, or buy an RST 55 call for $6, an investment of $600. If RST's price increases to $70, the stock investor will see a 20.7% profit, ($12 profit / $58 investment), whereas the option investor, with the call worth a minimum of $15 ($70 – $55), will have more than doubled the investment ($9 profit / $6 investment = 150%). The opposite is also true; if RST trades below $55, say at $48, when the option expires, the stock investor has a modest loss, but the option investor loses the entire investment. (What is the value of an option to buy stock at $55 per share when it is currently available to anyone at $48? Nothing.)

As you can see from the example, leverage works both ways—great when the stock is going your way, and a possible loss of everything when it doesn't. Of course, if, in the following example, RST had gone bankrupt leaving the stock worthless, the investor holding 100 shares would have lost the entire $5,800 while the option investor's loss would have been limited to the $600 premium paid.

Less Risk

When used properly, options can lower an investor's risk. The classic example is the covered call where the investor owns the stock and then writes a call option on it. Realize that there are only three things that can happen after you purchase a stock:

- The stock can increase in price
- The stock can remain stable
- The stock can decline in price

If you think about it, two of those possibilities are unfavorable. Certainly, you don't want the stock to fall in price. Even if the stock remains level, you've suffered from opportunity cost (you could have put it in the bank with no market risk and earned interest). Only if the stock increases by more than the risk-free rate do you emerge a winner.

However, if you write a call on that stock, you wind up better for sure in cases 2 and 3 and perhaps even in case 1. Let's look at an example:

Meredith purchases 100 shares of ABC at $50 per share. She then writes (sells) an ABC 50 call for a premium of 4 ($400). If the stock goes down to $47 by expiration date, the option she wrote will expire (who is going to call on her to sell stock at $50 when it is available for $47 in the marketplace)? In reality though, she hasn't lost $300, because she received $400 when she sold the option—she is still $100 ahead of the game, even though the stock dropped in price. It isn't until the stock falls below $46 that she begins to lose money, but, no matter how far it falls, she will still be $400 ahead of having just bought the stock without selling the option. If the stock price remains the same, the option will expire, and she will still own the shares, but will have $400 in her account from the sale of the option. Only in the first choice is it possible for her to be a "loser," but even that wouldn't happen until the stock rose above $54 per share. How is that? If the stock is $53, yes, her option will be exercised and she will have to sell her stock at the strike price of $50. She paid $50 for it, but also received the $4 premium so the total received on the sale of the stock plus the option is $54. Now, if the stock goes to $60, she would have been better off never writing the option. That is a risk you take in exchange for the chance that you'll win if the stock's price only rises a little, stays the same, or falls.

Alternative to Selling Short

As we will learn in Unit 22, one way to make money when an investor is of the belief that a stock's price will decline is to sell that stock short. At this juncture, to keep things simple, selling stock short involves putting up a deposit in a margin account, borrowing stock to sell, and carries with it the possibility of an unlimited loss. When you buy a put, you benefit when the stock's price declines, but all you pay is the premium and, if you guess wrong, that is all you can lose.

Having just mentioned the possibility of an unlimited loss when an investor sells a stock short, we would be remiss if we didn't discuss the parallel situation with options. When an investor writes an uncovered (naked) call option, the potential loss is unlimited. Here is how that works:

With the market price of ABC at $50 per share, Manny writes a 50 call option for a premium of 3. Manny does not own any ABC, but, as the seller of the call option, is obligated to deliver 100 shares of the ABC stock and receive $5,000 if the option is exercised. We use the phrase, "call up" to help us remember our objective when we *buy* a call. If the price of ABC should go up, the option will be exercised and Manny will have to buy it at its current market price and then deliver it. The question is, "how high can it go?" Theoretically (and that's the exam view), there is no limit—it can rise to infinity. That leaves Manny having to pay an infinite amount to buy stock for which he receives only the $5,000 strike price plus the $300 premium. Just in case you want to say, "but, because he receives $5,300, his loss can't be unlimited," remember, infinity minus any other number is still infinity. We know this is just theoretical, but, if you've watched some of the better known companies over the past few years, some of the price increases have been astronomical.

Hedging

In the example of writing the covered call, we showed one example of hedging (protecting) a position. In that case, the first four points of a market decline were absorbed by the premium received from the sale of the call. There is more to discuss on using options to hedge and we're going to cover that in Unit 20.

Time Decay

Have you ever heard an investor say, "I'm going to hold this stock until it gets back to what I paid for it"? We're not going to debate the logic of that statement other than to say, that doesn't work with options—they ultimately expire and, if the stock hasn't moved in the direction you're hoping for, you will run out of time. Time decay is the concept that, as the time to expiration gets closer, the value of the option decreases.

Taxation

In most cases, any profit realized from buying or selling options is treated as a short-term capital gain. As we will learn in Unit 21, those gains are taxed at ordinary income rates which are much higher than the long-term capital gain rate.

Much of what we've shown you here applies to forwards and futures as well, but other than some very basic questions, we don't expect the kind of detail we've presented here for options.

Here is the type of question that is basically easy, but, if you don't read carefully, you will waste time trying to figure it out.

EXAMPLES

1. Among the purposes of purchasing derivatives would be all of the following EXCEPT

   A. hedging

   B. income

   C. profits

   D. speculation

   Answer: B. Purchase of a derivative, whether an option, a forward, or futures contract, never generates income. Selling one does, but the question refers to a purchaser and that is why the correct answer is choice **B**.

2. The term derivative would not include

   A. futures on commodities

   B. interest rate swaps

   C. REITs

   D. LEAPS

   Answer: C. A derivative is something which derives its value from something else. REITs represent direct investment into real estate; the asset purchase is the actual asset (choice **C**). LEAPS are the options with the long-term expiry. Never heard of interest rate swaps? Well, on the real exam, there will occasionally be an answer choice that you've never heard of, but it should not affect your ability to choose the correct one.

UNIT 17

Alternative Investments and Other Assets

In the 1990s financial advisers began introducing their wealthy clients to **alternative investments**, now generally referred to as alts. These included, among other products, exchange-traded notes (ETN), Leveraged ETFs, and new, highly sophisticated financial derivatives. One thing that all of these had in common was that they were complex and not easy to understand, for both the investor and the person recommending the investment.

Although investing can be complex, standard investments are fairly easy to comprehend. Even new investors understand that stocks have more risk but hold out the chance of superior returns, while bonds generally have less risk with correspondingly lower returns. All investors dream of scoring a touchdown and not getting tackled for a loss. Alternative investments try to do just that. Some are successful, but many are not. Suitability determinations need to be made on a case-by-case basis considering each customer's objectives, circumstances, and sophistication. Securities professionals must take special care in recommending these complex products to the sophisticated customer and even more so to one with less financial acumen.

In addition to alternative investments, the exam will test your knowledge on other more traditional assets, such as investment real estate and commodities, including precious metals.

The Series 65 exam will include approximately four questions from this unit.

LEARNING OBJECTIVES

When you have completed this unit, you will be able to accomplish the following.

U17LO1: Identify the concept of "flow-through" (pass-through) of passive income and loss as it applies to DPPs.

U17LO2: Differentiate between the roles of the general partners and the limited partners in a DPP.

U17LO3: Recognize the characteristics of the pooled investment vehicles that are considered alternative investments.

U17LO4: Describe viatical/life settlements.

U17LO5: Contrast the difference between passive and active real estate investing.

U17LO6:   Identify the different types of commodities and precious metals that are popular investments.

U17LO7:   Describe the benefits and risks of alternative investments.

DIRECT PARTICIPATION PROGRAMS (DPPs)

U17LO1: Identify the concept of "flow-through" (pass-through) of passive income and loss as it applies to DPPs.

This is one class of alternative investment. DPPs, most of which are **limited partnerships**, allow the economic consequences of a business to flow-through to investors. Any income or loss is to the investor is considered passive because the investor does not take an active role in the management of the business—that is the role of the general partner as you will learn shortly. Unlike corporations, limited partnerships pay no dividends. Rather, they pass income, gains, losses, deductions, and credits directly to investors. Limited partnerships offer investors limited liability. Similar to a stockholder in a corporation, creditors cannot generally come directly to limited partners to collect on defaulted debt. In general, the maximum potential loss to a LP is the amount already invested plus any funds committed for which have not yet been submitted.

TAKE NOTE

In Unit 21, the topic of partnership taxation will be covered in greater detail, but, at this point, we want you to know that any income received by a partner is considered passive and the same is true for losses. The effect of this is that any passive losses can only be deducted as a loss against passive income.

INVESTORS IN A LIMITED PARTNERSHIP

U17LO2: Differentiate between the roles of the general partners and the limited partners in a DPP.

It is important to understand that a DPP is just a different way to invest in a business rather than buying the company's stock. There are certain tax advantages to being structured as a partnership with the flow-through of income or loss being one of them. That aside, this is merely an investment in a business, whether it be a RELP (Real Estate Limited Partnership), an oil and gas drilling program, or a movie production company.

Just like any other business, there are those who run the enterprise (management) and those who contribute the capital (investors). For DPPs, those roles are assumed by the general partner(s), usually referred to as GP, and the limited partner(s), the LPs. From a legal standpoint, there must be at least one GP and one LP.

Investing in a DPP requires analyzing the program just as one would analyze a stock or bond investment, just with a few different parameters.

An investor should choose to invest in a specific limited partnership because:

■   it is economically viable;

■   the investor can make use of the potential tax benefits;

- the GP(s) has (have) demonstrated management ability and expertise in running similar programs;
- the program's objectives match the investor's objectives and do so within a time frame that meets the investor's needs; and
- the start-up costs and projected revenues are in line with the start-up costs and revenues of similar ventures.

Promoters structure DPPs to meet various objectives. When a promoter's tax stance is too aggressive or is without economic purpose in the view of the IRS, the program is considered an abusive tax shelter. If the IRS judges the program to be abusive, it disallows deductions; assesses back taxes, interest, and penalties; and, in some cases, charges the promoter with criminal intent to defraud.

Investors should try to match their current and future objectives with a program's stated objectives.

EXAMPLE

A person seeking current taxable passive income should not invest in an oil and gas exploratory drilling program. Why not? Because these programs drill where oil (or gas) has never been found before (*exploratory*) and have a low success rate. Even when they do "hit," it may take years before any income is generated.

TAKE NOTE

Because most of these are privately placed, DPPs are considered illiquid, and investors must commit money for a long time. Even those which are publicly traded do not have the liquidity of other investments, frequently requiring authorization from the GP to be able to sell your unit(s).

General Partner (GP)

The GPs are the active investors in a limited partnership and assume responsibility for all aspects of the partnership's operations. A GP:

- makes decisions that bind the partnership;
- buys and sells property for the partnership;
- manages the partnership property and money;
- supervises all aspects of the partnership's business; and
- maintains a minimum 1% financial interest in the partnership.

Unlike LPs, who have limited liability, GPs assume unlimited liability, and are therefore personally liable for all partnership business losses and debts. A partnership's creditors may seek repayment from the GPs and may go after their personal assets.

A general partner has a fiduciary relationship to the LPs in that the GP has been entrusted with the LPs' capital and is legally bound to use that capital in the investors' best interests. The GP must manage the business in the partnership's best interest and avoid the appearance of improper use of assets and conflicts of interest. The GP cannot borrow from the partnership, compete with the partnership, or commingle personal funds with partnership funds. Finally, GPs do not generally receive any distributions from profits until after a payment has been made to the LPs.

Limited Partner (LP)

LPs are passive investors with no management or day-to-day decision-making responsibilities; therefore, they usually are not held personally responsible for the partnership's indebtedness. In fact, if an LP does take an active role, she faces the danger of losing the limitation on liability. LPs may receive cash distributions and capital gains from partnerships. The total yield of a partnership investment takes into account all potential rewards: tax deductions, cash distributions, and capital gains. Units of ownership in a partnership are called interests, rather than shares.

EXAMPLE

1. In a direct participation program, liability for the debts of the business falls upon the

   A. general partner(s)

   B. limited partner(s)

   C. shareholder(s)

   D. agent(s) selling the program

   Answer: A. DPPs consist of at least one GP and one LP. The liability of the LPs is limited to their investment, including commitments made but not yet fulfilled. On the other hand, the GPs, choice **A**, bear the liability for the debts of the entity.

ISSUING PARTNERSHIP INVESTMENTS

DPPs may be offered either as private placements, qualifying for an exemption from registration under state and federal law as described in Unit 4, or publicly registered either with the SEC, the state(s), or both. In either case, specialized documentation known as a subscription agreement is required from investors.

An investor who buys a limited partnership unit must complete and sign a subscription agreement, which includes a statement of the investor's net worth and annual income and a power of attorney form appointing the GP as the agent of the partnership. The agent is responsible to make certain that the information the potential investor provides in the subscription agreement is complete and accurate.

U17LO3: Recognize the characteristics of the pooled investment vehicles that are considered alternative investments.

The category of alts also includes a number of pooled investment vehicles. Probably the best known is the *hedge fund* (covered Unit 14), but there are a number of others. The following is a description of the pooled investment vehicles considered alternative investments that are most likely to appear on the exam.

Exchange-Traded Notes (ETNs)

Although similar in some regards, don't confuse ETFs with ETNs. It could be said that ETNs are cousins of ETFs. That said, just as with family members, there are some important differences. Most obvious is the difference in their basic structure. While ETNs are registered under the Securities Act of 1933, ETFs register under the Investment Company Act of 1940. Basically, this means that ETNs are made as debt instruments, while ETFs are looked at as investment companies. ETNs are a type of exchange-traded debt security offering a return linked to a market index or other benchmark rather than periodic interest payments as is the case with traditional debt securities. These are sometimes referred to as equity-linked notes (ELNs), which is a real misnomer because they are debt securities.

Issuers of ETNs issue and redeem notes as a means to keep the ETN's price in line with a calculated value, called the indicative value or closing indicative value for ETNs. This value is calculated and published at the end of each day by the ETN issuer. When an ETN is trading at a premium above the indicative value, issuing more notes to the market can bring the price down. Similarly, if an ETN is trading at a discount, redemption of notes by the issuer reduces the number of notes available in the market, which tends to raise the price. ETN issuers have primary control over the issuance and redemption processes which can become a conflict of interest.

Unlike ETFs, they do not buy or hold the assets replicating the performance of the underlying index. Some of the indexes and investment strategies used by ETNs can be sophisticated and very complex, carrying many different risks. They should be offered only to people who are knowledgeable and comfortable with the risks. Those risks, in part, include:

- credit risk (ETNs are unsecured debt obligations);

- market risk;

- liquidity risk (although exchange traded, a trading market may not develop);

- call, early redemption, and acceleration risk (ETNs may be called at the issuer's discretion); and

- conflicts of interest (the issuer may engage in trading activities that are at odds with note holders [shorting, for instance]).

Leveraged ETFs

These funds attempt to deliver a multiple of the return of the benchmark index they are designated to track. For instance, a 2x leveraged fund would try to deliver two times the return of whatever index it is tracking. With leveraged funds, there are no limits by rule or regulation as to the amount of leverage that could be applied to a portfolio. Currently there are numerous 2x and 3x leveraged funds available to investors. The risk associated with leverage is that it is always a double-edged sword; volatility is magnified. Therefore, the risk to be recognized regarding this fund strategy is that if the benchmark index is falling, then the fund's returns will be, in theory, the designated leverage amount (perhaps two or three) times the loss. In addition, most of these funds use derivatives products such as options, futures, and swaps to enable them to achieve the stated goal. Because these derivative products are not suitable for all investors, so too can it be said of the leverage fund portfolio containing them. Ultimately, as always, suitability becomes an issue when recommending these products.

Inverse (Reverse) Funds

Inverse funds, sometimes referred to as short funds, attempt to deliver returns that are the opposite of the benchmark index they are tracking. For example, if the benchmark is down 2%, the fund's goal is to be up 2%. As with leveraged ETFs, tools used to achieve the goal are options and other derivatives. In addition, inverse funds can also be leveraged funds, or said another way, two or three times the opposite of the indices' return.

EXAMPLE

A simple example of this would be an inverse fund tracking the S&P 500. If the index were to drop by 1%, the value of the inverse fund would rise by 1%. If this was a 3x inverse fund, then the fund's value would rise by 3%. Of course, if the index were to rise, the performance of the inverse fund would suffer, especially if it was leveraged.

TEST TOPIC ALERT

FINRA warns investors that most leveraged and inverse ETFs "reset" daily, meaning that they are designed to achieve their stated objectives on a daily basis. Their performance over longer periods of time—over weeks or months or years—can differ significantly from the performance (or inverse of the performance) of their underlying index or benchmark during the same period. Therefore, in most cases, these would not be suitable investments for *buy and hold* investors or those with other than a very short time horizon.

For the TVIX, (VelocityShares Daily 2x VIX ST ETN), one of the risk disclosures (page 28, PS-28) reads like this:

The long-term expected value of your ETNs is zero. If you hold your ETNs as a long-term investment, it is likely that you will lose all or a substantial portion of your investment.

TAKE NOTE

Both leveraged and inverse index funds (leveraged or not) can be traded on an exchange. When they are, they are known as ETFs. If the shares are exchange traded, they are priced by supply and demand, can be purchased on margin, and bought and sold throughout the trading day, like all exchange-traded products. For those that are not exchange-traded (e.g., inverse mutual funds), they would be priced, purchased, and redeemed like all investment company shares. Neither of these fund types carry any guarantee that they will achieve the stated goal or objective.

Structured Products

When you need something that doesn't yet exist, what do you do? You build it. That is the concept behind structured products; they are built (structured) to meet specific needs. In many cases, they involve structuring a debt issue in such fashion as to provide lower borrowing costs to the issuer while increasing potential returns to the lender. The goal is to give investors more reasons to accept a lower interest rate on debt in exchange for certain features.

In other examples, options and other derivatives are used to provide possible principal protection or other goals. Needless to say, for the most part these are highly complex products and should be limited to those investors who have the necessary financial sophistication to be able to understand the potential risks. When used properly, they can be useful tools to increase portfolio diversification.

Structured Notes With Principal Protection

FINRA defines the term "structured note with principal protection" as any structured product that combines a bond with a derivative component and that offers a full or partial return of principal at maturity. Structured notes with principal protection typically reflect the combination of a zero-coupon bond, which pays no interest until the bond matures, with an option or other derivative product whose payoff is linked to an underlying asset, index, or benchmark. These notes are promises to pay made by the product issuers. That is why any guarantee that the principal will be protected, whether in whole or in part, is only as good as the financial strength of the company that makes that promise. For those who can remember, this is what happened to investors who purchased structured notes with principal protection issued by Lehman Brothers Holdings which declared bankruptcy in September 2008.

Risks of Structured Products

There are several risks involved with structured products. Because of the customized nature of these products, there is little or no liquidity. Secondly, in most cases, these are structured so that the returns are not fully realized until maturity. As a result, these should appeal to buy and hold investors rather than short-term traders. There is also the matter of credit risk so it is important to know the strength of the financial institution who is the issuer. Finally, as with most alternative investments, there is a lack of efficient pricing. That is, the actual market price does not necessarily reflect the real value. This can lead to abnormal returns, good and bad. When good, the portfolio will generate positive alpha; when bad, the alpha will be negative.

VIATICAL/LIFE SETTLEMENTS

U17LO4: Describe viatical/life settlements.

The terms viatical and life settlement are often used interchangeably, but, they are technically not quite the same. The most significant (and testable) difference is that viaticals apply to those with a terminal illness and a life expectancy of 24 months or less regardless of their age, while life settlements apply to those who, although generally at least 65 years old, are in decent health with a life expectancy of at least 2 years that can run 10 years or longer. Health and life expectancy aside, the concepts are the same for both. In general, almost any kind of life insurance policy can be sold, although most companies will not purchase a straight (nonconvertible) term life policy.

Viatical settlements emerged in the early 1990s in response to the AIDS crisis to create opportunities for terminally ill patients to receive money by selling their life insurance death benefits for much more than the cash surrender value available, (but less than the death benefit), from insurance companies. The idea is that the money the person gets from the settlement is to go toward paying for medical expenses during this two-year period. Interests in the settled insurance policies are then sold to investors, with the promise of returns in the form of the death benefit (an amount higher than the purchase price) to be paid upon the death of the insured. As the market has expanded, viatical settlement providers turned to new classes of viators, those selling their life insurance policies, including the elderly and the chronically ill.

Selling a life insurance policy (or the right to receive the death benefit) to any person other than the insurance company that issued the policy, is a transaction known as a viatical or life settlement. NASAA concludes that these settlements, regardless of the health status or age of the insured, are securities. All persons involved in the offer and/or sale of viatical or life settlements should be aware of the nature and extent of the registration and antifraud provisions of state securities laws, as well as the applicability of these provisions to every offer and/or sale of a security. Because licensing is done on a state by state basis, there is little uniformity. Some states require just a life insurance license, some require both a life insurance and a life settlement license, and some require either or both of these and being licensed as a securities agent. As with so much else, the regulators are concerned about suitability and disclosure. When a life insurance policy is sold to an investor, the buyer is acquiring a financial interest in the insured's death. In addition to paying a lump sum, the purchaser agrees to pay any premiums that are necessary to support the cost of the policy for as long as the insured lives. In exchange, the buyer will receive the death benefit upon death of the insured. It is important to be aware of the risks involved in this activity:

- Because there is no active secondary market for these policies, it is difficult to arrive at a fair evaluation and the investor may wind up paying too much for the policy.

- There is always the chance that the insured will live longer than anticipated. The more the insured's life exceeds the projected expectancy, the lower the return to the investor.

- The possibility, remote as it is, that the insurance company will not be financially able to honor the claim.

- The intangible moral issue of the investor knowing that the sooner the insured dies, the greater the return.

INVESTMENT REAL ESTATE

U17LO5: Contrast the difference between passive and active real estate investing.

We have already discussed two methods of passive real estate investing. That is, investing in real estate where all of the work is done for the investor. That is the case with the REIT and the real estate limited partnership investment (RELP). Investing in real estate, whether it be single-family homes to flip or to rent, or commercial property, involves work on the part of the investor. Whether it is collection of rents, finding tenants, or doing repairs, the investor is responsible for doing the work (or hiring someone to do it).

One feature of real estate investment that is similar to the Section 1035 exchange available to annuities is the Section 1031 for real estate. An investor holding real estate may exchange that for another parcel and there are no immediate tax consequences.

COMMODITIES

U17LO6: Identify the different types of commodities and precious metals that are popular investments.

In the previous unit, we discussed futures. They are one of the methods by which individual investors can invest directly in commodities (forwards are used primarily by producers and industrial consumers). One can also invest indirectly through ETPs (exchange-traded products, such as ETFs that follow a commodity index) or mutual funds that invest in commodity-related businesses. For instance, an oil and gas fund would own stocks issued by companies involved in energy exploration, refining, storage, and distribution.

Historically, most commodity trading was of agricultural products (we were an agrarian society), and these commodities, such as corn, wheat, oats and soybeans, are still actively traded. There are animal-based commodities, such as beef, pork, and eggs. Today, the most commonly traded commodity is crude oil with coffee often claimed to be in second place. And, of course, for all of you Eddie Murphy fans (remember the movie *Trading Places*), there are frozen orange juice futures.

Active trading also takes place in industrial metals, such as aluminum, nickel, copper, and lead. Speaking of metals, it is hard to turn on the TV today without seeing a commercial for gold or silver investments. Whether you agree or not with the ads, for millennia, individuals and governments have stored their wealth in precious metals.

BENEFITS AND RISKS OF ALTERNATIVE INVESTMENTS

U17LO7: Describe the benefits and risks of alternative investments.

Most alternative investments share similar benefits and risks. Usually, these investments offer low or even negative correlation to the stock market, resulting in greater diversification of the portfolio. This can lead to greater overall long-term returns with reduced risk. In some cases, there are opportunities for abnormal returns, high and low.

As was done with pooled investment vehicles in Unit 14, we'll take these one at a time.

DPPs

The DPP investor enjoys several advantages, including:

- an investment managed by others;
- flow-through of income and certain expenses; and
- limited liability—the most the investors can lose is the amount of their investment plus any funds committed for, but not yet remitted.

The exam will probably give more attention to the following disadvantages.

Liquidity Risk

The greatest disadvantage is lack of liquidity. Because the secondary market for DPPs is limited, investors who want to sell their interests frequently cannot locate buyers.

Legislative Risk

When Congress changes tax laws, new rules can cause substantial damage to LPs, who may be locked into illiquid investments that lose previously assumed tax advantages.

Risk of Audit

Statistics from the IRS indicate that reporting ownership of a DPP results in a significantly higher percentage of returns selected for audit.

Depreciation Recapture

One of the tax benefits is the ability to depreciate most fixed assets, especially when that depreciation can be accelerated. The effect of the depreciation deduction is to lower the tax basis of the asset. If that asset is then sold for more than that basis, the excess is *recaptured* and subject to tax, possibly at ordinary income tax rates. You won't need to know anything more than the concept.

EXAMPLE

1. Benefits of investing in a DPP would include

   I.   high liquidity

   II. flow-through of operating losses

   III. limited liability

   IV. immunization against tax audit

   A. I and II

   B. I and IV

   C. II and III

   D. III and IV

   Answer: C. DPPs are structured as flow-through entities, giving their investors the opportunity to receive income without the partnership being taxed first. In addition, if there are losses, they get the opportunity to write off those losses against passive income from other DPPs. As limited partnership vehicles, they offer their investors liability limited to their investment. They generally have very low liquidity and, instead of reducing the tax audit risk, they increase it.

Real Estate

Real estate investing offers several benefits.

- Historically, real estate has been a hedge against inflation.
- It provides rental income, a portion of which may be tax-advantaged due to depreciation and interest deductions.
- It offers high leverage. Real estate loans generally require a relatively small down payment.
- Investment real estate is not generally correlated with stock market returns.
- It offers Section 1031 tax-free exchanges.

Investors should also be aware of some of the risks.

- In general, a lack of liquidity (certainly when compared to stocks, bonds, or mutual funds) is a risk.
- If purchased for rental, each month that the property is not rented is money lost.

- High leverage can work against the investor in a down market.

- The individual just might not have the skills necessary to manage the property and hiring someone else could eliminate or greatly reduce the profits.

Any good asset allocation program should have real estate, but, other than owning your own home, at least for most investors, REITs are probably the preferred option.

EXAMPLE

1. Among the reasons for investors to consider investing in real estate would be all of the following EXCEPT

    A. the ability to increase returns through leverage

    B. a high correlation with stock market returns

    C. possible tax advantages

    D. potential appreciation

    Answer: B. One of the investment advantages of real estate is that returns are generally negatively correlated with those of the stock market (option **B**).

Benefits of Investing in Commodities

- **Potential hedge against inflation.** One of the reasons for inflation is frequently an increase in the cost of basic commodities. During those periods, investors in those commodities should keep pace with or possibly exceed the inflation rate. However, investors should note that commodities can be much more volatile than other types of investments.

- **Diversification.** Commodities are generally not correlated with stock market returns. This negative correlation (see the next unit) offers diversification of returns (commodities up when stocks are down and the reverse) and can have the effect of reducing overall portfolio volatility. However, just as with any other assets, diversification does not ensure a profit or guarantee against loss.

- **Potential returns.** As with any other investment, those who buy low and sell high will make money (or the reverse if you take a short position). Commodity prices are subject to supply and demand on a global basis and can provide handsome returns to those who predict future shortages.

Risks of Commodity Investing

- **Principal Risk.** Commodity prices can be extremely volatile and the commodities industry can be significantly affected by world events, import controls, worldwide competition, government regulations, and economic conditions, all of which can have an impact on commodity prices. Because of the leverage involved in futures, investors can easily lose their entire investment virtually overnight.

- **Volatility.** Not only are the prices of the actual commodity volatile, but those investors seeking to lower their risk by investing in commodity mutual funds or ETFs will find that those vehicles reflect the volatility of the underlying commodity or index as well. This is especially so when the ETF or fund uses options or other derivatives.

- **Exposure to Foreign Markets.** In Unit 12, we discussed some of the risks of investing in foreign securities. Because commodities represent a global investment, in addition to the risks of the commodities themselves, there is also the vast array or risks that one faces when investing in foreign markets. Particularly prevalent here would be currency risk as well as the risks caused by political, economic, and currency instability.

- ▪ **High Cost.** This risk applies primarily to investing in the actual precious metal. For the small to average investor, the spread between what you pay for the bullion (or coins) and what you can resell for is significantly higher than the markup or commissions on stock or futures contracts.

- ▪ **Lack of Income.** No matter how long you hold gold or silver, you will never receive a dividend or an interest check. In fact, with any commodity, there is no income, only the chance for capital gains.

EXAMPLES

1. An investor is reading a report that industrial demand for copper is expected to double in the next five years. This might lead the investor to

    A. buy corn futures

    B. sell copper futures

    C. invest in several copper mining companies

    D. modify the investor's portfolio to take a larger cash position

    Answer: C. If the demand for copper increases, those companies producing the commodity should find their stock prices increase nicely (choice **C**). Selling copper futures would be when one expects the demand (and, therefore, prices) to fall.

2. Investors interested in adding precious metals to their portfolios would likely consider

    A. coal

    B. diamonds

    C. gold

    D. tin

    Answer: C. Of these choices, only gold, (**C**) is considered a precious metal. Diamonds are certainly precious, but they are not a metal. Tin, is a metal, but is not considered precious.

PART 4

Client Investment Recommendations and Strategies

This unit consists of seven units:

In total there will be 39 questions on this material, representing 30% of the Series 65 Exam.

UNIT
18

Type of Client

Generally, any competent person of majority age can open an account, and anyone declared legally incompetent cannot. Fiduciary or custodial accounts may be opened for minors or legally incompetent individuals.

In addition to individuals, accounts may be opened for anyone else meeting the definition of a person. That would include business and government entities. Some of these would be considered institutional accounts as defined in Unit 1.

The Series 65 Exam will include six questions on the material covered in this unit.

LEARNING OBJECTIVES

When you have completed this unit, you will be able to accomplish the following.

U18LO1: Recognize the different types of clients securities professionals service.
U18LO2: Identify the different ownership categories and the legal documentation required to open an account.
U18LO3: Distinguish between the different kinds of business entities capable of opening accounts.
U18LO4: Classify the special requirements for fiduciary accounts, including trust and estate accounts.
U18LO5: Identify estate planning options.

NEW ACCOUNT AGREEMENT

U18LO1: Recognize the different types of clients securities professionals service.

Securities professionals can serve a wide variety of clients. They range from the individual client to sovereign governments and everything in between. In this unit we'll cover accounts for natural persons, such as the various types of joint accounts. Accounts can be opened for all kinds of philanthropic endeavors including charities and foundations. We'll also spend time describing the various types of business accounts. Even though any type of government unit from municipalities to states to countries can employ the services of broker-dealers and investment advisers, the exam does not deal with those relationships other than when a broker-dealer acts as an underwriter for political issuer.

ACCOUNT OWNERSHIP CATEGORIES

U18LO2: Identify the different ownership categories and the legal documentation required to open an account.

Individual Account

An **individual account** may be for a natural person, a trust, or a deceased person through an estate account. There is one beneficial owner. When referring to investment advisers, normally an individual client is a natural person whose investments are managed by an adviser for a fee. When a business is organized as a sole proprietorship, that business account is also considered an individual account. The adviser should establish, in consultation with the client, a written statement of objectives and investment strategy before making recommendations to the client. This document is frequently referred to as an Investment Policy Statement (IPS). In the next unit we will examine the client profile and see the information necessary to prepare the IPS. In Unit 24, we will discuss the use of the IPS by those with fiduciary responsibility over qualified retirement plans.

The adviser must periodically review the client's investment profile to determine whether any changes in circumstances could alter the client's objectives.

Unless certain legal documents are procured, the account holder is the only person who can:

- control the investments within the account; or
- request distributions of cash or securities from the account.

Suitability for Individual Accounts

Both federal and state regulations require that any investment recommendation be suitable based upon the client's needs, objectives, and financial considerations. In the next unit, we will look at a number of those issues.

Joint Accounts

A **joint account** is owned by two or more persons, and each is allowed control over the account. Generally, suitability information is required on all of the tenants in the account.

On the new account form, the account must be designated as either **tenants in common (TIC)**, **joint tenants with right of survivorship (JTWROS)**, or **tenants by the entirety**. Account forms for joint accounts require the signatures of all owners. Trading activity (buying or selling) may be initiated at the request of any one of the parties. If a security is purchased, and a certificate is issued, it must be in the name of all of the tenants. Furthermore, when that security is sold, all of the tenants must sign that certificate, (or a stock or bond power). The check for the proceeds must be made payable to all of the tenants and it will be sent to the address designated in the account documents.

Tenants in Common (TIC)

TIC ownership (or JTIC), provides that a deceased tenant's fractional interest in the account is retained by that tenant's estate and is not passed to the surviving tenant(s). Ownership of a TIC account may be divided unequally. At the death of an account owner, that person's proportionate share of the cash and securities in the account is distributed according to the instructions in the decedent's will.

EXAMPLE

If a TIC agreement provides for 60% ownership interest by one owner and 40% ownership interest by the other, that fraction of the account would pass into the deceased owner's estate upon death. The TIC agreement may be used by more than two individuals.

Joint Tenants with Right of Survivorship (JTWROS)

JTWROS ownership stipulates that a deceased tenant's interest in the account passes to the surviving tenant(s). Regardless of contributions, each JTWROS account owner has an equal and undivided interest in the cash and securities in the account. Upon the death or declaration of incompetency of any of the account owners, account ownership passes to the survivor(s); a right of succession occurs and the other party or parties becomes sole owner(s) of the account.

TEST TOPIC ALERT

Whenever the test uses the term *joint tenants*, it means JTWROS (not tenants in common).

Tenancy by the Entirety (TBE)

This is the third type of concurrent ownership, or ownership by multiple persons. As with the other two we've described, each cotenant has an undivided interest in the account. Unlike the other two we've discussed, a tenancy by the entirety can created only by married persons. The most important difference between a tenancy by the entirety and a JTWROS or TIC is that in this form of ownership, the consent of the other tenant is required before the other tenant can sell or give away his interest in the property. As with JTWROS, upon the death of one of the spouses, the deceased spouse's interest passes to the surviving spouse. Because this form of ownership is restricted to spouses, it is considered similar to the community property laws found in some states. Tenancy by the entirety is most commonly used for ownership of real property (real estate).

Definition: Undivided Interest

In a joint account, all owners have an undivided interest in the account. What does that mean, especially when we see that TIC can have unequal shares? Simply stated, an undivided interest means that the no tenant has a designated interest in any specific asset in the account. Even when the shares are unequal, one tenant doesn't get stock A and the other stock B. Using our 60/40 example with the TIC account, one owner would have 60% of each of the holdings and the other 40% of each—the assets themselves are not divided between the owners.

TEST TOPIC ALERT

- Tenants in common can own unequal interests in the account, unlike joint tenants with right of survivorship, who always share equally. Tenants by the entirety are considered a single owner—no separate shares.

- TIC does not avoid probate.

- Checks or distributions must be made payable in the account name and endorsed by all parties.

EXAMPLES

1. A new account is opened for joint tenants with rights of survivorship. All of the following statements are true EXCEPT

    A. orders may be given by either party

    B. mail can be sent to either party with the permission of the other party

    C. checks can be drawn in the name of either party

    D. in the event of death, the decedent's interest in the account goes to the other party

    Answer: C. Although either party may enter an order, any money or securities delivered out of the account must be in the names of both owners, choice **C**. Rights of survivorship means that the surviving owner (or owners) receive the deceased's interest in the account.

2. If 3 individuals have a tenants in common account with a firm and one individual dies, then

    A. the account must be liquidated and the proceeds split evenly among the 2 survivors and the decedent's estate

    B. the 2 survivors continue as cotenants with the decedent's estate

    C. probate is avoided on the estate of the deceased cotenant.

    D. the account is converted to joint with rights of survivorship

    Answer: B. In the case of a TIC account, the decedent's estate, choice **B**, becomes a tenant in common with the survivors.

Suitability for Joint Accounts

The suitability requirements for a joint account follow the same basic rules as all accounts—you must have a reasonable basis to believe all recommendations presented are suitable based on the information gathered. Because a joint account is really nothing other than a collection of individuals, suitability information must be obtained on all of the account owners and any recommendations must be appropriate based upon that information. An example you might see on the exam has two brothers with a TIC account. One brother is an accredited investor under Rule 501 of the Securities Act, while the other is far from it. In this case, suitability is usually based on the lowest common denominator (the non-accredited brother).

EXAMPLES

1. Several investors open an account in joint tenancy. For suitability purposes, financial information is required on which of the following investors?

   A. The majority of the investors

   B. The largest investor only

   C. Only the one authorized to trade the account

   D. All of the investors

   Answer: D. When a joint account is opened, to be able to make suitable recommendations, financial information should be obtained on all of the account owners, choice **D**.

2. Which of the following individuals may not open a joint account?

   A. Two spouses

   B. Three sisters

   C. Two friends

   D. Parent and a minor child

   Answer: D. A joint account may be opened by two or more individuals who have legal standing. A minor may not be a party in a joint account because minors are not legally considered a person (think back to Unit 1). That makes choice **D** correct. A parent (or any other adult) can be custodian for a minor, but that is a single account, not a joint account.

What are the legal requirements for opening up these various accounts?

Opening an account for an individual requires the completion of the new account agreement. This is basically a contract between the broker-dealer or investment adviser and the customer explaining the rights and obligations of both and the charges for the services that will be rendered. Information that must be obtained from the client includes items such as:

- legal capacity—that is, is the client of full legal age in the state or jurisdiction or residence, and does she have the capacity to enter into the agreement;

- employment information; and

- the Customer Identification Program (CIP) notice. To help the government fight the funding of terrorism and money laundering activities, broker-dealers and investment advisers are required by federal law (The USA Patriot Act) to obtain, verify, and record information that identifies each person who opens an account. Customer identification requirements apply to all customers opening a new account as those terms are defined in the Bank Secrecy Act. That information includes:

  - name,

  - date of birth,

  - permanent physical address (no mail receiving or incorporation services),

  - tax identification number (if a U.S. citizen, this is typically the Social Security number),

  - citizenship or visa details, and

  - financial information about the client.

Unit 18

In the case of joint accounts, the information is the same except that details on all of the joint owners must be furnished. One of the joint owners is designated as the primary contact to receive statements and other communications.

We have not heard anything about the exam requiring you to know the account opening details for business accounts, although there is plenty about those accounts tested that will be covered shortly.

In Unit 16, we dealt with derivatives, especially options. There are some unique requirements to open those accounts. NASAA does not have a specific rule dealing with the opening of options accounts. Therefore, we will refer to the FINRA rules that are used as the guidelines for most states.

Because trading options (puts and calls) generally involves a higher degree of risk than stocks, bonds, or mutual funds, a designated supervisory person with knowledge about options must approve the account opening. In addition, there is a special Options Disclosure Document (ODD) that must be provided to any options customer at or prior to the time such customer's account is approved for options transactions.

In approving a customer's account for options trading, a broker-dealer, or agent associated with the broker-dealer, must exercise due diligence to ascertain the essential facts relative to the customer, his financial situation, and his investment objectives. One question asked on a new options account form that is not required on a normal brokerage account opening is investment experience and knowledge (e.g., number of years, size, frequency, and type of transactions) for options, stocks and bonds, commodities, and other financial instruments. Based upon such information, the designated supervisory person shall specifically approve or disapprove in writing the customer's account for options trading.

The account approval will indicate the:

- date the options disclosure document (ODD) is furnished to the customer;
- nature and types of transactions for which the account is approved (e.g., buying, covered writing, uncovered writing, spreading, and discretionary transactions);
- name of the agent assigned to the account;
- name of the supervisor approving the account;
- date of approval; and
- dates of verification of currency of account information.

Within 15 days after a customer's account has been approved for options trading, the broker-dealer must obtain from the customer a written agreement that the customer is aware of and agrees to be bound by FINRA rules applicable to the trading of option contracts and that the customer has received a copy of the current ODD. Part of the agreement states that she is aware of and agrees to be bound by the rules of the Options Clearing Corporation.

Finally, there are specific requirements for opening a margin account and those will be covered in Unit 22.

EXAMPLE

1. When an agent with a broker-dealer opens a new options account for a client, in which order must the following actions take place?

    I. Obtain approval from a qualified supervisor.

    II. Obtain essential facts from the customer.

    III. Obtain a signed options agreement.

    IV. Enter the initial order.

    A. I, II, III, and IV

    B. I, II, IV, and III

    C. II, I, IV, and III

    D. II, I, III, and IV

Answer: C. The steps in opening an options account occur in the following order: obtain essential facts about the customer; give the customer an ODD; have the manager approve the account; enter the initial order; and have the customer sign and return the options agreement within 15 days. That is the sequence in choice **C.**

ACCOUNTS FOR BUSINESS ENTITIES

U18LO3: Distinguish between the different kinds of business entities capable of opening accounts.

Sole Proprietorship

This is the simplest form of business organization and is treated like an individual account. Therefore, the same issues of suitability that apply to individual accounts apply to the management of sole proprietorship accounts. In a sole proprietorship, all income (or loss) is that of the individual. In fact, one of the risks of operating in this fashion is that all of the owner's assets are liable for the debts of the business—you can lose everything. Obviously, this is one of the major considerations when opening an account for this form of business.

General Partnership

A general partnership is an unincorporated association consisting of two or more individuals. In a general partnership, the partners manage and are responsible for the operation and debts of the business. Partnerships are easy to form and easy to dissolve, but are generally not suited for raising large sums of capital. Partnerships allow the business' profits and losses to flow directly through to the investors for tax purposes, thus avoiding double taxation of profits at the business and individual levels.

Because the income and losses flow through to the individual partners, an investment policy for a general partnership would have to consider the combined/collective objectives of all of the partners.

Limited Partnership

In the case of an enterprise organized as a limited partnership, the management (and liability) is assigned to the general partner(s) while the limited partner(s) are passive and have liability limited to their investment. This is the typical case with the Direct Participation Programs (DPPs) discussed in Unit 17. Suitability decisions are similar to a general partnership except that the limited partners do not have the full liability of the general partner(s).

Limited Liability Company (LLC)

A **limited liability company (LLC)** is a business structure that combines benefits of incorporation (limited liability) with the tax advantages of a partnership (flow-through of taxable earnings or losses). The LLC owners are **members** (not shareholders) and are not personally liable for the debts of the LLC.

Just as with the partnership clients described previously, the objectives and financial constraints of the individual members must be considered from a suitability standpoint.

S Corporation

An **S corporation**, although taxed like a partnership, offers investors the limited liability associated with corporations in general. The profits and losses are passed through directly to the shareholders in proportion to their ownership in the S corporation. Unlike an LLC, which can have an unlimited number of members, an S corporation may not have more than 100 shareholders, none of whom may be a nonresident alien, or more than one class of stock (presumably common).

Losses on S corporation stock may be claimed only to the extent of an investor's basis in the shares. The basis includes money contributed or lent to the corporation.

Any business organization client where the entity itself has no liability and is not subject to tax, such as the partnerships, LLC, and S corporation, requires the adviser to look through the entity to the owners to properly meet the suitability standards.

> **TAKE NOTE**
>
> Geraldine invested $25,000 in an S corporation, along with nine other investors who invested the same amount. Within a year, the corporation needed additional equipment, so Geraldine lent $10,000 to the business from her own funds. Her basis is now $35,000. If the corporation experiences a $400,000 loss, Geraldine's portion is $40,000. However, she may deduct only $35,000 of the loss because that is the amount of her basis.

C Corporation

A **C corporation** is a business structure that distinguishes the company as a separate entity from its owners. If a business expects to need significant capital, this form is almost always the preferred choice. Unlike the management of a partnership [the general partner(s)], in most cases, the corporation's officers and directors are shielded from personal liability for the corporation's debts and losses. Shareholders are also shielded from corporate creditors. That is the limited liability benefit of owning stock. Corporate income tax applies to the corporation as an entity rather than being passed through to the shareholder. If your client is a C corporation, you will only look at the corporation's financial needs and objectives when determining suitability.

TAKE NOTE

C corporation earnings are subject to double taxation. Before distribution, the earnings are taxable to the corporation and then are taxed again to the shareholder when paid out as a dividend. Distributions from LLCs and S corporations are taxed only once because there is no taxation at the business entity level.

CHOOSING THE RIGHT BUSINESS STRUCTURE

Here are some testable points to consider when a person is considering the most appropriate business form to use:

- The easiest business to set up, especially if you don't expect much liability, is the sole proprietorship. However, because the business and the owner are inseparable, there is unlimited liability and no limits to the amount of the loss (if any) that may be claimed on the proprietor's tax return.

- Partnerships and LLCs are generally easier to form and dissolve than a C corporation.

- Benefits of structuring a business as a general partnership, an LLC, or an S corporation would include no double taxation as is the case with a C corporation.

- However, a company that expects to be very profitable should be a C corporation instead of a partnership, an LLC, or an S corporation because in those three, all earnings pass to owners—nothing can be retained.

- Only the sole proprietorship and the C corporation are taxed on their income. The sole proprietorship's is on the owner's personal tax return and the corporation's is on a Form 1120.

- The only logical choice where a large amount of capital is to be raised is the C corporation.

- The business entities that have limited liability for owners as well as flow-through of income or loss are the limited partnership, LLC, and S corporation. The C corporation has limited liability but no flow-through; the sole proprietorship and general partnership have flow-through but unlimited liability.

- Corporations (including LLCs) survive the death of their owners (even if there is only one shareholder in an S corporation or C corporation, or one member of the LLC).

- When it comes to transferability of ownership, the corporate form, especially the C corporation, is the preferred choice (selling shares is usually pretty straightforward).

EXAMPLES

1. Three friends plan to start a new business. It is anticipated it will be several years before the business turns a profit. Which of the following types of business organization would be best if they wish to limit their liability while, at the same time, being able to receive favorable tax treatment for the expected losses?

   A. C corporation

   B. S corporation

   C. General partnership

   D. Sole proprietorship

   Answer: B. The only way to limit liability is through a corporation (or LLC or limited partnership—neither of which is offered here as a choice). The S corporation allows for the flow-through of operating losses to the shareholders while the C corporation does not.

2. Which of the following business structures is most appropriate for retaining money in the business?

   A. A C corporation

   B. A sole proprietorship

   C. An LLC

   D. An S corporation

   Answer: A. Only in the case of a C corporation, choice **A**, is money retained not subject to tax on the personal level. In all of the other choices, any income is passed through to the owners making it inefficient to accumulate funds in the business.

FIDUCIARY ACCOUNTS

U18LO4: Classify the special requirements for fiduciary accounts, including trust and estate accounts.

In a fiduciary account, the individual granted fiduciary responsibility enters trades for the account, makes all of the investment, management, and distribution decisions, and must manage the account in the owner's best interests.

Examples of fiduciaries include the following:

- **Trustee** designated to administer a trust

- **Executor** (f. **executrix**) designated in a decedent's will to manage the estate's affairs

- **Administrator** appointed by the courts to liquidate the estate of a person who died intestate (without a will), known as an administrator or trustee in intestacy

- **Guardian** (**conservator**) designated by the courts to handle the affairs of a minor's or a person judged incompetent

- **Custodian** of an Uniform Transfer to Minors Act (UTMA) account

- **Receiver** or trustee in a bankruptcy

A **fiduciary** is anyone legally appointed and authorized to represent another person, act on that person's behalf, and make decisions necessary to the prudent management of that person's account. The constraints placed on the actions of a fiduciary are described in detail in the Uniform Prudent Investors Act, (UPIA). For example, a fiduciary cannot use account contents for personal benefit but may be reimbursed for reasonable expenses incurred in managing the account. Do not confuse that with transaction costs. When determining appropriate investments, the cost of the transaction (trading commissions), is not nearly as important as how well the investment meets the needs of the account. The exam tends to focus its UPIA questions on those managing qualified retirement plans so we'll revisit the act in Unit 24.

TAKE NOTE

Any trades the fiduciary enters must be consistent with the trust's investment objectives.

Opening a Fiduciary Account

Opening a fiduciary account may require a court certification of the individual's appointment and authority. An account for a trustee must include a trust agreement detailing the limitations placed on the fiduciary. No documentation of custodial rights or court certification is required for an individual to open an UGMA or UTMA account (see Unit 24).

Power of Attorney

If a person who is not named on an account is to have trading authority, the customer must file written authorization with the broker-dealer giving that person access to the account. Without this power in writing, no matter how tempting the answer on the exam, activity in the account cannot be created by anyone other than the account owner(s). Trading authorization usually takes the form of a power of attorney. Two basic types of trading authorizations are **full** and **limited powers of attorney**.

Full Power of Attorney

A full power of attorney allows an individual who is not the owner of an account to:

- deposit or withdraw cash or securities; and/or
- make investment decisions for the account owner.

Limited Power of Attorney

A limited power of attorney allows an individual to have some, but not total, control over an account. The document specifies the level of access the person may exercise.

TEST TOPIC ALERT

Limited power of attorney, also called limited trading authorization, allows entering of buy and sell orders but not the withdrawal of funds. Entry of orders and withdrawal of funds is only allowed if full power of attorney is granted.

Durable Power of Attorney

A full or limited power may be made durable by the grantor of the power. It is designed to provide that a specifically designated person maintains power over the account even upon the grantor's incapacitation, whether due to physical or mental causes. Its most common use is when providing for aging parents. However, upon the death of either principal to the durable power of attorney, the power is terminated.

How does this differ from the living will we will discuss shortly? A living will is a written document making your specific end-of-life wishes known. The durable power of attorney (POA) appoints someone to act on your behalf and make the decisions. So, if you want to be sure your wishes, such as organ donation, are followed, prepare a living will.

TEST TOPIC ALERT

A durable power of attorney survives the physical or mental incompetence of the grantor but not the death of either party.

This means that orders entered after the time of death of the grantor, even if the purchase or sale was decided upon before death, are not accepted.

TRUST AND ESTATE ACCOUNTS

Two special kinds of accounts that may appear on the exam are those dealing with trusts and estates. What both of these have in common is that the person entering orders on behalf of the account is acting in a fiduciary capacity, whether it be the trustee of the trust or the executor (or administrator) of the estate. These fiduciaries are acting for the benefit of the beneficiary or beneficiaries of the trust or estate so it is necessary to look at the objectives of the trust and the needs of the heirs.

Trust Accounts

A **trust** is a legal entity that offers flexibility to an individual who wishes to transfer property. Trusts may be established for a variety of personal and charitable property transfers. Trusts are also established as the legal entity for a corporate retirement plan, but that will be covered in a later unit.

The subject of trust law is very complicated and should only be addressed by one who is competent in the subject, usually an attorney.

This exam will require you to know the basics of trusts, how trusts are taxed, trustee responsibility, and your obligations when acting as an adviser to the account.

Trust Parties

For a trust to be valid, three parties must be specified in the trust document (trust agreement). These parties are a settlor, a trustee, and a beneficiary. Under certain circumstances, the settlor, trustee, and beneficiary may be the same individual. For a trust to be valid, both the settlor and the trustee must be competent parties. However, the beneficiary may be a minor or a legally incompetent adult.

The Settlor

The **settlor** is the person who supplies the property for the trust. Trust property is also referred to as its principal or corpus. This party is also known as the maker, **grantor**, trustor, or donor.

Trustee

A **trustee** is an individual or other party holding legal title to property held for the benefit of another person (or persons). The trustee must administer the trust by following directions in a trust agreement or in a will. A trustee must perform certain duties relative to the trust property.

A trustee is a fiduciary and is obliged to perform in the interest of the beneficiaries. The trustee may be one or more adult individuals or an entity in the business of trusteeship that is responsible for investing, administering, and distributing trust assets for benefit of the beneficiary (or beneficiaries).

In many ways, a trustee's duties are like those of an **executor** (for an estate). However, a trustee's duties generally continue for more time than a typical estate settlement, and the trustee is charged with the greater duty of investing trust assets.

Beneficiary

A **beneficiary** is a person for whose benefit property is held in trust. A beneficiary is one who receives or who is designated to receive benefits from property transferred by a trustor. Beneficiaries to a trust include only those persons upon whom the settlor intended to benefit from the trust property or those who would succeed their interests.

EXAMPLE

Jill establishes a trust under which her husband, Julian, is to receive all income produced by the trust property for as long as he lives. Upon Julian's death, their daughter, Janet, will receive the trust principal. Julian is a primary beneficiary. However, until Julian's death, Janet is a contingent beneficiary because her benefit depends on the occurrence of an event, in this case, Julian's death.

TEST TOPIC ALERT

Although it doesn't happen often, the grantor of the trust can also be the trustee and/or the beneficiary.

Remainderman

When a trust has run its course and all expenses and distributions have been made, the person who receives the remaining balance is called the remainderman (no gender preference here, there's no such term as remainderwoman). The most common case involves real estate. For example, the husband dies and has arranged for his wife to have full use of their home until she passes away. At that time, any surviving children inherit the home. They are the remaindermen.

Simple Trusts vs. Complex

Simple Trusts

All income earned on assets placed into a **simple trust** must be distributed during the year it is received. If the trust does not distribute all of its net income at least annually, the trust is declared a complex trust. The trustee is not empowered to distribute the trust principal from a simple trust.

Complex Trust

On the other hand, a **complex trust** may accumulate income. A complex trust is permitted deductions for distributions of net income or principal. Capital gains are deemed part of the distributable net income of a complex trust unless reinvested. Furthermore, the trustee may distribute trust principal according to trust terms. We'll have more to say about these in Unit 21.

TEST TOPIC ALERT

The key difference between a simple and a complex trust is that the simple trust must distribute all of its annual income, whereas a complex trust is not obligated to do so.

Living vs. Testamentary Trusts

Living Trust

A **living trust**, also known as an **inter vivos trust**, is established during the maker's lifetime. When an individual sets up a revocable living trust, she maintains complete control over it. During the maker's lifetime, she can make changes to the trust as often as she wants to and can add or remove assets as desired. These trusts contain instructions for managing the trust upon the incapacity or death of the grantor.

Testamentary Trust

With a **testamentary trust**, the settlor retains control over assets until death (think "last will and testament"). The individual's will stipulates that, at death, the testator's property is to be placed in trust for the benefit of one or more beneficiaries.

The testamentary trust does not reduce the grantor's income or estate tax exposure. Furthermore, assets that pass to a testamentary trust do not avoid probate, because the validity of the will's instructions to pass property to the trust must be substantiated in probate court.

Living Will

Please do not confuse a living will with a living trust or even a will. The common name for these is an advance directive of medical care directive. This has nothing to do with assets or beneficiaries. It is the individual's instructions for end-of-life situations, such as withholding medical care or organ donation. The exam may show it something like this.

EXAMPLE

1. A living will is used to:

    A. avoid the cost and time of probate

    B. eliminate, or at least reduce, estate taxes

    C. ensure that the author's assets are properly distributed after death

    D. express the author's end-of-life wishes

    Answer: D. Sometimes referred to as a medical directive or advanced care directive, a living will is used to express the author's end-of-life wishes, such as organ donation, "pulling the plug," and so forth (choice **D**). It has nothing to do with living trust or a last will and testament describing the distribution of assets after death.

FOUNDATIONS AND CHARITIES

One of the discoveries of the Madoff affair was the large amounts lost by charities and foundations. In most cases, certainly true for charities, they should be dealt with as the fiduciary accounts described previously. In the case of foundations, because those are usually funded by the principals, a greater amount of investment flexibility may be called for.

Philanthropic Funds

Wealthy individuals may set up donor-advised funds that allow for flexibility and tax advantages. There are mutual fund sponsors and banks that offer these individuals the opportunity to donate a lump sum, take a current tax deduction, and then have the assets invested to earn over a period while allowing the donor to advise distributions to favored charities. If you are dealing with high net worth clients who are of a charitable bent, there could be great merit in advising them in this direction.

EXAMPLE

1. For which of the following types of clients would the suitability requirements be somewhat more relaxed?

    A. A guardian for an orphan

    B. A charity

    C. A foundation

    D. An executor

    Answer: C. Guardians and executors are fiduciaries controlling assets of those who cannot speak for themselves. Charities raise funds from donors expecting that the money will be invested wisely. Foundations, choice **C**, are generally funded by their founders who usually give those managing the money greater flexibility.

Impact Investments

Impact investing can be defined as "the intentional allocation of capital to generate a positive social or environmental impact that can be—and is—measured."

Charities and foundations usually have a specified goal, whether it be medical research (think American Cancer Society) or social goals (think Greenpeace). Impact investing is when the entity commits a portion of its funds to those companies or industries which align with those goals. I don't think the Cancer Society would have tobacco stocks in its portfolio and Greenpeace probably wouldn't invest in strip mining companies.

Impact investing is a subset of Socially Responsible Investing (SRI) that attempts to generate positive social good in addition to the goals typically outlined in an SRI approach. Where SRI fund managers are generally passive and adopt a "do no harm" approach, impact investing funds typically not only seek to create positive impact, but measure and report their impact in a transparent way. The acronym ESG is also frequently found. This stands for environment, social, and corporate governance.

EXAMPLE

1. A socially responsible mutual fund would probably invest in companies

    A. generating high returns

    B. acting with high ethics and morality

    C. located in a single geographic area

    D. with a major presence on social media

    Answer: B. SRI looks for companies with high ethical standards, choice **B**.

Here is a bit more about the topic, which should enable any student encountering this, or a similar question, to be confident in their choice of answer. The standards involved include corporate responsibility and concerns for society as valid parts of investment decisions. ESG criteria are used in an attempt to generate long-term competitive financial returns and positive societal impact.

Program-Related Investments

Although somewhat similar to impact investing, program-related investments are those where the foundation (more common for them than charities) makes a charitable distribution. Examples of this would be helping bring new drugs to market more quickly by providing necessary funding. One caution is that the investments must be consistent with the philanthropy's mission to get the same favorable tax treatment by the IRS as a regular charitable gift would.

Management Obligations

In general, these foundations are managed by a board of directors having the responsibility of selecting and overseeing the activities of the investment manager. The board prepares an investment policy statement (IPS) describing their goals and objectives and uses this IPS to monitor how well the investment manager(s) adhere to the plan.

As described in the specific IPS, these managers need to evaluate the expected returns and see that they outpace inflation without taking undue risk. Diversification is a key, both with the types of industry, types of security, and relative risk.

A special investment constraint applies to most private foundations. IRS regulations require a private foundation pay out each year an amount equal to 5% of its net investment assets in "qualifying distributions."

Account Opening Requirements

Opening an account for an organization is somewhat more complicated than an individual account. In addition to information about the entity, detailed information about those individuals in a control position (officers, 10% owners, etc.) must be supplied. Significant financial information about the organization is also required to help determine suitability. Most broker-dealers have special account opening forms, and investments advisers usually use a different contract when dealing with an organization. We don't expect you will see much in the way of detail on your exam.

ESTATE PLANNING OPTIONS

U18LO5: Identify estate planning options.

Although estate planning is best left for the specialists, the exam will cover several basic concepts which will enable you to assist your clients and help identify when to call in the attorneys.

Transfer-on-Death (TOD) Accounts

Using a transfer-on-death (TOD) account is the simplest way to keep assets held in brokerage accounts from becoming subject to probate upon a client's death and, at the same time, be distributed specifically as the account owner wishes. However, the TOD account does not avoid estate taxes if applicable. TOD accounts are available for most types of paper assets, such as savings and checking accounts in banks and credit unions, certificates of deposit, stocks, bonds, and other securities.

The owner, while alive, is the only person with any rights to the property. Upon the owner's death, the property is immediately transferred to the named beneficiaries, usually without any added cost. The owner has the right to change beneficiaries at any time and provide for unequal distribution of the assets if desired. One of the other attractive features of TOD accounts is that there is no legal documentation necessary. The only types of accounts that may be opened with a TOD designation are individual accounts, JTWROS, and tenants by the entirety accounts.

EXAMPLE

1. A client has an account where, upon her death, she desires that her only son will receive 50% of account value and her 4 daughters will receive 12.5% each. The easiest way to accomplish this would be to title the account

   A. TOD

   B. JWTROS

   C. tenants in common

   D. in trust for the children

   Answer: A. Transfer on death (TOD), choice **A**, requires no additional legal work and allows the account owner to designate beneficiaries in whatever percentages she wants. Furthermore, changes can be made at any time before death.

TAKE NOTE

You might also see this as payable-on-death (POD), although the term is used far more frequently for bank accounts.

Totten Trust

If you have a really old bank account you might have a Totten trust designation using language similar to "John Doe, in trust for Jane Doe," or perhaps, "John Doe as trustee for Jane Doe." Totten trusts, sometimes referred to as a poor man's will, allowed for the transfer of ownership of a bank account to a beneficiary after the owner's death. Totten trusts were the predecessor to POD or TOD designations, but a few states still recognize them.

Revocable vs. Irrevocable Trusts

For more elaborate estate planning, it is advised that the client consider the use of trusts. Terms of a **revocable trust** may be changed during the maker's lifetime. Terms of an irrevocable trust generally cannot be changed.

Revocable Trust

If the grantor retains the ability to revoke the trust and take back the trust assets, the trust is revocable, and the income is taxable to the grantor under the grantor trust rules. That means the grantor is subject to tax on trust income even when not receiving the income. Assets in a revocable trust are included in the grantor's gross estate for federal estate tax purposes—no estate tax benefits apply. Revocable trusts are also called living trusts. They are used primarily as a will substitute. Assets in trust avoid the cost, time, expense, and publicity of probate.

Irrevocable Trust

For a trust to be considered irrevocable, the settlor must give up all ownership in property transferred into the trust. Property placed in an irrevocable trust is usually not includable in the trustor's estate for federal estate tax purposes. Certain exceptions to the general rule can jeopardize the effectiveness of an irrevocable trust to reduce estate taxes, but are unlikely to be tested.

Grantor Retained Annuity Trusts (GRATs)

This is an estate planning tool designed to pass assets to beneficiaries (usually children) in a way to minimize gift and/or estate taxes. The topic is very complicated, but here are the basics you might need to know.

- The key is in the words—grantor retained. That tells you that any income from the trust is taxed to the grantor.

- The annuity portion is paid for a specified number of years. At the end of that term, the beneficiaries get whatever is left and that could be free of estate and gift taxes.

EXAMPLE

1. Sam Jones has been a successful businessman and is concerned that his youngest daughter will not be able to live within her means. To protect this from happening, Jones places a large sum of money into a trust for the benefit of the daughter. Because Jones knows he won't live forever, he arranges for the Fourth Fidelity Bank and Trust Company to have control over the assets. Which of the following statements is NOT true?

   A. Sam Jones is the grantor.

   B. Sam Jones is the trustee.

   C. Fidelity Bank and Trust Company is the trustee.

   D. Sam Jones's daughter is the beneficiary.

   Answer: B. The person (A) who funds the trust is the grantor or settlor. The bank has been appointed to be trustee (C), and the daughter is the beneficiary (D) of the trust. That makes choice **B** the untrue statement.

Estate Accounts

An **estate account** is an account that, like a trust account, is directed by fiduciary on behalf of the beneficiary or beneficiaries of an estate. In the case of one who prepares a will, there is a specified executor. In the case of one who dies without a will (intestate), these functions are performed by a court-appointed administrator. The executor or administrator makes the investment, management, and distribution decisions for the account.

Per Stirpes

One common way for people to provide for their descendants is to incorporate the phrase, "to my living issue, per stirpes" in their will. In fact, some states automatically distribute in that fashion when one dies intestate. Per stirpes (not a typo—it is not stripes) is from the Latin word meaning branch. When used, per stirpes means that the deceased intended that a beneficiary's share of the inheritance is to go to an heir.

EXAMPLE

A widow (or widower) had three children and wished the estate to be distributed equally. If one of those children died prior to the estate settlement, that child's children (the grandchildren of the widow or widower), would share their parent's one-third share (receiving 1/6th of the total each), while the two living children would each receive a one-third share.

It would look like this:

Child A	Child B	Child C (deceased)
		Grandchild 1 and 2
1/3rd	1/3rd	1/6th and 1/6th

Per Capita

Another Latin term, and this one means "by total head count." Let's take the example used previously, where the deceased left the estate to three children. If they are all alive, simple enough, each inherits one-third. But, if one of the three children, such as C in the previous example, has predeceased the parent and has two children, then the estate is split four ways (Child A, Child B and the two grandchildren each receive 1/4th of the estate).

TAKE NOTE

Some states have differing rules for per capita distributions, making it unlikely the topic will be tested.

TRUST SUITABILITY ISSUES

Just as with any other account, recommendations must be suitable when considering all of the relevant information. However, in the case of a trust or estate, there are several considerations that do not arise in other individual accounts. Some of these are as follows.

- In virtually all cases, the trust document declares the objectives of the trust. Generally, these can only be changed by the grantor or, once in receipt of the assets, the beneficiary. The trustee is obligated to invest the funds in accordance with those objectives. For example, if the objective is income until the death of the grantor, then that is the primary consideration in any recommended transaction. Always follow the terms of the trust.

- Unless specifically stated in the trust document, margin trading is not permitted.

- In the case of an estate, the terms of the will must be followed.

- If the investment adviser managing the account is also the trustee or executor, in addition to the normal fiduciary responsibility assumed by all investment advisers, there are the formal requirements of the Uniform Prudent Investors Act (UPIA). That Act is described in detail in Unit 24 dealing with retirement plans. "Wearing two hats" is an allowable practice, but not done very often because of the inherent conflict of interest. This, as with all potential conflicts of interest, must be disclosed to the client.

- There are unique tax considerations, which will be covered in Unit 21.

- In the case of trusts, conflicts between the grantor and the beneficiary may exist; in the case of estates, conflicts among the beneficiaries may arise.

EXAMPLE

A widow was left a trust with her children as contingent beneficiaries. She is to receive income from the trust, and her two children will receive the principal upon her death. To maximize their value, the children ask you to allocate half of the corpus to growth stocks while leaving the balance in bonds for their mother. Because the trust document calls for the widow to receive income, the adviser must pursue that objective and cannot follow the wishes of the children until the trust's assets become theirs.

UNIT
19

Client Profile

An adviser must be familiar with each client's circumstances, financial goals, and needs to formulate suitable investment recommendations. Without suitability information, the account cannot be opened. This is unlike broker-dealers that are permitted to open client accounts without suitability information.

The Series 65 exam will include seven questions on the material covered in this unit.

LEARNING OBJECTIVES

When you have completed this unit, you will be able to accomplish the following.

U19LO1: Describe the different methods of client data gathering.
U19LO2: Identify the client's current and future financial situation.
U19LO3: Contrast financial and nonfinancial investment considerations.
U19LO4: Discover the client's risk tolerance.
U19LO5: Distinguish between investment objectives and investment constraints.
U19LO6: Analyze a client's financial goals and objectives for suitable recommendations.

CLIENT FINANCIAL STATUS

U19LO1: Describe the different methods of client data gathering.

How is all of the information necessary to complete the customer profile obtained? Although there is no universal method, most firms rely on a combination of tools. The first step is usually having the client complete a detailed questionnaire. Optimally, this should be followed up by a personal interview, either in the office or home, on the phone, or online with one of the various video services currently available. There is only so much one can learn from a form, and both the client and the IAR benefit from the give and take of an interview, as that is the best way to discover qualitative information, such as risk tolerance and attitudes. As covered elsewhere in this course, confidentiality and security of this customer data is critical. Traditionally, data-gathering techniques for financial professionals involve asking clients or prospects to bring in account statements, insurance policies, 401(k) plan options, and maybe tax returns. Why is all of this information needed? Without it, there is no way to determine suitability. Furthermore, as learned in the previous unit, the CIP requires certain information.

FINANCIAL PROFILE

U19LO2: Identify the client's current and future financial situation.

A **financial profile** should include an assessment of the client's:

- current expenditures;
- debt obligations;
- tax status;
- income sources; and
- a balance sheet containing the client's assets, including
  - cash, CDs, and savings accounts (usually looked at as an "emergency fund," generally considered to be a primary requirement for investing in securities),
  - real estate holdings,
  - value and composition of securities holdings,
  - pension and retirement accounts,
  - cash value in life insurance policies, and
  - personal items such as jewelry and automobiles; and liabilities, including
    - current debt obligations (credit cards, estimated tax payments, etc.),
    - long-term debt obligations (auto loan, mortgage, etc.),
    - loans against insurance cash value, and
    - loans against 401(k) plan.

Using this information, the adviser will prepare a family balance sheet. This balance sheet reflects all of the client's assets and liabilities to determine the overall net worth and liquidity of that client, while a family income statement includes income and expenses and is used to determine the client's cash flow.

Taking into consideration all of this information indicates to the securities professional the extent to which the client is able to make a lump-sum investment (the balance sheet shows a large amount of net assets available), and/or periodic investments (the income statement reveals a positive cash flow—there is money left at the end of the month).

Because things can change, it is recommended that there be a follow-up meeting with the client at least annually.

TEST TOPIC ALERT

A family balance sheet only includes assets and liabilities, not income, such as salary, dividends, or interest, or amounts paid for expenses.

EXAMPLE

1. An individual's net worth is

    A. the difference between the individual's assets and the individual's liabilities

    B. best determined by examining the individual's personal income statement

    C. largely irrelevant in identifying the individual's investment objectives

    D. another term for discretionary income

    Answer: A. An individual's net worth is the difference between the individual's assets and the individual's liabilities, choice **A**. It is determined from the personal balance sheet rather than from the personal income statement. Net worth is relevant in determining an individual's investment objectives. Clients with a negative net worth might find it preferable to reduce their debt level before beginning an investment program.

NONFINANCIAL CONSIDERATIONS

U19LO3: Contrast financial and nonfinancial investment considerations.

The previous learning objective described a number of financial considerations. How do those contrast with nonfinancial ones? In its simplest form, the contrast is that one deals with monetary numbers and the other not. In the first case, we are gathering assets, liabilities, income and expense. Now, we will look at non-monetary items.

A client's nonfinancial considerations can be more important than the financial information. Relevant nonfinancial information includes the following:

- Age
- Marital status
- Investment experience
- Attitudes and values, such as "ESG" investing
- Number and age of dependents
- Employment stability
- Employment of family members
- Demographics (where clients live can affect their investment attitudes)
- Current and future family educational needs
- Current and future family health care needs

There is one other nonfinancial consideration that is gaining greater prominence after the 2017 Nobel Prize in economic sciences was awarded to Richard H. Thaler for his work in the field. Briefly the premise is that investors are irrational when it comes to making investment decisions. The study of this is known as *behavioral finance*.

The "dean" of behavioral finance, Daniel Kahneman, PhD, was awarded the Nobel Prize in this same field in 2002. In the announcement from the Royal Swedish Academy of Sciences, they stated, "his team's findings have countered some assumptions of traditional economic theory—that people make rational choices based on their self-interest—by showing that people frequently fail to fully analyze situations where they must make complex judgments. Instead, people often make decisions using rules of thumb rather than rational analysis, and they base those decisions on factors economists traditionally don't consider, such as fairness, past events and aversion to loss."

Today, it is accepted that behavioral biases can cause investors to make financial decisions that are irrational. Here are some of the more common examples:

- Overconfidence—Experienced (and even some "rookie") investors tend to overestimate their ability and the accuracy of the information available to them

- Conservatism—Many investors have a hard time changing their existing beliefs, even when new information is presented to them

- Herd behavior—A market drop may be followed by panic selling

- Anchoring—The tendency to base expectations upon the first information received which may, or may not be accurate. Once a thought has anchored in your mind, it is difficult to move away from it

- Regret aversion—The investor prepares himself in such a way as to avoid distress over an adverse outcome (think about a trip to Las Vegas where you know you will probably lose, but condition yourself to expect that)

RISK TOLERANCE

U19LO4: Discover the client's risk tolerance.

Investor **risk tolerance**—the attitude toward risk and safety—is an important part of a client's profile. Regardless of a person's financial status, the customer's motivation to invest and risk tolerance should shape the portfolio.

Selection of specific types of investments (e.g., stocks, bonds, annuities) depends on several factors including:

- Client's objectives

- Amount available for investing (client must use discretionary cash for investing, not the rent money)

- Client's aversion to risk (every investment involves some degree of risk because every investment requires transferring purchasing power from the present to the future and no one knows what the future holds)

To understand a customer's risk tolerance, an adviser should know information such as the following:

- How much of a loss the investor can tolerate (e.g., 5%, 50%, or 100%)

- The liquidity requirements for investments

- The importance of tax considerations

- Investment time horizon, either long term or short term

- Investment experience

- Current investment holdings

- Expectations regarding investment returns

■ Investment temperament (i.e., is the client bored with stable investments or anxious with volatile ones?)

■ Level of tolerance for market fluctuations

A person's risk tolerance is often characterized as either aggressive, moderate, or conservative.

Aggressive investors are willing to risk greater amounts and withstand market volatility in exchange for the chance to realize substantial returns. An aggressive investor may be willing to sustain losses of 10%, 25%, or even 50% on an investment. Moderate investors are in between the other two. They can tolerate some loss, but not nearly at the level of the aggressive investor. **Conservative investors** normally want the relative safety of guaranteed income with low risk to loss of principal. Very conservative investors are unwilling to sustain even modest losses on their investments. There is a full spectrum of risk profiles between these two extremes.

EXAMPLE

The following table is a sample of how a portfolio might be structured based on the three different risk tolerances.

Asset allocation	Conservative portfolio	Moderate portfolio	Aggressive portfolio
Stocks	30%	60%	80%
Bonds	50%	30%	15%
Cash	20%	10%	5%

TAKE NOTE

An investor who claims to be aggressive but is unwilling to sustain losses is actually conservative.

A client's tolerance for volatility and risk will often narrow the field of potential investments.

EXAMPLE

1. In designing an investment portfolio for a new client, one of the first things to do is determine the client's

    A. home address

    B. Social Security or tax ID number

    C. risk tolerance

    D. beneficiary

    Answer: C. One can't adequately present any investment recommendations without having an understanding of the client's risk tolerance, choice **C**. Home address and Social Security number are legal requirements for opening the account, but they don't enter into the decision-making process for portfolio design. Yes, you will want to know the beneficiary of any IRAs or qualified plans, but that has little to do with the nature of your recommendations.

INVESTMENT OBJECTIVES AND INVESTMENT CONSTRAINTS

U19LO5: Distinguish between investment objectives and investment constraints.

Within the parameters determined by a client's circumstances and financial resources, the adviser and client should establish financial goals. The most commonly specified goals include capital preservation, current income, capital growth, and speculation. The objectives behind these goals may be planning for college education, retirement, death, or disability.

However, in attempting to meet these objectives, there may be some obstacles, properly referred to as *investment constraints*, which must be considered. When an investment adviser or IAR prepares a plan for a client, all of these factors are used to prepare an investment policy statement (IPS) we described in the previous unit. The following chart may be helpful in your review of objectives and constraints.

Figure 19.1: Investment Policy Statements: Objectives and Constraints

Objectives	Description
Return requirements	Minimum current income requirements; accumulation amount needed to meet financial goals, preservation of capital, growth, and so forth
Risk tolerance	Investor's risk tolerance based on self-evaluation, objective questionnaire, and past experience

Constraints	Description
Time horizon	Time frame in which goals must be attained
Liquidity	What is the cash need? High if close to goals (retirement or education); low if long time horizon
Taxes	Tax characteristics of investor and desired level of tax management
Laws and regulations	Any legal prohibitions on types of investments or transactions—is the investor accredited?
Unique circumstances and/or preferences	Investor preferences or desires to avoid particular types of assets

Preservation of Capital

Many people are averse to any decline in value of their investments. For such investors, bank-insured CDs, savings accounts, and money market funds offer the safety they seek. However, by reducing market risk (there is little or no market price fluctuation in these instruments), the investor is sacrificing the opportunity for higher income. In addition, as fixed-income investments, they are exposed to inflation (purchasing power) risk.

Bank Insured Certificates of Deposit (CDs)

In addition to the questions about the jumbo, negotiable CDs that trade in the money market, there are questions on the exam about the certificates of deposit that you can get at your local bank. Here are some points that will help you get the right answer.

- Bank CDs eliminate interest rate risk (their value remains constant, even when interest rates change).

- They are *not* savings accounts with a maturity date.

- They would be included as an asset on a family balance sheet.

- They are the preferred answer when the question asks about a client who wants capital preservation with no risk of loss.

- They are insured by the FDIC up to the current limit (limits are not tested).

- Each bank sets the interest rate it will pay on those CDs with smaller banks typically offering more competitive rates.

TEST TOPIC ALERT

On the exam, the first choice for preservation of capital should always be bank-insured CDs. In addition, because they are not marketable (traded in any marketplace), bank CDs (we're referring to the ones retail investors purchase at their local branches, not the jumbo CDs traded in the money market), have no interest rate risk. That is, because their value is fixed, you can always redeem them at face value, regardless of the direction of interest rates. The exam will ignore the fact that there may be a penalty for cashing in before maturity.

Current Income

Investors seeking current income will normally focus on individual securities or mutual funds that invest in fixed-income investments such as:

- government bonds and notes, and agency bonds;

- corporate bonds;

- preferred stock; and

- utility company common stock.

When the investor's goal is income, a primary factor is the amount of risk the investor is willing and/or able to take. The risk/reward principle is quite clear—the more risk, the greater the potential reward and, logically, the lower the risk, the lower the potential reward. That is why, at least for those with a low risk tolerance, but with a time horizon that doesn't require money market instruments, U.S. Treasury and agency issues along with investment-grade bonds are usually the recommendations. On the other end of the spectrum are bonds of corporations with very low credit ratings (the high-yield, or junk, bonds). These bonds tend to yield high income with principal subject to credit (default) risk. In the middle might be those investing in preferred stock or public utility stocks.

Capital Growth

Common stock investments generally provide a means to preserve and increase the buying power of an investor's money over and above the inflation rate. Although subject to short-term volatility, the equity market tends to provide higher investment returns over time.

As with income, the term *growth* refers to a broad spectrum of investments. Aggressive growth stocks may be very appropriate for a person with a very high tolerance for risk and the ability to remain invested for many years. At the other end of the spectrum are large capitalization stock funds that invest in some of the largest and most respected companies. These funds may be a better choice for older investors, who may need to liquidate the investment in three to five years, or investors who are more comfortable knowing they have invested in a fund that is less risky.

Speculation

A customer may want to speculate with a portion of their investments. Speculative investments offer the opportunity to earn substantial returns but carry a commensurate amount of risk. Speculative investments may include:

- highly volatile stocks;

- high-yield (junk) bonds;

- options on stocks or stock indexes; and

- commodity futures.

EXAMPLE

1. An 83-year-old widower explains to you that he is risk averse and wishes to find an investment that will provide him with preservation of capital. Which of the following might you recommend?

   A. An index fund

   B. Bank-insured CDs

   C. Long-term U.S. government bonds

   D. Preferred stock

   Answer: B. This exam has two answers for preservation of capital. The strongest is a bank-insured CD, (choice **B**), followed by a money market fund (you'll never have both in the same question). But, aren't U.S. government bonds safe, you ask? Yes, but with maturities of 10 years or longer, that long duration involves interest rate risk. So, if the client needs money now and interest rates have increased, the principal has declined in value.

College Tuition

In addition to other types of investments, investors planning for college tuition often invest in zero-coupon bonds that mature when the tuition expenses are due. It may be advisable to establish college tuition investment programs such as Coverdell ESAs and Section 529 plans (covered in Unit 24) because of their tax advantages. The investments selected for either of these two have time horizon as a major constraint. That is, if the plan is started when the child is very young, the portfolio can be more aggressive than if started only a few years before the funds are needed.

Retirement

In determining a client's retirement needs, Social Security, company pensions, retirement savings accounts, and insurance (as well as investments outside of a retirement planning framework) should all be considered.

Once again, time horizon is an important constraint. The earlier an individual begins to save for retirement, the more time the investment assets are able to grow. A long-term retirement planning time horizon may enable an investor to assume additional risk in the portfolio, generally through equities. This helps a client accumulate significant funds to support a long retirement period. As life expectancy has risen, the topic of decumulation has come into focus. How do we make sure that the money accumulated lasts long enough? One way to minimize

Disability Insurance

Because workers' compensation only covers in limited cases and because Social Security's definition of disabled is relatively strict, most agree that it is wise to purchase a private disability insurance policy. Waiting and benefit periods can be adjusted based on the client's needs and finances. The amount of insurance can be determined by the information derived from the client's income, assets, and occupation.

TEST TOPIC ALERT

An application for disability insurance coverage can be denied in the case of a hazardous occupation.

Tax Planning

A client's tax situation is often an important factor in determining suitable investments. Taxes may be reduced by using the following three strategies: asset and income shifting, tax deferral, or tax-free income.

Asset and Income Shifting

A client can shift investment assets and income to a person in a lower tax bracket. Until early 2006, it was common to place income-producing assets in the name of a child aged 14 or older to avoid the "kiddie" tax, (see Unit 24), but because it now includes all children under age 19 and full-time students under age 24, the practice has lost much of its luster. However, with many of today's baby boomers supporting elderly parents, placing those assets in the parent's name will remove the income from your client and let the parent receive the income directly with little or no tax liability. As mentioned previously, trusts may also be used to shift assets and income.

Tax Deferral

Contributions to a qualified retirement plan or tax-sheltered annuity are not taxed until withdrawn. Investing funds that have not been taxed allows a substantially larger portion of the investor's money to earn income or capital gains, also not taxed until withdrawn.

Tax-Free Income

Most municipal bonds pay interest that is free from federal taxation, although they are generally subject to state income tax unless issued in the taxpayer's state of residence. Municipal bonds generally pay a lower interest rate than taxable bonds but, depending on the investor's tax bracket, may result in higher returns on an after-tax basis.

TAKE NOTE

Other potential sources of tax-free earnings are Section 529 plans, Roth IRAs, and Coverdell ESAs, all covered in Unit 24.

Unit 19

Time Horizon

An investor's time horizon and liquidity needs will determine the level of volatility the client should assume. Over a 20- or 30-year time frame, dramatic short-term volatility is acceptable, even to those who are risk averse. Money that will be needed within three to five years should be invested for safety and liquidity. Time horizon is a particularly important investment constraint when planning for college education and for retirement.

TEST TOPIC ALERT

The longer the time horizon, the more market risk the account can accept and vice versa.

EXAMPLE

1. A married couple is 55 and 57 years old. The older of the two plans to retire at 62 and the younger at 65, and both are healthy. What is the most appropriate estimate of the time horizon for their retirement portfolio?

    A. 5 years

    B. 7 years

    C. 8 years

    D. More than 20 years

    Answer: D. Time horizon does not end at retirement age. The portfolio will have to last them throughout their retirement until their death. On the basis of current life expectancy tables, the money will have to last them at least 20 years, choice **D**.

Life Cycle Considerations

An investor's goals may change over time. This is especially true as investors move from one phase of life to another. For example, a young couple may have a primary goal of funding a child's education. Later, the same family, having provided for their children's education, may turn their attention to the aggressive accumulation of wealth, perhaps to provide for an early retirement or a dream home. Upon retirement, this couple may need to move toward income-producing investments. Income and net worth change over time, as do investment goals and life cycle considerations. Because the adviser's responsibility to know his client is ongoing, the account form should be updated regularly to reflect the client's new goals and financial considerations.

As the baby boomer generation reaches retirement age, the regulators have increased their focus on protecting senior investors. Among the suggested practices is to take detailed notes of conversations and, when it becomes apparent that the client is not grasping as well as before, recommend that a family member or other competent person participate in all discussions.

HOW TO MAKE SUITABLE RECOMMENDATIONS

U19LO6: Analyze a client's financial goals and objectives for suitable recommendations.

Because the highest percentage of stock market investing by "Main Street America" is in pooled investment vehicles (mutual funds, ETFs, and variable annuities), whether through direct investment or an employer-sponsored retirement plan, such as a 401(k) or 403(b) plan, the exam tends to use these vehicles as proxies for meeting investor objectives.

Once a mutual fund or variable annuity sub-account defines its objective, its portfolio is invested to match it. The objective must be clearly stated in the fund's prospectus and can be changed only by a majority vote of the fund's outstanding shares.

Stock Funds

Common stocks normally provide the growth component of any mutual fund that has growth as a primary objective. Preferred, utility, and large-cap stocks are typically used to provide the income component of any stock mutual fund that has income as a primary objective.

Although there are other categories (to be covered in Unit 20), at this point you need to know the difference between large-cap and small-cap stocks. The term "cap" refers to the company's market capitalization (the number of outstanding common shares multiplied by the current market price per share). For example, a company with 30 million shares outstanding where the price per share is $30 has a market cap of $900 million. As you will see again in Unit 20, a market cap of $300 million to $2 billion is considered small cap, while that of more than $10 billion is considered large cap. It is generally felt that the larger the market cap, the more conservative the investment.

Growth Funds

Growth funds invest in stocks of rapidly growing corporations. Growth companies tend to reinvest all or most of their profits for research and development rather than pay dividends. Growth funds are focused on generating capital gains rather than income. Aggressive growth funds tend to concentrate more in small-cap stocks, while conservative growth funds have a preponderance of large-cap issues.

Income Funds

An income fund stresses current income over growth. The fund's objective may be accomplished by investing in the stocks of companies with long histories of dividend payments, such as utility company stocks, large-cap stocks, and preferred stocks.

Combination Funds

A combination fund (also called a growth and income fund) may attempt to combine the objectives of growth and current income by diversifying its portfolio among companies showing long-term growth potential and companies paying high dividends.

Specialized (Sector) Funds

Many funds specialize in particular economic sectors or industries. Others specialize in geographic areas such as the BRIC countries or the Pacific Rim. The funds have 25–100% of their assets invested in their specialties and are more likely than other funds to stick to a relatively fixed allocation.

EXAMPLE

Gold funds (gold mining stocks), insurance funds (insurance company stocks), technology funds, and utility funds are examples of sector funds. Sector funds offer high appreciation potential but may also pose higher risks to the investor because of their lack of diversification among industries or geographic areas.

Special Situation Funds

Special situation funds buy securities of companies that may benefit from a change within the corporations or in the economy. Takeover candidates and turnaround situations are common investments.

Index Funds

Index funds invest in securities to mirror a market index, such as the S&P 500. An index fund buys and sells securities in a manner that mirrors the composition of the selected index. The fund's performance tracks the underlying index's performance. This approach reflects the **passive** style of portfolio management, as opposed to **active** portfolio management (more on those in Unit 20).

Turnover of securities in an index fund's portfolio is minimal. As a result, an index fund generally has lower management costs than other types of funds. Furthermore, because index funds have little turnover, they frequently appeal to investors seeking minimal taxable capital gains.

Foreign Stock Funds

Foreign stock funds invest mostly in the securities of companies that have their principal business activities outside the United States. Long-term capital appreciation is their primary objective, although some funds also seek current income. Foreign investments involve foreign currency risks, as well as the usual risks associated with stock investments.

TAKE NOTE

There are two terms generally used to describe funds that invest in foreign securities.

- *International* funds have their entire portfolio invested in securities issued outside of the United States. The way to remember that is if you will be traveling internationally, you'll be outside the United States.

- *Global* funds have the portfolio invested around the globe, and that includes U.S. securities. Once again, using the travel example, if you were to travel around the globe, a portion of your trip would be in the United States.

EXAMPLE

1. An investor looking for an open-end investment company with an objective of providing current income to its shareholders, would most likely choose

    A. a common stock fund

    B. a growth fund

    C. an income fund

    D. a venture capital fund

    Answer: C. Income funds, choice **C**, have the goal of producing income; that is why they are named as such. This is a case where you "don't look a gift horse in the mouth."

Bond Funds

Bond funds have income as their primary investment objective. Some funds invest solely in investment-grade corporate bonds. Others, for enhanced safety, invest only in government issues. Others seek maximum income by investing in lower-rated issues that entail greater risk, but potentially higher returns.

Tax-Free (Tax-Exempt) Bond Funds

Tax-exempt funds invest in municipal bonds that produce income exempt from federal income tax. Tax-free funds invest in municipal bonds. Please note that any capital gains distributions from the fund are taxable just as with any other fund. A key to remember for the exam is that municipal bonds or municipal bond funds are only suitable for those in higher tax brackets.

U.S. Government and Agency Securities Funds

U.S. government funds purchase securities issued by the U.S. Treasury or an agency of the U.S. government, such as Ginnie Mae. Investors in these funds seek current income and maximum safety.

Foreign Bond Funds

These funds invest in foreign sovereign and/or corporate debt issues. Although they carry the same general risks as investing directly into foreign debt, these tend to be reduced because of the professional management and diversification offered by fund investing.

EXAMPLE

1. If ABC Fund pays regular dividends, offers a high degree of safety of principal, and appeals especially to investors in the higher tax brackets, ABC is

    A. an aggressive growth fund

    B. a corporate bond fund

    C. a money market fund

    D. a municipal bond fund

    Answer: D. Municipal bonds are considered second only to U.S. government securities in terms of safety. Furthermore, whenever you see a question about an investor in a high tax bracket, always look for the answer choice with municipal bonds; the tax-free income is the key. That is what makes choice **D** correct. On the other hand, when you see *growth*, dividends will probably not be part of the equation.

Balanced Funds

Balanced funds invest in stocks for appreciation and bonds for income. The exact mix is determined according to a formula used by the portfolio manager. These tend to be the most conservative of the stock funds.

EXAMPLE

A balanced fund's portfolio might contain 60% stocks and 40% bonds.

Asset Allocation Funds

Asset allocation funds split investments between stocks for growth, bonds for income, and money market instruments (or cash) for stability. The fund adviser switches the percentage of holdings in each asset category according to the performance, or expected performance, of that group. We will have more to say about asset allocation in Unit 20.

EXAMPLE

A fund may have 60% of its investments in stock, 20% in bonds, and the remaining 20% in cash. If the stock market is expected to do well, the adviser may switch from cash and bonds into stock. The result may be a portfolio of 80% in stock, 10% in bonds, and 10% in cash. Conversely, if the stock market is expected to decline, the fund may invest heavily in cash and sell stocks.

Money Market Funds

Money market funds are no-load, open-end investment companies (mutual funds) that serve as temporary holding accounts for investors' money. As the name implies, the portfolio of a money market fund consists of money market instruments having a maximum maturity of 397 days. The term *no-load* means that investors pay no sales or liquidation fees. Money market mutual funds are most suitable for investors whose financial goals require liquidity above all.

The interest these funds earn and distribute as dividends is computed daily and credited to customer accounts monthly. In general, money market mutual funds offer check-writing privileges making for extraordinary liquidity.

The net asset value (NAV) of money market funds is generally fixed at $1 per share. Although this price is not guaranteed, a fund is managed in order not to "break the buck," regardless of market changes. Thus, the price of money market shares does not fluctuate in response to changing interest rates.

EXAMPLE

1. An investor has a portfolio diversified among many different asset classes. If there was an immediate need for cash, which of the following would probably be the most liquid?

    A. Cash value from a universal life insurance policy

    B. CDL Common Stock Mutual Fund

    C. QRS Money Market Mutual Fund

    D. XYZ International Stock Mutual Fund

    Answer: C. Money market funds, choice **C**, generally come with a check-writing privilege offering investors the opportunity to convert the asset to cash at once. Although all mutual funds are readily redeemable, under the Investment Company Act of 1940, the fund has 7 days to redeem. One must request the cash value from the insurance company and, in many cases, that can take 30 days or longer.

TEST TOPIC ALERT

Be aware that an investment in a money market fund is not insured or guaranteed by the FDIC or any other government agency. Although a money market fund seeks to preserve the value of the investment at $1.00 per share, it is possible to lose money by investing in a money market fund.

Alternative Investments

As described in Unit 17, there are a number of alternative pooled investments. The risks and rewards were covered there, but, as a refresher, in almost all cases, these are speculative investments and will only be suitable on that basis. For example, ETNs can provide attractive short-term returns based on the performance of the selected index, but with a number of risks pointed out earlier. Leveraged or inverse ETFs or funds can offer dynamic profits, but only for those with a very short time horizon and high appetite for risk.

The following chart summarizes common investor objectives and appropriate recommendations. Be ready for a significant number of situational questions that require determining the best solution for the investor.

Investor Objective	Suitable Recommendation
Preservation of capital; safety	Insured bank CDs, money market instruments or funds, and T-bills
Growth ■ Balanced/moderate growth ■ Aggressive growth	Common stock or common stock mutual funds ■ Large-cap stocks, defensive stocks ■ Technology stocks, sector funds, or cyclical stocks
Income ■ Greatest safety ■ Tax-free income ■ High-yield income ■ From a stock portfolio	Bonds (but not zero-coupons) ■ U.S. Government bonds ■ Municipal bonds or municipal bond funds ■ Corporate bonds or corporate bond funds ■ Preferred stock and utility stocks
Liquidity	Money market funds ■ (DPPs, real estate, and annuities are not considered liquid)
Speculation	Volatile stocks, high-yield bonds, stock/index options, and leveraged and inverse ETFs

UNIT
20

Portfolio Management Styles, Strategies, and Techniques

Portfolio managers use a range of investment styles and strategies. Although each style attempts to generate superior investment returns and reduce investment risks, no single style is suited to every investor. Often, an investment adviser's role is to guide clients toward a mutual fund or private money manager that is consistent with the client's objectives and temperament.

The unit will conclude with a look at some of the techniques used by the various styles and strategies discussed.

The Series 65 exam will include nine questions from this unit.

LEARNING OBJECTIVES

When you have completed this unit, you will be able to accomplish the following.

U20LO1: Discriminate between the major asset classes used in an asset allocation program.
U20LO2: Identify the risk reduction benefits of diversification.
U20LO3: Describe the difference between active and passive management styles.
U20LO4: Compute a rebalancing problem.
U20LO5: Contrast the different portfolio management strategies, styles, and techniques.
U20LO6: Identify the major levels of market capitalization.
U20LO7: Compare the three techniques for minimizing interest rate risk.
U20LO8: Identify the components and goals of the Capital Market Theory.
U20LO9: Compute the expected return using the security market line.
U20LO10: Identify the three forms of the Efficient Market Hypothesis.
U20LO11: Illustrate how dollar cost averaging results in lowering an investor's average cost per share.
U20LO12: Describe the use of puts and calls to hedge positions.

ASSET ALLOCATION CLASSES

U20LO1: Discriminate between the major asset classes used in an asset allocation program.

Asset allocation (more accurately, but rarely stated, asset class allocation) refers to the spreading of portfolio funds among different asset classes with difference risk and return characteristics, based on the investment policy statement (IPS). Proponents of asset allocation feel that the mix of assets within a portfolio, rather than individual stock selection or marketing timing, is the primary factor underlying the variability of returns in portfolio performance. There are three major types (each with subclasses) of asset classes:

- Stock, with subclasses based on market capitalization, value versus growth, and foreign equity

- Bonds, with subclasses based on maturity (intermediate versus long-term), and issuer (Treasury versus corporate versus non-U.S. issuers)

- Cash, focusing mainly on the standard risk-free investment, the 91day (13 week) Treasury bill, but also including other short-term money market instruments

Proper asset allocation takes into consideration the investor's desire for preservation of capital, income, capital growth, or a combination of all of these.

In some instances, tangible assets, such as real estate (usually in the form of REITs), precious metals and other commodities, and certain collectibles (think fine art), are part of the asset allocation because these types of assets tend to reduce inflation risk. Increasingly, institutional investors (and some very high net worth individuals due to the high cost of entry) are using such alternative investment asset classes as ETNs, private equity, and venture capital. It is important to understand that asset allocation is not simply spreading the money around helter-skelter to different asset classes; there is a process, as described in the following question.

EXAMPLE

1. Which of the following best describes the steps of the asset allocation process?

   A. Determine the objectives and constraints; create the IPS, determine the asset allocation, allocate capital, monitor, and evaluate.

   B. Determine the objectives and constraints; determine the asset allocation, allocate the capital, create the IPS, monitor, and evaluate.

   C. Determine the objectives and constraints; perform asset allocation, create the IPS, monitor, and rebalance.

   D. Determine the objectives and constraints; determine capital market expectations, create the IPS, perform asset allocation, monitor, and evaluate.

   Answer: A. Steps in the asset allocation process are those in choice **A**:

   Step 1: Determination of the objectives and constraints of the asset owner.
   Step 2: Creation of the investment policy statement (IPS).
   Step 3: Determine the asset allocation based on the IPS.
   Step 4: Capital allocation.
   Step 5: Monitor and evaluate investments

BENEFITS OF DIVERSIFICATION

U20LO2: Identify the risk reduction benefits of diversification.

The term *diversification* has been used many times already in this manual. The term is a common one in our everyday life, not restricted to investing. As a technique in portfolio management, **portfolio diversification** (i.e., committing to an array of separate investments) reduces unsystematic risk, such as business risk, and enhances returns. The securities in a diversified portfolio are selected, in part, because they do not tend to move up or down in relation to each other; when some go down, the loss is offset by those that rise. That is the concept we covered with correlation coefficient. This kind of diversification is enhanced by the addition of foreign securities to a portfolio because they are usually not highly correlated with domestic equity.

There are many ways to classify investment and financial products. The investment pyramid, (shown following), for example, categorizes products according to their risk and return potential. Another way is to group similar products into specific classes. These classes are generally defined as the following:

- **Cash and cash equivalents**—passbook savings and checking accounts, money market accounts, money market funds, bank insured CDs, and T-bills
- **Fixed-income investments**—corporate bonds, municipal bonds, Treasury bonds, bond funds, and mortgage-backed securities
- **Equities**—preferred and common stocks of all kinds: growth, income appreciation, and stock mutual funds
- **Hard assets**—real estate, collectibles, precious metals, and stones

Each of these asset classes, as a whole, responds differently to different types of risk; therefore, diversifying or allocating investment resources among these classes is a proven way to reduce risk overall, dampen volatility, and improve the performance of one's portfolio. Fixed-income products, for example, are a hedge against deflation; equities are a hedge against inflation. To minimize market risk, one could diversify among all four asset categories (with additional diversification within the equities category). To minimize interest rate risk, one could diversify within the fixed-income category by staggering bond maturity dates. To minimize business risk, one could allocate among the four categories and purchase mutual funds. To reduce liquidity risk, one would keep a sufficient portion of assets in cash or cash equivalent assets.

Figure 20.1: Risk-Return Pyramid

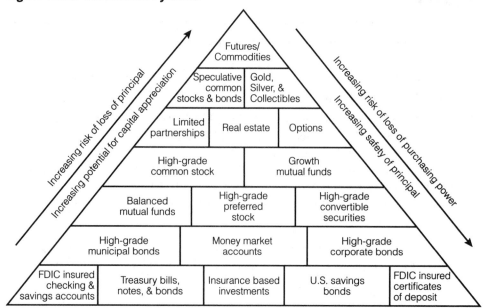

EXAMPLE

1. Simply adding more securities to a portfolio does not necessarily reduce portfolio volatility. For example, if the beta of a portfolio was 1.1, adding which of the following stocks would most likely increase the overall portfolio volatility?

   A. Stock A, beta 1.5

   B. Stock B, beta 1.1

   C. Stock C, beta 1.0

   D. Stock D, beta 0.7

Answer: A. The addition of a security with a beta higher (Stock A) than that of the current portfolio will increase overall portfolio volatility.

Diversification is not a synonym for asset allocation. For example, an aggressive young professional may invest almost exclusively in common stock. That would be a single asset class. But, within that asset class of common stock, the portfolio might consist of the shares of a dozen or more different companies in varied industries.

TACTICAL ASSET ALLOCATION

U20LO3: Describe the difference between active and passive management styles.

The two most common forms of asset allocation are tactical and strategic. You may see the terms *active* and *passive* management, referring to these two.

Tactical asset allocation refers to short-term portfolio adjustments that adjust the portfolio mix between asset classes in consideration of current market conditions and investor sentiment.

EXAMPLE

If the stock market is expected to do well over the near term, a portfolio manager may allocate greater portions of a portfolio to stocks. If the market is expected to decline, the portfolio manager may allocate greater portions of the portfolio entirely to bonds and cash. This is done in an attempt to create positive alpha for the portfolio.

An active (tactical) portfolio manager, using a particular stock selection approach, typically buys and sells individual securities. **Active management** relies on the manager's stock picking and *market timing* ability to outperform market indexes. Market timing is the strategy of making buy or sell decisions, generally regarding stocks, by attempting to predict future price movements. Usually, the focus is on timing the overall market rather than a specific security.

EXAMPLE

An active portfolio manager may position the portfolio in stocks within a few market sectors (such as pharmaceuticals and technology) frequently trading in and out of the stocks. An active manager may change the sector focus to capitalize on relative performance of different sectors during different stages of the business cycle. The goal is to successfully time the market. The term used to describe this process is *sector rotating*, sometimes called sector (or segment) rotation. Different sectors of the economy are stronger at different points in the economic cycle. Each industry sector follows its cycle as dictated by the stage of the economy. Portfolio managers attempt to buy into the next sector that is about to experience a move up. When an industry sector reaches the peak of its move as defined by the business cycle, it is time to start to sell the sector.

TEST TOPIC ALERT

One way to remember that tactical is active is by thinking of the word like this: t**ACT**ical where the act reminds you that it is *active* portfolio management.

STRATEGIC ASSET ALLOCATION

Strategic asset allocation refers to the proportion of various types of investments composing a long-term investment portfolio.

A **passive portfolio manager** believes that no particular management style will consistently outperform market averages and therefore constructs a portfolio that mirrors a market index, such as the S&P 500. In many cases, rather than construct a portfolio, those following this style will simply recommend index funds and/or ETFs. Passive portfolio management seeks low-cost means of generating consistent, long-term returns with minimal turnover.

When a portfolio is passively managed, it can happen that one asset class or even a single security can rise or decline in such a manner as to cause the portfolio to no longer mirror the targeted index (or portfolio balance). When that happens, the manager will *rebalance* the portfolio (we'll demonstrate how in the next learning objective.)

EXAMPLE

A standard asset allocation model suggests subtracting a person's age from 100 to determine the percentage of the portfolio to be invested in stocks. According to this method, a 30-year-old would be 70% invested in stocks and 30% in bonds and cash; a 70-year-old would be invested 30% in stocks with the remainder in bonds and cash.

TEST TOPIC ALERT

You may be asked about the relative commission expense when comparing active and passive management. It should be obvious that the more active the portfolio, the greater role commissions will play in determining overall portfolio performance. That is one reason why this style is more appropriate than strategic allocation for wrap-fee accounts.

REBALANCING

U20LO4: Compute a rebalancing problem.

A passive portfolio is **rebalanced** to bring the asset mix back to the target allocations. If the stock market should perform better than expected, the client's proportion of stocks to bonds would be out of balance. So, on some timely basis (perhaps quarterly but not less than annually), stocks would be sold and bonds would be purchased (or funds would be placed in cash) to bring the proportions back to the desired levels.

EXAMPLE

Using the 70% equity/30% debt model described previously, the investor's initial investment of $100,000 is split $70,000 into equity securities and $30,000 into debt securities. Let's say the account is to be rebalanced semiannually. Because of a bull market in stocks, six months later, the account value is $120,000. Analysis of the account indicates that the value of the equities is now $90,000, whereas the bonds have remained stable at $30,000. To rebalance—that is, to bring the account back to the 70/30 ratio—it will be necessary to sell $6,000 of the equity and invest those funds into debt. That will make the account $84,000 equity and $36,000 debt, our desired 70/30 ratio. The effect of this is that stocks are sold in a rising market and purchased in a falling market, following the old adage of "buy low and sell high."

Now, you try one:

EXAMPLE

1. A conservative client's portfolio is designed to have a 60/40 ratio of debt to equity securities. The initial investment was $250,000. One year later, the value of the portfolio is $260,000 with $90,000 of that represented by the equity portion. If the portfolio is rebalanced annually, this would require

    A. selling $14,000 of debt and buying $14,000 of equity

    B. selling $14,000 of equity and buying $14,000 of debt

    C. selling $6,000 of debt and buying $4,000 of equity

    D. buying $10,000 of equity and selling $10,000 of debt

    Answer: A. A 60/40 ratio will require that debt represent $156,000 (60% of $260,000) and equity represent the balance ($104,000). Thus, this portfolio will be rebalanced by selling $14,000 of debt and purchasing $14,000 of equity, choice **A**.

Constant Ratio Plan

An investment plan that attempts to maintain the type of relationship shown in our example between debt and equity securities (or other asset classes) is sometimes called a constant ratio plan. Periodically, the account is rebalanced to bring it back to the desired ratio.

Constant Dollar Plan

Under this investment plan, the goal is to maintain a constant dollar amount in stocks, moving money in and out of a money market fund when necessary. Using the last example, if the investor had a goal of a constant dollar of $70,000 in stock, the other $30,000 would be placed into a money market fund. When the stock value rose to $90,000, $20,000 would be liquidated and placed into the money market account. At this point, the account would have the desired $70,000 in stock and now have $50,000 in money markets. If the stock value should drop to $55,000, the money market fund would be tapped for $15,000 to get back to the $70,000 constant dollar.

EXAMPLE

1. Which of the following statements is correct regarding a portfolio manager employing a tactical style?

   A. The commission expense will likely be higher than one employing a passive style

   B. The portfolio will be rebalanced more often that would be the case with a passive style

   C. The manager is looking to create a positive beta

   D. The portfolio will contain a high percentage of index ETFs

   Answer: A. A tactical style is an active one with frequent trading. As such, commissions will be a larger portion of the operating expenses, choice **A**, than would be the case with a passive strategy. Rebalancing is an integral part of passive management. The very nature of tactical management makes rebalancing unnecessary. Tactical asset managers are looking to create positive alpha, not beta, and it is the passive manager who invests in indexes through ETFs and/or index funds.

LOW COST MANAGEMENT STRATEGIES

U20LO5: Contrast the different portfolio management strategies, styles, and techniques.

Money managers use a number of different styles and techniques. For the most part, these can be considered subsets of either active or passive management (or both).

Buy and Hold

A buy and hold manager rarely trades in the portfolio. This results in lower transaction costs and capital gains which are invariably taxed at the lower long-term rate (Unit 21). A low expense ratio in a mutual fund often may reflect a buy and hold approach. This is the classic passive strategy used by investors for many years and is probably the easiest of all to implement and follow.

With this strategy, there is always the question, "When do I sell?" As with most investment strategies, there are varying opinions. On an individual investor level, one of the most common reasons for unloading a position is a change in objectives. This is certainly true as one ages, or if one has a windfall, such as an inheritance. Of course, if there is a personal financial need, the asset will be sold to provide the necessary funds. Portfolio managers using this style may sell when the stock's fundamentals have weakened, such as a sharp decrease in earnings, or a change in the competitive arena (think of what digital cameras did to Kodak). Another case would be when the company's price to earnings ratio (P/E) has reached levels well above those for its competitors.

TEST TOPIC ALERT

Maybe you've owned a car that was a lemon. That generally means you had high maintenance costs. One point to know about the buy and hold style is that it is just the opposite—it is low maintenance.

Indexing

Investment portfolios constructed to mirror the components of a particular stock index, such as the S&P 500, will normally perform in line with the index. Because such portfolios are not actively managed, the costs of managing the portfolio are relatively low. With less frequent portfolio turnover, these funds have lower transaction costs and tend to be more tax efficient. Because most professional money managers are unable to consistently outperform market indexes, indexed mutual fund portfolios are a popular investment vehicle for investors. With the advent of index funds and ETFs, this has become a very popular passive strategy.

GROWTH VS. VALUE

One of the longest running arguments in investment analysis is, "Which is more successful, the growth style or the value style?" The father of value investing was Benjamin Graham and his text Security Analysis (co-authored with David Dodd in 1934) is still widely read today. The exam won't ask you about Graham and Dodd, but will want you to know the essential features of both styles.

Growth Style

Portfolio managers using the **growth** style of portfolio management focus on stocks of companies whose earnings are growing faster than most other stocks and are expected to continue to do so. Because rapid growth in earnings is often priced into the stocks, growth investment managers are likely to buy stocks that are at the high end of their 52-week price range. Therefore, in the eyes of some, they might be buying stocks that are overvalued.

TEST TOPIC ALERT

Growth managers are looking for **earnings momentum**.

Value

Portfolio managers using the **value** style of management concentrate on undervalued or out-of-favor securities whose price is low relative to the company's earnings or book value and whose earnings prospects are believed to be unattractive by investors and securities analysts. In fact, sometimes value managers think they can find a bargain with companies that are currently operating at a loss (no earnings, hence no P/E ratio). Value investment managers seek to buy undervalued securities before the company reports positive earnings surprises. Their primary source of information is the company's financial statements. Value investment managers are more likely to buy stocks that are at the bottom of their 52-week price range.

TEST TOPIC ALERT

In addition to the pricing models expressed previously, growth managers expect to see high P/E ratios (price to earnings ratios) or high price-to-book ratio with little or no dividends. On the other hand, value managers expect to see a low P/E ratio or low price-to-book ratio and dividends offering a reasonable yield. Another sign of a value stock is a large cash surplus, sometimes referred to as a *rainy day* fund.

EXAMPLE

ABC Co. is a metal processor for parts used in the automotive industry. Earnings per share have grown by a compounded rate of 8% per year for the past 15 years but are somewhat susceptible to downturns in the economy. The stock has paid a quarterly dividend that has increased five times in the past 10 years and the current market price of the stock is six times earnings. Conservatively managed, the company owns assets and cash that exceed the market value of its common stock. ABC would be attractive to *value* investors because its intrinsic value is higher than its market value, it appears to pay liberal dividends, and it is selling for a low earnings multiple.

OTHER PORTFOLIO MANAGEMENT STYLES

In addition to those already described, there are several other styles you should be familiar with.

Contrarian

A contrarian is an investment manager who takes positions opposite of that of other managers or in opposition to general market beliefs. In essence these managers buy when everyone else is selling and sell when everyone else is buying.

Income vs. Capital Appreciation

At first glance, this might appear to be a rehashing of growth versus value and, although there are some similarities, you should be aware of what each of these styles represents.

Capital Appreciation

Capital appreciation can take several forms, from moderate to aggressive. Although growth stocks will frequently be found in these portfolios, the hunt for appreciation will also involve options and/or futures, special situation stocks (potential takeover or merger candidates), futures, IPOs, and day trading. When recommending a manager using this style, it is critical to determine where on the risk scale, from lower to moderate to speculative, this manager's philosophy is. Then, and only then, can you attempt to match it with your clients.

Income

As the term implies, the income style focuses on generating portfolio income. When dividends on common stock offer better income opportunities than interest on debt securities, the portfolio will be overweighted in that direction. Frequently, the search for income will lead the portfolio manager to foreign securities and/or high-yield bonds. When recommending a manager using this style, it is important to evaluate the risks being taken to provide income. For the most part, an income style relies heavily on debt securities.

Monte Carlo Simulations

Stochastic modeling is a method of financial analysis that attempts to forecast how investment returns on different asset classes vary over time by using thousands of simulations to produce probability distributions for various outcomes. The term stochastic comes from the Greek word meaning, "to aim or guess."

When an investment adviser is called upon to provide advice on developing a plan for a client's funds to last throughout what might be a 30-year or even longer retirement, all the adviser can do is make an educated guess.

A popular form of stochastic modeling that uses computer-generated distributions is the Monte Carlo Simulation (MCS). This simulation is an analytic and risk management tool widely used in finance. MCS incorporates computer programming to generate thousands of different probabilities.

Consider the uncertainty in retirement planning. Small changes in the projected rate of return will make a dramatic difference in the outcome. Life expectancy is also another important variable that may be incorrectly approximated. MCS uses a random number generator to provide an output with specific probabilities of outcomes. The simulation provides insight into the range of outcomes and provides the user (the investor or adviser) with both a best-case and a worst-case scenario.

Advantages

- Can clearly display tradeoffs of risk and return. The paths can be ranked from best to worst to assess the probability of any given outcome.

- A clearer understanding of short-term and long-term risk can be gained. For example, reducing the holdings of risky stock would reduce the short-term variability of the portfolio but increase the long-term risk of not having running out of money.

- MCS can better model the real probability process where return over time depends not only on the starting value of the period but also on the additions or withdrawals to the portfolio at each future period.

- Points along the time line can be considered to answer questions such as, "Do savings need to be increased?" "Can I retire earlier?" "Must I retire later?" "Do I need to reduce my withdrawal rate?" "Can I increase my withdrawal rate?"

Disadvantages

- Simplistic use of historical data, such as expected returns, for the inputs. Returns change and have a major effect on projected future values of the portfolio.

- Models that simulate the return of asset classes but not the actual assets held. Simulating the return of the Wilshire 5000 or the S&P 500 when a fund with fees will be held could significantly overstate the future value or time period over which distributions can be sustained.

For an individual entering retirement, the timing of the cash flows out of the portfolio and the sequence of returns are critical.

EXAMPLE

Consider two clients, Mr. Jones and Ms. Smith. Both enter retirement with $1 million, both withdraw $50,000 per year from their portfolios, and both portfolios generate an average return of 10% over the life of the portfolios. Their yearly results are the same, but they come in different sequences. Jones experiences 15 up years followed by 5 down years. Smith experiences 5 down years followed by 15 up years. Jones will be better off than Smith, because Smith will deplete her portfolio in the early years, and hence her portfolio will not benefit fully from the positive return years down the line.

The concept of ill-timed cash flows may be easy for experienced advisers to grasp, but it is not one that clients readily understand. Through the use of MCSs, advisers can easily generate charts and graphs to educate clients about sequential return issues.

MARKET CAPITALIZATION LEVELS

U20LO6: Identify the major levels of market capitalization.

Definition: Market Capitalization

A company's market capitalization (usually referred to as market cap) is the product of the number of outstanding shares and the current market price per share. For example, if a corporation has 100 million shares of common stock outstanding and the market price per share is $50, the market cap is $5 billion.

Another portfolio management style is using market capitalization to influence security selection. Although the boundaries are imprecise, micro-cap companies are generally those with a market capitalization of less than $300 million; small-cap companies are generally those with a market capitalization of between $300 million and $2 billion; mid-cap companies are those with $2 billion to $10 billion; and large-cap companies are those with more than $10 billion.

It is generally assumed that small companies with a short history, small product line, and limited financial resources represent a larger degree of risk in an economic downturn. As revenues, product diversification, and financial worth increase, the relative risk the company carries in a weak economy diminishes. In Unit 23, we will match each level to its appropriate benchmark index.

TEST TOPIC ALERT

Look out for numbers written in long form. For example, where would you categorize a stock with a market capitalization of $5,000,000,000? Were you able to fight through all of those zeroes to see that this is $5 billion and is a mid-cap security?

TAKE NOTE

In a strong economy, small, fast-moving companies with a concentrated product line in a fast-growing sector can dramatically outperform larger, more bureaucratic companies.

MINIMIZING INTEREST RATE RISK

U20LO7: Compare the three techniques for minimizing interest rate risk.

Most of the substance of the exam will deal with strategies employed in equity investing, but you may be asked about several popular strategies used by bond buyers. Primarily, the goal in all of these strategies is to mitigate the effects of interest rate fluctuations on the value of the principal, the income received, or both. Three in particular are

- the barbell strategy;
- the bullet strategy; and
- the laddering strategy.

All three of these are considered active rather than passive, and we will look at them individually.

Barbells

Envision a barbell—what do you see? A thin bar with heavy weights of equal size on each end. That's what a bond portfolio using the barbell strategy looks like. The investor purchases bonds maturing in one or two years and an equal amount maturing in 10 (or more) years with no bonds in between.

Assuming a normal yield curve, the long-term end of the barbell contains bonds offering the higher long-term interest rates, while the short-term end provides you with soon to be realized cash (as they mature) that may be reinvested at higher rates if that is the direction the market takes. This is not a passive strategy like buy and hold—you will be actively buying new bonds as the old ones get closer to maturity.

Bullets

For what do you use a bullet? You use it to hit a target, and that is the concept behind the bullet strategy. Let's say the target is funds for a child's college education, and the child is currently six years old. This strategy would have the investor purchase bonds today that mature in 12 years (assuming college starting when the child is 18). Two years from now, the investor should purchase some more bonds, but those should have a 10-year maturity. In another two years, another purchase is made, this time of bonds that have eight years to go, and so forth. A picture of this active strategy would reveal bonds purchased at different times but all maturing at the same time. This tends to allow the investor to capture current interest rates as they change rather than having the entire portfolio locked into one rate.

Ladders

Picture a ladder. You see rungs at set intervals going from bottom to top. That is the concept behind a laddered portfolio. Unlike the bullet strategy described previously where the bonds are bought at different times but all mature together, in a laddered strategy, the bonds are all purchased at the same time but mature at different times (like the steps on the ladder). As the shorter maturities come due, they are reinvested, and now become the long-term ones. This has also been a very common strategy with those purchasing CDs at their local bank.

EXAMPLES

1. An investor in debt securities might elect to use any one of the following techniques to limit interest rate risk EXCEPT

   A. barbells

   B. bullets

   C. increasing the duration

   D. laddering

   Answer: C. The longer the duration, the greater the interest rate risk (choice **C**), so the investor would not want to do that. The others are useful strategies for reducing interest rate risk.

2. Which of the following statements regarding a bond ladder strategy is CORRECT?

   A. A bond ladder strategy involves the purchase of very long-term and very short-term bonds.

   B. A laddered portfolio of bonds will provide lower yields than a portfolio consisting entirely of short-term bonds.

   C. A bond ladder strategy is generally more aggressive than a bond barbell strategy.

   D. A bond ladder strategy is a relatively easy way to immunize a portfolio against interest rate risk.

   Answer: D. A bond ladder strategy, choice **D**, is a relatively easy way to immunize a portfolio against interest rate risk. By holding many positions across the yield curve, the individual is diversified in the event that yields behave differently in one part of the curve than in another. The laddered portfolio will generally provide higher (not lower) yields than a portfolio consisting entirely of short-term bonds. Choice A describes the bond barbell strategy, not the bond ladder strategy.

CAPITAL MARKET THEORY

U20LO8: Identify the components and goals of the Capital Market Theory.

Portfolio management theory builds on a foundation of assumptions about investors' behavior and was first introduced by Harry Markowitz in 1952. At its core, modern portfolio theory proceeds from the premise that investors will behave rationally. Pricing models have been introduced to determine what should be the proper market price for investment assets. The most familiar and useful of these models is the capital asset pricing model, known as CAPM, which derives from the work of Markowitz and others, including William Sharpe, after whom the Sharpe ratio was named.

Several capital market theories exist, all with the goal of maximizing returns while minimizing risks.

Capital Asset Pricing Model (CAPM)

CAPM is a securities market investment theory allowing the investor to determine an asset's expected rate of return, a form of risk-adjusted return encapsulating how much risk the investor should assume to obtain a particular return from an investment. The CAPM does so solely on the basis of the asset's *systematic* (non-diversifiable) risk.

William Sharpe first formulated the CAPM in the 1960s. The basic premise is that every investment carries two distinct risks; systematic, which cannot be diversified away, and unsystematic risk, which can be mitigated through appropriate diversification. As a result of this work, and its further refinements, Professor Sharpe was awarded the Nobel Prize in Economics in 1990 (that isn't tested). You will see several applications of the CAPM in upcoming paragraphs.

MODERN PORTFOLIO THEORY

Modern portfolio theory is an approach that attempts to quantify and control portfolio risk. It differs from a traditional securities analysis in that it emphasizes determining the relationship between risk and reward in the total portfolio rather than analyzing specific securities. Under the CAPM, the investor should be rewarded for the risks taken so it is proper to assume that the higher the risk, the higher the return.

Instead of emphasizing particular stocks, **modern portfolio theory (MPT)** focuses on the relationships among all the investments in a portfolio. This theory holds that specific risk can be diversified away by building portfolios of assets whose returns are not correlated.

MPT diversification allows investors to reduce the risk in a portfolio while simultaneously increasing expected returns.

Diversification reduces risk only when assets whose prices move inversely, or at different times, in relation to each other are combined. In other words, decreased correlation leads to decreased risk.

The theory is that, all factors being equal, the portfolio with the least amount of volatility would do better than one with a greater amount of volatility.

TEST TOPIC ALERT

The goal is to design the optimal portfolio. An **optimal portfolio** is one that returns the highest rate of return consistent with the amount of risk an investor is willing to take. In other words, an optimal portfolio is the portfolio that makes the best trade-off between risk and reward for a given investor's investment profile. Simply stated given a choice between assets with equal rates of expected return, the risk averse investor will always select the asset with the lowest level of risk.

EXAMPLE

1. Risk aversion means that if two assets have identical expected returns, a risk averse individual will choose the asset with the

   A. lower risk level

   B. higher standard deviation

   C. shorter payback period

   D. higher expected return

   Answer: A. *Risk averse* investors are those with a low tolerance or capacity for risk. Given a choice between assets with equal rates of expected return, the risk averse investor will always select the asset with the lowest level of risk, choice **A**. Standard deviation is a way to quantify risk—the higher the standard deviation, the greater the volatility. The payback period is used to evaluate capital projects, not investment returns.

Capital Market Assumptions

The capital market theory builds upon the Markowitz portfolio model. The main assumptions of the capital market theory are as follows.

- All investors can borrow or lend money at the risk-free rate of return.

- All investors are rationale and evaluate investments in terms of expected return and variability (standard deviation). Therefore, given a set of security prices and a risk-free rate, all investors use the same information to generate an efficient frontier.

- The time horizon is equal for all investors: when choosing investments, investors have equal time horizons for the chosen investments.

- There are no transaction costs or personal income taxes; investors are indifferent between capital gains and dividends.

- There is no inflation.

- All assets are infinitely divisible: this indicates that fractional shares can be purchased.

- There is no mispricing within the capital markets: it is assumed that the markets are efficient and that no mispricings within the markets exist. Another way to state this is that capital markets are in equilibrium.

Capital Market Line

One of the offshoots of the CAPM is the capital market line (CML). The CML provides an expected return based on the level of risk. The equation for the CML uses the:

- expected return of the portfolio;

- risk-free rate;
- return on the market;
- standard deviation of the market; and
- standard deviation of the portfolio.

TAKE NOTE

Note that the CML, like Markowitz's efficient frontier, uses standard deviation as the measure of risk.

TEST TOPIC ALERT

Please note that alpha and beta are not used in the CML equation while standard deviation is.

EFFICIENT PORTFOLIOS/EFFICIENT FRONTIER

The goal of MPT is to construct the most efficient portfolio. One selects the efficient set from the feasible set. The feasible set of portfolios represents all portfolios that can be constructed from a given set of equities. An efficient portfolio is one that offers:

- the most return for a given amount of risk; or
- the least risk for a given amount of return.

The collection of efficient portfolios is called the efficient set or efficient frontier. The universe of these portfolios is, in turn, plotted on a risk-return parabola known as the **efficient frontier**. Specifically, this curve represents that set of portfolios that has the maximum rate of return for every given level of risk. The objective is for the portfolio to lie on the curve. Then, by being **on** the efficient frontier, the optimal portfolio has been created. Any portfolio that is below the curve (not an efficient one) is said to be taking too much risk for too little return. A portfolio above the efficient frontier is impossible. In pictorial terms, the efficient frontier is depicted as follows:

Figure 20.2: Efficient Frontier

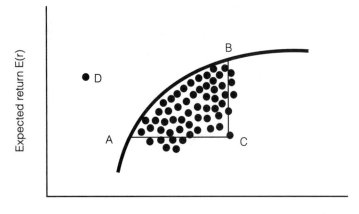

Every portfolio residing **on** the efficient frontier has either a higher rate of return for equal risk or lower risk for an equal rate of return than another portfolio below, (underneath), the frontier. For example, in the previous graphic, Portfolios A and B are both equally efficient and are more efficient than Portfolio C because:

- Portfolio A has an equal expected rate of return as Portfolio C but with a significantly lower level of assumed risk; and

- Portfolio B has an equal level of assumed risk as Portfolio C but with a significantly higher expected rate of return.

Therefore, Portfolio C is inefficient; it is attainable but not optimal.

Portfolio D is unattainable because it resides above the efficient frontier. As the graphic indicates, the expected rate of return is unattainable because it is located outside the universe of available portfolios.

In the figure, Portfolios A and B are both efficient, but Portfolio C is not.

EXAMPLE

1. According to modern portfolio theory, the optimal portfolio is one that

   A. lies above the efficient frontier

   B. lies below the efficient frontier

   C. lies on the efficient frontier

   D. provides the lowest return for the highest risk

   Answer: C. The efficient frontier is a curve representing the amount of return for a specified risk. Portfolios residing on that curve provide the highest return for that level of risk and are considered optimal or efficient portfolios, choice **C**. Below the efficient frontier is inefficient and a portfolio cannot lie above the curve.

THE SECURITY MARKET LINE

U20LO9: Compute the expected return using the security market line.

The CML provides an expected return for a portfolio based on the expected return of the market, the risk-free rate of return, and the standard deviation of the portfolio in relation to the standard deviation of the market. The CML is generally used to evaluate diversified portfolios. The security market line (SML), which is derived from the CML, allows us to evaluate individual securities for use in a diversified portfolio.

- The expected return for the asset

- The risk-free rate

- The return on the market

- The beta of the asset

The SML determines the expected return for a security on the basis of its beta and the expectations about the market and the risk-free rate. Basically, we want to determine how much over the risk-free rate we should earn for taking the investment risk. You may be asked to compute the expected return using the SML. It is done like this.

We start by comparing the market's return to the RF rate (expecting it will be higher because of the risk). Then we multiply that difference by the stock's beta and add that number to the RF rate. It is much easier to follow with the numbers.

EXAMPLE

If the beta of ABC Company is 1.2 and the market return is expected to be 13% with a risk-free return of 3%, then the expected return of ABC is 15%, as follows:

We begin with the difference between the risk-free rate and market rate (13% − 3) = 10%. Then we multiply the expected return in excess of the RF rate by the stock's beta, (10% × 1.2) = 12%. Finally we add the RF rate (3%) to the 12% and arrive at 15%.Therefore, on the basis of the level of systematic risk of ABC Company, it should earn a return of 15%. The SML helps identify how the characteristics of a portfolio will be impacted when a security is added to the portfolio. You should note that the SML accounts for the impact of systematic risk (as measured by beta) only and does not take into consideration unsystematic risk, which is assumed to have been diversified away.

THE EFFICIENT MARKET HYPOTHESIS (EMH)

U20LO10: Identify the three forms of the Efficient Market Hypothesis.

The **efficient market hypothesis** (EMH) maintains that security prices adjust rapidly to new information with security prices fully reflecting all available information. In other words, markets are efficiently priced as a result. This is sometimes referred to as the **random walk theory**. The random walk theory would suggest that throwing darts at the stock listings is as good a method as any for selecting stocks for investment.

Eugene F. Fama, professor at the University of Chicago, coined the term in a 1965 *Financial Analysts Journal* article entitled "Random Walks in Stock Market Prices."

There are three versions of the EMH based upon the level of available information. The more information available, the more likely it is that you should be able to beat the market. But, as we will see, under this theory the conclusion is, that under all circumstances, there is **no way** to accurately predict stock prices, and a passive strategy is probably the most suitable for investment success.

Weak-Form Market Efficiency

The *weak form* holds that current stock prices have already incorporated all historical market data and that historical price trends are, therefore, of no value in predicting future price changes. Although fundamental analysis and insider information may produce above-market returns under the weak form, technical analysis is of no value. Indeed, none of the forms of EMH attributes any value to technical analysis.

Semi-Strong-Form Market Efficiency

The *semi-strong form* holds that current stock prices not only reflect all historical price data but also reflect data from analyzing financial statements, industry, or current economic outlook.

Thus, even fundamental analysis is of no value in this form, and only insider information may produce above-market returns. Technical analysis is also of no value.

Strong-Form Market Efficiency

The strong form of the EMH states that security prices *fully reflect all information from both public and private sources.* The strong form includes all types of information: past security market, public, and private (inside) information. This means that no group of investors has monopolistic access to information relevant to the formation of prices, and none should be able to consistently achieve positive abnormal returns.

Although some would disagree, the prevailing opinion is that the only thing that will work in this case is random walk—just throwing darts because the market is totally efficient with market prices quickly adjusting to reflect new information.

TAKE NOTE

According to the EMH, if a financial market is weakly efficient, technical analysis will be useless, but it is still possible to use fundamental analysis to seek out mispriced investments. On the other hand, if a financial market is semi-strong-formly efficient, there is no point in using any fundamental analysis tools—all of that information is already in the hands of all investors. If a financial market is strongly efficient, then everything, including information generally only available to insiders is known and, without an edge, there is no benefit to be gained by using any analytical tools.

TAKE NOTE

As a base level knowledge of the EMH, you should know that the weak form is based on past security market information; the semistrong form is based on all public information (including market information); and the strong form is based on both public information and inside or private information.

The following chart may help you with EMH.

Figure 20.3: The Three Forms of EMH

Form	Won't work	Will work
Weak	Technical analysis	Fundamental analysis and Insider information
Semi-strong	Technical and fundamental analysis	Insider information
Strong	Technical and fundamental analysis and insider information	Random walk

TEST TOPIC ALERT

You may have to know that there is no such term as **semi-weak** EMH. Can't imagine what would be weaker than **weak** anyway.

EXAMPLE

1. Followers of the efficient market hypothesis believe that

   A. following the business cycle is the best way to maximize returns

   B. concentration rather than diversification will produce superior returns

   C. by following the pundits on TV, you'll wind up rich

   D. an efficient market is one that produces random results

   Answer: D. EMH is really just an extension of the Random Walk Theory, choice **D**, which states that throwing darts at the stock market page is as good as any way to select investments. If the market is truly efficient, no one has an edge.

One common fear of investors is buying at the top of the market. One can never know when a bull market will reverse its course. Conversely, we all want to get in at the bottom, but how do you know when the bear market is over? Because no one knows all of the answers, one popular technique is time-based investing to average your cost. Popular time-based investment programs used by investors include dollar cost averaging and income reinvestment.

DOLLAR COST AVERAGING

U20LO11: Illustrate how dollar cost averaging results in lowering an investor's average cost per share.

Investors use **dollar cost averaging** as a means to invest consistent amounts of money in a mutual fund or stock at regular periodic intervals, such as monthly or quarterly. This form of investing allows the individual to purchase more shares when prices are low and fewer shares when prices are high. This has the effect of reducing timing risk, the risk that all of your money will be invested at a market top. In a fluctuating market, the average cost per share is lower than the average price per share.

EXAMPLE

The following table illustrates how average price and average cost may vary with dollar cost averaging.

Month	Amount Invested	Price per Share	No. of Shares
January	$600	$20	30
February	$600	$24	25
March	$600	$30	20
April	$600	$40	15
Total	$2,400	$114	90

The average cost per share equals $2,400 (the total investment) divided by 90 (the total number of shares purchased), or $26.67 per share, whereas the average price per share is $28.50 ($114 / 4). With any market fluctuations, this strategy will produce a lower cost ($26.67) than average price ($28.50). This average cost of $26.67, not the average price paid of $28.50, is the investor's cost basis when the shares are subsequently sold.

TEST TOPIC ALERT

Although it is unlikely that you will have to compute the average price or average cost per share, a question may ask the purpose of dollar cost averaging. The purpose of dollar cost averaging is to reduce the investor's average cost to acquire a security over the buying period relative to its average price.

HEDGING WITH EQUITY OPTIONS

U20LO12: Describe the use of puts and calls to hedge positions.

The final strategy discussed in this unit is using options to hedge a position. In the real world, these are very popular tools to limit risk and the exam usually contains one question on their use.

An investor with a long position in a stock (she owns it) can use options to hedge the position's risks. Remember the term *hedge*, used in this context, means to protect.

Long Stock and Long Puts

What if the investor is concerned about a potential drop in the price of her stock? An investor who owns a stock can protect against a decline in market value by buying a put. Doing so allows the investor to sell the stock by exercising the put if the stock price declines before expiration which will offset the decline in the stock price. This strategy is called **portfolio insurance**. Any profits in the stock are offset by the cost of the put premiums.

EXAMPLE

A concerned (*afraid*) investor who owns 100 shares of stock with a current market value of $50 purchases a 50 put at $2.50 for protection. If the stock goes down to $40 per share, the investor has the ability to exercise the put, deliver the stock, and receive $50 per share. The only cost for this protection is the **premium** of $2.50 paid for the put. So, instead of losing $1,000 the loss was held to only $250.

TEST TOPIC ALERT

This strategy is also useful for managers of large portfolios, such as pension funds. If the portfolio consisted of large-cap stocks, a way to hedge against a down market would be to purchase put options on an index that mirrors the portfolio. In the case of large-cap stocks, that would generally be the S&P 500 index (more about that in Unit 23).

Long Stock and Short Calls (Covered Call Writing)

A **covered call** is a call written (sold) on a stock an investor owns. The covered call writer reduces the risk of that long stock position *and generates income* with the dollars received in premiums from selling the call. If the call is not exercised, the call writer keeps the premium. If the call is exercised, the covered call writer can deliver the stock owned. The covered call writer limits potential gain in exchange for the partial protection against a loss.

Unit 20

Partial Protection

By writing a covered call and receiving the premium, an investor, in effect, reduces the stock cost by the premium amount. If the stock price falls below the purchase price minus the premium received, the investor incurs a loss. Should the stock price rise dramatically, the stock will likely be called.

EXAMPLE

An investor buys 100 shares of RST at 53 and writes 1 RST 55 call for 2. The premium offsets the stock price by the $2 per share premium received. The maximum gain equals $400: if the stock price rises above 55, the call will be exercised; thus, the investor will sell the stock for a gain of $200, in addition to the $200 premium received. The $200 premium initially received lowers the true cost of the stock to $51 per share so the investor is protected against loss for the first 2 points of market decline. The maximum loss is $5,100 (instead of $5,300) should the stock become worthless.

TAKE NOTE

A covered call provides partial protection that generates income but reduces the stock's potential gain. Buying puts provides nearly total loss protection that costs money yet does not reduce the stock position's potential gain. The benefit of the covered call is that it does offer some hedging with no cost. In fact, the investor receives income in the form of the premium.

Short Stock and Long Calls

An investor who sells a stock short sells borrowed stock, expecting the price to decline. The short seller must buy stock to repay the stock loan and hopes to do so at a lower price. A short seller can buy calls to protect against a price rise. If you are not familiar with the concept of short selling, it will be covered in Part 4, Unit 22.

EXAMPLE

An investor sells short 100 shares of RST at 58 and buys an RST 60 call for 3. The maximum loss is no longer unlimited as it would normally be for a short sale. Instead, it is $500: no matter how high the stock price rises above $60, the investor will exercise the call to buy the stock for 60, incurring a $200 loss on the short sale, in addition to the $300 paid for the call.

TEST TOPIC ALERT

Most of our students report a question on protecting against loss on a short sale. As shown previously, the best way to hedge is to buy a call option on the stock underlying the short sale. This strategy offers full protection against loss. Please notice that in protecting the long or short position, the investor buys an option. It is useful to remember that you buy protection; you don't sell it.

21

Tax Considerations

Taxes on income and capital gains diminish the amount of money available to the person who earns it. As a result, personal and business investment decisions are often influenced by the tax implications. Please note: Because tax brackets generally change every year, they are not testable. We've included those for 2019 only for perspective.

The Series 65 exam will include two questions on the material covered in this unit.

LEARNING OBJECTIVES

When you have completed this unit, you will be able to accomplish the following.

U21LO1: Recognize income tax fundamentals for individuals.
U21LO2: Identify the different sources of income and loss.
U21LO3: Distinguish between income and capital gain, and how they are taxed.
U21LO4: Recall the preference items included in the AMT computation.
U21LO5: Describe the fundamentals of insurance, trust, estate, and gift taxation.
U21LO6: Identify the different types of business taxation.

INDIVIDUAL TAXATION

U21LO1: Recognize income tax fundamentals for individuals.

Taxes function as either **regressive** or **progressive**. **Regressive taxes** (e.g., sales, excise, payroll, property, and gasoline taxes) are levied at the same rate, regardless of income and thus represent a smaller percentage of income for wealthy taxpayers than for taxpayers with lower incomes. Because low-income families spend a larger percentage of their incomes than they save or invest, regressive taxes consume a larger fraction of the income of the poor than of the wealthy. **Progressive taxes** (e.g., estate, gift, and income taxes) increase the tax rate as income increases. Progressive taxes are costlier to people with high incomes than to people with low incomes. This unit will deal with taxation on the federal level with specific reference to state taxes when necessary.

TEST TOPIC ALERT

In a progressive tax system, the term used to describe the highest rate paid on income (sometimes referred to as the next dollar received, or the last dollar received), is the individual's *marginal tax rate*. For example, in 2019, a single individual with taxable income in excess of $214,100 is taxed on each dollar earned above that amount at a rate of 35% until reaching $510,300, at which time the excess is taxed at 37%. Therefore, if this individual reported earnings of $250,000, it is proper to say that the marginal tax rate is 35%. If the individual earned $525,000, then it would be 37%.

Please note: The actual tax brackets are *never* tested on the exam because they change every year—we are showing them only as examples.

EXAMPLE

Based on this information, a single taxpayer with taxable income of $220,000 is given a $10,000 bonus. The federal income tax on that bonus is taxed at the individual's marginal (or top) tax bracket rate of 35% so the tax would be $3,500. This individual won't move into another bracket until taxable income exceeds $510,300.

Besides the amount of income, the most important factor in determining an individual's income tax bill is the choice of filing status.

The choice of filing status one makes has a major impact on the amount of taxes levied. There are five different filing statuses:

- Single
- Married filing jointly
- Married filing separately
- Head of household
- Qualifying widow(er) with dependent child

Filing status is determined by your marital status as of the last day of the year. If more than one filing status applies to the taxpayer, the IRS suggests using the one resulting in the lowest tax obligation. Generally, that will be married filing jointly. For those who are not married, if qualifying, the lowest rate is usually obtained by filing as head of household.

TEST TOPIC ALERT

How you file a return can impact your taxes. Your tax filing status is based on your marital status as of the end of the year (December 31). In the case of a single parent with dependent children, it will generally be most advantageous to use the filing status, "head of household."

EXAMPLE

1. In most cases, the tax filing status that results in the highest income tax is

   A. head of household

   B. married filing jointly

   C. qualifying widower with a dependent child

   D. single

   Answer: D. In general, for the same amount of income, filing single, choice D, will result in the highest income tax while married filing jointly, the lowest. Head of household is usually the best for those who are not married, but do have children.

Other factors include:

Age: Taxpayers who are 65 or older receive an addition of $1,300 each if married and filing a joint return, or $1,650 if single, to the standard deduction. This additional amount is also available to those who are blind or disabled. This increased standard deduction can lower the tax bill.

State of residence: If the taxpayer lives in a state with a state income tax, up to certain limits, the amount paid can be taken as a deduction on the federal return, thus lowering the tax due.

Citizenship: An individual who is not a citizen of the U.S. may pay taxes at a different rate than citizens and may also receive certain tax credits due to tax treaties. Much of this depends on whether the individual is a resident alien or a nonresident alien and the details are beyond the scope of the exam.

EXAMPLE

1. Under current tax law, which of the following would NOT be a factor in determining an individual's federal income liability?

   A. Age

   B. Citizenship

   C. Filing status

   D. Sex

   Answer: D. One area in which the federal tax laws do not discriminate is the individual's sex, choice D. Those 65 and older are entitled to an additional exemption; non-U.S. citizens may pay more or less tax based on tax treaties and other factors; and filing status has a major impact on taxes.

SOURCES OF INCOME

U21LO2: Identify the different sources of income and loss.

Earned income includes salary, bonuses, tips, and income derived from active participation in a trade or business.

Alimony

Alimony is payment made under a (divorce) court order (or under a legal separation agreement) to an ex-spouse. Alimony may be paid directly to the ex-spouse or to a third party on the ex-spouse's behalf (e.g., to pay premiums on the ex-spouse's life insurance or contribute to the ex-spouse's IRA). Alimony payments, within limits, are generally deductible to the spouse making the payments and includable in income for tax purposes by the spouse receiving them.

TAKE NOTE

Effective January 1, 2019, the tax treatment of alimony is reversed. That is, the ex paying the alimony won't get to deduct the payment and the ex receiving the alimony won't report it as income. That will impact counting received alimony as income for IRA purposes. This change only applies to divorce decrees entered into after December 31, 2018, so any test question would have to specify a date.

Child Support

Alimony should not be confused with child support. **Child support** is a legal obligation of a parent to provide financial support for a child (typically occurring when the parent providing the support is not the parent with whom the child or children lives). Child support is not deductible by the parent who pays it, nor is it includable in income by the recipient, who is often the other parent receiving the support on behalf of the child of the dissolved marriage.

EXAMPLE

Chuck and Alice divorced on November 1, 2018, after a 10-year marriage that produced two children, Tim, age six, and Kim, age eight. Under a court order, it is decided that Chuck will pay Alice $1,000 per month in alimony and $600 per child per month ($1,200 in total child support). Chuck may deduct $12,000 for the tax year ($1,000 × 12 months) on his federal income tax return. Alice must report $12,000 for the tax year on her federal income tax return. Chuck cannot deduct any of the child support, nor is any of it reportable for income tax by Alice or their children.

Passive Income and Passive Losses

Passive income and losses come from rental property, limited partnerships, and enterprises (regardless of business structure) in which an individual does not actively participate. For the general partner, income from a limited partnership is earned income; for the limited partner, the income is passive, not earned. Passive income is netted against passive losses to determine net taxable income which is then taxed at ordinary income rates. Passive losses may be used to offset only passive income.

Portfolio Income

Portfolio income includes dividends, interest, and net capital gains derived from the sale of securities. No matter what the source of the income, it is taxed in the year in which it is earned. Capital gains and capital losses will be covered separately.

Dividend Income

If the dividend qualifies (you don't need to know the technical points that make a dividend qualify), the tax rate is generally a maximum of 15%. (It can be as high as 20% or more for very high-income taxpayers, but that is unlikely to be tested.) Otherwise, the dividend is taxed at ordinary income rates. For test purposes, assume that any dividend from a U.S. corporation, including stock mutual funds, is qualified, unless the question states otherwise.

EXAMPLE

1. An investor who would like to increase current income from investments and, at the same time, pay taxes on that income at less than his marginal tax rate, would probably find which of the following to be most suitable?

    A. U.S. Treasury bonds

    B. Public utility stock

    C. Growth stock

    D. Money market mutual fund

    Answer: B. The key to this question is that dividends paid on stock issued by American companies (and certain qualified foreign corporations) generally qualify for a reduced tax rate (maximum 15 to 20%). No such benefit accrues to money market funds (their dividends are generated from interest income) and government bond interest is always taxed as ordinary income (although state income tax free). The dividends on a growth stock would also qualify, but, because the question deals with increasing current income, public utility, choice **B**, is a more sensible approach. This is an example of how the test might present you with two answer choices that could be correct, and you must choose the one that is more correct.

Interest Income

Interest on any debt security (other than tax-free municipal issues) is always taxed at ordinary income rates. Please note that interest on U.S. Treasury securities (but not GMNA and FNMA debt) is exempt from state taxation, but not federal. Furthermore, income distributions from bond funds are not qualified dividends and are taxed fully as ordinary income.

TAKE NOTE

Although interest income from municipal bonds is tax free, capital gains are fully taxable. Capital gains occur when the bond is sold for a price that is greater than the investor's cost basis (investment) in the bond. This is also true of capital gains distributions from municipal bond mutual funds. While the income distributions may be tax free, capital gains from any source are always taxable.

TEST TOPIC ALERT

In the case of TIPS, the taxation is a bit different. Being Treasury securities, they are exempt from state and local income tax. However, the annual interest payment received is taxable on a federal basis as ordinary income and, what is reminiscent of the tax treatment of a zero-coupon bond discussed in Unit 13, the annual increase to the principal is taxed as well.

What about income from foreign issuers? Dividend and interest income received from foreign securities, including ADRs, is normally subject to withholding tax, typically about 15%, by the issuer's country of domicile. Current U.S. tax law allows many investors to reclaim the withheld tax as a credit against taxes owed on their tax returns and it is not a preference item for AMT (U21LO4). For example, if you purchased some Matilda (also called kangaroo) bonds (remember them from Unit 13); they are issued in the Australian marketplace by non-Australian entities. The Australian government requires that a withholding tax be placed on the interest, but U.S. taxpayers can take that tax withheld as a credit against U.S. income tax due on the interest. In almost all cases, income from foreign securities is taxed in the U.S. at all levels (federal and state).

Taxation of Reinvested Distributions

Stocks and bonds normally pay dividends and interest in cash, (taxable in the year of receipt), and the investor only realizes a capital gain or loss when the investment is sold. Mutual funds normally allow dividends, and capital gains to be automatically reinvested in the fund shares at the net asset value (NAV) per share. Reinvesting creates a compounding effect.

These distributions are taxable to shareholders whether the distributions are taken in cash or reinvested. The issuer must disclose whether each distribution comes from income or realized capital gains. **Form 1099**, which is sent to shareholders after the close of the year, details tax information related to distributions for the year. Dividends must be reported as dividend income and will be taxed either as ordinary income or as a qualifying dividend. Capital gains distributions from mutual funds are generally reported as a long-term capital gain and are taxed at the same reduced rate as qualified dividends.

TEST TOPIC ALERT

One term you might see on the exam refers to an interest-on-interest plan and it will be compared to a dividend reinvestment plan. What is the exam referring to? This is nothing other than a typical bank savings account where your interest compounds, usually quarterly. Therefore, you are earning interest on the interest. From a tax standpoint this interest, just like reinvested dividends, is taxable in the year received.

Dividend Reinvestment Plans (DRIPS)

Some corporations offer their shareholders the opportunity to purchase additional shares of the company's common stock using their cash dividend. Under most DRIPS, the shareholder automatically purchases the additional shares directly from the issuer paying little or no commission and often at a discount to market price. In fact, most companies permit investors in these plans to add money along with the reinvested dividend. They are taxed in the year of receipt as is any cash dividend. However, the amount of reinvested dividends increases the investor's cost basis, thereby reducing the amount of capital gains if the position is later sold at a profit.

The Effect of Reinvestments on Cost Basis

Because the taxes have already been paid on any income reinvested, when the investor sells the asset, the cost basis is increased so that the income is not taxed again.

EXAMPLE

An investor purchases 100 shares of KAPCO common stock for $100 per share and elects to participate in KAPCO's DRIP. During the next five years, the investor receives dividends totaling $2,200, which has allowed the purchase of 20 additional shares through the DRIP. With KAPCO selling at $110 per share, the investor liquidates the entire position. For tax purposes, the investor has a capital gain of $1,000, even though the proceeds are $3,200 more than the original investment. Here's the math:

Purchase of 100 shares at $100 = $10,000. Add the reinvested dividends of $2,200 to increase the cost basis to $12,200. Sell all the shares (100 + the 20 acquired through the DRIP) = 120 × $110 = $13,200. The proceeds exceed the adjusted cost basis by $1,000 and that is the amount of capital gain.

It might appear on the exam in question form like this:

EXAMPLE

1. An investor purchases 100 shares of DERP common stock at $50 per share and elects to have all cash dividends reinvested through the DRIP being offered by DERP. After holding the stock for 5 years, the investor has reinvested $1,200 and acquired 20 additional shares. If the market price of DERP is $55 per share and the investor liquidates the position, the tax consequence will be

    A. a loss of $700

    B. a gain of $400

    C. a gain of $600

    D. a gain of $1,600

    Answer: B. The investor establishes the position at a cost of $5,000. To that, we add the $1,200 cost of the reinvested dividends bringing the investor's tax cost basis to $6,200. When all of the shares are sold, the proceeds are $6,600 (120 shares × $55). Subtracting the $6,200 cost from the $6,600 proceeds results in a capital gain of $400 (choice **B**).

TEST TOPIC ALERT

Regardless of fluctuations in the market price, as long as a dividend is paid, investors participating in a DRIP will *always* have more shares in their account at the end of the year than at the beginning.

Retirement Plan Distributions

Qualified retirement plan distributions are, with few exceptions, taxed at the investor's ordinary income tax rate when funds are withdrawn from the plan. Distributions from a qualified plan before the investor reaches age 59½ are also subject to a 10% early withdrawal penalty. Distributions from a qualified plan must begin by April 1 following the year the participant reaches 70½. More on this in Unit 24.

Margin Expenses

Margin interest is a tax-deductible expense (margin accounts are covered in Unit 22). The one exception is interest expenses incurred in the purchase of municipal securities. Because municipal interest income is federally tax exempt, the IRS does not allow taxpayers to deduct the margin interest expenses for municipal securities. Investors can deduct interest expenses incurred when borrowing money to purchase other securities to the extent those interest expenses do not exceed their net investment income, which includes interest income, dividends, and all capital gains.

Effective Tax Rate

In an earlier Test Topic Alert, we introduced you to the term *marginal* tax rate. That should not be confused with the individual's effective tax rate. What is the difference? As stated earlier, the marginal tax rate is the rate you pay on each additional dollar you receive as income. The effective tax rate, however, is the overall rate of tax you pay on your total taxable income. The following example should help you visualize the difference.

EXAMPLE

In the Test Topic Alert, we showed you how a single person with $250,000 in taxable income was paying taxes at a marginal rate of 35%. That is, a bonus of $10,000 would result in an additional tax liability of $3,500. That 35% rate was in effect for all income in excess of $200,000. According to the tax tables (and absolutely not tested), the tax on that first $200,000 is $42,449 and then everything above that (until $500,000) is taxed at 35%. So, for the single individual with $250,000 of taxable income, the total tax bill would be $42,449 + (35% × $50,000) or $42,449 + $17,500, which is a total tax of $59,949. That means that out of $250,000 in income, slightly less than 24% of it ($59,949 divided by $250,000) went to pay tax. This works out to be an *effective* tax rate of 23.98%.

TAX TREATMENT OF CAPITAL GAINS AND CAPITAL LOSSES

U21LO3: Distinguish between income and capital gain, and how they are taxed.

Whereas income is generally money received from the ownership of an investment, e.g., dividends on a stock, interest on a debt security, or from personal work, such as salary, capital gains and losses always involve the sale of an asset. The sale of a security can result in a **capital gain** or a **capital loss**. A **capital gain** occurs when a security is sold for a price higher than its cost basis; if the selling price is lower than the cost basis, a **capital loss** occurs.

Capital Gains

A **capital gain** occurs when capital assets (securities, real estate, and tangible property) are sold at prices that exceed the adjusted cost basis. Usually, computing the capital gain or loss on an asset is a matter of comparing the purchase price with the selling price less commissions.

Adjusting Cost Basis

An investment's **cost basis** (total cost of the investment) is used to determine whether a capital gain or a capital loss occurs when an asset is sold. Because many factors affect an asset's cost basis, the IRS requires the cost basis to be adjusted for such occurrences as stock splits and stock dividends.

EXAMPLE

A client buys 100 shares of RST at $55. Later, the company declares a stock dividend and the investor receives 10 more shares. The client's total investment remains $5,500, but there are now 110 shares of RST in the account. The client's adjusted cost basis per share is now $50 ($5,500 / 110). When the securities are sold, the holding period is based upon the original purchase date; the date(s) of the acquisition of the shares through the stock dividend(s) or stock split(s) are of no consequence. If the sales price exceeds the adjusted cost basis, the investor realizes a capital gain; if lower, a capital loss.

TAKE NOTE

A lower cost basis results in a larger capital gain. The gain is determined by comparing the sales proceeds with the cost basis.

EXAMPLE

If the investor's cost basis in stock is $50 per share and shares are sold for $60, the investor has a capital gain of $10. However, if the investor's cost basis is $55 and the shares are sold for $60, the investor's capital gain is only $5.

Effects of Reinvesting on Cost Basis for Computing Capital Gains/Losses

A few pages ago, we discussed the fact that any distributions received, whether taken in cash or reinvested, were reported on the Form 1099 as taxable for that year. In the case of reinvestments, because they have already been taxed, when a sale takes place, they are not taxed again—the amount reinvested adds to the investor's tax basis (or cost). You may wish to go back and review the two examples shown there.

Capital Losses

A **capital loss** occurs when capital assets are sold at prices that are lower than the adjusted cost basis.

Net Capital Gains and Losses

To calculate tax liability, a taxpayer must first add all short-term capital gains and losses for the year. (Short-term gains are investments held 12 months or less and are taxed at the investor's ordinary income tax rate.) Then all long-term capital gains and losses are added. (A long-term capital gain or loss only occurs after the investor has held the investment at risk for a period exceeding one year.) Finally, the taxpayer offsets the totals to determine the net capital gain or loss for the year. If the result is a net long-term capital gain, it is taxed at the capital gains rate, currently at 15% for most taxpayers.

Capital losses that exceed capital gains are deductible against earned income up to a maximum of $3,000 per year. Any capital losses not deducted in a taxable year may be carried forward indefinitely as a deduction to offset capital gains in future years.

Determining Which Shares to Sell

An investor holding identical securities, each with a different acquisition date and cost basis, may determine which shares to sell by electing one of three accounting methods: first in, first out (FIFO); share identification; or average cost basis. If the investor fails to choose, the IRS assumes the investor liquidates shares on a FIFO basis.

When FIFO shares are sold, the cost of the shares held the longest is used to calculate the gain or loss. In a rising market, this method normally creates adverse tax consequences.

When using the **share identification** accounting method, the investor keeps track of the cost of each share purchased and uses this information to liquidate the shares that would provide the lowest capital gain. Share identification is used to identify the specific per-share cost basis when shares are sold. The investor keeps track of the cost of each share purchased and specifies which shares to sell on the basis of that investor's specific tax needs.

A shareholder may elect to use an **average cost basis** when redeeming mutual fund shares (but not shares of specific stocks). The investor would calculate average basis by dividing the total cost of all shares owned by the total number of shares. The shareholder may not change the decision to use the average basis method without IRS permission.

TAKE NOTE

Share identification may result in more advantageous tax treatment, but most accountants prefer the convenience of the averaging method for mutual fund shares. Share identification is most commonly used with stock sales.

Wash Sale

An investor may not use capital losses to offset gains or income if the taxpayer sells a security at a loss and purchases the same or a substantially identical security within 30 days before or after the trade date establishing the loss. The sale at a loss and the repurchase within this period is a **wash sale**. The loss that was disallowed, however, is added to the repurchased shares' cost basis.

EXAMPLE

An investor buys 100 shares of ABC for $50 per share. One year later, the investor sells the shares for $40 per share. Fifteen days after the sale, 100 shares of ABC are repurchased for $42 per share. The investor's new cost basis is $52 per share because the $10 loss that was disallowed is added to the repurchase price of $42.

Figure 21.1: Wash Sale

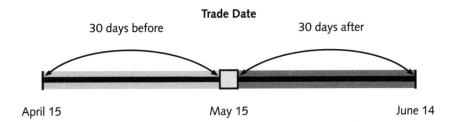

Trade Date

30 days before   30 days after

April 15   May 15   June 14

Substantially identical securities include stock rights, call options, warrants, and convertible securities of the same issue.

The IRS compares three qualities of debt securities in determining whether they are substantially identical: the maturity, coupon, and issuer. A bond is substantially identical if all three qualities of the bond sold at a loss and the newly purchased bond are the same.

After selling a bond, an investor can buy another bond with either a different maturity, coupon, or issuer without violating the wash sale rule.

EXAMPLE

An investor could sell an ABC 8% bond that matures in 2030 at a loss and buy back an XYZ 8% bond that matures in 2031 and claim the loss. This is commonly called tax-swapping.

TAKE NOTE

The wash sale rule applies only to realized losses—not to realized gains.

Sale of a Primary Residence

The final example of capital gain taxation deals with the unique treatment offered on the sale of a primary residence. There are special tax benefits available to those selling their primary residence as long as it has been lived in as the primary residence for at least two of the past five years. For a couple, the first $500,000 in profit is excluded from capital gains taxation; for a single person, it is the first $250,000.

EXAMPLE

Chloe and Edgar bought their home 30 years ago for $50,000. Now that the children are all on their own, they decide to downsize and move to a retirement village. If they sell their home for $600,000, what is the tax consequence?

Chloe and Edgar are selling their home for a profit of $550,000. However, the first $500,000 for a couple is excluded from taxation. Therefore, they will only have to report the remaining $50,000 as a long-term capital gain.

ALTERNATIVE MINIMUM TAX (AMT)

U21LO4: Recall the preference items included in the AMT computation.

Congress enacted the **alternative minimum tax (AMT)** to ensure that high-income taxpayers do not escape federal income taxes. Certain items that receive favorable tax treatment must be added back into taxable income to arrive at the AMTI (alternative minimum taxable income) and include the following:

- Accelerated depreciation on property placed in service after 1986.

- Certain costs associated with limited partnership programs, such as research and development costs and excess intangible drilling costs.

- Local tax and interest on investments that do not generate income.

- Tax-exempt interest on private purpose municipal bonds issued after August 7, 1986. Examples of these private purpose or private activity bonds that makes them subject to the AMT would be those issued to finance sports stadiums, hospitals, housing projects, and so forth.

- Incentive stock options (ISO) to the extent that the fair market value of the employer's stock is in excess of the strike price of the option, even when the stock is not sold in that year.

To determine if you owe AMT, you compute your regular tax and then you compute the AMT and pay whichever is the higher amount. The IRS has an unusual way of stating this. They say that the AMT is the regular tax plus the amount by which the AMT exceeds the regular tax. So, if the AMT computation shows $12,000 due and the regular shows $10,000 due, you take that $10,000 and add the amount by which $12,000 exceeds $10,000 ($2,000) to arrive at $12,000. Wouldn't saying, "Pay the higher of the two," be easier? It sure would, but then that might put some accountants out of business, just like simplifying the tax code would do.

 TAKE NOTE

Items that must be added back in for the purpose of the AMT computation are sometimes called **tax preference items**. If the tax liability computed under the AMT computation is greater than the taxpayer's regular tax computation, the taxpayer must pay the AMT amount.

TAXATION OF LIFE INSURANCE

U21LO5: Describe the fundamentals of insurance, trust, estate, and gift taxation.

Income Tax Implications of Life Insurance

Premiums for individually purchased life insurance are generally nondeductible for income tax purposes. Generally, proceeds from life insurance policies made to a beneficiary are exempt from federal income tax.

Estate Tax Implications to Owning Life Insurance

If someone named as the insured individual on a life insurance policy holds incidents of ownership in that policy, the entire death benefit payable under that policy is included for federal estate tax purposes in the insured individual's estate.

If a person retains the right to designate a beneficiary, transfer ownership of an insurance policy (assign), choose how dividends or policy proceeds will be paid out, borrow money from the accumulated cash value of the policy, or perform any other functions that are rights of ownership, then that person has incidents of ownership in the policy.

In light of the estate tax implications, it is frequently best that a party other than the insured own the life insurance policy in order to remove the proceeds from the estate of the insured. An effective alternative to ownership of a policy on one's own life is to have the life insurance acquired by or transferred to an irrevocable life insurance trust (ILIT). If certain provisions, known as Crummey powers, are included in the ILIT document, premiums paid by the insured may qualify for the annual gift tax exclusion (currently $15,000 per year, per beneficiary).

 TEST TOPIC ALERT

In those cases where the estate does have liquid assets such as stocks and bonds, life insurance still may serve a valuable need in that these income-producing assets will not have to be sold to cover the estate tax liability or other final expenses.

Policy Loans

When you borrow cash value from your life insurance policy, the funds received are nontaxable. This is the same as any other borrowed money—it isn't your money and must be paid back at some time in the future. Note that if you never pay it back, the amount of the loan will be deducted from the death benefit (the insurance company will finally get back the money).

Policy Surrender

If a variable life insurance policy is surrendered, any cash value in excess of the basis in the policy (the premiums paid) is taxable as ordinary income.

Withdrawal of Cash Value

If there is a partial withdrawal of cash value from a variable life insurance policy, the FIFO rules apply. This is unlike the LIFO treatment on an annuity. Therefore, there are no tax consequences until the amount withdrawn exceeds the cost basis in the policy.

EXAMPLE

1. Which of the following are possible sources of taxable income to an individual?

   I.   Owning a sole proprietorship

   II. Being a shareholder in a subchapter S corporation

   III. Owning stocks and bonds

   IV. Proceeds paid on a life insurance policy

   A. I and II

   B. I, II, and III

   C. I, II, III, and IV

   D. II and III

Answer: B. An individual can generate income from running a sole proprietorship or being a shareholder in an S corporation (the exam will probably use the obsolete term, Subchapter S). Of course, taxable income can be generated by investments in the form of dividends, interest, and capital gains. One very valuable feature of life insurance is that death benefits paid to the beneficiary of a life insurance policy are not subject to federal income tax so choice IV is not part of the correct answer **(B)**.

TAXATION OF SOCIAL SECURITY

Taxation of Social Security is included in this LO because The Old Age, Survivors and Disability Insurance program (*OASDI*) is the official name for Social Security in the United States. As much as 50% of Social Security benefits start becoming taxable once a single person's base income (IRS computation called "provisional income") exceeds $25,000 and a married couple's exceeds $32,000. Once that income exceeds $34,000 (single) or $44,000 (couple), it is likely that 85% of the Social Security benefit is subject to income tax.

Although we have not heard of this being tested, individuals claiming benefits before full retirement age will see a reduction in those benefits once earnings reach a certain point (changes every year).

CAPITAL GAINS TAXATION ON DONATED (GIFTED) AND INHERITED SECURITIES

Gifts

When a donor makes a gift of securities or virtually any asset, the cost basis to the recipient (the donee) is the donor's cost basis, (original cost and holding period beginning from the donor's date of purchase). This describes **carryover basis**.

EXAMPLE

In 2010, Joe Smith bought 1,000 shares of COD at $24 per share, for a total cost of $24,000. In 2017, when COD was trading at $32.50, Joe gave those 1,000 shares to his daughter, Sally. When Sally sells the shares, her cost basis is Joe's cost basis on the date of his original purchase—$24 per share, seven years ago—not the market value on the date of the gift. So, if Sally were to sell those shares for $33 per share one month after receiving the gift, she would be realizing a long-term capital gain of $9,000.

TAKE NOTE

It gets more complicated if the securities are worth less than the donor's cost at the time of the gift and we don't expect the exam to deal with that situation.

TAKE NOTE

If a gift of securities held more than one year (long-term), is made to a 501(c)(3) charity, (that is the IRS designation for qualifying nonprofit organizations), the tax treatment is more favorable. Under these circumstances, Joe's deduction is based on the fair market value on the date of the gift, not his cost basis. He would have received a $32,500 tax deduction and avoided capital gains taxes on the $8,500 profit.

Inherited Securities

When a person dies and leaves securities to heirs, the cost basis to the recipients is usually the **fair market value** on the date of the owner's death. In other words, the cost basis steps up to the date of death value. Furthermore, the IRS treats any gains to be long-term, regardless of when the deceased purchased the security.

EXAMPLE

In 2010, Joe Smith bought 1,000 shares of COD at $24 per share for a total cost of $24,000. In 2017, when COD was trading at $32.50, Joe died. His daughter, Sally, is Joe's sole heir and inherits the 1,000 shares upon his death. When Sally sells the shares, her cost basis is the fair market value on the date of Joe's death—$32.50 per share—not Joe's original purchase cost and any gain would be long term.

TEST TOPIC ALERT

The step up provision does not apply when inheriting an annuity.

Trusts are considered legal persons and may be subject to taxation. In fact, if not handled properly, the taxes can be quite onerous.

Trust Tax Rates

Taxation of trusts and estates is based on what is distributed and what is retained. In the case of non-distributed income, the tax consequences can be quite severe because the tax brackets are highly compressed. For example, although a joint return filed for 2019 would have to report income in excess of $612,350 to be subject to the highest tax bracket of 37%, that rate is reached once a trust or estate has non-distributed income in excess of $12,750. Obviously, this can have a major impact on investment planning.

TEST TOPIC ALERT

If the trust or estate has income, it must be reported on IRS Form 1041.

Distributable Net Income (DNI)

Because of the onerous tax implications described previously, most trusts and estates distribute their income. In the context of a trust or an estate, the taxable income is known as distributable net income (DNI). DNI determines the amount of income that may be taxable to beneficiaries (or the grantor in the case of a revocable trust), whereas the balance may be taxed to the trust as indicated previously. Commissions and other fees charged for buying and selling securities held in a trust are subtracted from the trust's DNI. Realized capital gains that are reinvested in the corpus (Latin for "body") of the trust are not considered part of DNI.

EXAMPLE

The Gordon Clark Trust had dividend income of $10,000 and interest income of $7,000. In addition, the trust realized capital gains of $3,000, half of which were reinvested in the corpus of the trust. Transaction costs for the year were $2,000. The Gordon Clark Trust has DNI for the year of $16,500 ($10,000 + $7,000 + $1,500 − $2,000). The $1,500 of realized gains reinvested is not part of DNI.

Tax-exempt interest from municipal bonds remains tax exempt to trust beneficiaries.

If the trust is revocable, all income, whether distributed or not, is taxed to the **grantor**. In the case of an irrevocable trust, distributed income might be taxed to the beneficiary and/or the grantor, but the topic is so complicated that we don't expect it to be tested.

Bypass Trust

A bypass trust is an estate planning tool used to take advantage of the lifetime estate tax exclusion. It is commonly used between spouses when both are U.S. citizens and takes advantage of the unified tax credit. The concept of the bypass trust is to enable a surviving spouse to take advantage of the unused lifetime exclusion (currently $11.4 million) of the first to die and add it to their exclusion. Tax legislation passed in 2010 has largely removed the need for this trust.

Portability of Unused Estate Tax Exemption Under ATRA

As mentioned previously, the bypass trust is no longer needed. This is because the Tax Act of 2010 contained the concept of portability, which permits the surviving spouse to take the unused portion of the first deceased spouse's federal exemption and aggregate it with the surviving spouse's unused portion.

To use an example, for 2019, each living spouse has a lifetime exemption from estate tax of $11.4 million. The husband dies in 2019, leaving his entire estate of $17 million to his wife. There would be no estate tax because of the unlimited marital deduction. Let's assume that the husband has not used any of his $11.4 million exemption by making taxable gifts in previous years. If the wife dies later with her estate value up to as much as $22.8 million, the executor of her estate can use all of her exemption of $11.4 million as well as the husband's unused portion (up to $11.4 million) needed to reduce the federal estate tax to zero.

EXAMPLE

Each individual in a married couple has a lifetime estate tax exclusion (2019) of $11.4 million. At the time of the first to die, the gross value of the estate is $15 million. If the provisions of the will stated that the estate was to be left to the surviving spouse, then, taking advantage of the unlimited marital deduction, all $15 million passes without estate tax and without impacting the deceased's lifetime exclusion. Therefore, the surviving spouse gets the $11.4 million "left over" from the deceased meaning that no estate tax will be due after the survivors' passing unless the estate's value exceeds $22.8 million.

Generation-Skipping Trust (GST)

Just as the name implies, a generation skipping trust is used to pass money from family members to other members more than one generation removed (grandchildren and/or great grandchildren). Therefore, instead of the assets being taxed upon the death of the parents and then again when their children pass them to the grandchildren, one level of estate taxation is eliminated. The combination of the marital portability and the greatly increased estate tax exclusion granted by the Tax Cuts and Jobs Act (TCJA) of 2017, will result in many fewer clients needing this kind of plan.

ESTATE TAXES

The federal government imposes a tax on a decedent's estate based on the value of the estate, at death. An individual may transfer an unlimited amount to a spouse who is a U.S. citizen without the imposition of federal estate tax. This is known as the marital deduction. In addition, an individual may transfer unlimited amounts of money and other property to an eligible charity with no federal estate tax. For heirs other than spouses, an estate tax credit will offset estate tax on transfers of up to $11.4 million in 2019, indexed for inflation of property. We have discussed some ways to reduce or eliminate estate taxes earlier in this unit.

The Gross Estate vs. the Taxable Estate

Federal estate tax is calculated using a formula that begins with the **gross estate**. The gross estate includes all interests in property held by an individual at the time of death. Although amounts of property transferred to a spouse or a charity will generally not be subject to federal estate tax, such amounts are includable in calculating the gross estate.

Certain expenses are then deducted from the gross estate to arrive at the **adjusted gross estate (AGE)**. Examples of deductions for the AGE include funeral expenses, charitable contributions, and debts of the decedent.

Once the amount of the AGE is determined, the unlimited marital and charitable deductions are subtracted to arrive at the **taxable estate**.

EXAMPLE

Caroline, who is unmarried, died in 2019, owning various property. The amount of her gross estate is $18 million. However, her estate incurred $20,000 in funeral expenses, she had made charitable gifts of $1,000,000, and she owed mortgages of $200,000 and $30,000 in credit card balances. Thus, her AGE is $16,750,000. In 2019, because of an estate tax credit that exempted the first $11,400,000 of property transferred after death, Caroline's estate will be taxed on the remaining $5,350,000 in transferred property.

Alternative Valuation Date

The Internal Revenue Code provides that the executor of an estate may choose to value the assets in the estate as of date of death or, alternatively, six months later. This is particularly beneficial if the estate consists of assets that have dropped substantially in value following the date of death of the deceased. What value is used if an asset that is appraised at the date of death is subsequently sold for a different price? The executor will use that sale price as long as it represents the fair market value.

In the case of mutual funds, FMV is the NAV, not the POP.

TEST TOPIC ALERT

If an asset is sold after death at a greatly reduced price from its appraised value in a transaction that does not meet the definition required under fair market value, the IRS will use the higher value.

Payment Date of Estate Taxes

Regardless of whether the date of death or alternative valuation date is used, estate taxes are due no later than nine months after death. Just as with personal income taxes, it is possible to get an extension to *file* the return, but the taxes are due at the nine months' time and interest will be charged on any amount owed that is not paid at that time.

TEST TOPIC ALERT

The computation of the estate tax is done on IRS Form 706. From the gross assets, certain expenses (such as the costs of administration of the estate, funeral expenses, payments of outstanding debts, and charitable bequests) are deducted and the tax is levied on the remaining taxable estate.

Taxation of Estate Income

During the time before the estate is liquidated (and estates that are contested can drag on for years), it is likely that the executor will manage the assets in such a fashion that the estate receives income and possibly capital gains. If this is the case, the taxation to the estate is at the same rates mentioned earlier regarding trusts and, as with trusts, Form 1041 is used to report the income. Furthermore, the income is taxed using the same compressed brackets as trust income (37% for everything in excess of $12,750).

TEST TOPIC ALERT

Just as you may have to know that the estate tax computation is done on Form 706, you may also have to know that the estate income tax computation is done on Form 1041.

DONOR'S GIFT TAX OBLIGATION

Gift tax is a progressive federal tax imposed on the transfer of property during the lifetime of the donor; up to $11.4 million (2019) in lifetime gifts may be made without incurring gift tax. Additionally, currently, an individual may give up to $15,000 per year, per person to any number of individuals without generating the federal gift tax. If a married couple joins in the gift, the allowable amount is doubled to $30,000 per person per year. Gifts of securities are valued as of the current market price on the date of the gift. Please don't confuse this with cost basis of a gift discussed earlier in this unit.

When a gift is made between spouses, the rule is somewhat different. Generally, there is an unlimited exclusion for these gifts. However, there are limits if your spouse is not a citizen of the United States. In 2019, a spouse may gift up to $155,000 to a noncitizen spouse. The number won't be tested because it changes each year, but the concept might be on your exam.

TEST TOPIC ALERT

Generally, a gift tax return must be filed whenever a gift in excess of $15,000 (or whatever the annual exclusion is at the time of the gift) is made to any individual (other than a spouse). Any excess over the annual exclusion is applied against the lifetime exclusion until it is used up.

The return is filed on *Form 709* and is due at the same time as the donor's income tax return, generally April 15.

TAKE NOTE

If a gift tax is due, it is the responsibility of the giver of the gift (donor), not the receiver of the gift (donee).

EXAMPLE

This concept is pretty simple: you have some stock worth $22,000 and give it to a child or grandchild; you've exceeded the $15,000 annual gift exclusion, so a gift tax return would have to be filed. However, it might look like this on your exam: "A grandfather received stock as a result of demutualization that is currently worth $22,000 and wishes to give it to his grandchild." Most students would waste their time trying to figure out what demutualization means and not realize how simple the question really is. It makes no difference how the stock was acquired, for gift tax purposes; the only thing that counts is the fair market value on the date of the gift.

TAKE NOTE

Taxation of estates and gifts are unified. That means that whatever is used of the lifetime gift exclusion before death, reduces the estate tax exclusion. Both have a lifetime exclusion (2019) of 11.4 million and both have a progressive structure with rates beginning at 18% and reaching a maximum tax rate (2019) of 40%. There are two testable differences:

1. the annual gift tax exclusion ($15,000 in 2019); and

2. gift taxes are due at the same time as the individual tax return (April 15) while estate taxes are due nine months after death.

TEST TOPIC ALERT

The concept of taxation relating to gifts and inheritances can be confusing. There are two separate taxable situations—taxes due on the proceeds of a sale of gifted or inherited property, and taxes due based on the amount of the gift or the estate.

The following comparison should help:

1. A client has received a gift of securities from someone, or has inherited securities.

   a. Gift: The client's cost basis for determining if there is a taxable capital gain is that of the donor. The client is considered to have acquired the security on the donor's purchase date and at the donor's purchase price.

   b. Inheritance: The client's cost basis for determining if there is a taxable capital gain is the fair market value (FMV) as of the date of death. The holding period is not a consideration because any gains are considered long-term.

2. Your client made a gift of securities to someone, or has died.

   a. Gift: The obligation to pay a gift tax is that of the donor. Anything over the annual exclusion (currently $15,000) may be subject to the gift tax (unless used against the lifetime exclusion of $11.4 million). The amount of the gift for tax purposes is the FMV as of the date of the gift.

   b. Estate: The obligation to pay an estate tax, is that of the deceased's estate. The value used to determine if there is an estate tax liability is the FMV either as of the date of death or, by using the alternative valuation date, the FMV six months after death. As with the gift tax, there is the unified credit of $11.4 million.

EXAMPLE

1. Bruno and Griselde have been married for 56 years. Bruno passes away in 2019 and leaves his entire estate of $10 million to his wife. During his lifetime, Bruno had used $2.2 million of his lifetime gift exclusion. Upon Griselde's death 2 years later, the estate is worth $22.2 million. The gross taxable estate is

   A. $0

   B. $1.6 million

   C. $2 million

   D. $11 million

   Answer: B. Because Bruno used $2.2 million, his estate tax exclusion is now $9.2 million. The portability provisions all that to be added to her exclusion making the total $9.2 million ($9.2 + $11.4 = $20.6 million). With a gross value of $22.2 million and a remaining exclusion of $20.6 million, before any deductions, the gross taxable estate is $1.6 million, choice **B**.

TAXATION OF BUSINESSES

U21LO6: Identify the different types of business taxation.

Sole Proprietorships

Sole proprietorships are the simplest business form but offer no liability protection to the owner. In fact, this is the only form of business where the potential loss is unlimited because the personal assets of the owner are at risk in addition to any assets owned by the business. The owner computes the earnings of the business on the Schedule C of her Form 1040 so anything made (or lost) by the business is reflected directly on her tax return—there is no separate tax return for the business entity.

Partnerships

Partnerships are relatively easy to form and dissolve and come in two types. Both offer flow-through of income and losses, the difference being in the degree of liability. General partnerships provide no liability protection to the partners. In other words, if the business goes under, they, collectively and separately, are liable for any losses. In a limited partnership, as the name implies, something is limited. In this case, it is the liability. A limited partner's maximum loss is what has already been invested plus any funds committed for but not yet contributed. That is why so many DPPs are organized as LPs.

Partnerships do not pay taxes. They file an information return, a Form 1065, and attach to that (and send a copy to each partner) a Schedule K-1 indicating the amount of income (or loss) to be inserted on the investor's personal Form 1040.

Limited Liability Company (LLC)

The LLC is somewhat of a hybrid between the partnership and the corporation. The federal government does not recognize an LLC as a classification for federal tax purposes. An LLC business entity must file as a corporation, a partnership, or sole proprietorship. Generally, a one-member LLC will use the Schedule C, just as if it were a sole proprietorship. Those with two or more members invariably file as partnerships using the Form 1065 to provide the IRS with the information and the Schedule K-1 for each member's share of income or loss. If filing as a corporation, they generally file as an S corporation, but it is unlikely, for test purposes, that you will have to know anything about an LLC filing as a corporation.

Corporations

As with partnerships, we have two types here as well—the C corporation and the S corporation. Of all the business entities we've discussed, the only one that actually files a tax return on which it must pay income tax is the C corporation. It files on Form 1120 and pays taxes at a rate that generally does not exceed 21%. The key fact about the C corporation is that its dividends are paid out after paying income taxes and then that dividend is taxable to the shareholder, hence the term *double taxation*.

The S corporation (sometime referred to by its ancient name, Subchapter S corporation, on the exam), is treated for tax purposes the same as a partnership except that the return filed is the Form 1120S. Shareholders receive a Schedule K-1 indicating their share of income or loss.

Just as with the LLC and the partnership, the business entity is not taxed; everything flows through to the owners. The TCJA of 2017 made a major change in the way that flow-through business entities are taxed. Subject to certain income limitations (not likely to be tested), there is a 20% reduction to operating business income. The effect of this is to lower the amount of taxable income to each partner/member/shareholder.

C corporations are major investors in securities. Some **Internal Revenue Code (IRC)** provisions affecting C corporations as investors include the following.

- **Dividend exclusion rule:** Dividends paid from one corporation to another are 50% exempt from taxation. A corporation that receives dividends on stocks of other domestic (and certain qualifying foreign) corporations, therefore, pays taxes on only 50% of the dividends received.

- **Municipal securities:** Like individual taxpayers, corporations do not pay federal taxes on interest received from municipal bonds.

FILING DATES FOR BUSINESS TAX RETURNS

Sole Proprietorship

A business organized as a sole proprietorship is an extension of the individual running the business, so its year-end is December 31, and the tax return due date is the same as the individual's—April 15 of the following year.

Single Member LLC

If the business is an LLC with only one member, it is taxed like a sole proprietorship, using Schedule C with a year-end of December 31. The tax returns are due and taxes payable on April 15 of the following year.

Partnership and Multiple Member LLCs

The tax filing requirements for a partnership and an LLC with more than one member are the same. An information return is filed on Form 1065, with a Schedule K-1 sent to the partners/members indicating the amount of income or loss attributable to each of them. Remember, the business entity pays no income tax—all reportable income/loss flows through to the partners/members. Form 1065 is due on March 15 of the following year. The year-end for these businesses is typically December 31. Because these are flow-through entities, they don't pay taxes. Taxes are due on April 15, when the individual partners/members file their Form 1040s showing their share of the business's income or loss that was reported on the Schedule K-1.

Corporations

A regular (C) corporation may choose any convenient date as their year-end (usually a quarter end date). C corporation tax returns are due and taxes are payable on the 15th day of the fourth month after the end of the company's fiscal (financial) year. So, a C corporation with a year-end date of December 31 must file and pay taxes by April 15; a C corporation with a year-end date of September 30 must file and pay taxes by January 15.

In the case of an S corporation, income/loss is taxed on individual income tax returns. Therefore, an S corporation must usually take a calendar year-end date (December 31) unless the corporation can establish a reasonable business purpose for a different date. The filing date of the Form 1120S due date is the same as for partnerships and multiple member LLCs (March 15 for a December 31 year-end). As with the other flow-through entities, the Schedule K-1 is sent to shareholders and is used in the preparation of their Form 1040 return.

TEST TOPIC ALERT

You may be asked about tax documents for each of these different forms of business organizations. Sole proprietors and single member LLCs file their business information on a Schedule C. Investors in partnerships, members of LLCs, and shareholders in S corporations receive a Schedule K-1 and C corporations report their income on a Form 1120.

TAKE NOTE

This chart should help:

Sole proprietorship - Schedule C - April 15

Single member LLC - same as above

Multiple member LLC, Partnership, S corporation - March 15. (LLC and partnership on Form 1065, S corp. on Form 1120S)

C corporation - April 15, or 15th day of the 4th month after the end of the fiscal year - Form 1120

EXAMPLE

1. Most new businesses operate at a loss the first year or so. If several of your clients were forming a group to fund a start-up enterprise but wished to limit their liability and, at the same time, be able to receive favorable tax treatment for the expected losses, you would suggest forming which of the following?

   A. C corporation

   B. General partnership

   C. LLC

   D. Sole proprietorship

   Answer: C. The only way to limit liability is through a corporation (C or S), LLC, or limited partnership. The LLC, choice **C**, allows for the flow-through of operating losses to the shareholders while the C corporation does not.

UNIT 22

Trading Securities

By this time in the course, you're probably itching to go out and try some of these great strategies and techniques and get active in the market. In this unit, we'll cover the first thing you have to do—decide what type of account you're going to open. Then, we'll discuss where the securities you wish to purchase or sell are traded. It isn't like you can visit your local Walmart and pick up a few hundred shares of stock. Nor can you go online to Amazon and, even if you have Prime®, order some bonds, and have them delivered in two business days.

The Series 65 exam will include approximately four questions on the material presented in this unit.

LEARNING OBJECTIVES

When you have completed this unit, you will be able to accomplish the following.

U22LO1:   Compare cash and margin accounts.
U22LO2:   Compute the margin account calculations.
U22LO3:   Contrast stock exchanges and the over-the-counter market.
U22LO4:   Identify the difference between functioning as a broker and acting as a dealer.
U22LO5:   Describe the costs of trading securities.
U22LO6:   Identify the features and uses of market, stop, limit orders and short sales.
U22LO7:   Describe high-frequency trading (HFT) and dark pools.

CASH AND MARGIN ACCOUNTS

U22LO1: Compare cash and margin accounts.

Customers can open either cash accounts or margin accounts, depending on how they choose to pay for securities. In cash accounts, customers pay the full purchase price of securities by the transaction settlement date. In margin accounts, customers may borrow part of a security's purchase price from the broker-dealer under terms set by Regulation T of the Federal Reserve Board. That power was given to the Federal Reserve Board (FRB) in the Securities Exchange Act of 1934.

Cash Accounts

A **cash account** is the basic investment account, and anyone eligible to open an investment account can open one. In a cash account, a customer must pay in full for any securities purchased. Although, as with almost everything in this course, there are exceptions, for exam purposes, certain accounts may *only* be opened as cash accounts, including:

- personal retirement accounts, such as IRAs;

- corporate retirement accounts;

- custodial accounts, such as Uniform Transfer to Minors Act accounts (UTMAs); and

- Coverdell ESAs.

Margin Accounts

Margin accounts allow customers to control investments for less money than they would need if they were to buy the securities outright because a margin account allows a customer to borrow money for investing. The term *margin* refers to the minimum amount of cash or marginable securities a customer must deposit to buy securities.

Margin also is a potential source of cash. If a customer has fully paid securities in an account and needs cash, a broker-dealer is permitted to lend money against those securities up to the margin limit that the FRB has set.

Customers who open margin accounts must meet certain minimal suitability requirements. The customer may then buy securities on margin and pay interest on the borrowed funds. The securities purchased are held in street name as collateral for the margin loan.

When buying on margin, investors are using financial leverage. That is, they are increasing the potential for gain (and for loss as well) by using borrowed funds. Leveraging can be beneficial when the security is moving up, but it can result in a loss greater than the original investment if the security goes against the investor.

Marginable Securities

In addition to prescribing the loan value of securities, Regulation T also identifies which securities are eligible for purchase on margin and which may be used as collateral for loans for other purchases. These are known as marginable securities. The following should be helpful:

Securities that may be purchased on margin/used as collateral:

- Exchange-listed stocks and bonds

- Stocks traded on the Nasdaq Stock Market

- Warrants traded on either of these

Securities that cannot be purchased on margin/used as collateral

- Options (puts and calls). LEAPS are an exception, but that is unlikely to be tested

■ Stock rights (preemptive)

■ Insurance contracts, e.g., variable annuities and variable life

Securities that cannot be purchased on margin, but may be used as margin collateral once owned at least 30 days:

■ Mutual funds

■ New issues

Finally, although exempt from Regulation T (they are exempt securities), the self-regulatory organizations, primarily FINRA, have established margin requirements for government and municipal securities. That means that they can also be purchased on margin and have value as collateral.

Documenting a Margin Account

Opening a margin account requires more documentation than opening a regular cash account. The customer signs a margin agreement, which includes the required credit agreement, hypothecation agreement, and an optional loan consent. Under NASAA policies, it is an unethical business practice to execute any transaction in a margin account without securing from the customer a properly executed written margin agreement promptly *after* the initial transaction in the account.

Margin Account Agreements	
Credit Agreement	Establishes the debtor/creditor relationship and discloses the terms under which credit is extended. SEC Rule 10b-16 requires firms to disclose the method of computing interest and the conditions under which interest rates and charges will be changed. Firms must send customers an assurance that statements accounting for interest charges will be sent with the same frequency that interest is charged (monthly or quarterly).
Hypothecation Agreement	Gives the firm permission to use the client's margin securities as collateral for the margin loan and pledge (re-hypothecate) securities held on margin to a lending institution; a mandatory part of a margin agreement.
Loan Consent (optional)	Gives the firm permission to lend securities held in the margin account to other brokers, usually for short sales. It is not mandatory for customers to sign the loan consent agreement.

TAKE NOTE

Although NASAA does not have one, FINRA rules (which most states view as practices to be followed by broker-dealers under their jurisdiction), do have a risk disclosure requirement for margin accounts. As part of opening a margin account, the broker-dealer must provide customers with a risk disclosure document. Unlike the "promptly after the initial trade" requirement that NASAA has for its required documentation, FINRA requires this document to be delivered no later than the time of opening the account. This information must also be provided to margin customers on an annual basis. The document discusses the risks associated with margin trading, some of which are listed here.

■ You can lose more funds than you deposit in the margin account.

- The firm can force the sale of securities or other assets in your account(s) and do so without contacting you.

- You are not entitled to choose which securities can be sold if a call for additional funds is not met.

- You are not entitled to an extension of time to meet a margin call.

- The firm can increase its house maintenance margin requirements at any time and is not required to provide advance written notice to the client.

TAKE NOTE

One of the agreements described previously is the hypothecation agreement. To finance the loan the broker-dealer makes to the client, the firm takes the newly purchased security and hypothecates (pledges) it to a bank to collateralize a loan made by the bank to the BD. The **broker call loan rate** is the interest rate banks charge broker-dealers on money they borrow to lend to margin account customers. The broker call loan rate is also known as the *call loan rate* or *call money rate*. The broker call loan rate usually is slightly higher than other short-term rates. Broker call loans are callable on 24-hour notice. Invariably, call loan appears on the exam as one of the incorrect choices.

MARGIN ACCOUNT CALCULATIONS

U22LO2: Compute the margin account calculations.

The term *margin call* is properly defined as the initial call for funds when making a margin transaction. For example, with the margin requirements of the FRB's Regulation T at 50% (as they have been since 1974), a purchase of $12,000 of stock will result in a margin call of $6,000. The broker-dealer lends the client the other $6,000 creating a debit balance in the account. The equity in the account is 50%, and the client's debt is the other 50%.

Maintenance Margin

The self-regulatory organizations (SROs) (e.g., FINRA and the NYSE), rather than the Fed through Reg. T, have established minimum levels of equity in a margin account below which a call will go out for additional funds. This is properly referred to as margin maintenance or a maintenance call. Current SRO levels are 25% for long margin accounts. For example, if, in the above purchase, the stock's price were to drop to $8,000, there would only be $2,000 of equity in the account (market value of $8,000 minus debit balance of $6,000 equals $2,000). At this point, the equity represents 25% of the current market value ($2,000/$8,000). If the stock should drop any further, a maintenance margin call would be sent with a request for immediate funds. You will not have to do any of these computations, but you will need to know the term. If the maintenance call is not met, the broker-dealer will liquidate enough securities in the account to bring the equity back to the maintenance level. If there is more than one security in the account, the firm can select which to sell—it does not have to be one whose decline triggered the call.

House Maintenance

This is the term used to describe stricter limits imposed by the broker-dealers themselves. Typically, instead of relying on the SRO maintenance level of 25%, the individual firm may require a minimum of 35% or even higher.

TAKE NOTE

This should help you remember the three terms we've just discussed:

Margin Call: Set by the Federal Reserve Board under Regulation T. This is the initial deposit required when purchase securities on margin (the broker-dealer lends the balance of the purchase price). For equity securities, the initial margin requirement is 50% of the purchase price.

Minimum Maintenance: Set by the SROs. This is the minimum equity that must be maintained in a margin account. Should the equity fall below the minimum required, a maintenance call (sometimes called maintenance margin) will go out demanding an immediate deposit of enough equity to bring the account above the required level. Currently, the minimum maintenance level for long positions is 25% and for short positions is 30%.

House Maintenance: Set by the individual broker-dealer firm. As a cushion, and to reduce the possible sellout caused by failure to meet a maintenance call, most firms set a minimum equity level above the SRO minimum. A common house requirement is 35%. Falling below triggers a *house call*.

None of these numbers will be tested, only the concepts.

Mixed Margin Account

Later in this unit, we'll describe the short sale. Short sales must take place in a margin account. When the margin account contains both long and short positions, it is said to be a mixed margin account. Computing the equity, sometimes called net equity, in one of these accounts is done by calculating the equity for both the longs and shorts and then combining them.

In a long account, the equity is what you own, minus what you owe. That would be the current market value of the long stock minus the debit balance. In the case of the short position, it is basically the same, except the terms are different. What you owe in a short position is the cost to buy back the stock you've borrowed. What you own is the credit balance representing what you received when you sold the stock in the first place. So, the equity in a short account is the credit balance minus the current market value of the short stock. Perhaps the following will make it a bit easier:

CMV long – debit balance = long equity

credit balance – CMV short = short equity

We have two positive numbers: the stock we own, and the credit balance (you know that when you get a bill and there is a credit balance, it means they owe you money—that's yours). On the other side, we have two negative numbers: the cost to buy back the stock we're short and the debit balance. If we add the two positives and then subtract the two negatives, we've got our net equity.

EXAMPLE

A client's mixed margin account shows the following. Current market value of the long positions is $50,000, while the current market value of the short positions is $25,000. There is a debit balance of $20,000 and a credit balance of $40,000. What is the combined, or net equity in the account?

Either find the equity in each account, Long: $50,000 − $20,000 = $30,000 and short: $40,000 − $25,000 = $15,000, so the total is $45,000. Or, take the two positive numbers, $50,000 + $40,000, which equal $90,000 and subtract the two negative numbers, $20,000 + $25,000, which equal $45,000 and you get the same $45,000.

Positive (Negative) Margin

The term *positive margin* simply means that your returns are higher than the cost of the borrowed money to carry the positions in a margin account.

For example, if you buy $10,000 of stock on 50% margin, you will be borrowing $5,000 of that purchase price from the broker-dealer. If, over the holding period, you pay $400 in interest and sell the stock for $11,000, you've made a profit of $1,000 against the cost of $400 for net winnings of $600. That would be considered *positive margin*.

If, however, you sold the stock for $10,300, your interest cost would have exceeded the profit by $100, and that would be considered *negative margin*.

There is one more fact we need to cover about margin accounts. **Margin interest** is a tax-deductible expense. The one exception is interest expense incurred in the purchase of municipal securities. Because municipal interest income is federally tax exempt, the IRS does not allow taxpayers to deduct the margin interest expenses for municipal securities. Investors can deduct interest expenses incurred when borrowing money to purchase other securities to the extent those interest expenses do not exceed their portfolio income, which includes interest income, dividends, and all capital gains.

TYPES OF SECURITIES MARKETS

U22LO3: Contrast stock exchanges and the over-the-counter market.

After the initial offering, many stocks and bonds are bought and sold on exchanges in a two-way auction process. The major exchanges include the New York Stock Exchange (NYSE), NYSE American LLC (formerly known as the American Stock Exchange [AMEX]), the Chicago Board Options Exchange (CBOE), and the Nasdaq Stock Market. Other trades take place in the nationwide network of broker-dealers known as the over-the-counter (OTC) market.

Securities Markets

There are two terms used to describe the market for securities. The **primary market** is the market in which the proceeds of sales go to the issuer of the securities sold. The **secondary market** is where previously issued securities are bought and sold between investors. This unit will focus on secondary market trading.

Exchange Market

The **exchange market** is composed of the NYSE and other exchanges on which **listed** securities are traded. *Listed security* refers to any security listed for trading on an exchange. Each stock exchange requires corporations to meet certain criteria before it will allow their stock to be listed for trading on the exchange. To operate in the United States, an exchange must be registered with the Securities Exchange Commission as called for in the Securities Exchange Act of 1934. Under that act, the SEC has many powers including enforcement of the laws. Two specific actions that the SEC can take that might be tested are:

■ suspend trading in any nonexempt security for up to 10 days without prior notice; and

■ suspend trading on an entire exchange for up to 90 days (to do this, the SEC must give prior notification to the President of the United States).

Location

Many stock exchanges, such as the NYSE, maintain central marketplaces and trading floors. Some, such as the Nasdaq Stock Market are strictly electronic markets. At one time, there were a number of regional stock exchanges, but they have either been closed or merged into the national ones.

Pricing System

Historically, listed markets operated as *auction markets*. Floor brokers competed to execute trades at the most favorable prices. That process still exists on some exchanges

Specialist

The **specialist** maintains an orderly market and provides price continuity. He fills limit and market orders for the public and trades for his own account to either stabilize or facilitate trading when imbalances in supply and demand occur.

The specialist's chief function is to maintain a fair and orderly market in the stocks for which he is responsible. An additional function is to minimize price disparities that may occur at the opening of daily trading. He does this by buying or selling, as a dealer, stock from his own inventory only when a need for such intervention exists. Otherwise, the specialist lets public supply and demand set the stock's price.

TAKE NOTE

The term *specialist* has been replaced with designated market maker (DMM), but you should expect to still see *specialist* on your exam.

Over-the-Counter (OTC) Market

The OTC market functions as an interdealer market in which **unlisted** securities—that is, securities not listed on any exchange—trade.

In the OTC market, securities dealers across the country are connected by computer and telephone. Thousands of securities are traded OTC, including stocks, corporate bonds, and all municipal and U.S. government securities. One of the best known of the OTC markets is the OTC Bulletin Board, where stocks that don't qualify for listing on the exchanges are traded. Another is the OTC Link, which, for many years was known as the Pink Sheets because the quotes were printed on pink paper. These tend to include those stocks which are thinly traded (little trading activity) with higher than normal spreads.

Location

No central marketplace facilitates OTC trading. Trading takes place over the phone, over computer networks, and in trading rooms across the country.

Pricing System

The OTC market is an **interdealer network**. Registered market makers compete to post the best bid and ask prices. The OTC market is a negotiated market.

Market Makers

Market makers are broker-dealers who stand ready to buy and sell at least the minimum trading unit, usually 100 shares (or any larger amount they have indicated), in each stock in which they have published bid and ask quotes. Market makers, acting in a dealer (principal) capacity, sell from their inventory at their asking price and buy for their inventory at the bid price.

TAKE NOTE

The differences between the OTC and NYSE markets are summarized here.

OTC	NYSE
Securities prices determined through negotiation	Securities prices determined through auction bidding
Regulated by FINRA	Regulated by the NYSE
Traded at many locations across the country	Traded on the NYSE floor on Wall Street

Exchange = Listed securities = prices determined by auction

OTC = Unlisted securities = prices determined by negotiation

Government and municipal bonds and unlisted corporate stocks and bonds trade in the OTC market.

BROKER VS. DEALER

U22LO4: Identify the difference between functioning as a broker and acting as a dealer.

Most securities firms act as both brokers and dealers but *never* in the same transaction. Let's examine the differences between these two terms.

Brokers

When a broker-dealer acts in the capacity of a *broker*, it is said to be acting in an agency capacity. That is, the firm represents clients who wish to buy a security by finding a seller, or finding a buyer for those clients with a security to sell. For this service, they charge a commission.

Brokers do not buy shares for inventory but facilitate trades between buyers and sellers.

Dealers

When a broker-dealer acts in the capacity of a dealer, it is said to be acting as a principal in the trade. Just as with any transaction, there are always two principals; the buyer and the seller. Dealers, acting as principals, buy and sell securities for their own account. When they receive a customer order to buy a security, they sell that security out of their inventory in the same manner as an automobile dealer sells you a car off the lot. When they receive a customer order to sell, dealers buy that security for their inventory, once again, similar to an automobile dealer who buys your old clunker from you.

TEST TOPIC ALERT

Disclosure of the capacity in which the broker-dealer acted is always required on the trade confirmation.

TRADING COSTS

U22LO5: Describe the costs of trading securities.

Buying and selling securities is not without cost. As described previously, there are two ways in which broker-dealers function; as brokers or as dealers. As brokers, they are acting as their client's agents and, as is typical in any business, agents charge a commission for their service. That means, when buying a security, the commission will be added to the purchase price. Likewise, when selling a security, the commission will be deducted from the proceeds.

When selling from their inventories, dealers charge the buying customers a markup rather than a commission. When buying for their inventory, dealers charge the selling customers a markdown (they buy for less than they can sell it for—think about what happens when the auto dealer buys your used car from you and what it sells for on the lot a week later after they've cleaned it up).

TAKE NOTE

The term *principal* has several meanings in the securities industry. A broker-dealer acts as a principal in a dealer transaction. A principal of a firm is a person who acts in a supervisory capacity. *Principal* can also mean the face value of a bond or asset in a trust.

A firm cannot act as both a broker and a dealer in the same transaction.

EXAMPLE

A firm cannot make a market in a stock, mark up that stock, and then add an agency commission. If the firm acts as a broker, it may charge a commission. If it acts as a dealer, it may charge a markup or markdown. Violation of this practice is called making a hidden profit.

Broker	Dealer
Acts as an agent, transacting orders on the client's behalf	Acts as a principal, dealing in securities for its own account and at its own risk
Charges a commission	Charges a markup or markdown
Is not a market maker	Makes markets and/or takes positions (long or short) in securities
Must disclose its role and the amount of its commission to the client	Must disclose its role to the client, but not necessarily the amount or source of the markup or markdown

TAKE NOTE

An easy way to remember these relationships is to memorize the following letters.

BAC/DPP—Brokers act as **A**gents for **C**ommissions/**D**ealers act as **P**rincipals for **P**rofits.

ABCD—Agents that are **B**rokers for **C**ommissions that must be **D**isclosed.

EXAMPLE

1. When viewing several of your client's trade confirmations, you notice that a recent purchase was made of ABC stock where there was no commission indicated while a sale took place of DEF stock in which the commission listed was $55. From this information you could determine that

    I.   ABC was purchased in an agency transaction

    II. ABC was purchased in a principal transaction

    III. DEF was sold in an agency transaction

    IV. DEF was sold in a principal transaction

    A. I and III

    B. I and IV

    C. II and III

    D. II and V

    Answer: C. Whenever a trade is made without a commission indicated on the confirmation, it means that a markup or markdown was charged. That makes it a dealer or principal transaction. Commissions are always disclosed on agency transactions. Therefore, we know that ABC (II) was purchased in a principal transaction and DEF (III) was sold in an agency transaction, so the correct match is choice **C**.

BIDS, OFFERS, AND QUOTES

A **firm quote** is a market maker's current bid and offer on a security. The **current bid** is the highest price at which the dealer will buy, and the **current offer** is the lowest price at which the dealer will sell. The difference between the bid and ask is known as the **spread**. A general rule is the more active the stock, the narrower the spread. This concept plays out in our everyday life because those products that move of the shelves quickly (think about milk, eggs, and bread in the grocery store) tend to have a lower retail markup than items which move slowly, such as antiques and fine art. We have mentioned earlier that higher markups or commissions on thinly traded (not highly active) securities would generally not be in violation as long as properly disclosed.

In most cases, a market maker's quote will also include the size. That indicates the number of shares the quote is good for. For example, a quote of (45 – 45.20)(8 × 10) means the dealer is offering 1,000 shares for sale at 45.20 and is ready to buy 800 shares at 45. If not stated, the quote is firm for a single round lot (100 shares). Remember, when acting in a principal capacity, no commissions are added.

EXAMPLE

If WXYZ is quoted as 43.25 to .50, it means that the bid price (the price that a customer would receive for his shares) is $43.25, and the ask price (the price that the customer would pay to buy shares) is $43.50. The $.25 difference is the dealer's spread. Alternatively, the exam might put it like this:

1. A broker-dealer quotes a stock 42 to a half. The difference between these two numbers is known as

    A. the broker's commission

    B. the dealer's markup

    C. the profit margin

    D. the spread

    Answer: D. The dealer's quote represents the bid and the offer (ask) prices. This quote is 42 bid and 42.50 offered. The difference between these two is the spread, choice D. Markup is added to the higher price (the ask or offering price).

TEST TOPIC ALERT

If a client has U.S. Treasury bonds she wishes to sell and receives a quote of 104.22, which represents the bid price (don't select an answer choice that says "a premium"). It is a premium, but that is not as specific an answer.

TYPES OF ORDERS

U22LO6: Identify the features and uses of market, stop, limit orders and short sales.

Many types of orders are available to customers. The type will be indicated on the *order ticket*. SEC rules require preparation of order tickets before order entry. Required disclosures include:

■ the account number;

- whether the order is solicited, unsolicited, or discretionary (including time or price);
- if a sale, whether long or short;
- the terms and conditions of the order (market, limit, or stop);
- the number of shares if a stock and if a bond, aggregate par value (but not rating or current yield);
- the time of order entry (execution time and execution price will be added); and
- the name of the broker-dealer and identity of the registered individual who accepted the order or is responsible for the account.

TEST TOPIC ALERT

Two items that would not be on an order ticket are the current market price of the security and the client's name or address.

Price

Orders that restrict the price of the transaction include the following:

- **Market**—executed immediately at the market price with no restrictions
- **Limit**—limits the amount paid or received for securities
- **Stop**—becomes a market order if the stock reaches or goes through the stop price
- **Stop limit**—entered as a stop order and changed to a limit order if the stock hits or goes through the trigger price

Time

Limit orders based on time considerations include the following:

- **Day**—expires if not filled by the end of the day
- **Good till canceled (GTC)**—does not expire until filled or canceled

Size

NYSE Rule 72 defines a "block" as at least 10,000 shares or $200,000 USD, whichever is less. Thus, for stocks priced at less than $20, a 10,000-share trade can be a block, but in higher-priced stocks even a 1,000-share trade could constitute a block.

EXAMPLE

1. Which of the following types of orders does NOT restrict the price at which an order is executed?

   A. Limit

   B. Stop

   C. Market

   D. Stop limit

   Answer: C. A market order, choice **C**, does not reflect or restrict the price at which a security is executed. A limit order limits the amount to be paid or received for securities. A stop order becomes a market order if the stock reaches or goes through the stop price. A stop limit order becomes a limit order if the stock hits or goes through the trigger price.

Market Orders

A **market order** is sent immediately to the floor for execution without restrictions or limits. It is executed immediately at the current market price and has priority over all other types of orders. A market order to buy is executed at the lowest offering price available; a market order to sell is executed at the highest bid price available. Those prices are usually referred to as the *inside market* or *inside quote*. As long as the security is trading, a market order guarantees execution.

Limit Orders

In a **limit order**, a customer limits the acceptable purchase or selling price. A limit order can be executed only at the specified price or better. *Better* means lower in a buy order and higher in a sell order. If the order cannot be executed at the market, the order is left with the specialist (now called the DMM), who records the trade in the order book and executes the order if and when the market price meets the limit order price.

Risks and Disadvantages of Limit Orders

A customer who enters a limit order risks missing the chance to buy or sell, especially if the market moves away from the limit price. The market price may never go as low as the buy limit price or as high as the sell limit price.

TEST TOPIC ALERT

If any part of an order can be filled at the limit price, it is done. For example, if a day limit order to buy 400 shares at $22.45 is turned in and all that can be executed at that price or better is 200 shares before the market closes, that sale is confirmed, and the order for the balance is canceled.

Definition: Short Sales

Selling short is a technique to profit from the decline in a stock's price. The short seller initially borrows stock from a broker-dealer to sell at the market. The investor expects the stock price to decline enough to allow him to buy shares at a lower price and replace the borrowed stock at a later date. Unless the stock price declines to zero, the short seller is obligated to buy the stock and replace the borrowed shares to close the short position. Because of this borrowing, a margin deposit is required. Therefore, short sales can only take place in a margin account.

Short sales are risky because if the stock price rises instead of falls, an investor still must buy the shares to replace the borrowed stock—and a stock's price can rise without limit. Therefore, the position has unlimited risk.

Stop Orders

A **stop order**, also known as a *stop loss order*, may be entered to protect a profit or prevent a loss if the stock begins to move in the wrong direction.

The stop order becomes a market order once the stock trades at or moves through a certain price, known as the **stop price**. Stop orders for listed stocks are usually left with and executed by the specialist (DMM).

A trade at or through (lower in the case of a sell stop; higher in the case of a buy stop) the stop price *triggers* the order, which then becomes a market order. As a market order, there is no assurance of any specific price. The order may wind up being executed at, above, or below the stop price.

A stop order takes two trades to execute:

- **Trigger**—the trigger transaction at or through the stop price activates the trade
- **Execution**—the stop order becomes a market order and is executed at the market price, completing the trade

Stop Limit Order

A stop limit order is a stop order that, once triggered, becomes a limit order instead of a market order.

Buy Stop Order

A **buy stop order** protects a profit or limits a loss in a short stock position. The buy stop is entered at a price above the current market and is triggered when the market price touches or goes through the buy stop price.

EXAMPLE

A customer has shorted 1,000 shares of XYZ stock at $55 with the expectation that the stock's price will decline. As we know, the investor will lose if the price rises and, because there is no limit on the upside, the potential loss is unlimited. As a form of protecting against extreme loss, the customer enters a buy stop order for 1,000 shares at $60. That way, if the price begins to rise, once it reaches (or goes above) 60, a market order will be entered, and, once the purchase is confirmed, the stock will be used to close the short position. Yes, it will be at a loss, but that is why these are called "stop loss" orders; they keep you from losing any more than you specify.

Sell Stop Order

A **sell stop order** protects a profit or limits a loss in a long stock position and is entered at a price below the current market.

EXAMPLE

Continuing the "stop-loss" theme, investors who own a stock will lose money if the price declines below the purchase price. These investors are hoping for a rising market but, just in case, to protect themselves, they can enter a sell stop order. A customer has purchased 1,000 shares of ABC stock at $55 with the expectation that the stock's price will rise. Unlike the short sale, the loss is not unlimited (the stock's price cannot fall below zero), but investors don't want to lose all of their investment. So, a sell stop order for 1,000 shares is entered *below* the current market at $50. As long as the stock's price goes up, they're making money, but, should it reach 50 or less, the order is triggered and a market order is automatically entered stopping the loss.

TAKE NOTE

In either of these examples, a stop limit order could have been turned in and the story would be the same except that, upon being triggered, a limit order at the limit price would be entered instead of a market order.

EXAMPLE

An order that reads, "sell 100 COD at 52 stop, 51.50 limit," means that the stop will be activated at or below 52. Because a 51.50 limit applies, the order to sell cannot be executed below 51.50.

TAKE NOTE

The uses of buy and sell stop orders are summarized here.

Buy Stop Orders (might be called stop-buy on the exam)

- Protect against loss in a short stock position

- Protect a gain from a short stock position

- Establish a long position when a breakout occurs above the line of resistance (i.e., stock prices rise above historic high levels)

Sell Stop Orders (might be called stop-sell on the exam)

- Protect against loss in a long stock position

- Protect a gain from a long stock position

- Establish a short position when a breakout occurs below the line of support (i.e., stock prices decline below low level)

Mechanics of a Stop Order

As stated previously, it takes more than one trade for a stop order to be executed. The first of those, the trigger, occurs whenever the subject security trades at or through the stop price. In the case of a buy stop order, *through* means *at a higher price*. In the case of a sell stop order, *through* means *at a lower price*.

Then, once the order has been triggered, unless it is a stop limit order, the next price in the market is the one at which the trade is executed. It will probably be easier to follow if we display an example.

EXAMPLE

A client enters a buy stop order for 100 shares of XYZ at 40. Trades then occur at 38, 39, 39.90, 40.05, 40.10, and 39.78. What price did the client pay for the stock? The order will be triggered as soon as the price gets to 40 or higher. That would be the trade at 40.05. At that time, a market order is entered and the client pays the next price (which could be more or less than 40). In this case, the next price is 40.10 and that is the price per share paid by the client (we're ignoring any commissions).

How is this different for a stop limit order? If we change the previous example to make the order, buy stop at 40, limit 40, then the client is stating that once the order has been triggered, enter a limit order, and do not pay any more than 40 for the stock. Once again, the order is triggered with the trade at 40.05, but now, because a limit order has been placed, we can't buy on the next trade—40.10 is too high. However, the following trade at 39.78 allows us to meet the client's limit of paying no more than 40 for the stock.

Let's try one in test format:

1. A client order is received with the following instructions: Buy stop 100 shares ABC at 34, limit 34.20. After the order is submitted, trades occur at 33, 33.90, 34.10, 33.85, 34.05, and 34.25. More than likely, the client paid

    A. 33.85

    B. 34.05

    C. 34.10

    D. 34.25

    Answer: A. This is two orders in one. The first does not become triggered until the price gets as high at 34. That happens at 34.10. Then, a buy stop order at 34.20 is entered (pay 34.20 or less) and the trade at 33.85, choice **A**, meets that requirement.

TEST TOPIC ALERT

There is a danger in using stop orders in that once they are triggered, the marketplace receives an increase of sell orders in a falling market and buy orders in a rising market. This can have the tendency to accelerate the direction of the market; sell stops in a bearish market, buy stops in a bullish one.

TAKE NOTE

An interesting legal question arises when an agent becomes aware of material nonpublic information (MNPI) after a stop order is triggered, but prior to execution. Unless the agent has reason to suspect that the client was acting on that information, the order can proceed as normal because it was received prior to the agent becoming aware of the information.

Market Manipulation Definitions

In Part 1, Unit 7, we discussed the prohibitions against market manipulation. Here are some additional cases that will make more sense now.

Capping

This is the act of entering sell orders in a stock for the purpose of keeping the stock from rising above the sale price when one is short the stock. If successful, the stock will stay below the strike price and the short position will be profitable. The opposite of this is **supporting** where purchase orders are entered in an attempt to keep the price of a stock from falling when one has a long position.

Pegging

This is a generic term that applies to any activity intended to keep the price of a stock from moving. This can involve entering either buy or sell orders or both. For example, a short straddle writer will profit most if the stock price and strike prices of the position are the same at expiration—that is, the short options are right at-the-money.

HIGH FREQUENCY TRADING (HFT)

U22LO7: Describe high-frequency trading (HFT) and dark pools.

Over the past 10 years, high-frequency trading (HFT) has gone from a small, niche strategy in financial markets to the dominant form of trading. It currently accounts for well over half of trading volume in U.S. equity markets, 40% in European equity markets, and is quickly growing in Asian, fixed-income, commodity, foreign exchange, and nearly every other market. Although a precise definition of HFT does not exist, it is generally classified as autonomous computerized trading that seeks quick profits using high-speed connections to financial exchanges. The objective of HFT is to take advantage of minute discrepancies in prices, and trade on them quickly and in huge quantities. As computers get more technically advanced, trading practices have increased in size and algorithms have become more sophisticated. The trades are done at close to the speed of light. In fact, HFT firms have moved their servers to be near an exchange computer to further increase trading speeds.

Regulators across the globe are spending considerable effort deciding if and how to regulate HFT. On the one hand, HFT appears to make markets more efficient. Algorithmic trading in general, and HFT specifically, increases the accuracy of prices and lowers transaction costs. On the other hand, HFT appears to make the financial system as a whole more fragile. The rapid fall and subsequent rise in prices that occurred in U.S. markets on May 6, 2010 (known as the Flash Crash, when the Dow Jones Industrial Average plunged about 1,000 point in a matter of minutes), was, in part, due to HFT. Because HFT firms do not openly disclose their trading activities, it has so far been unclear how and why HFT produces these outcomes; a circumstance that has greatly increased the controversy surrounding its existence.

A typical objective of high-frequency traders is to identify and capture minute price discrepancies present in the market. They do so with no human intervention, using computers to automatically capture and read market data in real-time, transmit thousands of order messages per second to an exchange, and execute, cancel, or replace orders based on new information on prices or demand. In most cases, the trades are executed before individual investors know the quotes of prices or that the trades happened at all. For example, a computer recognizes when one exchange quotes an ask price of one cent more than the quote on another exchange. This computer then trades in extraordinarily large volumes on this information, taking advantage of the arbitrage opportunity in a split second. Before individual and other investors who do not possess the same sophisticated technology realize, the one-cent spread between the two exchanges is erased and the stock price trades at the same level.

Benefits of HFT

- Increased liquidity in the markets, especially for more active stocks
- Market efficiency—price differences are arbitraged away leading to narrower spreads
- Reduced costs, especially for institutional purchasers such as mutual funds

Negatives of HFT

■ Market manipulation—with the huge volume that can be generated, HFT traders entering phony trades that are later canceled can prompt market activity that would not have happened had these HFT traders not manipulated the market to their advantage

■ Hurts small investors because they do not have access to the same trading information anywhere near as soon as the HFT traders

■ "Snowballing" effect of HFT—for years, one of the problems with stop orders was the acceleration of a downward move when sell stop orders were triggered. With HFT, the volume is so much greater that this movement, as we saw in the Flash Crash, is magnified.

TAKE NOTE

HFTs rely on very low latency for their algorithmic trading schemes. Low latency is just a fancy way of saying quick trading. It's not unusual nowadays to have a DMA (direct market access) customer enter and have executed 5,000 or 6,000 orders or more in one second. Trades are being executed and reported in microseconds. HFT customers are the most likely customers to be provided by their broker-dealer with DMA, which bypasses the firm's trading desk. This kind of DMA trading is called low or no-touch. No-touch doesn't mean no obligation; the broker-dealers still have an obligation to monitor their DMA customer's behavior. No broker-dealer can throw its hands up and say to the regulators, "We didn't know what they were doing."

DARK POOLS

Dark pools, sometimes referred to as dark pools of liquidity or simply dark liquidity, is trading volume that occurs or liquidity that is not openly available to the public. The bulk of this volume represents trades engaged in by institutional traders and trading desks away from the exchange markets. Generally, these are large volume transactions that occur on crossing networks or alternative trading systems that match buy and sell orders electronically for execution without routing the order to an exchange or other market where quote, last sale price, and volume information is displayed.

Institutional trading desks that choose to use dark pools are able to execute large block orders without impacting public quotes or price, or revealing their investment strategy regarding any of their holding accumulations or divestitures. Additionally, orders can be placed anonymously so that the identity of the entity placing the order is unknown to the general investing public along with the volume and price for the transaction. The concern with dark pools is that some market participants are left disadvantaged because they cannot see the trades, volume, or prices agreed upon within the pools, and thus market transparency is darkened.

Dark pools account for about 17% of the trading volume in the U.S. stock market.

EXAMPLE

1. A dark pool would most likely be used by

    A. a market manipulator

    B. a high-frequency trader

    C. an institution

    D. a retail investor

    Answer: C. Dark pools are favored by institutions, choice **C**, because of the anonymity it gives to their trading.

UNIT 23

Performance Measures

Ultimately, the judge of the value of an investment adviser is the performance of the client's account. There are a number of different ways to measure the performance and one must always keep in mind that it is how well the account meets the investor's objectives that counts. For example, an account that appreciated 10% in one year while distributing an income return of 1% is not meeting the goals of a client needing current income.

The Series 65 exam will include four questions on the material presented in this unit.

LEARNING OBJECTIVES

When you have completed this unit, you will be able to accomplish the following.

U23LO1: Define the difference between current yield, yield to maturity and yield to call.
U23LO2: Compute the investment return measurements most commonly found on the exam.
U23LO3: Match the appropriate benchmarks for various portfolios.

REVIEW OF BOND YIELDS

U23LO1: Define the difference between current yield, yield to maturity and yield to call.

Referring to the short example given in the introduction to this unit, for income oriented investors, probably the most important performance measurement is yield. In Part 3, Unit 13, we discussed the various types of yield on debt securities, so we'll just mention a few highlights here.

Current Yield

The current yield on any investment, debt or equity, is simply the annual income stream (interest or dividends) divided by the current market price. In the case of a debt security, the annual interest is always fixed as a percentage of the par value and doesn't fluctuate when the market price of the security changes. That means that a bond with a 5% coupon (interest) rate will always be paying $50 per year, divided into two semiannual payments of $25. If the market price of that bond is currently 80 ($800), the current yield (also called current return) is 6.25% (50 divided by 800). If the current market price of the bond is 125 ($1,250), the current yield is 4% (50 divided by 1,250). The arithmetic is the same when computing the current yield on a stock.

EXAMPLE

When asking for the current yield on a stock, the question will usually give you the quarterly dividend rate. Be sure to multiply that by 4 to arrive at the annual dividend payment. For example: ABC common stock's most recently quarterly dividend was $.36 per share. ABC expects to keep the dividend payments at that level. If ABC common stock has a current market value of $32 per share, the current return is? The first choice will probably be 1.1% which is incorrect because that is based on a single dividend. You must multiply the $.36 by 4 to arrive at the annual dividend of $1.44. Then, divide that by the current market price of $32 and the correct answer is 4.5%

Yield to Maturity

Yield to maturity would only apply to a debt security because they have a loan principal that is to be paid back at some future date (the maturity date). It is often referred to as the true yield because it is the most accurate reflection of the actual return to be received by the investor. Unlike our work in a previous unit, here you need merely understand the concept.

TEST TOPIC ALERT

The yield to maturity (YTM) of a bond is actually the bond's internal rate of return (IRR) because it represents the discount rate that equates to the discounted value of the bond's future cash flows to its current price.

Yield to call (YTC) is a subset of YTM in that, instead of using the maturity date, the call date is used to calculate the return. In almost cases, bonds are called when interest rates have fallen and the issuer can now borrow at a lower rate. Holders of those bonds with higher coupons do not want them taken away (called). The key facts to remember are:

- If the bond is selling at a premium, the YTC will be lower than the YTM, CY, and NY
- If the bond is selling at a discount, the YTC will be higher than the YTM, CY, and NY

INVESTMENT RETURN MEASUREMENTS

U23LO2: Compute the investment return measurements most commonly found on the exam.

There will probably be two computations on your exam dealing with different types of returns. We'll cover all of them and indicate which are the most (and least) likely to appear on your test.

TAKE NOTE

As you review these quantitative evaluation measurements, know that the exam is more concerned with the ability to identify what they measure than how to perform the calculation. One or two questions might require a relatively simple calculation on current yield, after-tax return/yield, inflation-adjusted return, or total return.

Total Return

Total return includes the income from dividends or interest plus any capital appreciation (or less any capital depreciation) over a given time period, usually one year. As such, total return is considered to be the best measure of how a security has performed for an investor.

EXAMPLE

A common stock purchased for $20 with an annual dividend of $1 is sold after one year for $24. The total return on the investment is $5: $1 in dividends plus $4 in capital appreciation. The total return, then, is 25% ($5 / $20 = 25%).

TEST TOPIC ALERT

The exam may require you to know how to calculate total return. Keep in mind that the total annual return on an investment includes income and capital appreciation. In the case of bonds held to maturity, this is the YTM. Otherwise, it is the coupon income plus any appreciation or less any price depreciation. In the case of stocks, one would use the dividend income plus or minus the appreciation or depreciation.

Mutual Fund Returns

Unlike other securities, an investor's total return from a mutual fund investment may include, in addition to income distributions in the form of dividends, distribution of realized capital gains. They are all added together, along with unrealized appreciation (or depreciation) to compute the total return.

Mutual funds must separate total return from current return. The SEC requires that **current return calculations** be based only on income distributions for the past 12 months divided by the current per-share price: annual dividend / current price = current yield.

EXAMPLE

1. The KAPCO Income Fund has a current public offering price of $10.50 and a NAV per share of $10.00. During the past 12 months, the fund has made four quarterly distributions from net investment income of $.15 and one distribution from capital gains in the amount of $.25. The fund's current yield would be?

   A. 1.1%

   B. 1.5%

   C. 5.7%

   D. 6.0%

   Answer: C. It is computed by dividing the annual income (4 × $.15 = $.60) by the POP (not the NAV) of $10.50. Only the dividends are used for current yield.

Holding Period Return

The length of time an investor owns an investment is called the **holding period**. The return for that period is called the **holding period return (HPR)**. HPR is the total return, income plus capital appreciation, of an investment over a specified period, the holding period. It is essentially the same as total return, but, whereas total return is usually computed on an annual basis, HPR can be for any period.

EXAMPLE

An investment purchased for $100 and sold three years later for $120 ($20 capital appreciation) after paying a total of $30 ($10 per year) in dividends has a HPR of 50% ($120 + $30 = $150). The total gain is $150 − $100 = $50. A $50 return on a $100 investment is 50% ($50 / $100 = 50%).

TAKE NOTE

HPR is not an annualized return. It is the percentage return over a defined period.

TEST TOPIC ALERT

We tend to focus on looking at the total return and holding period return for equities, but it is also a valid measurement for bond returns. In this case, we combine the interest received and any appreciation or depreciation. However, there is one other factor that is sometimes considered: the rate at which the coupons are reinvested. If we assume the bondholder will keep the bond until maturity date, in a period of rising interest rates, the bondholder should be able to reinvest the coupons at a higher rate than the coupon, thus causing the holding period return to exceed the yield to maturity. If, on the other hand, interest rates are falling, the coupons will only be able to be reinvested at a lower rate causing a holding period return that is less than the bond's YTM.

Annualized Return

Annualized return is the return an investor would have received had he held an investment for one year. Annualized return is determined by multiplying the actual return by an **annualization factor**. The annualization factor is the number of months in the year divided by the number of months an investment is held.

EXAMPLE

An investor receives $5 on a $100 investment held for six months. The annualized return is determined by multiplying the 5% return by the annualization factor of 2 (12 months / 6 months = 2) for an annualized return of 10%. Another investor has a capital gain of 30% from an investment held for 18 months. The annualized return is 20%, calculated as follows: 30 × (12 / 18) = 20.

TAKE NOTE

The formula we've shown you is only approximate (the computation has never been asked on the exam). In reality, because of compounding, the annualized return would actually be a bit different.

Inflation-Adjusted Return (Real Return)

Because inflation reduces the buying power of a dollar, investment performance measurements are often adjusted to provide a measure of the buying power earned from a given investment. Returns that have been adjusted for inflation are called **real rates of return**. This is a frequently required computation on the exam.

To determine the inflation-adjusted rate of return of debt security, reduce its nominal return by the inflation rate as reflected in the consumer price index (CPI).

To determine the inflation-adjusted rate of return of an equity security, reduce the **total return** (as taught previously), by the inflation rate as reflected in the CPI.

EXAMPLE

A bond with an 8% coupon has a nominal return of 8%. If inflation (as measured by the CPI) is 3%, then the inflation-adjusted return of the bond investment is 8% − 3%, or 5%.

Let's revisit the total return example from a couple of pages ago:

EXAMPLE

A common stock purchased for $20 with an annual dividend of $1 is sold after one year for $24. The total return on the investment is $5: $1 in dividends plus $4 in capital appreciation. The total return, then, is 25% ($5 / $20 = 25%). If the question asked for the "real rate of return" and told you that the CPI increase for the period was 6%, you would subtract that from the 25% total return to arrive at an inflation-adjusted return of 19%.

EXAMPLE

For fixed-income investors, inflation and taxes reduce the buying power of their dollars. For an investor in the 25% tax bracket in a 2.5% inflationary environment, an investment that yields 10% before taxes provides the investor with a 5% inflation-adjusted, after-tax return. To calculate the 5% after-tax inflation-adjusted return, first determine the after-tax return. In this case, 10% less 25% for taxes results in a 7.5% after-tax return.

The easiest was to compute the real rate of return is to reduce the return by the amount of inflation during the period. In this case, 7.5% less 2.5% inflation results in a 5% after-tax inflation-adjusted return. Even though a calculation of this type might not be on your exam, you need to understand the concept that your final returns are reduced by both taxes and inflation.

TEST TOPIC ALERT

The exam will require you to know how to calculate the approximate inflation-adjusted return by merely subtracting the CPI from the total return. What we've shown you is only an approximation—the correct formula is the sum of one plus the **nominal rate** divided by the sum of one plus the **inflation rate** which then is subtracted by one, but we've never heard of that being asked on the exam.

After-Tax Return/Yield

Capital gains and income are generally taxable; thus, taxes reduce the return of an investment. The **after-tax return**, also known as the **adjusted return**, is determined by reducing the investment's return by the client's tax rate.

EXAMPLE

The after-tax return of an investment that yields 10% for an investor in the 25% tax bracket is calculated by multiplying the return by (1 − 0.25), or 0.75. The investor retains 75% of the 10% yield, for a 7.5% after-tax return. Likewise, an investment that returns 45% over three years provides an after-tax return of 33.75% (0.75 × 45%).

The importance of after-tax return is realizing that any investor's return is going to be reduced by the effects of taxation whether it is the favorable capital gains tax or the higher ordinary income rate. That is the beauty of programs such as the Roth IRA or Section 529 Plan where it is possible to have totally tax-free returns. Remember, even though the interest on a municipal bond may be tax free, any capital gains are not.

Probable Return

Unlike historical or actual rates of returns, **probable returns** are estimates of the likely returns an investment may yield. To determine the probable return of an investment, the adviser assigns a probability to each return that the investment is likely to earn and then multiplies that return by the probability of it occurring. The sum of those probable returns is the expected return for that investment. The formula is as follows: expected or probable return = (probability of return #1 × possible return #1) + (probability of return #2 × possible return #2).

EXAMPLE

The probable (expected) return of an investment with a 30% probability of returning 15% and a 70% chance of returning 10% has a total expected return of 11.5%, calculated as follows: (0.30 × 15% = 4.5%) + (0.70 × 10% = 7.0%), or 4.5% + 7.0% = 11.5%.

In effect, this return reflects the arithmetic (mean) return of the portfolio. When one constructs a portfolio, there are usually securities with different grades of risk and, hence, different expectations of reward. Investors view the portfolio as a whole, looking to maximize for return for each level of risk. This overall view, or mean, of the entire portfolio is the expected or probable return of the portfolio.

TEST TOPIC ALERT

Don't be surprised to get a question similar to our previous example, but, with one of the possibilities being a negative. Suppose our example had said there was a 30% probability of returning 15%, a 40% chance of returning 10%, and a 30% chance of losing 8%. The expected return would be (0.30 × 15% = 4.5%) + (0.40 × 10% = 4.0%) + (0.30 × −8% = −2.4%) for a total of 6.1% expected return.

Risk-Adjusted Return (Sharpe Ratio)

Securities practitioners have developed many measures to quantify the risk characteristics of a portfolio. One such measure that may show up on the exam is called the **Sharpe ratio** or **Sharpe index**. The ratio is calculated by subtracting the risk-free rate (e.g., the 91-day Treasury bill rate) from the overall return of the portfolio. This result, which is the portfolio's risk premium, is then divided by the standard deviation of the portfolio. This ratio measures the amount of return per unit of risk taken. The higher the ratio, the better or more return per unit of risk taken.

TEST TOPIC ALERT

The Sharpe ratio measures risk-adjusted return.

TEST TOPIC ALERT

You must know that the three components of the Sharpe ratio are:

- the actual return minus;
- the risk-free rate (the 91-day T bill rate) divided by,
- the standard deviation.

Beta is not a part of this ratio.

Risk Premium

It should be clear that to have a positive Sharpe ratio, our actual return on an investment must exceed the risk-free return. Therefore, any investor would surely expect to achieve that higher return or the investment would not be made. This return is known as the risk premium.

The required rate of return on *any* investment is a combination of the risk-free rate plus a risk premium. For equity investments, the risk premium can be determined by using the capital asset pricing model (CAPM) discussed in Unit 20.

Internal Rate of Return (IRR)

IRR has been discussed previously in Unit 10. We're just going to list a couple of the points that are important for the exam:

■ IRR is the preferred method of measuring the return on a DPP;

■ IRR takes into consideration the time value of money; and

■ IRR is the way the yield to maturity of a bond is computed.

Time-Weighted Returns

Although time-weighted returns and dollar-weighted returns are both methods of determining a rate of return, they have very different purposes. A **time-weighted return** is determined without regard to any subsequent cash flows of the investor. As such, it measures the performance of the investment over a period (and not of the investor as in a dollar-weighted approach). Most returns reported on mutual funds are time-weighted because the portfolio manager does not have any control over the future cash flows to the fund with respect to investor dollars.

Dollar-Weighted Returns

In contrast, a **dollar-weighted return** considers subsequent contributions to and withdrawals from an investment, including sales of, for example, stock. As a result, the dollar-weighted approach focuses on the return of the investor (not the investment, as in the time-weighted approach) over a period, and usually results in a rate of return different than the time-weighted method.

Portfolio A

Period	Investor Deposits or Withdrawals	Beginning of Period Value	End of Period Value	Periodic Rate of Return
0	$1,000	$1,000	$1,200	20.00%
1	($400)	$800	$700	−12.50%
2	$300	$1,000	$1,400	40.00%
3	($200)	$1,200	$1,000	−16.67%
4	($1,000)	—	—	—
DWR = 8.2311%			TWR = 5.2034%	

Portfolio B

Period	Investor Deposits or Withdrawals	Beginning of Period Value	End of Period Value	Periodic Rate of Return
0	$1,000	$1,000	$1,200	20.00%
1	$400	$1,600	$1,400	−12.50%
2	($400)	$1,000	$1,400	40.00%
3	$400	$1,800	$1,500	−16.67%
4	($1,500)	—	—	—
DWR = 2.0245%			TWR = 5.2034%	

TEST TOPIC ALERT

The dollar-weighted return reflects the internal rate of return (IRR); the time-weighted return does not.

EXAMPLE

1. If you wanted to evaluate the performance of a portfolio manager, you would calculate the portfolio's

   A. dollar-weighted return

   B. holding period return

   C. portfolio return

   D. time-weighted return

   Answer: D. Because portfolio managers have no control over the deposits and withdrawals made by clients, the time-weighted return (choice **D**), is a more appropriate measure of performance.

PORTFOLIO BENCHMARKS

U23LO3: Match the appropriate benchmarks for various portfolios.

Tens of thousands of stocks trade in the stock markets. Stock indexes, such as the S&P 500 or the Utility Index, are smaller groups of stocks that serve as a benchmark for measuring the performance of the overall market or sectors of the market.

Indexes are generally weighted for the capitalization (number of outstanding shares times the market price per share) of the companies included. Therefore, a large company's stock price changes will have a greater effect on the index. Indexes are often used as benchmark portfolios against which managed portfolios are measured to gauge the performance, or added value, of the fund manager. In addition, index mutual funds and ETFs will invest in the securities that compose an index to specifically mirror the index's performance. Following is a listing of indexes or averages that may appear on the exam.

TEST TOPIC ALERT

The exam will want you to know which index serves as the benchmark for which type of portfolio:

- Large Cap—S&P 500
- Mid Cap—S&P 400
- Small Cap—Russell 2000
- International Stocks—EAFE

Dow Jones Industrial Average

The best known of all of the market indexes are those published by Dow Jones & Company. There are probably two reasons why the Dow Jones Industrial Average (DJIA) is so well known: first, because the 30 industrial stocks are among the 30 best-known corporations in the world and second (and some would say more important), the Dow Jones & Company also publishes *The Wall Street Journal*, the nation's leading financial newspaper. Because it is price weighted, the Dow Jones is truly an average. Originally it was computed by adding together the prices of one share for each of the 30 different companies and then dividing by 30. That had to be changed as soon as the first one of those 30 companies had a 2:1 stock split. Because a stock split will cause the market price of the stock to drop—that is, the average would be distorted by continuing to divide the 30 current market prices by 30—an adjustment had to be made to the 30 (called the divisor). Over the years, stock splits and other distributions have caused that original divisor of 30 to be adjusted. There are three other Dow Jones Averages: the 20 transportations, the 15 utilities, and the composite of all 65. On November 1, 1999, history was made when non-NYSE stocks were included in the DJIA for the first time. Added to the average were Microsoft and Intel, which are both listed on Nasdaq. The most recent addition (as of the date of this writing) was Walgreens, which replaced General Electric, an original member back in 1896.

Standard & Poor's 500

The composition of the Standard & Poor's 500 (S&P 500) Composite Index includes four main groups of securities: 400 industrials, 20 transportation companies, 40 public utilities, and 40 financial institutions. The S&P 500 is a cap-weighted index using a base period of 1941–1943 equal to 10. Although most of the stocks in the S&P 500 are listed on the NYSE, many of the highest priced issues—Google, Amazon, and Bookings Holdings (formerly known as Priceline)—are traded on the Nasdaq Stock Market.

New York Stock Exchange (NYSE) Index

The NYSE publishes a composite index that covers all of the common stocks listed on the NYSE, more than 3,000 different companies. This index provides the most comprehensive measure of market activity on the NYSE. The NYSE index is cap weighted, similar to the S&P 500, but the base is December 31, 1965, and the index for the base is 50.

Nasdaq Composite Index

The OTC market is represented by the Nasdaq Composite Index, which covers more than 3,000 OTC companies. The Nasdaq Composite Index is calculated in a manner similar to those used for the S&P and NYSE indexes, with a base period of February 5, 1971, and an index number of 100. These indexes, their subgroups, and several other popular indexes are quoted daily in *The Wall Street Journal.* As with the others (except for the Dow Jones), this is also a cap-weighted index.

Russell 2000 Index

The Russell 2000 index measures the performance of the small-cap segment of the U.S. equity universe. It includes approximately 2,000 of the smallest securities based upon their market capitalization (minimum market cap of $300 million). Like most of the others, it is market-cap weighted with the median market cap being something approximating $600 million.

EAFE

The EAFE, sometimes referred to as the MSCI EAFE (it was developed by Morgan Stanley Capital International), is an index of foreign stocks. The index is market capitalization weighted. The EAFE acronym stands for Europe, Australasia, and Far East.

The index includes a selection of stocks from 21 developed countries outside of the U.S. and Canada. The index has been calculated since the end of 1969 making it the oldest truly international stock index. It is probably the most common benchmark for foreign stock funds.

The Wilshire 5000

The Wilshire 5000 Total Market Index^{SM} measures the performance of all U.S. equity securities with readily available price data. This is another market or cap-weighted index that, when it was initially created in 1974, did contain approximately 5,000 issues. Now, as of December 31, 2017, the index contained only 3,492 components.

TEST TOPIC ALERT

If you are asked to identify the index that reflects the broadest coverage of the U.S. stock markets, it is the Wilshire 5000.

EXAMPLE

1. Which of the following is a price-weighted average?

   A. Dow Jones Industrial Average

   B. MSCI EAFE

   C. Russell 2000

   D. S&P 500

   Answer: A. The only major benchmark that is price-weighted is the Dow Jones, choice **A**. All of the others are market-cap weighted.

UNIT 24

Retirement Plans Including ERISA Issues and Educational Funding Programs

Retirement plans allow investors to accumulate resources to fund their retirement. Individuals accomplish this through business-sponsored retirement plans, personal plans, or individual and corporate retirement plans. To encourage Americans to save for retirement, Congress has passed legislation that allows investors to invest in certain retirement plans on a tax-deductible and/or tax-deferred basis.

Throughout this unit, we give you the contribution limits for all plans described that are current for those filing 2019 tax returns. It is highly unlikely that any of those numbers, other than perhaps the IRA contribution limit, will be asked on the exam. That new limit is $6,000 ($7,000 for those age 50 and older) and we will update our Qbank questions if we learn that the new limits are appearing on the exam. Therefore, you should consider these as included for reference purposes, not for testing. The exam will include approximately seven questions on the material presented in this unit.

LEARNING OBJECTIVES

When you have completed this unit, you will be able to accomplish the following.

U24LO1: Recall the features of traditional, Roth, and simplified employee pension plan individual retirement accounts.

U24LO2: Differentiate between the different types of employer-sponsored qualified retirement plans.

U24LO3: Contrast qualified and nonqualified retirement plans.

U24LO4: Identify the tax treatment of distributions from qualified plans.

U24LO5: Identify the purpose of the Employee Retirement Income Security Act of 1974 and its primary features including the fiduciary obligations under the Uniform Prudent Investor Act.

U24LO6: Compare the differences between the two major types of education funding programs.

U24LO7: Contrast UGMA and UTMA accounts.

U24LO8: Recall when health-savings accounts (HSAs) may be used.

INTRODUCTORY NOTE

U24LO1: Recall the features of traditional, Roth, and simplified employee pension plan individual retirement accounts.

As with so much in this course, there are similar terms with sometimes dissimilar meanings. Here is a useful list of terms used in the discussion of retirement plans:

Tax Deferred

Simply, income tax is put off (deferred) to a later time. In most retirement plans, tax on the amount of the contribution is usually deferred until withdrawal. Tax on the earnings is always deferred until withdrawal.

Qualified Plan

An employer-sponsored plan, such as a pension, 401(k), 403(b), where the contributions are made with pretax dollars and earnings in the account grow without any tax (tax deferred) until the funds are withdrawn.

Qualified

This term by itself means that contributions are made with pretax dollars and earnings in the account are tax deferred until the funds are withdrawn. This can apply to either a qualified plan or an IRA.

Nonqualified

An employer-sponsored plan, such as a deferred compensation plan, where there are no tax advantages other than that the pay is not received until sometime later when the individual should be in a lower tax bracket. Another advantage is that the employer can discriminate between employees. The term can also apply to an annuity purchased on an individual basis outside of a retirement plan as described in Unit 15.

Deductible Contribution

The contribution made by the individual, whether an employee contribution to a qualified plan such as a 401(k) plan, or by any individual to an IRA. This means the amount contributed is pretax or otherwise deductible on the tax return

Nondeductible Contribution

A contribution to a qualified plan or an IRA which is made with after-tax dollars. The funds do grow tax deferred, but there is no tax benefit derived from the contribution.

> **TAKE NOTE**
>
> Although *individual retirement arrangements* is the technical IRS term, (not tested), because everyone refers to these as individual retirement accounts (IRAs), we're going to use the common phrase to avoid confusion.

Individual retirement accounts (IRAs) were created to encourage people to save for their retirement. Most individuals with earned income (see U21LO2) may open and contribute to an IRA. Three types of IRAs are available, with different contribution, tax, and distribution characteristics: traditional IRAs, Roth IRAs, and simplified employee pension plan (SEP) IRAs.

IRAs are not to be confused with qualified plans or nonqualified plans used by businesses. Later in this unit we will cover topics such as pension plans, 401(k) plans, and deferred compensation plans. At this point, keep in mind that a qualified plan is employer sponsored and meets the IRS requirements for the contributions to the plan to be tax deductible and the earnings to grow tax deferred. Nonqualified plans do not enjoy most of the tax benefits of qualified plans.

TAKE NOTE

Although we may include some actual contribution limits, it is unlikely that you will have to know any other than the IRA and Coverdell numbers. The Coverdell numbers have not changed, but the IRA contribution is up to $6,000 for 2019.

TRADITIONAL IRAs

The first of the IRAs we'll cover is generally referred to as the traditional IRA, although there is no such term in the IRS regulations. This was the first IRA and as others have been introduced, this first one acquired its name. A **traditional IRA** allows a maximum *tax-deductible* annual contribution of the lesser of $6,000 per individual or $12,000 per couple, or 100% of taxable compensation for the taxable year 2019. The income and capital gains earned in the account are tax deferred until the funds are withdrawn.

Compensation for IRA Purposes

For purposes of contributing to an IRA, the IRS considers the following to be compensation:

- Wages, salaries, and tips
- Commissions and bonuses
- Self-employment income
- Alimony from pre-2019 divorce decrees
- Nontaxable combat pay

Not Compensation for IRA Purposes

For purposes of contributing to an IRA, the IRS does not consider the following to be compensation:

- Capital gains
- Interest and dividend income
- Pension or annuity income
- Child support
- Passive income from DPPs
- Alimony from post-December 31, 2018, divorces

Catch-Up Contributions for Older IRA Owners

The **Economic Growth and Tax Relief Reconciliation Act of 2001**, **(EGTRRA)**, was the source of the legislation permitting certain individuals to make additional contributions to their IRAs. Individuals aged 50 and older are allowed to make **catch-up contributions** to their IRAs above the scheduled maximum annual contribution limit, which will enable them to save more for retirement. These catch-up payments can go either to a traditional IRA or to a Roth IRA.

Year	Additional Catch-Up Amount Allowed
2006+	$1,000

TEST TOPIC ALERT

The exam may want you to know that EGTRRA is responsible for the catch-up provisions.

Any taxpayer younger than age 70½ who reports earned income for a given tax year may contribute to a traditional IRA. If one spouse has little or no earned income and a joint tax return is filed, a spousal IRA may be opened for that person and the contribution limits are the same as for any other IRA.

EXAMPLE

1. One member of a married couple in their 30s earns an annual salary of $45,000 while the other earns $2,000 annual from a home-based business. If they file a joint tax return, their maximum IRA contribution for the year is

   A. $6,000

   B. $8,000

   C. $12,000

   D. $14,000

   Answer: C. When one spouse's annual earnings are less than $6,000, the spousal IRA benefit permits that spouse to contribute the maximum as long as a joint return is filed showing combined income of at least $12,000. In this case, their income exceeds that, so they can each have an IRA with a contribution of $6,000 making for a total of $12,000 (choice **C**). Please note that when using the spousal IRA, the higher earning spouse cannot have more than the maximum contributed to their account (currently $6,000). One can't look at this and say the couple has $12,000 to be split however they wish. If this question had stated the couple was in their 50s, then, because of the catch-up provision, $14,000 would have been the correct choice.

IRA contributions for a specific taxable year may be made anytime from January 1 of that year through the required filing date of that year's return, (generally April 15 of the next year, unless the 15th falls on a holiday or weekend). If the individual obtains a filing extension, the deadline is still April 15.

TEST TOPIC ALERT

The exam may try to trick you into thinking that you can make a contribution later than April 15 if you have received an extension to file your taxes. You can't! You should know that an extension does not give you more time to **pay** your taxes, it only extends the time that you have to **file** your return.

Excess Contributions

Annual IRA contributions exceeding the maximum allowed are subject to a 6% penalty tax if the excess is not removed by the time the taxpayer files a tax return, but no later than April 15.

ROTH IRAs

Much of what has been stated about the traditional IRA applies to the Roth IRA—what is important are the differences. The most significant difference relates to the taxation of contributions and withdrawals. Contributions to Roth IRAs, unlike those of traditional IRAs, are **not** tax deductible. Earnings are not merely tax deferred; they can be tax-free.

Earnings accumulated may be withdrawn tax free, five years following the initial deposit, provided the:

- account holder is 59½ or older;
- money withdrawn is used for the first-time purchase of a principal residence (up to $10,000); or
- account holder has died or become disabled.

Regular contributions may always be withdrawn tax free because they are made with nondeductible contributions.

EXAMPLE

1. Among the requirements for accumulated earnings in a Roth IRA to be withdrawn free of tax is

    A. the owner of the account is at least 70½

    B. the money is withdrawn for a first-time purchase of vacation home

    C. the initial deposit to a Roth IRA was made at least 5 years ago

    D. the owner's spouse is declared disabled

    Answer: C. The first requirement for tax-free withdrawals from a Roth IRA is that the initial deposit to a Roth must have been made at least 5 years ago, choice **C**. The other primary requirement is that the owner must be at least 59½, not 70½. If the 5-year requirement is met, then owners under 59½ can receive distributions of accumulated earnings tax-free they wish to use up to $10,000 for a first-time purchase of a primary residence, not a vacation home. The disability requirement only applies to the owner of the Roth, not a spouse.

Contribution Limits

Contribution limits to Roth IRAs are the same as those for traditional IRAs with one important difference. Unlike a traditional IRA, contributions may be made past age 70½ as long as the taxpayer has earned income.

An individual may contribute to both a traditional and a Roth IRA. However, the maximum combined contribution is $6,000 (or $7,000, if 50 or older).

Eligibility Requirements

Unlike the traditional IRA, there are limits placed on Roth eligibility based on income. Anyone with earned income is eligible to open a Roth IRA provided the person's adjusted gross income (AGI) falls below specified income levels. The following numbers, (which are never tested), are effective for those filing a tax return for 2019. A single person with an AGI of less than $122,000 may contribute the full amount to a Roth IRA. The ability to contribute to a Roth IRA is gradually phased out if the taxpayer's AGI is between $122,000 and $137,000.

For married taxpayers who file joint tax returns, the AGI limit is $193,000, with the contribution phased out for couples whose income is between $193,000 and $203,000.

What is AGI?

Adjusted Gross Income (AGI)

Adjusted gross income, generally referred to as AGI, is computed on the bottom of the first page of your Form 1040. It might help you to take a look at yours. When you do your taxes, you begin by listing all of your earned income (salary, wages, and bonuses) plus other income such as interest and dividends, capital gains, alimony received, and profits from a business you may own. From that total, you deduct certain items to arrive at the AGI. Among the more testable items that are deductible are:

- traditional IRA contribution;
- alimony paid (if divorce decree was signed prior to January 1, 2019);
- self-employment tax; and
- penalties paid on early withdrawal from a savings account.

TEST TOPIC ALERT

Please note that although tax-exempt income from municipal securities is shown on the Form 1040, it is not included in AGI.

TAKE NOTE

These numbers will *not* be tested because they change every year. It is the concept that is important.

Roth Conversions

Anyone with a traditional IRA is permitted to convert it to a Roth IRA. However, there are income tax consequences. Basically, the entire amount converted is added to the investor's ordinary income. However, as long as the funds are transferred trustee to trustee, or, if distributed to the owner, are rolled over within 60 days, there will be no 10% early distribution tax penalty for those under age 59½. If some portion of the contributions to the traditional IRA were made with after-tax money, the IRS uses a proportionate system to determine how much is nontaxable, but that type of computation will not be tested. Conversions may also be done from any qualified employer plan such as 401(k) and 403(b) plans as well as Simple and SEP IRAs.

Key Points to Remember About the Roth IRA

- Contributions are not tax deductible.
- Distributions are tax free if taken after age 59½ and a Roth account has been open for at least five years.
- Contributions can be made after age 70½ as long as there is earned income.
- Distributions are not required to begin at age 70½.
- If due to death, disability, or first-time home purchase, the distribution is qualified and not subject to tax or the 10% penalty.
- A minor can be named as beneficiary.

SIMPLIFIED EMPLOYEE PENSIONS (SEP IRAs)

The third type of IRA is somewhat different in that is funded by an employer rather than the individual. **Simplified employee pension plans** (**SEPs**) offer self-employed persons and small businesses easy-to-administer pension plans. A SEP is a qualified plan that allows an employer to contribute money directly to an individual retirement account (IRA) set up for each employee, hence the name SEP IRA. Following is a list of the key points of which to be aware.

Eligibility

To be eligible, an employee must be at least 21 years of age, have performed services for the employer during at least three of the last five years, and have received at least $600 (for 2019) in compensation from the employer in the current year (the annual compensation figure is indexed for inflation).

Participation

SEP rules require the employer allow *all eligible employees* to participate.

Funding

A SEP allows the employer to contribute up to 25% of an employee's salary to the employee's SEP IRA each year, up to a maximum of $56,000 per employee per year in 2019. The employer determines the level of contributions each year and must contribute the same percentage for each employee, as well as the employer.

Catch-Up Provision

Unlike the IRA and most qualified plans, there is no catch-up provision for a SEP. However, and this is **unlikely** to be tested, if the SEP IRA permits non-SEP contributions, they can make regular IRA contributions (including IRA catch-up contributions if they are age 50 and older) to the SEP IRA, up to the maximum annual limit.

Vesting

Participants in a SEP IRA are **fully vested** immediately, meaning that once the money is deposited in an employee's SEP IRA, it belongs to the employee.

Taxation

Employer contributions are tax deductible to the employer. Contributions are not taxable to an employee until withdrawn, and earnings in the account accumulate tax deferred.

EXAMPLE

1. SEP IRAs

    A. are used primarily by large corporations

    B. are used primarily by small businesses

    C. are set up by nonemployees

    D. cannot be set up by self-employed persons

    Answer: B. Small businesses, choice **B**, and self-employed persons typically establish SEP IRAs because they are easier and less expensive than other plans for an employer to set up and administer.

WITHDRAWALS FROM TRADITIONAL IRAs AND SEP IRAs

Up until this point, we've discussed contributions; now let's look at taking the money out. When it comes to traditional IRAs and SEP IRAs, distributions without penalty may begin after age 59½ and must begin by April 1 of the year following the year an individual turns 70½. Distributions before age 59½ may be subject to a tax penalty and withdrawals less than the required minimum distributions (RMDs), after age 70½ may also incur tax penalties.

TAKE NOTE

When is the deadline for receiving a RMD from an IRA? An account owner must take the first RMD for the year in which the account owner turns 70½. However, the first RMD payment can be delayed until April 1 of the year following the year in which the account owner turns 70½. For all subsequent years, including the year in which the first RMD was paid by April 1, the account owner must take the RMD by December 31 of the year.

To the extent withdrawals are from tax-deductible contributions, they are taxable as ordinary income. When there are both deductible and nondeductible contributions, a formula is used whereby a portion of the withdrawal represents a nontaxable return of principal.

Taxable withdrawals before age 59½ are also subject to a 10% early withdrawal penalty unless they are due to:

■ death;

■ disability;

■ first-time purchase of a primary residence ($10,000 lifetime maximum);

■ qualified higher education expenses for immediate family members (including grandchildren, but not nieces or nephews); or

■ certain medical expenses.

These exceptions also apply in the case of a nonqualified (taxable) distribution from a Roth IRA.

EXAMPLE

1. Who of the following will NOT incur a penalty on an IRA withdrawal?

    A. A man who has just become totally disabled

    B. A woman who turned 59 a month before the withdrawal

    C. A woman, age 50, who decides on early retirement

    D. A man in his early 40s who uses the money to buy a second home

    Answer: A. Early withdrawals, without penalty, are permitted only in certain situations (such as death or qualifying disability, choice **A**).

As stated, withdrawals must begin by April 1 of the year following the year in which the account owner reaches age 70½, and they must meet minimum **Internal Revenue Code (IRC)** distribution requirements or incur a 50% penalty on the amounts falling short of the minimum required distribution (MRD).

One important respect in which the Roth IRA differs from other retirement plans is that the age 70½ is irrelevant. There are no RMDs and, as long as the individual has earned income, contributions may be made at any age.

There is one other way to tap your IRA before age 59½ without penalty—through the **substantially equal periodic payment** (SEPP) exception. The *substantially equal periodic payment exception* under IRS rule 72(t) states that if you receive IRA payments at least annually based on your life expectancy (or the joint life expectancies of you and your beneficiary), the withdrawals are not subject to the 10% penalty. The IRS has tables for determining the appropriate amount of each payment at any given age.

TAKE NOTE

For exam purposes, you can postpone beginning distributions until the later of:

■ April 1 of the calendar year after you turn age 70½, or

■ April 1 of the calendar year following your retirement (but only for qualified plans, not an IRA).

EXAMPLE

An IRA owner who reaches age 70½ on January 1, 2017, must begin withdrawals by April 1, 2018. However, if this individual is covered by an employer-sponsored plan, other than a SEP IRA, there are no RMDs from that plan (but there are from any traditional IRAs) until after retirement.

Nondeductible Capital Withdrawals

IRA investors who contribute after-tax dollars to an IRA are not taxed on those funds when they are withdrawn from the account, but taxpayers are taxed at the ordinary income tax rate when they withdraw funds resulting from investment gains or income. As stated previously, if the client is in the middle part of the phaseout range resulting in some of the contribution being pretax (deductible) and the rest post-tax, the IRS has a formula to determine how much of the money withdrawn is nontaxable.

EXAMPLE

A client has invested $25,000 in after-tax dollars in an IRA currently worth $75,000. If the client were to withdraw $75,000, only $50,000 would be taxable.

TAKE NOTE

The early withdrawal penalties for all IRAs are waived in the event of death or disability.

TEST TOPIC ALERT

Assume questions are about traditional IRAs unless they specifically state *otherwise*.

TEST TOPIC ALERT

Income and capital gains earned from investments in any IRA account are not taxed until the funds are withdrawn and, if a qualified withdrawal, are not taxed at all in the case of a Roth.

CHARACTERISTICS OF IRAs

IRA Investments

In most cases, IRAs at securities firms are set up as self-directed plans. That means the investment choices are determined by the account holder. Funds in an IRA account may be used to buy stocks, bonds, mutual funds, UITs, limited partnerships, REITS, U.S. government securities, gold or silver coins minted by the U.S. Treasury Department (American Eagles) as well as certain platinum coins and certain gold, silver, palladium, and platinum bullion, annuities, and many other investments.

IRA investments should be relatively conservative and should reflect the investor's age and risk tolerance profile. Because an IRA serves as a source of retirement funds, it is important that the account be managed for adequate long-term growth.

Ineligible and Inappropriate Investments

Collectibles, including antiques, gems, rare coins, works of art, and stamps, are not acceptable IRA investments. Life insurance contracts (such as whole life and term) may not be purchased in an IRA. Tax-free municipal bonds, municipal bond funds, and municipal bond UITs are eligible, but generally considered inappropriate for an IRA (or any tax-qualified plan) because their yields are typically lower than those of other similar investments, and the income generated is taxable on withdrawal from the IRA.

Ineligible Investment Practices

No short sales of stock, speculative option strategies, or margin account trading is permitted in an IRA or any other retirement plan. Covered call writing is allowed.

Ineligible Investments	Ineligible Investment Practices
Collectibles	Short sales of stock
Whole life insurance	Speculative option strategies
Term life Insurance	Margin account trading

Real Estate in an IRA (or Qualified Plan)

Legally, you may invest in real estate in your IRA or as a participant in a 401(k) or other qualified plan. It is not commonly something that is written into the documents, but it could be. Probably the biggest reason why the provision is rarely found is because of the extra care that must be taken when making a real estate investment. If done improperly, serious problems with the IRS can result. If it is done as a truly hands-off investment, it is unlikely that there will be an issue. However, the moment the participant derives any personal benefit from the property—such as staying in a condo purchased in resort area that is rented out most of the year, or allowing prohibited persons to use the property—look out.

TEST TOPIC ALERT

The IRS defines prohibited persons (people who can't benefit from real estate held in an IRA or qualified plan) as any member of the family. Who are they? A member of the family includes a spouse, ancestors (parents and grandparents), children, grandchildren, great grandchildren, and spouses of children, grandchildren, and great grandchildren. Believe it or not, a brother or sister of an individual is not a member of the family for this purpose, but a legally adopted child of an individual is treated as a child by blood.

Moving IRAs

Individuals may move their funds and investments from one IRA to another IRA through a one of three methods:

- 60-day rollover;
- direct rollover; or
- trustee-to-trustee transfer.

60-day Rollovers

If you just see "IRA rollover," it will be the 60-day rollover. An IRA account owner may take temporary possession of the account funds to move the retirement account to another custodian. The account owner may do so only once per 12-month period, and the rollover must be completed within 60 calendar days of the funds' withdrawal from the original plan. However, 100% of the withdrawn amount must be rolled into the new account, or the unrolled balance will be subject to income tax and, if applicable, early withdrawal penalty.

A participant in a business-sponsored qualified plan may move her plan assets to a rollover IRA if she leaves the company and elects to take a lump-sum distribution. If the participant does take possession of the funds, she must complete the rollover within *60 calendar days* of withdrawing the funds from the qualified plan.

When the participant takes possession of the funds from a qualified plan to make a rollover, the payor of the distribution must, by law, withhold 20% of the distribution as a withholding tax. The participant must, nonetheless, roll over 100% of the plan distribution, including the funds withheld, or be subject to income tax and, if applicable, early withdrawal penalty.

EXAMPLE

A 50-year-old individual with $100,000 in his company retirement plan changes employers. His pension plan may be distributed to him in a lump-sum payment, minus the mandatory 20% withholding of $20,000. He must then deposit $100,000 in an IRA rollover account within 60 days. Any portion not rolled over, including the $20,000 withheld, is considered a distribution subject to ordinary income tax and early distribution penalty. If he deposits the entire $100,000 into the IRA, he will apply on his next income tax return for a refund of the $20,000 withheld.

Direct Rollovers From Retirement Plans to IRAs

A direct rollover is a distribution from an employer-sponsored retirement plan to an IRA, either traditional or Roth. When you terminate employment (or retire), you have the option of moving your employer-sponsored plan assets to an IRA. In some cases, if you go to a new job, your new employer's plan may permit a direct rollover into the plan. The key to a direct rollover is that the money is never seen by the employee and moves directly from the current plan administrator directly to another administrator.

Trustee-to-Trustee Transfers

Sometimes simply referred to as an IRA transfer, this is when account assets are sent directly from one IRA custodian to another, and the account owner never takes possession of the funds. Unlike the 1 per 12 months with an IRA rollover, the number of IRA transfers an account owner may make per year is unlimited. Direct rollovers and transfers generally make better sense than 60-day rollovers because the 20% federal tax withholding does not apply to direct transfers of portfolios and, because there is no specified time limit, you don't have to rush to meet the 60-day requirement.

TAKE NOTE

How does a direct rollover differ from a transfer? A direct rollover is different from a transfer because it involves two different types of plans. For example, one would use a direct rollover to move funds from a 401(k) plan to an IRA while the transfer is from an IRA at one brokerage firm to an IRA at another.

Earnings Limitations for Tax Benefits

Traditional and certain SEP IRA participants may deduct contributions to their IRAs from their taxable income. The deductibility limits are lowered for individuals who are eligible for other qualified plans.

These AGI limits increase every year and will not be tested. Individuals who are ineligible to participate in qualified plans may deduct IRA contributions regardless of income level.

For those filing 2019 tax returns, the IRA deductibility phaseout range is expressed in the table here.

Year	Phaseout Range: Single Filers	Phaseout Range: Joint Filers
2019	$64,000–$74,000	$103,000–$123,000

TAKE NOTE

The limits are higher ($193,000–$203,000) if only one of the spouses is eligible to participate in a qualified plan, but, as with all of these numbers, it is only the concept that is tested, never the numbers themselves.

These limits only deal with the deductibility of contributions. If your client earns in excess of the limits, the full contribution can still be made, but part or none of it can be deducted. The test refers to those as *post-tax* or *after-tax* contributions. The earnings still grow tax deferred.

EXAMPLE

Two persons who are part of a married couple, each of whom is ineligible to participate in a qualified plan and whose combined income is $200,000, may contribute and *deduct* a total of $12,000 ($14,000 if both individuals are 50 or older). No *deduction* is allowed for a married couple where both are eligible to participate in a qualified plan and whose combined income is $123,000 (for 2019) or more. Nevertheless, their contributions are permitted and all earnings are tax deferred.

Inheriting an IRA

The rules on the treatment of an inherited IRA depend on whether the beneficiary is the spouse or is some other relative (or nonrelative) of the deceased. Another factor is if the deceased had already begun taking RMDs. This issue is very technical, and we will only cover points that might be tested.

Spousal Beneficiary

When the beneficiary is the spouse, there are two choices that can be made:

- Do a spousal rollover, meaning the amount of the inheritance is rolled over into the spouse's own IRA

- Continue to own the IRA as the beneficiary

When doing a spousal rollover, this is treated, logically, as your own with all of the normal rules applying (withdrawal ages, RMDs, and so forth). That means that if the spouse is younger than 59½, any distributions before then will be subject to the 10% penalty (unless meeting the exceptions).

If, however, the spouse elects to continue the account as the beneficiary, then there is no 10% penalty for withdrawals before age 59½. That's the good news. The bad news is that RMDs (from a traditional IRA or SEP IRA) must begin when the deceased would have had to take them, a disappointment if the survivor is the younger partner. However, the RMDs will be computed based on the beneficiary's age, not that of the deceased. Also, if it is a Roth IRA and the account hasn't been open for at least five years, any withdrawal of earnings will be subject to income tax but not the 10% penalty.

Nonspouse Beneficiary

Things are different when the person inheriting a traditional IRA is not the spouse of the deceased. For one thing, unlike the spouse, the beneficiary will not be allowed to rollover the inherited IRA into their own IRA, this is simply *not* an option. In general, there are four primary options available, the fourth of which probably won't be tested.

Take the cash now

The nonspouse IRA beneficiary can withdraw 100% of the IRA account immediately. If this option is chosen, then 100% of the amount withdrawn (assuming the IRA was funded completely with pretax contributions) will be included in taxable income during the year of withdrawal.

Cash out the IRA in five years

If the deceased was younger than 70½, (not obligated to take RMDs), the nonspouse IRA beneficiary is allowed to withdraw all of the funds from the IRA by December 31 of the fifth year following the IRA account owner's death. If this option is selected, then each withdrawal will be included in taxable income (once again, assuming all contributions were pretax) during the year the funds are withdrawn. Interestingly, the IRS does not require the payments to be made with any designated frequency. That is, you can take a portion the first year because you can use some cash, nothing for the next three years, and the balance no later than December 31 of the fifth year.

Take out required minimum distributions over the beneficiary's own life expectancy

Nonspouse IRA beneficiaries, may be able to take RMDs over their life expectancy, leaving the bulk of the account to continue to grow in the tax deferred account. Each distribution taken will be included in taxable income during the year the funds are withdrawn. To choose this option, a separate inherited IRA account in the deceased account owner's name for the benefit (FBO) of the beneficiary must be established and the first required minimum distribution must be taken by December 31 of the year following the year of the account owner's death. For example, the inherited IRA account would be titled "Sammy Jones, IRA (deceased 5/5/17), FBO Monique Gaillaird, beneficiary."

Take RMDs based on the life expectancy of the oldest beneficiary

If there are multiple beneficiaries and the decision is to stretch out the withdrawals, the IRS requires that the life expectancy of the oldest beneficiary be used. Obviously, this will result in a higher payout (and more tax revenue) than if the life expectancy of the youngest was an option. This can be avoided if separate inherited IRA accounts are set up for each beneficiary. In that case, RMDs are figured for each account.

If the beneficiary does nothing by December 31 of the year following the year of death, the default option used by the IRA is the five-year withdrawal option.

EXAMPLE

1. Grandma Abigail died at age 82 with a traditional IRA valued at $100,000. Her daughter Betsy, 53 years old, was the sole beneficiary. Betsy's choices would include

   A. rolling over this IRA to her own IRA

   B. taking distributions spread out over a 5-year period

   C. taking the cash by December 31st and paying the 10% tax penalty because she is under 59½

   D. leave the IRA in the name of the deceased and continue with the RMDs

   Answer: B. Among the options available to a nonspouse beneficiary is spreading the payout over 5 years (choice **B**). Betsy, being a daughter and not a spouse, could not roll over into her own IRA. Even though she is under 59½, inheritors of IRAs do not incur the 10% penalty tax on withdrawals.

TAKE NOTE

Just as with the spouse continuing the IRA as beneficiary, if the account were a Roth IRA and it had not been opened for the five-year minimum, any earnings distributed will be subject to ordinary income tax but not the 10% penalty.

TAKE NOTE

It is only in the case of nonspouse beneficiaries where the 10% tax penalty for withdrawals before age 59½ does not apply.

Disclaiming an IRA

Believe it or not, some people who inherit IRAs don't want the money. There are any number of reasons why (none of which will be tested), but what will be tested is what happens when the beneficiary **disclaims** the proceeds.

A disclaimer is a refusal to accept a gift or inheritance. Perhaps it is easier to understand like this: If you accept an item left to you by someone who has died, you are claiming that asset; if you refuse it, you are disclaiming it. In order for the disclaimer to be effective, it must be done within nine months of death, it must be in writing, and, of course, you cannot have taken any of the money.

If the named beneficiary of an IRA disclaims all or part of the inherited IRA, the disclaimer has the effect of changing the beneficiary of the retirement plan. In general, the assets pass to the contingent beneficiary(s). What if no contingent beneficiary has been named? Unless the IRA adoption document provides for it, the person disclaiming cannot decide where the money goes—it will follow the provisions of the deceased's will.

EXAMPLE

Joseph Miller passes away at the age of 72 and leaves his wife, Josephine, his traditional IRA with a value of $1,800,000. There are many other assets in the estate, and Josephine decides to disclaim the entire IRA. She would like to pass on the assets to her three grandchildren in equal shares with another share going to her favorite charity. Assuming the IRA adoption document permits the beneficiary to designate in this matter, the charity will receive $450,000 with no tax liability at all, and the three grandchildren will each receive $450,000 on which distributions may be stretched out over their life expectancy.

KEOGH PLANS

U24LO2: Differentiate between the different types of employer-sponsored qualified retirement plans.

Keogh plans are Employee Retirement Income Security Act (ERISA)-qualified plans intended for self-employed individuals and owner-employees of unincorporated business concerns or professional practices. Included in the self-employed category are independent contractors, consultants, freelancers, and anyone else who files and pays self-employment Social Security taxes. The term *owner-employee* refers to sole proprietors. A corporation cannot use a Keogh plan.

TAKE NOTE

Whenever the term *qualified plan* is used, it refers specifically to an employer-sponsored plan, not an IRA.

Contributions

Contribution limits for a Keogh plan are significantly higher than those for an IRA. For those filing tax returns in 2019, as much as $56,000 may be contributed on behalf of a plan participant. Those who are eligible for a Keogh plan may also maintain an IRA, but, as described previously, if the earning limits are exceeded, the IRA contribution will not be deductible. If the business has employees, they must be covered at the same contribution percentage as the owner in order for the plan to be nondiscriminatory.

TEST TOPIC ALERT

Only earnings from self-employment count toward determining the maximum that may be contributed. For example, if a corporate employee had a part time consulting job, only that income, not the corporate salary, could be included in the computation.

Eligibility

Employee participation in a Keogh plan is subject to these eligibility rules.

■ **Full-time employees** are employees who receive compensation for at least 1,000 hours of work per year.

■ **Tenured employees** are employees who have completed one or more years of continuous employment.

■ **Adult employees** are employees 21 years of age and older and, just as with traditional IRAs, not in excess of 70½.

Comparison of IRAs and Keogh Plans

Keogh plans and IRAs are designed to encourage individuals to set aside funds for retirement income. Although both IRAs and Keoghs are tax advantaged, an IRA does not involve employer contributions and, thus, is not a plan qualified by *ERISA*. The principal similarities between Keoghs and IRAs are listed in the following.

■ **Tax deferral of contributions to plans.** Taxes are deferred on contributions until the individual receives distributions.

■ **Tax sheltered.** Investment income and capital gains are not taxed until withdrawn at which time they are subject to taxation at ordinary income rates.

■ **Contributions.** Only cash may be contributed to a plan. In the event of a rollover or transfer, cash and securities from the transferring account can be deposited.

■ **Distributions.** Distributions without penalty can begin as early as age 59½.

■ **Penalties for early withdrawal.** The individual pays income tax on the total amount withdrawn, plus a 10% penalty. Early withdrawals without penalty are permitted in the event of death or disability.

■ **Payout options.** Distributions may be in a lump sum or periodic payments.

■ **Beneficiary.** Upon the planholder's death, payments are made to a designated beneficiary (or beneficiaries).

 EXAMPLE

1. Which of the following may participate in a Keogh plan?

   I.   Self-employed doctor

   II. Analyst who makes money giving speeches outside regular working hours

   III. Individual with a full-time job who also has income from freelancing

   IV. Corporate executive who receives $5,000 in stock options from his corporation

   A. I only

   B. I and II

   C. I, II, and III

   D. I, II, III, and IV

   Answer: C. A person with self-employment income may deduct contributions to a Keogh plan. Keogh plans are not available to corporations or their employees. That would make choice **C** the correct answer.

403(B) PLANS (TAX-EXEMPT ORGANIZATIONS)

403(b) plans are qualified tax-deferred retirement plans for employees of public school systems, (403(b) employees), and tax-exempt, nonprofit organizations such as churches and charitable institutions, (501(c)(3) employees). Qualified employees may exclude contributions from their taxable incomes provided they do not exceed limits.

Qualified annuity plans offered under Section 403(b) of the IRC, sometimes referred to as **tax-sheltered annuities (TSAs)**, are intended to encourage retirement savings. To ensure this objective, 403(b)s (like IRAs and other retirement plans) are subject to tax penalties if savings are withdrawn before a participant reaches age 59½.

Tax Advantages

The following tax advantages apply to 403(b)s.

- Contributions (which generally come from salary reduction) are excluded from a participant's gross income.
- Participant's earnings accumulate tax free until distribution.

Income Exclusion

If an eligible employee elects to make annual contributions to a 403(b), those contributions are excluded from the employee's gross income for that year. The amount of the contribution is not reported as income, resulting in lower current income taxes.

Tax-Deferred Accumulation

Earnings in a 403(b) accumulate with no current taxation of earnings or gains and do not increase the participant's taxable income until the dollars are withdrawn at retirement, usually when that person is in a lower tax bracket.

Investments

Historically, these plans were (and still are) referred to as tax-sheltered annuity plans (TSAs) because annuities were the only investment option. In 1974, a provision was made to permit the purchase of mutual funds as well, although it is estimated that more than 85% of all 403(b) money is invested in either fixed or variable annuities.

Guaranteed Investment Contracts (GICs)

Another option for 403(b) plans (as well as 401(k) plans), is the Guaranteed Investment Contract, almost always referred to by its initials, GIC. These are contracts issued by insurance companies that offer a guaranteed return of principal at a certain date in the future and come with a fixed rate of return that is generally a bit higher than that offered by comparable bank CDs. However, unlike CDs, GICs are not federally insured; therefore, despite the inclusion of the word guaranteed in the title, GICs carry slightly more investment risk than CDs and that is why their return is higher.

Eligibility Requirements

To be eligible to establish a 403(b), an employer must qualify as a:

- public educational 403(b) institution;
- tax-exempt 501(c)3 organization; or
- church organization.

Public Educational 403(b)

To qualify as a public educational institution, an organization must be state supported, a political subdivision, or an agency of a state. Private school systems have a separate set of qualifying rules. State-run educational systems include:

- elementary schools;
- secondary schools;
- colleges and universities; and
- medical schools.

Individuals employed by these school systems in the following job classifications may enroll in a 403(b) plan. These include:

- teachers and other faculty members;
- administrators, managers, principals, supervisors, and other members of the administrative staff;
- counselors;
- clerical staff and maintenance workers; and
- individuals who perform services for the institution, such as doctors or nurses.

Tax-Exempt 501(c)3

As stated earlier, 501(c)3 organizations are tax-exempt entities specifically cited in the IRC as eligible to establish 403(b)s for their employees. Typical 501(c)3 organizations include:

- private colleges and universities;
- trade schools;
- parochial schools;
- zoos and museums;
- research and scientific foundations;
- religious and charitable institutions; and
- private hospitals and medical schools.

Definition of an Employee

Only employees of qualified employers are eligible to participate in a 403(b) plan. Independent contractors are not eligible. It is the employer's responsibility to determine an individual's status or definition.

Eligibility

Similar to other qualified plans, if the employer either matches or makes nonelective contributions, a 403(b) plan must be made available to each full-time employee who has both reached age 21 and completed one year of service. Unique to the 403(b) plans is that if the plan only offers employee deferrals, then any employee, even one who started today, is eligible to participate.

Plan Requirements

A 403(b) plan must meet two requirements.

- The plan must be in writing and must be made through a plan instrument, a trust agreement, or both.
- The employer must remit plan contributions to an annuity contract, a mutual fund, or another approved investment.

Contribution Limits

An employer can make contributions to a 403(b) solely on behalf of the covered employee or in conjunction with an employee deferral.

Salary Reduction

403(b) Contributions are made by having the employee take a salary reduction. As such, the money is withdrawn before taxation. For 2019, the maximum is $19,000 with a $6,000 catch-up provision.

Employer Contributions

Employer contributions to a 403(b) are generally subject to the same maximums that apply to all defined contribution plans: the lesser of 100% of the participant's compensation or $56,000 per year.

EXAMPLE

1. A retirement plan that allows the employee to make pretax contributions (within certain limits), provides for tax deferral of earnings, and is available for employees of public school systems and certain tax-exempt organizations is

    A. a 403(b) plan

    B. a 401(k) plan

    C. an SEP IRA

    D. a payroll deduction plan

    Answer: A. The giveaway here is the public school employees—the 403(b), choice **A**, is their plan as well as being offered to employees of certain, but not all, tax-exempt organizations.

CORPORATE-SPONSORED RETIREMENT PLANS

In this section, we will be discussing qualified plans sponsored by corporations. These include pension plans, profit-sharing plans, and the highly popular 401(k) plans.

The **Employee Retirement Income Security Act of 1974 (ERISA)** is federal legislation that regulates the establishment and management of corporate pension or retirement plans, also known as **private sector plans**.

All qualified corporate plans must be established under a trust agreement. A trustee is appointed for each plan and has a fiduciary responsibility for the plan and the beneficial owners (the plan holders). We'll cover ERISA in greater detail later in this unit.

Defined Contribution and Defined Benefit Plans

All qualified retirement plans fall into one of two categories. Those that offer no specific end result, but, instead focus on current, tax-deductible contributions, are **defined contribution plans**. Those that promise a specific retirement benefit but do not specify the level of current contributions are **defined benefit plans**. It is important to distinguish between these two approaches.

Defined Contribution Plans

Defined contribution plans include money-purchase pension plans as well as profit-sharing plans and 401(k) plans. As with other business plans (as compared to an IRA), the maximum employer contribution is currently $56,000.

Defined contribution plan participants' funds accumulate until a future event, generally retirement, when the funds may be withdrawn. The ultimate account value depends on the total amount contributed, along with interest and capital gains from the plan investments. In this type of plan, the plan participant assumes the investment risk. The deduction for contributions to a defined contribution plan, such as a profit-sharing plan, (including 401(k)), or money-purchase pension plan, cannot be more than 25% of the total payroll for the year to the eligible employees participating in the plan.

Defined Benefit Plans

Defined benefit plans are designed to provide specific retirement benefits for participants, such as fixed monthly income or a specified sum at retirement (cash balance plan). Regardless of investment performance, the promised benefit is paid under the contract terms. A defined benefit plan sponsor assumes the investment risk. The benefit is usually determined by a formula that takes into account years of service and average salary for the last five years before retirement. Older, highly compensated employees are likely to have the largest annual contributions on their behalf. Because of the expenses and complexities involved (the Plan's annual return must be signed by an actuary), 3% of workers had defined benefit plans in 2011, whereas in 1979, that number was 28%.

TAKE NOTE

Because of the actuarial assumptions and computations, the maximum has to be figured by an actuary.

Contributory vs. Noncontributory Plans

In a contributory plan, both the employer and employee make contributions to the account. In a noncontributory plan, only the employer makes the contributions. Probably the most common example of a contributory plan is the 401(k) plan where the employee determines how much to contribute and the employer may match up to a certain percentage.

Employer Deductions

The employer can usually deduct, subject to limits, contributions made to a qualified plan. The deduction limit for those contributions to a qualified plan depends on the kind of plan in place.

TEST TOPIC ALERT

Unlike an annuity payout or life insurance premium, contributions to a defined benefit plan are not affected by the participant's sex.

TEST TOPIC ALERT

Employer contributions to defined benefit or defined contribution (money purchase), pension plans are mandatory. Although profit-sharing plans and 401(k) plans are technically defined contribution plans, they are not pension plans, and employer contributions are not mandatory. In all cases, allowable employer contributions are 100% deductible to the corporation. There is no tax obligation to the employee until withdrawal.

Profit-Sharing Plans

A **profit-sharing plan** established by an employer allows employees to participate in the business's profits. The benefits may be paid directly to the employee or deferred into an account for future payment, such as retirement, or a combination of both. This discussion concerns profit-sharing plans that defer benefits toward retirement.

Profit-sharing plans need not have a predetermined contribution formula. Plans that do include such a formula generally express contributions as a fixed percentage of profits. In either event, to be qualified, a profit-sharing plan must have substantial and recurring contributions, according to the Internal Revenue Code.

Profit-sharing plans are popular because they offer employers the greatest amount of contribution flexibility. The ability to skip contributions during years of low profits appeals to corporations with unpredictable cash flows. They are also relatively easy to install, administer, and communicate to employees.

401(k) Plans

In a **401(k) plan**, an employee directs an employer to deduct a percentage of the employee's salary which will be a contribution to a retirement account. 401(k) plans permit an employer to make matching contributions up to a set percentage of the employee-directed contributions, making this a type of defined contribution plan. All contributions are made with pretax dollars. In effect, participating employees are reducing their salary by the amount of their contribution and, therefore, their W-2 will show the actual salary less the 401(k) contribution. However, even though income taxes are based on this lower amount, FICA (Social Security) and FUTA (federal unemployment) taxes are levied against gross salary, not this reduced amount. In 2019, the maximum employee elective deferral is set at $19,000 with an additional catch-up contribution limit of $6,000.

TEST TOPIC ALERT

An employer-sponsored 401(k) plan may be established with no required employer or employee contributions. As we will shortly learn, there is one case where employer contributions would be mandatory, but for exam purposes, unless that case is specified, it is up to the employer to determine if it will incorporate matching contributions into the plan.

TAKE NOTE

When one includes the catch-up amount, the maximum combined employer and employee contribution in a defined contribution plan increases from $56,000 to $62,000 per year.

TEST TOPIC ALERT

One of the benefits of investing through a 401(k) plan is that it takes advantage of dollar cost averaging, the technique described in Unit 20, which always results in a lower cost per share in a fluctuating market.

Roth 401(k) Plans

Technically, there is no such thing as a Roth 401(k) plan. In reality, employers are permitted to add certain Roth features to existing 401(k) plans. Just as with a Roth IRA, these plans require after-tax contributions but allow tax-free withdrawals, provided the retiring person is at least 59½ years old at the time of the withdrawal. Once again, paralleling the Roth IRA, the account must be at least five years old to take tax-free withdrawals.

Like a regular 401(k) plan, it has employer-matching contributions; however, the employer's match must be deposited into a regular 401(k) plan and be fully taxable upon withdrawal. Thus, the employee must have two accounts: a regular 401(k) and a Roth 401(k). Employees may contribute to either account but may not transfer money between accounts once the money has been contributed.

Unlike Roth IRAs, Roth 401(k) plans have no income limit restriction on who may participate. One may have both a Roth 401(k) plan and a Roth IRA, but the income limits would still apply to the Roth IRA. Unlike Roth IRAs, Roth 401(k) plans require withdrawals to begin no later than age 70½, following the same rules that apply to all RMDs.

Section 457 Plans

A **Section 457(b) plan** is a deferred compensation plan set up under Section 457 of the tax code that may be used by employees of a state, political subdivision of a state, and any agency or instrumentality of a state. This plan may also be offered to employees of certain tax-exempt organizations (hospitals, charitable organizations, unions, and so forth, but *not* churches).

Unit 24

In a 457 plan, employees can defer compensation, and the amount deferred is not reportable for tax purposes. Therefore, the employee receives a deduction each year for the amount deferred.

There are several important facts to know about 457 plans.

- These plans are exempt from ERISA—nongovernmental plans must be unfunded to qualify for tax benefits while government plans must be funded.

- These plans are generally not required to follow the nondiscrimination rules of other retirement plans.

- Plans for tax-exempt organizations are limited to covering only highly compensated employees, while any employee (or even independent contractor) of a governmental entity may participate.

- Distributions from 457(b) plans of nongovernmental tax-exempt employees may be made at any age and there is no 10% penalty for early withdrawal.

- It is possible to maintain both a 457 and 403(b), or a 457 and 401(k) and make maximum contributions to both ($38,000 in 2019). As a result, those 50 or older, using the catch-up provision in each plan, could contribute as much as $50,000. You could also have an IRA along with the 457.

- Unlike 401(k) plans, loans from a 457(b) plan are available in governmental plans only, and only if the entity decides to include that feature in the plan. Furthermore, the requirements for unforeseen emergency withdrawals are much stricter than for hardship withdrawals under a 401(k) plan.

 EXAMPLE

1. A basic difference between a Section 457 plan established on behalf of a governmental entity and one established by a private tax-exempt organization is that

   A. a governmental plan must hold its assets in trust or custodial accounts for the benefit of individual participants

   B. a tax-exempt plan participant does not have to include plan distributions in his or her taxable income

   C. a governmental plan cannot make a distribution before the participant attains age 70½

   D. a tax-exempt plan's distributions are not eligible for a favorable lump-sum 10-year averaging treatment

   Answer: A. A governmental Section 457 plan must be funded, that is, it must hold plan assets in trusts or custodial accounts, choice **A**, for the benefit of individual participants. Conversely, a tax-exempt (nongovernmental) Section 457 plan may not be funded.

SIMPLE Plans

Savings Incentive Match Plans for Employees (SIMPLEs) are retirement plans for a business with 100 or fewer employees who earned $5,000 or more during the preceding calendar year. In addition, the business cannot currently have another retirement plan in place.

The plans are easy to set up and inexpensive to administer. The employee's contribution, up to $13,000 with a $3,000 catch-up provision (2019), is pretax and may be matched by the employer using either of the following two options.

- A 2% nonelective employer contribution, where employees eligible to participate receive an employer contribution equal to 2% of their compensation (limited to $280,000 per year for 2019 and subject to cost-of-living adjustments for later years), regardless of whether they make their own contributions.

- A dollar-for-dollar match up to 3% of compensation, where only the participating employees who have elected to make contributions will receive an employer contribution (i.e., the matching contribution).

For small business looking for a way to have an inexpensive retirement plan for their employees, the SIMPLE is the way to go.

TAKE NOTE

We've never heard of this being on the test, but, just in case, you might need to know about a penalty tax levied under these plans that is unique. Unless qualifying for an exception from the 10% penalty tax, such as that offered with traditional IRAs (over 59½, death or disability, etc.), withdrawals from a SIMPLE IRA within the first two years after beginning participation in the plan are subject to a penalty tax of 25%.

NONQUALIFIED RETIREMENT PLANS

U24LO3: Contrast qualified and nonqualified retirement plans.

A **nonqualified plan** does not allow the employer a current tax deduction for contributions. Instead, the employer receives the tax deduction when the money is paid out to the employee. Normally, earnings accumulate on a tax-deferred basis. A nonqualified plan need not comply with nondiscrimination rules that apply to qualified plans. The employer can make nonqualified benefits available to key employees and exclude others.

Nonqualified plans are not subject to the same reporting and disclosure requirements as qualified plans. However, nonqualified plans still must be in writing and communicated to the plan participants. Sponsors of nonqualified plans are fiduciaries.

Taxation

The corporation cannot deduct nonqualified plan contributions made on behalf of participants until paid to the participant. However, if the nonqualified plan is properly designed, contributions are not taxable to the employee until the benefit is received.

Contributions to nonqualified plans that have already been taxed make up the investor's cost base. When the investor withdraws money from the nonqualified plan, the cost base is not taxed. However, earnings are taxed when withdrawn.

Types of Plans

Three types of nonqualified plans are payroll deduction plans, deferred compensation plans, and supplemental executive retirement (or retention) plans.

Payroll Deduction Plans

A **payroll deduction plan** involves a deduction from an employee's check on a weekly, monthly, or quarterly basis as authorized by the employee. The money is deducted after taxes are paid and may be invested in investment vehicles, such as the employer's stock or U.S. Savings bonds at the employee's option.

Deferred Compensation Plans

A **nonqualified deferred compensation (NQDC) plan** is a contractual agreement between a firm and an employee in which the employee agrees to defer receipt of current compensation in favor of a payout at retirement. The agreement underlying a deferred compensation plan usually includes the following:

- Conditions and circumstances under which some or all of the benefits may be forfeited, such as if the employee moves to a competing firm

- A statement to the effect that the employee is not entitled to any claim against the employer's assets until retirement, death, or disability

- A disclaimer that the agreement may be void if the firm suffers a business failure or bankruptcy

TEST TOPIC ALERT

Because the employer can discriminate, one of the most common uses of deferred compensation plans is to provide benefits to retain key employees.

Business Failure

Generally, an employee enjoys no benefits from a deferred compensation plan until retirement. If the business fails, the employee is a general creditor of the business with no guarantee that he will receive the deferred payment.

Figure 24.1: Qualified Plans vs. Nonqualified Plans

Qualified Plans	Nonqualified Plans
Contributions tax deductible	Contributions not tax deductible
Plan approved by the IRS	Plan does not need IRS approval
Plan cannot discriminate	Plan can discriminate
Subject to ERISA	Not subject to ERISA
Tax on accumulation is deferred	Tax on accumulation is deferred
All withdrawals taxed	Excess over cost base taxed
Plan is a trust	Plan is not a trust

EXAMPLE

1. Which of the following objectives would NOT be met by an employer's use of a nonqualified retirement plan?

   A. The employer desires current tax savings.

   B. The employer desires an alternative to the qualified plan because of the complexity of legislative changes.

   C. The employer needs to bring executive retirement benefits up to desired levels by adding a second tier of benefits on top of the qualified plan.

   D. The employer desires a plan in which benefits may legally discriminate in favor of highly compensated employees.

   Answer: A. Tax benefits on a NQDC plan only result when the employee receives payment so choice **A** is correct. All of the other statements describe situations in which employers might benefit from establishing a nonqualified retirement plan.

SERP

A supplemental executive retirement plan (SERP) provides benefits to executives over and above the benefits available from a qualified plan and is funded entirely with employer funds. The plan can be either completely unfunded (like an excess benefit plan) or informally funded. The plan rewards an executive's continued employment or encourages the early retirement of the executive. A SERP also may be established to protect the executive from involuntary termination if the company changes ownership by awarding her increased benefits from the plan. The "R" sometimes refers to retention because these plans do encourage key employees to remain until they qualify for the benefit. These are frequently funded with cash value life insurance policies.

DISTRIBUTIONS FROM QUALIFIED PLANS

U24LO4: Identify the tax treatment of distributions from qualified plans.

If all of the funds were contributed by the employer, (known as a noncontributory plan), the employee's tax basis (cost) is zero. If the employee contribution were pretax, the basis for those is zero as well. Because everything above the cost is taxed at the employee's ordinary income rate at the time of distribution, in most cases all funds received are fully taxable.

Distributions from a 403(b) must follow the same rules as distributions from all qualified plans. Because the employee's 403(b) contributions are made with pretax dollars and all earnings were tax deferred, any distribution is subject to ordinary income tax rates in the year it is received. A normal distribution can start at age 59½. Premature distribution is subject to a 10% penalty tax. And, the RMD rules apply as well.

Hardship Withdrawals

401(k) plans are permitted to make hardship withdrawals available to participants facing serious and immediate financial difficulty. There are maximum limits; the amount withdrawn is not eligible for a rollover and, therefore, is taxable as ordinary income and possibly the 10% penalty. It differs from a 401(k) loan which is not taxable as long as the repayment requirements of the IRS are met.

401(k) Plan Loans

Somewhat different from the hardship withdrawal is the ability to borrow from the 401(k). This has the advantage of not being treated as a distribution so there is no tax. However, if certain IRS rules are not followed, it will be considered a premature distribution and taxed as such. The IRS maximum loan amount is 50% of the participant's vested share or $50,000, whichever is the smaller. All loans must carry what the IRS considers to be a "reasonable rate of interest." Other than if used for a home mortgage, the loan must be paid back on a regular schedule (usually through payroll deduction) in a period not to exceed 60 months.

 EXAMPLE

1. Susan participates in a Section 401(k) plan at work that includes loan provisions. Susan has recently enrolled in college and has inquired about the possible consequences of borrowing from the plan to help pay for her education. As her financial planner, what is your advice to her?

   A. The loan will statutorily be treated as a taxable distribution from the plan.

   B. The loan must be repayable within 5 years at a reasonable rate of interest.

   C. The 401(k) plan needs to be rewritten as loans are only available from qualified plans.

   D. The loan is not being made for reasons of an unforeseeable emergency and therefore is not possible.

   Answer: B. For a loan not to be treated as a taxable distribution for tax purposes, it must be repayable within 5 years at a reasonable rate of interest, choice **B**. The unforeseeable emergency requirements are found in a Section 457 plan.

Net Unrealized Appreciation (NUA)

Many employers enable employees to buy the stock or bonds of their company inside the 401(k) or other retirement plans. The distribution of employer securities is sometimes eligible for special treatment under the tax code. Those receiving a distribution of employer securities from a qualified retirement plan may be able to defer the tax on the net unrealized appreciation (NUA) in the securities. The NUA is the net increase in the securities' value while they were in the plan's trust. If taken as a lump-sum distribution, the participant has the option of deferring tax on all of the NUA. A lump-sum distribution is defined as the disbursement of the entire vested account balance within one taxable year as a result of a triggering event. Triggering events are limited to:

- separation from service,
- attainment of age 59½, or
- death.

To qualify for the NUA treatment, an employee must complete the entire distribution within the same calendar year. How does this work? Normally, the entire value of a distribution from a qualified plan is taxed as ordinary income. Even if rolled over into an IRA, when ultimately distributed, the entire value will be taxed as ordinary income. However, when using the NUA approach, only the original cost basis (as supplied by the employer) is subject to tax. Any unrealized appreciation will be taxed as long-term capital gain, whenever sold. And, to make things even sweeter, as long as held more than 12 months, any further appreciation is taxed as long-term capital gain. Let's take a look at an example.

EXAMPLE

George has been an employee of KAPCO Manufacturing Company for 20 years. He is turning 65 this year and plans to retire. In his 401(k) plan, he has assets of $600,000 of which $250,000 is KAPCO stock with a cost basis of $100,000. At retirement, George should transfer the $350,000 that is not KAPCO stock into an IRA. That will defer taxes on that money. Then, the $250,000 of KAPCO stock should be transferred into a regular, taxable brokerage account. In the year of retirement, George will have to report the $100,000 cost basis as ordinary income. However, the $150,000 in unrealized appreciation will receive the more favorable long-term capital gains rate when sold. If George holds on to the stock for another five years and it appreciates by another $50,000, then, upon sale, the entire $200,000 of gain is considered long-term.

SUMMARY OF DISTRIBUTION RULES FROM BOTH QUALIFIED PLANS AND IRAs

Qualified Plans and IRAs

Even though we have previously discussed IRA withdrawals, it is worth repeating them here to compare and contrast them with distributions from qualified plans.

Distributions from traditional IRAs must generally begin no later than April 1 of the year following the year in which the taxpayer attains age 70½.

In applying distribution rules, all traditional IRAs and SEPs are treated as a single account and must be liquidated at least to the extent of percentages specified on IRS tables. Qualified plans, however, are not aggregated; distributions from one qualified plan are not affected by distributions from another. What that means is an individual with multiple IRAs computes the RMD from each, but can elect to distribute the amounts from each IRA or select the IRA(s) from which to make the distribution. In the case of multiple qualified plans, (the individual worked for more than one employer and did not rollover the earlier employer's plan), the required RMD must be taken from each plan; there is no combining as there is with IRAs.

Lifetime Distributions

Early Withdrawal Penalties

In general, withdrawals from both IRAs and qualified plans are taxed as ordinary income. However, withdrawals from such arrangements occurring before owners turn age 59½ are subject to an additional 10% premature withdrawal penalty. Withdrawals from both escape the penalty when they are made on account of death or total disability, correcting excess contributions, or as a series of substantially equal payments over the life of the plan participant and beneficiary, if applicable. Only in the case of a *qualified plan* is the penalty avoided by using a qualified domestic relations order (QDRO).

TEST TOPIC ALERT

Although pre-59½ withdrawals from IRAs for education and first-time home purchase escape the early withdrawal penalty, withdrawals from qualified plans for those purposes do not.

The 10% tax will not apply on withdrawals from either of these before age 59½, however, if:

- the distribution is made to a beneficiary on or after the death of the employee/individual;

- the distribution is made because the employee/individual acquires a qualifying disability; or

- the distribution is made as a part of a series of substantially equal periodic payments under IRS Rule72(t), beginning after separation from service with the employer maintaining the plan before the payments begin, and made at least annually for the life or life expectancy of the employee/individual or the joint lives or life expectancies of the employee/individual and his designated beneficiary. (Excepting in the case of death or disability, the payments under this exception must continue for at least five years or until the employee/individual reaches age 59½, whichever is the longer period.)

TAKE NOTE

After a person begins taking distributions from an IRA under Rule 72(t), contributions, asset transfers, or rollovers are not permitted while receiving payments.

Penalty Tax on Failure to Make Required Minimum Distributions

As with IRAs, other than a Roth IRA, failure to distribute the required amount from qualified plans generates a 50% penalty tax on the shortfall in addition to ordinary income taxation. However, as mentioned earlier, and of particular importance as employees are working to much later ages than in previous generations, there are no RMDs from a qualified plan while still employed by the sponsor of that plan, regardless of your age.

Withholding on Eligible Rollover Distributions from Qualified Plans

Distributions paid to an employee are subjected to a mandatory federal withholding of 20% if the distribution is an eligible rollover distribution. Eligible rollover distributions (those which can be rolled over or transferred without current taxation) do not include the following:

- RMDs;

- hardship distributions;

- substantially equal lifetime payments (SEPP);

■ distribution of excess contributions; and

■ loans treated as deemed distributions.

TAKE NOTE

An employee may avoid the 20% withholding by having the distribution processed as a direct rollover to an eligible retirement plan. In a direct rollover the distribution check is made payable to the trustee or custodian of the receiving retirement plan.

Figure 24.2: 10% Early Distribution Penalty Exceptions by Plan Types

	Qualified Pension, Profit-Sharing, and TSAs (403(b) Plans)	401(k) and SIMPLE Plans	Traditional, Roth, and SEP IRAs
Death	X	X	X
Disability	X	X	X
Separation from service after age 55	X	X	
Certain medical expenses	X	X	X
QDROs	X	X	
To reduce excess contributions or deferrals	X	X	X
As substantially equal payments over life	X	X	X
First-time home purchase			X
Higher education expenses			X
Health insurance premiums while unemployed			X

SUMMARY OF ROLLOVER AND TRANSFER RULES

Following is a summary of the rules applying to moving money from one tax-deferred account to another. Here are the three key points:

■ **Direct rollover:** In the event the qualified plan calls for a distribution upon separation from service, a request can be made to the plan administrator to send the payment directly to another retirement plan or to an IRA. In this case, there are no taxes withheld from the amount transferred and no income is reported for tax purposes.

■ **Trustee-to-trustee transfer:** An investor who wishes to change trustees for an IRA, such as moving the account to another firm or mutual fund group, upon request, the trustee or custodian for the "old" IRA will make the payment directly to the trustee of the "new" IRA. In some cases, the IRA distribution may be made to the trustees of an employer-sponsored plan in the fashion. In either case, there are no taxes withheld from the amount transferred and no income is reported for tax purposes.

■ **60-day rollover:** In the event the distribution from an IRA or qualified employer plan is paid directly to the participant, there is the option to deposit all or any part of it to another IRA or qualified plan within 60 calendar days. However, there will be a 20% withholding tax on this distribution from the qualified plan (withholding is optional on the IRA distribution). That means, to avoid any tax, the individual will have to find other funds to deposit to cover the withheld amount. Any portion of the distribution that is not rolled over will be subject to tax and, if under age 59½, will be subject to the 10% (unless qualifying for one of the exemptions from the penalty tax).

EMPLOYEE RETIREMENT INCOME SECURITY ACT OF 1974 (ERISA)

U24LO5: Identify the purpose of the Employee Retirement Income Security Act of 1974 and its primary features including the fiduciary obligations under the Uniform Prudent Investor Act.

ERISA guidelines for the regulation of retirement plans include the following.

- **Eligibility.** If a company offers a retirement plan, all employees must be covered if they are 21 years old or older, have one year of service, and work 1,000 hours per year.

- **Funding.** Funds contributed to the plan must be segregated from other corporate assets. The plan's trustees have a fiduciary responsibility to invest prudently and manage funds in a way that represents the best interests of all participants.

- **Vesting.** Employees must be entitled to their entire retirement benefit amounts within a certain time, even if they no longer work for the employer.

- **Communication.** The retirement plan must be in writing, and employees must be kept informed of plan benefits, availability, account status, and vesting procedure no less frequently than annually.

- **Nondiscrimination.** A uniformly applied formula determines employee benefits and contributions. Such a method ensures equitable and impartial treatment.

TAKE NOTE

In the case of 403(b) plans, historically, they were totally exempt from ERISA. As Department of Labor regulations continue to make them increasingly similar to 401(k) plans, some 403(b) plans are now required to meet certain ERISA standards, such as nondiscrimination. Because it is not universal coverage, it is doubtful that the topic will appear on your exam.

ERISA regulations apply to *private sector* (corporate) plans only. Plans for federal or state government workers (*public sector* plans) are not subject to ERISA.

Fiduciary Responsibility Under ERISA

Because most retirement plans were set up under trust agreements, when it became time for ERISA to address fiduciary responsibilities of plan trustees, there was a long history of trust law to fall back on.

It all began with the Prudent Man Rule. That legal standard was established in 1830 by a Massachusetts Court decision (*Harvard College v. Amory*, 9 Pick. [26 Mass.] 446, 461 [1830]):

> All that is required of a trustee to invest is, that he shall conduct himself faithfully and exercise sound discretion. He is to observe how men of prudence, discretion and intelligence manage their own affairs, not in regard to speculation, but in regard to the permanent disposition of their funds, considering the probable income, as well as the probable safety of the capital to be invested.

Although it was possible to place common stock in a trust portfolio, the emphasis seemed to be on taking defensive positions that while preserving capital, did expose the portfolio to inflation risk. It was clear that some updating was necessary.

Beginning with the dynamic growth of the stock markets in the late 1960s, the investment practices of fiduciaries experienced significant change. As a result, the Uniform Prudent Investor Act (UPIA) was adopted in 1994 as an attempt to update trust investment laws in recognition of those many changes. One of the major influences on this legislation was the growing acceptance of modern portfolio theory. The UPIA (now used in almost every state) makes five fundamental alterations in the former criteria for prudent investing. Those changes are as follows.

- The standard of prudence is applied to any investment as part of the total portfolio, rather than to individual investments. In this context, the term *portfolio* means all of the trust's or estate's assets.

- The trade-off in all investments between risk and return is identified as the fiduciary's primary consideration.

- All categorical restrictions on types of investments have been removed; the trustee can invest in anything that plays an appropriate role in achieving the risk/return objectives of the trust and that meets the other requirements of prudent investing.

- The well-accepted requirement that fiduciaries diversify their investments has been integrated into the definition of prudent investing.

- The much-criticized former rule forbidding the trustee to delegate investment functions has been reversed. Delegation is now permitted, subject to safeguards.

With greater numbers of trustees delegating investment decisions to investment advisers, NASAA has determined that you must know how the UPIA affects your role. Here are some thoughts that will help you on the exam.

- A trustee must invest and manage trust assets as a prudent investor would, by considering the purposes, terms, distribution requirements, and other circumstances of the trust. In satisfying this standard, the trustee must exercise reasonable care, skill, and caution.

- A trustee's investment and management decisions about individual assets must be evaluated not in isolation but in the context of the total portfolio and as a part of an overall investment strategy with risk and return objectives that are reasonably suited to the trust.

- Among circumstances that a trustee must consider in investing and managing trust assets are any of the following that are relevant to the trust or its beneficiaries:
  - General economic conditions
  - The possible effect of inflation or deflation
  - The expected tax consequences of investment decisions or strategies
  - The role that each asset plays within the total portfolio, including financial assets, tangible and intangible personal property, and real property
  - The expected total return from income and the appreciation of capital
  - Other resources of the beneficiaries
  - Needs for liquidity, regularity of income, and preservation or appreciation of capital
  - An asset's special relationship or special value, if any, to the purposes of the trust or to one or more of the beneficiaries

- A trustee who has special skills or expertise, or who is named trustee in reliance upon the trustee's representation that the trustee has special skills or expertise, has a duty to use those special skills or expertise. This particular item led to the most stringent standard, that of the **prudent expert** for one acting as a professional money manager.

■ For those without special skills or expertise, a trustee may delegate investment and management functions as long as the trustee exercises reasonable care, skill, and caution in:

  — selecting the adviser,

  — establishing the scope and terms of the delegation, consistent with the purposes and terms of the trust, and

  — periodically reviewing the adviser's actions, to monitor the adviser's performance and compliance with the terms of the delegation. (However, something that cannot be delegated is the amount and timing of distributions. If it is for a trust, the trust document usually spells out those provisions and, in the case of a qualified retirement plan, the plan document accomplishes the same purpose.)

■ A trustee who complies with all of the previous is not liable to the beneficiaries or the trust for the decisions or actions of the adviser to whom the function was delegated.

■ In performing a delegated function, the adviser owes a duty to the trust to exercise reasonable care to comply with the terms of the delegation.

EXAMPLE

1. Which of the following would best describe a prudent investor?

  A. A person in a fiduciary capacity who invests in a prudent manner

  B. A trustee who invests with reasonable care, skill, and caution

  C. An investment adviser representative handling a discretionary account

  D. The custodian for a minor under the Uniform Transfers to Minors Act

Answer: B. Although all of these may have a fiduciary responsibility, the definition, as expressed in the Uniform Prudent Investor Act of 1994, requires reasonable care, skill, and caution, choice **B**.

Section 404 of ERISA

Specifically, there are a number of regulations that apply directly to retirement plan fiduciaries. The details are spelled out in ERISA Section 404.

Under Section 404 of ERISA, every person who acts as a fiduciary for an employee benefit plan must perform his responsibilities in accordance with the plan document specifications. Under ERISA, trustees cannot delegate fiduciary duties, but they can delegate investment management responsibilities to a qualified investment manager.

TEST TOPIC ALERT

Although the UPIA permits the delegation of portfolio management decisions, trustees cannot delegate certain fiduciary duties, such as determining the amount and timing of distributions.

Fiduciary responsibilities to the plan are explicit. With respect to the plan, fiduciaries must act:

■ solely in the interest of plan participants and beneficiaries;

■ for the exclusive purpose of providing benefits to participants and their beneficiaries and defraying reasonable plan expenses;

- with the care, skill, prudence, and diligence under the circumstances then prevailing that a prudent professional would use (known as the **prudent expert rule**);

- to diversify investments to minimize the risk of large losses, unless doing so is clearly not prudent under the circumstances; and

- in accordance with the governing plan documents unless they are not consistent with ERISA.

Under ERISA provisions, the fiduciary must be as prudent as the average expert, not the average person. To act with care, skill, prudence, and caution, the fiduciary must also:

- diversify plan assets;

- make investment decisions under the prudent expert standard;

- monitor investment performance;

- control investment expenses; and

- not engage in prohibited transactions.

TAKE NOTE

A plan participant or beneficiary who controls his specific plan account is not a fiduciary.

TEST TOPIC ALERT

You may be required to know that transaction cost is not a determining factor in security selection. That is, when the fiduciary is deciding what security will fit the needs of the portfolio, the amount of commission involved in the purchase is not considered when determining if that security is an appropriate addition.

Investment Policy Statement

Although it is not specifically mandated under ERISA, it is strongly suggested that each employee benefit plan have an investment policy statement (IPS), preferably in writing, which serves as a guideline for the plan's fiduciary regarding funding and investment management decisions. Investment policy statements address the specific needs of the plan.

For employee benefit plans that use outside investment managers (such as mutual funds), the fiduciary must ensure that the investment alternatives available to plan members are consistent with the policy statement.

A typical IPS will include:

- investment objectives for the plan;

- determination for meeting future cash flow needs;

- investment philosophy including asset allocation style;

- investment selection criteria (but *not* the specific securities themselves); and

- methods for monitoring procedures and performance.

TEST TOPIC ALERT

The IPS will NOT include specific security selection.

Unit 24

Prohibited Investments Under ERISA

It is important to differentiate between prohibited investments and prohibited transactions. Similar to IRAs, qualified plans cannot invest in art, antiques, gems, coins, collectibles, or alcoholic beverages. They can invest in precious metals, such as gold and silver coins minted by the U.S. Treasury, only if they meet various federal requirements. ERISA also limits how much some plans can invest in the employer's stock. Although not specifically prohibited under ERISA, the exam will never find writing *uncovered calls* in a retirement plan to be a prudent decision.

Prohibited Transactions by the Plan Fiduciary

ERISA allows for a wide range of investments and investment practices, but a plan fiduciary is strictly prohibited from any conflicts of interest, such as:

- self-dealing, dealing with plan assets in his own interest, or for his own account;

- acting in a transaction involving the plan on behalf of a party with interests adverse to the plan; and

- receiving any compensation for his personal account from any party dealing with the plan in connection with plan transactions.

TEST TOPIC ALERT

Under Section 407 of ERISA, a plan may not acquire any security or real (or personal) property of the employer, if immediately after such acquisition the aggregate fair market value of employer securities and employer real property held by the plan exceeds 10% of the fair market value of the assets of the plan.

Party in Interest

ERISA has a rather broad definition of the term *party in interest*, but it basically includes anyone who can have an impact on an employee benefit plan, including those who render advice to the plan. It is not an overstatement to say that all transactions involving parties in interest to an ERISA-covered plan are prohibited, unless there is an exemption for them.

TEST TOPIC ALERT

Anyone in the position of trustee over the assets of a qualified plan may not use the plan assets to make loans to the employer, even if failure to do so could lead to the company suffering a financial failure.

Safe Harbor Provisions of Section 404(c)

Several times, we have mentioned the requirement for the plan fiduciary to diversify the plan's investments. There is a particular part of ERISA, Section 404(c) dealing with 401(k) plans that provides a safe harbor from liability for the trustee if certain conditions are met. Under ERISA Section 404(c), a fiduciary is not liable for losses to the plan resulting from the participant's selection of investment in his own account, provided the participant exercised control over the investment and the plan met the detailed requirements of a Department of Labor regulation—that is, the 404(c) regulation.

There are three basic conditions of this regulation:

■ Investment selection

■ Investment control

■ Communicating required information

Let's look at these individually.

■ Investment selection—A 404(c) plan participant must be able to:

– materially affect portfolio return potential and risk level;

– choose between at least three investment alternatives; and

– diversify his investment to minimize the risk of large losses.

The practical effect of this is that it would be highly unlikely for the plan to meet the requirements by limiting the available choices to highly speculative funds, such as junk bond funds and highly aggressive growth funds.

TEST TOPIC ALERT

The trustee of a 401(k) would be able to reduce her ERISA fiduciary exposure and meet the safe harbor provisions of 404(c) if the plan offered a broad index fund, a medium term government bond fund, and a cash equivalent fund. It isn't the number of funds that counts; it is the different asset classes available. For example, if the plan offered 10 investment options, instead of three, but they were all of the same asset class, such as 10 equity funds, or 10 bond funds, that would not comply with 404(c).

■ Investment control—control is defined as:

– allowing employees the opportunity to exercise independent control over the assets in their account by letting them make their own choices among the investment options companies have selected (at least three);

– informing employees that they can change their investment allocations at least quarterly (a growing number of plans allow employees to make plan changes daily); and

– even though the employees maintain investment control, the plan fiduciary is not relieved of the responsibility to monitor the performance of the investment alternatives being offered and replace them when necessary.

■ Communicating required information means:

– making certain information available upon request, such as prospectuses and financial statements or reports relating to the investment options (included must be information such as annual operating expenses and portfolio composition);

– a statement that the plan is intended to constitute an ERISA Section 404(c) plan and that plan fiduciaries may be relieved of liability for investment losses;

– a description of the risk and return characteristics of each of the investment alternatives available under the plan;

– an explanation of how to give investment instructions; and

– allowing real-time access to employee accounts either by telephone or the internet.

TEST TOPIC ALERT

Although we have made extensive reference to **control** in the previous pages, that must be taken in context. Participants in a 401(k) do have a choice of investments, but that choice is limited to the package included in the employer's plan. Participants in a 403(b) plan have even fewer choices; annuities are the primary investment asset in those plans. If investment choice is the criteria, then the greatest control is with an IRA (see the earlier discussion on IRA investments).

EXAMPLE

1. To comply with the safe harbor requirements of Section 404(c) of ERISA, the trustee of a 401(k) plan must

    I.   offer plan participants at least 10 different investment alternatives

    II. allow plan participants to exercise control over their investments

    III. allow plan participants to change their investment options no less frequently than monthly

    IV. provide plan participants with information relating to the risks and performance of each investment alternative offered

    A. I and III

    B. I and IV

    C. II and III

    D. II and IV

    Answer: D. To comply with the safe harbor provisions of ERISA's Section 404(c), the plan trustee must allow each participant control over their investments and furnish them with full performance and risk information. Choice **D** contains both of these. The rule only mandates a minimum of 3 alternatives and quarterly changes.

Summary Plan Description (SPD)

Sometimes referred to as the summary plan document, one of the most important documents participants are entitled to receive automatically when becoming a participant of an ERISA-covered retirement plan or a beneficiary receiving benefits under such a plan is a summary of the plan, called the summary plan description (SPD). Under regulations of the U.S. Department of Labor (DOL), the plan administrator is legally obligated to provide to participants, free of charge, the SPD. The SPD is an important document that tells participants what the plan provides and how it operates. It provides information on when an employee can begin to participate in the plan, how service and benefits are calculated, when benefits become vested, when and in what form benefits are paid, and how to file a claim for benefits. Unlike the investment policy statement, it does not deal with the investment characteristics of the plan.

Top-Heavy Plan

Because all qualified plans must be nondiscriminatory, the IRS has defined a **top-heavy 401(k) plan** as one in which a disproportionate amount of the benefit goes to key employees. The plan must be tested on an annual basis to ensure that it complies with the regulations. On the exam, you may be asked to define a top-heavy plan and will have to choose between key employees and highly compensated employees. The easiest way to remember is to match the (k) in 401(k) with the word *key*.

Safe Harbor 401(k) Plan

Several years after the top-heavy rules were written, relief was offered in the form of the safe harbor 401(k). A plan does not have to undergo annual top-heavy testing if set up properly.

There are two basic choices for setting up a safe harbor plan. The employer will either match employee contributions or use a nonelective formula (the employees don't have to contribute) of eligible employee compensation to satisfy IRS requirements. If a matching formula is elected:

- the base formula is 100% of elective deferrals up to 3% of compensation and then 50% of elective deferrals on the next 2% of compensation. This means the maximum match is 4% (100% × 3% + 50% × 2% = 3% + 1%); or

- the employer may elect the nonelective formula (minimum of 3%) of all eligible participants' compensation. Under this formula, all eligible employees would receive this nonelective contribution whether making salary reduction contributions or not.

In either case, all employer contributions are immediately vested.

COVERDELL EDUCATION SAVINGS ACCOUNTS

U24LO6: Compare the differences between the two major types of education funding programs.

The examination will deal with two different types of programs designed to offer tax benefits when saving for education. We will begin with the Coverdell ESA and then move on to the Section 529 Plan.

The Taxpayer Relief Act of 1997 also created **Education IRAs** with a $500 annual contribution limit. In 2002, these were renamed **Coverdell ESAs**. ESAs allow after-tax contributions for student beneficiaries. Contributions must be made in cash and must be made on or before the date on which the beneficiary attains age 18 unless the beneficiary is a **special needs beneficiary**—an individual who because of a physical, mental, or emotional condition requires additional time to complete their education. Coverdell ESAs fund educational expenses of a designated beneficiary by allowing after-tax (nondeductible) contributions to accumulate on a tax-deferred basis. Probably owing to its heritage as an "IRA," these offer the same investment flexibility (and restrictions) as a self-directed IRA.

When distributions are made from a Coverdell ESA, the earnings portion of the distribution is excluded from income when it is used to pay qualified education expenses. Withdrawn earnings are taxed to the recipient (beneficiary) and subject to a 10% tax penalty when they are not used to pay qualified education expenses.

TAKE NOTE

If the money is not used by a beneficiary's 30th birthday (except for a special needs beneficiary), it must be distributed and the earnings are subject to ordinary income taxes and a 10% penalty.

Under EGTRRA, the maximum annual contribution limit to a Coverdell ESA was increased to $2,000 per beneficiary with a sunset provision in 2011 whereby the level would be reduced to the original $500 level. In 2013, Congress made the $2,000 limit permanent. In addition to qualified higher education expenses (postsecondary education), the account can also be used for elementary and secondary education expenses and for public, private, or religious schools.

The contribution to a Coverdell ESA may be limited depending on the amount of AGI and filing status.

Allowable Contribution	Single Filers	Joint Filers
Full contribution of $2,000 at AGI of and below	$95,000	$190,000
Partial phaseout begins at	$95,001	$190,001
No contributions may be made at AGI of and above	$110,000	$220,000

TAKE NOTE

There is nothing to prevent more than one individual from contributing to a Coverdell ESA; the annual limit applies to each beneficiary. Parents and grandparents can contribute to a single account, as long as the $2,000 limit per child is not exceeded in any given year.

Other changes made by the EGTRRA of 2001 include:

- provisions that allow contributions to continue past age 18 for beneficiaries with special needs;

- extending the period during which corrective withdrawals can be made to avoid the early distribution and excess contribution penalties; and

- allowing Coverdell ESA contributions, for any year, to be made up to April 15 of the following year (just like contributions to your IRA).

TEST TOPIC ALERT

Here are some key test points about Coverdell ESAs:

- Contributions can be made by parents and other adults; the total for one child is still $2,000.

- Contribution limit is $2,000 per year per child until the child's 18th birthday.

- Contributions are not tax deductible, but all earnings are tax deferred.

- Distributions are tax free if they are taken before age 30 and used for eligible education expenses.

- If the accumulated value in the account is not used by age 30 (except for special needs students), the funds must be distributed and subject to income tax and a 10% penalty on the earnings or rolled over into a different Coverdell ESA for another family member. Their definition of family is extremely broad and, in addition to the obvious, includes cousins, aunts and uncles, and even in-laws.

EXAMPLE

1. The maximum amount that may be invested in a Coverdell ESA in one year is

   A. $500 per parent

   B. $500 per couple

   C. $2,000 per child

   D. $2,000 per couple

   Answer: C. Only $2,000 may be invested in each child's ESA per year. If a couple has three children, they may contribute $6,000 in total, or $2,000 per child, per year, choice **C**.

SECTION 529 PLANS

Section 529 plans, legally known as qualified tuition programs (QTPs), are state-operated investment plans that were designed to give families a way to save money for college with substantial tax benefits. With the passage of Tax Cuts and Jobs Act of 2017, these plans extended the qualification to K–12 schooling as well. That change will be covered separately. There are two basic types of 529 plans: prepaid tuition plans and college savings plans.

Prepaid Tuition Plans

Prepaid tuition plans generally allow college savers to prepay for tuition at participating colleges and universities, and in some cases, room and board can be prepaid as well. Most prepaid tuition plans are sponsored by state governments and have residency requirements. The basic concept is that if you pay for the tuition at today's rates, the child will be able to attend in the future, regardless of how much higher the tuition is.

College Savings Plans

College savings plans generally permit the contributor, known as the account holder, to establish an account for a student (the beneficiary) for the purpose of paying the beneficiary's qualified college expenses. The typical plan offers a number of investment options including stock mutual funds, bond mutual funds, and money market funds. A very popular option is the age-based portfolio that automatically shifts toward more conservative investments as the beneficiary gets closer to college age. Withdrawals from college savings plans can generally be used at any college or university regardless of the state carrying the plan or the state of residence.

Differences Between the Two QTPs

The following chart outlines some of the major differences between prepaid tuition plans and college savings plans.

Prepaid Tuition Plan	College Savings Plan
Locks in tuition prices at eligible public and private colleges and universities	No lock on college costs
All plans cover tuition and mandatory fees only. Some plans allow families to purchase a room and board option or use excess tuition credits for other qualified expenses.	Covers all qualified higher education expenses, including the following: ■ Tuition ■ Room and board ■ Mandatory fees ■ Books, computers (if required)
Most plans set lump sum and installment payments before purchase based on age of beneficiary and number of years of college tuition purchased.	Many plans have contribution limits in excess of $250,000.
Many state plans guaranteed or backed by state	No state guarantee. Most investment options are subject to market risk. Your investment may make no profit or even decline in value.
Most plans have age/grade limit for beneficiary	No age limits. Open to adults and children.
Most state plans require either owner or beneficiary of plan to be a state resident	No residency requirement. However, nonresidents may only be able to purchase some plans through financial advisers or brokers.
Most plans have limited enrollment period	Enrollment open all year

Source: Smart Saving for College, FINRA®

EXAMPLE

1. One of your clients is a successful professional couple with earnings in excess of $500,000 per year. They are interested in providing a funding source for postsecondary education for their grandchildren. Which would be appropriate to discuss with them?

   A. The Coverdell ESA

   B. The Section 529 Plan

   C. Both the Coverdell ESA and the Section 529 Plan

   D. Neither the Coverdell ESA nor the Section 529 Plan

   Answer: B. Although both plans will help them with their objective, their earnings are above the Coverdell ESA limits so choice **B** is the best answer.

Tax Treatment of 529 Plans

A major factor in investing in a 529 plan is tax benefits. Although contributions are made with after-tax money, earnings in 529 plans are not subject to federal tax and, in most cases, state tax, so long as withdrawals are for eligible college expenses, such as tuition, and room and board, and even a computer.

However, money representing earnings that is withdrawn from a 529 plan for ineligible expenses will be subject to income tax and an additional 10% federal tax penalty. Unlike the IRS, many states offer deductions or credits against state income tax for investing in a 529 plan. But eligibility for these benefits is generally limited to participants in a 529 plan sponsored by your state of residence.

Withdrawal Restrictions

Both plans place restrictions on withdrawals. With limited exceptions, you can only withdraw money that you invest in a 529 plan for eligible college expenses without incurring taxes and penalties. However, you can rollover any unused funds to a member of the beneficiary's family without incurring any tax liability as long as the rollover is completed within 60 days of the distribution. Immediate family includes the following:

- Son, daughter, stepchild, foster child, adopted child, or a descendant of any of them

- Brother, sister, stepbrother, or stepsister

- Father, mother, or ancestor of either

- Stepfather or stepmother

- Son or daughter of a brother or sister

- Brother or sister of father or mother

- Son-in-law, daughter-in-law, father-in-law, mother-in-law, brother-in-law, or sister-in-law

- The spouse of any individual listed here

- First cousin

TEST TOPIC ALERT

The earnings portion of a nonqualified distribution is taxable to the individual who receives the payment, either the account owner or the designated beneficiary. If the payment is not made to the designated beneficiary or to an eligible educational institution for the benefit of the designated beneficiary, it will be deemed to have been made to the account owner.

TEST TOPIC ALERT

What if you don't like the 529 plan you are invested in? Can you make a change? Federal tax law allows a tax-free rollover of any or all of a 529 account from the current 529 plan to a different 529 plan, but only once in any 12-month period unless there is a change in beneficiary. Just as with an IRA, if the proceeds are distributed, they must be reinvested in the new plan within 60 days. Therefore, assets in the QTP may be moved from the plan of one state to the plan of another no more frequently than once per 12 months.

TEST TOPIC ALERT

As of the date of this question, there are approximately 330 institutions of higher learning located outside of the United States where Section 529 plans (and Coverdell ESAs) may be used to pay qualified expenses. The expense for room and board (residence cost) qualifies only to the extent that it isn't more than the greater of the following two amounts.

- The allowance for room and board, as determined by the eligible educational institution, that was included in the cost of attendance (for federal financial aid purposes) for a particular academic period and living arrangement of the student; or

- The actual amount charged if the student is residing in housing owned or operated by the eligible educational institution.

Impact on Financial Eligibility

Investing in a 529 plan (or Coverdell ESA) will generally impact a student's eligibility to participate in need-based financial aid. Both types of plans are treated as parental assets in the calculation of the expected family contribution toward college costs regardless of whether the owner is the parent or the student. This computation is done on the FAFSA Form (The Free Application for Federal Student Aid). Having money in a 529 plan is a better deal than if they were non-529 assets of the student because parental assets are assessed on the FAFSA at a maximum 5.64% rate in determining the student's expected family contribution (EFC) rather than the 20% rate on non-529 (or ESA) assets owned by the student, such as those in an UTMA account. These rates will not be tested, but the concept may be.

Contributions to a 529 Plan

Any adult can open a 529 plan for a future college student. The donor does not have to be related to the student.

With a 529 plan, the donor can invest a small or substantial lump sum or make periodic payments. When the student is ready for college, the donor withdraws the amount needed to pay for qualified education expenses (e.g., tuition, room and board, and books). Contributions are made with after-tax dollars, but qualified withdrawals are exempt from federal taxation. As stated previously, taxation varies from state to state. If any tax is due on withdrawal, it is the responsibility of the student, not the donor.

A donor (typically a parent or grandparent) may contribute a maximum of $75,000 ($150,000 if married) in a single year for each Section 529 Plan beneficiary without gift tax consequences. This represents a five-year advance on the (2019) $15,000 per recipient annual gift tax exclusion.

The donor of the 529 plan assets retains control of most 529 accounts and may take the money back at any time (although a 10% penalty tax may apply).

TAKE NOTE

Although it probably won't be tested, for those who bunch the annual gift exclusion allowing five years' worth at one time, this is not limited to one time per beneficiary. If started with a one-year-old grandchild, the grandparents can do this again when the child is six (five years have elapsed) and then again at 11, and so forth, as long as the total contribution does not exceed the state's limit. Sure would be nice to have grandparents like that, wouldn't it?

Offering Circular

These plans are considered municipal fund securities, and under the rules of the Municipal Securities Rulemaking Board (MSRB), require delivery of an official statement, sometimes called an offering circular, but never referred to as a prospectus. This leads to somewhat of a lack of flexibility because the investment choices are limited to the offerings provided in that offering circular.

Investment Options for 529 Plans

In general, these plans offer several different portfolio options ranging from aggressive (for those with a longer time horizon) to guaranteed (for those in college using the funds). In most cases, these portfolios are registered mutual funds, in others, they are separately managed accounts containing stocks and/or bonds. Some portfolios include insured bank CDs and some of the states offer managed fixed-income pools.

TEST TOPIC ALERT

However, U.S. Savings Bonds are not available as investment options in Section 529 plans.

Effect of TCJA 2017

The new rule permits K–12 withdrawals as qualified expenses for attendance at a public, private or religious elementary or secondary school. Virtually everything that applies to the pre-TCJA Section 529 Plan is the same with one major exception: qualified expenses are limited to $10,000 of tuition per student annually.

TAKE NOTE

Key points to remember about Section 529 plans include the following.

- The dollar amount of allowable contribution varies from state to state and may be as high as $300,000.

- Assets in the account remain under the donor's control even after the student is of legal age.

- There are no income limitations on donors making contributions to a 529 plan.

- Similar to Coverdell ESAs, these can be used for educational expenses incurred below the postsecondary level (post high school), but with expense limitations.

- There are no age restrictions. That is, if at any age, an individual desires to go back to school, a 529 Plan may be used.

- Earnings are exempt from federal taxes (as are withdrawals) if they go toward qualified postsecondary educational expenses.

- Most states hire experienced investment management companies to manage their accounts.

- In almost all cases, residents do not pay state income tax on qualified withdrawals from home-state plans.

- In a majority of the states with an income tax, residents are afforded an income tax deduction or credit for a portion of their contribution.

- If funds are withdrawn for purposes other than education, earnings are subject to a 10% penalty as well as federal income tax. States may assess their own penalties. The tax is the obligation of the distributee (student beneficiary or owner).

- A child can be a beneficiary of an ESA and a 529.

- Because of their legal status as municipal fund securities, it is required to deliver an official statement or offering circular when opening a 529 Plan account.

EXAMPLE

1. While in your office, you see that your firm is going to be holding a training session on municipal fund securities. You wish to attend because you are interested in being able to speak intelligently to your clients about

   A. the difference between GO bonds and revenue bonds
   B. the difference between using mutual funds or UITs to invest in municipal bonds
   C. Section 529 plans
   D. Section 457 plans

   Answer: C. The Securities and Exchange Commission has stated that certain Section 529 College Savings Plans established by states or local governmental entities are municipal fund securities. Accordingly, the purchase and sale of state-sponsored Section 529 plans are governed by the rules of the MSRB, choice **C**.

UGMA/UTMA ACCOUNTS

U24LO7: Contrast UGMA and UTMA accounts.

Long before there were Education IRAs and Section 529 plans, a favored way of saving for a child's education (or anything else for that matter), was by the use of a custodial account under the Uniform Gift to Minors Act. In a **custodial account**, the custodian for the beneficial owner enters all trades. UGMA and UTMA accounts require an adult or a trustee to act as custodian for a minor (the beneficial owner). Any kind of security or cash may be gifted to the account without limitation.

The Uniform Law Commissioners adopted the Uniform Gift to Minors Act (UGMA) in 1956 (the same year as the Uniform Securities Act). The primary focus then was to provide a convenient way to make gifts of money and securities to minors. Later, it became clear that a more flexible law was desirable. The Uniform Law Commissioners adopted the Uniform Transfers to Minors Act (UTMA) in 1986. UTMA expands the types of property you can transfer to a minor and provides that you can make other types of transfers besides gifts.

Nearly all states have adopted UTMA, but people still tend to refer to UGMA out of habit. For exam purposes, it doesn't matter which law is in effect in your state because the essential principles of both acts are the same.

Custodian

Securities in an UGMA/UTMA account are managed by a custodian until the minor reaches the age of majority, or in the case of UTMA, the age determined by the specific state. The custodian has full control over the minor's account and can:

- buy or sell securities;
- exercise rights or warrants; and
- liquidate, trade, or hold securities.

The custodian also may use the property in the account in any way the custodian deems proper for the minor's support, education, maintenance, general use, or benefit. However, the account is *not* normally used to pay expenses associated with raising a child, such as the three basic needs of food, clothing, and shelter.

Opening an UGMA/UTMA Account

UGMA/UTMA account applications must contain the custodian's name, minor's name and Social Security number, and the state in which the UGMA/UTMA is registered.

TEST TOPIC ALERT

The minor's Social Security number is used on the account.

Fiduciary Responsibility

An UGMA/UTMA custodian assumes fiduciary responsibilities in managing a minor's account. Restrictions are placed on improper handling of investments in an UGMA/UTMA. The most important limitations follow.

- UGMAs/UTMAs may be opened and managed as cash accounts only.
- A custodian may never purchase securities on margin or pledge them as collateral for a loan.
- A custodian must reinvest all cash proceeds, dividends, and interest within a reasonable period. Cash proceeds may be held in an interest-bearing custodial account for a reasonable period.
- Investment decisions must consider a minor's age and the custodial relationship; examples of inappropriate investments are commodity futures, naked options, and high-risk securities.
- Covered call writing is normally allowed.
- Stock subscription rights or warrants must be either exercised or sold.

A custodian may be reimbursed for any reasonable expenses incurred in managing the account. Compensation may be paid to the custodian unless the custodian is also the donor.

Donating Securities

When a person makes a gift of securities to a minor under the UGMA/UTMA laws, that person is the securities' **donor**. A gift under UGMA/UTMA conveys an **indefeasible title**— that is, the donor may not take back the gift, nor may the minor return the gift until the minor has reached the age of majority. Once a gift is donated, the donor gives up all rights to the property. When the minor reaches the specified age, the property in the account is transferred into the minor's name.

UGMA/UTMA Rules

Registered investment advisers should know the following UGMA/UTMA custodial account rules.

- All gifts are irrevocable. Gifts may be in the form of cash or fully paid securities.
- An account may have only one custodian and one minor or beneficial owner.
- A donor of securities can act as custodian or appoint someone to do so.

Unit 24

- Unless they are acting as custodians, parents have no legal control over an UGMA/UTMA account or the securities in it.

- A minor can be the beneficiary of more than one account, and a person may serve as custodian for more than one UGMA/UTMA, provided each account benefits only one minor.

- The minor has the right to sue the custodian for improper actions.

TAKE NOTE

Although an investment adviser representative is not responsible for determining whether an appointment is valid or a custodian's activities are appropriate, he should always be sensitive to the appearance of unethical behavior.

EXAMPLE

1. If a customer would like to open a custodial UGMA or UTMA account for his nephew, a minor, the uncle can

    A. open the account provided the proper trust arrangements are filed first

    B. open the account and name himself custodian

    C. open the account, but he needs a legal document evidencing the nephew's parents' prior approval of the account

    D. be custodian for the account only if he is also the minor's legal guardian

    Answer: B. The donor may name himself the custodian of an UGMA or UTMA account, choice **B**. No documentation of custodial status is required to open these accounts, and the custodian is not required to be the minor's legal guardian.

Registration of UGMA/UTMA Securities

Any securities in an UGMA/UTMA account are generally registered in the custodian's name for the benefit of the minor and *cannot be solely in the minor's name.*

So that transfers may be accomplished more expeditiously, securities may be held by custodians in street name.

EXAMPLE

In an account where Marilyn Johns, the donor, has appointed her daughter's aunt, Barbara Wood, as custodian for the account of her minor daughter, Alexis, the account and the certificates would read "Barbara Wood as custodian for Alexis Johns" (or a variation of this form).

When the minor reaches the age of transfer, all of the securities in the account are registered in her name. However, that change in registration is not automatic—the new adult must initiate the transfer.

Death of the Minor or Custodian

If the beneficiary of an UGMA/UTMA dies, the securities in the account pass to the minor's estate, not to the parents or the custodian. If the custodian dies or resigns, either a court of law or the donor must appoint a new custodian.

UNIQUE FEATURES OF THE UNIFORM TRANSFERS TO MINORS (UTMA)

Although UTMA and UGMA share many characteristics, there are a few important differences. First, although UGMA accounts may not hold real estate (real property), certain partnership interests, and other types of intangible property, UTMA accounts may. Thus, UTMA accounts offer greater investment choice.

In many states, UTMA account assets are not required to be transferred upon the age of majority of the beneficial owner (the child). In many UTMA states, the custodian may delay transferring the UTMA assets to the beneficial owner until he becomes age 21 or 25 (depending on the particular state statute).

EXAMPLE

1. One of the reasons you might suggest that a client with an 8-year-old child open an UTMA account rather than an UGMA is that the UTMA offers

   A. better tax advantages

   B. more investment flexibility

   C. more investment control to the parent

   D. greater flexibility in the appointment of a custodian

   Answer: B. UTMA has two testable advantages:

   - The money does not have to automatically transfer to the child once the age of majority is reached—it can be delayed, depending on the state, until as long as age 25.

   - The range of investments permitted under an UTMA is much larger giving the custodian greater flexibility in building the portfolio, which makes B the best choice.

   There is a problem with this question (although not one recognized by NASAA)—you can't select between an UTMA and an UGMA; clients can only use what is available in their state of residence. As of the print date, only 2 states have UGMA on their books; all of the rest plus D.C. use UTMA.

Taxation

The minor's Social Security number appears on an UGMA/UTMA account, and the minor must file an annual income tax return and pay taxes on any **earned** income produced by the UGMA/UTMA account as would any other taxpayer. However, in the case of **unearned** income, such as from dividends and interest, until the minor reaches age 19, or the individual is a full-time student under 24, that unearned income in excess of $2,100 is taxed using the trust tables where rates get as high as 37% when income exceeds $12,750. This is commonly referred to as the **kiddie tax**. This is a change brought about by the TCJA of 2017. Because a married couple doesn't reach the 37% rate until their taxable income exceeds $612,350, it may happen that children will be paying income tax at a rate higher than their parents.

Although the minor is the account's beneficiary and is responsible for any and all taxes on the account, in most states it is the custodian's responsibility to see that the taxes are paid from the account.

FAFSA and Custodial Accounts

In our discussion of educational funding programs, it was mentioned that money in Coverdell ESAs and Section 529 plans is only counted at a 5.64% rate when determining the family's financial contribution toward college. Assets held in a custodial account (UTMA or UGMA) are counted at a 20% rate—a true disadvantage when compared to the other plans.

HSAs

U24LO8: Recall when health-savings accounts (HSAs) may be used.

A health savings account (HSA) is a tax-exempt trust or custodial account individuals can set up with a qualified HSA trustee to pay or reimburse certain medical expenses they incur.

Benefits of an HSA

- You can claim a tax deduction for contributions you, or someone other than your employer, make to your HSA even if you do not itemize your deductions on Form 1040.
- Contributions to your HSA made by your employer (including contributions made through a cafeteria plan) may be excluded from your gross income.
- The contributions remain in your account until you use them.
- The interest or other earnings on the assets in the account are tax free.
- Distributions may be tax free if you pay qualified medical expenses.
- An HSA is portable. It stays with you if you change employers or leave the work force.

Eligibility for an HSA

To be an eligible individual and qualify for an HSA, you must meet the following requirements.

- You must be covered under a high deductible health plan (HDHP), on the first day of the month. That means you are considered to be an eligible individual for the entire year if you are an eligible individual on the first day of the last month of your tax year (December 1 for most taxpayers).
- You have no other health coverage except what is permitted under the rules.
- You are not enrolled in Medicare.
- You cannot be claimed as a dependent on someone else's tax return.
- Each spouse who is an eligible individual who wants an HSA must open a separate HSA. You cannot have a joint HSA.

High Deductible Health Plan (HDHP)

An HDHP has:

- a higher annual deductible than typical health plans, and

- a maximum limit on the sum of the annual deductible and out-of-pocket medical expenses that you must pay for covered expenses. Out-of-pocket expenses include copayments and other amounts, but do not include premiums.

Contributions to an HSA

Any eligible individual can contribute to an HSA. For an employee's HSA, the employee, the employee's employer, or both may contribute to the employee's HSA in the same year. For an HSA established by a self-employed (or unemployed) individual, the individual can contribute. Family members or any other person may also make contributions on behalf of an eligible individual. Contributions to an HSA must be made in cash, but the law permits investments to be made into stocks, bonds, and mutual funds. Contributions of stock or property are not allowed. There is a limit on the amount that may be contributed, but because it is a number that changes each year, it will not be tested. The only facts that could be important are that the contribution for those with family coverage is higher (logically) than that for self-only coverage, and that the amount the individual may contribute is reduced by any amounts contributed by the employer.

TAKE NOTE

Do not confuse an HSA with a FSA (flexible spending account). The FSA account holds money deducted from the employee's pay and remains with the company—it is not investible, and, if you don't use it, you lose it.

EXAMPLE

1. Among the eligibility requirements to open a health savings account is

   A. the individual must be on Medicare

   B. the individual must be claimed as a dependent on another individual's tax return

   C. the individual must have a HDHP

   D. if married, you must have a joint HSA

   Answer: C. To be eligible for a health savings plan, an individual must be enrolled in a high deductible health plan (HDHP), choice **C**.

APPENDIX A

FEDERAL VS. STATE COMPARISON CHART

Definition of Investment Adviser

Any person who, for compensation, engages in the business of advising others as to the value of securities or the advisability of investing in securities or, as part of a regular business, issues analyses or reports concerning securities.	Same as federal.

Exclusions from Above Definition

1. Banks 2. Lawyers, accountants, teachers, engineers 3. Broker-dealers 4. Publisher of any bona fide newspaper, news magazine, or other publication of general circulation 5. Any person whose advice relates solely to securities issued or guaranteed by the U.S. government	1. Banks 2. Lawyers, accountants, teachers, engineers 3. Broker-dealers 4. Publishers of any bona fide newspaper, news magazine, newsletter, or other publication that does not consist of the rendering of advice on the basis of the specific investment situation of each client 5. Investment adviser representatives

Exemptions

1. The Private Fund adviser exemption is available for advisers with less than $150 million in assets under management for private equity funds.
2. The only clients are insurance companies.
3. Intrastate business only and does not furnish advice with respect to securities listed on any national securities exchange, and do not have any private funds as clients.
	1. Private Fund adviser exemption more restrictive than federal law.
	2. Adviser has no place of business within that state and
	  a. The only clients are institutions such as investment companies, banks and trust companies, insurance companies, broker-dealers and other investment advisers, $1 million or larger employee benefit plans, governmental agency, or instrumentalities; or
	  b. Does not direct communications to more than five clients in the state (other than those above) during the previous 12 months (de minimis).

Registration

File Form ADV with the SEC and pay initial and renewal fees based on their fiscal year. Effective within 45 days. No net worth requirements. No surety bonds. Withdrawal of registration is on 60th day. Successor firm pays fee. No registration of investment adviser representatives.	File Form ADV with the Administrator and pay initial and renewal (12./31) fees. Effective at noon of the 30th day. There are net worth and/or surety bonds required (custody or discretion). Withdrawal of registration is on 30th day. Successor firm pays no fee until renewal. Registration automatically registers any adviser representative who is a partner, officer, director, or similar in status.

Recordkeeping

Investment adviser records must be kept easily accessible for five years.	Generally three years for broker-dealers and five years for investment advisers.

Fines/Penalties

$10,000 and five years in jail	$5,000 and three years in jail

Custody of Customer Funds/Securities

Kept by Qualified Custodian. It is custody if securities and/or checks are not returned or forwarded within three days. Third-party checks are not custody. An audited balance sheet would be required if adviser takes advance fees of more than $1,200, six months or more in advance, but not when the adviser maintains custody.	If not prohibited, with written notice to the Administrator. Requires minimum net worth or surety bond of $35,000. It is custody if securities or checks are not returned and third-party checks forwarded within three business days. An audited balance sheet would be required if adviser takes fees of more than $500, six or more months in advance or the adviser maintains custody.

Performance Fees

Prohibited unless: 1. contract with investment company 2. certain clients with at least $1 million under management or net worth in excess of $2.1 million.	Same as federal law, except must make risk incentive statement and other disclosures.

Statute of Limitations for Civil Action

Sooner of three years after the sale or one year after discovery.	Sooner of three years after the sale or two years after discovery.

A "Person"

A natural person or company (includes a corporation, a partnership, an association, a joint stock company, a trust, or any organized group of persons, whether incorporated or not).	An individual, a corporation, an association, a joint stock company, a trust where the interests of the beneficiaries are evidenced by a security, an unincorporated organization, a government, or a political subdivision of a government.

Filing of Advertisements

No filing with the SEC ever.	No filing for exempt securities or exempt transactions, otherwise filed with the Administrator.

Private Placement Exemption

Sold to up to 35 nonaccredited investors under Rule 506(b). Exclusively accredited investors under Rule 506(c).	Up to 10 offers within the state over a 12-month period. The term *accredited investor* is meaningless. Institutions are not counted nor restricted.

Miscellaneous

No assignment of the advisory contract may be made without the client's consent.	Same as federal.
The adviser, if a partnership, must notify the client of any change in the membership of the partnership within a reasonable period of time.	Same as federal.
The Brochure and Brochure Supplement Rule—120-day annual delivery.	Same as federal except 48-hour in advance rule.
The term *investment counsel* may not be used unless: 1. principal business is investment advice; and 2. substantial portion of his service is providing investment supervisory services (the giving of continuous advice on the investment of funds on the basis of the individual needs of each client).	An investment adviser representative is an associated person of an adviser firm (not clerical) who: 1. makes recommendations or otherwise gives advice; 2. manages accounts of clients; 3. solicits or negotiates for the sale of advisory service; and 4. supervises any of these.
May not use initials RIA or IAR on business card or letterhead. Professional or educational designations are okay.	Same as federal.
Insolvency is *not* a cause for revocation.	Insolvency is a cause for revocation.
$110 million or more under management registers with the SEC. $100–$110 million can do either.	Less than $100 million under management generally registers with the state.
Registration renewal for IAs within 90 days of fiscal year	Registration renewal for all securities professionals on December 31
Register as an IAR only if a place of business in the state; no de minimis	Register in the state if retail clients resident in the state; subject to five or fewer de minimis
Employee benefit plans $5 million—institution	Employee benefit plans $1 million—institution

APPENDIX B

NASAA MODEL RULE ON UNETHICAL BUSINESS PRACTICES OF INVESTMENT ADVISERS, INVESTMENT ADVISER REPRESENTATIVES, AND FEDERAL COVERED ADVISERS [WITH REVIEW ANNOTATION NOTES]

The North American Securities Administrators Association (NASAA) has adopted a Model Rule on unethical business practices of investment advisers and their representatives. This Model Rule is reproduced here, with review notes included.

An investment adviser is a fiduciary and has a duty to act primarily for the benefit of its clients. While the extent and nature of this duty varies according to the nature of the relationship between an investment adviser and its clients and the circumstances of each case, an investment adviser shall not engage in unethical business practices, including the following:

1. Recommending to a client to whom investment supervisory, management or consulting services are provided the purchase, sale or exchange of any security without reasonable grounds to believe that the recommendation is suitable for the client on the basis of information furnished by the client after reasonable inquiry concerning the client's investment objectives, financial situation and needs, and any other information known by the investment adviser.

    Review Note: *An investment adviser providing investment supervisory, management, or consulting services has a fundamental obligation to analyze a client's financial situation and needs before making any recommendation to the client. Recommendations made to a client must be reasonable in relation to the information that is obtained concerning the client's investment objective, financial situation and needs, and other information known by the investment adviser. By failing to make reasonable inquiry or by failing to make recommendations that are in line with the financial situation, investment objectives, and character of a client's account, an investment adviser has not met its primary responsibility.*

2. Exercising any discretionary power in placing an order for the purchase or sale of securities for a client without obtaining prior written discretionary authority from the client, unless the discretionary power relates solely to the price at which, or the time when, an order involving a definite amount of a specified security shall be executed, or both.

    Review Note: *This rule pertains only to investment advisers that place orders for client accounts. Before placing an order for an account, an investment adviser exercising discretion should have written discretionary authority from the client. In most cases, discretionary authority is granted in an advisory contract or in a separate document executed at the time the contract is executed. The rule permits oral discretionary authority to be used for the initial transactions in a customer's account within the first 10 business days after the date of the first transaction. An investment adviser is not precluded from exercising discretionary power that relates solely to the price or time at which an order involving a specific amount of a security is authorized by a customer because time and price do not constitute discretion.*

 TEST TOPIC ALERT

Be aware of the calendar. The 10-business-day period is equal to two normal work weeks. If a client opens a discretionary account and gives the OK orally, but three weeks has passed by since the initial trade and the written authorization has not been received, the IA can't exercise discretion in the account, even if not taking action would cause disastrous results to the client's portfolio.

3. Inducing trading in a client's account that is excessive in size or frequency in view of the financial resources, investment objectives, and character of the account.

    Review Note: *This rule is intended to prevent an excessive number of securities transactions from being induced by an investment adviser. There are many situations where an investment adviser may receive commissions or be affiliated with a person that receives commissions from the securities transactions that are placed by the investment adviser. Because an adviser in such situations can directly benefit from the number of securities transactions effected in a client's account, the rule appropriately forbids an excessive number of transaction orders to be induced by an adviser for a customer's account.*

4. Placing an order to purchase or sell a security for the account of a client without authority to do so.

    Review Note: *This rule is not new to either the securities or investment advisory professions. An investment adviser must have authority to place any order for the account of a client. The authority may be obtained from a client orally or in an agreement executed by the client giving the adviser blanket authority.*

5. Placing an order to purchase or sell a security for the account of a client upon instruction of a third party without first having obtained a written third-party trading authorization from the client.

    Review Note: *It is sound business practice for an investment adviser not to place an order for the account of a customer at the instruction of a third party without first knowing that the third party has obtained authority from the client for the order. For example, it would be important for an investment adviser to know that an attorney had power-of-attorney over an estate whose securities the adviser was managing before placing any order at the instruction of the attorney. Placing orders under such circumstances could result in substantial civil liability, besides being an unethical practice.*

6. Borrowing money or securities from a client unless the client is a broker-dealer, an affiliate of the investment adviser, or financial institution engaged in the business of loaning funds.

    Review Note: *Unless a client of an investment adviser is engaged in the business of loaning money, is an affiliate of the investment adviser, or is an institution that would engage in this type of activity, an investment adviser must not take advantage of its advisory role by borrowing funds from a client. A client provides a substantial amount of confidential information to an investment adviser regarding the client's financial situation and needs. Using that information to an investment adviser's own advantage by borrowing funds is a breach of confidentiality and may create a material conflict of interest that could influence the advice rendered by the adviser to the client.*

7. Loaning money to a client unless the investment adviser is a financial institution engaged in the business of loaning funds or the client is an affiliate of the investment adviser.

    Review Note: *Like borrowing money from a client, loaning funds to a client by an investment adviser should not be an allowable practice unless the investment adviser is a financial institution normally engaged in the business of loaning funds or unless the client is affiliated with the adviser. Loaning funds may influence decisions made for a client's account and puts the investment adviser in a conflict of interest position because the client becomes a debtor of the adviser after a loan is made.*

8. To misrepresent to any advisory client, or prospective advisory client, the qualifications of the investment adviser or any employee of the investment adviser, or to misrepresent the

nature of the advisory services being offered or fees to be charged for such service, or to omit to state a material fact necessary to make the statements made regarding qualifications, services or fees, in light of the circumstances under which they are made, not misleading.

> **Review Note:** *When an investment adviser offers its services to a prospective client or when it provides services to an existing client, the qualifications of the investment adviser or any employee of the investment adviser and the nature of the advisory services and the fees to be charged must be disclosed in such a way as to not mislead. Overstating the qualifications of the investment adviser or disclosing inaccurately the nature of the advisory services to be provided or fees to be charged are not ethical ways to either acquire or retain clients.*

9. Providing a report or recommendation to any advisory client prepared by someone other than the adviser without disclosing the fact. (This prohibition does not apply to a situation where the adviser uses published research reports or statistical analyses to render advice or where an adviser orders such a report in the normal course of providing service.)

> **Review Note:** *If an investment adviser provides a report to a client that is prepared by a third party, the adviser has a responsibility to disclose the fact to the client. By entering into an investment advisory agreement, the client relies on the expertise of the adviser to provide the advisory service. Thus, if the advice is provided by a third party, it is imperative that the adviser disclose this fact to the client so the client is not misled. The prohibition does not apply when an investment adviser gathers and uses research materials before making its recommendation to a client.*

10. Charging a client an unreasonable advisory fee.

> **Review Note:** *This rule is intended to prohibit an investment adviser from charging an excessively high advisory fee. Unreasonable as used in this rule means unreasonable in relation to fees charged by other advisers for similar services. Although no two advisory services are exactly alike, comparisons can be drawn. In those instances where an advisory fee is out of line with fees charged by other advisers providing essentially the same services, an investment adviser should justify the charge. It would be very difficult for a client to compare various advisory services to evaluate those services and the fees charged. This rule will allow state Administrators to research the competitiveness of an adviser's services and fees, and to determine whether the fees being charged are unreasonably high.*

11. Failing to disclose to clients in writing, before any advice is rendered, any material conflict of interest relating to the adviser or any of its employees which could reasonably be expected to impair the rendering of unbiased and objective advice including:

    a. Compensation arrangements connected with advisory services to clients which are in addition to compensation from such clients for such services, and

    b. Charging a client an advisory fee for rendering advice when a commission for executing securities transactions pursuant to such advice will be received by the adviser or its employees.

> **Review Note:** *This rule is designed to require disclosure of all material conflicts of interest relating to the adviser or any of its employees that could affect the advice that is rendered. The two examples cited in the rule pertain to compensation arrangements that benefit the adviser and that are connected with advisory services being provided. However, full disclosure of all other material conflicts of interest, such as affiliations between the investment adviser and product suppliers, are also required to be made under the rule.*

12. Guaranteeing a client that a specific result will be achieved (gain or no loss) with advice that will be rendered.

    Review Note: *An investment adviser should not guarantee any gain or against loss in connection with advice that is rendered. By doing so, the adviser fails to maintain an arms-length relationship with a client and puts himself in a conflict of interest position by having a direct interest in the outcome of the advice rendered by the adviser.*

13. Publishing, circulating, or distributing any advertisement which does not comply with the Investment Advisers Act of 1940.

    Review Note: *An investment adviser should not publish, circulate, or distribute any advertisement that is inconsistent with federal rules governing the use of advertisements. Rule 206(4)-1 of the Investment Advisers Act of 1940 contains prohibitions against advertisements that contain untrue statements of material fact, that refer directly or indirectly to anytestimonial of any kind, that refer to past specific recommendations of the investment adviser unless certain conditions are met, that represent that a chart or formula or other device being offered can, by itself, be used to determine which securities are to be bought or sold, or that contain a statement indicating that any analysis, report, or service will be furnished free when such is not the case. Third-party use of the "like" feature on an investment adviser's social media site could be deemed to be a testimonial if it is an explicit or implicit statement of a client's or clients' experience with an investment adviser or IAR. If, for example, the public is invited to "like" an IAR's biography posted on a social media site, that election could be viewed as a type of testimonial prohibited by the rule. These prohibitions are fundamental and sound standards that all investment advisers should follow.*

14. Disclosing the identity, affairs, or investments of any client unless required by law to do so, or unless consented to by the client.

    Review Note: *An investment advisory firm has a responsibility to ensure that all information collected from a client be kept confidential. The only exception to the rule should be in those instances where the client authorized the release of such information, or when the investment advisory firm is required by law to disclose such information.*

15. Taking any action, directly or indirectly, with respect to those securities or funds in which any client has any beneficial interest, where the investment adviser has custody or possession of such securities or funds when the adviser's action is subject to and does not comply with the requirements of the Investment Advisers Act of 1940.

    Review Note: *In instances where an investment adviser has custody or possession of client's funds or securities, it should comply with the regulations under the Investment Advisers Act of 1940 designed to ensure the safekeeping of those securities and funds. The rules under the act specifically provide that securities of clients be segregated and properly marked, that the funds of the clients be deposited in separate bank accounts, that the investment adviser notify each client as to the place and manner in which such funds and securities are being maintained, that an itemized list of all securities and funds in the adviser's possession be sent to the client not less frequently than every three months, and that all such funds and securities be verified annually by actual examination by an independent CPA on a surprise basis. The rule establishes very conservative measures to safeguard each client's funds and securities held by an investment adviser.*

16. Entering into, extending or renewing any investment advisory contract unless such contract is in ***writing*** and discloses, in substance, the services to be provided, the term of the contract, the advisory fee, the formula for computing the fee, the amount of prepaid fee to be returned in the event of contract termination or non-performance, whether the contract grants discretionary power to the adviser and that no assignment of such contract shall be made by the investment adviser without the consent of the other party to the contract.

Review Note: *The purpose of this rule is to ensure that clients have a document to refer to that describes the basic terms of the agreement the client has entered into with an adviser.*

The conduct set forth previously is not inclusive. Engaging in other conduct such as non-disclosure, incomplete disclosure, or deceptive practices shall be deemed an unethical business practice.

APPENDIX C

ABBREVIATIONS, DATES, AND CALCULATIONS FOR THE SERIES 65 EXAM

Common Abbreviations

ADR/ADS	American depositary receipt (share)
AIR	assumed interest rate
APO	additional public offering
AMTI	alternative minimum taxable income
AUM	assets under management
BCP	business continuity plan
BD	broker-dealer
BSA	Bank Security Act
BU	bushel
CD	certificate of deposit
CEF	closed-end fund
CEO	chief executive officer
CIP	customer identification program
CMO	collateralized mortgage obligation
CMV	current market value
CODA	cash or deferred arrangement
COGS	cost of goods sold
CPI	Consumer Price Index
CTFC	Commodity Futures Trading Commission
CY	current yield
DCF	discounted cash flow
DJIA	Dow Jones Industrial Average
DMA	direct market access
DMM	Designated Market Maker
DPP	direct participation program
EE	Series EE savings bonds
EIA	equity index annuity
ELN	equity linked note
EPS	earnings per share
ERA	exempt reporting adviser
ERISA	Employee Retirement Income Security Act of 1974
ESG	environmental, social, and governance investing
ETF	exchange traded fund
ETN	exchange traded note

FAC	face-amount certificate
Fed	Federal Reserve System
FDIC	Federal Deposit Insurance Corporation
FIFO	first in, first out
FINRA	Financial Industry Regulatory Authority
FMV	fair market value
FNMA	Federal National Mortgage Association
FOMC	Federal Open Market Committee
FRB	Federal Reserve Board
GIC	guaranteed investment contract
GNMA	Government National Mortgage Association
GDP	gross domestic product
GO	general obligation bond
HFT	high-frequency trading
HNW	high net worth
IA	investment adviser
IAR	investment adviser representative
IARD	Investment Adviser Registration Depository
IPO	initial public offering
IRA	individual retirement account
IRC	Internal Revenue Code
IRS	Internal Revenue Service
JTIC	joint tenants in common
JTWROS	joint tenants with right of survivorship
LIFO	last in, first out
LOI	letter of intent
MNPI	Material nonpublic information
MRD	minimum required distribution
MSRB	Municipal Securities Rulemaking Board
NASAA	North American Securities Administrators Association
Nasdaq	National Association of Securities Dealers Automated Quotation system
NAV	net asset value
NIRP	negative interest-rate policy
NL	no load
NYSE	New York Stock Exchange
OTC	over the counter
PE	price-to-earnings ratio
PII	personally identifiable information
POA	power of attorney
POD	pay on death
POP	public offering price
RAUM	regulatory assets under management
REIT	real estate investment trust

RF	risk-free rate
SEC	Securities and Exchange Commission
SEP	simplified employee pension plan
SERP	supplemental executive retirement plan
SIPC	Securities Investor Protection Corporation
SPO	subsequent public offering
SRO	self-regulatory organization
STRIPS	Separate Trading of Registered Interest and Principal of Securities
TBE	tenants by the entirety
TIC	tenants in common
TOD	transfer on death
TSA	tax-sheltered annuity
TVA	Tennessee Valley Authority
UGMA/UTMA	Uniform Gift (Transfers) to Minors Act
UIT	unit investment trust
UPIA	Uniform Prudent Investors Act
USA	Uniform Securities Act
UVL	universal variable life insurance
VLI	variable life insurance
YLD	yield
YTC	yield to call
YTM	yield to maturity
ZIRP	zero interest-rate policy
ZR	zero-coupon

Calculations

To Calculate...	Use Formula...
Current yield (stock)	$\dfrac{\text{annual dividend}}{\text{current market price}}$
Current yield (debt security)	$\dfrac{\text{annual interest}}{\text{current market price}}$
Number of shares for conversion	$\dfrac{\text{par value}}{\text{conversion price}}$
Parity	$\dfrac{\text{bond market value}}{\text{number of shares}}$
Tax-free equivalent yield	Corporate rate × (100% − tax bracket)
Tax-equivalent yield	$\dfrac{\text{municipal rate}}{(100\% - \text{tax bracket})}$
NAV of mutual fund share	$\dfrac{\text{fund NAV}}{\text{number of shares outstanding}}$

To Calculate...	Use Formula...
Dollar cost average	$\dfrac{\text{total dollars invested}}{\text{number of shares purchased}}$
Average market price	$\dfrac{\text{share price total}}{\text{number of investments}}$
Shareholders' equity	Assets − liabilities
Total return	income (dividends or interest) + gain or loss /original investment
Annualized return	Total return on an annualized basis
Inflation-adjusted (real) return	Total return minus the CPI
After-tax return	Total return minus the marginal tax bracket
Rule of 72	Divide 72 by known interest rate = number of years to double investment; or, divide 72 by known number of years = interest rate required to double investment
Arithmetic mean	Simple average of the numbers
Median	In a group of numbers, the one with an equal above and below, i.e., the number in the middle
Mode	In a group of numbers, the one appearing most frequently
Range	In a group of numbers the difference between the highest and the lowest one
Alpha (RF not given)	Actual return − (beta × market return)
Alpha (RF given)	(Actual return − RF) − (beta × [market return − RF]}
Sharpe ratio	$\dfrac{\text{actual return − RF}}{\text{standard deviation}}$

Dates

48 hours prior to contract	State IAs deliver initial brochure, or 5-day withdrawal without penalty
Entering advisory contract	Latest time to delivery IA brochure
Same day	Time limit for execution of a day limit order. Also, time and/or price discretion only good that day
Next business day	Notification to Administrator that IA's net worth is insufficient (send details the following business day)
2 business days	Maximum and minimum offering prices and underwriting discounts on file for coordination
3 business days	Securities or funds received by non-custody IA must be returned to client
3 business days	3rd party checks received by non-custody IA must be forwarded to the 3rd party (USA only)
4 business days	Filing Form 8-K
5 business days	Penalty-free cancelation of IA contract if brochure not delivered at least 48 hours in advance (USA only)
7 days	Time limit for open-end investment company (mutual fund) to redeem shares
10 days	SEC can summarily suspend trading in a security
10 business days after first trade	Investment advisers may use oral discretion
15 days after written request	Hearing must be granted - Summary order
15 days after first sale	File Form D (private placement Rule 506)
15 days after account approval	Receipt of options account agreement
18th birthday	Latest date for a Coverdell ESA contribution
20 days	Cooling off period under Securities Act of 1933. Also minimum time Administrator must have documents for coordination
30th day	State registration or withdrawal of securities professionals effective
30 days	Maximum residency under snowbird exemption
30 days	Time limit within which rescission offer must be accepted or rejected
30 days	Mandatory waiting time to retest (first two failures)
30 days	Wash sale rule
30 days	New issues eligible for margin once owned this long
40 days	Days after end of each quarter to file Form 10-Q
45th day	Federal registration of BDs and IAs effective
45 days	Days after end of each quarter to file Form 13F
60th day	Withdrawal of federal covered adviser on ADV-W
60 days	Time limit to appeal an order under both state and federal law
60 days	Maximum time for tax-free rollover
60 days	Maximum termination clause with mutual fund adviser
90 days	After end of fiscal year, IA must file annual updating amendment

90 days	State IA with AUM at $110 million or above, must register with SEC
90 days	Maximum time a letter of intent (LOI) backdated
90 days	SEC, with notice to U.S. President, can suspend all trading on an exchange
91 days	Maturity of T-Bill most commonly used as risk-free rate
120 days	Annual delivery of adviser brochure to clients (if material changes)
120 days	Time limit for an IA who expects to reach the required AUM to register with the SEC
180 days	SEC IA with AUM below $90 million must register with state(s)
180 days	Mandatory waiting time to retest (third and subsequent failures)
6 months	Alternative valuation date for estate taxes
9 months (270 days)	Maximum maturity of exempt commercial paper
9 months after death	Payment of estate taxes is due
13 months	Maximum time to complete a letter of intent
397 days	Maximum maturity of any holding in money market mutual fund
2 years	Records must be kept easily accessible
3 years	Time period for most records kept by broker-dealers
5 years	Time period for investment adviser recordkeeping

GLOSSARY

accredited investor   As defined in Rule 501 of Regulation D, any institution or individual meeting minimum net worth requirements for the purchase of securities qualifying under the Regulation D registration exemption. An individual accredited investor is generally accepted to be one who, individually or with spouse, has a net worth, excluding the net equity in the primary residence, of $1 million or more, or has had an annual income of $200,000 or more in each of the two most recent years (or $300,000 jointly with a spouse), and who has a reasonable expectation of reaching the same income level in the current year.

accumulation stage   The period during which contributions are made to an annuity account. *See* accumulation unit; distribution stage.

accumulation unit   An accounting measure used to determine an annuitant's proportionate interest in the insurer's separate account during an annuity's accumulation (deposit) stage. *See* accumulation stage; separate account.

acid test   *Syn.* acid test ratio. *See* quick asset ratio.

active management style   Unlike the passive style, analysts believe they can identify industries that are undervalued or overvalued in order to weight them appropriately and achieve returns in excess of the market. Some managers engage in sector rotation, which is overweighting or underweighting industries based on the current phase of the business cycle. *See* passive management style; sector rotation.

Act of 1933   *See* Securities Act of 1933.

Act of 1934   *See* Securities Exchange Act of 1934.

adjusted basis   The value attributed to an asset or security that reflects any deductions taken on, or capital improvements to, the asset or security. Adjusted basis is used to compute the gain or loss on the sale or other disposition of the asset or security.

adjusted gross income (AGI)   Gross income from all sources minus certain adjustments to income, such as deductible contributions to an IRA and net capital losses. It is basically the amount of income that will be subject to tax. *See* tax liability.

Administrator   An official or agency that administers a state's securities laws.

adoption   A social media term meaning that a securities firm links to a third-party site and indicates that it endorses the content on that site.

ADR   *See* American depositary receipt.

ADS   *See* American depositary receipt.

advertisement   Any notice, circular, letter, or other written communication addressed to more than one person, or any notice or other announcement in any publication or by radio or television, that offers (1) any analysis, report, or publication concerning securities, or that is to be used in making any determination as to when to buy or sell any security, or which security to buy or sell; or (2) any graph, chart, formula, or other device to be used in making any determination as to when to buy or sell any security, or which security to buy or sell; or (3) any other investment advisory service with regard to securities.

agency basis   *See* agency transaction.

agency cross transaction   For an advisory client, a transaction in which a person acts as an investment adviser in relation to a transaction in which that investment adviser, or any person controlling, controlled by, or under common control with that investment adviser, acts as broker for both an advisory client and for another person on the other side of the transaction.

agency issue   A debt security issued by an authorized agency of the federal government. Such an issue is backed by the issuing agency itself, not by the full faith and credit of the U.S. government (except GNMA issues). *See* government security.

agency transaction   A transaction in which a broker-dealer acts for the accounts of others by buying or selling securities on behalf of customers. *Syn.* agency basis. *See* agent; broker; principal transaction.

agent   (1) An individual who effects securities transactions for the accounts of others. (2) Under state law, a securities salesperson who represents a broker-dealer or an issuer when selling or trying to sell securities to the investing public; this individual is considered an agent whether he actually receives or simply solicits orders. *See* broker; broker-dealer; dealer; principal.

aggressive investment strategy   A method of portfolio allocation and management aimed at achieving maximum return. Aggressive investors place a high percentage of their investable assets in equity securities and a far lower percentage in safer debt securities and cash equivalents, and they pursue aggressive policies including margin trading, arbitrage, and option trading. *See* balanced investment strategy; defensive investment strategy.

AGI   *See* adjusted gross income.

algorithmic trading   Computerized trading using proprietary algorithms. There are two types of algorithmic trading. Execution trading is when an order (often a large order) is executed via an algorithmic trade. The program is designed to get the best possible price. It may split the order into smaller pieces and execute at different times. The second type of algorithmic trading is not executing a set order but looking for small trading opportunities in the market. It is estimated that more than 50% of stock trading volume in the United States is currently being driven by algorithmic trading. Also known as high-frequency trading.

all or none order (AON)   An order that instructs the floor broker to execute the entire order in one transaction; if the order cannot be executed in its entirety, it is allowed to expire.

alpha   The risk-adjusted returns that a portfolio manager generates in excess of the risk-adjusted returns expected by the capital asset pricing model (CAPM). Suppose an index return is 10%; the risk-free rate is 3%, the portfolio beta is 1.5, and the actual return is 25%. According to the CAPM, the portfolio should be expected to return 1.5 times the index after netting out the risk-free rate. This is because the portfolio is 1.5 times riskier than the market. If we take the index return after subtracting the 3% risk-free rate, we get 7%. Multiply that times 1.5 and the measured portfolio should have returned 10.5% for taking extra risk. It actually returned 22% over the risk-free rate giving us an alpha of 11.5.

alternative minimum tax (AMT)   An alternative tax computation that adds certain tax preference items back into adjusted gross income. If the AMT is higher than the regular tax liability for the year, the regular tax and the amount by which the AMT exceeds the regular tax are paid. *See* tax preference item.

American depositary receipt (ADR)   A negotiable certificate representing a given number of shares in a foreign corporation. It is issued by a domestic bank. ADRs are bought and sold in the American securities markets, and are traded in English and U.S. dollars. *Syn.* American depositary share (ADS).

anti-dilutive covenant   A protective clause found in most convertible issues (preferred stock or debentures) that adjusts the conversion rate for stock splits and/or stock dividends. This ensures that the holder of the convertible will not suffer a dilution in value.

appreciation   The increase in an asset's value.

arbitrage   A legal strategy that generates a guaranteed profit from a transaction. A common form of arbitrage is the simultaneous purchase and sale of the same security in different markets at different prices to lock in a profit. This is not considered market manipulation.

arithmetic mean   The average of a set of numbers, such as annual returns on an investment.

ask   An indication by a trader or a dealer of a willingness to sell a security or a commodity; the price at which an investor can buy from a broker-dealer. *Syn.* offer. *See* bid; public offering price; quotation.

assessable stock   A stock that is issued below its par or stated value. The issuer and/or creditors have the right to assess the shareholder for the deficiency. All stock issued today is nonassessable.

asset   (1) Anything that an individual or a corporation owns. (2) A balance sheet item expressing what a corporation owns.

asset class allocation   Dividing an investment portfolio among different asset categories, such as stocks, bonds, cash, and tangible assets such as real estate and precious metals and other commodities. *Syn.* asset allocation.

auction market   A market in which buyers enter competitive bids and sellers enter competitive offers simultaneously. The NYSE is an auction market. *Syn.* double auction market.

audited financial statement   A financial statement of a program, a corporation, or an issuer (including the profit and loss statement, cash flow and source and application of revenues statement, and balance sheet) that has been examined and verified by an independent certified public accountant.

average basis   An accounting method used when an investor has made multiple purchases at different prices of the same security; the method averages the purchase prices to calculate an investor's cost basis in shares being liquidated. The difference between the average cost basis and the selling price determines the investor's tax liability. *See* first in, first out; last in, first out.

back-end load   A commission or sales fee that is charged when mutual fund shares or variable annuity contracts are redeemed. It declines annually, decreasing to zero over an extended holding period—up to eight years— as described in the prospectus. *Syn.* contingent-deferred sales load.

balanced fund   A mutual fund whose stated investment policy is to have at all times some portion of its investment assets in bonds and preferred stock, as well as in common stock, in an attempt to provide both growth and income. *See* mutual fund.

balanced investment strategy   A method of portfolio allocation and management aimed at balancing risk and return. A balanced portfolio may combine stocks, bonds, packaged products such as investment companies, DPPs, or REITs, and cash equivalents.

balance of payments   An international accounting record of all transactions made by one particular country with others during a certain period; it compares the amount of foreign currency the country has taken in with the amount of its own currency it has paid out. *See* balance of trade.

balance of trade   The largest component of a country's balance of payments; it concerns the export and import of merchandise (not services). Debit items include imports, foreign aid, domestic spending abroad, and domestic investments abroad. Credit items include exports, foreign spending in the domestic economy, and foreign investments in the domestic economy. *See* balance of payments.

balance sheet   A report of a corporation's financial condition at a specific time.

balance sheet equation   A formula stating that a corporation's assets equal the sum of its liabilities plus shareholders' equity.

bank holding company   A holding company whose primary asset is a commercial bank. *See* holding company.

basis   Another term for yield to maturity (e.g., this bond is selling at a 5.78 basis).

basis point   A measure of a bond's yield, equal to 1/100 of 1% of yield. A bond whose yield increases from 5.00% to 5.50% is said to increase by 50 basis points. *See* point.

bear   An investor who acts on the belief that a security or the market is falling or will fall. *See* bull.

bear market   A market in which prices of a certain group of securities are falling or are expected to fall. *See* bull market.

benchmark portfolio   A model portfolio of a large number of assets, such as the S&P 500, against which the performance of a fund or portfolio is measured.

beta   A means of measuring the co-movement of the return of a security or a portfolio of securities to the return on the overall market. A beta of 1 indicates that the security's returns will be expected to move in tandem with the market. A beta greater than 1 indicates that the security's returns will be expected to exceed those of the market. A beta less than 1 means returns will be expected to be lower than those of the market. *Syn.* beta coefficient.

bid   An indication by an investor, a trader, or a dealer of a willingness to buy a security; the price at which an investor can sell to a broker-dealer. *See* offer; public offering price; quotation.

Black-Scholes   One of the most popular options pricing models. Appears frequently on the exam as an incorrect choice.

block trade   A large trading order, defined as an order that consists of 10,000 or more shares of a given stock or at a total market value of $200,000 or more. *Syn.* block sale.

blue-sky laws   The nickname for state regulations governing the securities industry. The term was coined in 1911 by a Kansas Supreme Court justice who wanted regulation to protect against "speculative schemes that have no more basis than so many feet of blue sky."

board of directors   Individuals elected by stockholders to establish corporate management policies. A board of directors decides, among other issues, if and when dividends will be paid to stockholders.

bona fide   From the Latin "good faith," something that is bona fide is genuine, authentic, and real. An example would be a bona fide quote.

bond   An issuing company's or government's legal obligation to repay the principal of a loan to bond investors at a specified future date. Bonds are usually issued with par or face values of $1,000, representing the amount of money borrowed. The issuer promises to pay a percentage of the par value as interest on the borrowed funds. The interest payment is stated on the face of the bond at issue.

bond fund   A mutual fund whose investment objective is to provide stable income with minimal capital risk. It invests in income-producing instruments, which may include corporate, government, or municipal bonds. *See* mutual fund.

bond quote   One of a number of quotations listed in the financial press and most daily newspapers that provide representative bid prices from the previous day's bond market. Quotes for corporate and government bonds are percentages of the bonds' face values (usually $1,000). Corporate bonds are quoted in increments of 1/8. Government bonds are quoted in increments of 1/32. Municipal bonds may be quoted on a dollar basis or on a yield-to-maturity basis. *See* quotation; stock quote.

bond rating   An evaluation of the possibility of a bond issuer's default, based on an analysis of the issuer's financial condition and profit potential. Standard & Poor's, Moody's Investors Service, and Fitch Investors Service, among others, provide bond rating services.

bond ratio   One of several tools used by bond analysts to assess the degree of safety offered by a corporation's bonds. It measures the percentage of the corporation's capitalization that is provided by long-term debt financing, calculated by dividing the total face value of the outstanding bonds by the total capitalization. *Syn.* debt ratio.

bond yield   The annual rate of return on a bond investment. Types of yield include nominal yield, current yield, yield to maturity, and yield to call. Their relationships vary according to whether the bond in question is at a discount, at a premium, or at par. *See* current yield; nominal yield.

book-entry security   A security sold without delivery of a certificate. Evidence of ownership is maintained on records kept by a central agency; for example, the Treasury keeps records of Treasury bill purchasers. Transfer of ownership is recorded by entering the change on the books or electronic files. *See* coupon bond.

book value per share   A measure of the net worth of each share of common stock is calculated by subtracting intangible assets and preferred stock from total net worth, then dividing the result by the number of shares of common outstanding. *Syn.* net tangible assets per share.

Brady bonds   Debt instruments, generally from third world countries, that may have a U.S. Treasury bond as collateral.

breadth-of-market theory   A technical analysis theory that predicts the strength of the market according to the number of issues that advance or decline in a particular trading day.

BRIC   An acronym referring to investments in Brazil, Russia, India, and China

bridge loan   A short-term loan made to bridge the gap until permanent financing is arranged.

brochure   A written disclosure statement that investment advisers must provide to most clients and prospective clients. The Form ADV Part 2A may be used for this purpose.

brochure supplement   A written disclosure statement containing information about certain of an investment adviser's supervised persons. This disclosure is usually accomplished by the delivery of Form ADV Part 2B to most clients and prospective clients.

broker   (1) An individual or a firm that charges a fee or commission for executing buy and sell orders submitted by another individual or firm. (2) The role of a firm when it acts as an agent for a customer and charges the customer a commission for its services. *See* agent; broker-dealer; dealer.

broker-dealer (BD)   A person in the business of buying and selling securities. A firm may act as both broker (agency) and dealer (principal), but not in the same transaction. Broker-dealers normally must register with the SEC, the appropriate SROs, and any state in which they do business. *See* agent; broker; dealer; principal.

bull   An investor who acts on the belief that a security or the market is rising or will rise. *See* bear.

bulletin board   *See* OTC Bulletin Board.

bull market   A market in which prices of a certain group of securities are rising or will rise. *See* bear market.

business cycle   A predictable long-term pattern of alternating periods of economic growth and decline. The cycle passes through four stages: expansion, peak, contraction, and trough.

business risk   The risk inherent in equity securities that poor management decisions will have a negative impact on the stock's performance. Can be reduced through diversification. *Syn.* unsystematic risk.

buy stop order   An order to buy a security that is entered at a price above the current offering price and that is triggered when the market price touches or goes through the buy stop price.

bypass trust   A trust that is funded with property in an amount equal to the exemption equivalent of the transfer tax credit amount applicable to the decedent ($11.4 million in 2019); thus, the property is not subject to federal estate tax. *See* generation skipping trust.

calendar year   For accounting purposes, a year that ends on December 31. When an accounting year ends any other time, it is called a fiscal year. *See* fiscal year.

call (1) An option contract giving the owner the right to buy a specified amount of an underlying security at a specified price within a specified time. (2) The act of exercising a call option. *See* put.

callable bond A type of bond issued with a provision allowing the issuer to redeem the bond before maturity at a predetermined price.

callable preferred stock A type of preferred stock issued with a provision allowing the corporation to call in the stock at a certain price and retire it. *See* call price; preferred stock.

call buyer An investor who pays a premium for an option contract and receives, for a specified time, the right to buy the underlying security at a specified price. *See* call writer; put.

call date The date, specified in the prospectus of every callable security, after which the security's issuer has the option to redeem the issue at par or at par plus a premium.

call feature *See* call provision.

call protection A provision in a bond indenture stating that the issue is noncallable for a certain period (e.g., 5 years or 10 years) after the original issue date. *See* call provision.

call provision The written agreement between an issuer and its bondholders or preferred stockholders giving the issuer the option to redeem its senior securities at a specified price before maturity and under certain conditions. *Syn.* call feature.

call risk The potential for a bond to be called before maturity, leaving the investor without the bond's current income. Because this is more likely to occur during times of falling interest rates, the investor may not be able to reinvest his principal at a comparable rate of return.

call writer An investor who receives a premium and takes on, for a specified time, the obligation to sell the underlying security at a specified price at the call buyer's discretion. *See* call buyer; put.

capital appreciation An increase in an asset's market price.

capital asset All tangible property, including securities, real estate, and other property, held for the long term.

capital asset pricing model (CAPM) A securities market investment theory that attempts to derive the expected return on an asset on the basis of the asset's systematic risk.

capital gain The profit realized when a capital asset is sold for a higher price than the purchase price. *See* capital loss; long-term gain.

capitalization The sum of a corporation's long-term debt, stock, and surpluses. *Syn.* invested capital. *See* capital structure.

capitalization ratio A measure of an issuer's financial status that calculates the value of its bonds, preferred stock, or common stock as a percentage of its total capitalization.

capital loss The loss incurred when a capital asset is sold for a price lower than the purchase price. *See* capital gain; long-term loss.

capital market The segment of the securities market that deals in instruments with more than one year to maturity—that is, long-term debt and equity securities. In contrast, the money market is the raising of short-term capital such as Treasury bills and commercial paper.

capital stock All of a corporation's outstanding preferred stock and common stock, listed at par value.

capital structure The composition of long-term funds (equity and debt) a corporation has as a source for financing. *See* capitalization.

capital surplus The money a corporation receives in excess of the stated value of stock at the time of first sale. *Syn.* paid-in capital; paid-in surplus. *See* par.

capping An illegal form of market manipulation that attempts to keep the price of a subject security from rising. It is used by those with a short position. *See* pegging.

cash account An account in which the customer is required by the SEC's Regulation T to pay in full for securities purchased not later than two days after the standard payment period set by industry practice codes. *Syn.* special cash account.

cash dividend Money paid to a corporation's stockholders out of the corporation's current earnings or accumulated profits. The board of directors must declare all dividends.

cash equivalent A security that can be readily converted into cash. Examples include Treasury bills, certificates of deposit, and money market instruments and funds.

cash flow The money received by a business minus the money paid out. Cash flow is also equal to net income plus depreciation or depletion.

CBOE *See* Chicago Board Options Exchange.

CD *See* negotiable certificate of deposit.

cease and desist order   Used by the Administrator when it appears that a registered person has or is about to commit a violation. May be issued with or without a prior hearing.

certificate of deposit (CD)   A traditional CD pays a fixed interest rate over a specific period of time. When that term ends, you can withdraw your money or roll it into another CD. These are insured up to $250,000 by the FDIC and are considered the best method of preservation of capital. *See* negotiable certificate of deposit.

chartist   A securities analyst who uses charts and graphs of the past price movements of a security to predict its future movements. *Syn.* technician. *See* technical analysis.

Chicago Board Options Exchange (CBOE)   The self-regulatory organization with jurisdiction over all writing and trading of standardized options and related contracts listed on that exchange. Also, the first national securities exchange for the trading of listed options.

Chicago Stock Exchange   Registered stock exchange located in Chicago's downtown "loop." Referred to with the initials CHX.

Chinese Wall   A descriptive name for the division within a brokerage firm that prevents insider information from passing from corporate advisers to investment traders, who could make use of the information to reap illicit profits. The preferred term today is *information barriers*. *See* Insider Trading and Securities Fraud Enforcement Act of 1988.

churning   Excessive trading in a customer's account by an agent who ignores the customer's interests and *seeks* only to increase commissions; violates NASAA's policies on unethical business practices. *Syn.* overtrading.

CHX   *See* Chicago Stock Exchange.

Class A share   A class of mutual fund share issued with a front-end sales load. A mutual fund offers different classes of shares to allow investors to choose the type of sales charge they will pay. Related item(s): Class B share; Class C share; front-end load.

Class B share   A class of mutual fund share issued with a back-end load. A mutual fund offers different classes of shares to allow investors to choose the type of sales charge they will pay. Related item(s): back-end load; Class A share; Class C share.

Class C share   A class of mutual fund share issued with a level load. A mutual fund offers different classes of shares to allow investors to choose the type of sales charge they will pay. Related item(s): back-end load; Class A share; Class B share.

closed-end investment company   An investment company that issues a fixed number of shares in an actively managed portfolio of securities. The shares may be of several classes; they are traded in the secondary marketplace, either on a stock exchange or over the counter. The market price of the shares is determined by supply and demand and not by net asset value. *Syn.* publicly traded fund; closed-end management company. *See* mutual fund.

closing purchase   An options transaction in which the seller buys back an option in the same series; the two transactions effectively cancel each other out and the position is liquidated. *See* opening purchase.

CMO   *See* collateralized mortgage obligation.

coincident indicator   A measurable economic factor that varies directly and simultaneously with the business cycle, thus indicating the current state of the economy. Examples include nonagricultural employment, personal income, and industrial production. *See* lagging indicator; leading indicator.

collateral   Certain assets set aside and pledged to a lender for the duration of a loan. If the borrower fails to meet obligations to pay principal or interest, the lender has claim to the assets.

collateralized mortgage obligation (CMO)   A mortgage-backed corporate security. These issues attempt to return interest and principal at a predetermined rate.

collateral trust bond   A secured bond backed by stocks or bonds of another issuer. The collateral is held by a trustee for safekeeping. *Syn.* collateral trust certificate.

collateral trust certificate   *See* collateral trust bond.

combination privilege   A benefit offered by a mutual fund whereby the investor may qualify for a sales charge breakpoint by combining separate investments in two or more mutual funds under the same management.

commercial paper   An unsecured, short-term promissory note issued by a corporation for financing accounts receivable and inventories. It is usually issued at a discount reflecting prevailing market interest rates. Maturities range up to nine months.

commingling   The combining by a brokerage firm of one customer's securities with another customer's securities and pledging them as joint collateral for a bank loan; unless authorized by the customers, this violates SEC Rule 15c2-1.

commission   A service charge an agent assesses in return for arranging a security's purchase or sale. A commission must be fair and reasonable, considering all the relevant factors of the transaction. *Syn.* sales charge. *See* markup.

common stock   A security that represents ownership in a corporation. Holders of common stock exercise control by electing a board of directors and voting on corporate policy. *See* equity; preferred stock.

complex trust   A trust that accumulates income over time and is not required to make scheduled distributions to its beneficiaries.

conduit theory   A means for an investment company to avoid taxation on net investment income distributed to shareholders. If a mutual fund acts as a conduit for the distribution of net investment income, it may qualify as a regulated investment company and be taxed only on the income the fund retains. *Syn.* pipeline theory.

confirmation   A printed document that states the trade date, settlement date, and money due from or owed to a customer. It is sent or given to the customer on or before the settlement date.

constant dollar plan   A formula method of investing that attempts to maintain a fixed dollar, rather than ratio, amount in a specific asset class. Periodically, the account is reviewed and the specified asset class is either sold or purchased in order to get to the fixed dollar level.

constant ratio plan   A formula method of investing that contemplates maintaining a fixed ratio, rather than dollar amount, between specific asset classes in the portfolio. Periodically, the account is reviewed and the specified asset class is either sold or purchased in order to get to the fixed ratio level.

Consumer Price Index (CPI)   A measure of price changes in a "market basket" of consumer goods and services used to identify periods of inflation or deflation.

consumption   A term used by economists to refer to the purchase by household units of newly produced goods and services.

contraction   A period of general economic decline, one of the business cycle's four stages. *See* business cycle.

contributory plan   A retirement plan to which both the employee and the employer make contributions. *See* noncontributory plan.

control person   (1) A director or an officer of an issuer. (2) A stockholder who owns more than 10% of any class of a corporation's outstanding securities. (3) Spouse or other immediate family of any of the previous. Under the Investment Company Act of 1940, a control person owns more than 25% of the voting securities and, under the Investment Advisers Act of 1940, it is 25% or more. *See* insider.

control security   Any security owned by a director or an officer of the issuer or by a stockholder who owns more than 10% of any class of a corporation's outstanding securities. Who owns a security, not the security itself, determines whether it is a control security.

conversion parity   Two securities, one of which can be converted into the other, of equal dollar value. A convertible security holder can calculate parity to help decide whether converting would lead to gain or loss.

conversion price   The dollar amount of a convertible security's par value that is exchangeable for one share of common stock.

conversion privilege   A feature the issuer adds to a security that allows the holder to change the security into shares of common stock. This makes the security attractive to investors and, therefore, more marketable. *See* convertible bond; convertible preferred stock.

conversion rate   *See* conversion ratio.

conversion ratio   The number of shares of common stock per par value amount that the holder would receive for converting a convertible bond or preferred share. *Syn.* conversion rate.

convertible bond   A debt security, usually in the form of a debenture, that can be exchanged for equity securities of the issuing corporation at specified prices or rates. *See* debenture.

convertible preferred stock   An equity security that can be exchanged for common stock at specified prices or rates. Dividends may be cumulative or noncumulative. *See* cumulative preferred stock; noncumulative preferred stock; preferred stock.

convexity   The most accurate way of indicating a debt security's sensitivity to changes in interest rates.

cooling-off period   The period (a minimum of 20 days) between a registration statement's filing date with the SEC and the registration's effective date. In practice, the period varies in length.

corporate account   An account held in a corporation's name. The corporate agreement, signed when the account is opened, specifies which officers are authorized to trade in the account. In addition to standard margin account documents, a corporation must provide a copy of its charter and bylaws authorizing a margin account.

corporate bond   A debt security issued by a corporation. A corporate bond typically has a par value of $1,000, its interest is taxable, and it has a term maturity.

corporation The most common form of business organization, in which the organization's total worth is divided into shares of stock, each share representing a unit of ownership. A corporation is characterized by a continuous life span and its owners' limited liability.

correlation The extent to which two or more securities or portfolios move together. The correlation coefficient is a number that ranges from –1 to +1. A perfect correlation would have a coefficient of +1, whereas two securities that move in total opposite directions would have a –1. A coefficient of 0 would reflect a totally random correlation between the two securities.

cost basis The price paid for an asset, including any commissions or fees, used to calculate capital gains or losses when the asset is sold.

coupon yield *See* nominal yield.

covered call writer An investor who sells a call option while owning the underlying security or some other asset that guarantees the ability to deliver if the call is exercised.

covered security *See* federal covered security.

CPI *See* Consumer Price Index.

credit risk The degree of probability that the issuer of a debt security will default in the payment of either principal or interest. Securities issued by the U.S. government are considered to have virtually no credit risk. Note: credit risk only refers to debt securities—common stock has no credit risk because there is no debt obligation to the owner. *Syn.* default risk; financial risk.

credit spread (1) A position established when the premium received for the option sold exceeds the premium paid for the option bought. *See* debit spread (2) The difference in yields between two securities. See yield spread.

cumulative preferred stock An equity security that offers the holder any unpaid dividends in arrears. These dividends accumulate and must be paid to the cumulative preferred stockholder before any dividends can be paid to the common stockholders. *See* noncumulative preferred stock; preferred stock.

current assets Cash and other assets that are expected to be converted into cash within the next 12 months. Examples include such liquid items as cash and equivalents, accounts receivable, inventory, and prepaid expenses.

current liabilities A corporation's debt obligations due for payment within the next 12 months. Examples include accounts payable, accrued wages payable, and current long-term debt.

current market value (CMV) The worth of the securities in an account. The market value of listed securities is based on the closing prices on the previous business day. *Syn.* long market value. *See* market value.

current ratio A measure of a corporation's liquidity; that is, its ability to transfer assets into cash to meet current short-term obligations. It is calculated by dividing total current assets by total current liabilities. *Syn.* working capital ratio.

current yield The annual rate of return on a security, calculated by dividing the interest or dividends paid by the security's current market price. *See* bond yield.

custodial account An account in which a custodian enters trades on behalf of the beneficial owner, often a minor. *See* custodian.

custodian An institution or a person responsible for making all investment, management, and distribution decisions in an account maintained in the best interests of another. Mutual funds have custodian banks responsible for safeguarding certificates and performing clerical duties.

custody Maintaining physical possession of a customer's assets. State-registered investment advisers must notify the Administrator if they intend to take custody, assuming the state law permits such.

customer Any person who opens a trading account with a broker-dealer. A customer may be classified in terms of account ownership, trading authorization, payment method, or types of securities traded.

customer statement A document showing a customer's trading activity, positions, and account balance. The SEC requires that customer statements be sent quarterly, but customers generally receive them monthly.

cyclical industry A fundamental analysis term for an industry that is sensitive to the business cycle and price changes. Most cyclical industries produce durable goods, raw materials, and heavy equipment.

dark pool This term refers to an alternative trading system (ATS) where a supply of shares exists that is not displayed for all to see. Dark pools are akin to members-only trading platforms for those desiring to execute larger trades without their interest being made known through an open book. A dark pool provides anonymity to investors and sensitivity of share prices to movement when any sizable demand appears.

day order An order that is valid only until the close of trading on the day it is entered; if it is not executed by the close of trading, it is canceled.

DCF See discounted cash flow

dealer (1) An individual or a firm engaged in the business of buying and selling securities for its own account, either directly or through a broker. (2) The role of a firm when it acts as a principal and charges the customer a markup or markdown. *Syn.* principal. *See* broker; broker-dealer.

debenture A debt obligation backed by the issuing corporation's general credit. *Syn.* unsecured bond.

debit spread A position established when the premium paid for the option bought exceeds the premium received for the option sold. *See* credit spread.

debt security A security representing an investor's loan to an issuer, such as a corporation, a municipality, the federal government, or a federal agency. In return for the loan, the issuer promises to repay the debt on a specified date and to pay interest. *See* equity security.

debt-to-equity ratio The ratio of total long-term debt to total stockholders' equity; it is used to measure leverage.

decumulation Disposal of something accumulated. Investors spend much of their working years accumulating for retirement; taking the funds out is decumulation.

default The failure to pay interest or principal promptly when due.

default risk *See* credit risk.

defensive industry A fundamental analysis term for an industry that is relatively unaffected by the business cycle. Most defensive industries produce nondurable goods for which demand remains steady throughout the business cycle; examples include the food industry and utilities.

defensive investment strategy A method of portfolio allocation and management aimed at minimizing the risk of losing principal. Defensive investors place a high percentage of their investable assets in bonds, cash equivalents, and stocks that are less volatile than average.

deferred annuity An annuity contract that delays payment of income, installments, or a lump sum until the investor elects to receive it.

deferred compensation plan A nonqualified retirement plan whereby the employee defers receiving current compensation in favor of a larger payout at retirement (or in the case of disability or death).

deficiency letter The SEC's notification of additions or corrections that a prospective issuer must make to a registration statement before the SEC will clear the offering for distribution.

defined benefit plan A qualified retirement plan that specifies the total amount of money that the employee will receive at retirement.

defined contribution plan A qualified retirement plan that specifies the amount of money that the employer will contribute annually to the plan.

deflation A persistent and measurable fall in the general level of prices. *See* inflation.

delta One of the four Greeks used by options analysts. An option's delta is the rate of change of the price of the option with respect to its underlying security's price. The delta of an option ranges in value from 0 to 1 for calls (0 to -1 for puts) and reflects the increase or decrease in the price of the option in response to a 1 point movement of the underlying asset price.

demand A consumer's desire and willingness to pay for a good or service. *See* supply.

demand deposit Demand deposit (DDA) refers to a type of account held at banks and financial institutions that may be withdrawn at any time by the customer. The majority of such demand deposit accounts are checking accounts, although many now include savings accounts in the definition as well.

demutualization Demutualization is the process through which a member-owned company becomes shareholder-owned. Historically, this has usually been done by mutual life insurance companies (think MetLife and Prudential), but, in recent years has been done by other member-owned entities such as the New York Stock Exchange.

depreciation (1) A tax deduction that compensates a business for the cost of certain tangible assets. (2) A decrease in the value of a particular currency relative to other currencies.

depreciation expense A bookkeeping entry of a noncash expense charged against earnings to recover the cost of an asset over its useful life.

depression A prolonged period of general economic decline.

derivative An investment vehicle, the value of which is based on another security's value. Futures contracts, forward contracts, and options are among the most common types of derivatives. Institutional investors generally use derivatives to increase overall portfolio return or to hedge portfolio risk.

designated market maker (DMM) *See* specialist.

dilution   A reduction in earnings per share of common stock. Dilution occurs through the issuance of additional shares of common stock and the conversion of convertible securities. *See* anti-dilutive covenant.

directed brokerage   The ability of an investment adviser or a client to determine broker-dealers to be used in the execution of transactions in their advisory accounts. *See* soft dollar compensation.

direct participation program (DPP)   A business organized so as to pass all income, gains, losses, and tax benefits to its owners, the investors; the business is usually structured as a limited partnership. Examples include oil and gas programs, real estate programs, agricultural programs, cattle programs, condominium securities, and S corporation offerings.

discount   The difference between the lower price paid for a security and the security's face amount at issue.

discount bond   A bond that sells at a lower price than its face value. *See* par.

discount rate   The interest rate charged by the 12 Federal Reserve Banks for short-term loans made to member banks.

discounted cash flow   Discounted cash flow (DCF) is a model or method of valuation in which future cash flows are discounted back to a present value using the time-value of money. An investment's worth is equal to the present value of all projected future cash flows.

discretion   The authority given to someone other than an account's beneficial owner to make investment decisions for the account concerning the security, the number of shares or units, and whether to buy or sell. The authority to decide only timing or price does not constitute discretion. *See* limited power of attorney.

discretionary account   An account in which the customer has given the agent authority to enter transactions at the representative's discretion.

disgorge(ment)   In legal usage, the forced giving up of profits made through illegal activity, most commonly insider trading.

disposable income (DI)   The sum that people divide between spending and personal savings. *See* personal income.

distributable net income (DNI)   Taxable income from a trust that determines the amount of income that may be taxable to beneficiaries.

diversification   A risk management technique that mixes a wide variety of investments within a portfolio, thus minimizing the impact of any one security on overall portfolio performance.

diversified common stock fund   A mutual fund that invests its assets in a wide range of common stocks. The fund's objectives may be growth, income, or a combination of both. *See* growth fund; mutual fund.

dividend   A distribution of a corporation's earnings. Dividends may be in the form of cash, stock, or property. The board of directors must declare all dividends. *See* cash dividend; dividend yield; stock dividend.

dividend discount model   The simplest model for valuing equity is the dividend discount model—the value of a stock is the present value of expected dividends on it. *Syn*, DDM.

dividend exclusion rule   An IRS provision that permits a corporation to exclude from its taxable income 70% of dividends received from domestic preferred and common stocks. The Tax Reform Act of 1986 repealed the dividend exclusion for individual investors.

dividend growth model   A valuation method which takes into consideration dividend per share and its expected growth. This model assumes that dividends grow at the same rate forever. Therefore, it is most commonly used to value companies belonging to for mature and stable industries, having steady dividend growth. It will show a higher valuation than the DDM. *Syn*. DGM.

dividend payout ratio   A measure of a corporation's policy of paying cash dividends, calculated by dividing the dividends paid on common stock by the net income available for common stockholders. The ratio is the complement of the retained earnings ratio.

dividends per share   The dollar amount of cash dividends paid on each common share during one year.

dividend reinvestment plan   Frequently referred to as a DRIP, the plan allows shareholders the option of having cash dividends automatically reinvested in shares of the issuer's stock, frequently at a discounted price and/or without commissions. In most plans, additional investments are permitted.

dividend yield   The annual rate of return on a common or preferred stock investment. The yield is calculated by dividing the annual dividend by the stock's purchase price. *See* current yield; dividend.

DNI   *See* distributable net income.

Dodd-Frank Bill The general term by which the Wall Street Reform and Consumer Protection Act of 2010 is known. Considered to be the most significant legislation impacting the securities industry since the 1930s.

dollar cost averaging A system of buying mutual fund shares in fixed dollar amounts at regular fixed intervals, regardless of the share's price. The investor purchases more shares when prices are low and fewer shares when prices are high, thus lowering the average cost per share over time.

donor A person who makes a gift of money or securities to another. Once the gift is donated, the donor gives up all rights to it. Gifts of securities to minors under the Uniform Gift to Minors Act provide tax advantages to the donor. *See* Uniform Gift to Minors Act.

Dow Jones averages The most widely quoted and oldest measures of change in stock prices. Each of the four averages is based on the prices of a limited number of stocks in a particular category. *See* average; Dow Jones Industrial Average.

Dow Jones Composite Average (DJCA) A market indicator composed of the 65 stocks that make up the Dow Jones Industrial, Transportation, and Utilities Averages. *See* average; Dow Jones Industrial Average; Dow Jones Transportation Average; Dow Jones Utilities Average.

Dow Jones Industrial Average (DJIA) The most widely used market indicator, composed of 30 large, actively traded issues of industrial stocks.

Dow Jones Transportation Average (DJTA) A market indicator composed of 20 transportation stocks. *See* average; Dow Jones Composite Average; Dow Jones Industrial Average; Dow Jones Utilities Average.

Dow Jones Utilities Average (DJUA) A market indicator composed of 15 utilities stocks. *See* average; Dow Jones Composite Average; Dow Jones Industrial Average; Dow Jones Transportation Average.

DRIP *See* dividend reinvestment plan.

durable power of attorney A document giving either full or limited authority to a third party that survives the mental or physical incompetence (but not death) of the grantor. *See* full power of attorney; limited power of attorney.

duration Duration is an approximate measure of a bond's price sensitivity to changes in interest rates. Duration can be used to compare bonds with different issue and maturity dates, coupon rates, and yields to maturity. The duration of a bond is expressed as a number of years from its purchase date.

EAFE The EAFE Index is designed to represent the performance of large and mid-cap securities across 21 developed markets, including countries in Europe, Australasia and the Far East, but not the U.S. or Canada.

earned income Income derived from active participation in a trade or business, including wages, salary, tips, commissions, and bonuses. Also included is alimony received. One must have earned income in order to make contributions to an IRA. *See* portfolio income; unearned income.

earned surplus *See* retained earnings.

earnings momentum A term used to describe that earnings are growing at an increasing rate. That is, if they grew at a rate of 10% in the first quarter, 11% in the second quarter and 14% in the most recent quarter, this shows earnings increasing at an accelerating rate. That is positive earnings momentum. Used by those following a growth style of portfolio management.

earnings multiplier Another term for the *price-to-earning (PE) ratio*. The earnings multiplier is the price of the stock divided by its earnings per share.

earnings per share (EPS) A corporation's net income available for common stock divided by its number of shares of common stock outstanding.

economically targeted investing (ETI) A form of impact investing in investments selected for the economic benefits they create apart from their investment return to the employee benefit plan.

effective date The date the registration of an issue of securities becomes effective, allowing the underwriters to sell the newly issued securities to the public and confirm sales to investors who have given indications of interest.

effective tax rate The overall rate paid on a taxpayer's total taxable income. It will always be less than the marginal tax rate. *See* marginal tax rate.

efficient market theory A theory based on the premise that the stock market processes information efficiently. The theory postulates that, as new information becomes known, it is reflected immediately in the price of a stock and therefore stock prices represent fair prices. There are three forms of this theory: weak, semistrong, and strong, depending upon the amount of information available. *Syn.* Efficient market hypothesis.

employee stock options A form of employee compensation where the employing corporation makes available the opportunity for employees to acquire the issuer's stock. There are two forms: nonqualified (NSOs) and incentive (ISOs).

enjoined This term includes being subject to a mandatory injunction, prohibitory injunction, preliminary injunction, or a temporary restraining order issued by a court of competent jurisdiction.

entangled A social media term meaning that a securities firm has participated in the development of content on a third-party site to which it publishes links.

environmental, social, and governance (ESG) A form of impact investing. It is a set of standards for a company's operations that socially conscious investors use to screen investments.

equity Common and preferred stockholders' ownership interests in a corporation. *See* common stock; preferred stock.

equity financing Raising money for working capital or for capital expenditures by selling common or preferred stock to individual or institutional investors. In return for the money paid, the investors receive ownership interests in the corporation. *See* debt financing.

equity security A security representing ownership in a corporation or another enterprise. Examples of equity securities include: common and preferred stock; interests in a limited partnership or joint venture; securities that carry the right to be traded for equity securities, such as convertible bonds, rights, and warrants; and put and call options on equity securities.

eurobond A long-term debt instrument of a government or corporation that is denominated in the currency of the issuer's country but is issued and sold in a different country.

Eurodollar U.S. currency held in banks outside the United States.

exchange-listed security A security that has met certain requirements and has been admitted to full trading privileges on a stock exchange. The NYSE and regional exchanges set listing requirements for volume of shares outstanding, corporate earnings, and other characteristics.

exchange privilege A feature offered by a mutual fund allowing an individual to transfer an investment in one fund to another fund under the same sponsor without incurring an additional sales charge. *Syn.* conversion privilege.

exchange traded fund An investment company originally designed to track a specific index that is traded on a stock exchange. Rather than basing the price on NAV, the ETF's market price is constantly changing as does the price of any other listed stock. ETFs may be purchased on margin and sold short. Although most ETFs still track indexes, there are a number of ETFs that are actively managed. *Syn.* ETF.

executor, (f. executrix) A person given fiduciary authorization to manage the affairs of a decedent's estate. An executor's authority is established by the decedent's last will.

exempt reporting adviser ERAs are advisers that are exempt from registration relying on either the venture capital fund adviser or the private fund adviser exemption. Although exempt from registration, an ERA is subject to certain reporting, recordkeeping, and other obligations.

exempt security A security exempt from the registration requirements (although not from the antifraud requirements) of the Securities Act of 1933 or the Uniform Securities Act. Examples include U.S. government securities and municipal securities.

exempt transaction A transaction that does not trigger a state's registration and advertising requirements under the Uniform Securities Act. Examples of exempt transactions include: nonissuer transactions in outstanding securities (normal market trading); transactions with financial institutions; unsolicited transactions; and private placement transactions. No transaction is exempt from the Uniform Securities Act's antifraud provisions

exercise price The cost per share at which an option or a warrant holder may buy or sell the underlying security. *Syn.* strike price.

expansion A period of increased business activity throughout an economy; one of the four stages of the business cycle. *Syn.* recovery. *See* business cycle.

expansionary policy A monetary policy that increases the money supply, usually with the intention of lowering interest rates and combating deflation.

expense ratio A ratio for comparing a mutual fund's efficiency by dividing the fund's expenses by its net assets.

face value *See* par.

Fannie Mae *See* Federal National Mortgage Association.

Farm Credit Administration (FCA) The government agency that coordinates the activities of the banks in the Farm Credit System. *See* Farm Credit System.

Farm Credit System (FCS)   An organization of 37 privately owned banks that provide credit services to farmers and mortgages on farm property. Included in the system are the Federal Land Banks, Federal Intermediate Credit Banks, and Banks for Cooperatives. *See* Federal Intermediate Credit Bank.

federal covered adviser   As defined by the NSMIA of 1996, either an investment adviser registered with the SEC or excluded from the definition of investment adviser by the Investment Advisers Act of 1940. Under Dodd-Frank, these advisers registering with the SEC must generally meet a threshold of $100 million or more in assets under management.

Federal covered security   Under the NSMIA of 1996, a new definition was created: covered security, generally referred to as federal covered security on the exam. State securities registration requirements were preempted with respect to covered securities, other than the ability to require notice filing, particularly in the case of registered investment companies. The most tested federal covered securities include those listed on the major U.S. exchanges and Nasdaq as well as investment companies registered with the SEC and securities offered pursuant to the provisions of Rule 506 of Regulation D under the Securities Act of 1933 (private placements).

Federal Deposit Insurance Corporation (FDIC)   The government agency that provides deposit insurance for member banks and prevents bank and thrift failures.

federal funds   The reserves of banks and certain other institutions greater than the reserve requirements or excess reserves. These funds are available immediately.

federal funds rate   The interest rate charged by one institution lending federal funds to another.

Federal Home Loan Bank (FHLB)   A government-regulated organization that operates a credit reserve system for the nation's savings and loan institutions.

Federal Home Loan Mortgage Corporation (FHLMC)   A publicly traded corporation that promotes the nationwide secondary market in mortgages by issuing mortgage-backed pass-through debt certificates. *Syn.* Freddie Mac.

Federal Intermediate Credit Bank (FICB)   One of 12 banks that provide short-term financing to farmers as part of the Farm Credit System.

Federal National Mortgage Association (FNMA)   A publicly held corporation that purchases conventional mortgages and mortgages from government agencies, including the Federal Housing Administration, Department of Veterans Affairs, and Farmers Home Administration. *Syn.* Fannie Mae.

Federal Open Market Committee (FOMC)   A committee that makes decisions concerning the Fed's operations to control the money supply.

Federal Reserve Board (FRB)   A seven-member group that directs the operations of the Federal Reserve System. The President appoints board members, subject to Congressional approval.

Federal Reserve System   The central bank system of the United States. Its primary responsibility is to regulate the flow of money and credit. The system includes 12 regional banks, 24 branch banks, and hundreds of national and state banks. *Syn.* Fed.

fiduciary   A person legally appointed and authorized to hold assets in trust for another person and manage those assets for that person's benefit.

filing date   The day on which an issuer submits to the SEC the registration statement for a new securities issue.

fill-or-kill order (FOK)   An order that instructs the floor broker to fill the entire order immediately; if the entire order cannot be executed immediately, it is canceled.

final prospectus   The legal document that states a new issue security's price, delivery date, and underwriting spread, as well as other material information. It must be given to every investor who purchases a new issue of registered securities. *Syn.* prospectus.

final order   A term used in both state and federal law to refer to a decision rendered by a regulatory body. The final order may result in a suspension, revocation, or denial of registration. It is analogous to the judge passing sentence in a trial.

Financial Industry Regulatory Authority (FINRA)   Organized in July 2007 as a joint effort of NASD and the NYSE to harmonize regulation in the securities industry.

financial risk   *See* credit risk.

FINRA   The acronym for the Financial Industry Regulatory Authority, the result of the cooperative effort of NASD and the NYSE to harmonize regulation in the securities industry.

firm quote   The actual price at which a trading unit of a security (such as 100 shares of stock or five bonds) may be bought or sold. All quotes are firm quotes unless otherwise indicated.

first in, first out (FIFO)   An accounting method used to assess a company's inventory, in which it is assumed that the first goods acquired are the first to be sold. The same method is used by the IRS to determine cost basis for tax purposes. *See* average basis; last in, first out.

fiscal policy   The federal tax and spending policies set by Congress or the President. These policies affect tax rates, interest rates, and government spending in an effort to control the economy. *See* monetary policy.

fiscal year   The term used to describe an accounting year that ends other than December 31st (calendar year accounting). *See* calendar year.

fixed annuity   An insurance contract in which the insurance company makes fixed dollar payments to the annuitant for the term of the contract, usually until the annuitant dies. The insurance company guarantees both earnings and principal. *Syn.* fixed dollar annuity; guaranteed dollar annuity.

fixed asset   A tangible, physical property used in the course of a corporation's everyday operations, including buildings, equipment, and land.

flat yield curve   A chart showing the yields of bonds with short maturities as equal to the yields of bonds with long maturities. *Syn.* even yield curve. *See* inverted yield curve; normal yield curve; yield curve.

flow-through   A term that describes the way income, deductions, and credits resulting from the activities of a business are applied to individual taxes and expenses as though each incurred the income and deductions directly. *See* limited partnership.

FNMA   *See* Federal National Mortgage Association.

FOK   *See* fill-or-kill order.

FOMC   *See* Federal Open Market Committee.

foreign currency   Money issued by a country other than the one in which the investor resides. Options and futures contracts on numerous foreign currencies are traded on U.S. exchanges.

foreign exchange rate   The price of one country's currency in terms of another currency. *Syn.* exchange rate.

Form 706   The IRS form used for the computation of estate tax. It must be filed within nine months of death unless an extension has been obtained.

Form 709   The United States Gift (and Generation-Skipping Transfer) Tax Return is filed on Form 709.

Form 1040   The IRS form used to file individual income tax. Schedule C of the Form 1040 is used to report business income for sole proprietorships.

Form 1041   The IRS form used by estates and trusts to report their income for tax purposes.

Form 1065   The information return filed by a partnership or LLC. Because income and losses flow through to owners, the entity pays no tax.

Form 1120 and 1120S   The tax returns filed by corporations. The "S" is for an S corporation.

Form D   The SEC form required to be filed when engaging in a Regulation D private placement.

forward contract   A forward contract is a direct commitment between one buyer and one seller for a specific commodity. Because forward contracts are direct obligations between a specific buyer and seller (unlike futures and options, they are not standardized), they are not easily transferred and are considered illiquid.

forward pricing   The valuation process for mutual fund shares, whereby an order to purchase or redeem shares is executed at the price determined by the portfolio valuation calculated after the order is received. Portfolio valuations occur at least once per business day.

fractional share   A portion of a whole share of stock. Mutual fund shares are frequently issued in fractional amounts. Fractional shares used to be generated when corporations declared stock dividends, merged, or voted to split stock, but today it is more common for corporations to issue the cash equivalent of fractional shares.

fraud   The deliberate concealment, misrepresentation, or omission of material information or the truth, so as to deceive or manipulate another party for unlawful or unfair gain.

FRB   *See* Federal Reserve Board.

Freddie Mac   *See* Federal Home Loan Mortgage Corporation.

front-end load   A mutual fund commission or sales fee that is charged at the time shares are purchased. The load is added to the share's net asset value when calculating the public offering price.

front running   The prohibited practice of entering an order for the benefit of a firm or a securities professional before entering customer orders.

Full Disclosure Act   *See* Securities Act of 1933.

full power of attorney   A written authorization for someone other than an account's beneficial owner to make deposits and withdrawals and to execute trades in the account. *See* limited power of attorney; durable power of attorney.

full trading authorization   An authorization, usually provided by a full power of attorney, for someone other than the customer to have full trading privileges in an account. *See* limited trading authorization.

fundamental analysis   A method of evaluating securities by attempting to measure the intrinsic value of a particular stock. Fundamental analysts study the overall economy, industry conditions, and the financial condition and management of particular companies. *See* technical analysis.

futures   Futures contracts are exchange-traded obligations for a specific commodity. A buyer goes long, or establishes a long position, and is obligated to take delivery of the commodity on the future date specified. A seller goes short, or establishes a short position, and is obligated to deliver the commodity on the specified future date. If the seller does not own the commodity, his potential loss is unlimited because he has promised delivery and must pay any price to acquire the commodity to deliver. Futures may be highly leveraged.

future value   The amount to which a current deposit will grow at a given rate of compound interest to a specific date in the future.

GAAP   The acronym for generally accepted accounting principles, the standard method used in the United States by professional accountants.

gamma   One of the four Greeks used by options analysts. An option's gamma is a measure of the rate of change of its delta. The gamma of an option is expressed as a percentage and reflects the change in the delta in response to a one point movement of the underlying stock price.

GDP   *See* gross domestic product.

general obligation bond (GO)   A municipal debt issue backed by the full faith, credit, and taxing power of the issuer for payment of interest and principal. *Syn.* full faith and credit bond. *See* revenue bond.

general partnership (GP)   An association of two or more entities formed to conduct a business jointly. The partnership does not require documents for formation, and the general partners are jointly and severally liable for the partnership's liabilities. *See* limited partnership.

generation skipping trust   A form of bypass trust that is designed to have assets pass to grandchildren (or great-grandchildren) in order to "skip" a generation of estate tax.

geometric mean   A type of average that indicates the central tendency of a set of numbers that, instead of finding the sum as with the arithmetic mean, takes the product of the numbers and divides that by the nth root (where n is the count of numbers). It will always be lower than the arithmetic mean [unless all of the numbers are the same (e.g., 6, 6, and 6)].

good-til-canceled order (GTC)   An order that is left on the specialist's book until it is either executed or canceled. *Syn.* open order.

goodwill   An intangible asset that represents the value that a firm's business reputation adds to its perceived value. It is not included in net worth for purposes of computing book value per share.

Government National Mortgage Association (GNMA)   A wholly government-owned corporation that issues pass-through mortgage debt certificates backed by the full faith and credit of the U.S. government. *Syn.* Ginnie Mae.

grantor   An individual or organization that gives assets to a beneficiary by transferring fiduciary duty to a third-party trustee that will maintain the assets for the benefit of the beneficiaries. *Syn.* settlor, trustor.

grantor trust   A trust that requires that the grantor be taxed on income produced by trust property if trust income is distributed to the grantor or to the grantor's spouse; trust income discharges a legal obligation of the grantor or grantor's family; and the grantor retains power to revoke or amend the trust.

gross domestic product (GDP)   The market value of all final goods and services produced within a country in a given period of time. GDP = consumption + investment + government spending + (exports – imports) investment. To account for inflation, GDP is based on a constant dollar, currently the value in 2005.

gross income   All income of a taxpayer, from whatever source derived.

gross margin Gross margin is the operating profit of a business prior to interest and taxes. It is computed by subtracting the cost of goods sold (COGS) from the company's sales (or revenues). Gross margin is frequently expressed as a percentage, called the margin of profit. The calculation is the gross margin divided by the sales (revenues). For example, a company has sales of $5 million and COGS of $3.5 million resulting in a gross margin of $1.5 million and a margin of profit of 30% ($1.5 million / $5 million).

gross revenues All money received by a business from its operations. The term typically does not include interest income or income from the sale, refinancing, or other disposition of properties.

growth fund A diversified common stock fund that has capital appreciation as its primary goal. It invests in companies that reinvest most of their earnings for expansion, research, or development. *See* diversified common stock fund; mutual fund.

growth industry An industry that is growing faster than the economy as a whole as a result of technological changes, new products, or changing consumer tastes.

growth stock A common stock that is believed to offer significant potential for capital gains. It often pays low dividends and sells at a high price-earnings ratio.

growth style investing A management style that attempts to find stocks with positive earnings momentum. These stocks typically sell at the upper end of their 52-week price range, have high P/E ratios and lower than average dividend payout ratios. *See* value style investing.

guaranteed security Under the Uniform Securities Act, the term guaranteed means guaranteed by a third party as to payment of principal, interest, or dividends, but not capital gains.

guardian A court-appointed fiduciary who manages the assets of a minor or an incompetent for that person's benefit. *See* fiduciary.

head and shoulders On a technical analyst's trading chart, a pattern that has three peaks resembling a head and two shoulders. The stock price moves up to its first peak (the left shoulder), drops back, then moves to a higher peak (the top of the head), drops again but recovers to another, lower peak (the right shoulder). A head and shoulders top typically forms after a substantial rise and indicates a market reversal. A head and shoulders bottom (an inverted head and shoulders) indicates a market advance.

hedge An investment made to reduce the risk of adverse price movements in a security. Normally, a hedge consists of a protecting position in a related security. *See* long hedge; selling a hedge; short hedge.

hedge clause Any legend, clause, or other provision that is likely to lead an investor to believe that he has in any way waived any right of action he may have.

hedge fund A fund that can use one or more alternative investment strategies, including hedging against market downturns, investing in asset classes such as currencies or distressed securities, and utilizing return-enhancing tools such as leverage, derivatives, and arbitrage. These funds tend to have very high minimum investment requirements.

high net worth individual An individual with at least $1 million managed by the IA or whose net worth the firm reasonably believes exceeds $2 million. The net worth of an individual may include assets held jointly with that individual's spouse. Performance-based fees may be charged to these clients.

High-yield bond A bond with a less than investment grade rating, characterized by a return commensurate with the higher risk. *Syn.* junk bond

holder The owner of a security. *See* long.

holding company A company organized to invest in and manage other corporations. Control can occur through the ownership of 50% or more of the voting rights or through the exercise of a dominant influence. It is sometimes referred to as the parent organization.

holding period A time period signifying how long the owner possesses a security. It starts the day after a purchase and ends on the day of the sale.

home state If an investment adviser is registered with a state Administrator (state-registered adviser), the firm's home state is the state where it maintains its principal office and place of business.

HR-10 plan *See* Keogh plan.

hypothecation Pledging to a broker-dealer securities bought on margin as collateral for the margin loan. *See* rehypothecation.

immediate annuity An annuity contract that provides for monthly payments to begin immediately after deposit of the invested funds. Payments usually commence within 30 to 60 days. *See* deferred annuity.

immediate-or-cancel order (IRC) An order that instructs the floor broker to execute it immediately, in full or in part. Any portion of the order that remains unexecuted is canceled.

impersonal investment advice Investment advisory services that do not purport to meet the objectives or needs of specific individuals or accounts.

incentive stock option A type of employee stock option. As long as stock purchased through exercise of an ISO is held at least two years after the date of grant and one year after the date of exercise, any profits are reported as long-term capital gains. If these time limits are broached, the ISO is taxed like an NSO. *See* nonqualified stock option.

income fund A mutual fund that *seeks* to provide stable current income by investing in securities that pay interest or dividends. *See* mutual fund.

income statement The summary of a corporation's revenues and expenses for a specific fiscal period.

indenture The agreement between a lender and a borrower that details specific terms of the bond issuance. The indenture specifies the legal obligations of the bond issuer and rights of the bondholders. It is sometimes called the deed of trust.

index *See* security market index.

index fund Investors who wish to invest passively can invest in an index fund, which *seeks* to replicate the performance of a security market index. There are index mutual funds and index exchange-traded funds. *See* security market index.

indication of interest An investor's expression of conditional interest in buying an upcoming securities issue after the investor has reviewed a preliminary prospectus. An indication of interest is not a commitment to buy.

individual retirement account (IRA) A retirement investing tool for employed individuals that allows an annual contribution of 100% of earned income up to a maximum of $5,500 ($6,500 for those 50 and older).

industrial development bond (IDB) A debt security issued by a municipal authority, which uses the proceeds to finance the construction or purchase of facilities to be leased or purchased by a private company. The bonds are backed by the credit of the private company, which is ultimately responsible for principal and interest payments. *Syn.* industrial revenue bond.

industrial revenue bond (IRB) *See* industrial development bond.

industry fund *See* sector fund.

inflation A persistent and measurable increase in the general level of prices. *See* deflation.

inflation risk *See* purchasing power risk.

initial public offering (IPO) A corporation's first sale of common stock to the public. *See* new issue market; public offering.

information barriers Policies and procedures created to prevent misuse of material nonpublic information (MNPI) are commonly referred to as information barriers. Formerly referred to as Chinese Walls.

inside information Material information that has not been disseminated to or is not readily available to the general public.

inside market When viewing the quotes of all of the market makers in a security, the inside market, or inside quote, is the best (highest) bid and the best (lowest) offer (or ask).

insider Any person who possesses or has access to material nonpublic information about a corporation. Insiders include directors, officers, and stockholders who own more than 10% of any class of equity security of a corporation.

Insider Trading Act *See* Insider Trading and Securities Fraud Enforcement Act of 1988.

Insider Trading and Securities Fraud Enforcement Act of 1988 Legislation that defines what constitutes the illicit use of nonpublic information in making securities trades and the liabilities and penalties that apply. *Syn.* Insider Trading Act. *See* Chinese Wall; insider.

institutional account An account held for the benefit of others. Examples of institutional accounts include banks, trusts, pension and profit-sharing plans, mutual funds, and insurance companies.

institutional investor A person or an organization that trades securities in large enough share quantities or dollar amounts that it qualifies for preferential treatment and lower commissions. An institutional order can be of any size. Institutional investors are covered by fewer protective regulations because it is assumed that they are more knowledgeable and better able to protect themselves.

intangible asset A property owned that is not physical, such as a formula, a copyright, or goodwill. *See* goodwill.

interactive content Social media content that can be added to by anyone with access to the link. A chat room is an example.

interest The charge for the privilege of borrowing money, usually expressed as an annual percentage rate.

interest rate risk The risk associated with investments relating to the sensitivity of price or value to fluctuation in the current level of interest rates; also, the risk that involves the competitive cost of money. This term is generally associated with bond prices, but it applies to all investments. In bonds, prices carry interest risk because if bond prices rise, outstanding bonds will not remain competitive unless their yields and prices adjust to reflect the current market.internal rate of return The discount rate that sets the net present value of an investment equal to zero. Syn. IRR

internal rate of return The discount rate that sets the net present value of an investment equal to zero. Syn. IRR

Internal Revenue Code (IRC) The legislation that defines tax liabilities and deductions for U.S. taxpayers.

Internal Revenue Service (IRS) The U.S. government agency responsible for collecting most federal taxes and for administering tax rules and regulations.

interstate offering An issue of securities registered with the SEC sold to residents of states other than the state in which the issuer does business.

intestate Dying without a legal will. Usually the probate court will appoint an administrator to handle the deceased's estate. For purposes of the Uniform Securities Act, transactions by this administrator (a fiduciary) are considered exempt transactions.

in-the-money The term used to describe an option that has intrinsic value, such as a call option when the stock is selling above the exercise price or a put option when the stock is selling below the exercise price. See at-the-money; intrinsic value; out-of-the-money.

intrastate offering An issue of securities exempt from SEC registration, available to companies that do business in one state and sell their securities only to residents of that same state. See Rule 147.

intrinsic value The potential profit to be made from exercising an option. A call option is said to have intrinsic value when the underlying stock is trading above the exercise price. See time value.

inverted yield curve A chart showing long-term debt instruments that have lower yields than short-term debt instruments. Syn. negative yield curve. See flat yield curve; normal yield curve.

investment adviser (1) Any person who makes investment recommendations in return for a flat fee or a percentage of assets managed. (2) For an investment company, the individual who bears the day-to-day responsibility of investing the cash and securities held in the fund's portfolio in accordance with objectives stated in the fund's prospectus.

investment adviser representative (IAR) Any partner, officer, director, or other individual employed by or associated with an investment adviser whose job function involves the rendering of advice, solicitation for clients, or supervision of those who do.

Investment Advisers Act of 1940 Legislation governing who must register with the SEC as an investment adviser. See investment adviser.

investment banker An institution in the business of raising capital for corporations and municipalities. An investment banker may not accept deposits or make commercial loans. Syn. investment bank.

investment banking business A broker, dealer, or municipal or government securities dealer that underwrites or distributes new issues of securities as a dealer or that buys and sells securities for the accounts of others as a broker. Syn. investment securities business.

investment company A company engaged in the business of pooling investors' money and trading in securities for them. Examples include face-amount certificate companies, unit investment trusts, and management companies.

Investment Company Act Amendments of 1970 Amendments to the Investment Company Act of 1940 requiring, in particular, that sales charges relate to the services a fund provides its shareholders. See Investment Company Act of 1940.

Investment Company Act of 1940 Congressional legislation regulating companies that invest and reinvest in securities. The act requires an investment company engaged in interstate commerce to register with the SEC.

investment constraints Limitations or restrictions that are specific to the adviser's client. Investment constraints include, among others, liquidity needs, time horizon, and personal ethical choices (no tobacco or alcohol stocks).

investment-grade security A security to which the rating services (e.g., Standard & Poor's and Moody's) have assigned a rating of BBB/Baa or above.

investment objective Any goal a client hopes to achieve through investing. Examples include current income, capital growth, and preservation of capital.

investment policy statement   Used by those administering employee benefit plans to set out the objectives, policies, investment selections, and monitoring procedures for the plan. May also be used by investment advisers to determine policies to be followed with their clients.

investor   The purchaser of an asset or security with the intent of profiting from the transaction.

IPO   *See* initial public offering.

IRA rollover   The reinvestment of assets that an individual receives as a distribution from a qualified tax-deferred retirement plan into an individual retirement account within 60 days of receiving the distribution. The individual may reinvest either the entire sum or a portion of the sum, although any portion not reinvested is taxed as ordinary income. *See also* individual retirement account; IRA transfer.

IRA transfer   The direct reinvestment of retirement assets from one qualified tax-deferred retirement plan to an individual retirement account. The account owner never takes possession of the assets but directs that they be transferred directly from the existing plan custodian to the new plan custodian. *See also* individual retirement account; IRA rollover.

IRR   *See* internal rate of return

irrevocable trust   A trust that cannot be altered or canceled by the grantor at any time.

issuer   The entity, such as a corporation or municipality, that offers or proposes to offer its securities for sale.

joint account   An account in which two or more individuals possess some form of control over the account and may transact business in the account. The account must be designated as either joint tenants in common or joint tenants with right of survivorship. *See* tenants in common; joint tenants with right of survivorship.

joint life with last survivor   An annuity payout option that covers two or more people, with annuity payments continuing as long as one of the annuitants remains alive.

joint tenants with right of survivorship (JTWROS)   A form of joint ownership of an account whereby a deceased tenant's fractional interest in the account passes to the surviving tenant(s). Used almost exclusively by husbands and wives. *See* tenants in common.

junk bond   *See* high-yield bond.

Keogh plan   A qualified tax-deferred retirement plan for persons who are self-employed and unincorporated or who earn extra income through personal services aside from their regular employment. *Syn.* HR-10 plan. *See* individual retirement account.

Keynesian economics   The theory that active government intervention in the marketplace is the best method of ensuring economic growth and stability.

lagging indicator   A measurable economic factor that changes after the economy has started to follow a particular pattern or trend. Lagging indicators are believed to confirm long-term trends. Examples include average duration of unemployment, corporate profits, and labor cost per unit of output. *See* coincident indicator; leading indicator.

large-cap   Stocks with a market capitalization of $10 billion or more.

last in, first out (LIFO)   An accounting method used to assess a corporation's inventory in which it is assumed that the last goods acquired are the first to be sold. The method is used to determine cost basis for tax purposes; the IRS designates last in, first out as the order in which sales or withdrawals from an investment are made. It is the system used for random withdrawals from a nonqualified annuity where the earnings are taxed first before receiving back a return of original principal. *See* average basis; first in, first out.

leading indicator   A measurable economic factor that changes before the economy starts to follow a particular pattern or trend. Leading indicators are believed to predict changes in the economy. Examples include new orders for durable goods, slowdowns in deliveries by vendors, and numbers of building permits issued. *See* coincident indicator; lagging indicator.

LEAPS   *See* Long-term Equity Anticipation Securities.

legal list   The selection of securities a state agency (usually a state banking or insurance commission) determines to be appropriate investments for fiduciary accounts such as mutual savings banks, pension funds, and insurance companies. This is used in states that do not have the prudent investor rule.

legislative risk   The potential for an investor to be adversely affected by changes in investment or tax laws.

letter of intent (LOI)   A signed agreement allowing an investor to buy mutual fund shares at a lower overall sales charge based on the total dollar amount of the intended investment. A letter of intent is valid only if the investor completes the terms of the agreement within 13 months of signing the agreement. A letter of intent may be backdated 90 days. *Syn.* statement of intention.

level load   A mutual fund sales fee charged annually and based on the net asset value of a share. *See* back-end load; Class C share; front-end load.

leverage   Using borrowed capital to increase investment return. *Syn.* trading on the equity.

liability   A legal obligation to pay a debt owed. Current liabilities are debts payable within 12 months. Long-term liabilities are debts payable over a period of more than 12 months.

LIBOR   LIBOR is a benchmark interest rate based on the rates at which banks lend unsecured funds to each other on the London interbank market. Published daily, the rate was previously administered by the British Bankers' Association (BBA). But in the aftermath of a scandal in 2012, Britain's primary financial regulator, the Financial Conduct Authority (FCA), shifted supervision of LIBOR to a new entity, the ICE Benchmark Administration, an independent subsidiary of the private exchange operator Intercontinental Exchange, or ICE.

limited liability   An investor's right to limit potential losses to no more than the amount invested. Equity shareholders, such as corporate stockholders and limited partners, have limited liability.

limited liability company (LLC)   A hybrid between a partnership and a corporation in that it combines the pass-through treatment of a partnership with the limited liability accorded to corporate shareholders.

limited partnership (LP)   An association of two or more partners formed to conduct a business jointly and in which one or more of the partners is liable only to the extent of the amount of money they have invested. Limited partners do not receive dividends but enjoy direct flow-through of income and expenses. *See* flow-through; general partnership.

limited power of attorney   A written authorization for someone other than an account's beneficial owner to make certain investment decisions regarding transactions in the account. *See* discretion; full power of attorney; durable power of attorney.

limited trading authorization   An authorization, usually provided by a limited power of attorney, for someone other than the customer to have trading privileges in an account. These privileges are limited to purchases and sales; withdrawal of assets is not authorized. *See* full trading authorization.

limit order   An order that instructs the broker-dealer to buy a specified security below a certain price or to sell a specified security above a certain price. These orders are entered either for the day or good-til-canceled (GTC). *See* stop limit order; stop order.

liquidation priority   In the case of a corporation's liquidation, the order that is strictly followed for paying off creditors and stockholders: (1) secured claims like mortgage bonds, equipment trust certificates, and collateral trust bonds; (2) unpaid wages; (3) taxes; (4) unsecured liabilities (debentures) and general creditors; (5) subordinated debt; (6) preferred stockholders; and (7) common stockholders.

liquidity   The ease with which an asset can be converted to cash at its fair market value.. A large number of buyers and sellers and a high volume of trading activity provide high liquidity.

liquidity risk   The potential that an investor might not be able to sell an investment when desired without adverse price disruption. *Syn.* marketability risk.

listed option   An option contract that can be bought and sold on a national securities exchange in a continuous secondary market. Listed options carry standardized strike prices and expiration dates. *Syn.* standardized option.

listed security   A stock, a bond, or another security that satisfies certain minimum requirements and is traded on a regional or national securities exchange such as the New York Stock Exchange. *See* over the counter.

living trust   A trust created during the lifetime of the grantor; also known as an inter vivos trust.

LLC   *See* limited liability company.

long   The term used to describe the owning of a security, contract, or commodity. For example, a common stock owner is said to have a long position in the stock. *See* short.

longevity annuity   A deferred income annuity that generally does not begin payout until the age of 85. If a QLAC (qualified longevity annuity contract), it is exempt from RMDs for up to 15 years in a qualified retirement plans.

Long-term Equity Anticipation Securities   LEAPS options have the same characteristics as standard options, but with expiration dates up to three years in the future.

long-term gain   The profit earned on the sale of a capital asset that has been owned for more than 12 months. *See* capital gain; capital loss; long-term loss.

long-term loss   The loss realized on the sale of a capital asset that has been owned for more than 12 months. *See* capital gain; capital loss; long-term gain.

loss carryover   A capital loss incurred in one tax year that is carried over to the next year or later years for use as a capital loss deduction. *See* capital loss.

make a market   To stand ready to buy or sell a particular security as a dealer for its own account. A market maker accepts the risk of holding the position in the security. *See* market maker.

Maloney Act   An amendment enacted in 1938 to broaden Section 15 of the Securities Exchange Act of 1934. Named for its sponsor, the late Sen. Francis Maloney of Connecticut, the amendment provided for the creation of a self-regulatory organization for the specific purpose of supervising the over-the-counter securities market. *See* National Association of Securities Dealers, Inc.

management company   An investment company that trades various types of securities in a portfolio in accordance with specific objectives stated in the prospectus. *See* closed-end management company; diversified management company; mutual fund; nondiversified management company.

margin   The amount of equity contributed by a customer as a percentage of the current market value of the securities held in a margin account. *See* equity; initial margin requirement; Regulation T.

marginal tax rate   The rate of taxation on any additional taxable income received. It is sometimes referred to as the tax on the "next" dollar or the "last" dollar of income. *See* effective tax rate.

margin of profit ratio   A measure of a corporation's relative profitability. It is calculated by dividing the operating profit by the net sales. *Syn.* operating profit ratio; profit margin.

marital trust   A trust that *seeks* to pass property to a survivor spouse while taking advantage of the marital deduction; also known as an A trust.

market capitalization   The number of outstanding shares multiplied by the current market price. Classed as large-cap, mid-cap, small-cap, and micro-cap.

market maker   A dealer willing to accept the risk of holding a particular security in its own account to facilitate trading in that security. *See* make a market.

market order   An order to be executed immediately at the best available price. A market order is the only order that guarantees execution. *Syn.* unrestricted order.

market risk   The potential for an investor to experience losses owing to day-to-day fluctuations in the prices at which securities can be bought or sold. *See* systematic risk.

market value   The price at which investors buy or sell a share of common stock or a bond at a given time. Market value is determined by buyers' and sellers' interaction. *See* current market value.

markup   The difference between the lowest current offering price among dealers and the higher price a dealer charges a customer.

matched orders   Simultaneously entering identical (or nearly identical) buy and sell orders for a security to create the appearance of active trading in that security. This violates the antifraud provisions of the Securities Exchange Act of 1934 and the USA.

material information   Any fact that could affect an investor's decision to trade a security.

maturity date   The date on which a bond's principal is repaid to the investor and interest payments cease. *See* par; principal.

mean   When referring to a series of values, such as portfolio returns, the average. A measure of central tendency known as the arithmetic mean. Could also refer to the geometric mean.

median   When viewing a series of values, such as portfolio returns, the number that has as many occurrences above as below. A measure of central tendency.

mid-cap   Stocks with a market capitalization of $2 billion to $10 billion.

mode   When viewing a series of values, the one that occurs the most frequently. A measure of central tendency.

modern portfolio theory (MPT)   A method of choosing investments that focuses on the importance of the relationships among all of the investments in a portfolio rather than the individual merits of each investment. The method allows investors to quantify and control the amount of risk they accept and return they achieve.

monetarist theory   An economic theory holding that the money supply is the major determinant of price levels and that therefore a well-controlled money supply will have the most beneficial impact on the economy.

monetary policy   The Federal Reserve Board's actions that determine the size and rate of the money supply's growth, which in turn affect interest rates. *See* fiscal policy.

money market   The securities market that deals in high quality, short-term debt. Money market instruments are very liquid forms of debt that mature in one year or less. Treasury bills, commercial paper, and jumbo CDs are examples of money market instruments.

money market fund   A mutual fund that invests in short-term debt instruments. The fund's objective is to earn interest while maintaining a stable net asset value of $1 per share. Always sold with no load, the fund may also offer check-writing privileges and a low initial minimum investment. *See* mutual fund.

Monte Carlo simulation   A statistical method to determine the return profile of a security or portfolio that recreates potential outcomes by generating random values on the basis of the risk and return characteristics of the securities themselves.

Moody's Investors Service   One of the best known investment rating agencies in the United States. A subsidiary of Dun & Bradstreet, Moody's rates bonds, commercial paper, preferred and common stocks, and municipal short-term issues. *See* bond rating; Standard & Poor's Corporation.

mortgage bond   A debt obligation secured by a property pledge. It represents a lien or mortgage against the issuing corporation's properties and real estate assets.

moving average chart   A tool used by technical analysts to track the price movements of a commodity. It plots average daily settlement prices over a defined period of time (for example, over three days for a three-day moving average).

MRD   Minimum required distribution. *See* required minimum distribution.

municipal bond   A debt security issued by a state, a municipality, or another subdivision (such as a school, a park, a sanitation, or another local taxing district) to finance its capital expenditures. Such expenditures might include the construction of highways, public works, or school buildings. *Syn.* municipal security.

municipal bond fund   A mutual fund that invests in municipal bonds and operates either as a unit investment trust or as an open-end fund. The fund's objective is to maximize federally tax-exempt income. *See* mutual fund; unit investment trust.

municipal note   A short-term municipal security issued in anticipation of funds from another source.

Municipal Securities Rulemaking Board (MSRB)   A self-regulatory organization that regulates the issuance and trading of municipal securities. The Board functions under the Securities and Exchange Commission's supervision; it has no enforcement powers. *See* Securities Amendments Act of 1975.

mutual fund   An investment company that continuously offers new equity shares in an actively managed portfolio of securities. All shareholders participate in the fund's gains or losses. The shares are redeemable on any business day at the net asset value. Each mutual fund's portfolio is invested to match the objective stated in the prospectus. *Syn.* open-end investment company; open-end management company. *See* balanced fund; contractual plan; net asset value.

NASAA   *See* North American Securities Administrators Association.

NASD   *See* National Association of Securities Dealers, Inc.

Nasdaq   *See* National Association of Securities Dealers Automated Quotation System.

NASD 5% markup policy   A guideline for reasonable markups, markdowns, and commissions for secondary over-the-counter transactions. According to the policy, all commissions on broker transactions and all markups or markdowns on principal transactions should equal 5% or should be fair and reasonable for a particular transaction. *Syn.* markup policy.

National Association of Securities Dealers, Inc. (NASD)   The self-regulatory organization for the over-the-counter market. NASD was organized under the provisions of the 1938 Maloney Act. *See* Maloney Act, FINRA.

National Association of Securities Dealers Automated Quotation System (Nasdaq)   The nationwide electronic quotation system for up-to-the-second on approximately 3,100 over-the-counter stocks trade information. Sometimes referred to as the Nasdaq Stock Market. All securities traded here are federal covered as defined in the NSMIA of 1996.

NAV per share   The value of a mutual fund share, calculated by dividing the fund's total net asset value by the number of shares outstanding.

negotiability   A characteristic of a security that permits the owner to assign, give, transfer, or sell it to another person without a third party's permission.

negotiable certificate of deposit (CD)   An unsecured promissory note issued with a minimum face value of $100,000. It evidences a time deposit of funds with the issuing bank and is guaranteed by the bank.

net asset value (NAV)   A mutual fund share's value, as calculated once a day on the basis of the closing market price for each security in the fund's portfolio. It is computed by deducting the fund's liabilities from the portfolio's total assets and dividing this amount by the number of shares outstanding. *See* mutual fund.

net investment income   The source of an investment company's dividend payments. It is calculated by subtracting the company's operating expenses from the total dividends and interest the company receives from the securities in its portfolio.

net present value   The difference between the present value of the future cash flows from an investment and the current market price. *Syn* NPV

net worth   The amount by which assets exceed liabilities.

new account form   The form that must be filled out for each new account opened with a brokerage firm. The form specifies, at a minimum, the account owner, trading authorization, payment method, and types of securities appropriate for the customer.

new issue market   The securities market for shares in privately owned businesses that are raising capital by selling common stock to the public for the first time. *Syn.* primary market. *See* initial public offering; secondary market.

no-load fund   A mutual fund whose shares are sold without a commission or sales charge. The investment company distributes the shares directly. *See* mutual fund; net asset value; sales load.

nominal yield   The interest rate stated on the face of a bond that represents the percentage of interest the issuer pays on the bond's face value. *Syn.* coupon rate; stated yield. *See* bond yield.

nominee   A person or company whose name is given as having title to a stock, real estate, and so forth, but who is not the actual owner. *See* street name.

nonaccredited investor   An investor not meeting the net worth requirements of Regulation D. Nonaccredited investors are counted for purposes of the 35-investor limitation for Rule 506(b) Regulation D private placements. *See* accredited investor; private placement; Regulation D.

noncontributory plan   A retirement plan to which only the employer makes contributions. *See* contributory plan.

noncumulative preferred stock   An equity security that does not have to pay any dividends in arrears to the holder. *See* cumulative preferred stock; preferred stock.

nondiversification   A portfolio management strategy that *seeks* to concentrate investments in a particular industry or geographic area in hopes of achieving higher returns. *See* diversification.

nonqualified retirement plan   A corporate retirement plan that does not meet the standards set by the Employee Retirement Income Security Act of 1974. Contributions to a nonqualified plan are not tax deductible. *See also* qualified retirement plan.

nonqualified stock option   A type of employee stock option. When NSOs are exercised, the difference between the current market price at the time of exercise and the strike price is reported as wages on the tax returns of the employer and the employee. *See* incentive stock option.

nonrecourse financing   Debt incurred for the purchase of an asset that pledges the asset as security for the debt but that does not hold the borrower personally liable.

nonsystematic risk   The potential for an unforeseen event to affect the value of a specific investment. Examples of such events include strikes, natural disasters, poor management decisions, introductions of new product lines, and attempted takeovers. This risk is diversifiable. *Syn.* unsystematic risk. *See* systematic risk.

no-par stock   An equity security issued without a stated value.

normal yield curve   A chart showing long-term debt instruments having higher yields than short-term debt instruments. *Syn.* positive yield curve. *See* flat yield curve; inverted yield curve; yield curve.

North American Securities Administrators Association   Organized in 1919, the North American Securities Administrators Association (NASAA) is the oldest international organization devoted to investor protection. NASAA is a voluntary association whose membership consists of 67 state, provincial, and territorial securities Administrators in the 50 states, the District of Columbia, Puerto Rico, the U.S. Virgin Islands, Canada, and Mexico.

note   A short-term debt security, usually maturing in five years or less. *See* Treasury note.

notice filing   (1) Method by which a registered investment company and certain other federal covered securities file records with state securities Administrators. (2) SEC-registered advisers (federal covered) may have to provide state securities authorities (the Administrator) with copies of documents that are filed with the SEC and pay a filing fee.

offer   (1) Under the Uniform Securities Act, any attempt to solicit a purchase or sale in a security for value. (2) An indication by an investor, a trader, or a dealer of a willingness to sell a security; the price at which an investor can buy from a broker-dealer. *See* bid.

open-end investment company   *See* mutual fund.

opening purchase   Entering the options market by buying calls or puts. *See* opening sale.

opening sale   Entering the options market by selling calls or puts. *See* closing purchase; opening purchase.

open-market operations   The buying and selling of securities (primarily government or agency debt) by the Federal Open Market Committee to effect control of the money supply. These transactions increase or decrease the level of bank reserves available for lending.

operating income   The profit realized from one year of operation of a business.

operating ratio   The ratio of operating expenses to net sales; the complement to the margin of profit ratio.

optimal portfolio   The optimal portfolio under modern portfolio theory assumes that investors *see*k a portfolio of assets that minimizes risks while offering the highest possible return.

ordinary income   Earnings other than capital gain.

OTC Bulletin Board (OTCBB)   An electronic quotation system for equity securities that are not listed on a national exchange or included in the Nasdaq system. These are not federal covered securities and generally require registration with both the SEC and the states.

OTC Link   An electronic inter-dealer quotation system that displays quotes from broker-dealers for many over-the-counter securities. Formerly known as the Pink Sheets, OTC Link does not require companies whose securities are quoted on its systems to meet any listing requirements.

OTC market   The security trading system in which broker-dealers negotiate directly with one another rather than through an auction on an exchange floor. The trading takes place over computer and telephone networks that link brokers and dealers around the world. Both listed and OTC securities, as well as municipal and U.S. government securities, trade in the OTC market.

out-of-the-money   The term used to describe an option that has no intrinsic value, such as a call option when the stock is selling below the exercise price or a put option when the stock is above the exercise price.

over the counter (OTC)   The term used to describe a security traded through the telephone-linked and computer-connected OTC market rather than through a stock exchange. *See* OTC market.

oversubscribed   The term used to describe a new security issue where the demand for the shares greatly exceeds the available supply. The issues usually appreciate rapidly on the first day of trading and failure to properly allocate them is a prohibited practice.

par   The dollar amount the issuer assigns to a security. For an equity security, par is usually a small dollar amount that bears no relationship to the security's market price. For a debt security, par is the amount repaid to the investor when the bond matures, usually $1,000. *Syn.* face value; principal; stated value. *See* capital surplus; maturity date.

parity price of common   The dollar amount at which a common stock is equal in value to its corresponding convertible security. It is calculated by dividing the convertible security's market value by its conversion ratio.

parity price of convertible   The dollar amount at which a convertible security is equal in value to its corresponding common stock. It is calculated by multiplying the market price of the common stock by its conversion ratio.

participation   The provision of the Employee Retirement Income Security Act of 1974 requiring that all employees in a qualified retirement plan be covered within a reasonable time of their dates of hire.

partnership   A form of business organization in which two or more individuals manage the business and are equally and personally liable for its debts.

partnership account   An account that empowers the individual members of a partnership to act on the behalf of the partnership as a whole.

partnership management fee   The amount payable to the general partners of a limited partnership, or to other persons, for managing the day-to-day partnership operations. *Syn.* program management fee; property management fee.

par value   The dollar amount assigned to a security by the issuer. For an equity security, par value is usually a small dollar amount that bears no relationship to the security's market price. For a debt security, par value is the amount repaid to the investor when the bond matures, usually $1,000. *Syn.* face value; principal; stated value. *See* capital surplus; discount bond; premium bond.

passive income   Earnings derived from a rental property, limited partnership, or other enterprise in which the individual is not actively involved. Passive income therefore does not include earnings from wages or active business participation, nor does it include income from dividends, interest, and capital gains. *See* passive loss; unearned income.

passive loss A loss incurred through a rental property, limited partnership, or other enterprise in which the individual is not actively involved. Passive losses can be used to offset passive income only, not wage or portfolio income. *See* passive income.

passive management style In a perfectly efficient market, investors should use a passive investment strategy (i.e., buying a broad market index of stocks and holding it) because active investment strategies will underperform due to transactions costs and management fees. However, to the extent that market prices are inefficient, active investment strategies can generate positive risk-adjusted returns. *See* active management style.

pass-through certificate A security representing an interest in a pool of conventional, Veterans Administration, Farmers Home Administration, or other agency mortgages. The pool receives the principal and interest payments, which it passes through to each certificate holder. Payments may or may not be guaranteed. *See* Federal National Mortgage Association; Government National Mortgage Association.

pattern A repetitive series of price movements on a chart used by a technical analyst to predict future movements of the market.

payment date The day on which a declared dividend is paid to all stockholders owning shares on the record date.

PE *See* price-earnings ratio.

peak The end of a period of increasing business activity throughout the economy, one of the four stages of the business cycle. *Syn.* prosperity. *See* business cycle.

pecuniary Of or relating to money, such as operating for pecuniary profit.

pegging An illegal form of market manipulation that attempts to keep the price of a subject security from falling. It is used by those with a long position. *See* capping.

pension plan A contract between an individual and an employer, a labor union, a government entity, or another institution that provides for the distribution of pension benefits at retirement.

Pension Reform Act *See* Employee Retirement Income Security Act of 1974.

PE ratio *See* price-earnings ratio.

performance-based fee An investment advisory fee based on a share of capital gains on, or capital appreciation of, client assets. A fee that is based upon a percentage of assets that the IA manages is not a performance-based fee. This fee may only be charged to certain high net worth clients.

person As defined in securities law, an individual, corporation, partnership, association, fund, joint stock company, unincorporated organization, trust, government, or political subdivision of a government.

personal income (PI) An individual's total earnings derived from wages, passive business enterprises, and investments. *See* disposable income.

Pink Sheets *See* OTC Link.

point A measure of a bond's price; $10 or 1% of the par value of $1,000. *See* basis point.

political risk The risk that an investment's returns could suffer as a result of political changes or instability in a country such as from a change in government, orderly or not, nationalization of industries, or military control.

portfolio income Earnings from interest, dividends, and all nonbusiness investments. *See* earned income; passive income; unearned income.

portfolio manager The entity responsible for investing a mutual fund's assets, implementing its investment strategy, and managing day-to-day portfolio trading. *Syn.* fund manager.

position The amount of a security either owned (a long position) or owed (a short position) by an individual or a dealer. Dealers take long positions in specific securities to maintain inventories and thereby facilitate trading.

preferred stock An equity security that represents ownership in a corporation. It is issued with a stated dividend, which must be paid before dividends are paid to common stockholders. It generally carries no voting rights. *See* callable preferred stock; cumulative preferred stock.

preferred stock fund A mutual fund whose investment objective is to provide stable income with minimal capital risk. It invests in income-producing instruments such as preferred stock. *See* bond fund.

preliminary prospectus An abbreviated prospectus that is distributed while the SEC is reviewing an issuer's registration statement. It contains all of the essential facts about the forthcoming offering except the underwriting spread, final public offering price, and date on which the shares will be delivered. *Syn.* red herring.

premium (1) The amount of cash that an option buyer pays to an option seller. (2) The difference between the higher price paid for a security and the security's face amount at issue. *See* discount.

premium bond A bond that sells at a higher price than its face value. *See* discount bond; par value.

premium mode Insurance companies give policyowners the choice to pay premiums annually, semiannually, quarterly or monthly.

present value The sum of money needed to invest now at a given rate of compound interest to reach a specified amount at a specified future date.

price-earnings ratio (PE) A tool for comparing the prices of different common stocks by assessing how much the market is willing to pay for a share of each corporation's earnings. It is calculated by dividing the current market price of a stock by the earnings per share. *Syn.* earnings multiplier.

primary offering An offering in which the proceeds of the underwriting go to the issuing corporation, agency, or municipality. The issuer *seeks* to increase its capitalization either by selling shares of stock, representing ownership, or by selling bonds, representing loans to the issuer. *Syn.* primary distribution.

prime rate The interest rate that commercial banks charge their prime or most creditworthy customers, generally large corporations.

principal (1) Every business transaction has two principals—the buyer and the seller. When a broker-dealer trades for its own account, it is acting in the capacity of a principal. (2) *See* dealer. (3) *See* par.

principal office and place of business The firm's executive office from which the firm's officers, partners, or managers direct, control, and coordinate the activities of the firm.

principal transaction A transaction in which a broker-dealer either buys securities from customers and takes them into its own inventory or sells securities to customers from its inventory. *See* agency transaction; agent; broker; dealer; principal.

private placement An offering of new issue securities that complies with Regulation D of the Securities Act of 1933. According to Regulation D, a security generally is not required to be registered with the SEC if it is offered to no more than 35 nonaccredited investors or to an unlimited number of accredited investors. *See* Regulation D.

profitability The ability to generate a level of income and gain in excess of expenses.

profitability ratio One of several measures of a corporation's relative profit or income in relation to its sales. *See* margin of profit ratio; return on equity.

profit-sharing plan An employee benefit plan established and maintained by an employer whereby the employees receive a share of the business's profits. The money may be paid directly to the employees or deferred until retirement. A combination of both approaches is also possible.

progressive tax A tax that takes a larger percentage of the income of high-income earners than that of low-income earners. An example is the graduated income tax. *See* regressive tax.

proscribed A term commonly used in legal situations to describe a prohibited action.

prospectus Any notice, circular, advertisement, letter, or communication, in written form or by radio or television, which offers any security for sale.

proxy A limited power of attorney from a stockholder authorizing another person to vote on stockholder issues according to the first stockholder's instructions. To vote on corporate matters, a stockholder must either attend the annual meeting or vote by proxy.

prudent expert rule A modern application of the prudent man rule to those with a fiduciary responsibility over qualified plans coming under the jurisdiction of ERISA.

prudent investor rule Legally known as the Uniform Prudent Investors Act (UPIA). A modern adaptation of the prudent man rule, which, as a result of the development of modern portfolio theory, applies the standard of prudence to the entire portfolio rather than to individual investments. It requires the fiduciary to measure risk with respect to return.

publicly traded fund *See* closed-end investment company.

public offering The sale of an issue of common stock, either by a corporation going public or by an offering of additional shares. *See* initial public offering.

public offering price (POP) (1) The price of new shares that is established in the issuing corporation's prospectus. (2) The price to investors for mutual fund shares, equal to the net asset value plus the sales charge. *See* ask; bid; mutual fund; net asset value.

purchasing power risk The potential that, because of inflation, a certain amount of money will not purchase as much in the future as it does today. *Syn.* inflation risk.

put (1) An option contract giving the owner the right to sell a certain amount of an underlying security at a specified price within a specified time. (2) The act of exercising a put option. *See* call.

QLAC A qualified longevity annuity contract. If certain limits prescribed by the IRS are met, RMDs do not have to include the value of these contracts until age 85.

QTIP trust A trust that is funded with qualified terminable interest property, meaning that the spouse's interest in the property terminates upon his death; also known as a Q trust, C trust, or current income trust.

QTP *See* qualified tuition program.

Q trust *See* QTIP trust.

Qualified Domestic Relations Orders (QDROs) Premature distributions that are taken pursuant to a qualified domestic relations order, or QDRO, are exempt from the 10% penalty. A QDRO is a court-issued order that gives someone the right to an individual's qualified plan assets, typically an ex- (or soon-to-be-ex-) spouse, and the QDRO is usually issued in the course of divorce proceedings or to satisfy child support obligations. A QDRO applies only to assets in a qualified employer plan; it would not be applicable to an IRA or a SEP.

qualified person Under both state and federal law, a client for whom an investment adviser may charge performance-based fees. Currently, the requirements are a minimum net worth of $2.1 million or at least $1 million in AUM with that adviser.

qualified retirement plan A corporate retirement plan that meets the standards set by the Employee Retirement Income Security Act of 1974. Contributions to a qualified plan are tax deductible. *Syn.* approved plan. *See also* individual retirement account; Keogh plan; nonqualified retirement plan.

qualified tuition program The technical name for Section 529 Plans. *Syn.* QTP.

quick asset ratio A more stringent test of liquidity than the current ratio. It is computed by taking the current assets, less the inventory, and dividing by the current liabilities. *Syn.* acid test ratio.

quick ratio *Syn.* acid test ratio, quick asset ratio.

quotation The price or bid a market maker or broker-dealer offers for a particular security. *Syn.* quote. *See* ask; bid; bond quote; stock quote.

quote machine A computer that provides representatives and market makers with the information that appears on the Consolidated Tape. The information on the screen is condensed into symbols and numbers.

rating An evaluation of a corporate or municipal bond's relative safety, according to the issuer's ability to repay principal and make interest payments. Bonds are rated by various organizations, such as Standard & Poor's and Moody's. Ratings range from AAA or Aaa (the highest) to C or D, which represents a company in default.

rating service A company, such as Moody's or Standard & Poor's, that rates various debt and preferred stock issues for safety of payment of principal, interest, or dividends. The issuing company or municipality pays a fee for the rating. *See* bond rating; rating.

real estate investment trust (REIT) A corporation or trust that uses the pooled capital of many investors to invest in direct ownership of either income property or mortgage loans. These investments offer tax benefits in addition to interest and capital gains distributions. However, unlike DPPs, these are not "flow-through" vehicles.

realized gain The amount a taxpayer earns when he sells an asset. *See* unrealized gain.

recession A general economic decline lasting from six to 18 months (at least two consecutive quarters of declining or negative DGP growth).

record date The date a corporation's board of directors establishes that determines which of its stockholders are entitled to receive dividend distributions or be eligible to vote.

redeemable security A security that the issuer redeems upon the holder's request. Examples include shares in an open-end investment company and Treasury notes.

redemption The return of an investor's principal in a security, such as a bond, preferred stock, or mutual fund shares. By law, redemption of mutual fund shares must occur within seven days of receiving the investor's request for redemption.

refunding Retiring an outstanding bond issue before maturity by using money from the sale of a new debt offering.

regional exchange A stock exchange that serves the financial community in a particular region of the country. These exchanges tend to focus on securities issued within their regions, but also offer trading in NYSE and Nasdaq-listed securities.

registration by coordination   A process that allows a security to be sold in a state. It is available to an issuer that files for the security's registration under the Securities Act of 1933 and files duplicates of the registration documents with the state Administrator. The state registration becomes effective at the same time the federal registration statement becomes effective as long as paperwork is on file with the Administrator for the required period, which ranges from 10 to 20 days depending on the state.

registration by qualification   A process that allows a security to be sold in a state. It is available to an issuer who files for the security's registration with the state Administrator, meets minimum net worth, disclosure, and other requirements, and files appropriate registration fees. The state registration becomes effective when the Administrator so orders.

registration statement   The legal document that discloses all pertinent information concerning an offering of a security and its issuer. It is submitted to the SEC (and/ or the Administrator) in accordance with the requirements of the Securities Act of 1933 and/or the Uniform Securities Act, and it forms the basis of the final prospectus distributed to investors.

regnant   Considered to be the ruling or general position, such as the regnant view on registration requirements.

regressive tax   A tax that takes a larger percentage of the income of low-income earners than that of high-income earners. Examples include gasoline tax and cigarette tax. *See* progressive tax.

regulated investment company   An investment company to which Subchapter M of the Internal Revenue Code grants special status that allows the flow-through of tax consequences on a distribution to shareholders. If 90% of its income is passed through to the shareholders, the company is not subject to tax on this income.

Regulation D   The provision of the Securities Act of 1933 that exempts from registration offerings sold in private placements. Rule 506(b) limits the sale to a maximum of 35 nonaccredited investors during a 12-month period with no advertising permitted, while Rule 506(c) permits advertising but requires that all purchasers be accredited investors. *See* private placement.

Regulation T   The Federal Reserve Board regulation that governs customer cash accounts and the amount of credit that brokerage firms and dealers may extend to customers for the purchase of securities. Regulation T currently sets the loan value of marginable securities at 50% and the payment deadline at two days beyond regular way settlement. *Syn.* Reg. T.

regulatory risk   The risk that changes in regulations may negatively affect the operations of a company.

reinstatement privilege   A benefit offered by some mutual funds, allowing an investor to withdraw money from a fund account and then redeposit the money without paying a second sales charge.

remainderman   A remainderman is the person who inherits or is entitled under the law to inherit property upon termination of the estate of the former owner. Usually, this occurs due to the death or termination of the former owner's life estate.

remuneration   Money paid for work performed or a service provided.

repurchase agreement   Sometimes just referred to as a REPO, this is widely used in the money market where the seller of a security agrees to buy it back (repurchase it) at a higher price (the imputed interest rate).

required minimum distribution (RMD)   The amount that traditional and SEP IRA owners and qualified plan participants must begin withdrawing from their retirement accounts by April 1 following the year they reach age 70½. Exceptions apply to those covered under a qualified plan who are still employed. RMD amounts must then be distributed by December 31 that year and each subsequent year.

reserve requirement   The percentage of depositors' money that the Federal Reserve Board requires a commercial bank to keep on deposit in the form of cash or in its vault. *Syn.* reserves.

residual claim   The right of a common stockholder to corporate assets in the event that the corporation ceases to exist. A common stockholder may claim assets only after the claims of all creditors and other security holders have been satisfied.

resistance level   A technical analysis term describing the top of a stock's historical trading range. *See* support level.

restricted security   An unregistered, nonexempt security acquired either directly or indirectly from the issuer, or an affiliate of the issuer, in a transaction that does not involve a public offering. *See* holding period; Rule 144.

retained earnings   The amount of a corporation's net income that remains after all dividends have been paid to preferred and common stockholders. *Syn.* earned surplus; reinvested earnings.

retiring bonds   Ending an issuer's debt obligation by calling the outstanding bonds, by purchasing bonds in the open market, or by repaying bondholders the principal amount at maturity.

return on common equity A measure of a corporation's profitability, calculated by dividing after-tax income by common shareholders' equity.

return on equity A measure of a corporation's profitability, specifically its return on assets, calculated by dividing after-tax income by tangible assets.

return on investment (ROI) The profit or loss resulting from a security transaction, often expressed as an annual percentage rate.

revenue bond A municipal debt issue whose interest and principal are payable only from the specific earnings of an income-producing public project.

reverse churning The prohibited practice of parking assets that will only be traded infrequently in a fee-based advisory account.

reverse split A reduction in the number of a corporation's shares outstanding that increases the par value of its stock or its earnings per share. The market value of the total number of shares remains the same. *See* stock split.

revocable trust A trust that can be altered or canceled by the grantor. During the life of the trust, income earned is distributed to the grantor, and only after death does property transfer to the beneficiaries.

right A security representing a stockholder's entitlement to the first opportunity to purchase new shares issued by the corporation at a predetermined price (normally less than the current market price) in proportion to the number of shares already owned. Rights are issued for a short time only, after which they expire. *Syn.* subscription right; subscription right certificate.

right of accumulation A benefit offered by a mutual fund that allows the investor to qualify for reduced sales loads on additional purchases according to the fund account's total dollar value.

risk-adjusted return Return from a security adjusted for the market risk associated with it. Usually measured by the Sharpe ratio.

risk-free rate Generally refers to the interest rate of 13 week (91-day) U.S. Treasury bills.

risk premium The amount in excess of the risk-free rate demanded by investors to compensate for the additional risks inherent in the specific security being described.

risk tolerance Risk tolerance is an investor's ability and willingness to lose some or all of the original investment in exchange for greater potential returns. An aggressive investor, or one with a high risk tolerance, is more likely to risk losing money in order to get better results. A conservative investor, or one with a low-risk tolerance, tends to favor investments that will preserve the original investment.

RMD *See* required minimum distribution.

Roth 401(k) As with a Roth IRA, contributions are not tax deductible, but qualified withdrawals are free from income tax. There are no earnings limits in order to participate, but it is required that distributions begin no later than age 70½.

Roth IRA Funded with after-tax contributions, but, if qualified, withdrawals are tax-free. There are earnings limits but no required distributions at age 70½.

Rule 144 SEC rule requiring that persons who hold control or restricted securities may sell them only in limited quantities, and that all sales of restricted stock by control persons must be reported to the SEC by filing a Form 144, Notice of Proposed Sale of Securities. *See* control security; restricted security.

Rule 147 SEC rule that provides exemption from the registration statement and prospectus requirements of the 1933 Act for securities offered and sold exclusively intrastate.

safe harbor A provision in a regulatory scheme that provides protection against legal action if stated procedures are followed. In this exam, it may apply in three different cases: (1) Section 28(e) of the Securities Exchange Act of 1934 describes those research and brokerage activities that may be received by an investment adviser in exchange for directed brokerage transactions; (2) Section 404c of ERISA describes what a fiduciary of a qualified plan must do to minimize personal responsibility; and (3) top-heavy 401(k) concerns are minimized if the employer covers all employees with immediate vesting. *See* soft dollar compensation; top heavy.

sales load The amount added to a mutual fund share's net asset value to arrive at the offering price. *See* mutual fund; net asset value; no-load fund.

Savings Incentive Match Plan for Employees A form of employer sponsored IRA for businesses that have 100 or fewer employees who earned $5,000 or more during the preceding calendar year. In addition, the employer cannot currently have another retirement plan.

S corporation A small business corporation that meets certain requirements and is taxed as a partnership while retaining limited liability. *Syn.* Subchapter S corporation.

Schedule K-1 The form supplied by a partnership, LLC, or S corporation to owners indicating their proportionate share of income/loss to be reported on their Form 1040 tax returns.

secondary distribution A distribution, with a prospectus, that involves securities owned by major stockholders (typically founders or principal owners of a corporation). The sale proceeds go to the sellers of the stock, not to the issuer.

secondary market The market in which securities are bought and sold subsequent to their being sold to the public for the first time. *See* new issue market.

secondary offering A sale of securities in which one or more major stockholders in a company sell all or a large portion of their holdings; the underwriting proceeds are paid to the stockholders rather than to the corporation. Typically, such an offering occurs when the founder of a business (and perhaps some of the original financial backers) determine that there is more to be gained by going public than by staying private. The offering does not increase the number of shares of stock outstanding. *See* secondary distribution.

Section 457 Plan A deferred compensation plan set up under Section 457 of the tax code that may be used by employees of a state, political subdivision of a state, and any agency or instrumentality of a state. This plan may also be offered to employees of certain tax-exempt organizations (hospitals, charitable organizations, unions, and so forth), but *not* churches. Even independent contractors may be covered under these plans.

Section 28(e) A code section of the Securities Exchange Act of 1934 hat deals with soft dollar compensation. *See* soft dollar compensation; state harbor.

sector fund A mutual fund whose investment objective is to capitalize on the return potential provided by investing primarily in a particular industry or sector of the economy. *Syn.* industry fund; specialized fund.

sector rotation An active portfolio management technique that attempts to take advantage of the fact that different sectors of the economy rise and fall in the business cycle at different times. Rotating from one to the other at the right times can lead to investment success. *Syn.* Sector rotating. *See* active management style.

secured bond A debt security backed by identifiable assets set aside as collateral. In the event that the issuer defaults on payment, the bondholders may lay claim to the collateral. *See* debenture.

Securities Act of 1933 Federal legislation requiring the full and fair disclosure of all material information about the issuance of new securities. *Syn.* Act of 1933; Full Disclosure Act; New Issues Act; Prospectus Act; Trust in Securities Act; Truth in Securities Act.

Securities Amendments Act of 1975 Federal legislation that established the Municipal Securities Rulemaking Board.

Securities and Exchange Commission (SEC) Commission created by Congress to regulate the securities markets and protect investors. It is composed of five commissioners appointed by the President of the United States with the advice and consent of the Senate. The SEC enforces, among other acts, the Securities Act of 1933, the Securities Exchange Act of 1934, the Trust Indenture Act of 1939, the Investment Company Act of 1940, and the Investment Advisers Act of 1940.

Securities Exchange Act of 1934 Federal legislation that established the Securities and Exchange Commission. The act aims to protect investors by regulating the exchanges, the OTC market, the extension of credit by the Federal Reserve Board, broker-dealers, insider transactions, trading activities, client accounts, and net capital. *Syn.* Act of 1934; Exchange Act.

Securities Information Processor (SIP) A system that consolidates quote and trade data for U.S. stocks.

Securities Investor Protection Corporation (SIPC) A nonprofit membership corporation created by an act of Congress to protect clients of brokerage firms that are forced into bankruptcy. Membership is composed of all brokers and dealers registered under the Securities Exchange Act of 1934, all members of national securities exchanges, and most FINRA members. SIPC provides brokerage firm customers up to $500,000 coverage for cash and securities held by the firms (although cash coverage is limited to $250,000).

security Other than an insurance policy or a fixed annuity, any piece of securitized paper that can be traded for value. Under the Uniform Securities Act, this includes any note; stock; treasury stock; bond; debenture; evidence of indebtedness; certificate of interest or participation in any profit-sharing agreement; collateral-trust certificate; preorganization certificate or subscription; transferable share; investment contract; voting-trust certificate; certificate of deposit for a security; certificate of interest or participation in an oil, gas, or mining title or lease or in payments out of production under such a title or lease; or, in general, any interest or instrument commonly known as a security, or any certificate of interest or participation in, temporary or interim certificate for, receipt for, guarantee of, or warrant or right to subscribe to or purchase, any of the foregoing.

security market index A security market index is used to represent the performance of an asset class, security market, or segment of a market. They are usually created as portfolios of individual securities, which are referred to as the constituent securities of the index. An index has a numerical value that is calculated from the market prices (actual when available, or estimated) of its constituent securities at a point in time. An index return is the percentage change in the index's value over a period of time. Popular examples are the S&P 500 and the Russell 2000.

self-regulatory organization (SRO) One of eight organizations accountable to the SEC for the enforcement of federal securities laws and the supervision of securities practices within an assigned field of jurisdiction. For example, the National Association of Securities Dealers regulates the over-the-counter market; the Municipal Securities Rulemaking Board supervises state and municipal securities; and certain stock exchanges, such as the New York Stock Exchange and the Chicago Board Options Exchange, act as self-regulatory bodies to promote ethical conduct and standard trading practices.

sell To convey ownership of a security or another asset for money or value. This includes giving or delivering a security with or as a bonus for a purchase of securities, a gift of assessable stock, and selling or offering a warrant or right to purchase or subscribe to another security. Not included in the definition is a bona fide pledge or loan or a stock dividend if nothing of value is given by the stockholders for the dividend. *Syn.* sale.

selling away An associated person engaging in private securities transactions without the employing broker-dealer's knowledge and consent. This violates the NASAA Policy on prohibited practices.

selling dividends Inducing customers to buy mutual fund shares by implying that an upcoming distribution will benefit them. This practice is illegal.

sell stop order An order to sell a security that is entered at a price below the current market price and that is triggered when the market price touches or goes through the sell stop price.

senior security A security that grants its holder a prior claim to the issuer's assets over the claims of another security's holders. For example, a bond is a senior security over common stock.

separate account The account that holds funds paid by variable annuity contract holders. The funds are kept separate from the insurer's general account and are invested in a portfolio of securities that match the contract holders' objectives. *See* accumulation unit; annuity.

settlor An individual or organization that gifts assets to a beneficiary by transferring fiduciary duty to a third-party trustee that will maintain the assets for the benefit of the beneficiaries. *Syn.* grantor, trustor.

Sharpe ratio The Sharpe ratio measures the risk adjusted return of an investment. It is calculated by dividing the excess return of an asset over the 91-day Treasury bill rate by its standard deviation. It measures the reward per unit of risk so the higher the ratio, the better.

short The term used to describe the selling of a security, contract, or commodity that the seller does not own. For example, an investor who borrows shares of stock from a broker-dealer and sells them on the open market is said to have a short position in the stock. *See* long.

short sale The sale of a security that the seller does not own, or any sale consummated by the delivery of a security borrowed by or for the account of the seller.

short-term capital gain The profit realized on the sale of an asset that has been owned for 12 months or less. *See* capital gain; capital loss; short-term capital loss.

short-term capital loss The loss incurred on the sale of a capital asset that has been owned for 12 months or less. *See* capital gain; capital loss; short-term capital gain.

side-by-side management The practice of managing accounts that are charged performance-based fees while at the same time managing accounts that are not charged performance-based fees.

SIMPLE Plan *See* Savings Incentive Match Plan for Employees.

simple trust A trust that accumulates income and distributes it to its beneficiaries on an annual basis.

small-cap Stocks with a market capitalization of $300 million to $2 billion.

socially responsible investing (SRI) Also known as sustainable, socially conscious, "green" or ethical investing—is an impact investment strategy which seeks to consider both financial return and social good. In general, socially responsible investors encourage corporate practices that promote environmental stewardship, consumer protection, human rights, and diversity.

soft dollar compensation Noncash compensation received by an investment adviser from a broker-dealer, generally in exchange for directed brokerage transactions. Must always be disclosed and should come under the safe harbor provisions of Section 28(e). *See* safe harbor.

solicitor A person either contracted or employed by an investment adviser for the purpose of bringing in advisory business. If an employee, registration as an IAR is required. If contracted, the person must not be statutorily disqualified from registration and is subject to the terms of a written agreement between the IA and the solicitor.

solvency The ability of a corporation both to meet its long-term fixed expenses and to have adequate money for long-term expansion and growth.

specialist Stock exchange member who stands ready to quote and trade certain securities either for his own account or for customer accounts. The specialist's role is to maintain a fair and orderly market in the stocks for which he is responsible. *Syn.* designated market maker, DMM.

special situation fund A mutual fund whose objective is to capitalize on the profit potential of corporations in nonrecurring circumstances, such as those undergoing reorganizations or being considered as takeover candidates.

speculation Trading a security with a higher than average risk in return for a higher than average profit potential. The trade is effected solely for the purpose of profiting from it and not as a means of hedging or protecting other positions.

spousal IRA A separate individual retirement account established for a spouse with little or no earned income. Contributions to the account made by the working spouse grow tax deferred until withdrawal.

spread In a quotation, the difference between a security's bid and ask prices.

Standard & Poor's Composite Index of 500 Stocks (S&P 500) A value-weighted index that offers broad coverage of the securities market. It is composed of 400 industrial stocks, 40 financial stocks, 40 public utility stocks, and 20 transportation stocks. The index is owned and compiled by Standard & Poor's Corporation. *See* index; Standard & Poor's Corporation; Standard & Poor's 100 Stock Index.

Standard & Poor's Corporation (S&P) A company that rates stocks and corporate and municipal bonds according to risk profiles and that produces and tracks the S&P indexes. The company also publishes a variety of financial and investment reports. *See* bond rating; Moody's Investors Service; rating; Standard & Poor's 100 Stock Index; Standard & Poor's Composite Index of 500 Stocks.

standard deviation A measurement of a security's or a portfolio's total risk. The greater the standard deviation, the more the security's returns deviate from its average return, hence indicating greater volatility. *See* total risk.

standardized contract A futures contract in which all the contract terms are set by the exchange except for price.

standardized options Options contracts trading on a national securities exchange, or an automated quotation system of a registered securities association, which relate to options classes the terms of which are limited to specific expiration dates and exercise prices.

static content Social media content that rarely changes and can only be changed by the author of the content. Examples would be an investment adviser's website.

stock certificate Printed evidence of ownership in a corporation.

stock dividend A dividend paid in additional shares of the issuer's stock rather than in cash. Unlike cash dividends, stock dividends are not taxable when received. They lower the cost basis of the current shareholdings and are only subject to capital gains tax when sold.

stock exchange Any organization, association, or group of persons that maintains or provides a marketplace in which securities can be bought and sold. Examples include the New York Stock Exchange (NYSE), the London Stock Exchange (LSE), and the Tokyo Stock Exchange (TSE).

stock split An increase in the number of a corporation's outstanding shares, which decreases its stock's par value. The market value of the total number of shares remains the same. The proportional reductions in orders held on the books for a split stock are calculated by dividing the stock's market price by the fraction that represents the split.

stop limit order A customer order that becomes a limit order when the market price of the security reaches or passes a specific price. *See* limit order; stop order.

stop order (1) A directive from the SEC or the Administrator that suspends the sale of new issue securities to the public when fraud is suspected or filing materials are deficient. (2) A customer order that becomes a market order when the market price of the security reaches or passes a specific price. *See* limit order; market order; stop limit order.

street name   Term used in the industry to refer to customer securities held in the name of the broker-dealer as nominee.

subordinated debenture   A debt obligation, backed by the general credit of the issuing corporation, that has claims to interest and principal subordinated to ordinary debentures and all other liabilities. *See* debenture.

successor firm   A new entity which takes over (succeeds) an existing one and continues the business, generally under a new name.

suitability   A determination made by an agent as to whether a particular security matches a customer's objectives and financial capability. The agent must have enough information about the customer to make this judgment.

supply   The total amount of a good or service available for purchase by consumers. *See* demand.

supply-side theory   An economic theory holding that bolstering an economy's ability to supply more goods is the most effective way to stimulate economic growth. Supply-side theorists advocate income tax reduction insofar as this increases private investment in corporations, facilities, and equipment.

support level   A technical analysis term describing the bottom of a stock's historical trading range. *See* resistance level.

systematic risk   The potential for a security to decrease in value owing to its inherent tendency to move together with all securities of the same type. Neither diversification nor any other investment strategy can eliminate this risk. Systematic risks are sometimes referred to as external risk factors because they take place outside of the company being analyzed. *See* market risk, unsystematic risk.

taxable gain   The portion of a sale or distribution of mutual fund shares subject to taxation.

tax credit   An amount that can be subtracted from a tax liability, often in connection with real estate development, energy conservation, and research and development programs. Every dollar of tax credit reduces the amount of tax due, dollar for dollar. *See* deduction.

tax-equivalent yield   The rate of return a taxable bond must earn before taxes in order to equal the tax-exempt earnings on a municipal bond. This number varies with the investor's tax bracket.

tax-exempt bond fund   A mutual fund whose investment objective is to provide maximum tax-free income. It invests primarily in municipal bonds and short-term debt. *Syn*. tax-free bond fund.

tax liability   The amount of tax payable on earnings, usually calculated by subtracting standard and itemized deductions and personal exemptions from adjusted gross income, then multiplying by the tax rate. *See* adjusted gross income.

tax preference item   An element of income that receives favorable tax treatment. The item must be added to taxable income when computing alternative minimum tax. Tax preference items include accelerated depreciation on property, research and development costs, intangible drilling costs, tax-exempt interest on municipal private purpose bonds, and certain incentive stock options. *See* alternative minimum tax.

tax-sheltered annuity (TSA)   An annuity contract that entitles the holder to exclude all contributions from gross income in the year they are made. Taxes payable on the earnings are deferred until the holder withdraws funds at retirement. TSAs are available primarily through a 403(b) plan to employees of public schools, church organizations, and other tax-exempt organizations. *Syn*. tax-deferred annuity.

technical analysis   A method of evaluating securities by analyzing statistics generated by market activity, such as past prices and volume. Technical analysts do not attempt to measure a security's intrinsic value. *See* chartist; fundamental analysis.

Telephone Consumer Protection Act of 1991 (TCPA)   Federal legislation restricting the use of telephone lines for solicitation purposes. A company soliciting sales via telephone, facsimile, or email must disclose its name and address to the called party and must not call any person who has requested not to be called.

tenants in common (TIC)   A form of joint ownership of an account whereby a deceased tenant's fractional interest in the account is retained by his estate. *See* joint tenants with right of survivorship.

tenants by the entirety   A form of joint ownership only available to married couples. Unlike other forms, it requires consent of both parties in order to effect transactions.

tergiversation   The practice of continually changing one's mind, attitude, or opinion.

testamentary trust   A trust created as a result of instructions from a deceased's last will and testament.

testator   The legal term for a person who makes a will.

testimonial   An endorsement of an investment or service by a celebrity or public opinion influencer. The use of testimonials by investment advisers is prohibited.

theta   One of the four Greeks used by options analysts. An option's theta is a measurement of the option's time decay. The theta measures the rate at which options lose their value, specifically the time value, as the expiration date draws nearer. Generally expressed as a negative number, the theta of an option reflects the amount by which the option's value will decrease every day.

time horizon   Time horizon is the expected number of months, years, or decades over which the investments will be made to achieve a particular financial goal. An investor with a longer time horizon may feel more comfortable taking on a riskier, or more volatile, investment because that investor can wait out slow economic cycles and the inevitable ups and downs of our markets. By contrast, an investor saving up for a teenager's college education would likely take on less risk because of the shorter time horizon.

time value   The amount an investor pays for an option above its intrinsic value; it reflects the amount of time left until expiration. The amount is calculated by subtracting the intrinsic value from the premium paid. *See* intrinsic value.

tombstone advertisement   A printed advertisement that is used to generate interest in a securities offering. The text is limited to basic information about the offering, such as the name of the issuer, type of security, names of the underwriters, and where a prospectus is available. A tombstone ad is not considered to be an offering of the subject security.

top heavy   The term used to describe a 401(k) plan that offers a disproportionate benefit to key employees. Topheavy testing must be done on an annual basis unless the plan qualifies as a safe harbor 401(k). *See* safe harbor.

total capitalization   The sum of a corporation's long-term debt, stock accounts, and capital in excess of par.

total risk   (As measured by standard deviation) can be broken down into its component parts: unsystematic risk and systematic risk. That is, total risk = systematic risk + unsystematic risk.

toxic debt   Debt whose quality has dropped and is now indicating a high likelihood of default. This can be toxic for the investor's portfolio.

trading authorization   *See* full trading authorization; limited trading authorization.

tranche   A class of bonds. Collateralized mortgage obligations are structured with several tranches of bonds that have various maturities. It comes from the French word for *slice*.

transfer agent   A person or corporation responsible for recording the names and holdings of registered security owners, *see*ing that certificates are signed by the appropriate corporate officers, affixing the corporate seal, and delivering securities to the new owners.

Treasury bill   A marketable U.S. government debt security with a maturity of less than one year. Treasury bills are issued through a competitive bidding process at a discount from par; they have no fixed interest rate. *Syn.* T-bill.

Treasury bond   A marketable, fixed-interest U.S. government debt security with a maturity of more than 10 years. *Syn.* T-bond.

Treasury note   A marketable, fixed-interest U.S. government debt security with a maturity of between 2 and 10 years. *Syn.* T-note.

trendline   A tool used by technical analysts to trace a security's movement by connecting the reaction lows in an upward trend or the rally highs in a downward trend.

trough   The end of a period of declining business activity throughout the economy, one of the four stages of the business cycle. *See* business cycle.

trustee   A person legally appointed to act on a beneficiary's behalf.

trustor   An individual or organization that gifts assets to a beneficiary by transferring fiduciary duty to a third-party trustee that will maintain the assets for the benefit of the beneficiaries. *Syn.* settlor, grantor.

12b-1 asset-based fees   Investment Company Act of 1940 provision that allows a mutual fund to collect a fee for the promotion or sale of or another activity connected with the distribution of its shares. This fee will not exceed .75%.

underlying securities   The securities that are bought or sold when an option, right, or warrant is exercised.

underwriter   An investment banker that works with an issuer to help bring a security to the market and sell it to the public.

underwriting   The procedure by which investment bankers channel investment capital from investors to corporations and municipalities that are issuing securities.

unearned income   Income derived from investments and other sources not related to employment services. Examples of unearned income include interest from a savings account, bond interest, and dividends from stock. *See* earned income; passive income; portfolio income.

Uniform Gift to Minors Act (UGMA)   Legislation that permits a gift of money or securities to be given to a minor and held in a custodial account that an adult manages for the minor's benefit. Income and capital gains transferred to a minor's name are usually taxed at the minor's rate. However, if the child is under a specified age and has unearned income above a certain level, those earnings are taxed at trust rates. *See* Uniform Transfers to Minors Act.

Uniform Securities Act (USA)   Model legislation for securities industry regulation at the state level. Each state may adopt the legislation in its entirety or it may adapt it (within limits) to suit its needs.

Uniform Transfers to Minors Act (UTMA)   Legislation adopted in most states that permits a gift of money or securities to be given to a minor and held in a custodial account that an adult manages for the minor's benefit until the minor reaches a certain age (not necessarily the age of majority). Income and capital gains transferred to a minor's name are usually taxed at the minor's rate. However, just as with UGMA, if the child is under a specified age and has unearned income above a certain level, those earnings are taxed at trust rates. *See* Uniform Gift to Minors Act.

unit   A share in the ownership of a direct participation program that entitles the investor to an interest in the program's net income, net loss, and distributions.

unit investment trust (UIT)   An investment company that sells redeemable shares in a professionally selected portfolio of securities. It is organized under a trust indenture, not a corporate charter.

unit of beneficial interest   A redeemable share in a unit investment trust, representing ownership of an undivided interest in the underlying portfolio. *Syn.* share of beneficial interest. *See* unit investment trust.

unrealized gain   The amount by which a security appreciates in value before it is sold. Until it is sold, the investor does not actually possess the sale proceeds. *See* realized gain.

unsystematic risk   The potential for an unforeseen event to affect the value of a specific investment. Examples of such events include strikes, natural disasters, poor management decisions, introductions of new product lines, and attempted takeovers. This risk is diversifiable. Unsystematic risks are sometimes referred to as internal risk factors because they deal with risk arising from the events taking place within the company *Syn.* nonsystematic risk. *See* systematic risk.

U.S. government and agency bond fund   A mutual fund whose investment objective is to provide current income while preserving safety of capital through investing in securities backed by the U.S. Treasury or issued by a government agency.

value style investing   A management style that looks for stocks currently selling at distressed prices that have solid underlying fundamentals. These stocks typically sell at the lower end of their 52-week price range and have low P/E ratios and higher than average dividend payout ratios. *See* growth style investing.

vega   One of the four Greeks used by options analysts. An option's vega is a measure of the impact of changes in the underlying volatility on the option price. Specifically, the vega of an option expresses the change in the price of the option for every 1% change in underlying volatility.

vesting   (1) An ERISA guideline stipulating that employees must be entitled to their entire retirement benefits within a certain period of time even if no longer employed. (2) The amount of time that an employee must work before retirement or before benefit plan contributions made by the employer become the employee's property without penalty. The IRS and the Employee Retirement Income Security Act of 1974 set minimum requirements for vesting in a qualified plan.

volatility   The magnitude and frequency of changes in the price of a security or commodity within a given period.

volume of trading theory   A technical analysis theory holding that the ratio of the number of shares traded to total outstanding shares indicates whether a market is strong or weak.

voting trust certificate   A certificate issued by a voting trustee to the beneficial holders of shares held by the voting trust. It is readily transferable and is considered a security.

warrant   A security that gives the holder the right to purchase securities from the warrant issuer at a stipulated subscription price. Warrants are usually long-term instruments, with expiration dates years in the future.

wash sale   Selling a security at a loss for tax purposes and, within 30 days before or after, purchasing the same or a substantially identical security. The IRS disallows the claimed loss.

wash trade   A wash trade occurs when a customer enters a purchase order and a sale order for the same security at the same time. It is done to create a false appearance of activity in a security. This is a prohibited practice.

Wells notice A Wells notice indicates that the regulator intends to bring an enforcement action against an individual or a business. If the notice is against a publicly traded company, it usually has the effect of depressing the current market price.

Wilshire 5000 The Wilshire 5000 Total Market Index represents the broadest index for the U.S. equity market, measuring the performance of all U.S. equity securities with readily available price data. As of the date of printing, it includes some 3,700 issues.

withdrawal plan A benefit offered by a mutual fund whereby a customer receives the proceeds of periodic systematic liquidation of shares in the account. The amounts received may be based on a fixed dollar amount, a fixed number of shares, a fixed percentage, or a fixed period.

working capital A measure of a corporation's liquidity—that is, its ability to transfer assets into cash to meet current short-term obligations. It is calculated by subtracting total current liabilities from total current assets.

wrap fee program Any advisory program under which a specified fee or fees not based directly upon transactions in a client's account is charged for investment advisory services (which may include portfolio management or advice concerning the selection of other investment advisers) and the execution of client transactions. The exclusion from the definition of investment adviser available under both state and federal law to broker-dealers is not in effect for those offering wrap fee programs.

yield The rate of return on an investment, usually expressed as an annual percentage rate. *See* current yield; dividend yield; nominal yield.

yield curve A graphic representation of the actual or projected yields of fixed-income securities in relation to their maturities. In most cases, the securities of a single issuer are plotted over varying maturities. *See* flat yield curve; inverted yield curve.

yield spread The difference in yield between two debt securities, usually with similar quality and different maturities or similar maturities and different quality. Syn. credit spread.

yield to call (YTC) The rate of return on a bond that accounts for the difference between the bond's acquisition cost and its proceeds, including interest income, calculated to the earliest date that the bond may be called by the issuing corporation. *See* bond yield.

yield to maturity (YTM) The rate of return on a bond that accounts for the difference between the bond's acquisition cost and its maturity proceeds, including interest income. *See* bond yield.

zero-coupon bond A debt security usually issued at a deep discount from face value. The bond pays no interest; rather, it may be surrendered at maturity for its full face value. The duration of a zero-coupon bond is equal to its maturity.

INDEX

Notes

Notes

Notes

Notes

Notes

Notes

Notes

Notes

Notes